Goosepool

The History of
RAF and RCAF Middleton St George
and Teesside Airport

by

Stanley D Howes

PUBLISHED BY

Stanley BOOKS

First Published in the United Kingdom in 2003
by
Stanley D Howes (Stanley Books)
7, Station Road
Darlington
DL3 6TA
UK

British Library Cataloguing in Publication Data.
A catalogue record for this book is available from the British Library

ISBN 0-9545427-0-3

Typeset in Times 10/12,
Futura, and Helvetica.

Printed by:
Marford Lithographic
Victoria Road
Darlington DL1 5SF
UK

Dedication

This book is dedicated to the 1,266 airmen
who took off from Goosepool,
never to return.

Contents

Contents

Forewords
Larry Donnelly DFM 76 Squadron

When my fellow Aviator/Author asked me to write the foreword to his book I was both flattered and embarrassed, because I was under the impression there were others more qualified. However, I am privileged to accept.

Reading his tome revealed that he has written a painstakingly researched and definitive history of Middleton-St-George, covering the period from when it opened as an RAF aerodrome in 1941 to its present day status as a thriving International Civil Airport.

The 'War Diaries' chapters, graphically and starkly presented, recall the epic years when the aerodrome was used as a heavy bomber base by the RAF during 1941/1942 and the Royal Canadian Air Force from 1943 to the cessation of hostilities. The major air battles over Germany are described in detail, The Battle of the Ruhr, The Battle of Berlin and the special operations such as the daylight attacks on the major German Naval Units and the night attacks on the Rocket Establishment at Peenemunde. Also, during the invasion of the Continent and the final defeat of Germany the Middleton squadrons were well to the fore.

Stan has included precise and comprehensive details of the aircraft involved, the Armstrong Whitworth Whitley, the Handley Page Halifax and the Avro Lancaster.

The present Airport Hotel was the RAF and RCAF Officer's Mess. In front of it is a memorial to the squadrons who operated and in the hotel itself there is a wealth of photographic memorabilia. It is used as the venue for annual pilgrimages by RAF and RCAF survivors and their relatives to pay their respects and revere the memory of those who took off from Middleton-St-George never to return.

After the fall of France and the Battle of Britain the 'poisoned chalice' of taking the fight to Germany was thrust upon the RAF, on Bomber Command in particular. Subsequently they were ably and unselfishly assisted by Commonwealth Air Forces, especially the Royal Canadian Air Force, who formed their own bomber Group at Middleton- St-George.

The cost of taking the fight to Germany was high, For any given one hundred aircrew of Bomber Command during 1939/1945, the daunting casualty breakdown was, Fifty one killed on operations, Nine killed in crashes in the UK, Three seriously injured, Twelve taken prisoner, One evading capture. Only twenty-four out of the hundred survived unharmed.

The post war history of Middleton- St-George has also been well researched and presented. At the end of the war when the RCAF left Middleton-St-George, the RAF resumed tenure, and it was subsequently used by a variety of Units. These included an Air Navigation School and an Advanced Flying Training School.

When the RAF entered the 'Jet Age', it was used by a Jet Flying Training School. Later it became the home of 264 Squadron equipped with Meteor NF.14's and 92 Squadron equipped with Hunter F. Mk 6's.

In 1964, RAF Middleton- St-George was 'demobbed' after twenty-three years of active service, because of Defence cuts, but it wasn't long before it was operating as a Civil Airport, the first Commercial flight taking place in October 1964.

From this small beginning it has developed over the years into Teesside International Airport. It is also the home of Cleveland Flying Club; (the author is a keen and active member).

To conclude, this book is a book which I am sure will appeal to anyone who had/has an interest in Goosepool/Middleton-St-George over the years.

Reading it transported me back to 1941/1942 when I flew at Middleton St George with 76 Halifax Bomber Squadron on my second operational 'tour', and to the early sixties when I flew communications flights during 'alerts' and exercises when the airfield was used as a 'V' Force Dispersal.

I am certain that this unique well written book will grace many a bookshelf in Canada belonging to our Canadian comrades who flew from Middleton- St-George to preserve our freedom from Nazi tyranny during World War two.

Larry Donnelly DFM

Having spent a period of aircrew service with 428 (RCAF) Ghost Squadron at Middleton- St-George, from Peenemunde until 'D' Day, I found the history of MSG most interesting and enjoyable reading; it revived many memories, both happy and sad.

Many books have been written and published about the Wartime Bomber Command, it's strategy and bombing policy, but the real story lays with the people who actually participated in the Command's activities be they aircrew or groundcrew. The author has put together a first class record of the No.6 (RCAF) Group Bomber Command Canadians taken from personal correspondence with former Canadian airmen and from an exhaustive research of official documents.

Readers will find this section of the book most excellent reading on what the Royal Canadian Air Force did in Bomber Command. The many, many Canadians who now lie below ground, both in Europe and the United Kingdom bear witness to their contribution.

Robbie Robson

Glossary of Terms

None-Commissioned RAF/RCAF ranks
A/C. Aircraftsman
LAC Leading Aircraftsman
Cpl. Corporal
Sgt. Sergeant
F/S. Flight Sergeant (often called chiefy, slang)
W/O. Warrant Officer
W/O2. Warrant Officer 2nd class
M/P. Master Pilot
WAAF. Womans Auxiliary Air Force

Commissioned ranks
P/O. Pilot Officer
F/O. Flying Officer
F/L. Flight Lieutenant
S/L. Squadron Leader
W/C. Wing Commander
G/C. Group Captain
A/C. Air Commodore
AVM. Air Vice Marshall
AM. Air Marshall
ACM. Air Chief Marshall
Marshall of the Royal Airforce
C-in-C. Commander in chief
AOC. Air Officer Commanding

General terms
AFC. Air Force Cross.
Aileron. Elevator and rudder. Control surfaces on wings, tailplane and fin respectively.
ASR. Air Sea Rescue launch.
BFX. Message to divert to alternate airfield, because of bad weather at base.
Course/Fine pitch. Aircraft take off in fine pitch (high revs with prop blades at smaller angle to airflow), and cruise in course pitch, lower revs due to prop blades being at a greater angle to airflow, (more fuel-efficient)
DFC. Distinguished Flying Cross.
DSO. Distinguished Service Order.
Feather. To feather prop blades on failed engines, rotate blades fore and aft at minimum angle to airflow, to reduce drag and prevent airflow from windmilling/over speeding of engine.
GCA. Ground Controlled Approach.
Instrument Basher. Instrument fitter.
Nav. Navigator.
Peri track. Perimeter track.
Prang. Crash.
Prop. Propeller
Rigger. Airframe fitter.
Second Dickie. Co-Pilot.
Trolley Acc. Two-wheeled trolley with cable to plug into aircraft, containing bank of batteries used to start engines.
U/S. Unserviceable, faulty, not able to fly due to technical reasons etc.
Viz/Vis. Visibility, relating to mist, fog or cloud.
WOP/AG. Wireless Operator/ Air Gunner.

Introduction

If you had told me right at the start that writing this book would take five years you would not be reading these words now. However, once underway, the task became compulsive. I set out to tell the definitive story of Goosepool, from the commencement of its construction in late 1938, throughout the war and Jet years and right up to the present day, as Teesside International Airport. I decided from the outset to write about the people who have made the history of Goosepool, although the hardware follows close behind.

One thing I thought I could do was enlarge on the usual method of identifying the wartime aircraft by the pilot's name. I decided to try and include the other equally heroic flak dodgers sitting in the back. Fairly soon I realised that this was impossible. To do so would have probably made the book even thicker and much more laborious to read. I have however included from the best of available records the names of every single man who was killed, taken prisoner, injured, evaded capture or was interned. Along the way, I have also included the names of as many aircrew and groundcrew as the storyline would allow.

I am fortunate enough to have been directly involved with the airfield from 1960 as a young teenage Air Cadet, and after April 1964, as a member of the various flying clubs. I have met many wonderful people along the way, although not all have found their way into these pages. To those people I apologise, although their words are indelibly written in my heart and memories.

The biggest problem was what to do with Croft, it was after all Middleton's satellite airfield. Croft has its own story to tell, which will fill another book. Therefore I have not covered Croft in the same depth as Middleton. However because 78 squadron were first footers at both airfields I have included their time out at Croft from October 1941 to their return to Middleton the following spring. I have also covered some aspects of Croft as 419 Squadron RCAF began their time there prior to moving the 6 miles over to Goosepool. During the war Croft's squadrons, including; 427, 431 and 434 would often accompany Middletons crews to the same targets and this must be remembered. - I feel another book coming on.

Stanley D Howes

CHAPTER ONE

Ab Initio (From the beginning)
Goosepool
Construction
Why
78 Squadron
76 Squadron
4 Group

AB Initio

At 19:01 hours on the night of March 1st 1941, Sgt J W Quincey of 78 Squadron RAF opened the throttles of his Armstrong Whitworth Whitley bomber. Once the engines had developed full take-off boost, he released the brakes and the laden aircraft began to accelerate along Dishforth's main runway. Keeping the aircraft straight with judicious use of rudder and throttles, Quincey attempted to correct the drift from the strong starboard crosswind.

Pressing forward on the control column he lifted the tail. The full weight of the now streamlined Whitley was held firmly on the two main wheels. In the darkness his four-man crew sat silently at their individual stations within the aircraft, unable to do anything, other than to hope that all would go smoothly.

Whilst keeping an eye on the luminescent needle of the airspeed indicator, Sgt Quincey allowed the aircraft to accelerate. Soon it was passing 80 mph, and with a gentle but firm pull on the control column, she momentarily and reluctantly began to unstick. No sooner had the rumbling of the tyres ceased, than she settled back onto the runway. He and the rest of the crew were painfully aware that the airfield's boundary hedge, hidden by the darkness, was rushing towards them as they used up what little remained of the runway.

Whitley Mk. V taking off at sunset   Photo: Imperial War Museum (IWM). CH251

Quincey, with greater urgency, pulled again on the wheel. The crosswind suddenly lifted the starboard wing slightly, simultaneously trying to yaw the aircraft's nose to the right. This momentarily placed the overloaded Whitley in a most precarious position, balanced only on its port main wheel. With a firm clockwise pressure on the control wheel, he counteracted the lifting wing with right aileron, and at the same time he fed in a small amount of left rudder to keep her straight. Both throttles were fully forward, the engines were straining to give full boost, there was nothing left. To start jockeying with the throttles at this point to keep her straight would have been suicide. After what seemed like an eternity, both tyres reluctantly left the runway. She was airborne! With a small but positive climb-rate established, Quincey immediately encouraged the struggling bomber to weathercock herself from the runway's heading and into wind. Climbing slowly at first, the laden Whitley eventually gained a little height. Having completed a gentle climbing turn to the right, Quincey was able to overfly the airfield and set course for the first leg of their journey.

Watching from the side of the runway was the usual gaggle of WAAFs and groundcrew. They were there to see the squadron off on yet another raid, this time to Cologne. Their hopes and good wishes were with the departing crews, each one silently praying for the safe return of their friends. Little did they know that the small dot receding into the night, containing Sgt Quincey, Pilot Officer M J David, Sgt R Clark, Sgt R Bradbury and Sgt J G Earley, would never be seen again. They did not realise it at the time, but when the crew of the Whitley closed the hatch that evening, they were also closing the book on their young lives.

The doomed 78 Squadron Whitley Mk V, serial number N1525, had the identification letters EY-E painted on the side of the fuselage. The letters EY denoted 78 Squadron, the letter E identified this particular aircraft as E for Echo.

Steering a straight-line course of 161° and flying at an indicated airspeed of 135 mph, the bomber's crew were headed for their first turning point, Peterborough, some 119 statute flying miles to the south. From here, 66 minutes later, a new bearing of 113° would have them heading southeast, towards the small coastal town of Aldeburgh, near Orfordness on the Suffolk Coast. This leg of the journey covered 84 miles, which was covered in 28 minutes. Aldeburgh's prominent river features, nestling close to the Suffolk Coast, provided a clear landmark for the Whitley's navigator. Unknowingly leaving their homeland for the last time, the crew of EY-E sped out to sea. Their next port of call was the Dutch Island of Schouwen, 30 miles southwest of Rotterdam. This small island was found after a sea crossing of 98 miles. Now over enemy territory, they turned onto the final leg, heading 112°. This would take them the last 150 miles to the target, which they reached at 21:56 hours. The total distance to Cologne was 472 miles, time taken, 2 hours and 55 minutes. Their average ground speed - just 154 mph.

Of all the people waiting for the Whitley's safe return, only the Wireless Telegraphy (W/T) operators of Bomber Command would have a hint of her current situation. Sometime during that cold March night, one of these operators heard a faint Morse code transmission crackling in her headphones. It was from the wireless operator of EY-E, still over enemy territory. The coded message was brief, and to the point, 'EY-E Mission completed.' Nothing further was heard.

The Runnymede Memorial site, placed on Cooper's Hill, overlooks the Thames and the meadow where the Magna Carta was sealed by King John on June 15th 1215.

The Runnymede Memorial is dedicated to the 20,041 Airmen who lost their lives in WWII and have no known graves.
The total is made up of RAF 15,315, RCAF 3,045, RAAF 1,396, RNZAF 576, SAAF 17, RIAF 7, ATC 4, WAAF 13, ATA 10, BOAC 7, Ferry Command 9, War Correspondents 2.

The tablets of stone commemorating the names of the lost airmen were designed to represent the pages of a book.
Photos: Author

[1] Flak - Flieger Abwehr Kanone (Anti-Aircraft fire)

[2] Last heard of on W/T at 21:37 hrs, the crew of EY-G were shot down by a night fighter. This was later identified from German records as being flown by Ober Fieldwebel Herzog of 3./ NJG1 (Night Fighter Squadron No.1)

The next morning, the Whitley had not returned and was posted 'Overdue'. Later this was amended to 'Missing'. No one will ever know what got her on the way home. It could have been a German night fighter, flak,[1] bad weather, icing or even mechanical problems. The bomber and her crew had vanished without trace. Even today their fate and final resting-place is unknown. As with so many other airmen who simply disappeared forever, they are commemorated on the Runnymede Memorial.

The loss of Sgt Quincey's crew was not by any stretch of the imagination an isolated incident. On the night of the 27/28th of March, 78 Squadron were to lose another crew. F/O K F Seager, flying Whitley EY-G Z6470 on Ops to Dusseldorf, took off from Dishforth[2] at 19:29 hours. Sadly, the crew of G-George were to have the unfortunate distinction of being 78's last Whitley crew to go missing from Dishforth. Within a fortnight, 78 would move from Dishforth to Bomber Command's newest and most northerly airfield, RAF Middleton St George.

Goosepool

Situated at 54° 30' North - 01° 25' West, the former RAF Station Middleton St George, now Teesside International Airport, is located exactly half way between Darlington and Stockton-On-Tees in the northeast of England. Its elevation is 120 feet above mean sea level (AMSL). The airfield covers an area of over 740 acres. It is positioned close to the Durham-North Yorkshire border, so close in fact, that an aircraft taking off from the northeast end of the main runway, which is in Durham, enters Yorkshire when flying over the River Tees at the other end. This is because everything south of the Tees is in Yorkshire. Today, the border between Durham and Cleveland passes straight through the control tower. Whilst in military hands during WWII, and after, its Pundit code was MG. Better known to the locals as 'Goosepool', the airfield was, however, referred to by its inhabitants as either Goosepool or Middleton. On the Radio Telephone (R/T), Middleton's crews during the war sometimes made references to Goosepool. The German listening posts, having heard this, reported back to Luftwaffe HQ that a thus far unidentified airfield called Goosepool was to be found somewhere in the North of England. The location of this covert airfield was never found by Luftwaffe aircraft or its spies during the war, but it was suspected that it lay somewhere not too far from Middleton St George.

Construction

The records show that various contractors were appointed to construct the airfield. Building work commenced in late 1938, just before the outbreak of World War II. Although not fully completed due to wartime shortages of materials, needs must, and the airfield was officially opened on January 15th 1941.

The area was called Goosepool, as was a farm that occupied the site. However, Goosepool may have derived its name originally from more than one source. One version is that in olden days Irish farmers may have walked their flocks of geese the 60 miles or so to the area, having landed them at ports in Cumberland (now called Cumbria). Once at

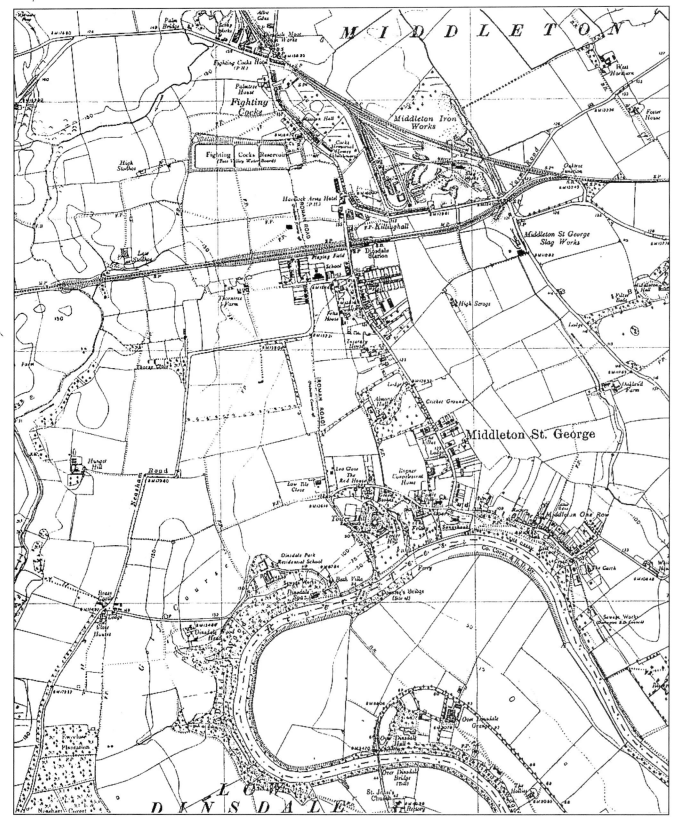

Map of Middleton-St-George dated 1938.

Photo:
Kind permission of Durham County Hall Archives

Goosepool, which was wet and marshy ground, they would be recuperated and fattened prior to being taken to local markets. Another theory is that Canadian geese would frequent the marshy ground as they migrated. An amazing coincidence that Canadian flyers of a different type would later populate the area.

The Old Goosepool Farmhouse, from which the name Goosepool derives. Even today those that were around during the war still know the airfield as Goosepool; it was never referred to as RAF Middleton St. George by the wartime civilian population.
Photo: Via Geoff Hill

Today the foundations of the farmhouse are still visible on the south side of the runway, along with the old stone gateposts which indicate the former entrance to the farmyard. During a dry summer, the track from the farm to the Yarm Road is still visible. The grass that has overgrown the farm track is not the same colour or texture as the more recent airfield variety.

Although there were various contractors involved with the construction of the airfield, the St Albans firm of Miskins was one of the main ones. At Goosepool, major problems with the semi-flooded ground prevented the start of construction proper. Lawrence Logan, who worked for Miskins, was the first onto the site. His initial task was to do something about the excess water, which not only hampered construction but also actually prevented it. The name 'Goosepool' was apt in more ways than one; geese had in fact adopted the partially flooded marshland and claimed it as their own. On arrival, and after surveying the proposed site, Lawrence initiated some research. He had a chance meeting with a very old man who had lived in the area for most of his life. This man had extremely good knowledge of the local countryside and he immediately came to the rescue. Escorting Mr Logan to the southwest side of the site, the old man began to search for something. There had been an old drain dug on the land years before, but this had been overgrown and forgotten. Eventually the old Victorian brick lined drain was found with its entrance completely blocked by undergrowth and mud. Sloping down to the River Tees, its outfall cleared the flooded land in a few days, once a couple of men had been put to work clearing the entrance.

The second problem for the constructors was the workforce. Old or medically unfit men, unsuitable for the military, were bussed in from all over South Durham and North Yorkshire. They had no proper clothing for the job and Wellington boots had to be purchased by the companies involved in the construction. The problem was that in war torn England, 'Wellies' were not readily available for anyone to buy with their ration cards. Rubber is not indigenous to England and during the war had to be shipped in, via the German U-boat blockade. In a bid to solve the problem, the Air Ministry was approached, and the situation explained. The Ministry pulled a few strings and the boots duly arrived, along with a bill for Miskins to pay. Work conditions were very hard. Four men died whilst the airfield was under construction. This was due to the extreme working conditions, the appalling weather, and lack of proper food and clothing. There were no Donkey Jackets or waterproof anoraks in those days, nor were there any JCBs. The work was extremely hard, practically all of it manual labour. Drotts, large Bulldozers, and crane type excavators were about the only powered technology of the day, and they were in very short supply. The railway brought building materials to be unloaded at Dinsdale sidings. Situated close to the Fighting Cocks pub in Middleton St George village, alas, today the sidings are no more. Nearly one hundred men worked non-stop in the siding, unloading hardcore with shovels.

The hardcore was brought from quarries situated all over the North, including Shildon, Sacriston, Scorton, and Urpeth near Beamish. Craig Brothers of Sacriston and a large contingent of hired transport brought thousands of tons of sand and gravel.

Because this haulage was defined as 'Essential war works', the trucking companies were given an extra petrol allowance, which was dyed red. Frequent checks were made on private vehicles. Any unauthorised car or lorry showing red dye seepage around the carburettor bowl had the owners prosecuted. Also, special allowances were given for tyres and spare parts. At the outbreak of war, all lorries less than 2 years old were requisitioned by the Government to provide transport until greater numbers of military vehicles became available. Hardcore from the site of the old iron works at Middleton St George was provided for the construction of the runways and hardstandings The power stations at Darlington and Middlesbrough were also supplying the contractors with black ash and cinders from the coal-fired boilers, to mix with the top layer of concrete. This, and a liberal spraying of black tar, prevented the light coloured concrete runways and dispersals being seen by enemy bombers on moonlit nights.

The latest civil engineering technology circa 1938.
Today the principle is the same, only bigger.
Photo: IWM CH.9498

Photograph of Darlington F.C.'s new partly complete football ground taken by the Author during September 2001.   Photo: Author

Even today, the main sections of the runways and the old panhandle shaped bomber dispersals are still black, just as they were during the war. Only the extensions on either end of the main runway are of lighter coloured concrete. Added during the fifties, these extensions were provided for the introduction of faster and heavier aircraft. Because of this strategy, even today, under certain conditions the airfield is often dark and quite hard to find, even though you know it is there. For years the Germans tried in vain to find Goosepool. When approaching visually, my fellow pilots and I tend to rely on certain landmarks to locate the airfield. The reservoirs east of Sadberge are situated just to the north of the airfield and provide a good orbit point for waiting circuit traffic. Another good visual reference point is the Urlay Nook Chemical Works chimneys, affectionately known to pilots and the air-traffic lads and lasses

as 'Smoky Joe's'. Situated close to the end of the main 23 runway, the chimneys are one of the best airfield locators going. The smoke from the chimneys doubles up as a wind speed/direction indicator. If the smoke goes straight up there is no wind, if it is horizontal, a pilot can expect an interesting approach and landing. The white aircraft hulks in the airfield's Fire Training Area also enable us to find our way home. During late September 2001, as this book was under construction, so was Darlington's new football stadium. Only 4 miles from the airfield, it became our latest landmark and navigation aid.

On May 16th 1940, Squadron Leader Crosbie from HQ Bomber Command landed at RAF Thornaby in an Airspeed Oxford. Goosepool's neighbour, Thornaby, which opened for business in 1930, was just 5 flying miles due east of Goosepool. Thornaby's main role during WW II was that of a Coastal Command airfield. Sadly it is no more. The land it once stood on has been turned into a large housing development. Now, Thornaby New Town and nearby Ingleby Barwick occupy the site of this historic airfield.

The runways at Goosepool were at that time unfinished and not able to take aircraft, not even something as small as an Oxford. Crosbie had been sent to see the state of play at Middleton and possibly chase things up a bit. The airfield was one big construction site with builder's rubble everywhere. Having met with the construction engineers he returned by car to Thornaby and departed in the Oxford to report back. Britain's Prime Minister, Winston Churchill, took a personal interest in the building of the airfield and progress was improved by introducing a 24-hour shift system. This allowed most of the work to be completed by April of 1941, in time for the RAF's heavy bombers to arrive.

Shuttering and pouring of concrete during construction of perimeter track and taxiways   Photo: IWM CH.21486

During the latter part of the airfield's construction, soldiers guarding the perimeter of the airfield departed, because the wet and muddy conditions were so bad. Other perils besetting the workforce included the farmer's wife, at Goosepool Farm. She had to be warned by the police on more than one occasion for brandishing a shotgun at the workmen each time they came near. Mr Logan tried the diplomatic approach several times to no avail. He eventually died a few years ago at the ripe old age of 94, so she must have been a rotten shot.

Three runways were constructed, as per the norm for wartime RAF bomber airfields. The main runway (240°/060°) was 2,000 yards in length and orientated as close as possible to the prevailing wind directions, (southwest/northeast). To allow for westerly (and on occasion easterly) winds, the second runway, which was 1,400 yards long, was set at 280°/100°. Teesside does get its fair share of northerly winds, especially during the winter months, and so the 1,400-yard

Runways taking shape. The Euclid grader towed by a caterpillar tractor has been superceded today by a self propelled version.
Photo: IWM CH.21493

Middleton's Officers' Mess (now the St George Hotel) under construction. Note on the horizon, the old Middleton ironworks. On the extreme right hand side, the garage complex and squash court, still there in 2003.

Photo: Via Geoff Hill

third runway (010°/190°) was aligned as close to North/South as the available terrain would allow. This 10° offset from magnetic-north probably came about because of the proximity of the end of the runway to the Darlington to Eaglescliffe railway line, which forms the northern boundary of the airfield. This layout ensured that maximum crosswind conditions could never exceed 45°.

A contract to extend the runways was awarded to McAlpines, and later in the war, a further extension was sanctioned to accommodate the heavier bombers coming into service. During the latter part of 1940, due to delays and shortages, the construction of the airfield had still not been fully completed. Urgent necessity demanded however, that, although somewhat premature, the RAF should begin to prepare the site for habitation. At first there were only 2 hangars, hangar 1, a C1 type, and hangar 2, a J type. Work began during 1942 to erect 3 more, a B1 and two T2s.

Prior to the laying of the road surface leading from the guardroom to the Station HQ building, a large underground tunnel capable of carrying vehicles was constructed beneath it. This tunnel linked the Station Sick Quarters, located on the opposite side of the road to the guardroom, and the Station Headquarters building some 200 feet away. The idea was that during an air raid personnel could be taken from SHQ to the SSQ without injury. It also doubled up as a large air-raid shelter.

Why

To build an airfield such as RAF Middleton St George cost the taxpayer millions of pounds, even at 1939 prices. It is worth noting that this was just one of many built during the late thirties and forties. By the end of the war, Bomber Command had 172 bomber airfields at its disposal.

To understand why the Government chose to bless Teesside with the airfield of RAF Middleton St George one must undertake a short history lesson. Without the Germans there would probably have never been a wartime bomber station called RAF Middleton St George. It is interesting to note that most modern British airports, with the exception of Newcastle, have been built on existing wartime Bomber airfields. Therefore, if not for Adolph Hitler, there probably would never have been a Teesside International Airport.

To see how, and why, Bomber Command, and at least two of our protagonists, 76 and 78 Squadrons, came about, let us first turn the clock back to 1914. During this year, Germany's first aggressive attempt at world domination began, which culminated in the First World War.

Strategic bombing, as we know it, started in 1915, when German Zeppelin airships bombed the Midlands and the North of England. Some also bombed London, which understandably was their main objective. Close to home, West Hartlepool, with its connections with the British Fleet, was one target for these huge leviathans of the air. With a foothold in Belgium, the Germans soon had the range to send Gotha bomber aircraft to military targets in southeast England. Their bombs, however, did not always hit their military mark. During one such raid on Folkestone on May 25th 1917, 95 civilians were killed and twice that number injured. British home defence fighters were sent up but were unable to find the high-flying German intruders easily. Only one Gotha was shot down.

More raids followed, including two on London. One in June killed 162 and injured 432. Following raids on the British capital in July of 1915, the Prime Minister, Mr. Lloyd George, had urgent meetings with General Smuts. They suggested recommendations to the cabinet that would, it was hoped, alleviate the situation. Thus far, the over-stretched Royal Naval Air Service had carried out Britain's Home Defence. They, it was decided, would eventually join with the Royal Flying Corps to become a single body. Subsequently this did not actually happen until April Fool's Day, April 1st 1918, when the Royal Air Force was officially born.

When first formed, the RAF came under the command of Chief-of-Staff Sir Hugh Trenchard, better known to history as the Father of the Royal Air Force. The second recommendation provided for the upgrading of Britain's Home Defence fighters. It was decided that after the German raids of 1915, ten Home Defence squadrons were to be formed to combat the Zeppelin and Gotha raids. The build-up leading to the Somme offensive during the summer of 1916 reduced the eventual number of Home Defence squadrons to six. Situated between Edinburgh and Dover, these squadrons formed the backbone of Britain's air defence.

78 Squadron

78 B Squadron was to form one sixth of the envisaged Home Defence fighter force and was formed at Hove on November 1st 1916. It was assigned to Home Defence duties from that date to protect the south coast. A calendar of events appertaining to 78 Squadron's first formation is detailed below.

1.11.1916 - Under the command of Major H A Van Ryneveld, 78 Squadron HQ was initially based at Hove, (Brighton).

20.4.1917 - Flying BE 2C aircraft, A Flight under Major J C Halahan began operating from Telscombe Cliffs, Newhaven, 6 miles E/S/E of Brighton.

5.7.1917 - B Flight began flying from Gosport, Hampshire, to protect Portsmouth, their commanding officer being Major C R Rowden.

26.4.1918 - Major G Allen formed C Flight at Chiddingstone Causeway, west of Tonbridge, Kent.

12.8.1918 - Under Major C D Truran, B and C Flights were moved to Penshurst, 13 miles N/N/E of Eastbourne.

1.4.1918 - The Royal Flying Corps and the RNAS combined to become The Royal Airforce.

31.12.1919 - Following the end of World War One, 78 Squadron RAF was disbanded at Sutton's Farm, Hornchurch, to the east of London.

From November 1916 until disbanded, 78 Squadrons A, B, and C Flights flew a variety of aircraft. These included: BE 2C, BE 12, Sopwith Two strutter, and Sopwith Camel and Dolphin aircraft.

78 Squadron's crest
NEMO NON PARATUS
translates to 'Nobody unprepared'.
Photo: Courtesy of Alan Austin, Copyright MOD reproduced with permission of Her Majesty's Stationery Office.

76 Squadron

76 Squadron was formed at Ripon, North Yorkshire on September 15th 1916, also as a Home Defence Squadron. Under the Command of Major E M Murray DSO MC, the Squadron consisted of three flights. Their aircraft were dispersed at airfields around Yorkshire, with 'A' Flight being located at Copmanthorpe[3], 'B' Flight at Helperby[4], and 'C' Flight at Catterick[5]. After the cessation of hostilities, the squadron, then under the command of Major A C Wilson, became superfluous to requirements and was disbanded on the 13th of June 1919 at Tadcaster, 9 miles southwest of York. During this period (1916 - 1919), the Squadron was equipped with BE 2C, 2E, BE 12, 12A, 12B, RE7, DH5, Bristol fighter, RE 8, and Avro aircraft.

In France, Trenchard had already formed, albeit unofficially, a British Strategic Bomber Force on October 17th 1917. This was to be the third and final recommendation of Lloyd George and Smuts to combat the German bomber offensive. This force actually carried out over 50 raids on German targets up to the time that it became official on June 5th 1918.

Trenchard's determination ensured that despite attempts by the British Army and Royal Navy Chiefs to dissolve Britain's Air Arm after the war, Britain was able to retain its Air force. This was just as well, as during the early 1930s, Adolph Hitler came to power, and Germany's mass rearmament program began, in total disregard for the Treaty of Versailles, signed by the Germans at the end of the First World War.

Soon, alarm bells began sounding in Whitehall. New aircraft specifications were drawn up and urgently distributed to the various aircraft manufacturers. Britain had been caught with its proverbial trousers down and time was of the essence. In keeping with this wakeup call, Bomber Command was formed on July 14th 1936. It was based at Hillingdon House in Uxbridge, Middlesex, under the Command of Air Chief Marshall Sir John Steel. When formed, it had already been preceded by the formation of three of its Groups.

76 Squadron's crest
Photo: Courtesy of Alan Austin, Copyright MOD reproduced with permission of Her Majesty's Stationery Office.

Earlier, on March 20th, 2 Group had been formed with their HQ at Abingdon. Their first airfield was at Abbotsinch, Scotland. Such was the obsolescence of equipment at the time that both 21 and 34 Squadrons, which were based there,

were equipped with two-seater Hawker Hind biplanes. 1 and 3 Groups were formed two months later, on May 1st 1936. This early arrangement also accommodated 6 Group, which were made up from 12 squadrons of the Royal Auxiliary Airforce. They would soon be absorbed into the RAF and would change their role to one of training new aircrew. 6 Group had 13 group pool squadrons, which would ensure a steady stream of trained crews that would be available to populate an ever-growing Bomber Command. They provided crews trained on Battles, Blenheims, Hampdens, Wellingtons and Whitleys.

[3] Southwest of York on the York to Tadcaster Road
[4] Northwest of York, near Boroughbridge. [5] S/S/W of Darlington, by the side of the Great North Road.

November 1st 1936 also saw the re-formation of 78 Squadron at Boscombe Down. They were born of C Flight of 10 Bomber Squadron. Equipped with Heyford III aircraft, they would remain at Boscombe Down under the Command of W/C M B Frew. They were born of C Flight of 10 Bomber Squadron. Equipped with Heyford III aircraft, they would remain at Boscombe Down until they moved to Dishforth, Yorkshire on February 1st 1937. This was in preparation for the formation of 4 Group. One month later, on March 2nd , W/C R Harrison was posted in to 78 Squadron as a supernumerary officer. As W/C Frew was to be posted to Hornchurch on March 8th, W/C Harrison was to take over command of the squadron. During the first few days of April a second flight was formed under the Command of F/O M Hallam. B Flight's equipment consisted of aircraft that were immediate reserves to A Flight.

4 Group

It was actually not until April 1st 1937 that 4 Group was formed. Initially the Group HQ was at Mildenhall, Suffolk. They had been born out of 3 Group and were under the command of a certain Air Commodore A T Harris, about whom we will hear much more later. Departing on June 2nd, the Heyfords of 78 flew in loose formation to their practice camp at RAF Aldergrove, near Belfast, returning to Dishforth on the 25th. They began converting onto the Tiger IX engined version of the Armstrong Whitworth Whitley Bomber and were destined to remain at Dishforth until 1939. Yorkshire, and especially Linton-on-Ouse, became 4 Group's new home on June 29th. 51 and 58 Squadrons, who were equipped with Virginias, arrived there shortly after, having flown up from Boscombe Down. 51 also operated a small number of Avro Ansons. 4 Group's strength began to grow, with 75 and 215 Squadrons arriving at Driffield; they too operated Virginias. 97 and 116 Squadrons at Leconfield flew Heyfords. 7 Squadron, who also operated Heyfords, were based at Finningley, along with 76, who were flying Vickers Wellesleys. 78 at Dishforth had Heyfords and Ansons. They shared the airfield with 10 Squadron, which was the first RAF unit to fly the Armstrong Whitworth Whitley.

CHAPTER TWO

The Whitley
Armstrong Whitworth Whitley

The Whitley

Armstrong Whitworth Whitley Mk. V.   Photo: IWM *via Geoff Hill*

The Whitley took its name from Coventry's Whitley Abbey aerodrome, which had been purchased in 1920 for the princely sum of £5,000. Built by German POWs during 1917-18, the airfield was used as a RAF stores depot to receive aircraft that were delivered from the manufacturers. The site had several Belfast type hangars, but was limited in size, and therefore not really suited for use as an airfield. Although the works did not move there until 1923, a flying school was formed, whilst the aircraft drawing office remained at the Parkside site. They were to remain there even up to the time that the Whitley flew. By the 1930s it was realised that Whitley aerodrome was becoming unsuitable for the larger types of aircraft under development.

An Air Ministry order for 80 Whitleys during August 1935 finally convinced the Armstrong Whitworth Company that it needed premises elsewhere. A 99-year lease on 460 acres of land, adjoining the new Municipal Airport being laid out 2 miles away at Baginton, was taken out with Coventry City Council. The construction of a new factory was commenced, this however was not completed by the time the Whitley was ready for its first flight. On March 17th 1936, Alan Campbell Orde, the chief test pilot of Armstrong Whitworth, took off in the prototype, K4586. The first flight did not take place from Baginton as everyone has stated previously, but in fact from the old Whitley Abbey airfield just down the road.

The production jigs arrived at Baginton during the latter part of that year. Despite production being shared between Baginton, Whitley, and other dispersed sites, all further final assembly and test flying was carried out from Baginton. The Whitley was the first of the RAF's heavy bombers. 1,466 Whitleys were built at Baginton. Today, thanks to post-war indifference, not a single one is left. A section of Whitley rear fuselage is the only remnant of this once fine piece of history. It can be seen at the Midland Aircraft Museum at Baginton (Coventry Airport). The only reason this is still in existence is due to the fact that the aircraft crashed on a Welsh mountain top. So remote was its location that recovery and disposal by the RAF was not deemed practical at the time. Therefore it became a sheep shelter and survived. In recent times, the fuselage section was recovered and presented to the museum. The pilot of the Whitley, who had survived the crash, was invited to the opening of this exhibit at the museum. During his speech, he sympathised with the sheep, as he knew how cold a Whitley could be in winter.

Armstrong Whitworth Whitley Mk. 1

Whitley undergoing 100 hour check in R&I hangar.   Photo: IWM CH.689

The first production Whitley left the production line in March 1937 and was issued to 10 Squadron based at Dishforth. The Mk 1 had nose and tail turrets, each being fitted with one .303 VGO[6]. Unlike most modern bombers of the time, the Whitley did not have hydraulic or electrically operated bomb doors. Simple bungee rubber bands kept the bomb-doors closed. When the bombs were dropped, they fell onto the doors, which opened under the weight. After the bombs had departed the aircraft, the bungees pulled the doors closed again. This was a very simple system, but it worked.

In response to specification B21/35, 34 Mk 1s and 46 Mk IIs were built to complete an order for 80 aircraft. They went to 10, 58 and 78 Squadrons in January 1938. 78 at the time was stationed at Boscombe Down. 7, 51 and 97 Squadrons followed in July. The Whitley Mk II was equipped with two 920hp Tiger VIII engines, which were fitted with two-speed superchargers. This provided an unloaded cruising speed of 177 mph and maximum speed of 215 mph at 15,000 feet. Maximum range was increased to 1,315 miles.

80 Mk IIIs were ordered after B20/36 was issued during 1936. The Whitley's armament was upgraded to include a Nash and Thompson powered nose turret. The addition of a ventral dustbin turret in the belly subsequently turned out to be flop. Armed with two .303 Browning machine-guns, this drag inducing half-ton encumbrance was eventually removed. However, its mounting ring in the fuselage bottom was retained for the paratroop-dropping role. Larger bomb racks were added, and wing dihedral increased. The range increased to 1,315 miles and the service ceiling to 23,000 feet.

10 Squadron at Dishforth received the first Mk IV Whitleys in May 1939. They were upgraded with Rolls Royce Merlin IV engines, turning Rotol constant-speed propellers. Producing 1,030 hp at take-off, these power plants developed 990 hp at 12,500 feet. Fuel capacity was increased to over 700 gallons and the bomb aimer's window was changed to accommodate the famous 'chin' modification. Maximum cruise speed went up to 220 mph at 15,000 feet, whilst the maximum speed increased to 245 mph at 16,000 feet.

A Nash and Thompson power turret, sporting four Browning .303 machine-guns, replaced the old manual rear turret. Up to this point, the gunner had sat on a motorbike style seat, which was attached to the rotating part of the turret. The rear gunner's feet pressing against the aircraft's structure provided the only motive power to rotate the turret from side to side. His legs had to resist the increasing force being applied to the side of the turret as it was buffeted by the slipstream. This force increased proportionally as the turret was moved from rearwards to sideways where it lost the shielding effect of the fuselage. The fitting of the new power operated four-gun turret gave the Whitley the best defended rear end of any aircraft of that time.

[6] Vickers Gas Operated machine gun

*With its 4 .303 Browning machine guns and better visibility this turret gave the Whitley one of the best
defended rear ends of any contemporary bomber*   Photo: IWM CH.678

The normal range was 1,250 miles, but by fitting extra internal fuselage tanks the range could be increased to 1,800 miles. Empty weight was 17,250-lbs. With a normal load of bombs and fuel, the weight was increased to 25,900-lbs. The Merlin powered Mk IV was, on occasions, a bit tricky to keep straight during takeoff. The original rudder design had not kept pace with the various increases in engine power. With a strong tendency to swing to port, the Mk IV often required judicious throttle twiddling to keep the aircraft straight on the runway. Under certain crosswind conditions the rudders were not always powerful enough to counter the increased engine torque. The last 7 Mk IV Whitleys were fitted with Merlin X engines, which developed 1,075 hp at takeoff and 1,130 hp at 5,250 feet. These 7 aircraft, K9049 to K9055, changed their designation from Mk IV to Mk IVa and were earmarked for 78 Squadron.

Next came the Mk V, which was fitted with the same Merlin X engines as the Mk IVa. An increase in fuselage length by 15 inches gave the rear gunner a less restricted view and a better field of fire. To combat the directional stability problems brought about by the increased engine power, Armstrong Whitworth took the opportunity to redesign the tail. The main modifications were to the twin fins and rudders, which were enlarged and reshaped. The drag increase brought about by the modifications to the Mk V reduced its speed slightly in comparison with the Mk IV. Maximum speed was now 230 mph, and in the cruise, 210 mph. To alleviate some of the increased drag brought about by the enlarged tail surfaces, small drag reducing exercises were carried out. One such mod in this regard was to the D/F Loop[7], which was reduced in size and faired over. To reduce the problems brought about by icing, rubber de-icing boots were fitted to the wing leading edges.

The Whitley Mk V (as flown by Goosepool's crews) had a fuselage of light-alloy monocoque construction, the skin being stiffened by continuous fore-and-aft stringers supported by transverse hoops. The fuselage was built in three parts, the front and rear bodies, which were pin jointed to the main wing spar, and the stern body, which was bolted to the rear body, aft of the tail wheel. This stern body carried the rear gun turret. The wings were of cantilever construction and were tapered in plan and elevation with a single box main spar, which was covered with light-alloy sheet from the leading edge to the rear of the main spar web. From this point aft the wing was fabric covered. Various bomb loads were carried in four cells in the underside of the fuselage and in six cells in the wings on each side. The tail plane was of similar construction to the wings and was fitted with a fabric-covered elevator, the twin fins and rudders were also fabric covered. A horizontal strut braced each fin to the stern body. Both the elevator and the rudder had servo trim-tabs fitted. Hydraulically operated split-trailing-edge flaps extended from the fuselage sides outwards to the ailerons. The flying controls were of the standard type, and attached to the ailerons, elevators and rudders by chains and cables. A Mk IV autopilot was fitted and dual controls could be fitted side by side with the main pilot's controls. The main point of entry into the Whitley was via a door on the port side of the fuselage. This was positioned equidistant between the wing trailing edge and the tail wheel. The door opened upwards and outwards and was supported in the open position by a tubular alloy stay. An entrance ladder hooked to the doorstep when the door was in use. This ladder was stowed inside the fuselage immediately aft of the doorway, within easy reach of the crew from outside.

[7] Direction Finding Loop, used to obtain radio navigational fixes from known radio beacons

Entering by this hatch, forward of the tailplane, required the members of the crew, sitting in the front of the aircraft, to have to negotiate a small opening in the wingspar to reach the cockpit   Photo: IWM CH.229

There was also an emergency exit door in the floor just aft of the front turret. This could also be used as an entrance, providing that the engines were not running. This hatch was reached with the aid of a special ladder, which was normally stowed inside the fuselage. A tunnel type gangway led through the open bracing of the centre portion of the main wing spar, and gave access to both ends of the fuselage, providing dual controls were not fitted.

Heaters in one or both engine nacelles provided hot air for internal cockpit heating; this was delivered through branch ducts to all crew stations except the rear turret. The heating system could also be employed for ventilation when heating was not required. The rear gunner was warmed by electrically heated clothing. Armour plating was fitted for the protection of the pilot, wireless operator, rear gunner and main fuse panel, in the event of gunfire from the rear. If not of the protected type,[8] the fuel and oil tanks were also armoured. The undercarriage consisted of two retractable units, one under each engine nacelle, and a non-retractable castoring tail wheel. A single hydraulic jack operated each main undercarriage unit, and when retracting, moved forward and upwards into the engine nacelle. A system of levers and links compressed the Oleo shock-absorber legs during the last portion of this movement in order to increase the amount of retraction. The gap in the bottom of the nacelle was faired-in by spring-loaded doors, but a small amount of the tyre was left protruding. The undercarriage could be lowered mechanically if the hydraulic system failed. A car type horn, located behind the pilot's head, sounded if the throttles were closed below a certain airspeed while the undercarriage was retracted. Coloured lights indicated green when the undercarriage was locked down, red during retraction, and off when locked up.[9] The two Merlin X engines were equipped with two-speed superchargers and two-speed constant-speed variable-pitch propellers. The engines were mounted on nacelle structures built out from the wing spar. They were fitted with ejector type exhausts, and were Glycol cooled. The oil and coolant radiators were mounted together in a duct under each engine, and a hydraulically operated shutter at the outlet end controlled the flow of cooling air.

Hydraulic pressure for the undercarriage retraction system, flaps, and radiator shutters was provided by a twin action pump; mounted on the starboard engine. An identical pump, also on the starboard engine, supplied pressure for both gun turrets. Mounted on the port engine were two air compressors, one supplying high-pressure air for the brakes and the other low-pressure air for the autopilot. Each engine had a vacuum pump fitted, to operate the instruments on the blind flying panel and the de-icing system. The engines were started electrically, but hand-starting gear was also provided. General electrical services were provided by a 12 volt 500 Watt type A generator, fitted on the port engine and working in conjunction with a 12 volt 40 amp-hour accumulator[10] mounted on the starboard side of the wireless operator's compartment. A 12 volt 500 Watt type 'L' generator on the starboard engine, in conjunction with a second 40 amp-hour accumulator sited next to the main accumulator, supplied electrical power for engine starting and general purpose wireless loads.

[8] Self sealing
[9] This system is still standard today
[10] Battery

Prior to the end of 1939, the Whitley's crew had consisted of a pilot, who was seated on the left of the cockpit and assumed the role of captain. His job was to fly the aircraft and co-ordinate the actions of the rest of the crew. The second pilot (affectionately known as the second dickie) sat to his right and was there mainly to gain experience, before moving on to a command of his own. Up to the end of 1939, his tasks would have included navigation and bomb aiming. A navigation table facing sideways was placed down the side of the cockpit behind the pilot for his use. To the rear of this table and facing forward was the 1st wireless operator/air gunner (WOP/AG) who normally manned the radios. On operations the 2nd WOP/AG would be expected to man the retractable mid-under turret (or drop leaflets as required), whilst a ground tradesman gunner operated the rear turret.

At the end of 1939, new crewing arrangements were introduced. The new operational aircrew position of observer (later to be called navigator) was created. Seated behind the co-pilot, he took over the roles of navigation and bomb aiming previously carried out by the second pilot. The 1st WOP/AG continued in his role as wireless operator, whilst the 2nd WOP/AG replaced the former tradesman rear gunner, who was taken off flying duties and returned to his ground trade. Until its removal in later marks of the Whitley, this left the mid-under turret for use by the 1st WOP/AG as required.

In the Mk V the wireless operator's position remained in the usual place, sitting behind the pilot at the rear of the navigator's table, facing forward. To his right, on the other side of the cockpit, were the fuse boxes and two 12-volt accumulators. Originally the radio equipment consisted of a standard T1154 radio transmitter and R1155 receiver, with provision for using a crystal monitor unit.

In this view, taken from the side facing navigator's seat, one can see the opening below the instrument panel, leading down into the nose
Photo: IWM CH.700

Mounted on the starboard side of the wing spar gangway was the TR9.F transceiver, operated by remote control in the pilot's cockpit. This was better known as the R/T set. Each installation had its own fixed aerial and a trailing aerial was also provided for use with the general-purpose transmitter and receiver. The trailing aerial winding drum was located on the left-hand side of the cockpit wall, adjacent to the wireless operator's left knee. Beneath the wireless operator's table was the A1133 amplifier; this was used for the aircraft's intercom system. Above the wireless operator's compartment, on the outside of the aircraft, was the DF loop; protected within a streamlined fairing, this was used in conjunction with the general purpose receiver and was operated by the wireless operator. The Whitley Mk V had the Lorenz beam-approach equipment installed, and both its receivers had independent aerial systems mounted on the port side of the wing spar gangway, within the rear fuselage body. The system was operated remotely by a control box located next to the pilot's left shoulder. The beam approach visual indicator resided in the top left-hand corner of the pilot's blind flying instrument panel. Finally, an R3002 wireless installation was mounted aft of the entrance door on the port side of the fuselage; this was remotely controlled by the wireless operator. The aerials for this system ran from the tips of the tailplane to the fuselage. The bulkhead behind the wireless operator's back divided the cockpit from the rear of the aircraft. A small 2-foot square opening in the bulkhead allowed passage between cockpit and rear of the fuselage.

Passage from the cockpit area through the tunnel and back to the side hatch forward of the tailplane was partially blocked by the wing main spar, and had to be negotiated. Pulsing-tube de-icing over-shoes were fitted to the leading edges of the wings, tailplane, fins and wireless masts. An electrically driven distributor valve in the fuselage operated the system. The previously mentioned engine driven suction pumps were used to supply vacuum to the instrument panel. Propeller anti-icing was by way of a slinger ring on each propeller hub. De-icing fluid was fed to the slinger ring by an electric pump, which was positioned adjacent to the de-icing fluid reservoir close to the wing root inside the starboard wing spar. Provision was made for de-icing of the pilot's and bomb aimer's windows by way of pumps and flow regulators at their respective stations, fluid being drawn from a reservoir adjacent to the one used for propeller de-icing.

Fuel was supplied from one main fuselage tank and four other tanks, two in each wing. For increased range, 2 auxiliary tanks could be fitted in the front bomb cells in place of the bombs. In addition, 2 or 4 auxiliary tanks could be added inside the fuselage. The oil tanks were fitted inside the engine nacelles. Later models had protected fuel and oil tanks fitted.

.303 Brownings being loaded into the Whitley's tail turret through the open doors at the rear, prior to operations later that day. The doors were also the standard escape method for most rear turrets fitted to British Bomber aircraft during the war. To abandon the aircraft; the gunner would first point his turret rearwards, open both doors behind him to provide access into the rear of the fuselage, reach in and grab his parachute pack, then pull it into the turret and clip it onto the front of his harness. Having then closed the doors, he would rotate the turret 90° to the left or right, open the doors again, fall out backwards and when clear, pull the D-handle on his chute (ripcord)   Photo: IWM CH.246

The tail gunner sat for anything up to 10 hours in his cramped unheated habitat. Dressed in a heavy flying suit, it took him some considerable time to ensconce himself into his tiny workspace. Once the Whitley returned to base, the gunner took even longer to get out. Try sitting in a dustbin sized compartment for eight to ten hours, unable to get up and stretch your legs, (Deep Vein Thrombosis was not recognised in those days). Now have the dustbin (with you in it) put into a freezer, set for minus 35°. For good measure, ask several hundred very unfriendly German flak gunners to fire at you with 88 mm high explosive shells, along with other lethal bits of ironmungary. When they get tired there is always the nightfighter pilots, who will be happy to creep up behind you and pump 20 mm cannon shells into your aircraft. Don't worry, you are protected all round by paper-thin aircraft aluminium. Now you are getting some idea of what RAF aircrew had to endure, at least 30 times every tour. Having sat immobile for so many hours, the gunner's circulation would suffer terribly. To extricate himself from the turret and walk to the waiting truck after landing was often a major task, let alone jumping out quickly when the aircraft was crashing. Much stamping of feet on tarmac was witnessed after every raid.

At the beginning of the war, rather than antagonize the Germans, Bomber Command was only instructed to carry out nickeling raids.[11] Dropping bombs came later, and only after the Germans began to bomb civilian targets such as Rotterdam. Over the target, the 1st WOP/AG would be found kneeling on the floor assisting the 2nd WOP/AG. He would open the brown paper packs, which contained the bundles of leaflets. The bundles were then thrown down the flare chute. The slipstream conveniently removed the retaining elastic band and scattered the literature over the required area. The rear gunner would be used to confirm that the 'Bumf' was evenly distributed. It was generally agreed throughout Bomber Command at the time that the dropping of leaflets had little practical use, other than to provide the Germans with sufficient bog[12] paper to see them through the war.

5 Group was formed at Mildenhall on the 1st day of September 1937. One month later it moved its HQ to Grantham. Out of all the types initially operated by 4 Group, during the late 1930s only the Whitley would still be in service by the beginning of hostilities. When war with Germany was declared at 11am on Sunday September 3rd 1939, all 4 Group squadrons would be equipped with the Whitley. The same month, 78 found themselves on the move again, this time to Ternhill on detachment. September also saw them become 4 Group's reserve Squadron. They were to train crews onto the Whitley, and become a crew reservoir for operational squadrons and group pool airfields. During October 1939, they flew to Linton-on-Ouse for a further detachment. In December the whole squadron became based there. February 1940 saw 78 on detachment again, this time to Brackley where they remained until May. At the outbreak of war, 1 Group, which was equipped with ten squadrons of Fairey Battles, found themselves in France supporting the British Expeditionary Force. They were soon to realise the unsuitability of this aircraft in combat with the latest German fighters. Many Battle crews were to be decimated before this aircraft was removed from its front line bomber roll. At the same time, seven squadrons of Bristol Blenheims equipped 2 Group, whilst 3 Group possessed eight squadrons of Vickers Wellingtons. By now 4 Group had six squadrons of Whitleys, while 5 Group had eight squadrons of Handley Page Hampdens. This is how Bomber Command went to war with Germany in 1939.

The wheel turned full circle when, in July 1940, 78 Squadron's Whitleys touched down once again at Dishforth to be based there with 51 squadron. Apart from a couple of detachments, here they would remain until April 1941.

[11] Leaflet dropping
[12] Airman's slang for toilet

CHAPTER THREE

Royal Air Force Station Middleton St George
Goosepool welcomes its first flock
The weather

Royal Air Force Station Middleton St George

Five months later on October 29th 1940, came the very first RAF uniform to enter through the portals of Goosepool. It was worn by F/O S V Lock, the Equipment Officer. His job was to take over the brand new buildings and facilities and turn them into one fully functioning entity. The task included everything from trucks to toilet paper, kitchen equipment to mattresses, filing cabinets to light bulbs. With the first anniversary of the beginning of WWII just passed, the RAF was in a hurry to get as many bomber stations operational as possible, as soon as possible. Many of the stations were, at that time, unfinished due to shortages of everything. Even though the British Government had started its expansion plan back in the mid 1930s things were not progressing quickly enough.

Water was initially pumped into the two tanks at the top, which then supplied adequate water pressure on demand, for the whole of the camp Photo: Author

Next to arrive at Goosepool was Acting F/L H Dear. He came a few weeks later than F/O Locke, on December 28th. F/L Dear was responsible for Airfield Defence. Eventually, on January 15th 1941, RAF Middleton St George opened on a care and maintenance basis under Headquarters 4 Group, preparatory to opening up as a Bomber Station. Acting S/L D G Singleton was posted in the next day to become the first Commanding Officer. On the same day, P/O A S Newman arrived from RAF Leeming and was attached to the station for Messing duties. Later in the day P/O R E W Stroud also arrived; he had been posted in for accounting duties in the Station HQ building.

At 15:00 hours on the 17th, an intake of 305 airmen was posted in from 9 Recruitment Centre, Blackpool. Included in the intake were 19 MT[13] drivers and 280 airmen (General Duties). This party of men had no sooner settled in when, two days later, most of them departed again. Owing to the severe winter conditions, and the freezing of the water system, both domestic and heating, 253 of these airmen had to be sent on 7 days leave. On the morning of January 22nd, the resident engineer, P/O J Jackson, had the situation under control, and reported that the water supply was now back in working order. The next day two more officers were posted in to take up their duties. These were Acting S/L E K Brownrigg, the Station Medical Officer, and P/O P C Pearson who joined the Station Defence Section. January 26th saw the arrival of Major J W Bell of the Durham Light Infantry, who was to become the Local Defence Commander.

And so it went on, with personnel being posted in to bring the Station to life. The new arrivals included the Assistant Adjutant, P/O A K C Morley, who arrived from RAF Leeming on February 1st. He was followed two days later by F/O D R Goudie reporting in from RAF Topcliffe for Messing duties.

Having joined the RAF, Norman Thompson left Leeds on January 30th for Padgate. Here he received his inoculations and was kitted out. Induction training began next and continued over the next couple of months. Like the airmen at Middleton St George, Norman and his roommates had their fair share of inhospitable weather. It was very cold indeed. Inside the billets, water froze in the fire buckets. Learning how to make a bed with the minimum number of blankets served him well during the remainder of his service life.

In February 1941, 78 Squadron at Dishforth flew to Malta for Operation 'Colossus', returning a few days later. Meanwhile, on the afternoon of February 4th, Middleton had a visit from Air Vice Marshall (AVM) Arthur (Maori) Conningham DSO MC DFC AFC. He was the Air Officer Commanding (AOC) 4 Group, and was accompanied by Major J R Theobalds. They had arrived from Croft, where in the morning they had reviewed its position as Middleton's satellite aerodrome. Due to the urgent emphasis on getting the station ready, the normal working routine of Station personnel was not allowed to be affected by this visit. After an inspection of the airfield and its buildings the visitors left at 14:00 hours. Visitors were many to the embryonic station, including, on February 16th, the Senior Equipment Officer of 4 Group, W/C Fry. He was followed two days later by the Bishop of Jarrow, Dr Leslie Owen DD, who had lunch in the Officers' Mess. The morning of the same day saw the first officer reporting for permanent pilot duties; this was P/O A L A Petty who arrived from 10 Elementary Flying Training School. He was followed a few minutes later by W/C Corner, the Senior Medical Officer for 4 Group. The afternoon brought yet another visit by a high ranking official; this was Group Captain Jago who was the Assistant Chaplain-in-Chief. The contractors were still in full swing hurriedly trying to complete the construction of the runways, roads and buildings. This work had to cease on the 19th, due to 36 hours of continuous snow. They anticipated that work could not recommence until the March 3rd. The winters of the late thirties and early forties had been the worst to be experienced for 45 years. Meanwhile, the Air Ministry Works Department Resident Engineer, Pilot Officer J Jackson, was posted in from Catterick. He was in charge of construction and took up duties with No.2 Works Area.

At Middleton, disaster struck during the night of 27/28th when a rapid thaw set in. This caused severe flooding of the runways and ducts, and left extensive areas of the camp under feet of water. F/O Hennessy, who arrived that day for Adjutant duties, wondered if he had joined the RAF or the Navy. 'A' Company of the 70th Battalion, Durham Light Infantry, arrived on March 1st for Station defence duties. By now the floods had subsided, and the contractors had returned

[13] Motor Transport

that morning to recommence construction of the airfield. In the afternoon came the Signal Officer P/O LT Wright, who was immediately attached to HQ 4 Group. The Intelligence Officer, Acting F/L H J C (Skip) Seymour, was posted in from Linton-on-Ouse and he was followed by P/O Slater (Equipment) and P/O Morley (Admin). Acting F/L Dear left on the 16th for RAF West Kerby in Lincolnshire, pending embarkation to the Middle East. Although still very much under construction, the airfield was beginning to look as if at long last it might be able to accept its first aircraft, providing the crews had a penchant for builder's rubble and earth moving equipment. March 20th 1941 welcomed an advance working party from 78 Squadron who had driven up from Dishforth. They came to deal with the squadron's flight equipment.

By March 21st, Norman Thompson found himself posted to Morecambe. Foot drill and marching skills had been practiced up and down the sea front. Rather than send him and his fellow recruits to a formal training camp, the RAF utilized the redundant facilities of Morecambe's holiday industry. Now lacking its pre-war customers, this once bustling resort found itself minus holiday makers who were off doing something else, like fighting a war for instance.

Norman outside his home in Leeds
Photo: Norman Thompson

The RAF had noticed that all the lovely boarding houses were just sitting there, doing nothing, and considered that was a waste. So they filled them with new recruits and utilized the local promenade to teach the embryonic airmen the rudiments of service life. At Morecambe, Norman was accommodated in various billets. The first one was ok although meals were mostly made up of potatoes. This was fine, except that Norman began to pile on the weight. A second boarding house was run by two sweet old ladies, who could not do enough for Norman and his fellow guests. Following a move to a different boarding house the opposite was the case. The landlady resented having to take in airmen. Everyone had to use the back basement door and remove their boots before entering. The rooms were cheerless, cold and very bare. The food was barely adequate. Whilst at Morecambe, he earned two shillings and sixpence[14] per day, better known as half a Crown. Somehow he managed to lend his oppos[15] cash, for a small charge of course. Eventually Norman and his oppos were deemed to be airmen and ready for their trade training to begin. Marching down to Morecambe's town centre, they congregated inside what had been a large car showroom and garage. Due to the U-boat blockade, an extreme shortage of petrol for anything non-military prevailed, hence the availability of the aforesaid garage. Some civilians were requested to hand over their cars for use by the military, so this particular establishment was somewhat surplus to requirements until after the cessation of hostilities.

The garage had been turned into a rudimentary classroom and was decorated with various aero-engines and associated components. Despite these austere beginnings, Norman and his chums were given a good working knowledge of their trade. In typical military fashion, much later in the war (when he had become a proficient engine fitter and knew everything there was to know about aero engines) he was allowed to attend courses at the Rolls Royce factory in Derby and the Bristol aero engine factory. Whilst at the Rolls Royce factory, Norman was aware of a strange building with a huge pipe sticking out of one end. Every now and again this pipe would spit out a long blast of flame for about 5 minutes, accompanied by a strange, piercing, whistling noise. Everyone wondered what this thing was. Today we all realise that Norman was witnessing the birth of Frank Whittle's jet engine, something we take so much for granted these days. Norman remembers that for his stay at the Bristol aero engine factory he was accommodated in a

Trainee engine fitters being demonstrated the finer points of a Bristol Hercules engine Photo: IWM CH.1990

civilian billet that served Yorkshire Pudding with jam for sweet. The course was very good, but for the first week they did nothing but write; they wrote and wrote until they got cramp in their arms. The second week involved stripping the Bristol Hercules engine down and rebuilding it. The final test to see if one had rebuilt the engine correctly was to insert two metal bars into holes in the engine. If one bar went in all the way and the other didn't, the engine had been put together correctly.

And so, with the runways and most of the buildings useable, March 1941 saw Goosepool almost ready for its intended role. The first 2 WAAF Officers arrived, Assistant Section Officers M Elliot and D L Carmichael. They had arrived from RAF Leighton Buzzard for Code and Cipher duties. Two major events for the station took place on March 30th. The first was when Lieutenant Colonel Theobald of HQ 4 Group visited the station. He was to discuss with the Station Commander the date of acceptance of Goosepool's first bomber squadron. It was agreed that all being well this would be on April 7th,

---

[14] Twelve and half new pence, he had to work 8 days to earn one pound
[15] Friends, mates, pals, colleagues ....

subject to the approval of AVM Conningham. Whilst these discussions were taking place, the second major event for Goosepool occurred. Lorry loads of bombs started arriving on the other side of the airfield. During the next few days, the Armament Officer, P/O A W L Burke, began supervising the stocking of the bomb store. Now things were really starting to happen.

Meanwhile on April 7th, 78 Squadron at Dishforth prepared for a night raid on Kiel. At the same time, a large contingent of 78's ground personnel departed Dishforth by road. Their destination was a brand-new 4 Group bomber station 25 miles to the north, called Middleton St George. They would be the very first RAF squadron to be based at Middleton and would introduce the good people of Teesside to Bomber Command. A steady stream of lorries trundled up the Great North Road. Loaded with everything from paperclips to spanners the lorries disgorged their contents into offices and hangers alike. All the paraphernalia of a great bomber station was distributed to every nook and cranny of the airfield.

The same night, Sergeant R J Freas was approaching Kiel in Northern Germany. He had lifted Whitley Z6492 from Dishforth's westerly runway at 21:00 hours. He and his crew of four took just over three hours to cover the 470 miles from Dishforth to Kiel, at an average ground speed of 145 mph. They had left the English Coast just north of Whitby and had hit land at the northern Friesian Island of Suddorf-Amrum. From there they had flown due east to the small German town of Damp where a turn to the south took them the final 20 miles to the target. The co-pilot was Pilot Officer Christopher Cheshire, younger brother of the famous to be bomber pilot, Leonard Cheshire. Other members of the crew were Sgt Unwin observer, Sgt Brown 1st WOP/AG, and Sgt Hall 2nd WOP/AG. This aircraft was one of 229 aircraft dispatched to Kiel that night, comprising 61 Hampdens, 2 Stirlings, 49 Whitleys and 117 Wellingtons. 78 had contributed 9 Whitleys for this, the biggest raid on a single target thus far in the war. Sgt Freas leveled off at 11,000 feet and ran into the primary target, which was the shipbuilding yard. As the aircraft came over the target, it lifted as the bombs were released. Now free of its heavy load, the Whitley became a different animal, more agile, more manoeuvreable. Turning away from the bomb-run, they were suddenly coned by searchlights so no results were observed. The flak became intense and the crew felt a hit on the aircraft. Fortunately no serious damage was done and they were able to return to Dishforth safely after nearly 7 hours in the air.

Another Whitley from Dishforth, Z6466, was commanded by Flight Lieutenant Lawrence. His crew consisted of Sergeants Gibson, Wood, Cook and Chadwick. They too had reached Kiel unscathed and had bombed from 15,000 feet. Their first stick of bombs made a direct hit on the shipyards. Their second stick fell short to hit only the edge of the target area. The flak was moderate and they turned for home. Their troubles were not yet over, as they left the target area they discovered that a container of incendiaries had hung up in the bomb bay. On the route home, which was by a more direct route, they had a 55-mile wide spit of enemy territory to cross before reaching the coast. Meanwhile they searched their charts for a place to off-load their unwanted cargo.

Some 17 minutes flying time from Kiel was the town of Heide, situated just 11 miles from the coast and the safety of the North Sea. Heide was the only reasonable sized enemy town on their route home so this seemed as good a place as any. A slight detour off track was necessary to reach their sleepy target. The bombs found their mark, and a few minutes later the Whitley had left the enemy coast behind. Returning safely to Dishforth at 03:45 hours, they had been in the air for 6 hrs 45 minutes.

Having taken off some 37 minutes after the other two Whitleys, Sergeant Thorp, along with Sergeants Bird, Nolan, Moodie and Bailey were in T4147. When they reached the target, fires were already burning. Bombing from a height of 14,000 feet, they added their contribution to the conflagration below. On their return to base at 04:27 hours they reported that the flak was slight, and the weather over the target was good.

Sergeant Dunlop and Harry Drummond were flying Z6490 at a height of 15,000 feet when their bombs went down. No results were observed, as they were too busy contending with the flak, both light and heavy. Several concentrations of searchlights were in the target area, but the bright moonlight reduced their intensity. With Pilot Officer Jones and Sergeants Fraser and Smith being told to watch out for fighters, they turned for home.

Of 78 Squadron's 9 Whitleys that departed Dishforth that night, all returned, including one Fresher crew[16] whose primary target had been Emden. Sadly, two Wellingtons and three Whitleys from other squadrons were lost. One of the Whitleys was from 51 Squadron, who were also based at Dishforth. The crew of this aircraft, MH-K T4298, piloted by Sgt Bowyer, became POWs. They had survived an earlier incident in mid February when they had to bail out due to poor weather whilst returning from Bremen.

The raid on Kiel lasted for 5 hours and inflicted much damage. The city's electricity supply was cut off and numerous fires were started. The fire service could not cope and outside reinforcements were called in to assist. Widespread damage to industrial and naval housing was reported, also many civilians were made homeless. The eastern dock was the area that sustained the worst damage. The nightshift workers of the Deutsche Werke and the Germania Warf were sent home. Both these U-boat production yards were put out of action for several days. A fire in a naval armament depot burned for two days. German casualties for this raid were 88 killed and 184 injured. The next night saw a further raid on Kiel. This time, 160 aircraft, including 44 Whitleys, 29 Hampdens, 74 Wellingtons, one Stirling and 12 Manchesters, claimed another successful raid. Only four aircraft were lost; 2 Wellingtons, one Hampden and one Manchester. 10 aircraft from 78 Squadron bombed the primary target and returned safely. This second attack concentrated on the town of Kiel rather than the docks. Many buildings were hit including a museum, a bank and an engineering college. The gasworks was hit and the supply cut off, as again was the electricity supply. In some areas the water supply was also disrupted, making fire-fighting even more difficult. One hundred and twenty five people were killed and three hundred injured. This was believed to be the heaviest casualty list of any air raid thus far in the war. Eight thousand civilians and three hundred naval personnel were

---

[16] A Fresher crew were a crew flying on their first operations. As already stated the pilot would have already gained some operational experience whilst flying as co-pilot with a more experienced pilot.

bombed out. A large number of the civilian population left the city by as many means as possible, even on foot. It was accepted that these two consecutive raids on Kiel were probably the most successful of the war up to that time.

The next day was Wednesday April 9th, no operations or standby were ordered. The remaining ground staff, flying personnel and aircraft completed 78 Squadron's move from Dishforth to Middleton St George.

Goosepool welcomes its first flock

The first ever squeal of rubber on Goosepool's runway came on April 9th 1941. This was from a Whitley of 78 Squadron under the command of W/C B V Robinson. They had just flown the 25 miles from Dishforth. Within a short period of time the remainder of the squadron's 16 Whitley Mk Vs had landed and taxied to their dispersal points. W/C Robinson assumed command of the station and S/L D G Singleton became Station Admin Officer.

Whitley landing at Goosepool.   Photo: IWM via Geoff Hill

Wing Commander Basil Vernon Robinson was a pre-war pilot born in Gateshead. He was awarded the DFC in July 1941 whilst commanding 78 at Middleton. Later, during 1942, he served at Linton-on-Ouse, and whilst flying a 35 Squadron Halifax on a raid to Turin one night, a load of flares ignited in the aircraft. He ordered the crew to bale out and so they opened the hatch and jumped. This turned out to be fortuitous for Robinson, as the blast of air rushing into the fuselage from the open escape hatch somehow blew the fires out. Robinson managed to bring the aircraft home single-handed and landed safely. Later he was shot down whilst leading 35 Squadron during an attack on German cruisers in Brest harbour on December 18th 1941. He maintained control of the aircraft and made the first ever successful ditching of a Halifax. Having vacated the sinking aircraft he astounded his fellow crewmembers by re-entering the Halifax to retrieve his pipe. He later went on to win the DSO and rose to the rank of Group Captain. He became the Station Commander of RAF Graveley and despite his high rank, continued to fly on operations when his duties allowed. Sadly he was killed during a raid on Berlin on the night of the August 23/24th 1943 whilst flying with a novice crew. By then he had been awarded the DSO, DFC and bar and the AFC.

On the same day as 78 landed at Goosepool, a message was received from Air Vice Marshal A Conningham, the AOC of 4 Group, which read, 'Congratulations on the opening of RAF Middleton St George as an active operational station, it also welcomed 78 Squadron thereto.'

As the aircrew prepared to make themselves comfortable in their new accommodation, they were acutely aware that Goosepool had one or two less than desirable attributes. The first topic of concern was that most of the time, on operations; they had much farther to fly there and back than anyone else in Bomber Command. It should be remembered that Middleton was the most northerly of the Bomber Stations. Along with Croft, Dalton, Dishforth, Leeming, Skipton-on-Swale, Topcliffe and Wombleton, its crews had to operate within the potentially hazardous Vale of York. The second and greater point of concern was the proximity of the surrounding hills. To the east lay the Cleveland Hills, which rise to a height of 1,491 feet above sea level (Cockyne Ridge). At their closest point at Ingleby Arncliffe, the hills are only 9 miles from the airfield. For the crew of a heavily laden and under-powered bomber struggling for height, the proximity of these huge obstacles was to say the least, disconcerting. Even in good weather, a route out over the flatter terrain of Teesmouth to the north of the hills was preferred if one had to use Goosepool's northeasterly runway. It took quite a while to claw one's way up to a safe height after take-off. There was insufficient time available given the closeness of the hills so other routes had to be adopted. Night operations in the dark, in the blackout, were a very dangerous occupation for bomber crews. Just for good measure, the barrage balloons situated over ICI's complex and the docks at Middlesbrough were at first an added danger. Unwittingly placed in the paths of the bombers heading out over Teesmouth, they were later lowered whilst Middleton was operating.

Like all bomber crews during WWII, Goosepool's crews often had to let down through low cloud and fog to reach home. This prospect was made all that more dangerous as they had to avoid high ground on each side of the Vale. As stated, to the east lies the Cleveland hills, and to the west, the Yorkshire Dales and the Pennines. In the Yorkshire Dales, Great Whernside rises to a height of 2,308 feet, and this part of the Pennines Chain is only 18 miles west of Ripon. To the west of Goosepool lies Mickle Fell, height 2,691 feet. The author has had some experience of this bit of Cumulous Granite and its effect on aviation, as you will read later. The Vale is quite a small area, and the prospect of flying around in zero visibility at 200 mph, knowing, or rather not knowing, ones proximity to the high ground was to say the least, hairy. Many a tired crew, having just spent eight or nine hours dodging fighters, flak, and ice, had the extra hazard of finding base in these conditions. Many aircraft wrecks littered these hilly outcrops, sadly only minutes from home.

The Weather

As this is a history book written over a 5 year period at the turn of the new millenium (1998-2003), it is the author's view that, with the recent mutterings about global warming, a contrast between the wartime weather experienced by Goosepool's crews and their modern day civilian counterparts should be recorded. As a northeast lad, the author is only too aware of the huge North/South divide experienced in the UK up to this point in history, not only in social and financial terms, but also in the marked difference in weather patterns.

Dishforth, on a parallel with the southerly end of the Cleveland Hills, has the slight advantage of flatter ground to the southeast, providing one lets down south of the airfield. Having flown in this area for many years I have often experienced a strange weather phenomenon north of Wetherby. It seems strange that the ancients named Wetherby thus. Although spelt only slightly differently, its pronunciation is exactly the same as weather-b. Perhaps they too were acutely conscious of the weather differentials of this area. One can often draw a horizontal East/West weather line from the southeastern end of the Cleveland Hills via Dishforth to the high ground of the Yorkshire Dales and Pennines in the west. To the north of this line the visibility (Viz), even in summer, can deteriorate drastically in a short space of time, whilst to the south it may remain Gin clear.

Located in the narrowest part of mainland Britain, the North Yorkshire airfields do not enjoy the best flying weather. If one draws a line from Teesmouth in the east, to the nearest point on the West Coast, (Morecambe Bay), the furthest one can get from the sea is only 36 miles. It is interesting to note that there is nowhere in the British Isles that is greater than 70 miles from the sea. Thus, with the permanently cold North Sea on one side and the Irish Sea/Atlantic on the other, fog and haze is common. With no large landmass to dry out the wind, one may as well be in the middle of the ocean. Along with the associated weather problems caused by the merging of the Polar and southerly winds together with the Atlantic and European winds, Northern England's weather is a melting pot of Hubble, Bubble and Trouble.

Consistent good flying weather in this area was, and still is, only a dream. On a recent visit to Middleton for a reunion, a WWII Canadian Air Force veteran described Teesside's weather to me as 'nine months of winter, and three months of bad weather.' He continued, 'During your so called summer, if we woke and saw out of the window that they were using runway 06, we would often turn over and think about going back to sleep, there would probably be no Ops tonight.' He explained, 'If you couldn't see the hills in broad daylight, you sure as hell wouldn't see them flying home at 3 in the morning.' This observation by the veteran pilot, describes the effects experienced by airman, both then and now, when easterly winds blow sea fog, sea-frets and general haze inland over Teesmouth, and on towards the airfield. Farewell good visibility. His colleague went further, and chirped in, 'If Britain has the backside of the world's weather, and it does, Darlington is the sphincter. On our way home we always knew where to find the place, we just looked for the blackest cloud, and headed for it and there it was, right underneath.'

This reminded me of the time I had been watching Billy Connolly on TV. During the show he talked about the time he had returned to England from his home in California, where he now lives. Apart from coming for a holiday, the main reason for his trip was to visit Glasgow, and show his young kids (who were born and raised in California) where Daddy was born. He hired a car at Heathrow, and headed north up the A1 to Scotland. As they were bypassing Darlington, his children sitting in the back of the car, looked out and asked, ' Daddy! Why is the sky so low?'

During the year 2000, private pilots operating from Teesside Airport had to wait until June 15th before seeing the real start of the summer. There were a few days previously when the deckchair brigade could have got a tan of sorts, but in the air the visibility was severely curtailed by a bad dose of the hazes. When the Viz was ok, strong winds or incessant rain took over. The winter gives the best visibility by far in the northeast, if one can stand the cold. During the summer, some local pilots have learned the trick of sneaking a flight in during the early morning, before the sun can boil up the haze and turbulence. Another good time to fly is after about 7pm, when hopefully it all calms down again, but not always. The only problem is that in the evening in the summer, and from 15:00 hours onwards during the winter, the blinding sun (270° magnetic) sometimes sits low, virtually on the end of the main East/West runway (230°). This causes a large dose of the squints for pilots on final approach, despite a good pair of Ray Bans.

Spring 2000 supplied some atrocious weather for the people of the Northeast. April was the wettest since weather records were started in the early part of the 19th century, the recorded rainfall being shown as 142 mm, 219% of the average. May turned out to be similar. On Sunday June 4th, due to flooding, the A1 Motorway at Catterick was closed to traffic. I was in the huge queue of cars that ground to a halt a mile north of Scotch Corner. One had to take a long and precarious detour around Middleton Tyas and Scorton to regain the A1 Southbound at Leeming. That day, some parts of Bishop Auckland to the west of Darlington were under 8 feet of water. Croft and Neasham, only 5 miles from the airfield, were flooded up to a height of 6 feet. To my recollection, this was the first time that the main arterial motorway of Britain had been closed by flooding.

The rain persisted month on month, there was no let up from the rain until winter arrived. 2000 broke all records for floods and rain. Flying was a joke for most of the time. Summer 2001 was dryer and had the weather presenters and newspaper headlines raving over several heat waves in the South. During one such period, which was typical, London and the South enjoyed 30°; during the same period Darlington at best only reached 18°. It is not the fact that the airfield is in the North, which causes the problem. In fact, if one looks at the map, it sits near the centre of the British landmass. The most northern tip of mainland Scotland is 290 miles north of Middleton St George, as the crow flies. Lands End lies 349 miles to the south (same crow), a difference of only 59 miles. For several days in mid May, although it is located 120 miles to the north of Teesside, Edinburgh had temperatures of 22° C. At the same time, Ireland had the same temperature, London recorded 26° C, Darlington however had only 8° C.

Even Moscow was enjoying 30° C at that time. So, as can be seen, latitude and longitude have little to do with the Northeast's weather. The culprit is most definitely the Cold - North - Sea. The people of Teesside have a question for the scientists who are predicting global warming - when? WHEN?

The normal ploy of the northeastern winds is to strike at Teesmouth and be funneled into the Vale of York between the Cleveland Hills and the Pennines, which acts as a sump. Bagby airfield is situated at the bottom of the Cleveland Hills near Thirsk. If the visibility is poor at Teesside, one usually expects the weather (and Viz) to improve dramatically south of this point. The good people of Darlington and Teesside are often oblivious to the fact that during the summer, the weather (and sunshine) is usually much better almost everywhere else in the UK. To the non-aviator the weather is secondary, unless it spoils the barbecue. It often goes unnoticed and the effect of the poor Teesside weather on the pilot is somewhat irrelevant to most earthbound types. During the war, returning aircrew were able to reach airfields as close as Leeming (15 miles) and even Croft (6 miles), but be unable to find Goosepool.

During wartime, the Blackout and Teesside's heavy industry often contributed to a distinct lack of visibility. Chimneys, belching out thick black smoke, often turned fog into Smog. This problem persisted well into the 1970s, when smokeless zones became effective. ICI, placed near the coast between Middlesbrough and Billingham, has often been blamed for contributing to Teesside's bad weather. During its hey-day ICI employed up to 25,000 people, its myriad of chimneys belching smoke and steam skywards. During the 60s, after the opening of Teesside Airport, we took some photographs one lovely July day, from a flying club aircraft flying at 8,000 feet. The photos showed three large chimneys at ICI, from which smoke emanated. All three sets of smoke fanned out and amalgamated to the west of the plant to completely cover Darlington and beyond. It was a lovely cloudless hot summer's day, but for the people to the west of Teesmouth it was dull and overcast. That day, the weathermen spoke of a heatwave for everyone in the British Isles. Today things are much better, but several large gas fired generating plants can sometimes cause their exhausts of steam to form clouds above the complex, which, when the conditions are right, form into huge cloud masses which can blow westwards. These man-made sun-blockers often seem to affect Darlington's and Bishop Auckland's chances of a sunny day. Surprisingly enough however, sunny conditions can sometimes be found at points east of Hartburn, which seems to be a mini weatherpoint for Teesside. Places like Ingleby Barwick, Stockton, Middlesbrough and Hartlepool can enjoy some lovely summer days when the area stretching from the Dales to the west of Darlington and across to Hartburn can be having the most atrocious weather.

The weather in the northeast during the summer of 2001 was a non-starter. From May 1st to the end of September, the number of dawn to dust cloud-free days totalled zero. There were a few hot and sunny days but always with a covering of scattered clouds and/or haze. It is an indictment on the region that if the clouds and haze ever roll away, and a blue-sky hot and sunny weather trend should ever descend over the northeast for more than two days in a row, newspaper banner headlines would certainly be pre-occupied with the unusual nature of it all, and proclaim a heatwave.

2002 was identical to 2001, with the amazing exception of all of April being warm and sunny, unusually so for this time of the year. It was the best spring that anyone could remember for many a decade, warm bright sunny days that went on for weeks. As soon as the last days of April approached and the sun began to get a bit of bite in it, everything changed. Each morning one was encouraged out of bed with sunshine from the early hours until 9am, by which time the cloud had bubbled up and it was goodbye sky, hello cloud cover. 2002 represented the worst year for the airfield's flying clubs. In terms of GA flying hours lost to the weather, it has, to date, no parallel. June and July developed into days of partial and total cloud cover, it rained most nights and quite a lot of days too.

As far as the summer was concerned, by August, Darlington had enjoyed only one dawn to dusk blue sky and sun day. There were a few partially sunny days, with the cloud bubbling up to represent 25-75% coverage. Many warm days were hazy, with up to 75%+ humidity. They were horribly muggy, causing the smallest of exertions to bathe one in sweat; the type of conditions formerly experienced only by tropical countries. August began with a whole month's average rainfall falling in a single night, the most rainfall in a single day since records began. The monsoon style showers were so heavy that traffic was brought to a virtual standstill, vehicle windscreen wipers being inundated. One man died when he was washed away at Durham. Parts of Durham and North Yorkshire were under several feet of water; some villages were completely flooded, and cut off to motor transport for several days (yes, in August?).

The cloud cover persisted, until the 12th of the month, with very little blue sky or sun, while in other parts of the country, summer continued. As it turned out, most of the remainder of August/ September was short on sunlight, as cloud blanketed Darlington. By the 26th, with the onset of wind and rain, it was realised that summer 2002 was well and truly over, and that it would be another 8 months before one was likely to feel the hot sun on one's face again. After that, there was only cloud and unprecedented amounts of rain, which persisted right through to January 2003. One counted the clear days on one hand. If Middleton's wartime bomber crews had encountered the kind of weather endured in the Teesside area during 2002, they would have only been able to carry out a fraction of the raids they did during the war.

During the first week in January 2003 a colleague flew to Iceland for a one day shopping trip. On departure the temperature at Teesside Airport was -1°, on arrival in Iceland (950 miles to the N/N/E) a short time later, it was +8°. Some of the Icelanders on the south of the island said that they have not had snow for over 3 years, due to global warming.

The last comment on Darlington's summers I will leave to Croft's Operational Record Book. The entry for August 25th 1943 reads 'The WAAFs are complaining that the very damp weather is taking the curl out of their hair.'

After it opened on March 26th 1944, Carnaby Airfield, near the seaside town of Bridlington on the Yorkshire coast, became a haven for many returning aircraft that were low on fuel, damaged, or had simply become lost in the fog. With a 9,000ft long and 750ft wide extra large emergency runway, this airfield saved many lives. It even had 1,500-foot grass covered undershoot / overshoot extensions at each end.

Located just to the south of Bridlington, RAF Carnaby was equipped with FIDO (Fog Investigation and Dispersal Operation) as it was called during the war. Burning petrol in channels alongside the runway dispersed fog and providing visibility for pilots to land. Carnaby's Bitumen runway offered hope to countless fog-bound airmen. As it was only an emergency landing ground, like its other two sisters at Woodbridge, Suffolk and Manston, (now Kent International Airport). Carnaby had no real accommodation for large numbers of aircrew. It was simply a place to land when the excrement hit the rotary cooling device. Carnaby's runway is there today, used by Bridlington Council. Its size from the air is still an awesome sight.

Carnaby's massive runway shown heading NE. Ahead and to the left can be seen Bridlington Bay   Photo: PRO AIR 24/286

CHAPTER FOUR

Reformation of 76
Halifax

Reformation of 76

About the time that 78 were packing their bags for the move to Goosepool, Squadron Leader Tom Sawyer, who had already completed 20 operations with 10 Squadron at Leeming (better known as shiny 10), heard that he was posted. His new home was to be with 35 Squadron at Linton-on-Ouse, a bomber airfield northwest of York. Tom was also accompanied by four of the most experienced crews from 10 Squadron who, like him, were to convert onto the Halifax.

At Linton, 35 was under the command of Wing Commander Willie Tait, who would come to fame later in the war with 617, the Dambusters' Squadron. At this time Willie Tait had already acquired a DSO and a DFC; he later went on to be the only person to be awarded the DSO four times and he also ended up with two DFCs. Later in the war Tait would lead 617 Squadron in the famous raid to sink the Tirpitz. 35 had been at Linton since December 1940, having been the first unit to convert onto the Handley Page Halifax Mk 1 in November of that year.

At Linton-on-Ouse, Willie Tait gave Tom Sawyer his first dual circuits and bumps on the Halifax. After some practice, Tom was able, along with Willie and Flight Lieutenant Lane, to convert the rest of the new pilots onto the Halifax. Tom and the other crews from 10 Squadron became C Flight of 35 whilst converting onto the new type. On April 12th 1941, orders were received to form a new squadron, and so C Flight of 35 now became the nucleus of a re-formed 76 Squadron.

76 B Squadron had been originally re-formed at Finningley, South Yorkshire on April 10th 1937 as a heavy bomber squadron. Under the command of Wing Commander E J George, the squadron consisted of personnel from B Flight of 7 B Squadron. On its strength the squadron had 5 officers, 6 airman pilots and 36 airmen. Its aircraft consisted of 4 Vickers Wellesleys, general-purpose medium bombers. The Squadron was the first to be equipped with the Wellesleys.

June 26th of that year saw a flight of 5 aircraft from the squadron take part in the set piece of the RAF display at Hendon. Squadron strength by August 31st had grown to 11 officers, 37 airman and 12 aircraft. It was with some irony that, in connection with the visit of a German mission to Mildenhall on October 19th 1937, a fly-past of new types was arranged. Six aircraft from 76 Squadron were selected to take part. Despite all the practices, which were carried out, the formation was unable to take its place in the program owing to bad weather conditions. They were attached to 5 Group at Finningley, the Squadron Commander being Wing Commander D S Allen, with P/O H V Matthews as Adjutant. October 23rd saw 76 with its Handley Page Hampdens and Avro Ansons move to Upper Heyford on attachment to HQ 6 Group as a group pool training squadron for 5 Group. The squadron was reorganized and A Flight was merged with B Flight to form a flying flight and a maintenance flight. During April 1940 the squadron's nomenclature disappeared as it was absorbed into 16 OTU.

Now, with their rebirth at Linton in April 1941, 76 became only the second unit of Bomber Command to operate the Halifax. Soon 'The Squadron' began working up to operational standards as more experienced crews arrived.

Halifax

During 1935 Specification B1/35 was issued to aircraft manufacturers in a bid to create a replacement for the Whitley. Along with other British plane makers, Handley Page (HP) submitted their design to fulfil this specification. Their particular offering was better known to Handley Page employees as the HP 55. This aircraft followed the trend of their contemporaries and had two power plants. HP favored the Bristol Hercules engines although Merlin and Vulture engines were also considered. Unfortunately the contract was awarded to Vickers for the Warwick, which became the predecessor to the Wellington.

During the build up of the RAF during 1936, the possibility of acquiring four engined bombers was considered. The extra two engines meant greater lifting power and therefore a larger bomb-load. This was more cost effective, as for the same number of sorties one could deliver more bomb tonnage onto the target. To this end, bomber specifications from the Air Ministry abounded. Short Brothers developed the Stirling from specification B12/36, the first four-engined heavy bomber to enter service with Bomber Command. Of revolutionary design, initially this aircraft had great potential. Unfortunately, due to no fault of Short Brothers, the Air Ministry specifications of the time severely restricted the wingspan of bomber aircraft to less than 100 feet. The reason for this requirement was to allow the bombers to pass through the RAF's standard 100-foot hangar doors for servicing. The designers had envisaged a much larger wingspan for the Stirling. This would have allowed a greater bomb load, along with a higher service ceiling. Clipping the Stirling's wings was to cost many lives, and relegate this potentially fine aircraft to third place, behind the Halifax and Lancaster.

The ill-fated Avro Type 679, better known as the Manchester, came about from P13/36, as did Handley Page's offering, which became the HP 56. Subsequently a development contract for the ill-fated Manchester was granted to Avro. Handley Page was also awarded a contract on April 30th 1937; this was for two prototypes of the HP 56. Despite their misgivings, both Avro and Handley Page were requested to install Rolls Royce Vulture engines in both these aircraft. It soon became apparent that producing enough Vulture engines to satisfy the requirements of both manufacturers could not be achieved. Along with this, the engine was slow in realizing its full power requirement. Reliability, too, was giving much cause for concern. Therefore on the September 3rd of that year, Handley Page was requested to produce two prototypes to be fitted with four Rolls Royce Merlins. This development became the HP 57, later to be known as the Halifax.

To accommodate the two extra engines, the wingspan was increased from 88 feet to 98 foot 8 inches. This was also to give the Halifax a better service ceiling. Handley Page would have preferred an even larger wingspan but they too were restricted by the 100-foot hangar door problem. The Halifax prototype was made at Cricklewood and fitted with 1,145hp Rolls Royce Merlin X engines and De-Havilland VP propellers. Given the choice, Handley Page would have fitted radial engines. Their choice would have been the Hercules HE 65M, which used 100 Octane fuel. Instead they were requested by the Air Ministry to utilise the Merlin after running tests with the less powerful 87 Octane Hercules 15M. This gave the Halifax a longer range but reduced its speed. Major J Cords flew the first (unarmed) prototype, L7244, from RAF Bicester on October 25th 1939. The Halifax had been awarded a production contract in January of the same year.

The second (armed) prototype flew on August 17th 1940. The Halifax's test program began at Boscombe Down in October 1940. Two prototypes, L7244 (unarmed) and L7245 (armed), along with the first production aircraft, L9485, that first flew on the 11th were used in extensive testing of the type. Such was the urgency to get the Halifax into service that a month later, on November 5th, 35 Squadron was reformed under 4 Group to convert onto the new type. Commanded by W/C R W P Collings, 35 wasted no time. On the 13th, they collected their first Halifax from the factory and flew it to Boscombe Down to begin training.

During the war the Halifax was manufactured by an organization called the Halifax Group. This consisted of Handley Page, English Electric and The London Aircraft Production Group, which included Chrysler Motors, Duple Bodies and Motors, Express Motor and Body Works, Park Royal Coach Works, the London Passenger Transport Board, Rootes Securities and the Halifax Group was spread over 40 sites; they also utilized 600 sub-contracting during a normal working day, one Halifax left the production line every

Halifax Mk 1. The letters MP denote this aircraft as belonging to 76 squadron.
The letter L denotes the individual aircraft identification
Photo: IWM via Geoff Hill

The Mk 1 Halifax had a Boulton Paul rear turret fitted with four .303 Browning machine guns, there were also two in the front turret. To complete the armament package, two waist gunners, one each side, equipped with Vickers VGOs were added in the rear fuselage forward of the tailplane.

The first operation to be carried out by the Halifax was on the night of March 10/11th 1941. On this raid, six 35 Squadron Halifaxes and eight Blenheims attacked Le Havre. So new (and secret) was the Halifax, that on their return to England the crew of TL-F L9489 were accidentally shot down by an RAF Beaufighter. Five crewmembers were killed, only the pilot S/L Gilchrist and the engineer Sgt Aedy survived. The Halifax had been mistaken for an enemy bomber. The existence of the Halifax was not made public until July of 1941. After completing 84 Mk 1s, work started on the Mk II, the first being L9609. The engines were upgraded to the Merlin XX for greater power.

Halifax Mk 1

Wingspan	98ft 8 in (30.12m)
Length	71ft 1in (21.36m)
Height	20ft 9in (6.33m)
Engines	4 Rolls Royce 1,220 hp Merlin X (series 3)
Weight	Empty 34,000 -lbs (series 1) and 35,000 -lbs (series 2/3)
	Loaded 55,000 -lbs (series 1) and 60,000 -lbs (series 2/3)
Service Ceiling	18,000 feet
Range	1,860 miles
Crew	7
Max Bomb-load	13,000 -lbs (5,890kg)
Fuel load	2.243 Gals (12,336 ltrs)
Max Speed	255 mph (426 km/ph) at 7,000 ft (5,300m)
Cruising speed	195 mph
Number built	84

The Boulton Paul E turret equipped many of Bomber Command's heavy bombers   Photo: IWM via Geoff Hill

To this new version of the Halifax came the addition of a Boulton Paul C Mk II mid-upper turret. This was fitted with two .303 Brownings, the waist guns being deleted. Unfortunately the extra weight and aerodynamic drag created by this overlarge mid-upper turret cancelled out any power advantage.

The early Halifaxes had smaller and dissimilar shaped rudders to later marks. If the aircraft was flown below 120 mph and the rudders were taken beyond a certain point in their travel, for example whilst taking evasive action, they could stall and become locked over by the airflow causing the aircraft to drop its nose and flip over into an uncontrollable spin. Another problem was that the rudders were not very effective during the take off run.

The turret and the triangular shape of the rudders were identified as one of the contributory factors. Eventually the rudders were modified to a squarer D shaped profile with increased area. The Halifax had also collected quite a lot of extra weighty and drag inducing bits and pieces up to this stage. These included large exhaust shrouds and a rough Matt Black paint finish that surprisingly created lots of drag. The little used nose turret was removed and replaced with a streamlined Perspex nose with provision for a single VGO.

Norman Frankish came from Middlesbrough. At 19, he had volunteered to join the RAF. Late in 1940 he was posted to Padgate. He had no sooner arrived there, when, 48 hours later; he was on his way to Blackpool and the comforts of a seaside landlady's boarding house. Like many an RAF recruit early in the war, he learned his basic drill and square bashing at a pre-war holiday resort where accommodation was readily available. When his basic training was over, he left Blackpool and travelled to Kirkham, near Preston, for his trade training as a flight mechanic. Once his training was over he was posted in April 1941 to 35 Squadron at Linton-on-Ouse in Yorkshire, Norman was put to work in the Halifax R and I hangar[17]. As a rookie, Norman was used as a gofer. He was not entrusted with major tasks until he became more *au fait* with the way things were done. As C Flight broke its umbilical with 35 and became an embryonic squadron in its own right, Norman became one of the first groundcrew members of the reformed 76.

---

[17] Repair and Inspection

CHAPTER FIVE
Goosepool War Diaries 1941

Goosepool War Diaries April 1941
May 1941
June 1941-76 on the move
Ops June 1941
Operation Sunrise
78 Squadron - July 1941
Sgt Hafferden
Manoeuvres July 1941
76 Squadron - August 1941
78 Squadron - August 1941
September 1941
October 1941
Sgt Roland Whitehorn
78 arrive at Croft
November 1941
The Bats arrive
December 1941

Goosepool War Diaries April 1941

As 78 settled into life at their new station they didn't waste any time. Although no operations or standbys were detailed, the Squadron ORB (operations record book) indicated that on April 11th they were ready for operations. The next night, Sgt W G Rogers was detailed to fly Whitley Z6490 on operations to Ostend. His Fresher crew consisted of Sgt R W Bird second pilot, Sgt J W R Boggis 1st WOP/AG, Sgt C F Cook 2nd WOP/AG, and Sgt T Hall tail gunner. However, due to adverse weather conditions in the target area, this operation was later cancelled. On April 14th, F/L W R Williams assumed command of 78 Squadron's A Flight, his Vice being S/L R K Wildly DFC. On the same day the first operation from Goosepool took place. Eight aircraft from 78 were detailed for a raid on Mannheim. Later this order was amended and the main target was changed to German cruisers in Brest harbour. Although 8 Whitleys were detailed, only 7 attacked. Due to engine trouble, one aircraft, flown by Sgt Alcock, abandoned and returned after 90 minutes flying. The remainder, led by F/L G M Lawrence, experienced 4-6/10ths cloud cover over the target area. Sgt Marshall dropped three sticks of bombs in the target area from a height of 12,000 feet. Due to the cloud cover, flak and heavy concentrations of searchlights, the results of the bombing were not observed. Ground haze added to the poor visibility and Sgt Davies's crew experienced similar conditions. Dropping two sticks of bombs across the docks from 14,000 feet they observed light flak up to 13,000 feet. The crews of the aircraft flown by Sergeants Ennis, Stobbs, Freas and Dunlop all carried out similar attacks with similar results. All landed safely back at Middleton, each having been airborne for over seven and half-hours.

That night 78 had formed part of a total of 20 Whitleys, along with 46 Wellingtons, 25 Hampdens and 3 Stirlings from other squadrons. Bombing was poor because of thick cloud, but at least there were no losses from this group of aircraft. Whilst this raid was taking place, 16 Blenheims bombed Leiden and Haalem power stations on the Dutch coast. A further 14 Blenheims were dispatched on shipping patrols. A convoy off the coast of Holland was bombed with the loss of one Blenheim. This aircraft, R2784 of 21 squadron, took off from Watton at 15:14 and crashed 1 hour 31 minutes later at Oegstgeest, Holland, 2 km N/W of Leiden. The crew, consisting of Sgts E Newhouse, V A Cobb and J M C Bougin are all buried at Oegstgeest cemetery.

When 78 arrived at Goosepool there was still much constructional activity going on. A week or so after the arrival of the first aircraft, the contractors began to complain about building materials going missing. The main complaints came from the firm responsible for laying the drains. Large numbers of 4-inch drainpipes could not be accounted for. Security was tightened up in respect to people leaving the camp. In an attempt to solve the mystery, the guardroom carried out random checks on vehicles leaving the airfield. Nothing was found but still the drainpipes continued to disappear. Meanwhile, 78 Squadron's crews during their nights off would go into the local pubs for a few well-earned pints. At the end of the night they would hang on to a few empty beer bottles and bring them back to camp. The bottles would be safely kept until a raid was planned and then smuggled into their aircraft. The idea was that these bottles would be thrown out of the aircraft whilst over enemy territory on the way to the target. The high pitched scream created by these missiles would, it was hoped, put off the German's delicate sound locators. A spin-off was that when dropped out of the aircraft's flare chute, the bottles sounded just like falling bombs. This, it was hoped, would demoralise the enemy population and have them running for the shelters. The bottles made a fantastic din as they fell to Earth, but evidently not as fantastic as 4-inch drain pipes. Eventually someone on high found out what was happening to the drainpipes and the practice was stopped. The crews however, continued to distribute their empty beer bottles liberally around the Fatherland.

On April 15th, Group Captain T C (Tommy) Traill OBE DFC arrived from Bomber Command to assume command of RAF Middleton St George. He was a very popular commander and well thought of by all ranks. Kind and considerate, he took great interest in the wellbeing of aircrew and ground staff alike. When he arrived, the airfield was nothing more than a building site. As the Whitleys moved around the airfield there was precious little clearance between building materials stored close to the edges of the taxiways and runways and the bottom of their tailplanes.

April 16th saw the continuation of Ops as the squadron dispatched 9 Whitleys on operations. These aircraft under the command of F/L G M Lawrence were first detailed for a raid to Berlin, but at 16:50 an order was received changing the target to Bremen. The official report stated that only six aircraft bombed Bremen as three had abandoned this target due to mechanical problems. One of these attacked its alternate, Oldenburg, whilst another bombed Wilhelmshaven and the third bombed an airfield on the Friesian Island of Texel. All returned safely.

F/L Lawrence reached Bremen and despite thick ground haze attacked the primary target from 12,000 feet. This attack resulted in a fire being started, this was observed by the second pilot Sgt Gibson and the rear gunner Sgt Emmett. At de-briefing the observer Sgt Wood and wireless operator Sgt Chadwick reported that accurate searchlight and flak activity prevailed in the target area. Sgt Blackwell flying Z6484 had been over Oldenburg when he experienced engine failure. His second pilot Sgt Marks had jettisoned their bomb load on the town. As they were leaving the area it was realised that a 500-lb bomb had hung up in the bomb bay. Sgt Blackburn decided that failed engine or no, they would visit Bremen after all and present the original target with the offending bomb. Having shaken off the unwanted ironmongery, he returned to Middleton and landed safely at 05:15.

Sgt Dunlop in Z6435 experienced Exactor trouble (Brand name of remote feathering control system) and it was his aircraft that had abandoned the operation and bombed Wilhelmshaven. Second pilot Sgt R W Bird reported at de-briefing that they were lucky to make it back. This was due to the fact that the oil temperature gauges for both engines had been off the clock. Sgt Freas was running in for the target when two fighter flares were dropped in front of their Whitley. One lit 4,000 yards ahead of them whilst the other ignited 3,000 feet above and ahead of them. Fortunately these were avoided by a bit of skilful flying from Sgt Freas. Despite the heavy flak and searchlights they went on to bomb the primary, where fires were observed resulting from their attack. Having bombed Bremen with two sticks of HE and incendiaries, Sgt Alcock in Z6492 and his second pilot Sgt Hatcher observed that six separate fires were started. Rear gunner Sgt Ward reported that later, whilst they were vacating the target area, three of these exploded.

An enemy fighter was seen approaching them but fortunately they managed to lose it. Sgt H J Davies and his crew in Z 6555 were not able to locate Bremen so Texel aerodrome became their target. The airfield was bombed from a height of 12,500 feet. Second pilot P/O Lowry, observer Sgt R A Gibson and rear gunner Sgt W H Hunt observed that the bomb bursts straddled the flarepath and that two fires were started. Despite the ground haze the weather was fairly good with some searchlights operating in the vicinity of the airfield. Enemy fighters were observed in the area, one in particular was seen circling the runway. Fortunately none of these aircraft attacked the Whitley.

The remaining Whitleys, flown by Sgt Marshall, Sgt Lewin and Sgt Ennis, all bombed Bremen with similar results. Four Whitleys from Middleton were sent on the 17th to two separate aiming points in Berlin, but haze prevented concentrated bombing. Only two bombed the primary target whilst one attacked Hannover and Cuxhaven, and another returned early due to mechanical problems.

S/L J (Jock) Mercer in Z6560 led the raid but did not reach the target due to the fact that both his engines failed to develop full power. Despite the poor visibility he was able to drop one stick of bombs on Hannover and a second on Cuxhaven. Bursts were observed by the rear gunner P/O R T Hunter, in spite of the intense flak and searchlight activity. Incendiaries were seen starting small fires by his second pilot P/O J C McWaters and observer P/O J L Wagland. F/L G K Williams in Z6483 attacked Berlin from 12,000 feet. Second pilot Sgt H Gibson reported that their bombs started many fires. An enemy nightfighter was seen stalking the Whitley by the tail gunner Sgt V M Coull. He instantly gave the order to corkscrew and they managed to give the fighter the slip. Sgt P Alcock in Z6492 had a spot of bad luck, as when outbound to the enemy coast, the contents gauges of the fuselage auxiliary fuel tanks showed only 20 gallons in each tank. The Whitley was turned for base and the bomb load was jettisoned safe[18] out to sea, 60 miles east of Whitby.

For P/O A E Lewin and the crew of Whitley Z6493 the raid was considered straight forward. On the way to the target, they saw the demise of another squadron's aircraft as it was shot down in the vicinity of Hamburg. They reached Berlin and bombed from 12,000 feet. However, although their incendiaries were seen to start two large fires, the results of their HE (High Explosive) bomb hits were not observed.

Of the 50 Wellingtons, 39 Hampdens, 28 Whitleys and 1 Stirling taking part, 5 Whitleys from other squadrons, 2 Hampdens and 1 Wellington were lost, along with the 3 Wellingtons that failed to return from a second raid to Cologne. This total of 11 aircraft posted missing represented the largest number of aircraft lost during night operations thus far in the war.

Three nights later a fresher crew in Z4147, flown by P/O T C Richards, was sent to a nursery target at Rotterdam to bomb the oil storage depot. It joined 17 Wellingtons and 7 Whitleys sent from other squadrons. As the cloud cover extended to 8,000 feet, Richards dived down from 10,000 feet to get below the cloud before P/O D Lake released the bombs. Good strikes on the oil storage tanks were observed and a large concentration of fires were started. The Whitley returned and landed safely at 02:45.

For a raid to Brest on the night of the 23rd, 9 aircraft were dispatched by 78. Joining 16 Whitleys, 30 Wellingtons, 10 Hampdens and 2 Stirlings from other squadrons, they bombed the Scharnhorst and Gneisenau which were sitting in the harbour. Hits on these two capital ships were claimed but could not be confirmed as low cloud and haze joined with the heavy concentrations of searchlights. Again the old favourites of Mercer, Lewin, Richards, Freas, Dunlop, Alcock, Davies, Marshall and Blackwell took part in this raid.

The next evening, 78 sent one aircraft, Z6483, to Wilhelmshaven; here it joined 8 Whitleys sent by other squadrons. A new name entered into the battle order at Middleton, Sgt Hatcher. Bombing from 16,000 feet in a glide attack, the second pilot Sgt R W Bird and observer Sgt H Buttell saw five bursts in the target area causing one dull red fire. The Whitley's incendiaries started small fires but the tail gunner Sgt E C Gurmin reported that they were soon extinguished. The weather over the target had been perfect with no cloud cover.

The following night a further three fresher crews were dispatched to Bremerhaven. Two of these aircraft bombed the primary (Harry Drummond in Z6577 and Sgt Marks in Z6555). The third aircraft, flown by P/O J C McWatter, attacked Wilhelmshaven. All returned safely to Middleton. 12 aircraft of 78 Squadron were detailed on the 26th to attack Hamburg. However, due to adverse weather over the target area at 20:17 the stand down order was given and the operation cancelled. The next night 8 operational and 4 fresher crews were briefed for Ops but again the weather, this time over England, prevented their departure.

The final operation for 78 during their first month at Middleton came on the 29th, and involved 10 operational and 4 fresher crews. Originally the primary for the operational crews was Hamburg but it was subsequently changed to Mannheim. The target for the freshman was Rotterdam. Only eight operational crews took off for Mannheim, as one was accidentally damaged and unable to start. The other was grounded when the captain fell ill. Of the operational aircraft, 7 bombed their primary target, Mannheim, with one abandoning operation due to bad weather. P/O Richards reported that the IFF[19] equipment in his aircraft was switched on and off whilst over the target. At the time as it was thought that by so doing the German Ant-aircraft radar could be adversely affected. However, on this occasion, there were no observable results. All crews reported accurate searchlight and flak concentrations in the target area.

Of the freshman, three abandoned operations due to adverse weather condition over the target. One of these aircraft was flown by Sgt Hatcher who reported that he could not identify his target, Rotterdam, as there was 9/10ths cloud cover. One aircraft, flown by Harry Drummond, successfully attacked Rotterdam. On their return, he and his crew stated that their tail gunner, SGT F L Fewkes, could see their fires 40 miles away. They and the operational crew, who had abandoned their operation, jettisoned their bombs safe in the sea. Only one aircraft failed to return to Middleton. However this Whitley had put down at Waddington and the crew was safe. April had been kind to 78, as no aircraft were lost that month.

[18] Unfused

[19] Identification, "Friend or Foe"

May 1941

May 3rd 1941 dawned warm and sunny. On hearing that Ops were on for that night, Sgt L Hatcher and his crew walked out across the airfield to test their Whitley, Z6483. Briefing was not until late in the afternoon, so some of the time was passed playing snooker in the Sergeants' Mess. At briefing, Cologne was revealed as the target. After the C/O and the Intelligence Officer had passed their 'Gen' it was the turn of the civilian Met man. He painted an optimistic picture of the weather to and from the target.

Middleton's station headquarters (SHQ) behind which can be seen the water tower. The first floor windows show the main briefing room   Photo: Author

Armourers prepare to bomb up a Whitley V   Photo: IWM CH.227

They took off at 20:45 and set course for the 940-mile round-trip. As the Whitley gained height, Sgt Hatcher turned the laden bomber onto 164°, the course that would take them the 141 miles to Peterborough, their first turning point. On reaching Peterborough 66 minutes later, the navigator (Nav) gave a course change that would take them directly to the coast. ' Steer 114 skip', called Sgt Shandos. The Whitley banked to port until the compass swung around to the new heading.

Depending on what the wind did to them, their next leg to Aldeburgh on the Suffolk Coast would cover 83 miles and take 28 minutes. Once out to sea, Sgt Hatcher lifted his right hand to the front of his oxygen mask and flicked the intercom switch, 'Pilot to gunners, test your guns.' A few seconds later his earphones crackled into life, it was the tail gunner, 'Rear turret ok Skip'. The 1st WOP/AG came forward from his radio position. The second pilot tried the best he could to move out of his way, after folding up his retractable foot rest. The gunner squeezed past him and ducked below the right hand side of the instrument panel and slid down into the nose. Soon after came the sound of the front turret as he opened fire. 'Front gunner to captain, front guns ok Skipper', came a different voice in the crew's earphones.

Now far out over the North Sea, they began to curse the Met man; as the night developed, so did the cloud. Having crossed the enemy coast at the Dutch Island of Schouwen, the Whitley's route took them on to Cologne. As there wasn't the usual flak, the rear gunner Sgt Hall was told to keep a good lookout for fighters, as the flak gunners were quiet for some reason. With nine/tenths cloud cover over the target area, bombing was poor. Although 11 people on the ground were killed and 14 injured, the Germans recorded that 8 to 10 bomb loads were observed, with only minor damage to property being sustained. It is unclear if the Whitley's bomb aimer was one of the few to hit the target, as the heavy cloud prevented accurate identification of the bomb-bursts.

Shortly after leaving the target area for the long flight home, it became apparent that the W/T equipment in the aircraft had failed. Along with this and the poor weather, the flight home was made that much more difficult by a change in the forecast wind direction. Once over the Continent, there was little chance to gain accurate wind vectors, and under these circumstances crews had to rely on a variety of tenuous clues, such as smoke. At this stage in the war, navigators still relied mainly on DR[20]. This employed the Dalton computer, carried by each navigator. This was, and still is, nothing more than a round disc of Perspex, which one rotates over a graticule of drift lines to show the effects of the wind on one's course. This was all very well, providing you knew the correct wind direction and speed in the first place. This was not an easy task over enemy territory. For some strange reason, the Germans were not very accommodating in this regard, and at the time did not offer the Air Traffic Information Service to British airmen that they do today. And so, with a combination of drift error, bad visibility and with no W/T set to give navigational assistance, they became unsure of their position. Having drifted many miles off course, the Whitley; having used up all of its fuel, crashed near Leominster, Herefordshire, after the crew abandoned the aircraft.

The Squadron records indicate that this, the first ever aircraft to be lost on operations from Middleton St George, came down without injury to the crew. Sergeant Hatcher was later commissioned and reached the rank of Squadron Leader, gaining a DFC and an AFM. Sadly he died on December 22nd 1944 whilst flying a Lancaster of 83 Squadron. Taking off at 16:36 from Coningsby, he and his crew were diverted to Matheringham on their return from a raid on Politz, as the weather at base was not good. Unfortunately the weather conditions at the alternative airfield were just as bad, and whilst descending to land through the fog, the Lancaster crashed at 02:46. Only one crewmember, F/L Ingmire survived the crash. S/L Hatcher is buried in his hometown of Woolwich.

If you take the straight line distance from MSG to Cologne (430 miles), the return trip from Cologne to Leominster (425 miles) and compute this with the time taken (9 hours 45 minutes), less the time on target, say 20 minutes. The result is an average ground-speed of 92 mph. Given that on a good day the maximum airspeed of an unloaded Whitley V was 230 mph, and the maximum cruising airspeed was about 210 mph, one could be forgiven for asking why average operational ground-speeds could be as low as 92 mph. Little wonder that some Whitley operations took over 10 hours to complete.

In reality a fully loaded aircraft complete with 700 gallons of fuel and a load of bombs would probably have an indicated cruising airspeed of no more than 125/135 mph. This was a more acceptable and economical airspeed. To open the throttles further may indeed give a higher indicated airspeed, but an increase in engine power does not come cheap and the aircraft would then suffer from much greater and disproportionate fuel consumption figures. The aircraft then may not have had enough fuel to get home. No two aircraft are exactly the same. Many Whitleys were clapped out flying wreaks and would have been even slower than 125/135 mph. If the airspeed indicator was showing 130 mph and the aircraft was flying into a 30 mph headwind, its speed over the ground would only be 100 mph. Only the ground-speed decided how long the trip would take, not what was shown on the airspeed indicator on the pilot's instrument panel.

Often on long trips, fuel conservation was the number one priority over speed. The crews were given enough fuel for the trip, plus 200 gallons for a reserve. One could not anticipate the many possible pitfalls awaiting one in the dark. These were myriad. Flak could puncture one or more tanks, leaking much precious petrol. Under these circumstances the crew could operate the transfer cocks and pump some of the leaking fuel to other tanks, if they were available to receive it. Unexpected diversions due to bad weather at base were yet another unknown, along with getting lost.

One must remember that flights were seldom in a straight line. Doglegs to prominent landmarks for navigational reasons increased the length and time of the journey. Also the aircraft were often overloaded with bombs and fuel, which caused the pilot to fly at higher angle of attack to maintain height. This increased drag, and so decreased speed. If extra power and fuel was available there was no problem, if not, up went the airborne time. On some aircraft the extra power made the exhausts glow hotter and helped the German night fighters to see them even better.

[20] Dead Reckoning Navigation principles

Given that an aircraft often had to battle against a headwind, it would be expected that this headwind, that decreased one's ground speed, would yield a reciprocal advantage on the way home. This was not always the case. Due to a heavy bomb and fuel load, many aircraft were unable to gain sufficient height on the outward flight to get above the flak and/or icing levels. Having dropped their bombs and reduced their fuel loads, they would be able to climb to a much higher (and safer) height for the return journey.

Winds aloft vary at different heights, not only their speeds, but also their direction. It is possible to have, for example, a northerly wind at say, 1,500 feet, and a wind direction that is 90° to this at 15,000 feet. Icing plays a large part in affecting speed, and sometimes flying in icing cloud was unavoidable if it was at such a height that one could not get above it. Some lunatic during the development of the Stirling bomber requested that the wingspan be reduced to 99ft 1in, to allow the aircraft to pass through the standard 100-foot RAF hangar doors for servicing. This reduced the ability of this basically fine bomber to operate at heights above 17,000 feet. Thus, when fully loaded, it would often be unable to climb above the icing level and flak as most other aircraft could (well, sometimes). Ice forming on the wings, for example, accumulates mostly at the leading edge. The tremendous weight penalty aside, this changes the shape of the wing and its ability to create lift. It also reduces the aircraft's speed, due to drag, plus its ability to remain at height, let alone climb. The extra power used to try and combat this problem also plays havoc with fuel consumption, but sometimes icing is unavoidable, as the ice-forming clouds can be very deep. Propellers too can accumulate ice and have their thrust efficiency reduced. Large chunks of ice that break off the airframe and props sound frightening as they hit the side of the fuselage. This would only add to the uneasiness of the hapless aircrew. A direct track that was used en-route to the target may not always have been flown on the return trip. The hornet's nest one stirred up on the way out would, if at all possible, be avoided on the way back, even if it required a long detour.

Another factor was the time it could take to assemble a formation of several squadrons over the collection point before setting off. This was in addition to the time taken wandering about trying to find and accurately identify the target. Often the bomb-run had to be undertaken several times due to the inability of the bomb-aimer to see the target through cloud and smoke. He also had to ensure that the bomb-load fell only on the correct target and did not kill innocent civilians in occupied countries. This was also very important in the early part of the Bomber Offensive over Germany due to the risk of Luftwaffe reprisals. When bombing French factories a warning was usually given by the RAF to the French underground, who passed it on to the workers just before a raid. Hopefully this gave them the chance to head tout de suit for the air raid shelters.

Diversions to avoid known intensive flack and searchlight areas played yet another part. And when all this was taken into account one still had the long trek home. This could possibly be with the loss of more than one engine due to enemy action, or 'Gremlins'. The evading of fighter attacks to and from the target could use up much fuel, height and time. In an attempt to shake off an attacking night fighter, a bomber pilot might corkscrew down from 15,000 feet to a height possibly as low as 2,000 feet. Fog, low cloud, heavy rain and even snowstorms caused diversions as home airfields were closed due to bad weather.

Even good weather at base could cause problems. Overloading could take place, if your base was the only one in the area that was still open to other squadrons as well as your own. Crashes that closed runways, having to circle to allow the lame ducks to land, possibly with wounded aircrew on board, all these problems and more could present themselves to the unlucky airman. Many aircraft, having done eight or nine hours, were pushed away by the controllers to allow damaged aircraft to land first. When finally called, some did not answer, they had flown into high ground whilst circling in marginal conditions, victims of fatigue and the weather.

At Middleton on May 5th, 13 aircraft had been prepared for Ops to Mannheim. 12 attacked the docks and one of the crews brought their bombs back as they were unable to find the target. On Saturday the 7th, the squadron put up 15 Whitleys for a raid on battleships at Brest. All squadron aircraft found and bombed their primary target, including P/O Christopher Cheshire in Z6625. All aircraft returned safely.

On the same day, Sergeant Michael Renaut, and several other pilots, travelled to their final training camp, which was 19 OTU at RAF Kinloss on the Moray Firth. Here they were to receive their final operational training during an eight-week course. At Kinloss they were converted onto the Armstrong Whitworth Whitley, which was found to be gentle and viceless. One had to get used to the size but it was easy to fly. With a total of 114 flying hours, Michael Renaut went solo after two and a half hours dual instruction. This had been at night, but in northern Scotland the summer nights do not get very dark. Single engined landings had proved difficult; these occupied a large amount of the time during circuits and bumps. The Whitleys they flew were clapped-out old rejects from operational squadrons.

Having learned about bombing large white triangles from 10,000 feet with eleven and half-pound practice smoke bombs, they honed their skills for the operations that would shortly come. Next came much bigger bombs, more like the ones they would eventually drop in anger. These were 250-lb variety. They also had to learn how to photograph the results of their bombing.

About this time, the crews became uneasy as they realised that at this stage, the training was almost over and soon it would be time to begin operations. The thought of the impending flak, fighters and the weather, all enemies of the airman, niggled away at them. Although they felt unique in this growing fear, none had actually cornered the market in uneasiness. This fear had secretly manifested itself in almost everyone, although one would never know it. Each one, regardless of rank, aircrew position or background, suspected that he was the only one who was apprehensive and worried about the future. Unlike today, it was politically correct at the time to omit the words 'him' or 'her' when discussing aircrew, for there were no operational female aircrew in Bomber Command during WWII. This was a man thing, and the admittance of fear to your fellow aircrew was unthinkable. Everyone suspected that they were the only one who was scared, and yet they all did the job. Unfortunately over 56,000 of them eventually confirmed their fears and were killed between September 1939 and May 1945.

Most of them were schoolboys. If you reached the age of 21 you were an old man amongst the younger aircrew, many were Wing Commanders at that age. Leonard Cheshire became a Group Captain at the tender age of 25.

On May 6th, Germany's second largest city was host to 115 aircraft, including 4 Manchesters, 3 Stirlings, 27 Hampdens, 50 Wellingtons and 31 Whitleys. Due to poor visibility few aircraft were able to identify their targets. Whilst 81 crews reported that they had attacked Hamburg, 22 others chose to bomb their alternative targets. Hamburg's recorder stated that only 4 fires were started with 2 people injured and 33 bombed out. All aircraft returned safely.

On the morning of Sunday the 8th, AVM Conningham, the Air Officer Commanding of 4 Group, arrived at Goosepool from Group HQ in York. He inspected the aerodrome and talked to the crews of 78 Squadron. Of the 16 Goosepool Whitley crews detailed that night for an attack on the shipyards at Bremen, 15 successfully attacked their primary targets. One was a non-starter due to engine trouble. The crew of T4147, flown by Sgt L Thorpe, failed to return, having sent the operation-completed signal. This aircraft had crashed at Heisfelderfeld, just north of the outskirts of the German town of Leer, 12 miles southeast of Emden.

Meanwhile at Linton-on-Ouse, 76 Squadron continued training on the Halifax as more experienced crews arrived. The squadron's aircraft were sometimes dispersed in a large open field at Tholthorpe, a few miles to the east. This landing ground would itself become a 6 Group bomber airfield in June of 1943. It was just as well that they were so well dispersed, as on the clear moonlit night of May 11/12th 1941, the Luftwaffe paid a visit to Linton in the form of 3 Junkers Ju88 bombers. Fortunately, 35 Squadron were also well dispersed around Linton's perimeter and no aircraft were hit. Some fragmentation bombs were dropped and a few buildings close to the control tower were damaged. Fires were started when incendiaries were dropped on the hangar roofs. The Station Commander, Group Captain F F Garroway OBE, was killed. He was struck by shrapnel from a fragmentation bomb. Only posted in the day before, he had been leading a team that was fighting a serious incendiary fire. Three airmen were also killed and 10 injured during the attack, which lasted half an hour. Although every able-bodied airman was called out to fight the fires, two in particular were noted in the squadron's records. Sergeant Saunders and Aircraftsman Macleod were commended for their exceptional courage and initiative whilst under fire.

Back at Goosepool, on the 15th, five of 78 Squadron's aircraft were detailed for operations. Having been loaded for the first time with the new 1,000-lb bombs, they joined 4 Whitleys from another squadron to attack the docks at Boulogne. All returned safely. During the preparations for a raid to Cologne on the 16th, a lorry damaged the tailplane of F/L Lawrence's Whitley. This accident and the failure of a generator on another aircraft reduced the night's tally to 12. The number of available aircraft was depleted further as one of 78's Whitleys received the undivided attention of the flak gunners as it crossed the Dutch coast. The captain was injured which necessitated an immediate return to Middleton. Having jettisoned their bombs in the sea, the crew of this aircraft managed to reach base and land without further incident. At 22:43 the ground personnel of Middleton had watched the departure of P/O J A T Jarrould in EY-V Z6493. Nothing further was heard from this aircraft. It later transpired that it was shot down by Uffz[21] Pross of 3 NJG/1, and crashed at 02:34 between Helenaveen and Maasbree, Holland. All on board were killed. On the 27th thirteen aircraft were detailed for Ops to Cologne. Eleven bombed their primary, whilst another attacked Aachen. One aircraft returned to base with a faulty compass having been airborne for two hours.

The following night saw the last raid for Middleton's Whitleys during May as 14 aircraft were detailed for Ops to Kiel. The primary was the Battleship Tirpitz, with 78 being the only protagonists. Due to extremely bad weather conditions only 3 aircraft claimed to have bombed Kiel. On their return to Middleton the crew reported that they had experienced severe icing and electrical storms. The cloud was so thick that the searchlights could not penetrate it. Sgt Blackwell and his crew stated that, so bad were the icing conditions, they had to jettison their bombs when ice clogged the starboard engine intake, causing it to overheat. Blackwell went on to state that these were the worst conditions he had experienced in his five months of operational flying. Unable to see the target Sgt Dunlop dumped his bombs on the town of Husam whilst on the way home. This was a medium sized town 45 miles to the northwest of Kiel, the last bit of enemy real estate before flashing out to sea and safety. His was the only aircraft to get anywhere near Middleton, landing at Linton-on-Ouse. On their return, most squadron aircraft were diverted to Abingdon, including P/O Lake complete with his full load of bombs. This operation cost the squadron Whitley Z6484. No details of the fate of Sgt A T Copley and his crew are available, only that they are buried in Soltau's Becklingen War Cemetery.

At Linton on the same day, Wing Commander S O Bufton, who had taken command of the reborn 76 Squadron on April 12th, was promoted to Group Captain. W/C G T Jarman DSO DFC replaced him as 76's commander on the 28th.

June 1941 - 76 on the move

S/L Bickford was posted in to Linton-on-Ouse on June 2nd to command 76 squadron's second flight. Tom Sawyer gave him his initial training on the Mk 1 Halifax. Two days later, on the 4th, the day dawned with low stratus cloud persisting until late morning. During the afternoon it became fine, with just a little haze. By mid afternoon flying conditions had improved sufficiently to allow Wing Commander Jarman to lead 76 Squadron and its 6 Halifax Mk 1s on a 33 mile flight to their new home at RAF Middleton St George.

---

[21] Unteroffizier (Under Officer)

Halifax Mk1 landing   Photo: via Geoff Hill

Cyril Tuckwell arrived at York railway station. He was to join 76 Squadron at Linton-on-Ouse. When he reached Linton he was informed that the squadron had just left for Middleton St George. He spent the night in temporary accommodation and set out the next day by the usual RAF transport, a three-ton lorry. Cyril Tuckwell recalled that Middleton was an extremely nice camp, with the usual H shaped two-story brick buildings for sleeping quarters. This was the same as Dishforth and Linton-on-Ouse. Middleton was centrally heated in the winter months with radiators. As in all these types of camps, along the roadside were paths of concrete slabs, under which were all the water and lagged heating pipes and electric and telephone cables. There was a central boiler house, which supplied all the domestic and heating hot water for every building in the camp. There was also a water tower up to which water was pumped to give the necessary pressure throughout the camp. This system worked very well and these camps were just like small towns.

On his arrival at Middleton, Norman Frankish was accommodated in one of the 6 H-blocks on the domestic site. The next morning, having had breakfast, he set off just before 8am to walk around the perimeter track, (affectionately known as the peri-track) to find the Flight Sergeant in charge (I/C) Admin, who resided in the Technical Flight hut on the south side of the airfield. There were quite a few other groundcrew bods also taking this route to work. The Technical Flight hut was the Administration Centre for all the various trades responsible for servicing the squadron aircraft out on the flights. On arrival, Norman knocked on the door and entered. He introduced himself to Flight Sergeant Horsefall, who was affectionately known to the ground staff as 'Donkydrop' (but not to his face!). The trades also had their own Flight Sergeants, who ensured that their section carried out the tasks required out on the flights. These included the engine fitters, airframe fitters (better known as riggers), electricians, radio mechanics, instrument fitters (affectionately know as instrument bashers), and the armourers. Their individual Flight Offices were on the north side of the runway, located in rooms constructed along the outside walls side of the hangars. From these offices general orders were issued. All the flight offices were in communication with the Engineering Officer who also had an office on one side of the squadron hangar.

Both hangars 1, 2 & 3 at Middleton had external offices, locker rooms and debriefing rooms along each side   Photo: Author

Today, hangars 1 and 2 are still in daily use, just as they were during the war. Hangar 1 was the home of 76 Squadron and was also used as the R and I hangar. Hangar 2 was the flight hangar, used to carry out minor repairs. Out on the flights, Norman's day would consist of working on the engines of the Halifaxes. During the war, the normal practice was to service the aircraft outside, regardless of the weather; they only went into the hangars for major repairs and inspections such as 50 and 100-hour checks. When the aircraft returned from operations or training flights there was usually a snag list. The riggers would have patches to put over holes provided courtesy of the Luftwaffe and flak batteries. Armourers, too, would spring into action and remove the hundreds, possibly thousands of empty cartridge cases from the floors of the aircraft and gun turrets. Norman and the rest of the engine fitters would have a variety of things to do. Leaking coolant radiators to change for example, their fragile cores were usually one of the first things to sustain flak damage, even by tiny pieces of shrapnel. Spark plugs had to be changed on rough running or underpowered engines. Header-tanks were another common engine accessory to need attention. This involved the removal and replacement of 32 x 2BA nuts, often with numb fingers that did not want to work properly outside on a freezing winter's morning. For everyone on the flights, the NAFFI van was their salvation on cold winter mornings, on any morning come to that. A cup of tea and a wad was most welcome to one and all, a pick me up that would last until lunchtime. Many went on to re-muster as fitters to get away from the flights and into the dryer hangars (not that they were much warmer).

Norman Frankish, front row second from left, kneeling   Photo: Norman Frankish

People were always required on the flights and Norman enjoyed his job. He felt that he only wanted to do his duty, and was not really interested in moving very far up the promotion ladder. His interest was for the duration only; a career in the Air Force was not really on his agenda. When the repairs were done, the main job was to ensure that the aircraft were always serviceable and ready for operations. Oil was topped up, as was the coolant level in the header tanks, then the engine covers were fitted after the run-ups and final adjustments. There were no courses to attend during this period; one had to figure out any new procedures for oneself, even on new engines. This included the new versions of the Merlin and its accessories. When the Hercules came into service, it, also, did not come complete with training or introduction courses. Later came the Taurus and the same applied. Just get on with it and figure it out.

Interspersed with the fitter's normal duties were spells of guard duty. This involved sleeping in the aircraft, often on freezing cold nights. One was supplied only with a blanket, rifle and a cheese sandwich. It got very spooky trying to sleep on the quiet side of the airfield. The dispersals were a long way from the domestic site nestling in civilization on the north side. Windy nights were the worst. The engine covers flapped, and the sound of the wind whistling and shrieking as it passed through orifices in the airframe did nothing for the wellbeing of Norman and his oppos.

In the early days at Middleton, the aircraft earmarked for a raid later that day would first be prepared for flight by the groundcrew. Once this was completed, the aircraft would be lined up on the end of the runway, not nose to tail facing up and down the runway, but in a row with all their noses facing across the runway and wingtip to wingtip. One enemy bomber could have taken the lot out with a couple of hits. It has to be said that the art of dispersing aircraft around the airfield was somewhat embryonic at this time. A heavy raid at nearby Middlesbrough one night soon educated the powers that be at Middleton to think again. The practice of dispersing the aircraft around the perimeter of the airfield until ready to taxi out was soon adopted by the whole of the RAF and remained the standard throughout the remainder of the war.

One very cold night Norman Frankish was taken to a dark, cheerless and very remote area up in the Cleveland hills. A Halifax from another squadron had crashed up there while returning to Middleton. His job was to guard the wreckage; its secret electronic equipment could have been very useful to the enemy. All but 3 of the crew had baled out prior to the crash. Fortunately those left on board managed to unstrap the bits and walk away. Although it was lonely and very cold, Norman was unofficially well looked after by the people from a nearby farm. Life on a busy wartime airfield was not all work and no play.

The NAFFI was the hub of the social side for the lower ranks. Although the Corporals had their own Mess, they would on occasion pay a visit if the mood took them. The Sergeants and officers were expected to remain within their own Messes and were rarely invited into the NAFFI except on very special occasions. If remaining on the camp, there was nowhere else for the airmen to go except their own billets or to those of their friends.

There was also a NAFFI shop. Cyril Tuckwell remembers that they were something like modern mini-markets. They were mainly for those airmen and their families who were living out of the camp. Cyril recalls that quite a few of them did. His bed was on the ground floor of one of the H-blocks. In charge of Cyril and his oppos was Sgt Perry, who came from Essex. He had been a postman in civilian life. He had also been in the RAF Volunteer Reserve when he was called up at the start of hostilities. One morning Sgt Perry came to the block to see if the airman were ready for work. Cyril and the majority of his colleagues had returned from breakfast and were washed, dressed and shaved. One airman was still in bed, wrapped in his blankets. Sgt Perry gave him a shake and called, 'Wakey Wakey.' The airman promptly threw back the blankets and leapt out of bed. He was fully dressed, right down to his oilskin coat and Wellies. He just walked straight out of the billet, leaving everyone staring in amazement. Sgt Perry was speechless.

About the only job Cyril helped to do at this time was to assist in removing part of a Halifax undercarriage, which he remembers went drastically wrong. It turned out that he unbolted the wrong part first. A heavy elastic return mechanism sprang back; swiping him across the head with a metal plate that was attached to the bungee elastic. Although not knocked out he was taken to the station sick bay to have the necessary repairs carried out. Cyril had not been trained for the job he was doing when injured, it should have been done by a fitter IIA, Cyril's trade being that of fitter II E. Cyril Tuckwell also thought that he would try his hand at flying. One of the jobs he and his oppos had to do was to wheel the Station Commander's Tiger Moth from one end of the hangar up to its parking place by flying control. One of Cyril's colleagues suggested that as he was an engine fitter the easiest way to do this was for him to get in, start the thing up and taxi it. This it was hoped would save them much work. Cyril climbed into the cockpit and they started the engine. Everything was going really well until they were passing between the two hangars. Cyril thinks that he must have opened the throttles too far. Suddenly there was a gust of wind. The next thing he knew was that he was airborne with about six feet between him and the ground. He could see all sorts of charges being made against him as he gently eased the stick back and gingerly closed the throttle. Once on the ground he cut the engine and his oppos caught up with him. It was a much mortified Cyril that climbed from the cockpit. The good news was that they didn't have so far to push it now, so needless to say the job was done in record time.

At this time there was not much work to do, as 76 was not operational. Having observed Cyril's antics at fixing Halifaxes undercarriage legs and taxiing Tiger Moths, the powers that be were informed that Cyril had now also grown a boil on a portion of his anatomy that he sat upon. This meant that he was only able to sit partially on a chair. Due to this problem he was delegated to light duties only. Kershaw, the Engineering Officer's clerk was due for a fortnight's leave, and from somewhere a temporary replacement had to be found. A question was asked, 'Who can use a typewriter?' Cyril's hand went up and he was in.

Part of Cyril's job was to send off the daily Q form signals[22] to 4 Group HQ in York and to Bomber Command. His typing left a bit to be desired, as he was self-taught. Things were a bit slow, what with the one fingered typing and all. But accuracy was the main requirement and at that he was fine. Two weeks later, Kershaw returned from leave and as the work situation had not changed, Cyril was asked if he would like to help out in the squadron's maintenance office. He was told that he could make himself useful with typing and general office duties. It was about this time that the idea of a Technical Records Office was conceived. The duty of this office was to collate the information from each aircraft's form 700[23] and enter the information into the appropriate logbook. The office would also run and keep up-to-date the aircraft publication manuals, and enter in them the modifications and amendments, which continually arrived from various sources. Even today, over 60 years on, Cyril still remembers that the Bible for the Halifax Mk I aircraft was AP 1719A, and for the Merlin X engines it was AP 1519E. Eventually he was put in charge of the Technical Records Office and was given a helper, ACH/GD Robin Roll. Robin came from Hepscott near Morpeth in Northumberland, and they became great friends, which they are even up to the present day.

The Office was located on the left-hand side of 76 Squadron's hangar, looking from the camp end. At the start there was just Cyril and Robin, but soon it grew and grew until it became a very well organized facility and it was constantly used by many people. As far as cleaning was concerned, one simply put out one's laundry and it was taken away, washed and returned. Despite the odd loss of kit which was cursed profusely the system worked surprisingly well.

Cyril Tuckwell Photo: Cyril Tuckwell

[22] Aircraft Serviceability

[23] The Aircraft daily servicing record

Located along the back road leading from the railway bridge at the bottom of Middleton Village and along to the end of 06 runway and Middleton-One-Row, the WAAF block was quite a distance from the main domestic site. The WAAF block and the area around it were definitely 'verboten' to the male population of the airfield, and anyone else for that matter. However, before lights out, the WAAFs could be found in the NAFFI, and with tea, wallop and fags available as a bonus, the airmen and WAAFs used it as a home from home. Norman Frankish was quite an accomplished and sought after singer. He would accompany the station band that often performed in the NAFFI. He and the band would travel to Stockton and other towns to perform with the famous Jack Marwood band. The main venue for dancing was the Maison-de-Dance in Yarm Road, Stockton and people would come from Middlesbrough and miles around to see and hear them. Sunday concerts at the Odeon, Middlesbrough were yet another venue for Norman and the band, along with the Kendrew Baths in Gladstone Street, Darlington. Here the main swimming baths were boarded over for dancing and a wooden stage erected for the band. This was a practice that continued through the 60s and 70s until the building was demolished.

The train from Dinsdale station was one of the main forms of transport on days and nights off. One practice employed by simply hundreds of Middleton's inhabitants involved the cutting up of Woodbine cigarette packets to form look-alike railway tickets. These were put to good use at night in the blacked-out wartime railway carriages. For a while this worked very well, until the ticket collectors were eventually issued with torches that is. Pulling the communication cord to stop the train was another ploy, just as the train reached the airfield. This saved a long walk back from Dinsdale station, but was highly illegal of course, the penalty – a £5 fine. However, Mr. Nobody, who actually pulled the chord, was very elusive, and was never brought to book.

There were many pubs that were frequented by Goosepool's personnel, the ones in Darlington included the Wheatsheaf Hotel on Yarm Road and the Imperial, which was, and still is, on the corner of Grange Road and Coniscliffe Road. The Imperial is now known as the Imperial Centre, but on the outside it still looks exactly the same today as it did then. Bondgate offered the Freemasons, whilst Brunswick Street, which today is the home of a large Ford garage, was the location for the long-gone Golden Lion, a favorite venue for the airmen of Goosepool.

There was no purpose built Church on the airfield. Services were carried out in a variety of buildings depending on one's religious beliefs. The NAFFI was pressed into service for many a church parade. Norman remembers visiting the church of St George, which is located just outside the southern perimeter of the airfield. This is reached by taking the Aislaby back road out of Middleton-One-Row. Norman recalls that the church was not locked up and when he and his colleagues entered it was empty. For quite a while Norman played the beautiful organ, which sounded very loud within the confines of this tiny house of God. Today, alas, locks have become mandatory, even for churches.

St George's church tucked away beyond Middleton-one-Row on the Aislaby road   Photo: Author

Ops - June 1941

In June, operations for 78 had begun on the 8th with a raid to Dortmund. The bombing turned out to be poor, due to industrial haze. This raid involved 37 Bomber Command Whitleys and cost 78 Squadron the lives of Sgt D R Simm and his crew. They had been one of 10 aircraft detailed for Ops that night. Having bombed the target they had sent the 'Ops completed' signal, and whilst over Yorkshire on the way home had begun their descent through the clouds prior to landing. With his eyes glued to the instruments, Sgt Simm descended through the cloud, hoping that the height of the ground did not exceed the height of the cloud base. He was of course very conscious that the Vale of York and its high ground was all around him. There was no approach radar in those days, no instrument landing system, no auto-land, or GPS,[24] only rudimentary radio bearings and DR navigation. Oh yes, and guesswork. Having reached Wyton (Huntingdon) on the way back, they would have turned north gaining radio 'fixes' on the way. These do not allow for wind and so errors of many miles can be achieved. In the narrow constraints of the Vale of York this can be fatal and in this case it was. Whilst descending through the cloud at about 1,000 feet, the aircraft met the earth at Ellingstring, south of the A6108 Masham to Middleham road. All on board were killed.

Sgt Hollingworth, the wireless operator in Z6655, flown by Sgt Hudgell, was hit by flak whilst he was dropping flares over the target area. The crew were bombing the primary from 16,000 feet when the flak struck. It also cut the intercom to the tail gunner and put the HF radio out of action. Despite the damage to the wireless operator and the aircraft, they were able to return and divert into Linton-on-Ouse, as the weather at Middleton was extremely poor. F/L Lawrence and his 3-man crew in Z6466 attacked the target from 13,000 feet, having just taken evasive action to avoid an enemy fighter. They returned safely and landed at Linton using the Lorenz, which was described by Lawrence as extremely effective. At de-briefing the 1st wireless operator, Sgt Bisset, who was on his first operation, was described as excellent. Sgt Hutchin's crew dropped their bombs about two miles north of the railway station. A large fire was started, and as they left the target area the flames were seen to burn with a bluish white flame. Owing to a delayed take-off, P/O McWatters attacked the centre of Duisburg. The docks and river were seen clearly by the observer Sgt Franklin and the tail gunner Sgt Barker. Turning for home, the large fire that they had started was still visible 20 minutes after leaving the target area. On their return, the weather over the northeast of England was most unsuitable. Due to a navigational error, this aircraft over-shot the East Coast and landed 80 miles beyond Middleton at Silloth, Cumberland.

Whitley Z6495, flown by Sgt Blackwell, managed to attack the primary from 14,000 ft, despite having to jettison 'safe' one of his 1,000-lb bombs due to faulty wiring. On their return to Middleton the weather was found to be extremely poor, however they did manage to land safely. Having dropped his bombs, P/O Stobbs and his crew watched in horror as their bombs fell towards an unknown Whitley that was circling some incendiaries below. Just as the bombs seemed to reach the low flying aircraft it moved to the north out of the defended area and clear of danger. The captain of this Whitley was not aware of the bombs falling from above but had obviously decided, fortuitously, to move clear of the intense flak that was bursting all around him.

Christopher Cheshire in EY-L Z6625 was also on this raid, he, too, would have his fair share of problems. Having taken off with his crew at 22:55, their route to Dortmund would take them via Wyton, Orfordness, Over Flakee on the Dutch Coast and on to the target, hopefully returning by the same route. On reaching the primary target they started their attack at 15,500 feet. Their bombs were seen to burst in the target area by the observer Sgt Slim Smalley and tail gunner Sgt Tug Wilson[25]. On the way home, the 2nd WOP/AG, Sgt Tommy Hall, manning the radio, received a signal reporting that due to fog at Middleton they were to divert to Prestwick. Later whilst on the way to their diversion airfield, they received a second instruction by radio that the Viz had improved and Middleton was now open. They changed course for Middleton, cursing the detour that had cost them much precious fuel. Like Sgt Simm and his crew, it was almost time to drop below the cloud and find terra firmer, the less terra and more firmer the better. Concerned about the proximity of high ground, they had no choice but to continue down. Whilst Cheshire flew on instruments, his second pilot, ex Canadian Mountie Sgt Sid Lang, watched for any breaks in the cloud. Fortunately for Chesh and his crew they had more luck than Sgt Simm did, the cloud began to break and below them were green fields. The problem was that the hole in the volatile cloud base was only temporary, it was beginning to diminish and time was of the essence.

Cheshire reefed the bomber around and stuck its nose down. The windscreen was filled with the only bit of green for miles around. They popped out below the cloud before it slammed shut behind them, the altimeter reading only 500 feet. They were flying around in a valley surrounded by high ground that disappeared up into the clag[26], but at least they had sight of the surface. The needles of the fuel gauges had long since reached empty but still the Merlins sang. There wasn't much to choose from in the way of a landing area. The fields were very small, not really long enough to accommodate a bomber. Chesh picked what he thought was the longest one and began his approach. He was heartened by the fact that it was devoid of cattle and had a few less trees than most of the others. On landing it was realised that the field's surface was much rougher than had been expected, its retarding effect proved to be somewhat advantageous. After a very bumpy ride the crew breathed a sigh of relief as they stopped only feet from a stone wall. Chesh moved his hand to the port throttle lever to begin shutting down the engines. There was no need, somewhere during their unceremonious landing run the port engine had drunk the last of its fuel and stopped. It would have been only seconds before the starboard engine followed suit. With the tanks empty, the Merlin would have been burning only what was left in the fuel lines. It had been a very close thing indeed. They had landed at 06:15, having been airborne for 7 hours and 20 minutes. Whilst taking stock of their situation they were joined by the local policeman who informed them that the field was only 400 yards long.

---

[24] Global Positioning System (Satellite navigation)

[25] Their normal rear gunner, Taff Gurmin, was on leave

[26] Poor visibility, low cloud or fog etc.

When asked where they were he told them, 'Clapham.' None the wiser, Cheshire and his crew must have looked bemused. 'Where?' they choroused.

Clapham is found 6 miles northwest of Settle in the Western Pennines, 15 miles from what is now the M6 Motorway, and only 18 miles from Morecambe on the West Coast. If they had not landed when they did, or had carried more fuel, even at a reduced speed of 150 mph they had only 7.2 minutes of land left. After that they would have probably crashed into the Irish Sea or even the Atlantic. Having reported the situation to his Flight Commander S/L Walter Williams at Middleton, Cheshire waited for help to arrive. About three hours went by, after which a truck and a fuel bowser turned up, along with a contingent of 78 Squadron's groundcrew. They removed everything that was removable to lighten the aircraft as much as possible. This way the aircraft might, and only might, be coaxed out of what was a very short field.

They refuelled the Whitley with just enough petrol to get it to Liverpool, 56 miles to the south. In the afternoon Wing Commander Robinson and Walter Williams, along with the Squadron Engineering Officer, arrived. Having paced out the field, W/C Robinson entered the Whitley, fired up the engines, released the brakes and took off. With only inches to spare he managed to clear the wall at the far end of the field. The last time the good people of Clapham saw the Whitley it was heading South for Liverpool.

Whitley crew preparing to enter via the nose hatch. Note the entrance ladder and homing pigeon box next to the airman shown on the left hand side   Photo: IWM CH.235

On Wednesday June 11th, 78 were off to Duisburg in the Ruhr (better known as Happy Valley). This raid employed 13 of Middleton's Whitleys, 5 of which were freshers. As take-off time approached, one of the fresher crews discovered that their oxygen system was U/S[27] and became non-starters. Including the 12 aircraft from 78 Squadron, 4 Group's contribution on that night amounted to 36 Whitleys and 9 Halifaxes. Just for good measure, 35 Hampdens from 5 Group went along for the ride. When reached, the target was identified easily as the conditions were ideal. Bright moonlight and good weather allowed Sgt Gourley in Z6661 to bomb from a height of 12,300 feet. Explosions and fires were seen by his observer Sgt Harper and second pilot Sgt Jones. On the way home the fires raging in the target area were still visible by the tail gunner Sgt Bee from over 80 miles away. Sgt Jepson on Z6658 attacked from a height of 15,500 feet and the bombs were seen to explode south of the main docks. P/O Lowry and his crew brought similar reports. They had attacked from 14,000 feet and watched as their bombs fell dead on the aiming point. Also during debriefing, Sgt Blackwell described how he and his crew had scored a direct hit on the target with a 1,000-lb bomb. His two sticks of bombs were right on the money and were confirmed by his camera. Sgt Blackwell described this raid as 'a most successful operation.'

Also on this raid was Christopher Cheshire; short of a second pilot, his crew were reduced to four. Having taken off at 23:45 in his usual L for London (or as Taff Gurmin the radio operator preferred, L for Leather), he had a particularly uneventful evening. Despite the heavy flak concentration they bombed the target from 14,000 feet and returned home to Middleton at around 06:00.

As Cheshire went off for a well-deserved week's leave, his observer Sgt Smalley was given a variety of captains to fly with. These included Wing Commander Robinson. This trip was to Schwerte on the 12th to bomb railway installations. The weather was bad, with 10/10ths cloud right down to 2,000 feet. Diving down below the cloud base they hastily dropped their bombs and even more hastily climbed back up to the sanctuary of the cloud cover, next stop Middleton.

The first operation at Middleton for 76 Squadron was to the Ruhr Valley on the night of June 12/13. F/L Hillary, P/O Lewin and P/O Richards were to join a force of 399 aircraft from various squadrons on raids to Soest, Hamm, Osnabruck and Schwerte. These were some of the main railway marshalling yards in Germany and responsible for the movement of

[27] Unserviceable

men and material vital to the war effort. Also Huls was on the battle order that night. This town sported a huge chemical factory, which was an important target to Bomber Command. This was not an auspicious start to the squadron's stay at Middleton. Haze protected the Ruhr valley that night. Targets were hard to find, and due to engine problems both F/L Hillary and P/O Lewin returned to base without any great measure of success, their bomb loads still on board. Only P/O Richards managed to bomb. Having failed to find Huls, he managed to find Essen where he decided to jettison his bomb load.

On June 15th, 76's Sgt MacDonald was trying to land his Halifax in a crosswind on runway 24 at Middleton. As he flared for a landing, the aircraft swung from its path down the runway and tried to become agricultural. MacDonald was wresting with the controls and trying to keep the Halifax on the runway and at the same time avoid hitting a ground obstruction. In typical Halifax fashion, the undercarriage collapsed and the aircraft slued to a halt in the middle of the runway. With the main into-wind flarepath now closed to business, P/O Lewin in Halifax L9514 elected to land on runway 19. As he touched down cross wind, his aircraft veered to the right off the runway, where the starboard wheel dug into the soft ground, again causing the undercarriage to collapse. Later, MacDonald's aircraft was repaired and flew again. The distinction of being the first pilot to have his Halifax written off since 76 Squadron was reformed went to P/O Lewin. His aircraft was struck off charge and became an instructional airframe for the training of riggers. He had only recently joined 76, having been transferred over from 78 Squadron on May 15th. It was the practice at the time to detach aircrew from 76 over to 78 for experience on the smaller (and less complicated) Whitley, before returning them to 76 for conversion onto the Halifax.

76 Squadron was building up steadily. On the night of the 16th, they sent three of their Halifaxes to join with 47 Hampdens, 39 Whitleys, and 16 Wellingtons, which were attacking Cologne.

Once again the weather was poor and so was the bombing. 55 high explosive bombs and 300 incendiaries were dropped. This caused scattered damage and 19 people were killed on the ground and 17 injured. After take off, the escape hatch on S/L Bickford's Halifax blew off, taking the astro hatch with it. P/O Ireton, the observer, sustained damage to his hand. The aircraft had to be turned around and brought back without completing the operation. The other two 76 aircraft, flown by Sgts McHale and MacDonald, completed their Op and returned safely to Goosepool.

Also taking part that night were Sgt McGreggor and his crew, flying Wellington LQ-Q W5522 of 405, based at Pocklington. They were last heard on W/T at 03:03. It is presumed that they lie beneath the waves of the North Sea somewhere between Holland and England. They are commemorated on the Runnymede Memorial. This particular crew was the first all Canadian crew to be lost by an RCAF squadron.

That night Cologne was also the target for 78. They detailed 13 operational and one fresher crew to attack this historic German city. From his old crew, Tom Sawyer had brought Sgt Grenyer his navigator, Sgt Heaton his wireless operator, and Sgt Phillips his rear gunner, having lost his second pilot who had moved on to gain an operational command of his own. There was sadness that night as Middleton lost Whitley EY-K Z6492. Having taken off at 22:32, P/O D S Lake and his crew were lost without trace and today are commemorated on the Runnymede Memorial. Due to engine trouble, one Whitley returned early to Middleton and did not take part in the evening's activities.

Bremen was the target on the 18th, when Cheshire, back from his leave, was again behind the wheel of EY-L. That night his crew included the usual, Sid Lang as second pilot, Slim Smalley as observer and Taff Gurmin manning the radios. A new rear gunner, Sgt Burgess, became the Whitley's tail end Charley. Thick industrial haze prevented accurate identification of the target by the 100 Bomber Command aircraft. Whilst stooging around, EY-L was hit in one of its wings by flak, but this did not prevent Chesh and his crew from returning safely to Middleton. Unfortunately this was not the case for two other 78 Squadron crews that night. Also operating without second pilots were the crews of Z6560 and Z6661. The latter was flown by P/O T C Richards who, along with his crew, died when the Whitley crashed at Lorup, 80 km southwest of Bremen.

On their return from the target, this aircraft had called for, and received, a QDM[28] from Linton at 05:35. After this transmission nothing further was heard. All are buried in the Reichswald Forest War Cemetery. As for Z6560, flown by F/S V H Marks, all on board were lost without trace and are commemorated on the Runnymede Memorial. As can be seen, at this juncture 78 were suffering a shortage of second pilots, which is represented by the last three crews lost. Pilot Officer Cheshire was carrying out the duties of Flight Commander at this time with the acting rank of Flight Lieutenant. The Tirpitz was the target on the night of June 20th, as 78 sent 10 Whitleys to Kiel. P/O Bob Cant with Cheshire's observer Sgt Smalley had an eventful night in T6490. Due to thick cloud cover they diverted their attention from the battleship and concentrated on the city itself. Hit by intensive flak, P/O Cant's aircraft received hits to the port engine, and the cowling was blown off. The undercarriage was also damaged along with the port wheel. They managed to return to Middleton but as they landed the port undercarriage collapsed causing the Whitley to end the operation slithering off the runway in a lazy left-hand arc. Everyone managed to evacuate the aircraft safely.

The remainder of the squadron's aircraft bombed through 10/10ths cloud cover on ETA and BFX'd[29] to Driffield where they landed safely.

On June 20th, Sawyer flew his last mission with 76 when he led five crews from Middleton on a raid to Kiel. On this occasion his crew consisted of Sergeants Hindshaw, Butler, Heaton, Brotherton, Grenyer and Sanderson. They were searching for the Tirpitz, but if it could not be found the city of Kiel would become the alternative target. Taking off at 23:27, he was heading for the transporter bridge at Middlesbrough, a good landmark from where he would turn south onto his first track. Having just gained a bit of height and breathing a sigh of relief at getting off ok, Tom soon encountered a major problem. Besides the usual AA guns and searchlights, Middlesbrough was protected from enemy air attack by huge

---

[28] Magnetic course to steer for home without making allowances for wind

[29] Estimated Time of Arrival and Divert Signal

barrage balloons. As it was dusk, Sawyer was concentrating on his instruments, with his head down in the cockpit, preparing to set course, when the radio operator Sgt G Heaton, sounding very startled, shouted over the intercom, 'We are heading into the balloon barrage Skipper.' Sawyer had also heard the high pitched buzz of the squealers in his earphones. This was a radio system in the aircraft, which indicated the close proximity of friendly barrage balloons. The balloon crew transmitted this warning from the ground on the same frequency as the R/T; this showed that balloons were being flown nearby. Unfortunately the range was short and in this case the Halifax was amongst the balloons before they knew it. The Halifax was at 4,000ft and looking up Tom vaguely saw the huge obstacles 7-800ft above them. The ground below was dark so the thick steel cables that were meant to slice off a wing were not visible. Fortunately they were not too closely spaced, and were all pointing into wind. With his eyes straining upwards Tom kept them in sight. He also flew into wind to ensure that the cables were straight ahead and not sloping across his path. After what had seemed a lifetime they eventually passed the last two, but it had been close.

After this raid an agreement was made with the balloon commander to lower the Middlesbrough balloon barrage when Middleton was operating. After this nerve racking start the raid to Kiel was fairly uneventful. It turned out to be a long flight over the sea followed by a short run over enemy territory. The flak was heavy as from 12,500 feet Sawyer and his crew bombed the Germania shipyards on ETA. Soon after, the glow from the resultant fires was seen burning through the 10/10ths-cloud cover. Due to fog in the Vale of York, on the way home they received a message ordering them to divert to Driffield. This they did, landing safely at 06:17. Having taken off at 23:30, Sgt McHale in L9517 attacked Kiel with two sticks of bombs, which he dropped from a height of 11,000 feet in a gliding attack. The searchlights were ineffective but he encountered heavy flak. Due to the cloud cover the results of the bombing could not be observed. They returned safely to Middleton 05:03. This crew managed to beat the fog forming in the Vale of York. The majority of 76 Squadron's aircraft operating that night arrived after 06:00 to bed and breakfast at Driffield.

Sgt Bryne and his crew left Middleton in Halifax L9592 at 23:59. Their evening was almost a mirror image of the others. Attacking from 11,000 feet they too were unable to observe their bomb hits. Leaving the heavy flak and searchlights behind them they landed at Driffield at 06:32. Sgt Smith in L9523 landed back at Middleton at 06:15, having somehow found a gap in the fog. His night had been identical to the other crews with no bombing results being observed. The final crew, commanded by F/L Hillary had taken off at 23:22. They landed safely at Driffield at 06:18 to supply the de-briefing officer with yet another account of the 10/10ths cloud, heavy flak and unobserved bomb hits. All crews dispatched returned safely and the diverted aircraft flew the 53 miles from Driffield to base later in the day after the sun burned off the fog. The weather in June 1941 had been very unkind to Bomber Command.

The 23rd saw 78 detail 11 Whitleys to attack Cologne. All of 78's aircraft returned safely to Middleton. On the same night, 76 were unlucky enough to suffer the loss of the first ever Bomber Command Halifax bomber to go missing on ops. This was L9492, shot down by Oblt Reinhold Eckardt of II /NJG1, and flown by P/O W K Stobbs and his crew. They had left Middleton St George at 23:09, as part of a 4 aircraft raid to bomb Kiel. They crashed at 02:32 at Eilendorf, 20-km SW of Hamburg. P/O Stobbs and four members of his crew were killed. Only Sgt Lipton the mid-upper gunner survived to become a POW. Meanwhile, Sgt McDonald and his crew were at 11,000 feet over Kiel in Halifax L9517. They dropped their bombs in a single stick close to the aiming point. Having turned from the bomb run, many searchlights coned them. Although two fires appeared to have been started, they were unable to see the true results of their attack. They returned safely to Middleton at 05:08. Sgt Smith and his crew in L9517 had better luck. Having adopted a gliding attack they bombed from 11,000 feet and saw many bursts over a wide area of the target. Sgt Byrne located and identified the target in good visibility. Bomb bursts across the target were clearly observed. This started a huge fire, which was seen to spread. As they flew home, the crew of L9510 could still see the flames from the fire 80 miles from the target. They too returned safely back to Middleton, landing at 05:18.

Middleton was visited by the Inspector General of the Air Force on June 26th. Having arriving by air at 14:00 he went straight to the Mess for lunch, after which he had a conference with 76 and 78 Squadron commanders and their adjutants. Later he went out onto the airfield to inspect a Halifax, talking to its crew for over 20 minutes. He went on to carry out inspections of both the Sergeants' and the Airmen's Mess. Finally he spoke to the Station Armourer, F/L Burk, before having tea and leaving by air for Linton at 17:25. This was a very busy time for the Inspector General; many airfields were being completed or were still under construction. On reaching Linton he immediately left by car for Grantham for a conference with the AOC of 5 Group.

The 26th also saw Cologne visited again by 7 Whitleys belonging to 78. Although 10 aircraft had been detailed for this raid, one scrubbed due to engine trouble whilst another that had taken off returned shortly afterwards with similar problems. The fresher crew taking part in this raid returned with its bombs as both the primary and secondary targets could not be found. All aircraft returned safely to base.

The final operation of the month for 78 took place that evening. 12 Whitleys, including 2 freshers, were detailed to attack Bremen. 9 attacked the primary, whilst one bombed Bremerhaven. One aircraft, Z6658 flown by Sgt R S Green, failed to return. This aircraft was presumed lost over the North Sea. It is thought possible that this aircraft was the one tracked by 4 Group operators, They gave its position as being 65 to 100 miles off Alnmouth, Northumberland. Middleton sent 4 Whitleys to search for this aircraft but nothing was found. The body of the rear gunner Sgt Hird was recovered later. The remaining crewmembers are commemorated on the Runnymede Memorial.

July saw 76 Squadron practicing daylight formation flying. Most of this was over water and caused rumours to abound. Norman Frankish recalls that the thought of rehearsing for a daylight raid did not inspire the aircrew, who were very uneasy about the prospects for their survival. Bremen was the target on the 2nd for 4 of the squadron's aircraft. All returned safe. The next day, 76 welcomed S/L WR Williams who had been posted to them from 78. He was to take over from S/L Sawyer who would leave to assume command of 78 Squadron the next day. The 5th saw an operation to Magdeburg and on the 7th, Frankfurt was the target. The same day Christopher Cheshire was posted in from 78 Squadron. His regular wireless operator Sgt Gurmin had also been posted to 76 the day before, their observer Sgt Smalley would take until the 29th to find his way to 76.

Christopher Cheshire, younger brother of the famous Leonard Cheshire, in his Halifax Mk1, MP-L. Note pseudo-Cheshire coat of arms, denoting Cheshire: cheese; cats - and bombs! Photo: IWM CH.3426

Photo taken next morning of damage to Bickford's instrument panel. Badly injured he was taken to hospital Photo: PRO AIR28/542

A trip to the oilfields at Leuna on the 8th nearly cost the squadron S/L Bickford. A successful attack on the primary was carried out from 9,000 feet, after which the Halifax was caught in a concentration of searchlights and holed in several places. On the way home they were attacked by an enemy fighter, which caused considerable damage to the Halifax. Part of the windscreen was shattered and many of the instruments were put out of action. The compass was shot from its mountings. One of the crew picked up the compass and it was put on Bickford's lap, where by the light of a torch strapped to his harness he was able to steer a course home. The flight engineer Sgt Kenworthy was wounded by shrapnel, whilst Bickford was wounded by shell splinters. It was by sheer skill and determination that he was able to fly the badly damaged aircraft back to Middleton where they landed safely at 05:45.

Flight Sergeants Larry Donnelly and Chas Armstrong, having completed a tour on Whitleys with 10 Squadron at Dishforth had been screened in October 1940 and posted to 19 Whitley OTU at Kinloss as instructors. After persistently trying to escape from Kinloss by hook or by crook, they finally swung it during July 1941 and were subsequently posted to 76 at Middleton on the 12th. Arriving at Darlington's railway station in the middle of the night after the long and tedious train journey from Kinloss, they spent the night on settees in the Sergeants' Mess.

Next morning they were interviewed by W/C Jarman, after which they set off to see the sights of Goosepool. As WOP/AGs they reported to the W/T and Gunnery Sections for the low-down on the Halifax. S/L Bickford had been Larry's skipper on Whitleys and had played a not insignificant part in short circuiting Larry's escape from Kinloss. To hear that Bickford was in hospital suffering from shell splinters was a bit of a shock for Larry, who rather hoped that he could once again team up with his old skipper. Sadly this was not to be. Meanwhile both Larry and Chas began their conversion onto the Halifax. Gone were the old T1083/R1082 W/T radios, so familiar to Whitley crews. Now they had new toys to play with in the form of the upgraded Marconi T1154/R1155 radio equipment. Next to be learned were the intricacies of the Halifax's Boulton Paul turrets. Larry related to the author about some of the recreational exploits at Goosepool at the time, like the marathon card schools for instance. Far-be-it that Larry had anything to do with the Very pistol cartridges that were 'accidentally' dropped down the chimneys of Nissen huts frequented by the squadron's card sharks. Larry and Chas were to remain at Middleton until February 1942, taking part in many of 76's operations. Larry then completed a third tour, this time on Short Sunderlands, operating against German U-boats and long-range aircraft in the Bay of Biscay.

Far be it from me to cover Larry's exploits during this time, better the reader picks up copies of 'The Whitley Boys' and 'A Quest for Wings'. Both books cover in great detail Larry's exploits during and after WWII.

Larry went on to re-muster as a pilot later in the war and fulfill a lifetime of aviation related professions. I had the great honour of first meeting Larry in 2000 and flying with him on his 80th birthday in the spring of that year at Teesside International Airport (Middleton St George). I was supposed to fly him in the flying club's PA28 Warrior, as a birthday treat, but ended up being shown 'how to do it' by the master himself. Today we are great friends, 'A true kindred spirit', to quote Larry. His books are a must to read. His current (3rd) book entitled 'The Other Few' covers Bomber Command's little known and little appreciated involvement during the Battle of Britain.

On the 18th, Wing Commander G T Jarman was attending an investiture at Buckingham Palace to receive the DFC. The day before, Goosepool had welcomed Sir Richard E C Pierce KCB DSO AFC, who in his official capacity as the Air Officer Commanding (AOC) Bomber Command had arrived in style by Halifax at 11:45 am. He was late landing as a stray barrage balloon was spotted drifting towards the airfield. He joined Wing Commander Fieldon and his crew in the cockpit and instructed them to shoot down the wayward airborne obstacle. Sir Richard and the crew of the Halifax had an enjoyable 10 minutes sport stalking the balloon before it was dispatched by the Halifax's gunners. The deflated blimp fluttered to earth harmlessly 4 miles from the camp. Having visited the SHQ buildings[30] the AOC gave a pep talk to all aircrew after which he was introduced to the officers in the anti-room of the Officers' Mess. After lunch with the SASO[31] from 4 group and the Station Commander, he was driven around the airfield where he visited various sections. His inspection complete he bade everyone farewell and re-boarded the Halifax before taking off for Pocklington. A few days later on July 21st a farewell message was received from Air Vice Marshall A Conningham DSO MC DFC AFC expressing his regret on relinquishing his command of 4 Group. Conningham was handing command over to AVM C R (Roddy) Carr CB CBE DFC AFC.

During the morning three of the squadron's aircraft had been engaged on a fighter affiliation exercise with Hurricanes from Catterick. At 12:45, after the exercise was over, one of the fighters followed the Halifaxes back to Middleton. As P/O Blackwell in L9533 was overflying the airfield at about 500 feet the Hurricane began a mock diving attack on the bomber. Blackwell over-banked the Halifax, which immediately entered into a very steep turn, after which control was lost and the aircraft spun into the ground, killing all on board. It is possible that the bomber suffered rudder lock-over; from such a low altitude, recovery would have been impossible. Norman Frankish remembers this tragedy. He recalls that at the time the squadron had but a few Halifaxes and the groundcrew were working overtime to prepare them for operations. Norman and his oppos took great pride in their work and the squadron, and they were devastated by this incident.

Norman Frankish and his oppos doing daily inspection of MP-L   Photo: IWM CH.3393

[30] SHQ - Station Headquarters
[31] Senior Air Staff Officer

Operation Sunrise

On the 24th, 76 joined the Halifaxes of 35 for a 'daylight raid to the docks at La Pallice in the Bay of Biscay. The target was to be the Scharnhorst, which had left her sister ship the Gneisenau and their support ships in Brest harbour. Wing Commander Jarman of 76 Squadron led the raid, which was to be without fighter escort, and involved a total of 15 aircraft. This operation followed a raid the night before, which included aircraft from other squadrons including 77 who were based at Topcliffe. They had lost Whitley V Z6643 flown by F/L Dury. He and his crew of three were injured when they crashed near Swindon after 7 hours in the air.

The raid was to commence from an advance base, Stanton Harcourt in Oxfordshire. This was Abingdon's satellite airfield and was situated 190 miles nearer to the target. Taking off from this more southerly airfield allowed the aircraft extra fuel and reduced the distance to be flown from approximately 1,400 miles to 1,020. Taking off from Stanton Harcourt at 10.35, the first flight was led by W/C Jarman. S/L Walter Williams, who had just replaced Tom Sawyer as 76 Squadron's A Flight commander led the second. One of his aircraft had experienced engine problems whilst running up, and they lost about 10 minutes whilst the crew ran to a spare aircraft and prepared it for flight. Jarman and Williams agreed over the R/T that the first flight would not waste any more time and would take off. It was decided that both flights would rendezvous over Swindon before setting off together. When S/L Williams and his second flight eventually reached Swindon they did not meet up with W/C Jarman. As they were now well behind schedule Williams decided that rather than waste even more time they would set out for La Pallice alone.

The Lizard was reached about lunchtime and this heralded a change of course onto the next leg of the journey. To foil the enemy radar operators they flew at 1,000 feet and headed on a course that would take them west of Brest. On the second leg to the target F/L Hillary had to turn back with engine trouble leaving only two aircraft in Walter William's formation, his own and F/O McKenna's. As they approached La Pallice they flew over the seaside resort of L'Aiguillon-sur-Mer. They were unaware that as W/C Jarman's flight had passed this position a few minutes earlier, fighters had shot down F/L Lewin, in L9529. Ahead, and already over the target, W/C Jarman's flight was taking a pasting. F/S Greaves of 35 Squadron was hit by flak and in quick succession attacked by a fighter. Having straddled the target he and his crew baled out over the island of Saint-Martin-de-Re, off La Rochelle, all were to become POWs. Another crew from 35, under F/S Goodwin, were shot down northwest of the target area, only the radio operator P/O Eperon and the engineer Sgt Balcombe managed to bale out. S/L Bradley's Halifax was also hit; the wireless-op was killed and the second dickie was hit in the leg. The bomb-doors were jammed but they managed to get them open on their first run and save themselves a second suicidal trek through the flak. And so the carnage went on.

As the bomb-aimer of W/O Holden's aircraft was about to press the tit, an explosion below the nose wrecked the release mechanism, punctured the port tyre and damaged the wings. A fighter attacked with machine-gun fire and badly injured both waist gunners. Showing great courage and tenacity, Sgts Smith and Perriement quickly returned to their guns and fired on their attacker. Later Sgt Smith fell into a coma. The flak barrage was extremely intense, and there were many fighters on the way to the target, but when he arrived, Walter Williams saw no other aircraft over the target area, not even any of the Halifaxes from the other flight. Now down to two aircraft, he began to make his bomb run. Because the bomb-aimer was not sure that he had the Scharnhorst correctly in his bombsight, he asked for another run to be carried out. So with P/O J F P J McKenna still following, they continued over the target area accompanied by a curtain of flak. Having flown through the jaws of Hell, Williams circled around to the start point to make another run-in. Looking around for the other Halifax, L9517, he realised that he alone had made it through the flak. McKenna had been shot down. There were no survivors.

For Williams, the second run-in was better and the bomb-load was dropped, but not before they received hits to the starboard side of the aircraft. Streaming Glycol from one engine on that side, they headed out to sea. Seconds later a second engine on the starboard side failed after an attack from a Me109. Walter Williams called to his crew on the intercom to tell them that he was unable to maintain height on the two port engines and they were to prepare for ditching. No one had ever successfully ditched a Halifax before, so tensions were high as the bomber began its descent to the sea below. They were about eight miles off the French coast when they hit the water. The wireless operator Norman Kershaw had used the minutes before ditching to good use. He had rattled off a SOS on the W/T, stating that they had been hit by flak and fighters. He also reported that the Scharnhorst had been hit. The next thing he remembers is lying in the fuselage with water lapping around him. He shed his harness and found himself up on the wing. He jumped into the sea next to the dinghy, once in the water he tried to remove his heavy flying boots but he passed out. He was dragged unconscious into the dinghy by his crewmates who had all survived the ditching. His nose had to be lifted back into place although he recalls feeling no pain. A few tense minutes passed as the fighter made several passes over their heads, fortunately without firing at them. The pilot must have been on the radio to his base reporting their position. They had been in the water for about half an hour when a French fishing boat hove into view altered course and came alongside. Once inside the fishing boat it headed for La Rochelle but a German patrol boat appeared on the scene and took them to the shore. Having carried out the first ever successful ditching of a Halifax they, unlike many of their fellow airmen who set of for La Pallice that day, would spend the rest of the war as POWs.

Harry Drummond had been following the lead aircraft when his rear gunner Sgt Begbie spoke on the intercom. The gunner had just returned fire on a fighter, and was reporting to Harry that he had hit the 109, when he too was hit. Almost at the same moment another fighter came in for a head-on attack. The enemy aircraft opened fire and Harry's windscreen shattered, sending an icy blast of air through the cockpit. The salvo had missed him by inches. Sgt Hutchin, who had been standing at the astrodome behind him, picked himself up from the cockpit floor, amazed that he was not injured. Harry's hands were peppered with Perspex wounds from the shattered windscreen, but he kept Jarman's aircraft in sight and followed suit when he saw the bomb-doors open and the load fall from the Halifax in front. Harry's bombs fell about 300 yards short of the Scharnhorst. As the Halifaxes cleared the area the flak subsided. The fighters began to disappear back to their bases to count the loss of four of their number shot down. W/C Jarman had delayed his landing at Stanton Harcourt so Harry Drummond, who had fallen behind and limped back on three engines, was able to carry out a straight in approach. There were five Halifaxes lost on this raid and a further 10 damaged. The bombs used were armour piercing, and although five hits were made on the ship, three of the bombs passed through the hull without exploding and only made small holes. The remaining hits also did not cause major damage. Despite her hull being heavily flooded with thousands of tons of water, she was able to sail back to Brest that night under the cover of darkness.

At Brest repairs began that would take over four months to complete. The repair facilities were much better there and she could be better defended. Thus ended a raid that was branded a complete success. This raid had come at a time when Bomber Command had already learned the stark lessons of sending unescorted bombers on daylight raids. Despite enduring extreme flak and fighter opposition, the crews of 35 and 76 carried out this operation with gallantry of the highest order.

At 13:00 hrs on July 30th came great news. German radio announced via X group, quoted by BUP, that the following were prisoners of war: 39359 Squadron Leader Williams W R and his crew.

78 Squadron – July 1941

July for 78 Squadron began on the 2nd, when 14 aircraft were detailed for a raid on Cologne. They were to join 19 other Whitleys and 9 Wellingtons from other squadrons. Only 10 Whitleys of 78 Squadron actually reached the target. One was a non-starter due to brake pressure trouble, a second aircraft landed at Hemswell in Lincolnshire with its bombs, having returned with engine trouble. Yet another Whitley, Z6491 flown by Sgt Jones, developed engine trouble on the way to the target, and attacked the airfield at Flushing instead. Finally a fourth aircraft failed to return. This was Whitley Z6658 flown by Sgt A Jepson. Having taken off from Goosepool at 23:24, this aircraft was shot down by Lt Reinhold Knacke of 11./NJG1. It crashed at Itteren, 3 miles from the centre of Maastricht in Holland. Along with Sgt Jepson, his observer P/O G M Kennedy, WOP/AG Sgt G A Avory, and tail gunner Sgt J F Hollingworth, were killed. They are buried in Jonkerbos War Cemetery.

Sgt McLean's crew bombed from a height of 12,000 feet through 2/10ths cloud. When the bombs hit, the second pilot Sgt Muttart and the observer Sgt Millard-Tucker saw a huge green flash but due to ground haze identification of the target was impossible. The flak was intense and the rear gunner Sgt Byrne reported that his turret was U/S. On the way home the Whitley felt a bit sluggish. It later transpired that two of the 250-lb bombs had hung up in the bomb bay. Christopher Cheshire in Z6625 bombed from 12,000 feet. Sgt Lang the second pilot and Slim Smalley the observer saw the flashes of their HE as it hit, along with incendiaries as they, too, landed on the target. They saw a building resembling a warehouse burning fiercely. On their return during de-briefing they reported that opposition was light flak and moderate searchlights. All crews reported not being able to identify the target due to the ground haze and 8/10th cloud between 2-3,000 feet.

On the 3rd, Squadron Leader Sawyer took command of 78 Squadron when Wing Commander Robinson was posted to 35. F/L Lawrence then became 78 Squadron's A Flight Commander, as S/L 'Willie' Williams was posted over to 76. The 5th saw 13 aircraft detailed for a raid on Munster although due to engine trouble one was cancelled. All aircraft dispatched returned safely to Middleton. After a raid on Osnabruck on the 7th, the Whitleys of 78 were detailed to attack Hamm on the 8th. One aircraft became a non-starter as its rear turret and oxygen system became U/S. On their way home the crew of Z6555 had transmitted an FGQ at 23:03 before disappearing forever beneath the cold waters of the North Sea. The reason for their demise is unknown. Only the body of Sgt K Noddle, the wireless operator, was washed up on the Danish Island of Romo where he is buried in the Kirkeby Cemetery. The rest of the crew have no graves. The aircraft's captain, Sgt McLean RAAF, second pilot Sgt C McMartin RCAF, observer P/O H H Mountain and rear gunner Sgt L Byrne are all commemorated on the Runnymede Memorial.

On the Hamm raid, P/O Wright was flying Christopher Cheshire's Whitley, Z6625 EY-L). Chesh did not need it anymore, as the day before he had left 78 to be posted over to fly Halifaxes with 76 on the other side of the airfield. Wright and his crew had bombed Hamm and were on their return flight when the port engine failed. After 5 hours of flying and low on fuel, Chesh's pride and joy was diverting to Bircham Newton when, during a forced landing, it collided with a haystack at Shernborne, Norfolk. The crash was timed at 04:04, fortunately the crew escaped without injury.

Sgt Hafferden

At 23:00 hours on the same night, yet another Whitley, EY-W T4209, had taken off from Middleton St George. Its destination was also the railway marshalling yards at Hamm, 18 miles northeast from the centre of Dortmund in the Ruhr Valley. This raid involved a minimum round trip of 1002 miles. The first leg of the flight took the crew on a direct track of 165° to RAF Wyton, a distance of 158 miles, that would take them one hour and thirteen minutes into their journey. The navigator, or rather the observer as they were called at that time of the war, was Sgt J F Hafferden. During the flight to their first turning point he calculated the Whitley's ground speed to be 128 mph.

As they approached Peterborough, Sgt Hafferden informed the pilot, Sgt W M McQuitty RAAF, that they had 17 miles to run to Wyton, which is three miles due east of Huntingdon. Having reached Wyton, the Whitley was swung around to port and its nose pointed almost eastward onto a track of 096°. This course would take them to the coast at Dunwich, on the south side of the river Blyth. Dunwich is a small coastal town in Suffolk, just 4 miles below Southwold and 22 miles south of Great Yarmouth. The river Blyth was a very good coastal pinpoint for navigators, as it snakes from Blythburgh to Walberswick on the coast. As they began to leave Wyton behind, WOP/AG, Sgt D J Clow looked down at the Stirling bombers of 15 Squadron parked at their dispersals. 'Lucky sods, all tucked up in their beds, they are', he said over the intercom. 'Alright for some', replied Sgt Hafferden, distantly, without looking up from his charts. As they flew over the final 75 mile stretch of English countryside, little did the crew know that for some of them, this was the last time they would gaze down on England. As Dunwich was reached, again Hafferden checked their progress. Having taken 27 minutes to fly from their last turning point, this had given them a ground speed of 166 mph, thanks to the strong westerly wind. Now it was time to leave England behind and set course for the Dutch coast - and the flak. As they were turning, he watched the compass; as it came around to 101°, McQuitty straightened the Whitley and they thundered out to sea.

Sgt McQuitty opened the throttles wider as they crossed the coast. He had been nursing fuel whilst over friendly soil, but now he let the Whitley have its head and the speed began to pick up. Their ground speed rose to 181 mph. Just over 110 miles separated them from the friendly skies of England and the reception committee waiting at the flak intensive Dutch coast after the flight over the cold inhospitable North Sea.

On reaching the small hamlet of Monster on the Dutch coast, Sgt Hafferden checked their position. This should have been about 6 miles southwest of the Hague, and about 5 miles northeast of Hoek Van Holland (Hook of Holland). 'Spot on', he murmured to himself. 'Course change Skipper', he called on the intercom, 'turn left one degree to one zero zero, distance to target 157 miles.' 'Don't be bloody stupid', called back the incredulous voice of the skipper, 'I can't fly to within one bloody degree.' 'Well what can you fly to?' enquired Hafferden, smirking to himself. 'You know damn well, two or three degrees' said the skipper. 'OK', said Hafferden, 'turn left three degrees', and as the bomber began to turn, he added, 'now back two degrees.' The reply from McQuitty is unprintable.

Just over forty-nine minutes later they were approaching the target area. Although there were also 45 Hampdens and 28 Whitleys involved in the raid, only one or two were visible to the crew of EY-W. It would transpire that for one reason or another, only 31 aircraft would successfully attack the main target. By now McQuitty had reached his bombing height of 12,000 feet. As they clearly identified the target and its Initial Point (IP) they turned onto 025° and began their run-in. In order to obtain accurate bombing, they gritted their teeth, defied the flak, and flew straight and level towards the bomb release point. The bomb-aimer had the target in his bombsight. With only a few seconds left before he released the bombs they were coned by searchlights, followed in quick succession by the flak.

One shell struck the side of the front turret. This was not allowed to deter the bomb run and they pressed on with their attack. Still with no evasive action to upset accurate aiming they continued through the murderous flak. After what seemed like an eternity, the call 'Bombs gone' was heard over the intercom. The Whitley lifted, as she was relieved of her full weight of bombs. Soon after, the rear gunner, Sgt W Forster, reported that they had burst accurately on the target. Now free of the duty to precisely lay the bombs on the target, severe evasive action was the order of the day. Still with its mantle of light, courtesy of many searchlights, Sgt McQuitty hauled the Whitley around the sky in an attempt to shake off the beams and also the intense flak barrage that accompanied them. The aircraft received repeated hits, some were absorbed without hitting anything vital, but one shell removed the Pitot tube, rendering the Airspeed Indicator useless. This hit was followed shortly after by another that struck the starboard engine, setting it alight. The fire quickly burned itself out but soon after - the engine stopped. Despite attempts by McQuitty and the second pilot P/O E A Scott, it was not possible to restart the engine. Due to the situation he found himself in, McQuitty had great difficulty in flying the bomber accurately. Now in a mad dash for the Dutch Coast and safety, they pressed for home. As they took a direct route for Middleton their course led them northwest. After only 53 miles they were down to 8,000 feet and still losing height. At this point on the Dutch/German border they had only to fly another 110 miles to clear enemy held territory.

The flak was still niggling at them as at 5,000 feet they reached the east of Lemmer, a small coastal town on the Ijsselmeer, some 48 miles northwest of Amsterdam. Fortunately the gunner's aim was off, and they were not hit. As they crossed the last small spit of land and passed over the coast at Hendeloopen, there was hope at last as they saw beneath them the waters of the Waddenzee. One final obstacle lay in their path. Waiting some 28 miles ahead of them in the inky darkness of the night was a gap, but not just any gap. As they left the enemy coast for the relative safety of the North Sea, one last card could be dealt against them by the Grim Reaper. This was his last chance to get them, just when they thought they were safe. Invisible to them as yet were the Friesian islands and one in particular called Texel. Lying off the Dutch mainland, these islands were famous for their heavy flak batteries. It almost seemed that they were placed there by fate, to allow the Germans to guard the entrance and exit to and from Holland and beyond into Germany. Crews had a healthy respect for these Islands that were lying directly in their flight paths, and the flak ships, which also took their toll of many an allied bomber. The Whitley continued on its direct track, a track that hopefully would lead it, all being well, through the small gap between the islands of Texel to the south and Vlieland to the north. The gap is no more than 2.24 miles wide, and at the bomber's height of 4,000 feet this was practically nothing. To make things worse a flak ship had been placed halfway between the islands to close the gap to would be enemies of the Reich. The Whitley was a sitting duck at such a low altitude, but for some strange reason the flak ship did not open fire. Nor did the main flak guns located on each of the two islands open up.

The crew wondered at their luck, were the gunners asleep? Soon the answer came as Sgt Forster in the rear turret sent a shiver through the crippled bomber, 'There's an aircraft coming up astern Skip, I can't identify it yet though.' McQuitty called back, 'Alright, keep an eye on him.' Soon after, the rear gunner identified the aircraft as being a Me110 night fighter, probably from the airfield on Texel itself. The aircraft opened fire on the Whitley. Forster returned fire, and the enemy aircraft dived away steeply heading off for the safety of the night. Amazingly it appeared that no damage had been inflicted and at last they were free of the guns and the fighters to wend their weary way home. In a change of plan McQuitty asked Hafferden for a new course, this time to Bircham Newton, East Anglia. Although 170 miles to the west this would shorten the sea crossing considerably as the remaining engine was working overtime to keep the failing bomber in the air.

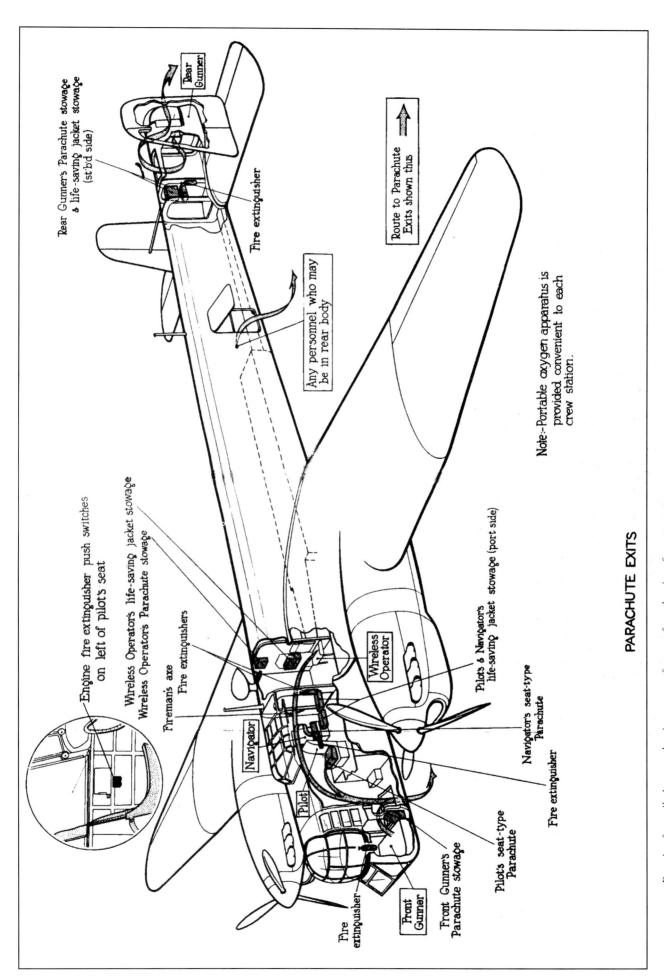

Rear Gunner's Parachute stowage
& life-saving jacket stowage
(st'b'd side)

Rear Gunner

Fire extinguisher

Route to Parachute
Exits shown thus

Any personnel who may
be in rear body

Note:- Portable oxygen apparatus is
provided convenient to each
crew station.

Engine fire extinguisher push switches
on left of pilot's seat

Wireless Operator's life-saving jacket stowage
Wireless Operator's Parachute stowage

Fireman's axe
Fire extinguishers

Wireless
Operator

Navigator

Pilot

Pilots & Navigator's
life-saving jacket stowage (port side)

Navigator's seat-type
Parachute

Fire extinguisher

Pilot's seat-type
Parachute

Front Gunner's Parachute stowage

Front
Gunner

Fire
extinguisher

PARACHUTE EXITS

Drawing from pilot's notes showing means of escape from the aircraft   Photo: © crown copyright/MOD, reproduced with the permission of the Controller of Her Majesty's Stationery Office

By the time they were approaching the Wash and had reached a position some 9 miles from the English Coast, the engine was overheating badly, and they were down to about 800 feet. McQuitty ordered the second pilot P/O E A Scott to go aft and get the dingy ready, as it was inevitable that they would have to ditch. Soon after, at 400 feet, the engine seized. Not knowing his airspeed, Sgt McQuitty had great difficulty flying the aircraft. Now in a semi-stalled condition, he was unable to flare the aircraft and the Whitley fell into the sea.

Hafferden remembered that the aircraft seemed to go right under the water but it soon surfaced and floated in a nose-down attitude. The tanks, now five and a half hours lighter in fuel, provided some temporary buoyancy. The front section began filling with water very quickly. Looking at his watch he could see that they had crashed at 04:29. McQuitty and Hafferden crawled their way back through the, by now, almost completely water filled fuselage. Reaching the escape hatch in the side of the aircraft they found it jammed by the impact of the crash.

The crew proceeded aft, the water already up to their chests. They were hoping to escape via the rear turret. Sgt Hafferden picked up the dinghy and took it with him. He also found the crash axe and was able to use this to free the rear gunners top escape hatch, which was situated just forward of the rear turret. The gunner was by now sitting on the top of the fuselage at the extreme end of the tail. He was wounded with blood pouring from his eyes. However the gunner was able to assist Sgt Hafferden, who was the last to leave the aircraft, in pushing the dinghy out through the hatch. Once out of the aircraft and into the sea, Hafferden pulled the chord and the dinghy inflated and, almost immediately, deflated. It must have been holed by flak or by the attacking fighter, who might, after all, have sealed their fate. The rest of the crew were in the water and the rear gunner said he could not inflate his Mae West, (life Jacket, named after the famous and frontally well endowed film star). Sgt Hafferden gave his life jacket to the gunner and told the rest of the crew to hang onto the dinghy, which was still just afloat.

Sgt Hafferden began to strip off his heavy flying gear, and with a promise to return with help, set off to swim towards a light they could see. After some time he realised that it was a lightship and was too far to the east of him. The strong current would prevent him reaching it. He turned around and swam in the opposite direction. Presently he came across the waterlogged dinghy, floating nearby was the Mae West he had given to the gunner. Of the rest of the crew there was no sign. By now dawn was approaching and in the pale gathering light he put the life jacket under his chest and chin and began to swim to the darkest part of the horizon, which he hoped was land and with a little luck, safety. After a while his Mae West became partially waterlogged and he decided that he would be able to swim better without it. Twice he discarded the jacket but each time returned for it as he felt he was unable to swim to land without it. The third time he decided to leave the jacket as the light had improved and he could now see land. He was swimming the breaststroke but he became stricken with cramp. Changing to the crawl he managed to reach the shore, exhausted after swimming 9 miles. But his ordeal was not completely over, as when he had recovered his strength, he had to walk through the barbed wire up the beach. Having cleared the beach he began to walk along a path, which after a couple of miles led to a Coast Guard Cottage. Once there, he relayed his story to the Coast Guard, who immediately enquired how he had got there. 'You walked up the beach you say? What! Straight through the minefield?' Hafferden looked at him in disbelief. It had been a close call. It seamed that all beaches were mined against German invasion. After he had recovered from that, the Coast Guard assisted him in telephoning the switchboard at Bircham Newton. An immediate search for the rest of the crew began both by sea and air, but failed to find any trace of his missing crew. They were never seen again and are today commemorated on the Runnymede Memorial.

July 10th saw 78 detail 8 aircraft, including 1 fresher, for operations to Oldenburg. One Whitley never left Middleton, its port wheel seized whilst it taxied out to the runway. After the first three aircraft had taken off the 'Cancel Operation' Order was received and the Whitleys were recalled.

Meanwhile, for Michael Renaut and the other trainee pilots at Kinloss, the Whitley conversion course ended on July 14th. Michael was due seven days leave prior to going to an operational squadron, but this was short lived as half way through it he received orders to head north. Michael was to be posted to 78 Squadron based at Middleton St George. When Michael Renaut arrived at Darlington's Bank Top railway station on the 23rd, he remembered from his history lessons that the town was famous for its railway heritage. The world's first ever railway journey had taken place between Darlington and Stockton. But now the railway had brought him to his first operational squadron.

On his arrival at Goosepool/Middleton, Michael was informed that he was to be posted from 78 Squadron to 76. This 'posting' was to last a whole 3 days, as on the 26th, along with Sgts Lambeth, Thomas, Beardmore and Herbert, he was to be detached to 78 Squadron.

Manoeuvres July 1941

The airfield was attacked by 1,000 crazed enemy soldiers on July 29th, or, rather, by a contingent of the Divisional Durham Light Infantry (DLI). This was part of an airfield defence exercise, and they were fortunately repulsed by the defenders. The exercise was not without its casualties however. The M/O[32] was gainfully employed throughout the day, treating a small number of cuts and bruises. He also had some stitching up to do, but everyone seemed to enjoy the chance to let off a little steam.

Dawn had heralded the beginning of the exercise. All methods of communication were tested and found to be in good working order. Instructions received from DLI Brigade HQ were read out to the waiting airfield defenders. These included the golden rule that no blank ammunition would be fired at anyone at less than 50 yards range. No sooner had the defenders received their briefing than the air-raid sirens began to sound. Simultaneously a signal was received from BHQ[33] that enemy

[32] Medical Officer
[33] Brigade Headquarters

aircraft were approaching the station. The station's AA guns opened fire on the enemy aircraft (Ansons, Hurricanes and a Lysander). Word came through that the airfield perimeter was being heavily dive-bombed, the order came for all guns to open fire. The Airfield defenders did themselves proud and reported that they had shot down the Lysander. Airfield police reported that enemy paratroopers were landing in the vicinity of the aerodrome. Then came the order to stand-to, followed by word that the enemy paratroopers had been shot by a sniper.

Meanwhile, in the woods to the north of the airfield, Pilot Officer Taylor in the Armadillo reported that the enemy had been sighted and he was opening fire. BHQ signalled, 'We are sending up a reconnaissance that will fire a red Very light on sighting the enemy.' P/O Taylor sent a signal that he was sending a patrol of four men in Indian file into the woods, to ascertain the strength of the enemy. A short time later he signalled that he was engaging the enemy in small numbers at 200 yards range, due north of Y post. This was confirmed by a friendly aircraft that signalled with a red light the position and number of the enemy in the location given by P/O Taylor. A mobile platoon patrolling the road on the northern perimeter of the airfield (the Darlington to Yarm road), signalled that they had sighted the enemy north of the railway line, strength unknown. The enemy was then covered by machine guns and the defenders inflicted heavy casualties. Another section of enemy personnel were approaching the Battalion HQ, they were engaged by No.1 post. Meanwhile two casualties (Station personnel) were taken by ambulance from the Armadillo to the Station Sick Quarters (SSQ).

The enemy was then sighted by the NCO in charge of the Bomb Dump. They were entering the camp via the dump to create a pincer movement. Following this, Wing Commander Jarman reported that he had captured two lorry loads of prisoners, and was then instructed to escort them to SHQ. His work completed, P/O Taylor returned to patrol the camp with the Armadillo. The enemy had occupied the pillbox east of the bomb dump and was advancing in single file towards the airfield. Meanwhile, at Oaktree Farm, the enemy attacked under the cover of a smokescreen. The attack was repulsed by the defenders but not without heavy losses.

Next the enemy attacked and captured the guardroom as one of their number was shot in front of the Sergeants' Mess. Meanwhile at the bomb-dump, A Company succeeded in wiping out the enemy. Soon after, the enemy sent reinforcements to the bomb-dump; these were taken prisoner by A Company. After this, the order was received from BHQ to 'Cease fire.'

During the exercise a 78 Squadron Whitley, Z6838, had taken off for a routine training flight. Flown by Sgt Turnbull RCAF, this aircraft crashed at the end of its take-off run, just beyond the airfield's boundary, fortunately without serious injury to the crew. The subsequent enquiry attributed the accident to jammed ailerons.

That night, 78 carried out its last raid during July, as 3 fresher crews were detailed to attack nursery targets at Boulogne. One was a non-starter due to a defective rear turret, whilst the other 2 jettisoned their bombs in the sea and came safely home, after finding the target covered by 10/10ths cloud.

76 - August 41

August 1st 1941 started with a slight mist during the early morning, followed later in the day by 10/10ths-cloud cover at less than 1,000 feet. For this reason no Ops were called. The morning of the 2nd found the cloud still in place. By lunchtime it dispersed, leaving a clear blue sky. However, during the afternoon the visibility deteriorated, due to the onset of industrial haze. During the morning four crews had been briefed for an attack on Bremen. This raid was led by S/L Bickford; all 4 of Middleton's Halifaxes bombed the target and returned safely.

Karlsruhe was the target on the 5th, despite frequent heavy showers and very strong west-northwesterly winds. Sgt McHale found the target and bombed from a height of 7,000 feet in a shallow dive. On the way home from the target existing fires, along with those from his bomb-load, were visible from over 80 miles away.

Christopher Cheshire in MP-L comes in close for the photographer Photo: IWM CH.3383

The next night, 76 lost Halifax L9516, flown by Sgt T A Byrne, whilst on a raid to Karlsruhe. This aircraft crashed in Belgium near the town of Glebeek, 25 miles east of Brussels. With the exception of the front gunner, Sgt R Brown, the crew survived. Sgt Brown is buried in Germany's Durnbach War Cemetery. Later in the war, after taking part in the mass breakout from Sagen POW camp, the rear gunner, F/L T B Leigh, was shot in cold blood by the Germans on March 30th 1944,[34] along with about 50 other British POWs. He is buried in Poznan Old Garrison Cemetery, in Poland.

On the night of the 7th, four crews were briefed for a raid on the Krupps works at Essen. However, this was reduced to three just prior to take off, when one of the Halifaxes shed its bomb-load all over its dispersal whilst taxiing out. Fortunately the 4,000-lb 'Cookie' languishing within the bomb bay decided to stay put. The aircraft had been carrying an army officer in the second dickie's seat, who was along for the ride. He was most dis-chuffed when told that they could not go.

Next day, Wing Commander G T Jarman was awarded the DSO, whilst F/L Bastin and F/O Brisbain received the DFC. Also decorated were Sgt Frazer and Sgt Bell, who both received the DFM.

The night of August 12th was to prove very eventful for 76. Led by Christopher Cheshire, seven crews were detailed for a raid on Berlin. The first Halifax airborne was Sgt McHale's, which was logged off at 21:29. Eight hours later this aircraft was seen approaching Middleton. The bomber turned onto final approach, the crew no doubt looking forward to some well-earned sleep. As the aircraft began to reduce speed ready for touchdown, possibly as the flaps were lowered, the bomber stalled, hit the ground and burst into flames, killing all on board. An investigation into the crash was carried out. After the wreckage was examined, it was thought that the Halifax had been damaged by enemy action.

P/O Dobson, Sgts Dunlop, Hutchin and Drummond returned safe. Dobson had attacked Berlin, having taken 3 hours and 50 minutes to get there. Hutchin had failed to climb above a weather-front sitting over the Friesian Islands and elected to attack Bremen instead. Over the target area the flak had been intense. Harry Drummond's Halifax had been holed by flak in several places. Due to engine trouble, Dunlop had jettisoned his bombs at 53° 26 North - 07° 36 East, which turned out to be 3 km N/E of the sleepy little German hamlet of Wrisse, 9 km S/E of Aurich. Of the two remaining aircraft, flown by Sgt Whitfield and F/L Christopher Cheshire, nothing further was heard. It later transpired that Leutnant Hans Autenrieth of NJG1 had shot down MP-R L9531, flown by Sgt Whitfield. The Halifax had come down 500 metres east of Wittstedt, some 15-km S/S/E of Bremerhaven. All of the crew were able to bail out. However, out of the seven-man crew, only Sgt Kenworthy and F/S Bone survived to become POWs. The remaining five drowned when they fell into a swamp.

As for the loss of Christopher Cheshire and his crew, this story is best told in Ken Marshall's excellent book, 'The Pendulum and the Scythe', The History of 4 Group. During the research for his book, Ken had the good fortune to be able to interview both Christopher and Leonard Cheshire, before they both passed away (Christopher died after Leonard during 1999). As my research began after the death of Christopher, Ken has been kind enough to allow me to relate verbatim to the reader from his book, the events surrounding the loss of Christopher Cheshire and his crew during the fateful night of August 12th 1941.

One of the friendships that Christopher Cheshire made when he first arrived on 78 Squadron in January 1941 was with a jovial army officer, who had been seconded to the unit as an advisor on air defence matters. In the Officers' Mess one evening, he spoke of his love of game shooting and invited Christopher up to his shoot in Scotland on the 'Glorious Twelfth'. Chesh had, however, already booked his annual leave for earlier in the summer and, realising that it would be very difficult to arrange for more so soon afterwards, he thanked his would-be benefactor but had to decline his generous offer. The army officer replied that he quite understood but added that he was sure it would be far more enjoyable taking pot shots at grouse than being potted by German flak, a sentiment with which Christopher wholeheartedly agreed.

At Middleton St George, Tuesday August 12th dawned with mist and early morning showers. There were variable amounts of cloud all day, and westerly winds in the region of ten to twenty mph. The showers returned briefly during the early evening, but, by half-past-eight, as 'Chesh' and his crew walked across the tarmac to 'L for London', it was a lovely evening. At the briefing earlier that evening, the crew had learned that they were to fly L9530 as one of six Halifaxes from 76 Squadron that were to form part of a seventy aircraft force detailed to attack the German Air Ministry buildings in Berlin. The crew comprised of all six of the 'regulars'; Chris Cheshire – 1st pilot and aircraft captain, on his 25th operation with Bomber Command, Paul Horrox – 2nd pilot, on his 5th operation, Slim Smalley – observer, on his 26th, Taff Gurmin - wireless operator, on his 29th Reggie Wash - flight engineer, on his 6th, and rear gunner Timber Woods, on his 6th. The 7th crewmember for this trip was a new WOP/AG about to undertake his very first operation; Sergeant Geoff (Jock) Niven would occupy the front turret.

As the crew walked to L9530, Christopher Cheshire's thoughts were far removed from shooting grouse in Scotland. Having just been reminded that he was due to be screened from operations shortly, he was in fact, thinking more about where he was likely to be posted at the end of his tour. Having reached the Halifax however, all such thoughts vanished as the crew began to carry out their pre-flight checks. Chesh and Slim checked out the enormous 4,000-lb Cookie that had been winched up into the aircraft's belly. Unfortunately the Halifax bomb bay had not been designed to accommodate such a large bomb, and the only way it could be fitted in was to leave the bomb doors partly open, with the bomb protruding into the slipstream, adding a considerable amount of drag to the airframe. The crew climbed into MP-L, started the four Merlin engines, and completed their internal pre-flight checks. Then, with the usual 'thumbs up' from their groundcrew chief, Flight Sergeant Brown, and his lads, they taxied out in line to the end of the runway. As usual when carrying a 4,000-pounder, Chesh found the take-off a very tense time, but he felt much more at ease once he had lifted the Halifax off the runway and cleared the hedge on the airfield boundary.

---

[34] As depicted in the film "The Great Escape"

The Duty Officer logged L9530 as airborne at 21.35 hours. Having set course on the briefed route for Berlin, they climbed slowly but steadily to an altitude of 12,000 feet, and settled down for the long haul to the 'Big City'. It was not until 1986, when Christopher and his brother Leonard were talking 'old times', that he learned that Leonard had tried to telephone him several times prior to take-off to warn him against following the briefed route to Berlin, as he was convinced that it would be disastrous. Leonard Cheshire was at that time a Squadron Leader on his second tour (he'd somehow managed to stretch his first to fifty operations) and a Flight Commander with 35 Squadron stationed at Linton-on-Ouse. Had the call reached Christopher, he would certainly have followed his brother's advice. Squadron Leader G L Cheshire followed his own hunch and took a more southerly route to that briefed. He and his crew had a trouble-free trip, while watching aircraft to the north of them getting hammered by flak. As it was, L for London was steadily cruising along the official route, heading for the enemy coast that they were to cross roughly mid-way between Bremen and Hamburg, both of which had been offered as secondary targets.

When MP-L was about thirty minutes flying time from the German coast, Reggie Wash, the flight engineer, who by his very nature was unflappable, informed Chesh that their fuel consumption was all to hell and they'd already used so much that they couldn't possibly make it to Berlin and have enough to be able to return to base. Neither Washy nor Chesh could think of any reason why the consumption should have been so high, so, in case it was just the fuel gauges messing about they agreed to continue on their present course for another fifteen minutes and check again. A quarter of an hour later, the Skipper handed control over to Paul Horrox and joined Washy at the flight engineer's panel behind the pilot's seat. Sure enough, the gauges showed that a little over half their fuel load was already gone. Chesh realised that Washy's dismal forecast was right and asked Slim to work out a course for the nearest alternative target. He returned to his seat and took control back from Paul. Seconds later, Slim came back with a course for Hamburg, which was marginally closer than Bremen, so, on a cloudless night with good visibility, Chesh turned the Halifax to port and headed for Germany's second largest city. They met very little flak until they were on the outskirts of Hamburg itself and then all hell broke loose around them. Being the only RAF bomber over the City, every Luftwaffe anti-aircraft gun crew in Hamburg was able to give MP-L its undivided attention. Lying on his belly in the nose of the aircraft, Slim Smalley released the bombs over the centre of the city, and Chesh then held the Halifax straight and level for the one-and-a-half minutes required to take their aiming point photograph. Miraculously the enemy flak gunners missed this heaven-sent opportunity to blast them out of the sky. Hearing Slim say 'Bombs gone', Taff got on the radio to transmit back to base the 'Operation completed' signal. Chesh operated the lever to close the bomb doors, and was waiting to feel them clunk shut when the first flak shells hit them. Initially, Chesh still had control of the bucking Halifax but then there was an almighty crash at the rear of the aircraft and both his and Paul's control columns went totally limp in their hands. Neither control column had any effect whatsoever on the aircraft's behaviour, nor did either of the trim wheels. The Halifax went into a gentle nose down position and Christopher Cheshire had little option but to order his crew to abandon ship. Taff Gurmin had just received Base's acknowledgement of his signal and plugged back into the intercom as Chesh said, 'Jump for it boys.' Taff couldn't believe his ears, 'Do you mean bale out Skipper?' he asked. 'Yes', said Chesh, 'And make it quick!' Although the Halifax was at 11,000 feet when it was so badly hit, time was still of the essence. Slim Smalley's seat was directly over the nose compartment escape hatch, so he folded his seat away in preparation to open the hatch. Taff tried to get to the hatch as quickly as possible, but in his rush he'd forgotten to disconnect his oxygen tube from the economiser. He lunged forward only to be almost catapulted back to his radio set as the oxygen tube reached its limit of elasticity and then recoiled. He ripped his mask and helmet off, threw them onto the radio table and then dived forward and opened the escape hatch while Slim shook the legs of Geoff Niven in the nose turret.

As the hatch was opened a blast of icy cold air shot in through the aperture and the interior of the Halifax was filled with swirling papers and dust. Taff clipped on his parachute and stood by the open hatch, thinking that he should be second last out, just before his Skipper. He was about to try to move aside but then realised that all he would achieve would be to get in everybody else's way. He stepped forward over the hole, turned around, sat on the edge and taking his ripcord in his right hand, launched himself into space. He was closely followed by Paul Horrox and Slim Smalley, who shook hands before jumping. Thinking that all of his crew who could do so had now left the aircraft, Cheshire found himself with a small problem - he couldn't locate his parachute. After two minutes frantic searching he found the missing item close to the escape hatch and clipped it to his harness. He was sitting on the edge of the hatch with his legs dangling out of the aircraft, just about to jump, when he noticed a movement in the centre fuselage. Pulling his legs back inside the Halifax he saw Reggie Wash coming towards him, clipping on his 'chute as he made his way forward. Washy, who had dropped the photo flash flare down the flare chute for the bombing photograph, had been knocked end over end by the big flak explosion and just managed to pick himself up and find his parachute. Having wished Reggie 'Bon voyage' and seen him off the premises, Chesh once again sat on the edge of the escape hatch before launching himself out into the cold night sky. As soon as his parachute had opened Chesh looked up and saw that L9530 had got itself into a slow spiral descent and was circling around him. The Halifax had taken on the sinister appearance of a large and ugly vampire, and the German flak was still banging away at it - and consequently at Christopher too. In true British fashion, Chesh considered this to be very un-sporting of his enemy and was greatly relieved when MP-L finally gathered speed and took itself off in an almost westerly direction, finally crashing at Parnewinkel, near the small town of Wenzendorf some twenty-five miles northeast of Bremen. It was not until 1992 that Christopher discovered why his Halifax had suddenly appeared like a vampire as it circled around him. As Paul Horrox, who was second to leave the aircraft, was floating down on his parachute, he looked up to see the Halifax sailing on quite serenely - but with no tail! The complete tail unit, from in front of the leading edge of the tailplane, had been blown off by the last direct flak hit, killing Timber Woods outright, and explaining why neither pilot had any control over the aircraft after the loud explosion. Sergeant Geoff Niven's body was found by the Germans the following morning.

Having watched his aircraft heading off to the west, Cheshire then had time to look downwards and see the type of terrain on which he was going to land. Directly below him was what looked like a large village. Remembering his classroom instruction on parachute descent, he pulled on one of the chute straps and side-slipped, changing his direction towards open fields. By luck rather than judgement, he found himself in a field in the middle of a herd of Friesian cows, who paid not the slightest attention to the interloper. Lying where he had landed for a few moments, Chesh took stock of his position. He felt very much alone and wondered what had happened to his crew. He thought about shouting out their names but realised that they were more likely to be separated by miles rather than yards, and decided that all his shouting would achieve would be to bring German soldiers to his location. He suddenly felt very hungry and reached into his flying suit pocket for the small food parcel with which he'd been issued before take off. It wasn't there. It must have fallen out, either in the aircraft or during his parachute descent. Sadly it dawned on him that the whole course of his war career had changed in a very short space of time and he wondered how his parents and brother would take the news that he was 'missing', that his aircraft had 'failed to return'. In short, Flight Lieutenant Christopher Cheshire and his crew had become a statistic. The prospect of becoming a prisoner-of-war for the duration was not one that particularly appealed and thoughts of escape were at the forefront of his mind. Still in the field in which he had landed, Christopher estimated that he was somewhere west of Hamburg and decided that his best chance of escape lay in heading west towards Holland, where he might be able to make contact with the Dutch Resistance Movement. His attention was suddenly drawn to the night sky above him where a Wellington was receiving the same treatment that he and his crew had experienced such a short while ago. The searchlights stuck to the Wimpy like a leech, flak was exploding all around it, and within seconds the Wellington was nose-diving towards the earth. Chesh had not seen anyone bale out of the stricken aircraft. Feeling very downhearted, he gathered himself together, took off his flying suit and hid it and his parachute in the ditch that separated his field from its neighbour.

Despite being a few minutes ahead of Chesh, Taff was also in the line of fire as the Germans continued to shoot at MP-L, and each near miss made his chute flap and sway. Nearing the ground Taff realised that the wind was blowing him backwards. He also remembered the advice given by 'Parachute Pete', his instructor at Yatesbury. The theory was to side-slip the chute by pulling hard on one of the straps. Taff was about to do this when he remembered the subsequent warning, 'Pull too hard and spill too much air from the chute, it will collapse and you'll end up seriously dead!' Taff decided that he would be quite happy to land backwards. Other advice came back to him as he noticed a line of trees in his probable landing area. 'When you land by parachute, its like jumping off a twelve foot wall, lad. So brace yerself!!' Working on an average tree height of forty feet, Taff decided to brace himself when level with the treetops. The next thing her knew, he was lying in a heap on the ground. The trees were actually bushes, no higher than six feet. Taff lay still for a minute, listening. All he could hear was his heart, beating more loudly and faster than usual. He stood up, released his parachute harness and took a step forward, only to sink up to his knees in a bog. (76 Squadron lost another aircraft in this same area later that night. This was L9531 flown by Sergeant C E Whitfield. He and four of his crew also landed in this same bog and tragically all were drowned. Taff Gurmin's guardian angel was certainly working overtime this night.) Using the branches to pull himself out of the mire, he climbed up onto the roots of the bushes and took a look around in the moonlight. He thought he could see a pathway about thirty feet away, so taking a deep breath, he ran like the wind towards it. The second man to walk on water reached the pathway and started to walk along it, whistling softly 'There'll always be an England' and hoping to meet up with one of the crew. No such luck. He walked straight into the arms of a Luftwaffe officer and ten men, who had watched him descend on his parachute and had come hunting for him.

Flight Lieutenant Cheshire started walking in a westerly direction. He was using the stars as a guide and progress across country was slow. At about 2 am, he found himself on a main road with an amazing amount of traffic on it for that time in the morning. In particular there seemed to be a lot of cyclists, which gave Chesh the idea of trying to 'borrow' a bicycle to help speed him on his way, supposing, of course, he could find one unattended. He decided to follow the road, hoping to find a bike standing outside a house or a garage. The first house he came to had a dog that started to bark ferociously the minute Chesh approached, so he moved on rapidly. Five minutes further down the road he came to another house with a garage attached. He crept up the path and tried the garage door but it was securely locked, so he quietly retraced his steps and carried on down the road. At the third house it looked as if his luck was in. There, leaning against an outhouse, was exactly what he was looking for. Overjoyed, he moved towards his prize when, totally out of the blue, a gun was pushed against his ribs and a husky voice said, 'For you the war is over.' Christopher found himself face to face with a German Gefreiter (corporal), who promptly handcuffed him and marched him a hundred yards or so to a Kubelwagen containing two more German soldiers. He had been caught by a patrol specifically sent out to round up RAF airmen who, like Christopher, had been unfortunate to have been shot down but fortunate enough to have survived. Flight Lieutenant Cheshire was driven in the direction of Hamburg where he was deposited at the local Luftwaffe Headquarters approximately thirty minutes later. Chris was placed in a large room, which, to his surprise, contained a large map showing all the flak gun emplacements from the Elbe Estuary to a point north of Hamburg. Each gun position had a number written inside a red circle, and not having much else to do for the moment, Chesh started to count all the emplacements. Having reached a total of 247, he was trying to assess, by means of the numbers in red circles, what this total meant in terms of individual guns when one of the doors into his room was opened and a familiar figure was led into the room.

Having been picked up by the search party, Taff Gurmin was taken to the flak post that had been responsible (so they claimed) for shooting down L9530. The Luftwaffe officer started to question the wireless operator, but Taff was not feeling particularly co-operative and the only answer he would give was, 'I don't know.' The 88mm flak guns outside the building were still banging away and Taff could hardly hear himself think. Suddenly a German soldier ran into the office in which the little Welshman was being questioned, gabbled something in an excited manner and everyone rushed outside. One of the soldiers had the presence of mind to grab Taff and pulled him along behind them. As he was being hustled outside, Taff grabbed a German steel helmet from a table and put it on his head.

He'd had enough excitement for one night and didn't fancy being brained by falling shrapnel. When he got outside everybody was looking skywards. The guns were shooting at the Wellington that Cheshire was also watching from his landing field. One of the German soldiers took a sideways glance at Taff, just to make sure he was behaving himself, saw him wearing the coal-scuttle helmet and drawing his comrades' attention to this strange sight they all fell about laughing. Even Taff managed to raise a tired smile. Sometime later Taff, now carrying his inner and outer Sidcot suits, was taken down a pathway to a road. After a minute or so a car drew up and Taff was ordered to sit next to the driver. As he walked around the car, someone in the darkness of the back seat put two fingers up to him against the rear side window. Being too tired to even wonder who it might be who was being so impolite to such a likeable chap as himself, Taff simply returned the reversed Churchillian sign, saying as he did so, 'And you mate!' He opened the front passenger door and was wondering where to put his Sidcot suits when a pair of hands emerged from the darkness of the rear of the car and took Taff's flying clothes from him. Taff climbed in and the car moved off, stopping some ten minutes later at a Luftwaffe camp. Taff was ordered out of the car and taken into a building. Seeing Chesh sitting there alive and well, Taff was so overjoyed that he momentarily forgot that they were supposed to ignore each other in enemy company and almost rushed up to his skipper to shake his hand. He remembered just in time and he and Chesh just winked at each other.

At this point the door opened again and in limped 'Washy' Wash (he had banged his leg on landing), carrying not only his own flying gear but also Taff's Sidcot suits. It had been Washy in the back of the car that had delivered Taff. Poor Reggie Wash! By this time both Chesh and Taff had regained their composure and both studiously ignored their flight engineer. They were all questioned individually and then Taff and Washy were taken to separate cells in the guardroom. Cheshire's ensuing interrogation was most civilised and basically conformed to the standards laid down in the Geneva Convention. Christopher was asked for his name and rank, information that he readily gave. After a pause, the Hauptmann (Captain) conducting the interrogation asked for Chesh's Squadron number and aircraft type. He refused point-blank to supply these details and his interrogation was terminated. He was then taken down a long corridor to a small room containing only a single bunk bed and was informed that he would shortly be going by train to an unspecified town in Germany. It seemed that he had only just dropped off to sleep when he was awoken by a shout of 'Heraus!', which can be loosely translated as the German equivalent of 'Rise and shine!' Having received a slice of black bread and a cup of ersatz coffee (made from acorns), Cheshire was handcuffed to a Feldwebel (Sergeant) and they were taken by car to Hamburg's main railway station where they met up with Taff, Washy and their guards, and boarded a train for the Dulag Luft near Frankfurt-am-Main. The journey was a long and tedious one, with the train seeming to stop at every station it came to, no matter how small it was. The Luftwaffe guards were pleasant enough, considering the circumstances, and at midday they produced black bread and wurst (sausage) for each prisoner. These were gratefully received and soon devoured, as it was some considerable time since any of them had had anything substantial to eat. At one point during the journey, a Luftwaffe pilot passed the prisoners' reserved compartment, probably on his way to the toilet. On his return he opened the compartment door and spoke to the guards, obviously checking with them that it was all right to speak to their charges. In pretty fair English he told them that he had been shot up over England and only just managed to nurse his damaged aircraft back across the Channel to crash-land in France. The burn scars on his face and hands bore testimony to this event and he'd been lucky to survive his ordeal. He then looked at Taff, smiled and said, 'Are you still going to hang out the vashing on the Siegfried Line?' 'There's still plenty of time for that, mate', replied Taff, 'you wait and see.' A little later, Cheshire apologised to Taff and Washy for landing them in their current predicament. Taff replied for both of them when he said, 'No apologies necessary, Skipper. If we'd been with anyone else we'd have bought it ages ago.'

Arriving at Frankfurt in the late afternoon, his guard bundled Cheshire into a taxi and they were driven the six miles to the Frankfurt Dulag Luft, a clearing centre to which all RAF and allied airmen prisoners were taken and processed before being sent to an Oflag (Officers' camp) or a Staling Luft (primarily for captured aircrew), both of which were fully fledged POW camps. Chesh was not taken into the Dulag itself, but was locked in a small room in a nearby building. He was given a plate of totally unpalatable food that he tried to eat sitting on the iron bedstead that was the only item of furniture in the room. Christopher was very tired and despite his surroundings, he slept until daylight. All that day he was kept in his small room, having no communication with anyone other than a somewhat taciturn guard who twice accompanied him to the nearest lavatory.

When Taff and Washy arrived at Dulag Luft, they were put into solitary confinement while their clothes were taken away to be searched. As was the practice at this time, they both had a silk map of Germany hidden in one shoulder of their battledress jackets, another of France in the other, and a small compass was sewn into the waistband of Taff's jacket. Only the compass remained when their clothes were returned. A Luftwaffe Feldwebel entered Taff's cell, opened a packet of English 'Gold Flake' cigarettes and offered one to the prisoner. 'No thanks', said Taff smugly, 'I don't smoke.' The Feldwebel then gave Taff a pencil and a form bearing the International Red Cross symbol on the top and asked him to fill it in. Taff looked at the form, seeing questions about his squadron, aircraft type, bases, etc. and he said, 'This isn't a Red Cross form, its one of yours and I'm not putting anything on it!' Taff got very annoyed at the attempted trickery and told his inquisitor exactly what he could do with his form. A blazing row ensued and Taff refused to even write his name, rank and number on the bogus form. The Feldwebel about turned and marched to the door of Taff's cell. He opened the door and faced the prisoner once more. 'You know what this means, don't you?' he asked. 'No', said Taff, 'What does it mean?' 'Without your details on this form we cannot inform the Red Cross of your whereabouts', he said with a sadistic smile, 'Your parents will think that you are dead!' Taff Gurmin was only twenty years old and the thought of his Mum and Dad not knowing what had happened to him was not a pleasant one. 'Alright', he said, 'Give me the bloody form.' The German closed the cell door and returned to the table, putting the form upon it and handing Taff the pencil, rubbing his hands with glee. Taff sat down at the table, wrote his number, rank and name and then put the pencil down. 'Go on', said the Feldwebel, 'Keep writing!' Taff looked him straight in the eye and with as much feeling as he could muster said, 'Get stuffed, mate.' The Feldwebel realised he was beaten, picked up the form and stamped out of the cell.

Cheshire's second morning at Frankfurt was, however, completely different. He was given a more generous breakfast, and shortly after he had finished this repast, his door was opened by a distinguished looking grey-haired Oberst (Colonel), who took Chesh along to his office for further interrogation. Offering him a cigarette and coffee, the Oberst opened the proceedings by telling Cheshire of the great advances made at Leningrad by the victorious Wehrmacht, how this Russian city was already surrounded, and that its surrender was imminent. He then, in a roundabout manner, attempted to find out where Flight Lieutenant Cheshire had been stationed and which type of aeroplane he had been flying when he was shot down. Christopher repeated at least three times that, under the terms of the Geneva Convention, he had no obligation to supply such information. After an hour of similar questions and answers, the Oberst had Cheshire returned to his room, informing him as he did so that he would shortly be taken to a camp where he would find somewhat better accommodation than he'd had during the past thirty-six hours.

And so it was. The next morning Taff and Washy were taken into the main camp and shown into a small room containing three two tier bunks. They still did not know if any of the other crewmembers had survived and their non-appearance seemed ominous. Taff was particularly concerned about his best friend Slim Smalley. He asked another prisoner if he had seen a chap called Smalley and to his great joy the answer was, 'Yes, he's in the mess room.' Taff ran into the room looking for his six feet two inch friend but couldn't see him anywhere. 'Smalley!' he shouted, and a total stranger walked up to him and asked him what he wanted. 'You're not Smalley', said Taff. 'Yes I am', he said, 'I'm Geoff Smalley.' And a friendship was started that was to last for the duration. Much to Taff's great relief, Slim and Paul Horrox arrived the next day, although their pleasure at being reunited was saddened by the final realisation that Timber Woods and Jock Niven would not now be joining them. Paul Horrox was captured shortly after landing and was taken to a farmhouse where he was reunited with Slim Smalley. They were then both taken to a Hitler Youth Barracks where they spent their first night in captivity. The following day they were taken to the same Luftwaffe base where Chris Cheshire and Taff Gurmin had spent the previous night. Paul was also left alone with the flak positions map and was studying it when a Luftwaffe Officer entered the room. 'Ah. So you find that map of interest, yes? Well come over here and look at this one, it's much more interesting.' It was a map of the Eastern Front, and Paul, like Cheshire before him, was treated to a German overview of how well the Russian campaign was progressing. From this base they were taken to a Police Station in Hamburg and then by train to the Dulag Luft at Frankfurt. Oflag seemed to be efficiently serviced by orderlies and the accommodation and food was, to Cheshire's mind, more than adequate for those of POW status. The Senior British Officer (SBO) was a Squadron Leader and appeared to be there in permanency. He interviewed every new arrival at the camp and Cheshire was no exception. Chris was aware that most POW camps had managed to establish clandestine communications with London, so he wasted no time in telling the SBO about the map showing all the Hamburg gun positions and told him about the total figure of 247. The SBO responded by saying that this information was of very little importance, because the number and position of these emplacements would probably change from day to day and were therefore not worth passing on to London! Christopher Cheshire is still convinced to this day that, even if this information had saved only one RAF bomber from being shot down in the Hamburg area, then it would have been worth transmitting. With the interview with the SBO at an end, Christopher got up to leave. 'Oh Cheshire', said the SBO, 'I don't seem to have written down the date of your last sortie. What was it?' 'The twelfth of August, Sir', said Christopher. 'Bad luck old chap', came the response, 'not to have been shooting grouse instead.'

During the remainder of August, 76 carried out raids on Magdeburg, Cologne, Kiel, Dusseldorf, Duisburg and a further raid on Cologne. On the 30th, the airfield saw the arrival of Wing Commander J J A Sutton, who had been posted in from HQ 4 Group. That night the squadron carried out its final raid of the month, when Frankfurt became the target. Squadron Leader R Bickford and his crew had taken off from Middleton at 21:13 in L9518. Bickford was noted for his conscientiousness and would often circle the target area longer than most, to ensure the success of the operation. It was suggested that Bickford might have dallied over the target area a little too long during this raid, using up much precious fuel. Eventually, when happy with the proceedings, Bickford turned for home and left the target area. Seven hours later, Bickford's aircraft had reached Yorkshire and was almost home. The Halifax had only 72 miles and 27 minutes to go before reaching Middleton. Having reached the vicinity of Finningley near Doncaster, it began to suffer engine trouble. Thirty miles further north, the engines began to splutter, showing all the signs of running out of fuel. Both engines on one side suddenly stopped and the Halifax dropped a wing. The aircraft was at 2,000 feet when the order to bale out was given. Five of the crew abandoned the aircraft immediately, whilst Bickford remained behind to hold her steady. Unfortunately the tail gunner Sgt Duckmanton took some time to bale out, when he did jump it was too late and he was killed. Thinking all the crew had left the aircraft, Bickford tried to escape out of the top hatch, but was struck by the windmilling propellers and killed. Squadron Leader Bickford was a much-loved officer, and this was reflected in the words written at the time in Middleton St George's Operational Record Book.

'The Loss of this fine officer has come as a severe blow to his squadron and this station. His skill and experience as a pilot were of immense value to the squadron and his pleasing personality made him genuinely popular and esteemed by his brother officers.'

Squadron Leader Richard Bickford DFC of Wimbledon   Photo: IWM CH.1220

78 Squadron - August 1941

Michael Renaut's first flight at Middleton was with P/O Jock Calder, who would later in the war join the famous 617 Dam Buster Squadron. One's first flight when arriving at a new station was to familiarize one with the local area. At Goosepool, pilots were shown the main navigational landmarks, which included Durham Cathedral and the balloon barrage at ICI and Billingham. They were also shown the long straight railway line linking Darlington and York. The Sergeants' Mess was very comfortable and the food was excellent, but the first thing that struck everyone was that there was always an atmosphere of urgency about the place. As Darlington was only five miles away the crews nearly always went there for entertainment. One of their favorite haunts was the Imperial Hotel and its good food.

As already stated, at this time, 78 Squadron was commanded by W/C Tom Sawyer, with F/L Lawrence I/C A Flight and S/L Jock Mercer, B Flight. Jock Mercer was a small man and a bit shy. However he was a brilliant and capable pilot who taught Michael Renaut a great deal. Sadly Jock Mercer was killed a few months later, on November 1st 1941. Jock took off from Croft at 17:32 for Ops to Kiel in Whitley Z9152. Transmissions from his aircraft were last heard on W/T at 01:16, by an operator at Linton-on-Ouse. At the time, Jock Calder and his crew were in contact with Bircham Newton. Presumed lost over the North Sea, they were never seen again. It was suspected that a German night fighter shot them down. The crew, who consisted of S/L J Mercer, Sgt R F Duggan, F/L J R Campbell, SGT T P Woodhouse and F/S V G Wright, are all commemorated on the Runnymede Memorial. If the reader looks carefully, Jock Calder's name can be made out on the tablet of stone shown in one of the Runnymede photographs found at the beginning of this book.

Training continued for Renaut and the other new pilots, and included formation flying, flying on one engine, and homing on beacons. The crews did not relish formation flying because they knew it was training for daylight raids, and these were bloody dangerous.

For 78, Ops for August began on the 2nd, when Hamburg was the primary. This particular summer had thrown some unseasonable weather at Goosepool's bomber crews. An operation on the 4th was cancelled after the briefing at 17:00 hrs, due entirely to adverse weather.

Michael Renaut's first Op was on the night of August 6th. He was second pilot to Pilot Officer Lowry, who was an experienced pilot who had already done 20 trips. The target was Frankfurt, the aircraft, Whitley Z6742. Apart from P/O Lowry, Michael's fellow crewmen that night were Sgt Alexander - navigator, Sgt Fudge - wireless operator, and Sgt Wyatt - rear gunner. Occupying one's mind before a raid was a problem. Playing snooker, cards, table tennis and writing letters were the most popular pastimes that would allow one to take one's mind off the impending danger. The day would have begun with a list of names being posted on a board, showing the crews who would be operating that night. Often, briefing would not take place until as late as 9 or 10 pm, followed by takeoff around midnight. The target was not officially announced until briefing, although the bush telegraph on some squadrons often filtered the target down before lunch. This left anything up to 12 hours for the crews on Ops to brood about the risks and dangers. Sometimes they were stood down at the last minute, and ended up not going. This anticlimax did nothing for the nerves or moral of the aircrews involved. Most felt uneasy all day.

The Met man painted a bleak picture of the weather over the Continent that night. There would be a good deal of cloud. Take off was to be at midnight, so there was plenty time to kill, all the while wondering what would it be like. Would there be fighters, what would the flak be like? They had their 'Last Supper', as some of the irreverent aircrew called it. Bacon and eggs for those on Ops, a great treat, as these wartime luxuries were in short supply for the remainder of the population. When the time came, the crews began to head for the locker-room. Once there, they collected their flying kit and parachutes. Having put on their flying clothing they would join the gathering throng outside. There would be quite a few other crews sitting or standing outside, many of them grabbing the chance to have a last fag. Whilst they waited for the transport to arrive, there was time to enter into the usual nervous half hearted tittle-tattle that came just before departure.

Whitley crew enter by way of the nose hatch   Photo: IWM CH.241

Presently, with a skip of a heartbeat, the engine noises coming from the general direction of the MT section brought more than a few choruses of, 'Well, here we go then.' Those that were seated rose to their feet. Like the others, they picked up their parachutes, navigation bags, thermos flasks, homing-pigeon boxes and other assorted paraphernalia, whilst waiting for the approaching trucks or busses. Having got everyone on board, the WAAF driver of Renaut's truck moved off, after the usual grinding of gears, (there were no synchronous gearboxes in those days). Double de-clutching was an art form, even for the best of wartime drivers. In the gathering darkness, the truck, with its gearbox whining, began its short journey around the peri-track to 78's dispersal. The other trucks were out there somewhere, dropping off the other crews at their respective aircraft.

On reaching their Whitley, Michael, along with the rest of Lowry's crew, descended from the tailboard and walked towards their aircraft. They gathered by the Whitley's nose and began to sort out their flying kit. Once they were ready to board the aircraft, they headed for the ladder leading up into the nose hatch.

On this occasion the wireless-operator Sgt Fudge climbed up first, as he had the furthest to go. Once inside the nose he made his way aft and upwards and emerged from under the instrument panel into the right hand side of the cockpit. He continued rearwards past the navigators table which was on his right. He sat right at the back of the cockpit, in the radio operator's position on the port side, just forward of the wing spar. On entering the Whitley's cockpit, Pilot Officer Lowry swung into his seat, which was also on the port side, and made himself comfortable. Sgt Alexander came up next and settled down in the navigators position, facing towards the port side of the cockpit. He was the only one in the cockpit who didn't face forwards. The navigation table was in front of him, the wireless operator to his left facing forward, the pilots on his right. The tail gunner Sgt Wyatt had entered by way of the side door, just forward of the port tailplane. He sat facing rearwards in the rear turret, normally looking back at where the aircraft had just been.

When ready, with Renaut's help, Lowry began his cockpit drill. The first thing to ensure was that the undercarriage selector lever was in the neutral position and the safety catch locked. To do this, he moved his right hand to the centre lever of a group of three, placed on the floor to the right of the trim wheels. They all had knobs or handles of a different shape, thus allowing them to have their own tactile feel and be individually identified in the dark of the cockpit without having to look at them. The undercarriage lever had a circular knob, with its safety catch positioned on the left-hand side.

Automatically his experienced hands continued their work. He switched on the flap and undercarriage indicators; the lights came on, the 'two greens' confirming that the undercart was locked down. Next came the pre-engine start checks,

Wing tanks balance cock. ------------------------------SHUT
Left and right wing fuel tanks. ----------------------Selected
Throttles. ---1/2 inch open
Mixture. ---RICH
Propeller control. -----------------Fully forward (Fine pitch)
Superchargers. --------------------------------LOW (lever up)
Carburettor heat. --------------------------------------COLD
Radiator shutters. ------------------------------------OPEN

Looking out of the window, Lowry could see that the groundcrew of Z6742 had taken up position ahead of the Whitley and in view of the cockpit. Presently, there was the squeal of drum brakes behind the trailing edge of the port wing, announcing the arrival of the trolley-acc.[35] Out of one end of the trolley-acc protruded several yards of thick black cable. On the other end of the cable was the ground power plug. Having paid out enough cable, the driver dragged it over to the Whitley and pushed the plug into the aircraft's ground power socket. He gave a hand signal to indicate that it was plugged in and ready to go. Earlier, on his arrival in the aircraft, the wireless operator had checked that the Ground Power Switch had been placed in the

'Ground' position. Lowry gave the thumbs-up in recognition. Now they waited for the Very pistol to be fired from flying control. This would inform all squadron pilots to start their engines. Lowry looked at his watch. From the details given at the briefing, he realised that they had a full five minutes to wait for the expected signal. He spent the time rechecking everything in the cockpit, including the intercom. Whilst checking in with the radio operator he asked him to prime the port engine. The priming pump, and a two-position selector cock for left or right engines was located on the starboard side of his radio compartment. The wireless operator turned the selector-cock to the 'PORT' position, and unscrewed the priming pump lock. As the engines were cold, he pushed the pump in and out 4 or 5 times.

When the Very pistol was eventually fired, Lowry had his head down in the cockpit setting his compass for the first course to steer after take-off. 'That's it Skipper', said Michael on seeing the green pyrotechnic arcing through the sky. Lowry had in fact heard the crack of the Very cartridge through his open sliding side window. He looked out at the groundcrew, who were still in view, kicking their heels a few yards forward of the port wing. He pointed at the port engine and twirled his vertical left forefinger round and round. He received a thumbs-up from the engine fitter in return. The airframe fitter nipped under the wing and joined the trolley-acc driver behind the trailing edge of the wing. Lowry reached forward of the control wheel and flipped up the port engine's twin magneto switches, which were located on the lower section of the instrument panel. Next, his left hand reached up to the top of the instrument panel. He was aiming below the autopilot control for the port starting magneto switch. He hesitated, and his hand withdrew as he suddenly remembered that he hadn't double-checked that the parking brake was on. It was!

Again his left hand went to the switch. Taking hold of it with his second finger he clicked it on. His forefinger found the adjacent starter button, which he then pressed. The port engine turned slowly; after half a dozen blades it almost came to a stop as the fuel arrived at the cylinders and the increasing compression created more resistance. With a chuff the exhausts shed a small amount of white smoke, but the Merlin did not fire. Keeping his finger in place he coaxed the reluctant power plant to continue turning. After a few more seconds, with the compression almost getting the better of the starter motor, the inhibited engine spluttered into life, accompanied by a larger cloud of smoke, which was whisked away by the propeller blades.

Once the port engine was running smoothly, Lowry switched off its starting magneto. Having checked that the oil pressure gauge had moved from its stop and had now reached 60 psi[36], within the prescribed 30 seconds, Lowry left the engine to warm up. Whilst starting the starboard Merlin, Lowry, Renaut, the groundcrew and the wireless operator went through a similar ritual with the other engine. Soon both engines were running smoothly. Sgt Fudge then re-locked the priming pump, and having checked that the ground power plug had been removed after start-up by the groundcrew, he clicked the Ground/Air Power switch from 'Ground' to 'Air'. Now the Whitley's own accumulators provided all necessary internal electrical power. As the engines warmed up, Lowry and Renaut continued with the after start checks.

---

[35] A wheeled trolley, carrying accumulators (12-volt batteries). Wired in parallel for greater current output, the accumulators in the trolley-acc were used for starting the engines on the ground. This saved the aircraft's accumulators for emergency airborne engine starts.

[36] Pounds per square inch pressure

GENERAL VIEW OF COCKPIT

Photo: © crown copyright/MOD reproduced with the permission of the Controller of Her Majesty's Stationery Office

25. Camera indicator wedge plate
31. Engine data plate
32. Engine boost gauges
33. Landing lamp switch
34. Rudder pedal leg-reach adjuster
35. Rudder pedal footrest (starboard)
36. Main magneto switches
37. Undercarriage position indicator switch
38. De-icing system pressure gauge
39. Selector switch and pushbutton for main plane fuel tanks contents gauge
40. Main plane fuel tanks contents gauge
41. Compass
42. Automatic boost cut-out control
43. Hot and cold air intake control
44. Switches for (left to right) head lamp (independent and signalling), navigation lamps and flaps position indicators
45. Oxygen supply bayonet socket
46. Pilot's clock mounting (if fitted)
47. Auto-controls speed and steering levers
48. Compass deviation card holder
49. Oxygen regulator
51. Dimmer switches for cockpit lamps
52. Beam approach visual indicator
53. Instrument-flying panel
54. Engine-speed indicators
55. Fuel pressure gauges

56. Electrical starting push-switches
57. Starting magneto switches
58. Auto-controls main control cock
59. C.S.B.S. steering indicator
60. A.S.I. pressure head heating switch
61. Signal pistol stowage
62. Oil temperature gauges
63. Oil pressure gauges
64. Suction gauge
64A Bomb jettison remote control handle
65. Suction pump change-over cock control
66. Auto-controls "nose-heavy", "tail heavy" and main pressure gauge
67. Air temperature gauge
68. Flaps position indicators
69. Undercarriage position indicator
70. Pneumatic system and brake triple pressure gauge
71. Undercarriage dimmer mask stowage (if fitted)
72. Coolant temperature gauges
73. D.F. loop setting indicator
74. Airscrew anti-icing system control rheostat
75. Radiator shutter position indicators and switch (if fitted)
76. Signalling switchbox for upward and downward identification lamps
77. Signalling switchbox for formation-keeping lamps
78. Engine control friction adjuster

Photo: © crown copyright/MOD reproduced with the permission of the Controller of Her Majesty's Stationery Office

1. Navigator's seat rails

2. Airscrew controls

3. Hydraulic handpump lever

4. Undercarriage control lever

5. Radiator shutters control lever

6. Main plane flaps control lever

7. Elevator trimming tabs control lever

8. Rudder trimming tabs control handwheel

9. Pilot's seat

10. Safety harness release gear

11. Armour plating for back protection

12. Armour plating for head protection

13. Signal istol cartridge stowage

14. Direct-vision windows and catches

15. Brake operating lever

16. Control column

17. Aileron control handwheel

18. Landing lamp dipping control

19. Throttle control levers

20. Mixture control lever

20.A Special panel for taking sextant readings

21. Door to front turret

22. Cockpit lamp

23. Sliding window

24. Window latch

25. Height and airspeed computer

26. Hydraulic system instruction plate

27. Footrest for dual control (shown hinged back)

28. Bomb door control handle (if fitted)

29. Fuel system diagram and instruction plate

30. Hydraulic handpump handle (shown stowed)

Next they checked the operation of the hydraulic engine pump by lowering and raising the flaps. The engine temperature gauges were then checked, to see that they were now above the required minimum of 15° Centigrade for take-off.

Now the after warm-up checks could be completed.

Brake pressure. -------------------------------------100 psi

Propeller controls. --- Primed.
Propeller constant speed units at +1- lb/psi boost.----------------Checked.
Test each magneto at +4 lb/psi. boost, Maximum drop----------- 80 rpm.
Open the throttles fully, check boost, rpm. And oil pressure.

With the after warm up checks complete, Lowry signaled for the chocks to be removed. Immediately, two of the groundcrew disappeared from sight under the wings to carry out this task. Having received the chocks-away hand signal from the re-appearing groundcrew, Lowry opened the throttles slightly and the Whitley began to move forward. Having advanced a few yards he tested the brakes by bringing the aircraft to a halt, with the associated 'Hiss' of the brake's pneumatic system.

They waited at the dispersal until it was their turn to taxi around the peri-track towards the duty runway. This was determined by the location of their individual dispersal site, relevant to the end of the runway in use. Eventually it was time to move off. Lowry moved his hand to the right of the Magneto switches. As it was very dark, he selected the outboard landing lamp by turning the switch to the up position. Next he dipped the lamp's beam for taxiing by moving the lever on the left-hand side of the throttle box forward. As it was usual to taxi without the use of landing lights, having checked the way ahead was unobstructed, he turned it off quickly, to preserve his night vision. As they moved off, they saw the other

Whitley V running up prior to take-off   Photo: IWM CH.695

squadron Whitleys that were ahead and behind them in the queue. Eventually the number of aircraft ahead of them diminished, as, one by one, they reached the flarepath, and took off. Soon there were only two aircraft ahead. In turn, the first one moved forward to take its place on the flarepath. Lowry commenced his pre-takeoff vital actions. As they were heavily loaded, he re-checked that he had moved the trim wheel to the prescribed position, just forward of neutral. Lowry pulled the throttle levers back to the fully closed position. This ensured that the automatic interlock system in the throttle-box had set the fuel mixture to the 'Fully Rich' position. Having done this, he moved the throttles forward again, to the optimum idle position. Next he felt below the throttle and mixture lever quadrant. Both propeller pitch controls were already pointing up, in the 'Fine Pitch' position for take-off, (He was just double-checking).
Lowry looked down at the levers of the fuel cocks, located on the floor to the left of his seat. He checked that the levers for the wing tanks were pointing forward to the 'On' position. This was the requirement, as under no circumstances were the fuselage tanks to be used for take-off. He checked that the balance cocks, fuselage tank cock and auxiliary tank cocks were pointing aft to the 'Off' position. The fuel contents gauges were double-checked. As they were hauling a heavy load, flaps would be required for takeoff. Lowry moved his right hand to the cylindrical flap handle, which was situated to the left of the undercarriage lever. He moved the lever forward, whilst watching the flap position indicator on the starboard side of the instrument panel. When the pointer reached the required 15° position, he stopped them there, by returning the lever to the neutral position. Between the elevator trim hand wheel and his seat was the two-speed supercharger control lever. This was checked to ensure that it was in the 'Up' position, indicating that low gear was selected for take-off. The two final checks were to ensure that the engine's coolant radiators were fully open and there was full and free movement of the flying controls[37] .

37 Elevators, ailerons and rudders

Lowry had time to glance up and see the Whitley in front turn onto the runway. At the beginning of the runway, better known as the first flare in those days, stood the control caravan. This was positioned on the grass to the left-hand side of the flarepath. On the top was a semi-circular Perspex astrodome, glowing in the pale yellow light permeating up from inside the caravan. In the dome, one could see only the head and shoulders of the duty dispatcher. He was equipped with an Aldis lamp, with which he could signal to the aircraft. He could select a red or green lens to cover the bulb. This would allow him to indicate stop or go as required. Throughout the war, all Bomber stations used this silent signaling method. The use of radio (R/T) for taxi and take-off instructions, as we do today, would have invited the unwanted attention of the German listening posts. Not even a telegram, phone-call or spot on the 6 o'clock news would have alerted the Germans quicker of an impending raid, and the number of aircraft taking part. Throughout the war, many of Middleton's crews used 'Goosepool' as a code word on the R/T, rather than Middleton, as they knew that the German radio operators would not identify it with the airfield.

Having received his 'Green', the captain of the Whitley on the runway ahead took both engines up to full power. Although unseen by the crew in the dark, the grass by the side of the runway shimmered, as the aircraft's slipstream tried to press it flat against the ground. Suddenly, with a hiss of compressed air, the Whitley's brakes were released. The dark shape ahead disappeared into the night, the bomber's progress marked only by its navigation lights and four receding jets of blue flame, emanating from the exhaust stubs of its Merlin engines.

Even before the other Whitley was half way through its take-off run, the Aldis lamp again came to life, glowing green. Now it was Lowry's turn to enter the runway. He opened both throttles, and the Whitley began to move forward. He immediately closed the starboard throttle, and opened the port one further, thus assisting Z6742 to swing to the right and onto runway 06. At the same time as he operated the throttles, Lowry operated the differential braking system, by pressing on the starboard rudder pedal, and briefly depressing the brake lever on his control column. Moving a few yards down the runway, Lowrey ensured that the tailwheel was straight and that he was lined up and facing straight down the flarepath. He then closed the throttles fully and applied the brakes. The light of the Aldis had by now extinguished. When the bomber had come to a halt, he continued to depress the brake lever, whilst he engaged the parking brake catch, located near the brake lever's pivot point.

'Ready for the off lads', Lowrey said into his mask, not really expecting any reply. To reduce the possibility of a swing developing, due to uneven responses from the engines, Lowry decided that he would hold her on the brakes until full power from both Merlins was attained. Having pulled out the boost cutout control knob on the left-hand side of the instrument panel, he rotated it 90° to the 'Locked' position. Although scanning the cockpit in a last minute double check of the fuel and magneto systems, Lowry was suddenly aware that out of the corner of his eye, the Perspex on the left-hand side of the cockpit was again glowing green. It was time to open the throttles up to the gate. Having done this, he checked the rpm and boost gauges; they indicated 3,000 rpm[38] and +5³/₄ lbs/psi of boost. Now that full take-off power was being developed, he released the brakes. She started to move, slowly at first, but then she got her wind. With a firm pressure on the rudder bars and judicious use of the throttle levers, he kept her straight. Now with gathering speed, the tail came up, and she became more streamlined. In the fuselage, despite their helmets, the noise from the engines was deafening. Touching the vibrating metal of the aircraft was just like getting an electric shock, even through thick flying gloves. The rest of the crew, sitting in the dark, always felt tense. For most of them, there was nothing to do but cross their fingers, and hope. There was always the chance of a swing on takeoff that might end up with the aircraft leaving the runway. This could cause them to strike something lying unseen in the inky blackness of the airfield, possibly collapsing the undercarriage. The prospect of slithering along on the bomb doors, with a full load of high explosives and incendiaries a couple of feet below them in the bomb-bay, along with over 700 gallons of petrol in the wing and fuselage tanks, was a thought that they would rather do without.

Fortunately there was no crosswind, and she did not swing. Nor did the Whitley suffer catastrophic engine failure during take-off, as so many aircraft did during WWII. The loss of one engine would guarantee certain disaster. At over 30,000-lbs, the Whitley's stall speed with flap and undercarriage down was 70 mph. Now indicating over 80 she was beginning to feel for the sky. Gentle backpressure was applied to the control column, and slowly the Whitley began to unstick. Michael had been taught the trick of leaving the bomber on the runway for a couple of seconds more, if it was at all possible. Better to unstick cleanly at a higher speed than to leave the flarepath in a series of bounces as she felt for the ground effect air under her wings. Sometimes at night, with little wind, a short runway, and a heavy fuel and bomb load, she would have to be pulled off to clear the unseen and quickly approaching perimeter fence or trees.

Now airborne, Lowry released the safety catch for the undercarriage lever. He then pulled the lever back to raise the undercarriage. The lights on the indicator changed from two greens to one red whilst the wheels were retracting. When the undercarriage was fully up and locked, the red lamp was joined by two amber lights. The undercarriage lever was then checked to see that it had returned automatically to the neutral position. Michael reached over to the starboard side of the cockpit just aft of the instrument panel. Here there was a bracket, which held the night flying dimmer mask. This he fitted over the undercarriage indicator lights to reduce their glow to a mere pinprick of light. Later aircraft would have a different system of lights, which fully extinguished once the wheels were locked up, a practice still with us to this day.

Now above the single engine safety speed of 95 mph, she was held until her best climbing speed was attained. At 30,000 -lbs, this was 115mph. At 500 feet Lowry raised the flaps and again checked that the lever had returned itself to the neutral position. Michael checked his watch, it was dead on midnight. Getting on with the navigation, the observer Sgt Alexander checked their course for Dunwich. The wind had been calculated and the drift corrected.

---

[38] Revs per minute

Climbing slowly to 8,000 feet, all was quiet, save the sound of the synchronized engines. Presently there was the exchange of verbal checks over the R/T, 'Captain to rear gunner, everything OK?' 'Ok Skipper', came the reply from Wyatt. The rest of the crew were also involved in the systematic check of the intercom, as without it the mission could not take place. After 1 hour and 22 minutes they reached Dunwich and the Suffolk coastline receded behind them. At this point the navigation lights were turned off. At 8,000 feet the Whitley began to suffer severe icing in the dense cumulus cloud, reducing the aircraft's rate of climb. To the uninitiated the sound of huge chunks of ice breaking off the propeller tips and hitting the sides of the fuselage was disconcerting. Lowry appeared oblivious to this alarming occurrence. On reaching 10,000 feet over the North Sea, they were ordered to put on their oxygen masks. Lowry called over the intercom, 'Captain to Navigator, how long to the enemy coast?' After only a few seconds came the reply, 'Navigator to Skipper, 12 minutes.' They continued on.

Some time later, they began to hear the sound of flak, and they felt the shock as it burst close by. Enemy gunfire needed to be pretty accurate. A shell had to explode within 20 feet of an aircraft to cause real damage and bring it down. A box barrage was the most feared. This was when several guns were trained onto the same bit of sky, directly on an aircraft's track, through which it had no choice but to fly.

Once inland, their course would take them over Gouda, then north of Eindhoven. Once past this flak hot spot, they would fly over Venlo, on the Dutch-German border. Passing south of Krefeld and Dusseldorf. A direct track would have taken them over northern Cologne, so a diversion to the left was necessary, to avoid this very well defended city. Their final leg to the target was via the north of Koblenz and on to Frankfurt, 550 miles from Goosepool. Soon they were clear of the coastal batteries and things settled down again, but they were still in broken cumulus cloud and icing conditions. As if they didn't have enough to worry about, an electrical storm was observed ahead, and after a few minutes they were in it. 'Captain to Navigator, ETA target?' 'Navigator to Skipper: 04:20 hours.' At that there was almighty bang and a crash, and the cockpit lights went out. Lowry spoke; 'Captain to crew - prepare to bale out.' The Whitley had been struck by lightning, or rather the W/T trailing aerial had. It had burned completely off, right up to the reeling-in drum adjacent to the radio operator's left knee. The wireless operator was in a panic and thought that he had done his wedding tackle a power of no good. After a few moments they calmed down and everything returned to normal, except for the pilot's compass, which was spinning erratically, and the sound of the de-synchronized engines running out of phase. They had lost a considerable amount of height and this precious commodity could not be economically regained. Climbing up through the icing conditions had taken its toll on fuel consumption, and Lowry took the decision to jettison the bombs and return to base. This was done over German territory, about 20 miles from Luxembourg. As the bombs left the Whitley, she lifted, grateful to be free of the weight of the bombs. Lowry climbed to 20,000 feet. This allowed them to clear the warm front and the icing layer they had been in for most of the trip. They headed for home, with only a few bangs being heard from the flak gunners as the Whitley passed over the enemy coast and out to sea. They began to descend on the return trip across the North Sea, and the remainder of Michael's first Op passed uneventfully. Touching down at Middleton at 05:40, they were the first crew back, well ahead of the rest.

They turned off the runway and began to taxi in. After the engines were stopped, Renaut sat next to Lowry, as his skipper passed on some advice appertaining to the trip. Eventually, with a 'Let's go' from Lowry, they climbed out of their seats and headed for the hatch. They joined the crew, who were waiting on the Tarmac. Having been cooped up in the tail turret for so long, Sgt Wyatt was stamping his feet on the tarmac in an attempt to regain some circulation. After nearly six hours in his cramped turret he could feel nothing but pins and needles in his feet and legs. Having given up on the stamping, he lit a fag. As they waited for the transport to arrive, he relieved himself on the tyre of the Starboard undercarriage leg; this was a superstition he always pandered to. Many aircrew had their own superstitions, which they would religiously adhere to before or after a raid. Some carried a piece of wood to knock on, or a lucky penny. Some held rosary beads, or kept a small Teddy bear inside their flying jackets, this gunner just had a pee on the starboard wheel. Not just any old wheel, but always the starboard one.

Eventually a truck arrived and the WAAF driver took them around the peri-track to the locker room to dump their flying kit. From there it was off to de-briefing. Once there they passed through the blackout curtains into the brightly-lit room. The first job on their arrival was to pour themselves a cup of tea from the large white cylindrical tea urn on a table by the door and grab a fag from the box nearby.

One aircraft had not returned. Later the circumstances of its demise came to light. P/O Atchison and his crew had taken off in Whitley T4158 and on their way home had to ditch. They came down 8 miles North of Dunkirk. They were picked up by an RAF Vosper high-speed launch (No.145) out of Dover, which rescued them despite being shot at by the German shore batteries. Sitting in wicker chairs at one of the de-briefing tables, Lowry's crew listened as he, tea mug in hand, related the night's events to the WAAF de-briefing officer, who was filling in the report sheet. Occasionally, the skipper would turn to one or more of the crew to confirm a particular answer to a question, sometimes the crew would join in at a particular juncture, to add their view of events. With the de-briefing at an end, they put out their cigarettes, and with a screech of chair legs on linoleum, stood up and shuffled out of the building and went off for some food and sleep.

Two days later Renaut was off on his second trip, once again as second pilot to Lowry. The target was Kiel, which was popular with the crews as most of the trip was over the sea, they only spent a relatively short time flying the 52 miles or so over enemy territory. Fifteen aircraft had been detailed for this raid, including 3 freshers. At 17:30 the freshers were cancelled. This time the weather conditions were much better, and the moon was full. As the crews approached Kiel, the flak and searchlights could be seen from miles away, as they attended to the bombers already overhead. When Lowry arrived, the flak barrage at Kiel was like an inferno. The German gunners were firing from the ships as well as the shore batteries. Other aircraft could be seen 'coned' by the searchlights. As they started their approach, the crews came under heavy ground fire and were caught in the glare of many searchlights, which were absolutely blinding. Several aircraft were coned for several minutes as they made their bombing run over the target, which was the dock area.

Although a few of the bombs ended up in the harbour, some also straddled the buildings and dock installations. At this stage of the war, bombing accuracy was not very good, some bombs were only getting within five miles of the target, if they were lucky. On this occasion however, the bombing was fairly accurate. Having completed his attack, Lowry turned for home.

Once well clear of the enemy coast, the crews reduced height to 2,000 feet for the trip back. Having removed their oxygen masks, out came the thermos flasks. A well-deserved cup of coffee was enjoyed. All of 78's crews had hit the primary, except one, which had dropped their bombs on a built up area on the West Bank. The squadron suffered no losses on this raid, but Sgt J W Bell's Whitley had Exactor[39] trouble over the target, and at one point both propellers were on fire. This attracted the flak gunners, who added insult to injury and popped away at them. The aircraft was quite badly hit, and despite a valiant effort to reach home, at 06:00 the Whitley ditched, 80 miles off Blyth, Northumberland. The crew scrambled into the dinghy, which had sprung a small leak. This caused the crew some discomfort, as they had to sit in freezing cold water for several hours. At 07:45 they saw a Hudson (probably out of Thornaby), which dropped a bag of provisions. The bag fell about 20 yards from the dinghy, which by now was fairly waterlogged. Unfortunately because the dinghy was heavy with water and unmaneuverable, the waves carried it away faster than the crew could paddle towards the bag. Thanks to the crew of the Hudson, Bell and his crew were picked up unharmed, by an Air Sea Rescue Launch at 10:30 and taken to Blyth. When they arrived they were merry, as the boat's crew had broken out the rum on the way back. For good measure, the naval folk at Blyth invited them to their bar for further refreshments. By the time they departed for Goosepool, some of Bell's crew had, for some reason, a bit of difficulty in remaining upright.

After this raid the weather deteriorated. It was not until the 14th that 78 mounted another operation. Originally 16 Whitleys were earmarked for this raid to Hannover, later the 6 freshers were cancelled. One aircraft did not take-off, as it had a broken contact breaker arm in the magneto of one of its Merlins. Another had to land back, as the pilot could not retract the undercarriage. A third returned with propeller trouble. The remainder managed to attack the primary, with the exception of one that could not locate the target.

In his book 'Terror by night', Michael Renaut tells of one of the squadron's pilots, Sergeant Beardmore, who had been with him on the OTU course at Kinloss. Beardmore had, before the war, owned and raced greyhounds. Every day they would see him with a stack of form letters, sent by his trainer who lived in the south. They used to pull his leg and say that he knew absolutely nothing about greyhounds. On the August 16th, Michael Renaut, Beardmore and a few others decided to go to Stockton dog track by car. They got there in plenty of time for the first race, which began at 2.30pm. However, they had to be back for 5.30pm, in time for briefing, as there were Ops on for that night. Beardmore did indeed seem very knowledgeable about Greyhound racing, and bet in pounds, whilst the rest of them bet in shillings. In the end, thanks to Beardmore's expertise, they all backed the winners of all six races. Michael won £18, which was a large amount of money in those days. Beardmore himself won about £100. They were all quite ecstatic as they made their way back to Middleton. As they had all been so lucky they agreed that it would be a good idea to go to Stockton for every meeting. Beardmore was the happiest; he said that he had been the luckiest of them all that day. Sadly this was not so. He was killed that night whilst on Ops to Cologne.

Having taken off from Middleton St George at 23:05, Sgt Beardmore, in Whitley V EY-F (F for Freddie) Z6754, was flying as second pilot to Sgt J H Malet-Warden. The rest of the crew consisted of Sgt A J R Millard-Tucker, Sgt G H P Buchanan RCAF and F/S A Brown. They crashed at 03:50 at Buggenum (Limburg), 12 miles southwest of Venlo, Holland. They are all buried in Jonkerbos war Cemetery. Michael and his friends never did go back to Stockton dog track.

This raid was something of a disaster. Of the 13 operational and 3 fresher crews detailed, one had not taken-off due to defective bomb doors, 5 did not reach the target due to mechanical problems, 4 jettisoned their bombs, whilst one attacked Rotterdam. Only 4 aircraft managed to hit Cologne. Three aircraft went missing. Apart from Sgt Beardmore and the crew of Sgt Malet-Warden's aircraft, 78 lost Sgt T A Sherman RCAF and his crew in EY-F Z6577. Having taken off at 23:44, they crashed at 02:47 near Hoe, 3 miles N/E of Maaseik, Holland. They also rest in the Jonkerbos War Cemetery.

The third Whitley to be lost that night was EY-B Z6823, flown by F/L J A Cant. This aircraft took off from Middleton just 4 minutes after Sgt Sherman, and crashed four hours and nineteen minutes later at Velddriel, 3 miles from Zaltbommel, Holland. The second pilot, P/O J L Asprey RAAF, joined the other two crews in Jonkerbos War Cemetery, whilst Sgt Wills, the wireless operator, is buried in Woensel General Cemetery, Eindhoven. F/L Cant and the two other remaining crewmembers survived and became POWs.

Yet another Middleton pilot who would eventually become famous was Pilot Officer Calder. He was another airman destined to join the famous 617 Dam Busters Squadron later in the war. Calder and his crew were detailed for Ops to Dusseldorf on the night of the August 24th. This stretch of real estate provided the greatest concentration of flak and searchlights in Germany. It was better known to the aircrew of Bomber Command as 'Happy Valley'. During the day there was some distraction from the apprehension brought about by this choice of target, as the station slipped into bullshit mode in advance of the arrival of AVM Roddy Carr, the new AOC of 4 Group. Carr himself was a great character, very popular with the aircrews as he always had their best interests at heart. He arrived at 15:30 in time for the evening's briefing. As the crews prepared for departure, Carr was down at the dispersals, wishing the crews luck. He watched and waited until the last aircraft had disappeared into the distance.

Crossing the coast at Dunkirk, Calder's crew were at 9,000 feet, and after 10 minutes of heavy flak they decided to fire off the enemy colours of the day using the Very pistol. British Intelligence would pass on to the aircrews the German colours to be used that night, having received them earlier that day from agents who had risked life and limb to secretly acquire them from the Germans.

---

[39] Propeller feathering equipment

These might be for example, two reds and a green, or a white and a yellow. These codes were only to be used by German aircraft in real emergencies. Once fired, the effect was startling – the German defences shut shop, and left Calder's crew to it.

It was only a short run from the French Coast to the Ruhr, with its battery of eight hundred searchlights and countless flak batteries. An unknown aircraft flew towards the lights and was coned. Within a second, one could have walked upon the flak surrounding the hapless bomber. Suddenly, the aircraft, which was probably a Wellington, first burst into flames and then exploded. Calder got through the defences whilst the flak and searchlights picked on someone else. Having bombed the target he returned safely to Goosepool. Roddy Carr was still there, to greet the crews as they returned. He remained at Middleton all night, until the last man had landed. He joined some of them in the de-briefing room, to hear the accounts of the night's activities first hand. He left for 4 Group HQ at 08:00 the next morning, long after the last crew had gone to bed. Some of Middleton's airmen would not be greeted by Roddy Carr that night. Sgt W G Rogers and his crew would not have been removed from the wreckage of EY-A Z6466 by the time that Roddy Carr had departed Middleton; the twisted metal would have been far too hot to touch. The defenders of Wavre would have to wait many hours for the Whitley's aluminium, duralumin and magnesium alloys to cool, before they would be able to extricate and transport the bodies of the crew to the town's Communal Cemetery.

A second Whitley crew to miss de-briefing that night was that of P/O Fransden. Whilst over Essex on their way home they had to abandon Z6742, which was on fire. At 02:27 the aircraft came down on the south bank of the river Stour near Mistley, some 8 miles S/S/E of Ipswich. The second pilot, Sgt Sinclair RCAF, had been receiving instruction from Fransden and was sitting in the pilot's seat, having been allowed to fly the plane home. There was insufficient time for them to swap seats, so Sgt Sinclair held the bomber steady, whilst the rest jumped. Later his body was found in the wreckage of the Whitley.

Although seven of 78's crews were detailed for operations to Mannheim on the 27th, four were later cancelled. Of the three Whitleys dispatched, only two bombed the primary. The third aircraft was flown by Sgt Woodhatch, who had taken off in Whitley Z6872. With him were Sgts Childs, Olley and Davidson. Having bombed their alternative target, which was Bruges, they headed for home. All was well until they were approaching the Dutch Coast. Suddenly the flak gunners opened up on them, hitting the Whitley in the tail section. Woodhatch realised that he had suffered serious damage as the aircraft was very difficult to control in pitch.[40] He ordered the wireless operator to send a message back to base, informing them of their predicament. In his book 'Only Owls and Bloody Fools Fly at Night', Tom Sawyer recalled that they received the transmission from the Whitley, which said, 'Hit by flak at Dutch coast - returning - damage to elevators.' Tom was Duty Officer that night, and having received this distress message, he ordered the crash tender and blood-wagon out to the first flare.[41] He then remained in the tower so he could speak on the radio to Woodhatch on his return.

When within R/T range, Sgt Woodhatch repeated that he had elevator control problems. He was told by Sawyer to make a wide circuit and to carry out a long low approach. It was also suggested to Woodhatch that he would be better off flying the Whitley onto the ground with engine power. This was preferential to trying to use the practically useless elevators to flare the aircraft in the normal way. Whilst flying the aircraft a few feet above the runway with its wheels down, all that was necessary was for Woodhatch to close the throttles and let the Whitley sink onto the ground. He could then simply bring the bomber to a stop with the brakes. Having passed on these instructions, Sawyer then left the tower and hurried off to join the others, who were waiting for the Whitley to land.

Sgt Woodhatch did quite a good job of obeying his instructions, and despite an erratic approach, the aircraft was soon passing about 20 feet over the heads of Tom and the crash crew, waiting at the first flare. The aircraft was porpoising up and down, with very little elevator control being available to the pilot. Woodhatch throttled back and the Whitley began to settle onto the runway. Unfortunately the tail would not come down. Woodhatch must have gone for the brakes, as suddenly the aircraft pivoted forward on its main wheels and with a crunch its nose hit the runway. It did not bounce, but slithered forwards for a short distance accompanied by the sound of screeching metal. As the aircraft came to a sudden stop, it burst into flames as the ruptured fuel tanks spilled petrol onto the hot engines. As Tom Sawyer and the crash wagon crew raced to the now blazing wreck, he looked at his watch; it was 00:45. By the time they pulled up at the crash-site, the injured crew had all managed to vacate the aircraft. Sgt Woodhatch had the worst injury; he came staggering back from beyond the front of the Whitley with a large gash across his forehead. Surprisingly, despite the fact that the bone was exposed, there was no blood. He had not been wearing his seat belt. Woodhatch and the navigator had been catapulted out through the Perspex windscreen and had landed in a heap on the runway. Sgt Woodhatch and his crew were taken to the SSQ, where he was stitched up. Fortunately they would soon recover from their injuries, unlike the Whitley, which was burned out. The rest of the crew had all been in their correct crash positions. If Sgt Woodhatch had also been strapped in, he too would have got out unscathed. However he was praised for doing an exceptional job of flying the almost uncontrollable Whitley back from the Dutch coast, and for saving his crew. He would of course be forgiven for having more important things on his mind at the time than seat belts.

The following night, 3 fresher crews were sent to Dunkirk. Two successfully bombed the primary and returned safely to base. The third Whitley, Z6508 flown by P/O K W Davies, crashed into the sea off Dunkirk. The bodies of Sgt G T Harper the observer and Sgt P Gennon RNZAF the tail gunner were washed ashore. They are buried in Dunkirk War Cemetery. P/O Davies, Sgt S E Rowed RCAF the second pilot, and Sgt J W Bills the wireless operator, have no known graves.

Frankfurt, Saarbrucken and Mannheim were attacked by 7 of Goosepool's Whitleys on the night of the 29/30th, all returned safe. The final effort by 78 during August came on the 31st when Essen was the target for 6 of their Whitleys. Nine aircraft had originally been dispatched, but one returned early and landed at Leeming with wireless trouble.

---

[40] The elevator control allows the aircraft to climb or dive, i.e. pitch the nose up or pitch the nose down
[41] Touch-down point at the beginning of the runway

View of Whitley formation. Note standard nose down flying attitude of type   Photo: IWM via Geoff Hill

A second aircraft had its starboard engine fail whilst over the Dutch Coast. After jettisoning its bombs, flares and ammunition, it reached Coltishall, where it landed safely. The third wayward bomber did not reach its intended target. Whilst north of the Ruhr Valley, it attacked the flarepath at Hunxe airfield, 6 miles southeast of Weasel, before heading back to Middleton.

And so ended August 1941. One of the note-worthy events of the month was the operational testing by the RAF of their new radio navigation aid, Gee, more of which we shall learn later.

September 41

An operation on the night of September 2nd /3rd saw two of 76's Halifaxes join with five more from 35 Squadron at Leeming to take part in a 49 aircraft raid on Berlin. The remainder of the force consisted of 32 Hampdens, 6 Stirlings and 4 Manchesters. Norman Frankish remembers that the squadron had only four operational aircraft available at this time. S/L Bouwens led this raid; he was the new commander of B Flight and had only been posted in from 51 Squadron the same day. Two Hampdens and 1 Manchester were lost, along with two out of the five 35 Squadron Halifaxes sent from Leeming.

Wing Commander G T Jarman bad a sad farewell to 76 Squadron on the 4th, having been being posted to 4 Group Headquarters at York.

Huls was the target for 78 on the night of September 6/7th. This raid on the town's large chemical works saw 9 Whitleys from Middleton join 32 from other squadrons. Also taking part were 18 Hampdens and 27 Wellingtons. Although good results were observed, 2 Wellingtons and 5 Whitleys were lost, including 2 Whitleys from Middleton. S/L Lawrence bombed the primary from 17,000 feet. The target was identified due to nil cloud and bright moonlight, and by Lake Steuer Stausee at Haltern. Incendiaries were seen burning on the target and HE bombs were planted on them. Other bursts were not seen due to very active searchlight concentrations. F/L Snow and his crew could not identify Huls so they attacked what appeared to be a railway marshalling yard E/N/E of the Ruhr. Having bombed from 15,000 feet, large fires were started, and large flashes were seen to erupt 10 minutes after the attack. Due to overheating and Exactor trouble,[42] Huls was abandoned by Sgt Snider, his crew elected to mooch about, bombing the flarepath of any enemy airfields that came into view. One was attacked at 52° 15 North - 05° 15 East. This lies just to the east of Lauren in Holland. The second was at 52° 32 North - 04° 40 East, which is 15 miles northwest of Amsterdam.

Sgt Herbert and his crew in Z6817 had a narrow escape when his Whitley was hit several times by intense flak over the target. The aircraft was holed in several places but they managed to limp back to Middleton. P/O Calder in Z6825 hauled

[42] Exactor equipment provided a remote control facility linking the throttle box with the propellers

his bomb-load all the way to Huls and all the way home again. It was only found out over the target that the main fuse had blown in his aircraft, thus preventing the bombs from being dropped. Sgt Muttart had an interesting night as he and the second pilot, P/O Layland, fought to keep Whitley Z6977 in the air. Having attacked the target from 10,000 feet, they were twice attacked by Me110 fighters and the port engine was hit. Along with this, the aircraft's 250-lb bombs hung up in the bomb bay. With diligent flying from both pilots the aircraft was landed safely at Martlesham at 02:15. Whitley Z6881, flown by P/O Thorpe and his crew, had taken off from Goosepool at 20:37. The squadron record state, 'Nothing has been heard from this aircraft since take off.' It later transpired that this aircraft was shot down by a night fighter flown by Oblt Helmut Lent of 4./NJG1. It had crashed at 01:25, near Bergum in Holland, killing all of its crew. They are buried in Bergum's Tietjerksteradee Protestant Churchyard.

The second Whitley to be lost from Middleton was Z6864. Having searched for over an hour, Sgt Jones and his crew eventually found and bombed the target from a height of 12,000 feet. On the way back to base whilst over Yorkshire, this aircraft was attacked by an enemy intruder. The Whitley crash-landed at Markington, 4 miles S/W of Ripon, injuring 3 members of the crew. The aircraft was burned out.

The following night, Sgt Simmonds and his crew took off from Middleton at 20:43. They were one of three 78 Squadron Whitleys to attack Berlin. Having bombed the target from 10,000 feet, they, in return, received much attention from the city's defences. Holed by heavy flak, they limped home, only to crash-land, out of fuel, at Houghton-Le-Spring on the A690 near Sunderland. No injuries to the crew were reported. At the time of their crash (06:20) the crew of this aircraft had been airborne for 10 hours and 3 minutes.

Berlin was again the target on the 8th, when 76 sent a lone Halifax to the Big City. It joined with 196 aircraft sent by other squadrons. Most of the bombs fell to the north and east of the city centre, in the Licktenberg and Pankow districts. Four factories employed in producing war material were badly damaged, along with 10 transport and 13 public utilities, 2 public buildings, a zoo, 16 farms and 200 houses. Casualties on the ground consisted of 36 dead and 212 injured. 2,873 people were bombed out of their homes. 8 Wellingtons, 2 Hampdens, 2 Whitleys, 2 Stirlings and 1 Manchester were lost.

A long haul to Italy took place on the 10/11th when four of 76's Halifaxes were sent on a raid to Turin, using Stradishall as their advanced base. This operation by a total of 76 Bomber Command aircraft successfully attacked the centre of the city and the Fiat Steel Works. The navigators used the Rhone valley, Geneva and the Alps as pinpoints. All crews returned safely to Stradishall, and reported that they had seen their bombs burst in the town, starting many fires.

The following night saw nine of 78's Whitleys detailed for operations, this time it was the docks at Warnemunde, 6 miles north of Rostock. However, most crews bombed the town itself. This raid highlighted one of the main problems with Bomber Command during the early years of the war, poor navigation facilities available to the bomber crews. All eleven Whitleys dispatched from Middleton that night took off during a narrow time band, 21:09 to 21:35. This represents a 26-minute period between the first and the last aircraft to take off. The first one landed back at 05:11 after 8 hours in the air. Within a 30-minute bracket all eleven aircraft performed similarly. Therefore, it is reasonable to suggest that they all would have experienced the same weather conditions. Let us take a look at the de-briefing reports of the crews returning to Middleton from this particular raid. The first to take off at 21:09 was Sgt Muttart in Z6640, He and his crew reported that no bombing results were observed due to 10/10ths cloud cover over the target. They also reported 10/10ths-cloud cover all the way to the target and back. Having taken off some 7 minutes later, P/O Calder reported, 'Weather 3/10ths-4/10ths cloud over the target.' They were able to bomb from a height of 14,000 feet and observe bomb bursts and fires started by other aircraft. Obviously this was not the same target as Sgt Muttart. One of them had bombed somewhere else thinking it was the correct target.

Let us digest the differing reports supplied at de-briefing by the various crews.

Sgt Herbert	Good visibility.
Sgt Snider	Bright Moon, bombs seen bursting on docks.
Sgt Bird	10/10ths cloud, attacked Rostock instead.
P/O Calder	3/10ths-4/10ths cloud.
Sgt Muttart	10/10ths cloud.
Sgt Newborn	10/10ths cloud inland from the coast.
F/L Snow	Bursts seen across target, 8/10ths cloud.
P/O Dunlop	Fires seen in dock area, 8/10ths cloud.
Sgt Simmonds	Unable to locate target 10/10ths cloud.

Some crews report quite different weather conditions, although they supposedly flew to and attacked the same target. It is more likely that some crews may have bombed the wrong targets/towns. One crew reports total cloud cover all the way there and back, whilst one crew states good visibility and others 10/10ths cloud.

During the middle of 1941, Bomber Command sought out a civil servant called Mr D M Butt, and asked him to carry out an investigation into bombing accuracy. He went away and having scrutinised large numbers of aiming point photographs produced a report, better known to aviation history as the Butt Report. Its findings were, to say the least, startling. Although a very in-depth report, the gist stated that only one third of bomber crews were able to get their bombs within 5 miles of the intended target. This was not an aiming problem per se, but more a navigational one. DR navigation was taking its toll, some crews were bombing the wrong targets altogether, not only the wrong targets but even the wrong towns. This was not entirely the crew's fault and some form of alternative navigation was certainly required.

The 13/14th saw 10 Whitleys detailed to attack the Scharnhorst and Gneisenau in Brest harbour. Sgt Simmonds's Whitley Z6490 never got away, It returned to its dispersal, having turned back from the runway with engine problems. The remainder managed to take off, but two more returned with mechanical problems. The first, Z6825 flown by Sgt Thomas, came back after only 16 minutes with an inoperative airspeed indicator. After carrying out a nerve-racking landing, Sgt Simmonds taxied the Whitley to its dispersal, where the Pitot cover was found to be still in place. Someone had forgot to remove it during the aircraft's pre-flight inspection. At 03:32, Sgt Jones returned in Z9127 due to failure of the trimming gear on the W/T equipment.

Due to low cloud and a very efficient smoke screen, reports of the bombing were vague. Having bombed the target from 16,000 feet, Sgt Bell in Z6978 turned for home and was attacked by a night fighter. Although the enemy aircraft itself could not be seen, the tail gunner Sgt Davidson observed tracer as it passed below the Whitley. He immediately opened fire in the general direction of the tracer's source, whereupon the fighter became illuminated as its fuel tanks burst into flames. It then fell away and disappeared into the cloud below. Having landed for a short time at Kirton-In-Linsey for fuel, this Whitley returned to Middleton soon after. All of 78's aircraft operating that night returned safely to base. 76 also contributed to the attack on Brest. They sent four aircraft, 3 of which returned safe. The fourth was Halifax L9567, flown by P/O R E Hutchin. Having taken off from Middleton at 01:42, this aircraft crashed one hour and thirty minutes later whilst outbound to the target. It crashed near the River Ousse at Water End Renhold, 3 miles N/E of Bedford. P/O Hutchin died in the crash, the remainder baled out.

Roddy Carr was back at Goosepool on September 14th, this time it was to join RAF Viscount Lord Trenchard GCB GCVO DSO DCL and LLD, who had arrived at 12:07 hours. After visits to the hangars they had lunch, after which Middleton's Station Commander, Group Captain Tommy Trail presented squadron and station officers to Lord Trenchard. At 14:00 Lord Trenchard inspected the Ops room and the Intelligence Section. He then went on to address the crews in the briefing room before departing by air at 14:40 for Mackmerry. Next day, two of 76's Halifax crews were briefed to attack Hamburg, both returned safe.

Four Whitleys were detailed to attack Stettin on the 19th. Only 3 reached the target as Sgt Simmonds brought Z9129 back to base with Exactor trouble. The other 3 aircraft bombed Stettin successfully but had to land at Driffield due to fog in the Vale of York. The single 76 Halifax crew captained by Sgt Turnbull also returned safe from the same target.

The following night, a further 9 Whitleys were dispatched to targets at Ostend. Sgt King was bringing Z6948 in to attack when the aircraft was hit by heavy flak. The auxiliary pipelines were cut, along with the auxiliary ammo tank. Damage was also caused to the rear turret and W/T set. The observer, Sgt Jupp, jettisoned the bombs 'safe' from 15,000 feet, whereafter the Whitley was flown back to Middleton where it landed safely at 00:30. All of 78 Squadron's aircraft, having attacked Ostend, returned safely to base. This included P/O Bickerdike who taxied in sporting several large holes in Z9129's port engine and cowling. Also on the 20th September, owing to bad weather over the continent, all 4 Group aircraft were recalled after take-off. That night, Middleton St George was acting as the Chief Diversion Area. Three Hampdens of 5 Group were diverted to Goosepool. The captain of one Hampden praised the control tower staff at Middleton for the speedy and efficient way that he and his crew were brought in to land.

September drew to a close for 78 with 16 sorties being flown to various targets on the 29th and 30th. The targets attacked over these two nights included Stettin, Warnemunde, Cherbourg and Hamburg.

Three of 76's Halifaxes, flown by S/L Bouwens, F/L Wright and Sgt Morin, were detailed to attack Stettener Haxen on the 29th; all returned safe. During the same night, a radio transmission calling for help was received from Sgt Bird and his crew in Whitley Z9126, who had been detailed to attack Stettin. Bearings taken at the time indicated that the Whitley was close to the Island of Sylt. Nothing further was heard from this aircraft and it is presumed that it came down in the sea. Sgt Bird and his crew are commemorated on the Runnymede Memorial.

Whitley being bombed up, note wing bomb bay doors open   Photo: IWM CH.224

October 1941

On October 3rd, 78 detailed two fresher crews for a raid on a nursery target at Dunkirk. Due to mechanical problems one aircraft was unable to take off and so the other crew went it alone. They formed part of a 7 aircraft raid on Dunkirk and Boulogne and were able to start several fires in the Dunkirk area before returning safely to Goosepool.

October's Ops began the same night for 76, with a two aircraft raid to bomb German cruisers in Brest harbour. Both F/L Wright and Sgt Banclark attacked the primary from a height of 15,000 feet. MP-C suffered some accurate heavy flak, which punched 10 separate holes in the aircraft, fortunately no one was injured. Having completed their attack, bursts were seen on the target. Just prior to their bomb run a smoke screen was lit, which began to reduce the excellent visibility. 15 minutes later the target area was completely obscured. Both aircraft turned for Boscombe Down where they landed safely at 22:04 and 22:25 respectively. A third aircraft, MP-T, flown by Sgt Morin, did not attack the target, owing to a Glycol coolant leak. Having set course for home the bomb-load was jettisoned in the sea and the Halifax was landed safely at Exeter. The weather during October was quite bad, providing a persistent mixture of high winds, drizzle, mist and fog. A series of cancellations and stand-downs was to plague Goosepool for the next few days. On the 9th, F/L Buck arrived from the Air Ministry to begin his investigation into the loss of P/O Hitchin's Halifax

At six minutes past midnight on the 10th, S/L Mercer taxied 78 Squadron Whitley Z9152 onto Goosepool's runway 24. The target that night was to be the Krupps Works at Essen; the total number of Bomber Command aircraft to be employed on this raid totalled 78. Applying the brakes, he began his final take-off checks. Individually he cut the magneto switches on each engine, and checked for any mag drops[43]. Ts and Ps were checked next[44]. The final check was 'full and free'. This involved moving the flight controls to ensure that they were free to move throughout their full travel and were not jammed. There were, and still are, fatal crashes caused by spanners left behind by groundcrew, also control rods and cables incorrectly routed. Roy Chadwick, designer of the Lancaster, was killed after the war whilst flying in an aircraft that allegedly had the aileron push rods incorrectly re-assembled. With the pre take-off checks complete, S/L Mercer opened the throttles and began his take-off run. Once airborne, the Whitley was turned onto a track of 144°; this would involve a direct flight to Dunwich on the Suffolk coast, some 199 miles to the southeast. Behind him, P/O King in Z6948 had begun his take-off run. Whilst gaining speed down the runway, his port engine lost power and the aircraft swung. The Whitley eventually came to a halt undamaged, but it was scrubbed from the operation.

Having been airborne for about 20 minutes, Sgt Wilson, the observer in S/L Mercer's aircraft, passed a note to the second dickie, Sgt Whitehorn. Having read the note, Whitehorn then passed the 'Gen' onto Mercer. 'Ground speed is about 153, should be at Dunwich about - erm - twenty-five past one Skip.' Mercer did not speak but simply acknowledged that he had heard by glancing across the cockpit. Dunwich lay sleeping as the Whitley passed overhead. The observer spoke on the intercom, 'New course Skipper, steer 111°, its about 98 miles to the Dutch Coast.' Mercer increased speed. Having checked the guns, the crew settled down for the short flight over the North Sea. Twenty-five minutes later Sgt Wilson spoke again; 'I estimate about five minutes to the Dutch Coast, Skip.' 'Pilot to crew, keep a good look-out for our land-fall.' At 01:54 the enemy coast was crossed and the final 142-mile leg to the target began. Essen lies slap-bang in the middle of Happy Valley; there was no easy route to Essen. They would pass to the north of Eindhoven, a major hot spot in its own right. This was not as bad as the next section of the journey, as they went on to pass between Duisburg and Krefeld, better known to some bomber crews as the Jaws of Hell.

Just 42 minutes after leaving Schouwen they arrived over Essen at 11,000 feet, after checking their course by the Dortmund-Emms canal. Having bombed the primary target through 10/10ths-cloud cover, no results of the attack could be observed by the rear gunner F/S Wright. It was now time to go home. They reached the Dutch Coast safely without incident and headed out to sea. Sgt Simpson, the WOP/AG manning the radio, received a transmission on the W/T that they were to divert to Dishforth. This they did and landed safely at 07:23. For Mercer's second pilot Sgt Roland Whitehorn, this operation to Essen was to be his last. As will be revealed shortly, unexpected events that were to take place 6 nights later would conspire to end his flying career altogether. P/O Knox and his crew in Z6817 dropped their bombs despite intense flak, and again Sgt Thorn in the tail turret reported that no results were seen due to total cloud cover. They too returned safely, only to see the Whitley damaged when it collided with an obstruction on Oakington's[45] runway.
Sgt Snider in Z9132 reached Essen and bombed from a height of 14,000 feet on ETA. Although plagued by the same 10/10ths-cloud cover, his rear gunner Sgt Freeman saw reddish fires glowing through the clouds. Similar results were reported by Sgt Lambert on his return in Z6978. These results were confirmed by Sgt Simmonds and his crew in Z9131, who on the way home had dropped two 250-lb bombs on searchlight concentrations at Pipsen. The crews of P/O Kirkpatrick, Sgt Hobbs, Sgt Moorfoot and Sgt Thomas also bombed Essen, but again, due to the cloud were unable to confirm any results of the bombing.

Out of the 12 Goosepool Whitleys earmarked for this operation, only 9 had actually taken off to attack the target.

As the above mentioned aircraft returned, they received a W/T message diverting them to Dishforth, as it was not possible for them to land back at base. They thought this a bit strange. The weather on departure, along with the forecast, had been very good. Flying back over the North Sea, the crews had no idea what was going on, but back at Middleton during their absence there had been much excitement. Having all returned safely to spend the night at a Gin clear Dishforth, Mercer and the others would have to wait until the next day to find out what had been 'up' at Middleton the night before.

---

[43] For safety purposes, aero engines have two spark plugs per cylinder and two magnetos to supply the sparks. One plug in each of the cylinders is fed with sparks supplied by the first magneto, the second magneto feeds the second set of plugs. Should a magneto fail, the engine can still run on one set of plugs, albeit with reduced power. The Mag check involves turning off each Magneto in turn to see how many revs are lost. If the mags (and plugs) are OK only a small drop in engine revolutions will be observed on the RPM gauges, if a large drop occurs the aircraft will be grounded.
[44] Temperature and Pressures
[45] North of Cambridge

It later transpired that, as the last two Whitleys on the Essen raid had been taking off, they had collided on the flarepath and burst into flames. In his excellent book 'Only Owls and Bloody Fools Fly at Night', Wing Commander Sawyer, as he was at the time, remembered that this incident took place on a really dark night. The nine aircraft had already taken off when Whitley Z6825 started its take-off run. Suddenly the pilot, P/O Fransden, throttled back when half way down the runway. He appeared to have stopped right at the end of the runway close to the perimeter track. Standing on the balcony of flying control, Tom Sawyer thought the pilot was turning off the 06 end of the runway and onto the peri-track before taxiing round towards the starting point again. Meanwhile, before Tom and his colleagues could call the pilot on the R/T to ask what was going on, the flare-path controller at the first flare, who could not see what was going on at the other end, gave the all clear for the next Whitley to take off. After a few moments, the small group standing on the balcony realised that the first Whitley was still on the flarepath and had turned around to taxi back along the runway. This was not approved by the RAF under any circumstances. The second Whitley, Z9127, was by now half way down the runway, tail up, almost airborne. Both aircraft collided, hitting port wing to port wing. The ensuing crash pirouetted the aircraft around each other in a half circle, bits flying off in all directions.

As they came to a halt, about 30 yards apart, small fires started in both aircraft. By the time the rescuers arrived, the aircraft were well alight. Luckily all the crewmembers got out ok, although Sgt Taylor from P/O Fransden's crew and Sgt Dench from P/O Leyland's crew were slightly injured. The crew from the first aircraft were P/O Fransden, Sgt Dennis, Sgt Bowden, Sgt Young, and Sgt Taylor; the crew from the second were P/O Layland[46], Sgt Dench, P/O Geddes, Sgt Donaldson, and Sgt Vere. Meanwhile the fires were getting out of hand, as each Whitley carried over 700 gallons of petrol. The crash tender crew was ordered to return to the M/T section to refill their foam tanks. Before they could even get there, both aircraft blew up almost simultaneously. The bomb-loads followed soon after, blowing two large craters, 20 feet deep, in the main runway, 24/06. This effectively closed the airfield. As already stated, the aircraft already airborne were signalled to divert to other airfields on their return from ops. The main runway was out of use for several days, whilst civilian contractors carried out repairs. Two of 76's crews were due to take off after the Whitleys for the same raid on Essen. Larry Donnelly was in one of the Halifaxes as it taxied around the peri track towards the duty runway. It had a 4,000-lb Cookie in its bomb bay, along with many other assorted bang makers. His captain promptly turned the Hally around and put as much distance as he could between his aircraft and the burning Whitleys. With the closure of the main (longest) runway, for 76, the war was over, well for a few days anyway. Both Halifax crews simply taxied back to their dispersals, parked up, and went to bed.

Earlier that day, Norman Thompson had stepped from his railway carriage onto platform 4 of Darlington's Bank Top Station. He was dressed in best blues and wearing white webbing and full packs. Struggling with his heavy kit bag, he reported to an RAF corporal who was stood talking with some other airmen outside the station café. The corporal pointed to the northern entrance and informed Norman that he would find transport waiting for him there. Having found an RAF 3 ton truck, Norman threw his kit up onto the tailgate and quickly followed it. There were a few other airmen on the truck, and as it left the station ramp and turned right onto Yarm Road, Norman got his first glimpse of wartime Darlington. Some of the airmen were returning from leave, they painted a rosy picture of life at Goosepool. Unlike many camps, this one had warm and dry accommodation. Norman didn't know any different, as this was his first operational posting, and it was all new to him.

Having reported to the guardroom, he presented his movement orders to the SP[47]. Norman waited for someone to collect him and take him to his barrack block. Whilst waiting he found the 'Snowdrop' friendly enough,[48] and they chatted until the Orderly Corporal arrived. Norman picked up his kit and followed the corporal up the road and to the left of Station Headquarters. He was taken into one of the six H-blocks on the domestic site. Norman followed the corporal up to a 24-bed dormitory on the first floor. There were several spare beds, so he chose one by a window. The corporal told Norman to dump his kit and follow him to the bedding store. Here he was issued with his bedding, and the corporal left him to find his own way back to his billet. Norman's bed was just like all the others in the room. Made of tubular steel, it was flanked on one side by the usual wooden bedside locker and a tall blue/gray locker on the other. He unpacked his kit and went off to the cookhouse for tea. For Norman, it had been a very long day, so he decided to have an early night. Climbing into bed after his tiring wartime train journey, he pulled up the covers and closed his eyes. Whilst dozing, he reviewed the events that had led him to Goosepool.

Everyone on the course had celebrated the last night at Morecambe in style. It was deemed compulsory to have a drink in every pub on the main road leading back to the billet. Norman remembers there were quite a few pubs on the route, and many bodies littered the trail back to the billets. Although they only lived about a hundred yards from the last pub, it took Norman and his fellow drinkers about an hour to carry each other home. Norman very nearly didn't make it back, but he managed it somehow. At the billets they all said their goodbyes, wished each other luck, and duly passed out. Norman eventually woke and with a bit of a struggle reached his room. Norman's last recollection was - that the next time his bed came around, he was going to try and jump on it. What a night!

Meanwhile, back at Middleton, the whole airfield was awakened by the sounds of several huge explosions. Norman sat up in bed. The building was in chaos, he could also hear shouting coming from outside. It seemed that practically the whole camp was running for cover. Presuming that an air raid was taking place, people were running everywhere, banging into each other, some were diving out of windows, even from the first floor. Everyone was frantically heading for the shelters, everyone that is except Norman. He was far too tired and comfortable to move. Later, when Norman's griping roommates noisily returned, he awoke again. Many were soaked to the skin. In the dark and the confusion, some of them had dived

[46] To Norman Thompson and his oppos, better known as "Crasher" Layland
[47] Service Police
[48] SPs were nicknamed Snowdrops because of their white-painted helmets

head first into the underground air raid shelters, which unfortunately had been half-full of water. It later transpired that the explosions were not from an air raid at all, but from the two Whitleys that had collided on the flarepath. 'What a welcome to one's first station', thought Norman, as he rolled over and went back to sleep.

The following day, the Station Armament Officer, F/L Burke, carried out controlled explosions on the bombs that had been on the two crashed Whitleys and had failed to explode in the heat of the fires. The only damage to the rest of the airfield had been a couple of broken widows.

The same day saw a visit to the airfield of a group of work people from Messrs Boulton Paul Ltd, who came to carry out adjustments to the gun turrets on some of the squadron's Halifaxes.

The following night was the 12th, and 78 Squadron sent 7 Whitleys to take part in the first large-scale raid on Nuremberg. Led by W/C Sawyer in Z9152, Goosepool's Whitleys were to swell the ranks of a force of 152 bombers, comprising 54 Whitleys, 7 Stirlings, 82 Wellingtons, and 9 Halifaxes. 76's contribution was 4 Halifaxes. They also briefed one fresher crew to attack Bremen. There should have been 8 Whitleys sent from Goosepool on the Nuremberg trip, but one was unable to take-off due to mechanical problems. Air Vice-Marshall Roddy Carr was present at briefing. He stated to the gathered aircrews that this raid was to be one of Bomber Command's greatest efforts thus far. Nuremberg was Germany's largest medieval city, situated in Bavaria. Famous for its Nazi's rallies during the early and mid 30s, it would later become the venue for their war crimes trials after the war. Meanwhile it played a large part in providing the German war machine with material. The raid to Nuremberg involved a 1,332-mile round trip, across some of the most inhospitable real estate one could ever imagine. The first leg was to Orfordness, some 199 miles from Goosepool. S/L Sawyer already had the first compass heading ready from briefing, a direct track of 148° corrected for wind drift.

Just before the flight, the navigator, P/O Middlemass had been given a wind vector of 240° at 10 knots. Using his navigation calculator, he worked out his heading and ground speed. To conserve fuel whilst over friendly territory, the first leg to Dunwich would be flown at 145 mph (126 knots).[49] The direct track without wind was 144°. He deduced that at a heading of 148° the wind would be almost directly on the wingtip and therefore would not effect their ground speed unduly.

During each leg, upgrades to the heading would be made as the effects of the wind were observed. At this stage in the war, Dead Reckoning (DR) was the main form of navigation for the RAF. Later, new radio navigation aids would came into service, which would improve the navigator's lot tremendously.

There were of course some rudimentary radio aids available at this time but they were limited to finding a cross plot from 2 or more radio beacons. This employed the use of a rotatable loop aerial which, when turned end on to a radio beam, provided a null and thus a bearing to the transmitting station. During the war, DR navigation was the main method of getting about. Even on the darkest nights the sea, rivers, canals, lakes, blast furnaces and a variety of other large objects could be seen quite clearly (if there wasn't too much cloud cover). One could at times even orientate one's direction of travel by the lights of neutral countries, as not everyone in the civilised world was blacked out. These countries included Denmark, Sweden, Portugal and Spain to name but a few.

For Tom Sawyer in Z9152, take-off came at 18:48. His crew that night, apart from the observer P/O Middlemass, were second pilot Sgt Attwell, wireless operator Sgt Bradford and rear gunner F/S Bee. Once out to sea beyond Dunwich, their next landmark would be Blankenburge on the Belgian coast, 8 miles northwest of Bruges. From here they would fly a semi-direct route to the target, avoiding the flak hot spots of Aachen, Koblenz and Frankfurt, amongst others. When Sawyer arrived at the target area, several scattered fires were already burning. Some 78 Squadron aircraft had arrived earlier, including Sgt Thomas and his crew. Throughout the war, many crews had a preference to get to the target that bit earlier, preferably before anyone else. The reason for this was that most towns preferred to keep a low profile until they knew for certain that they were the target. Relying on the blackout for protection, the flak and searchlights would not announce the location of the target until the bombs were practically falling from the aircraft. This must have been the strategy of Sgt Thomas in Z9157, as, due to the lack of flak when first on the target, he carried out his attack from only 3,000 feet. Moonlight, the absence of cloud, and the extremely low altitude afforded P/O Forbes in the nose an excellent view. The target was easily identified and Sgt Morrison in the rear turret saw their bombs burst dead on the aiming point. So low were the crew of Z9157, that after they dropped their bombs, they could feel the concussions from the explosions from inside the aircraft. Close behind came P/O Kirkpatrick in Z6977. His bomb aimer, Sgt Smythe, dropped their bombs from 11,000 feet. As the visibility was still good, Sgt Vere in the tail turret and the second pilot, F/L Packe, observed the bomb bursts. The glow of the fires started by their incendiaries was also visible in the target area.

S/L Bouwens in 76 Halifax MP-Y L9523 bombed the primary from 16,000 feet. Although the river was identified, pinpointing the target was impossible. A myriad of incendiary fires were dotted all over the countryside, up to a radius of 30 miles from Nuremberg. F/L Wright's crew attacked the primary from 13,000 feet at 23:04. They scored some direct hits. Very little flak was encountered on the way out but over Mannheim on the way back it was a very different story, with some very accurate flak in evidence. They managed to shake off the unwanted attentions of the flak gunners, only to be coned by five searchlights over the French coast. After trying every trick in the book, Wright was able to shake off the lights and head out to sea. Sgt Turnbull's crew dropped their incendiaries from 15,000 feet, noticing German Barrage Balloons, which were up to 8,000 feet. They encountered no flak problems in either direction. Sgt Morin's crew also had a flak free trip. Good pinpoints were achieved on the Rhine and the river northwest of the city's aerodrome. The northern part of the town was well alight by the time they got to the target. Their bursts were seen in the built-up areas, which started fires that began burning well. As they focused in, a second stick dropped by another aircraft swelled the conflagration they had started.

---

[49] 1 nautical mile = 1.1414 statute miles, i.e. 10-kts. = 14.14 mph

By now smoke haze was forming, and Sgt Bell in 78's Whitley Z6978 was running in at 12,000 feet. Sgt Webb dropped the H E bombs and incendiaries, which were seen to fall on the target by Sgt Hanna in the rear turret. The second pilot, P/O Shattock, and Sgt Boucher the WOP/AG, saw many scattered incendiary fires around the target area. At 17,000 feet, Sgt Hobbs and his crew in Z6491 dropped their bombs on a large fire located on the northwest edge of the aiming point. Two large white explosions were observed by Sgt Strang the rear gunner. Sawyer attacked next from a height of 13,000 feet. Sgt Middlemass in the nose dropped the bombs, which were seen to burst on the fires below. It was not possible to identify the target with any great accuracy due to the increasing ground haze. P/O King in Z9151 bombed the primary aiming point from 12,000 feet. Sgt Campbell in the rear turret, the second pilot P/O Pruden and observer Sgt Jupp all saw that their incendiary bombs had started fires in many buildings. All crews returned to base safely, but the last two aircraft flown by Sawyer and King diverted to Abingdon as they were low on fuel.

78's crews passed their report to the Intelligence Officer during debriefing back at Middleton. They firmly believed that their testimony was totally correct and depicted events just as they saw them happen. How different they were to the accounts written that night by the Germans. First of all, it must be remembered that there were 152 aircraft from various squadrons operating to Nuremberg that night. 78 contributed only 7 aircraft and presumably their descriptions of the evening's proceedings were totally accurate. However, it looks like navigational difficulties were experienced by some aircraft that night as the accounts by German record keepers differ greatly from those of the RAF. German officials in the city recorded that only a small number of bombs had fallen in the Nuremberg area. Only one person was reported killed, and six injured.

Admittedly, on reaching their bases, one or two bomber crews reported seeing villages burning up to 10 miles away from Nuremberg. Some 8 miles to the southwest of Nuremberg is the small river-side town of Schwabach, which, at the exact time of the raid, experienced the destruction of about 50 buildings and the deaths of approximately 10 people. Also, over 65 miles to the southwest of Nuremberg, is the small village of Lauingen, which also endured a raid that night which lasted for over 4 hours. Just like Nuremberg, this small town was situated on a wide river, in this case the Danube. This hamlet suffered the loss of 44 houses and 4 killed. During the following few days, hundreds of people came from all over the region to see the devastation and wonder why such a small insignificant village had been attacked. Over 200 bomb craters were counted, both in and around the village. It had been realised by the town folk at the time that this was not the intended target, as there were no factories or workshops in or around the village. Instead they believed, incorrectly, that the intended target was the larger industrial town of Ingoldstadt, 46 miles to the northeast. Some 21 miles north of Stuttgart lies yet another town astride a wide river, in this case the river Neckar. Lauffen-am-Neckar also became an accidental recipient of the attentions of Bomber Command that night, when 46 houses were damaged. This small town was positioned over 88 miles from Nuremberg and close to one of Stuttgart's main decoy sites.

Many crews, having found burning towns, simply joined in and added to the distraction, believing that this was the correct target. After all, the towns and villages affected were all situated on large rivers, just as Nuremberg straddles the river Pegnitz. Such were the failings of DR navigation over a blacked out Germany during the early part of WWII.

All four of 76's aircraft sent to Nuremberg returned safely, Bouwens and Morin to base, Wright to South Cerny and Turnbull to Docking. Of the two Halifaxes that landed back at Middleton, MP-U L9563, flown by Sgt Morin, crashed on landing, fortunately without injuring any of the crew. Two nights later, Sgt Banclark and his crew in MP-B were the only contribution provided by Middleton in another raid on Nuremberg. Having bombed through the thin cloud on ETA, they landed safely on the grass runways of RAF Swanton Morley, Norfolk, after seven hours airborne.

Two hours and four minutes after leaving Middleton, Flight Sergeant E B Muttart in MP-H L9561, who was on his way to Bremen, fell to the guns of Lt Leopold Fellerer of 4. /NJG1. His aircraft crashed near Wons, 7 miles south of Harlingen, Holland. Muttart remained at the controls long enough for his crew to jump out. He paid the ultimate price to ensure their survival. They became POWs, whilst he rests in the local General Cemetery. The squadron lost another aircraft during the morning, happily in less unfortunate circumstances, as MP-Q, one of the old Mk Is, was transferred to Linton-on-Ouse, to join the Halifax conversion flight.

Six of 78's Whitleys, including four fresher crews, were assigned to operations on the night of the 13th but due to poor weather this order was later rescinded. The next night, 10 more were detailed for another 80 bomber raid on Nuremberg. Unfortunately, due to 10/10ths-cloud cover over the target area and much of Germany, only five of 78's aircraft managed to bomb the primary, and even then only on ETA. For 78 this raid was somewhat problematic. Two Whitleys were non-starters due to mechanical problems. One aircraft attacked flak and searchlight batteries at what the crew believed to be Karleshuhem. Due to 10/10ths-cloud cover and icing, one aircraft returned to Middleton with its bomb-load. Also on its return, one of the squadron's Whitleys taxied into a pole on the airfield and was damaged. Another returned early due to engine trouble. To finish off an eventful night, P/O D S King and his crew flying in Z9213 had run out of fuel near Hythe, Kent. P/O King, along with P/O Pruden and Sergeants Jupp, Lyndon and Campbell baled out. They all landed safely[50].

A lone Halifax, MP-B L9565, flown by Sgt Bunclark, was the only contribution from 76 to this raid. On reaching the target it attacked on ETA from 14,000 feet through thin cloud cover. Bunclark's bombs seem to open up a veritable hornet's nest of flak and searchlights. Discretion being the better part of valour, he and his crew high-tailed it out of town and returned safely to land at Swanton Morley.

Although at this time 76 still had few operational crews and aircraft, it was slowly beginning to expand. During the morning of the 15th, two new Mk II Halifaxes were delivered. At 13:00 the first to arrive was MP-M L9583, which had been flown in from 45 MU at Kinloss. Two hours later MP-H L9608 landed from 24 MU at Ternhill.

---

[50] This story does not have a totally happy ending. P/O King RCAF, having been posted to 76 Squadron, went missing on the 30th of December 1941 whilst flying Halifax L.9615 (MP-X) on operations to Brest. Hit by flak, he and his crew have never been found. They are recorded on the Runnymede Memorial.

Still the October weather dogged 78's attempts to mount operations. On the 16th, four fresher crews were sent to a nursery target at Ostend. Due to the persistent 10/10ths-cloud cover, only two of the crews were able to bomb the target. The other two jettisoned their bomb-load over the sea off the Belgian coast and came home.

Halifax MP-L flying close to the western side of the Cleveland Hills, south of Yarm   Photo: IWM CH.3380

For the groundcrew at Goosepool, life went on as usual. One of the less appealing occupations for Norman Thompson and his fellow airman was guard duty. This often included walking around the full perimeter of the airfield late at night. Round and round one would go walking for miles. The only soul to bump into (hopefully) was one's counterpart on a reciprocal beat. This was spooky to say the least, especially the deserted area to the south of the main runway 24/06, the bomb dump and the aircraft being the main reason for the guard. This was the furthest and most far-flung part of the airfield. Remember that the blackout was in full force at this time, unlike today when the place is lit up like Blackpool. The best bit was when one reached the north side of the airfield, and habitation.

On their days off, Norman and his oppos would walk up to the railway station at Middleton St George, this was better known as Dinsdale station. Boarding the train from, the small seaside town of Redcar, they would alight at Darlington's Bank Top railway station.

Sgt Roland Whitehorn

Whitley V overflies airfield to set course for first leg of outbound flight
Photo: IWM CH.244

Sgt Roland Whitehorn had been posted in to 78 Squadron on September 21st. When he arrived he was informed that he was to be transferred to 76 as they had urgent need of him. He was immediately despatched to the Halifax conversion flight. Once his training was over he was assigned to the duties of second pilot and instantly thrown into the operational deep-end. His first raid was to Berlin, followed a few nights later by a second. Having carried out these two raids, little time was lost and soon he found himself visiting the French port of Brest. During the next three weeks he added Turin and Boulogne to his tally of targets. Having just returned from the Boulogne raid, he awoke the next day to find that he was again to fly Whitleys with 78 Squadron.

His first flight was to Essen on October 10th with S/L Mercer. This was the operation previously mentioned, during which, the 2 Whitleys had collided on the runway. On the evening of the 16th, Sgt Whitehorn and P/O B O Smith were detailed to fly a Whitley from Croft airfield, and brush up on their night flying skills. Croft was expected to open for operations as Goosepool's satellite in the near future, and its facilities were being used occasionally for crew training. They were assigned a gash wireless operator, Sgt Duffort, and a rear-gunner, Sgt Kidd RCAF. With P/O Smith acting as captain, they took-off at 20:10 in Whitley Z6646 to practice a couple of night circuits and bumps. As this aircraft had quite a reputation for frequent engine changes, they were not at all happy at being assigned to this particular crate. Their misgivings were soon confirmed. Just after they had taken off, the port engine started banging and began losing power. They tried to reduce drag by retracting the undercarriage, but it would not budge. The aircraft had not even reached its single engine safety speed of 95 mph when the engine failed. They tried to carry out a wide circuit and bring the Whitley back to the airfield. Unfortunately, due to the drag of the undercarriage, they were unable to maintain height on one engine. Before they could reach Croft, the aircraft hit the ground near Stillington, 10 miles N/N/E of Croft, and some 3.5 miles S/S/E of Sedgefield. The Whitley immediately caught fire. The rear gunner was able to turn his turret sideways, open the rear doors, and fall out backwards before the fire reached him. He then ran around to the front of the aircraft to assist the rest of the crew. Inside the aircraft, the other three crewmembers were scrambling for the nose hatch, their clothes on fire. By a miracle they fell out of the Whitley, to the accompaniment of exploding flares, ammo and petrol tanks. Running to a small tributary of the river Tees, which ran near by, they quenched their burning clothes. They then painfully waded back to the riverbank to rejoin the rear gunner.

Alerted by the crash and the subsequent fire, several local people had rushed to the scene. They took the burned airmen to a nearby doctor for treatment. He telephoned Sedgefield hospital and an ambulance collected them. Unsurprisingly, the subsequent RAF enquiry confirmed that the accident was due to engine failure. After spending some time at Sedgefield, all three airmen were moved to The Queen Victoria Hospital at East Grinstead, where they became some of the famous Guinea Pigs, under the care of pioneering plastic surgeon Sir Archibold McIndoe. Here Sgt Whitehorn spent the next two years undergoing plastic surgery. Roland Whitehorn wrote to me in May of 1999 and relayed his account of that fateful evening. Such was his modesty that he told me that he hasn't much of interest to portray to me about life at Middleton St George during his time there, I beg to differ. He told me that he still attends the annual Guinea Pig reunions each September. Of the 649 original members of the Guinea Pig Club, who came from Britain, Canada, Australia, New Zealand and the Czech Republic, 155 still attend the annual reunions. As for the rear-gunner, he went back to Canada and they never met again.

The 17th saw no operations or standbys. On the 18th, a single 78 fresher crew was detailed for operations, but this was later cancelled, due to exceptionally strong winds. The wind persisted throughout the next day. The weather improved steadily over the next 24 hours, just in time to allow 78 Squadron's ground staff, flying personnel and aircraft to move the 6 miles southwest to RAF Station Croft.

78 arrive at Croft

Having moved to Croft, 78 once again found themselves as first footers. For the second time in seven months they were to initiate a brand new station. The ground staff had arrived in the vehicles normally used to ferry the aircrew out to the dispersals. On jumping to the ground with his kit, Norman Thompson took one look at his new home. 'Where the bloody 'ell's the hangars?' he complained in his strong Yorkshire accent, to anyone who was listening. 'Supposed to service aircraft outside in all weathers again are we?' he continued. In actual fact that is exactly what they had to do, as when they arrived in October 1941, there were no hangars. They would be built later. The construction of Croft was still in progress. Just for a change there was builder's rubble everywhere, just as there had been when 78 first arrived at Goosepool. Croft had more surprises for its new inhabitants. Not only were there no hangars but also there was only rudimentary accommodation. The cozy centrally heated H-block dormitories at Middleton were replaced by cold damp Nissen huts made from concrete and corrugated steel.

For Norman and his oppos things only got worse. It was promptly announced that there was no water, well in the mornings anyway. The small diameter water pipe feeding the airfield was proving to be totally inadequate. The water was only turned on for a couple of hours in the afternoons. Life was primitive. The WAAFs were bussed in from Middleton each morning, and returned there in the evening after finishing work. Croft Village and its railway station was a 15-minute walk from the camp, about the same distance as Dinsdale railway station was from Middleton. There was also another railway station a couple of miles to the south at nearby Cowton, although this was little used by the in habitants of RAF Croft. Later the old station at Eryholme junction, close to the southeast boundary of the airfield, would be reopened, Croft's personnel for the use of. The London to Edinburgh railway line passed by the eastern end of the airfield. It was used by the London and North Eastern Railway (LNER). Although RAF Croft is no more and became a motor racing circuit in the early 60s, the line is still in use today. It continues to carry passengers and freight from London to Edinburgh and beyond. The trains these days however have different names on them, like GNER (Great North Eastern Railway) and Virgin for example.

Croft railway station was built in the mid-1800s to accommodate the thousands of people who came from around the globe to bathe in the world famous Croft Spa. Now a private dwelling, this once busy place sported many natural chemical and sulphur pools. People would come from all corners of the world to avail themselves of the healing powers of the spa waters. During the war, the main buildings and café along with the beautiful walks attracted many an off-duty airman. During the summer months, British and Canadian airmen would be found at Croft Spa, often walking with their lady friends at their sides. In recent years it was discovered that the site may have been eligible for listed building status, but before this could happen it was bulldozed to the ground and the site cleared by its former owner. Only a house and one small pool remains today.

Croft-in-the-mud, as it was called, presented Norman and his oppos with many problems, one of which was hygiene. Such were the difficulties, what with the limited water supply and all, that he had to take things into his own hands. The situation called for him to exercise his initiative and fortunately Darlington was not too far away. For Norman on his days off, his first port of call was the Chinese laundry in Bondgate to collect his clean laundry.[52] This was followed by a short walk to the public baths in Gladstone Street. Above the swimming baths, was a first floor area where one could, for a couple of pennies, have a wash or a bath. Having bathed and refreshed himself, Norman would change into his clean clothes. He would then return to the laundry to drop off his dirty clothes. Now smartly dressed, his next stop was usually the Green Dragon pub in Post House Wynd.

In June of 1999, I drove Norman back to Darlington from his home in Horseforth, Leeds. Whilst spending a very pleasant summer's day we visited the Green Dragon. To Norman, Posthouse Wynd the name of the little narrow street where the pub is located, and the outside of the pub itself, were exactly the same as they were when he last saw them in 1942. The inside however, had surrendered to the inevitable modern plasticized conversion. Now in an open plan configuration, internally it bore little resemblance to the Green Dragon he remembered. The standard 1940s pub was made up of many little rooms, the Snug, the Bar and the Lounge to name but a few. Norman couldn't resist dragging me in for a nostalgic pint. With his great sense of humour still in evidence, he asked the very young barman if he could still purchase a pint for the same price as he paid last time he was in. The barman said that that shouldn't be a problem, he had worked there for just over a year and the beer prices hadn't been put up once in that time. Unfortunately for Norman (and me) it soon became evident that one can no longer drink all night in the Green Dragon, have a fish supper and still have change left from a pound. 'Oh well!'

One of Norman's friends whilst he was at Middleton was Bill Shaw, who came from Blackpool and was rather a good singer. Having purchased the first round of beers in a pub, Bill and his assistant (Norman) would spend the rest of the night drinking the free beer sent over by a grateful audience. The only problem for Norman was that Bill always thought that his companion was called Tommy. It was a long time before he eventually started to call Norman by his real name, but fortunately this little error didn't stop the flow of beer. Also still in Posthouse Wynd is a building, opposite the Green Dragon, that during the war was a Gent's hairdressers. Here they would have 5 or 6 men cutting hair all day. He remembers that it was always a very busy place.

Whilst roaming around Darlington, Norman remembered that on nights off, a visit to the pictures, perhaps with a young lady, was also an option. In the year 2003,[53] Darlington has but one Cinema, the Odeon, in Northgate. In its heyday the town sported not only the Regal, but also the Royal Astoria, better known as the 'Fleapit'. This picture house was on the southern corner of Station Road and North Road. Today it has been replaced by a petrol filling station. The Gaumont Cinema was located on the southern corner of Gladstone Street and Northgate; a huge tower-block office complex has now replaced it. The Empire is now Wilkinson's Supermarket in Crown Street. Eldon Street had the Scala and Cobden Street the Regent. The Court Arcade in Skinnergate housed the Arcade cinema, and the original Odeon was situated in Bondgate. It has now become a snooker hall. There were others, including one just off the Market Square in Bull Wynd, but you get the picture (pun intended).

Sometimes Norman's companion was a young lady who worked in the Railway station café. Norman remembers that she had a bit of a limp, but was a very nice girl. She was engaged to a soldier so, to use Norman's vernacular, there was never any hanky panky. They just kept each other company during those dark times. However, she would always have a bag of sweets for Norman to take back to camp with him.

Croft in October 1941, when 78 arrived there, was, to use Norman's description, a dump. All aircraft servicing was carried out in the open. As they were there during the wintertime, things were especially bad. From October 1941 until they left in June 42, the only buildings were the billets, which were dispersed well away from the airfield.[54]

One had a bit of a trek in the blackout through the snow to reach the billets, especially after spending most of the night running up engines before a raid. Keeping the Merlins warm, ready for late night/early morning take-off, was one of the engine fitter's tasks. Ice was one of the biggest problems. Norman would have to go over to the runways to do the warm-ups, sometimes as late as 4 am. The winter weather did bring some advantages however, as they were able to boil pans of snow on the stove in their huts to wash with, this to some extent made up for the aforementioned water shortage.

As 78 were moving over to Croft on the 20th, two more Mk II Halifaxes arrived at Middleton destined for 76, one from Kirkbridge and the other from Kinloss. Later that day two crews were briefed for operations, one for Emden and the other Wilhelmshaven. Pilot Officer Calder flew the Emden trip, whilst Sgt Morin went to Wilhelmshaven. Both crews returned safe.

On the 21st, 78 opened the batting from their new home at Croft, and detailed 10 aircraft to bomb Bremen. This raid involved 136 aircraft of different types from different squadrons. The airfields of Lincolnshire had a bad night of it when a Hampden and 2 Wellingtons were lost. One of the Wellingtons lost that night had been W5393 of 12 Squadron. Tragically, having returned safely to their base at Binbrook, five members of the six-man crew were killed when they crashed into a section of the station's married quarters, only the rear-gunner survived, despite being injured. RAF Waddington mourned the crew of 44 Squadron's Hampden AE257 when informed that P/O Budd and his crew had crashed into the North Sea. The second Wellington, GR-W Z1217, belonged to 301 Squadron at Hemswell. The members of its all Polish crew were more fortunate and survived to become POWs.

The bombing was scattered with most of it landing in housing areas, although one bomb fell in the Vulcan shipyard. The Germans recorded that 17 people were killed, 29 injured and 70 made homeless.

---

[52] The laundry and the block of buildings it was in has now gone. Situated to the right of the old Odeon cinema in Bondgate, it has been knocked down and replaced by the entrance to the dual carriageway, which leads down to Northgate.
[53] Formerly the ABC and before that the Regal
[54] Some are still there today used by a market garden

The raid was hampered by heavy industrial haze, which made the identification of targets difficult. One of 78's aircraft returned early and landed at Middleton due to engine trouble. Another was jumped on the way home by a night fighter; the Whitley's rear gunner opened fire and claimed the fighter as destroyed. All aircraft dispatched returned safe. Meanwhile at Middleton, 80 of 76's Maintenance Flight were transferred to Station HQ to form a Station Maintenance Unit.

On the 22nd, 76 sent 3 crews to Mannheim. Most crews encountered thick cloud and icing conditions and only 58 out of a total of 123 aircraft managed to reach the primary. The remainder were forced to find alternative targets. Damage to Mannheim was classed as minimal. All of Goosepool's aircraft returned safe. The ninth aircraft turned back with a faulty compass.

On the night of the 23/24th, 78 sent nine Whitleys to bomb the shipyards at Kiel. Only eight bombed as one had compass failure and had to return early. The remainder returned safely having bombed on ETA. Due to bad weather, out of the 114 aircraft detailed to take part in this raid only 69 reached the target. Kiel was attacked by 6 Manchesters, 27 Whitleys, 43 Wellingtons and 38 Hampdens, one of which, AE256 based at Swinderby, was shot down over the target area. At the time of its demise, the pilot, P/O Cooper of 50 Squadron, was trying to dive clear, having been coned by searchlights and flak.

Kiel suffered damage to the Deutsche Werke Submarine yards, the Navel base, a bakery, a dancehall and several houses. 78 continued through October with raids on Cherbourg and Dunkirk. Although they suffered no losses during their first month at Croft they knew it was just a matter of time.

76 sent 2 crews to Hamburg and 3 to Cherbourg on the 26th. The same night, 78 briefed 3 fresher crews, who also attacked Cherbourg. All returned safe. Bad weather over the next few days put paid to Ops but during the remainder of the month more of the old Mk Is were transferred to Linton's conversion unit, whilst 3 more Mk IIs were delivered, one each from Kinloss, Ternhill and Handley Page Ltd (Radlett).

Halifax MP-N L9602, flown by F/S C S O'Brien RCAF was lost on the 31st. After it took off at 19:17 for fresher operations to Dunkirk, no further signals were received from this aircraft, it simply vanished. Lost without trace, its crew are commemorated on the Runnymede Memorial.

The last entry for October 1941 goes to 78, who sent 8 fresher crews to Dunkirk. Only 4 out of the 8 aircraft dispatched were able to locate the target and drop their bombs. Of the remainder, 2 couldn't find the target, and 1 had magneto trouble and jettisoned its bombs in the sea. A fourth suffered a lack of boost from its port engine, and landed back at Croft, having circled the drome a few times to use up fuel.

November 1941

On the night of November 1st, S/L J (Jock) Mercer, 78's B Flight commander, led nine Whitleys on a raid to Kiel. The operation turned out to be somewhat of a disaster. Out of the 9 aircraft detailed for this raid, only five attacked the target, bombing on ETA. Two aircraft had experienced wireless trouble and returned to base, another was a non-starter due to mechanical problems. Out of the 134 aircraft sent that night only 70 actually made it to the target. German records show that no bombs fell on Kiel but the aircraft were heard to the east. This was just as well for the defenders as their searchlights could not penetrate the thick low cloud. S/L Mercer and his crew never came home. Mercer, in Whitley Z9152, had taken-off from Croft at 17:32. In his crew that night was Sgt R F Duggan, second pilot, F/L J R Campbell, navigator, Sgt T P Woodhouse, wireless operator and F/S V G Wright, rear gunner. Although in contact with Bircham Newton, they were last heard on W/T at 01:06 by Linton-on-Ouse. It is presumed that they met their fate somewhere in the cold North Sea. They are all commemorated on the Runnymede Memorial. A second 4 Group Whitley fell that night. Based just 20 miles away at Topcliffe, 102 Squadron lost Z6749 when it was shot down by a night fighter. P/O V M Albrecht and his crew were killed when they crashed into the sea just off the coast of Holland. Like S/L Mercer and his crew, their resting-place is unknown; they are commemorated at Runnymede.

The weather during November 1941 was atrocious, practically curtailing operations for the whole of the month. Despite the continuation of extremely bad weather Berlin was the primary on the 7th. The day dawned with a cloudless sky, however a strong gusty wind developed during the early afternoon. This may have played some part in the heavy landing of 76's Halifax MP-R L9574, which tore its tail-wheel off whilst landing after an air test. Earlier in the day the squadron increased its stock of new Mk II Halifaxes, with the arrival of MP-B V9980 from 8 MU at Little Rissington. During the day, 76 detailed 6 crews for operations to Berlin. Subsequently one was a non-starter and only five departed for the target. The weather was against Bomber Command that night and in all, 37 aircraft from various squadrons were lost. 76 were to be lucky with all five aircraft returning safely, 3 to base, one to Docking and one to South Rynham. On the other hand, 78 were to lose aircraft flown by Sgts Sargent and Bell.

Z6948 flown by Sgt Bell transmitted a task-abandoned signal at 02:25. This aircraft did not return.[55] Nor did Z9151, flown by Sgt E J Sargent. His crew baled out and became POWs. Sgt Sargent didn't have time to escape and was killed, he rests in the 1939-1945 War Cemetery in Berlin. For 78 this was the last visit from the Grim Reaper during 1941. Six Whitleys had been sent from Croft on this, the last raid on the German capital to be carried out until January 1943. A total of 244 aircraft were detailed for this major effort. This raid was ordered despite the Met man's prediction of thick cloud, hail, icing conditions and storms over the route. On seeing this forecast, 5 Group withdrew their 75 aircraft from this raid and sent them to Cologne instead. All returned safely. The remaining 169 aircraft sent to Berlin consisted of 42 Whitleys, 101 Wellingtons, 9 Halifaxes and 17 Stirlings. These aircraft were provided by Nos. 1, 3, and 4 Groups. Many areas of Berlin were damaged and various buildings hit. These included 46 houses, 2 public buildings, a factory, 2 railway installations and a gasometer. Of the 6 aircraft sent from Croft, only three bombed Berlin, without being able to observe the results. One Whitley bombed Kiel.

---

[55] Having taken off from Croft at 22.31 Sgt J W Bell and his crew were shot down by Oblt Ludwig Becker of 4./NJG1 and crashed at 06.30, 6 miles west of the Dutch town of Lemmer.

Halifax Mk 1 being fuelled prior to operations   Photo: IWM CH.6643

Over the next couple of days two more Mk Is were delivered to 76, the first being L9609, flown in from 37 MU, Burton Wood. The second was L9581, earmarked to become MP-Q. On the 9th, it was announced that Wing Commander J J Sutton, DFC and F/L G M Brisbane DFM DFC were to be posted to HQ Bomber Command. That night 76 sent 3 crews to Hamburg. Two of the aircraft, flown by P/O Hank Iveson and Sgt Morin, attacked the target at 20:17, from a height of 13,000 feet. The flashes of their exploding bombs could be seen as they hit the target but due to the intensity of the searchlight and flak barrage, along with the ground haze, the results could not be observed. However, Hamburg's Norder Elbe and docks were identified on the way home. P/O Calder was unable to reach the target and had to make do with bombing the Isle of Sylt from 17,000 feet. Again, due to low cloud and intense searchlight activity, no results of their bombing could be seen. Goosepool's weather was its usual inhospitable self. P/O Calder had to land at Catterick, whilst Leeming was the closest Iveson and Morin's crews could get to home. The following day, S/L Bouwens assumed command of 76 Squadron. He was immediately informed that he was to accompany F/L Bastin to an investiture at Buckingham Palace on the 24th, where they were both to receive the DFC.

Meanwhile, on the 15th, Middleton was to receive a most distinguished visitor in the form of the Secretary of State for Air, the Right Honourable Sir Archibald Sinclair Bart KT CMG MP. He asked for the operational pilots to sit by him at lunch. During the afternoon he went out onto the airfield where he spent a considerable amount of time sitting in a Halifax surrounded by its crew. He questioned them on various operational matters and took a great interest in their answers.

The Bats arrive

November 18th 1941 saw Goosepool welcome the arrival of a brand new unit. During the day, N0.1516 BAT Flight arrived with their Airspeed Oxfords. The BAT Flight, better known by their official title as The Beam Approach Training Flight, were responsible for the training of pilots in the art of lining the aircraft up on the correct approach path for a landing at night or during bad weather using electronic approach aids. The Lorenz system, actually developed in Germany during the 1930s, was one such system used by the RAF. The 1516 BAT Flight were to remain at Middleton until December 12th 1942 when they moved to Hampstead Heath.

Operations during the remainder of the month were to be seriously curtailed by the bad weather. Operation 'Scuttle' began on the 25th. Its objective was to attack any identifiable targets in the Emden, Hamburg, Osnabruck and Hannover area. Separate to this, a raid to Brest for four of 76's Halifaxes took place that evening. The crews that night were flown by F/L Wright and Sgts Harwood, Herbert, and Morin. The weather conditions to the target were ideal, with a clear sky, a good moon and excellent visibility. All attacked the primary from 14 -16,000 feet at around 19:00 hours, through what was described as a very effective smoke screen. Sgt Herbert's Halifax was hit in the front turret but no one was injured. Sgt Morin suffered a failure to one of his port engines but was able to reach Boscombe Down. The 3 remaining aircraft returned safely to Goosepool.

The rotten weather went on and on, cancelling Op after Op. On 28th November, a telegram was received from the Air Ministry informing 78 Squadron that Sgt Pilot A J Mott, missing since December 28/29th 1940, had arrived safely at Gibraltar. He and his crew had taken off from Dishforth on that date in Whitley P4950 for a raid on Lorient. The aircraft did not return, but word was received later that the crew (less Sgt Mott) were POWs. He was reported to have evaded capture. It had taken him 11 months to travel from France through neutral Spain and on to Gibraltar.

Mechanical problems reduced the fighting capabilities of 78 Squadron on the 30th when 9 aircraft were detailed to attack Hamburg. One aircraft was a non-starter owing to its D/F loop not being swung. A second collided with drainpipes whilst taxiing to the runway. A third returned to base when its starboard undercarriage failed to retract, its captain also reported that the starboard boost gauge was U/S. Three of 78's Whitleys joined forces with 178 aircraft of other squadrons to successfully attack the shipyards and 3 aiming points in the city. Out of the total force, 122 aircraft claimed good results due to the moonlit conditions. In this raid 22 separate fires were started including two large ones. Casualties reported included 65 dead, 176 injured and over 2,500 bombed out of their homes. On the debit side, 4 Whitleys from other squadrons, 2 Hampdens, 6 Wellingtons and 1 Halifax were lost. A further 3 Whitleys, flown by fresher crews, were dispatched from Croft that night. They joined with other squadrons to form a force of 50 aircraft to attack Emden. Two bombed successfully, and one returned with generator trouble. All of 78's Whitleys dispatched that night returned safely. One aircraft bombed a German airfield, 11 miles northwest of Bremerhaven. Another attacked in the region of the Kiel Canal, whilst a third bombed an unknown German town.

Five of 76's Halifaxes were ordered to take part in this raid, all returned safe, but due to the good old Teesside weather had to land at Linton-on-Ouse. MP-W L9604, flown by Sgt Herbert, overshot whilst landing, fortunately the crew were unhurt. Subsequently, this Halifax was written off and having been re-classified as 3161M, spent the remainder of its days firmly on the ground as an instructional airframe. This proved to be the only aircraft lost by 76 during November.

December 1941

The first two weeks in December were plagued by bad weather; it had been very windy, some days had seen gusts in excess of 30 mph. On December 7th the weather over England relented a little to allow five of 78's fresher crews to attack nursery targets at Dunkirk. Due to the moderate weather and heavy cloud cover only one aircraft bombed. The 4 remaining crews jettisoned their bombs in the sea on the way home. All returned to Croft safely. Meanwhile at Pearl Harbour, the weather was perfect, and allowed aircraft of the Japanese battle-fleet to change the course of the Second World War forever, ultimately to Britain's advantage, by bringing America into the war.

The training of fresher crews continued the following night when two crews were detailed to attack Le Havre. Again one of the aircraft dropped its bombs in the sea having failed to clearly identify the target. P/O H G Bedford and his crew, having taken-off from Croft at 16:43 in Z9129, were on their way to the target when the Gremlins struck. The Whitley had just passed Portsmouth and was over the Solent flying south at a height of 6,000 feet when the starboard engine suddenly burst into flames. The crew managed to extinguish the fire and successfully ditch off Spithead at 18:50. They were rescued by the Isle of Wight lifeboat. Sharing the dingy with P/O Bedford that night were Sgt Howell - second pilot, P/O Ponds - nav, Sgt Oliver - wireless operator, and Sgt Parks - rear gunner. They returned to Croft a few days later.

On the 15th, thirteen of 78's Whitleys were detailed for a raid on Wilhelmshaven, later this was cancelled prior to take-off. However, 3 fresher crews were briefed for this raid. One went U/S and did not take-off, the other 2 Whitleys failed to identify the target and jettisoned their bombs 'safe' in the sea. The next night, 3 fresher crews took-off to attack Dunkirk. Owing to the glare of the searchlights only one was able to bomb. The remaining two turned for home and added their bomb-loads to Davy Jones's locker, also on the 15th, 76 Squadron were to have another change of Boss, in the form of Wing Commander David Young. He was posted in from 77 squadron at Leeming. Two days later as a security precaution, the camp was sealed at 16:00 hours. This was in preparation for a daylight raid on the German Cruisers Scharnhorst and Gneisenau in Brest Harbour, that was to take place the following day.

At 09:45 the next morning, 6 of 76's Halifaxes led by W/C Young began to taxi out in preparation for take off. On his way to the active runway, F/L Calder's Halifax developed brake trouble necessitating a last minute transfer to the reserve aircraft.

Despite this technical hitch, Calder and his crew were able to become airborne within a few minutes of their scheduled take off time. Their first rendezvous was to be over Linton at 4,000 feet. Calder was able to catch up and take his correct place in 76's formation before getting there. This operation was to employ a total of 47 Bomber Command aircraft, including some from 35 Squadron, hence the rendezvous over Linton. Their contingent was commanded by Wing Commander B V Robinson, who, as you will remember, had commanded 78 Squadron when they landed at Middleton from Dishforth. Coincidentally, during the afternoon, 78 at Croft would also take off to attack Brest but in an entirely separate operation. The timings were carefully synchronised, to ensure perfect co-ordination with the protecting screen of British fighter patrols, which would join the bombers near the French coast. S/L Packe in MP-L had to leave the formation when his Halifax suffered engine trouble whilst near Lundy Island. He landed at Boscombe Down, after first jettisoning his bombs. The weather was excellent, visibility was near perfect. The target was reached without opposition, the flak only starting during the run in, which was carried out from 16,000 feet in two tight Vic formations to ensure pattern bombing. The first Vic was flown by W/C Young, F/O Iveson and Sgt Herbert, whilst the second contained S/L Packe, F/L Calder and Sgt Morin. Several sticks of bombs were seen to explode right across the docks. The Cruisers were seen to be damaged in the attack, this was confirmed later by some very good aiming point photographs. W/C Robinson's Halifax TL-A had been hit by flak over the target and badly damaged, his tail gunner F/O Rivas being injured. Robinson turned for home, but at 13:15 the bomber had to ditch whilst still about 60 miles from the English coast. The aircraft floated for about 20 minutes, enabling the crew to launch the dinghy and paddle away. During the attack, enemy fighters had been seen, but these were engaged by the British supporting fighters, allowing all of 76's aircraft to return safely. Although 4 Stirlings, 1 Halifax and 1 Manchester were lost, the attack was considered to have been very successful. This was reflected in a congratulatory message being received from the AOC and AOC-in-C Bomber Command at Middleton the next day.

Out of the 12 Whitleys detailed on the 18th for a raid on Brest, only 7 managed to attack the target. Failing to find its target, one Whitley jettisoned its bombs in the sea. Another was a non-starter due to faulty valves in one of its engines. A third had Exactor trouble and had to land at Boscombe Down. A fourth did not go, as a major inspection was not completed in time. The fifth and final lame duck was Z9308 flown by Sgt Attwell RCAF. Having just taken off at 16:07 this Whitley began to lose power on one engine. Attwell began circling the drome to allow the remainder of the aircraft to take-off. Whilst orbiting, the offending engine caught fire. Losing height all the time, Sgt Attwell, rather than compromise the operation, carried out a successful forced landing at Keanley Sides farm near Hurworth. The crew were unhurt. Whitley EY-S Z9277 took off from Croft at 15:53 en-route to Brest. Having returned to the Vale of York after completing the mission the pilot P/O Beadle called on the R/T for a bearing to steer for Croft. The radio must have been faulty as no reply was received.

76 squadron Halifaxes attack harbour installations at Brest　Photo: IWM C.4109

As they were lost there was little option but to gingerly ease down through the cloud in an attempt to check their position. At the same time as they found the cloudbase they also found the ground. They came down on a stretch of remote moorland, called Simon's Seat, high up in the Yorkshire Dales. Having slithered to a stop, the crew, who were unhurt, unstrapped the bits and walked away.

Goosepool's Station Commander G/C Trail had become ill during late 1941. Whilst recovering in Hospital his place was taken by Group Captain Bradbury, C/O of RAF Marsden Moor. On December 20th G/C Bradbury departed Middleton and returned to Marsden Moor, leaving W/C Young in temporary command of Middleton until G/C Trail's recovery was complete. S/L Bouwens said his goodbyes also, and left to take up his post at 6 Group HQ. Three days later, S/L Hillary DFM was posted to 102 Squadron, who were based at Dalton, 2 miles east of Topcliffe.

On Christmas Eve, 9 of 78's aircraft were detailed for operations but to the relief of all at Croft the order was cancelled before take-off. The operation was reinstated on Boxing Day only to be cancelled once more. Finally, on the 27th, the weather relented and again 9 aircraft were prepared for Ops. One Whitley was a non-starter due to mechanical problems whilst another returned after only one hour with W/T trouble. Three Whitleys managed to attack the primary target and one hit a built up area in the vicinity of the main target. These were the only aircraft of 78 to reach Dusseldorf. Out of the 3 remaining Whitleys, one attacked an aerodrome near Den Helder,[56] whilst a second aircraft attacked docks on the Rhine. Whitley Z9276 flown by P/O Shattock had left Croft at 17:40. Whilst flying to the west of Bridlington and only 50 miles from Croft, they experienced severe airframe icing. One of the engines overheated, probably due to ice restricting the Merlin's radiator air intake. So severe was the icing that an emergency landing had to be undertaken. Whilst trying to carry-out a forced landing in the dark, the Whitley struck high-tension wires and crashed near the village of Foxholes, 10 miles northwest of Bridlington. The aircraft burst into flames and injured 3 of its crewmembers.

And so 1941 drew to a close.

[56] About 40 miles north of Amsterdam and still in use today

CHAPTER SIX

76 and 78 Squadrons - January 1942

On January 1st 1942 Wing Commander Corbally assumed command of 78 Squadron at Croft, whilst Wing Commander Tom Sawyer was posted from Middleton to HQ 4 Group at York. The following day, ten of 78 Squadron's Whitleys were briefed for a raid on St Nazaire; five aircraft were later cancelled. Of the five aircraft that took-off, one returned to base with engine trouble, one successfully attacked the primary target but had to divert to Exeter because of bad weather. Another landed at Exeter having failed to find the target. One of the Whitleys suffered engine trouble and diverted to Pershore, Worcestershire. The fifth Whitley, Z6656, flown by Sgt Attwell and his crew, had also successfully attacked the target but crashed on Woogill Moor, whilst descending through low cloud. The crash site, 14 miles W/N/W of Ripon, North Yorkshire, is 1,500 feet above sea level. All of the crew were injured. Three nights later, eight of 78's crews were briefed for operations to Cherbourg. Only two crews successfully identified the target and attacked. The remaining six jettisoned their bombs and returned safely to land at Croft.

On the 6th, F/L Burdett arrived from 10 Squadron, based at Leeming, to become 76 Squadron's A Flight commander. The following night 3 of 76's Halifaxes carried out the squadron's first operation of 1942 when they attacked St Nazaire. All returned safely to Middleton. Out of the seven Whitleys sent by 78 to Emden on the 10th, four found the target and were able to bomb. A fifth aircraft bombed short of the target area whilst a sixth attacked flak positions on ETA. The seventh Whitley suffered Exactor trouble and rather than spend time searching for the target it also bombed flak positions. All returned safely. Emden was the target again on the 15th for 3 of 78's fresher crews. One did not take off due to a problem with a faulty tail trimmer. The second Whitley had an engine overheat and returned early, having jettisoned its bombs in the sea. The remaining aircraft was able to bomb the target, all three returned safe.

During the day, one of 76's Halifaxes crashed on the airfield after a training flight. At about 16:00 hours, Sgt Stark and his crew in MP-C L9578 were returning from a training flight. The wind during the day had been light, slightly backing, but during the afternoon it had increased significantly. As the Halifax touched down in a crosswind at Middleton, it veered to the left. Stark fought vainly to keep the Halifax under control but the strain on the undercarriage was too much and it collapsed. The aircraft slithered off the runway in a cloud of dust and flying grass, coming to a halt in the middle of the airfield. Fortunately there were no injuries to the crew but the Halifax was written off. The next day there was further bad news for 76, as Sgt Anderson's crew, who were also on a training flight, crashed in MP-J L9611. They were taking off from Middleton at 11:00 hours when the Halifax lost height and crashed. Meanwhile on the same morning another of 76's Halifaxes, L9379, crashed whilst landing at Dishforth. Both crews escaped without injury.

With still no operations for 76 during the month, they were heartened on the 25th by the arrival of three new Halifaxes. Two had been delivered from 35 Squadron at Linton-on-Ouse (R9364 and R9386), the third, R9420, was flown in by a female ATA pilot who had collected the bomber from the Handley Page factory at Radlett, 3 miles N/E of Watford. The squadron was continuing with its build up and many air-tests and training flights were carried out. On January 26th, so bad was the weather that all available airfield personnel were employed in snow clearance. The 27th saw five of 76 Squadron's operational crews proceeding, between persistent snow showers, to an advanced base at Lossiemouth, Scotland. On arrival they were informed that they were to wait there for further orders. They had been accompanied by a party of ground personnel who were flown up in a separate aircraft.

At Croft conditions allowed 78 to carry out an eight aircraft operation to Rotterdam two days later. Having taken-off at 17:20, contact was lost with Whitley Z9305 flown by Sgt Williams. Later a message was received at Middleton that it had been shot down by the Royal Navy.

It later transpired that the Whitley had been hit by anti aircraft fire from Royal Navy trawlers off the Essex Coast. The aircraft crashed into the sea at 19:05 near to the Cork lightship, off Harwich, killing all on board. Only two bodies were recovered from the water but the remains of F/S D R Campbell RCAF were committed back to the sea. He and the remainder of the crew are commemorated on the Runnymede Memorial.

By the morning of the 29th, snow clearance had become a daily necessity. Fortunately, as the day progressed a thaw began, and the snow turned to sleet and then rain. By the next day the conditions at Middleton had improved enough to allow some air-tests to take place. It also allowed a visit by Air Commodore HRH the Duke of Kent, who visited Middleton during the morning. He was escorted by G/C Trail, who by now had recovered from his illness. His Highness visited 76 Squadron and talked to the aircrews, he then had lunch in the Officers Mess before leaving for Croft. On his arrival at Croft, the Duke of Kent was welcomed by the Station Commander, W/C Corbally, who escorted him on his tour of the airfield. The visit included a talk with some of 78's aircrews. Prior to leaving the camp at 17:30, tea was taken by His Royal Highness in the Officers Mess.

During the same day, five of 76's Halifaxes took off from Lossiemouth to carry out a raid on the battle cruiser Tirpitz, which was holed up in a fjord near Trondjheim, Norway. Aircraft flown by W/C Young, S/L Burdett and F/L Iveson did not attack the Tirpitz owing to 10/10ths cloud cover. They returned to Lossiemouth, jettisoning their bombs in the sea on the way home. Sgt Herbert in MP-V had better luck. Although he and his crew had the same problem with 10/10ths-cloud cover over the target, they were able to bomb from a height of 8,000 feet. Although the Tirpitz was not clearly observed, a barrage of light flak indicated the position of the cruiser. Sgt Street in the rear turret was able to observe that their bombs burst between the ship and the shore. Four out of the five Halifaxes returned safely to Lossiemouth. The crew of MP-Q, flown by Sgt J W Harwood, was not quite so fortunate. Having found the target totally covered by cloud, it was realised that pinpointing the Tirpitz was impossible. No attack was carried out and Harwood turned for home. During the flight back to Lossiemouth they suffered icing and radio problems for most of the trip. A build up of ice on the engine air intakes caused the failure of the port inner. Despite jettisoning the bombs, the Halifax failed to maintain height. The crew could see Aberdeen only three miles away when the aircraft crashed into the sea. Two of the crew were slightly injured when the aircraft hit the water. Eventually, they were all rescued by the Aberdeen lifeboat. The last day of January 1942 saw most of the airfield's personnel employed in their favourite pastime - snow clearing. For 76 Squadron the build up went on. The end of January showed 76's squadron strength as; 37 Officers, 147 NCO aircrew, 35 NCOs, 538 Corporals and Airmen.

Halifax bomb load. The special bomb containers (SBCs) on the second trolley back contain large numbers of small incendiary bombs
Photo: IWM CH.6594

76 & 78 - February 1942

The first of February dawned overcast; the cloud base fell from 3,000 feet to 1,000 feet by mid morning. The fog cleared slowly, but visibility remained poor with a slight snowfall continuing throughout the day. The 1,000-foot cloudbase persisted until the 5th, accompanied by varying amounts of fog, rain and snow. On the 6th, despite only a slight improvement in the weather, two of the Tirpitz raiders returned from Lossiemouth, along with some of the groundcrew. Still poor weather persisted, covering Goosepool with frozen drizzle and poor visibility. The bad weather continued until the morning of February 11th. Two new Halifaxes were delivered to 76 during the afternoon, one from Preston and the other from Radlett.

That night, 78 attacked Le Havre. Of the four aircraft detailed for this attack only three were able to successfully bomb the target. The fourth Whitley had port and starboard Exactor trouble and had to divert to Boscombe Down, having jettisoned its bombs in the sea. Over at Middleton, 76 attacked Mannheim, all six aircraft dispatched returned safely. Two nights later, three of 78's fresher crews set off to give Le Havre a second helping, but due to heavy cloud cover had to jettison their bombs in the sea. All returned safely. That night 76 sent four Halifaxes to Cologne, all returned safely.

On the 14th, six of 76's crews were sent by truck to Darlington Railway Station. Four of them were off to the factory at Radlett to collect new Halifaxes for the squadron. The other two crews were similarly tasked, but they were headed for the English Electric aircraft factory at Worton near Blackpool. That night seven of 78's aircraft were dispatched from Croft to attack Mannheim. No sooner were they airborne when two of them returned with engine trouble. Of the remaining Whitleys, four were able to bomb the primary. Minus its W/T, the last aircraft, Z9320 flown by Sgt Stevens, had to carry out its attack by bombing through cloud on ETA. During the return journey it was suspected that the compass was U/S. Short of fuel after eight and a half-hours in the air, the Whitley had to be ditched, 20 miles off Bournemouth. The crew, who were suffering from shock and abrasions, were rescued by an Air Sea Rescue launch and taken to Portsmouth's Haslar Hospital for treatment. Thus ended 78's last operation during February. Next day 76 celebrated the opening of its brand new Operations Room, Pilot Officer Cole being in charge. On the 18th, two more crews were despatched by rail to Radlett to collect more new Halifaxes. During the afternoon the Teesside smoke haze developed and that night's operations were cancelled.

Three nights later, Lista aerodrome on the south West coast of Norway was the target for three of 76's Halifaxes. Led by S/L Burdett they took off at 04:11 during a very heavy fall of snow. Total cloud cover persisted until the aircraft were about 6-10 miles off the Norwegian Coast. After that, the visibility was quite clear, through large gaps in the cloud. The target, which was 330 miles E/N/E of Aberdeen, was attacked at 06:53 from 11,000 feet in good daylight. The bomb bursts from S/L Burdett's Halifax were seen to explode across one of the runways. Sgt Lambert had dropped his bombs five minutes earlier from 3,000 feet. During the run up, two unidentified aircraft were spotted directly ahead. Fearing fighters, Lambert's crew were somewhat distracted. Unsurprisingly they were unable to report where their bombs burst.

As Lambeth and his crew flew over the enemy airfield, the front and rear gunners opened fire on anything they could see. Owing to a late take-off and insufficient boost from the engines, P/O Michael Renaut could not make up for lost time. As he was unable to reach the target before daylight, he elected to turn back from position 57° 02 North - 03° 45 East (216 miles east of Aberdeen) as instructed during briefing. His bombs were jettisoned safe into the sea. There should have been five aircraft taking part in this raid, but due to crewing shortages only three took-off.

On the 22nd Air Marshal Sir Arthur Harris took over as Commander-in-Chief (C-in-C) of Bomber Command, a position he would hold until the end of the war. He replaced Sir Richard Pierse who had been posted to a new command on January the 8th. The position of Bomber Commands C-in-C was temporarily filled by Air Vice Marshal J E A Baldwin who became acting AOC-in-C until Harris arrived.

During the afternoon of the 24th, three brand new Halifaxes from Radlett, R9447, R9482 and R9484 flew in to Goosepool. They were flown in by the 76 squadron crews despatched by rail 10 days earlier. Two days later four more arrived. The first to arrive were W1035 and W1036, both from English Electric at Worton. Next to arrive during mid afternoon was R9485, flown in from Radlett. The final new Halifax to land that day was W1018 from 12 MU. Still the weather was diabolical; during the night of the 27th, after several sleet and snow showers, the temperature fell to ten degrees of frost by dawn. 76's strength by the end of February 1942 was 36 Officers, 142 NCO aircrew, 36 NCOs, 559 Corporals and airmen, a total strength of 773.

March 1942 for 76 and 78

Operations started for 76 on the night of March 3rd when three crews attacked the Renault works in Paris. All aircraft returned safely. During the 5th it snowed all day, there was over 2 inches of snow by midnight and the temperature fell to 6 inches of frost. By the 7th, the same 2 inches of snow persisted. Next day one of 76's Halifaxes along with three crews was despatched to Waterbeach to collect two squadron aircraft, which landed there from a previous raid. These aircraft, along with the ferry aircraft tasked to take the crews down to Waterbeach, returned during the afternoon. During the day fighter affiliation exercises were carried out with Hurricanes from Catterick. At the same time, three of 76's Halifaxes were flown over to Croft. By now 78's conversion onto the Halifax was well under way, the squadron's Conversion Flight was hard at it and the days of their Whitleys were numbered. The following morning saw more fighter affiliation exercises and three crews undertaking Lorenz beam approach practice. During the day a further three Halifaxes were ferried over to 78 squadron at Croft. During the evening of the 10th, a night flying program was organised; this was cancelled due to a sudden closing in of the weather. A thick industrial haze came in on the sea breeze reducing the visibility to below fog level. Meanwhile over at Croft, due to the fickleness of the Teesside weather, 78 were still able to fly. They carried out their first operation of the month when four fresher crews were briefed for a raid on Boulogne.

On the 11th an air firing exercise was organised for one of 76's Halifax crews. When they got to the rendezvous point over Driffield aerodrome the drogue towing aircraft had failed to turn up. The crew of the Halifax made the most of a bad job and fired their rounds into the sea in Filey Bay.

Back at Middleton the planned fighter affiliation exercise failed miserably, as no fighters from Catterick were available. On the night of the 13th, 78 sent another four fresher crews to nursery targets at Boulogne. Whilst in the target area at 11,000 feet one of the Whitleys flown by Sgt Dennis experienced heavy flak. The pilot put the aircraft into a steep dive only pulling out at about 2,000 feet. The rear gunner Sgt Copeland had been busy on the way down; coolly he fired at, and extinguished, four searchlights that had coned the bomber. Sgt Wilson and his crew in Z6817 did not attack the target but managed to drop their nickels at Ardres, about 10 km inland of Calais.

The oil temperature gauge on the port engine began to read low, and as a precaution Wilson elected to divert to Donna Nook. On landing, the Whitley overran the runway and ran into a hedge, fortunately without injury to the crew. One of the Whitleys taking part was Z9214, flown by Pilot Officer Hockaday. This aircraft took off from Croft at 18:08 after which nothing further was heard. Hockaday and his crew were lost without trace; they are all commemorated on the Runnymede Memorial.

Taking off one minute after Hockaday was P/O Ferris and his crew. They arrived back at base at 00:04, Ferris made five attempts to land and on the fifth the Whitley overshot, stalled and crashed. P/O Ferris, Sgt Bell and Sgt Gander were found dead in the wreckage, The wireless operator Sgt Davies died later in Darlington's Memorial Hospital, the rear gunner Sgt Hentall was badly injured and was also taken to the Memorial. This was the last Whitley operation for 78 Squadron, and their last Whitley crews to be lost. Two days later, on the 16th of March, 78 discontinued operations on the Whitley, in preparation to completing their conversion onto the Halifax. For the remainder of March and most of April the squadron would remain non-operational.

For 76 flying practice continued throughout the month of March, with fighter affiliation, gunnery practice, air-tests, night flying, cross country navigation exercises and bombing practice taking up most of their time.

The Tirpitz in her berth at Faettenfjord near Trondheim   Photo: IWM C.4126.A

85

The Tirpitz

During the afternoon of March 25th, all 76 Squadron personnel were ordered to assemble in No.1 hangar. W/C Young addressed the parade and announced that a number of ground personnel would be proceeding to an advanced base, from where the aircrew would take off for an operation. He stressed to the gathering the need for utter secrecy. Only the senior officers were privy to the location of the advanced base and ultimate target. On the 27th, twelve crews were briefed for a 14:00 take-off for the advanced base. The advanced base turned out to be RAF Tain in Scotland, 25 miles north of Inverness. The weather that day was partly cloudy but with very good visibility, which became more moderate as the day progressed. By early afternoon the wind had increased to about 10 mph. The aircraft took-off between 14:00 and 14:40 in two flights of six, flying in close formation. The first flight landed at Tain between 16:22 and 16:33, the second between 16:52 and 17:18. At Tain, no flying was ordered for the next day as the aircraft were prepared for an operation.

On the 29th, operations were ordered but due to the weather they were later cancelled. During the morning the crews were addressed by the AOC. The following day 12 crews were briefed for a raid on the Battleship Tirpitz, which was residing in Aas Fjord, Norway. They were given secondary targets of the Admiral Scheer or Prinz Eugen, which were skulking in Lo Fjord. Originally it was anticipated that ten of 76's Halifaxes would take part, but later permission was given to fly the two reserve aircraft.

Details of the crews and timings are as follows:

W/C Young DFC.
Up at 8:07 - down at 02:40. MP-R R9447.
P/O Moorhouse.
P/O Miller.
Sgt Brooks.
Sgt O'Reilly.
Sgt Spriggs.
Sgt Greenwood.

Sgt Lloyd-Jones.
Up at 18:08 - Down at 02:52. MP-M (Unknown).
P/O Culmsee.
P/O Fairclough.
F/S Hawksworth.
Sgt Hothersall.
Sgt Wheeldon.
Sgt Moule.

F/L Warner.
Up at 18:13 - Down at 02:58. MP-X R9487.
Sgt Bassom.
F/O Collins.
F/S Gook.
Sgt Herbert.
Sgt Waddington.
Sgt Greenway.

Sgt Harwood.
Up at - 18:16 - Down at 01:45. MP-S R9454.
Sgt Wood.
F/S Scott.
F/S Roche.
Sgt Potus.
Sgt Petch.
Sgt Glover.

F/S Clack.
Up at 18:16 - Down at 02:44. MP-P R9485.
P/O Anderson.
F/S Thompson.
Sgt Williams.
Sgt Oram.
Sgt Lawes.
Sgt Payne.

F/L Iveson.
Up at 18:19 - Down at 02:15. MP-A R9457.
Sgt Willmott.
Sgt Lloyd.
F/S Craine.
Sgt Elliot.
Sgt Morrell.
Sgt Holmes.

P/O Renaut.
Up at 18:22 - Down at 02:22. MP-L R9452.
Sgt Kitchin.
P/O Collins.
Sgt Hall.
Sgt Webb.
Sgt Ellis.
F/L Croft.

F/S Lambeth.
Up at 18:23 - Down at 02:35. MP-G R9484.
Sgt Gathercole.
P/O Connoly.
Sgt Swain.
Sgt Gowers.
Sgt George.
Sgt Reynolds.

Sgt Borsberry.
Up at 18:26 - Down at 02:23. MP-F R9456.
P/O Norfolk.
F/L Newsham.
F/S Pearce.
Sgt Smith.
Sgt Van Schaick.
Sgt Hoskins.

F/S Anderson.
 Up at 18:28 - Down at 02:26. MP-C R9455.
Sgt Aston.
Sgt Ilian.
Sgt Heaton.
Sgt Redding.
Sgt La Franchise.
Sgt Southward.

F/S Hobbs.

S/L Burdett.

Up at 18:30 - Down at 02:30. MP-D R9482.

Up at 18:32 - Missing   MP-K R9453.

Sgt Butler.

P/O Bowsher. RCAF

F/S Roony.

F/S Cadger. RCAF

Sgt Charlsworth.

F/S Fletcher. RCAF

Sgt Roberts.

Sgt Davis.

Sgt Jones.

Sgt Martin.

Sgt Davison.

Sgt Hanson. RAAF

Due to the poor weather conditions and the risk of being detected by enemy radar, or RDF as it was called then, the crews were ordered to fly at a height not greater than 1,000 feet. Once at a certain position near the Norwegian coast they were to climb to their attack height of 6,000 feet. The weather below the 2,000-foot cloud base was good, and assisted the navigators to check the Met winds, given to them earlier. This was done by making a landfall near Wick aerodrome and Sumburgh Head on the Shetland Isles. This proved to be a good idea, and allowed the navigators to ensure that all aircraft reached the Norwegian coast successfully. To assist any returning aircraft that might be low on fuel, four Royal Navy destroyers were on station, 25, 50, 75 and 100 miles from Tain.

On reaching the Norwegian coast, the crews found the visibility to be very good and map reading was very easy. This was partly due to the fact that at this latitude it never really gets very dark. Unfortunately, by the time they reached Trondjheim Fjord, 10/10ths fog was encountered, making identification of the target impossible. All captains remained over the target area for as long as their fuel supplies would allow, in the hopes that a break in the weather would eventually occur. Young, Warner, Hobbs, Anderson, Renaut and Clack jettisoned their bombs as ordered in Aas Fjord from 5,000 feet. Apart from 76's twelve Halifaxes, a further 22 aircraft belonging to other 4 Group squadrons were also there to attack the Tirpitz. 35 Squadron based at Linton-on-Ouse had used Kinloss as their advanced base, whilst Leeming's 10 Squadron had taken off from Lossiemouth.

Iveson, Borsberry, Lambeth, Lloyd-Jones and Harwood bombed searchlights and flak concentrations. Due to sea fog, damage could not be assessed, although the bomb bursts could be seen through the haze. This had the desired effect and the defences ceased to operate. Of the twelve 76 Squadron Halifaxes operating that night, 9 returned safely to Tain.

Renaut and his crew had to divert to Lossiemouth, where they landed with their fuel gauges reading zero. F/L Iveson, also low on fuel, landed at Wick, having suffered heavy airframe icing. Later, when the aircraft was checked by the groundcrew, they discovered that there was only 18 gallons of fuel remaining in the tanks of his aircraft. Even at the most economical settings of 2,000 rpm @ minus 4 inches of boost, in a Halifax one could at best expect a fuel burn of approximately 124 gallons per hour. Eighteen gallons of fuel would have represented a maximum of eight minutes flying time before the engines would have stopped. At a cruising speed of 150 mph this would have taken them only 20 miles further.

Lost somewhere over the North Sea, the wireless operator of S/L Burdett's Halifax, MP-K, asked for, and was given, a radio fix at 23:52. Later, at 02:10, 14 Group reported that this aircraft had passed over Sumburgh on a heading of 170°. Later it was believed that Burdett and his crew had forced-landed in the sea, about 18 miles to the south of Sumburgh. Despite an immediate search of the area by nearly twenty aircraft and two destroyers, nothing was found. Squadron Leader Burdett's body was later recovered from the sea. The remainder of the crew were never found, and are commemorated on the Runnymede Memorial.

Losses for 35 Squadron were 3 Halifaxes, whilst Leeming's 10 Squadron lost 2. There were no survivors from any of these seven man crews. Including S/L Burdett and his crew, the operation cost the lives of 42 airmen. Of those who perished, only 14 bodies were ever accounted for, the remainder are commemorated on the Runnymede Memorial.

76 and 78 - April 1942

At Tain, for the next few days the weather would have the last word. From the 1st to the 3rd, operations were ordered, only to be cancelled each day due to adverse weather. On the 4th, Ops were again ordered. At 09:50 a cancellation order was received, along with instructions to return to base. The next afternoon, 11 aircraft took-off for the return trip to Goosepool. Sgt Harwood in S turned back to Tain with engine trouble. A further 8 Halifaxes also returned to Tain due to bad weather conditions. Whilst trying to land in a strong crosswind, F/S Anderson in MP-C swung off the runway and damaged the Halifax's undercarriage. Only 2 aircraft, MP-G and MP-Q made it back to Middleton that day. A further seven[57] arrived there the next afternoon, having left MP-S and D at Tain for repairs. The 7th saw the return by train of forty-seven groundcrew and one officer. A further twenty-four groundcrew, this time with three officers, returned the following day by train with the aircraft equipment.

During the absence of what amounted to the bulk of the squadron, things at Middleton had been quiet operationally. An opportunity to continue training had been seized and many cross-country training flights had been carried out. On the 4th of April, P/O Kofoed ferried MP-D W1016 to Handley Page Ltd at Warton. This was to allow adjustments to be made. The crew returned to Middleton by train. The next Op for 76 was on the 8th, when eight aircraft were detailed for a trip to Hamburg. By take-off time, only the aircraft of Renaut, Lloyd-Jones, Harwood, Lambeth, Hobbs and Anderson actually took part in the raid. For most of 76's crews, the load was two four thousand pound Cookies.

Carrying these bombs, the shape of overgrown dustbins, required the bomb bay doors to be left ajar. This was made possible by the use of the selective closing cock. This was fitted in the hydraulic pipeline of the fuselage bomb-door

[57] A, C, D, F, L, P and R

jacks. Operated by the engineer, it was located aft of the pilot's bulkhead. This cock was closed when bombs with a larger diameter than the bomb bay were carried, necessitating the aircraft to be flown with the doors partially open. The principle was simple. The doors were partially closed to the required position by the bomb door hydraulic hand-pump, after which the selective closing cock was closed. This procedure was carried out before the engines were started and subsequent hydraulic pressure was built up.

The crews had a fairly easy trip past the Dutch coast. At their height of 16,000 feet, the night was clear and starry. Hamburg and its intense flak and searchlight barrage could not be seen due to 10/10ths cloud cover. The crews bombed on ETA. The flak was intensive and accounted for the fact that no enemy night fighters were seen. Renaut's aircraft suffered flak damage to its port wing and fuselage. Fortunately nothing vital was hit and they were able to turn for home. Despite severe icing and electrical storms all squadron aircraft returned safely.

The next day Renaut was summoned to the office of Tommy Trail the Station Commander. He was introduced to Air Commodore Hoskins, who was blind. An expert on bomb design, Hoskins had been blinded in London earlier in the war, whilst watching an air raid. Hoskins was involved with the prototype 'Two by Four', a new 8,000-lb bomb that was now ready for a test drop. Renaut felt a job coming on, and sure enough he was right. When asked if he would like to carry out the first test dropping, he said he would.

Renaut was briefed by Hoskins as to what was required. He was to take part in a squadron raid the following night (the 10th) to Essen, where he would drop the bomb, but only if the results could be observed. If cloud cover over Essen prevented this, he was to take it to Duisburg instead. So big was the new bomb that the Halifax had to be flown with the bomb doors fully open. Later, they attended the usual briefing with the other four crews, who would be carrying a normal bomb load. Three fresher crews were to be sent to bomb Le Havre and five other operational crews were briefed for Ops

View of interior of Halifax looking aft. On the right can be seen the ammo tracks leading from the centre section back to the rear turret. Also note the Elsan toilet in the foreground   Photo: IWM CH.6640

to Essen. Renaut told later that he had been doubtful about the extra weight and drag. The aircraft required full boost to get off, normal take-off boost proving to be inadequate. The aircraft was barely able to become airborne and required 2,000 yards of Middleton's main runway.

The book stated that one was only allowed a maximum of five minutes at full revs and boost, and as soon as they had struggled to 1,000 feet, Renaut quickly brought the throttles back through the gate to cancel max boost. Immediately the Halifax began to lose height. He had no choice but to re-apply max boost, and he was unable to cancel it until one hour later, when they reached 8,000 feet. The Halifax refused to climb higher. The engines were being thrashed, and the crew were expecting them to seize at any moment. Still at 8,000 feet, they crossed the Dutch coast. By now they had used so much fuel that the aircraft was becoming lighter. Slowly she began to gain height. By the time they approached Essen they had somehow managed to coax her up to 15,000 feet. Now it was the turn of the searchlights and flak to add to the crew's problems. Due to only 5/10ths-cloud cover, Collins the navigator could see the target quite clearly, and so the bomb run was instigated. Renaut had to fly on instruments as they were suddenly coned by a huge number of searchlights.

The flak was intense. After what seamed an eternity, Collins in the nose called 'Bombs gone' and the Halifax reared up like a homesick angel. Collins watched the huge bomb go down by the light of the searchlights. When it exploded there was a tremendous orange flame in the middle of the town. There was little time to hang around as the flak and searchlights suddenly became even worse. There were now about forty searchlights, and it seemed that everyone was firing at them. Inevitably they took some hits, and the port inner burst into flames. The engineer operated the fire extinguisher and as the propeller was feathered the flames abated. The mid-upper gunner, Sgt Webb, had been hit. He had a large lump of shrapnel in his thigh. The wireless operator tried to get him out of his turret, but the internal lights had been put out of action, and in the dark the situation was that much more difficult. Collins was sent back to assist, and eventually, by torchlight, they both managed to get Webb out of his turret. The gunner was in agony and the wireless operator injected the Morphia into his own thumb by mistake. His fingers had become numb after he had removed his fleece-lined gauntlets. Eventually they managed, and were able to apply a tourniquet to the gunner's thigh. He never lost consciousness despite bleeding profusely. The wireless operator transmitted a radio message to RAF Docking, Norfolk, asking for an ambulance to be standing by. Collins provided a course to steer to the Norfolk Coast whilst they reduced height rapidly. On three engines, and with their mouths dry from sheer terror, they dodged and weaved their way through the enemy defences over Holland. Eventually they reached Docking where they were met at the end of the runway by an ambulance. While a new engine was fitted to MP-A, the crew went over to Newmarket to see the gunner who was in hospital. The surgeons had removed a four-inch piece of jagged shrapnel from his leg. While they operated, they also removed from the wound a half crown and two pennies that had been in his pocket. Sgt Webb was to make a good recovery, and was able to leave hospital, just in time to join another crew and be killed a few months later.

When they flew back to Middleton the next day, they were saddened to hear that one of the squadron aircraft sent with them to Essen had failed to return. Having taken-off at 21:02, nothing further was heard from F/S Lambeth and his crew. It later transpired that they were all killed when their Halifax crashed at Oer-Erkenschwick, 16 miles N/E of Essen. They all rest in the Reichswald Forest War Cemetery. When Renaut and his crew checked their aircraft later in daylight, it was discovered that they had collected 79 holes during their visit to Essen, including one just above the elevator control cable. They had been extremely lucky to get back, especially when the groundcrew told them that the three remaining engines had to be replaced as they were almost seized. Renaut had a de-briefing with Tommy Trail, who spent much time asking questions about the raid and the bomb. They asked him if he would do it all again that night. Michael told them that he would, but pointed out the problems they had experienced with the engines and what they had been through. Michael and his crew were not required for Ops that night and slept well in their beds.

About this time Renaut had a difference of opinion with W/C Young over the handling qualities of MP-L, which was the Halifax he normally flew. Unlike any others that Michael had flown, it had a tendency to swing to port on take off. He was sure that it was not he who was at fault but the aircraft. Michael had already suffered one narrow escape, despite judicious use of engines and brakes, whilst trying to take off with two 4,000-lb cookies on board. Young was adamant that it was the pilot and not the aircraft that was at fault.

On the night of April 12/13th, Renaut had the night off, and MP-L was being used by F/S Hobbs RCAF and crew. They were to be part of a six aircraft raid on Essen. Michael had warned Hobbs what to expect, and rather than go to bed he decided that he would go out onto the airfield around 21:30 to see the aircraft off. Standing at the take off point of the runway, Renaut watched the departure of the laden Halifaxes. Eventually, along came MP-L, which, having received a green, began to move off down the runway at 21:59. As it went, it was accompanied by the hiss of air as Hobbs used the brakes in an attempt to keep the aircraft straight. Twice the Halifax veered to the left onto the grass and back onto the runway. Hobbs was in trouble, and when he reached the far end of the runway there was an awful bang as the aircraft hauled itself into the air. The engines were making strange banging noises whilst emitting huge showers of sparks. Michael grabbed a car and quickly drove at top speed to the end of the runway. There he found that the Halifax had struck a 10-foot tall dispersal platform used by groundcrew when working on aircraft engines. It also had shattered a groundcrew hut and a shed with its undercarriage, parts of which were found by a hedge at the airfield boundary.

By torchlight, Michael and some of the groundcrew followed the path taken by the Halifax as it crossed a ploughed field. They found most of the propeller tips, each about 8 inches long. They also found undercarriage doors, along with various small bits of aeroplane. Meanwhile, the aircraft was circling low over Middleton. Renaut drove back to the control tower to hear the R/T conversation between flying control and the Halifax. The aircraft was suffering from severe vibration, due to the now unbalanced propeller blades. Hobbs reported that he was having great difficulty in gaining height with his full bomb load. Young had arrived in the tower and instructed Hobbs to jettison his bombs in the sea off Bridlington and return inland using up as much fuel as he could.

He was then to fly back out to the coast, point the Halifax in an easterly direction, and having engaged the autopilot, he and his crew were to jump out. Hobbs complied with his instructions and all the crew parachuted to safety, although the second pilot, Sgt Butler, was reported as being injured. At 00:30 the Halifax, now without crew, and with a mind of its own, crashed not in the sea, but at Hunmanby, 2 miles S/S/W of Filey, Yorkshire.

The second Halifax, MP-X R9487, flown by Sgt K F Lloyd-Jones, took off one minute later. This aircraft was hit by flak at 16,000 feet and crashed at Buer, 9 miles north of Essen. The navigator, P/O R Fairclough, baled out and became a POW. The remainder of the 7-man crew including Keith Loyd-Jones were killed. At first, the crew were buried at Gelsenkirchen. After the war they were exhumed and are now resting in the Reichswald Forest War cemetery.

On the 21st, three officers from Middleton arrived at Tain by road. The next day saw the arrival of two more, along with 85 other groundcrew ranks that had proceeded by rail from Middleton to await the arrival of the air party. Between 12:32 and 13:14 on the 23rd twelve Halifaxes from 76 Squadron arrived at Tain from Middleton. In addition to the crews were four officers and 22 other ranks that were carried as passengers. At 10:00 on the following day, a serviceability signal was passed to Group over Tain's teleprinter, to the effect that 12 aircraft and crews were available for operations. Two hours later 76 was informed that there would be no operations that night. The AOC arrived by air from Lossiemouth during the afternoon to give the crews a pep talk. When he had finished, W/C Young flew him back to Lossi. A Whitley belonging to 78 Squadron arrived at Tain on the 25th, carrying necessary spares.

On the morning of the 27th, eleven crews were briefed for a second raid on the Tirpitz. Briefing took place at 16:00, with 11 Halifaxes of 76 taking off between 20:15 and 21: 01. After two hours, Young in MP-Y had to turn back, as his starboard inner went U/S and he found it impossible to retain height with the engine feathered. He jettisoned his bombs in the sea and returned to Tain. The remaining 10 aircraft carried on to the target where the Viz was extremely good. The crews found it possible to map read right up to the target area. Unfortunately the Germans had covered the target area with smoke, which obscured the Tirpitz. The crews of Iveson's, Kofoed's, Anderson's and Warner's aircraft reported that they had definitely seen the Tirpitz as they released their bombs. Three of them also stated that their bursts were observed landing very close to the ship. Other crews saw Renaut's bombs as they burst between the Tirpitz and the shore. F/S Kenny Clack in MP-Q arrived too late to attack the Tirpitz, but bombed the estimated position of the secondary targets, the Admiral Scheer and Prinz Eugen, in Lo Fjord. This aircraft was hit by flak and lost its port inner engine and some of its hydraulics. Having jettisoned four of its 250-lb general-purpose bombs at 01:10 in the Trondjheim area, Kenny turned for home. An SOS was sent out by this aircraft at 02:35, but was later cancelled. All crews returned to Tain and landed safely. The crews reported that due to the northerly latitude, the outward trip was carried out in daylight and the target area was lit by twilight. All the aircraft carried one 4,000-lb Cookie, just as they did in the previous Tirpitz raid.

Back at Middleton, in their absence, two 76 fresher crews were briefed to attack nursery targets at Dunkirk. One of them was captained by Sgt West, who, you will remember, had flown as second dickie with Michael Renaut on the disastrous 8,000-pounder raid to Essen. They returned safely, having bombed the target. The second Halifax was flown by Sgt P C Morris in MP-T W1017, which was engaged by heavy flak over the target area. Whilst taking evasive action, Morris lost control and crashed, possibly due to rudder lockover. Three of the crew managed to bale out and became POWs. Sgt Morris, Sgt G A Simpson, P/O J Potts and F/S G Sanderson were killed. They are buried in Dunkirk town cemetery.

The following day was the 28th, when a further nine crews were briefed for Ops against the Tirpitz. Conditions were similar to the previous days. Again they were easily able to map read to the target, but smoke was again in evidence over the target area, and only three crews reported that they definitely saw the Tirpitz. F/L Warner's crew stated on arrival back at Tain that their Cookie might not have exploded. On their return in MP-R, Young's crew reported that they had attacked from a height of 6,700 feet but were not certain that they had bombed the primary. The navigator believed that their Cookie was dropped by error in Stranden fjord, as the visibility on the ground at the time was obscured by smoke. During their time over the target area, the rear gunner F/L Croft saw an enemy fighter and reported it on the intercom. Young took evasive action and it was successfully avoided. All of 76's aircraft returned safely to Tain.

Also taking part in this raid were the lads from 35 Squadron at Linton-on-Ouse. Their involvement in the raid was marred by the loss of two of their Halifaxes. Having taken off from their advance base at Kinloss, F/L D Petley and his crew were hit by flak at 4,000 feet whilst flying near the target. Their aircraft, TL-P W7656, which was set on fire, crashed at high speed in a fjord near to the target. The nose of the Halifax broke off on impact and sank immediately, taking two members of the crew, Sgt A B Columbine and Sgt A W Evans RNZAF, with it. Their bodies were never recovered, both are commemorated on the Runnymede Memorial. The remainder of the crew survived and became POWs.

The second aircraft, flown by P/O J R Roe RCAF, had taken off from Kinloss two minutes earlier than F/L Petley. One side of the fjord rose to a height of 400 feet above the water, on the other side it towered up to 1,000 feet. Johnny Roe flew his Halifax, TL-G W1053, down the fjord at only 150 feet. Reg Williams the navigator shouted, 'She's swung at 90 degrees across the fjord.' Johnny shouted 'Ok, we'll go round again.' Hardly had the words left his lips when he spoke again, adding, 'We're on fire.' The Halifax had been hit on the wing by flak. Bill Parr RCAF in the rear turret shouted, 'Make for Sweden, its only 40 miles.' If Johnny Roe had an answer he didn't voice it, he simply flew on, aiming for a small exit point at the end of the valley, which they just managed to scrape over. The aircraft was well and truly on fire, Sweden might as well have been 400 miles away, there was no possible chance of reaching it. Roe saw a flat snow covered area some 5 miles further on, and decided that, if they could reach it, he would put the blazing Halifax down on it. Although impossible to ascertain from the air, it was in fact a frozen lake. At 00:30 hours, the Halifax touched down and skated along on the ice, which offered little retardation to the bomber's speed. The Halifax ran out of lake and overshot into a small wood where it came to a sudden halt. Sgt Rusty Russell, the second wireless operator in the mid-upper position, was killed in the crash when his turret was crushed. John Morrison, the first wireless operator, awoke after a few moments to find blood on his face from a deep wound. (John, whose wife lived on the corner of Bates Avenue in Darlington, had only recently been posted to 35 after spending the previous few months with 76 at Goosepool). He was joined by Reg Williams, the navigator. Both tried to make it to the rest position but elected to escape from the burning aircraft by way of the top escape hatch. Flames were leaping high into the air.

Williams left the hatch first, but as he did so a flashover engulfed him, and although he still had his helmet on, he received burns to his hands and face. John left the hatch second and had more luck, and missed the flames. They both managed to reach a safe distance, from where they looked back at the blazing Halifax. Flames were shooting about 100 feet into the air. The sound of exploding ammo from the turrets encouraged the two airmen to keep their heads down. As they looked on, a figure appeared at the front of the plane. This was the engineer, Danny Boutchart, who had sustained a broken arm and ribs. They both ran over and moved him to safety. Unbeknown to the three of them gathered on the port side of the aircraft, Johnny Roe and Bill Parr had also escaped from the blazing aircraft, out of sight on the opposite side, from where they struck off into the woods before the Germans arrived. The trio on the port side did likewise and moved off in the opposite direction.

Roe and Parr managed to get within 5 kilometres of the Swedish border before being captured. John Morrison and Reg Williams were helped by a Norwegian family, who took them to their cottage. They couldn't speak English but knew of a young lady who lived close by who could. She was sent for and was able to use the little English she had to converse with the airmen. Due to the low height of the operation the crew had no heavy flying clothing, and were wearing only trousers and their battle-dress tunics. The Norwegians gave John and Reg some sandwiches and a couple of civilian jackets to wear, after which they set off for the Swedish border. Boutchart, who was too badly injured to accompany them, remained behind to await the arrival of the Germans, who, it was hoped, would take him for hospital treatment. John and Reg were helped on their way by other Norwegians, who gave them more sandwiches. By the first of March, having trudged through 6-foot snowdrifts, they were within 10 kilometres of the Swedish border. Up to that point they had managed to stay off the roads, which they could see below them, as they were patrolled by the Germans. Reg Williams's wounds were getting worse and so they decided to get down onto the road. Having done so they continued along until they came across a little village, where they decided to rest. Soon after, two workmen came along on bikes and saw the airmen's footprints in the snow at the side of the road. At that they hurried off. About 10 minutes later they returned with German soldiers.

The unlucky duo were taken by truck to Trondjheim, and then on by train to Oslo, where they were kept in the Staffel HQ, which was located in a former hotel. Here they joined two airmen from Coastal Command, who had also been shot down. Surprisingly they were not interrogated whilst there, and only had to give their name, rank and number. Next day their number increased to 6 when Johnny Roe and Bill Parr were brought in. This was the first time that Morrison and Williams had seen anyone else from their crew, it was good to see that they were safe. Next day all six of them were put aboard a Junkers 52 for a flight to Copenhagen. There was an armed guard on the plane, which discouraged them from trying

anything. From Copenhagen they flew to Berlin and were taken by passenger train to Frankfurt. Here their uniforms were taken from them and they were given some other uniforms to wear, either Polish or French. By the time John Morrison got his own uniform back, it was minus his escape aids, including the compass buttons from his battledress. Here the interrogation began. They were kept in solitary confinement over the next few days. The Germans tried the usual good guy/ bad guy method of trying to gain information from them. One would shout at them and later the other one would have a go whilst offering them British Gold Leaf cigarettes in the usual yellow packets. They never gave them a packet, only single cigarettes. Then it was the turn of the bad guy again, and so on. After about 3 or 4 days the Germans gave it up as a bad job and moved them on to Stallag Luft 3 at Sagan, about 80 miles southeast of Berlin.

Johnny Roe and Bill Parr after their capture. Their German captors seeming quite friendly.
Photo: John Morrison

Sagan at the time was quite new, and had only been built to hold British aircrew. When Johnny Roe and his other three crewmembers arrived, there were only 2 compounds, one for the NCOs and the other for officers. Eventually, as the numbers of shot down allied aircrew increased, the camp became an officers only establishment. John Morrison, Bill Par and Doug Williams, along with all the other NCOs, were moved north to Stallag Luft 6 in Poland, close to the Baltic port of Danzig (now Gdansk). During late 1944, when the Russians began to advance towards Berlin, it was time for the Germans to vacate the premises. They marched the POWs to camp 357 at Thorn, some 90 miles to the south of Danzig, where they stayed for 3 or 4 weeks. After this they were moved on again, to Fallingbostel, 370 miles to the west and 50 miles S/S/W of Hamburg. They remained here until April 19th 1945, when the Allies began to approach from the west. The Germans then marched the POW column in batches to the east again. John Morrison and his group were in the first batch. They would march all day and at night were herded into barns and other farm buildings. There was little to eat and only straw to sleep on. To say the least, the guards were not front line troops; they were old men belonging to the home guard. One day, the column was stopped as they marched along a tree-lined avenue where there was a store of Red Cross parcels. As they sat under the trees eating the food from the parcels, there came a mighty roar as 4 Hawker Typhoons strafed the column. John Morrison dived for cover to one side of a tree, whilst his pal took refuge on the other side of the same tree. After the first pass the aircraft came around again for a second go, but some brave members of the column had moved out into the fields surrounding the road and were waving frantically at the approaching aircraft. The Typhoons pulled up without firing and flew off. After the noise of the aero engines had receded, John Morrison took stock of his situation and realised that his pal, who had dived for cover on the other side of the tree, had been killed. It turned out that 42 people, most of them allied POWs, had been killed, whilst a further 100 were injured. Everyone attended to the wounded, after which the Germans took the injured to hospital. The march continued, but after a short while, the Germans, who much preferred to be captured by the Allies rather than the Russians, decided to about turn and head west again. The guards were in no great hurry and trailed behind, whilst the younger lads in the column quickened their step and after a while left them behind.

Eventually John and the rest of the POWs stopped at a small hamlet for a rest. Here they heard the sound of not too distant gunfire. The hamlet was on a bit of a rise, and after a while, hearing the sound of an engine, they looked down the road towards the noise, which was coming from the crossroads at the base of the hamlet. Stopped at the crossroads was a British Army scout car. Everyone shouted enthusiastically and waved. Slowly and gingerly the scout car turned into the road and edged its way over the short distance towards them. It was 12:30 on May 2nd 1945, and John and his group were free. Their liberators turned out to be a small group of soldiers belonging to the 5th Wiltshire regiment, who had no time to hang around, and told them to wait there whilst they promptly left to get on with the war. They would, of course, radio back to tell their HQ that the POWs were there, and so everyone waited. At the bottom of the hamlet, on the other side of the crossroads, was a large field, and this became a stopgap POW camp for captured Germans. By now the Wiltshires has arrived in greater numbers, and as the British POWs had some experience in these matters they were asked to help search the German POWs. Eventually John and his group were told to make their way to Luneburg Heath, and so, having walked far enough, they began to find something to get them there. Everyone broke up into smaller groups and John and 7 others soon found a German staff car, which they commandeered.

Today one takes for granted that most people can drive, but at this point in history there were very few cars on British roads and therefore, with the exception of military trained drivers, only the relatively well off tended to be able to drive. Thousands of young men, who were able to pilot a Lancaster or a Spitfire during the war, could not actually drive a car. Motor bikes were more likely to satisfy the transport needs of the less well off. However, John's group did manage to find someone who could drive and off they set for Luneburg Heath. When the petrol ran out, the car was ditched, and the transport problem reared its ugly head once again. They all set off to search for something else and one of them found a wood-burning lorry. They soon mastered the intricacies of its steam engine and off they set again. The lorry, being larger than the staff car, allowed them to pick up more passengers and eventually they reached Luneburg. When they arrived, in a puff of steam and smoke, the guard at the barrier walked around to the back of the lorry and lifted the canvas cover. Looking in at the motley bunch sitting on the floor he enquired, 'Who the hell are you lot?' 'We're POWs!' came the reply. The guard looked bewildered for a moment. 'You're allies aren't you?' 'Yes', came the reply. 'You silly buggers!' he replied, 'you're ex-POWs.' It was at that point that, for John and his fellow travellers, the penny dropped, as they realised that at last they really were free. They no longer had to worry about finding their own way about as the army would handle that side of things from then on.

After being fed and taken care of they were moved further west. At one point they stopped for the night somewhere where there was a cinema. They were given the treat of a film show, which starred Esther Williams. It opened with her standing in a tight swimming costume on the top of a diving board. For John and some of the others who had spent over 3 years in the bag, the first few moments of the sound track were drowned under a cacophony of wolf whistles and yells of delight. Eventually they arrived at an airfield, which contained thousands of POWs, all waiting in line for the trip home. There was the constant arrival and departure of aircraft, many of them Lancasters. Having had a detailed lecture on emergency drills by one of its crewmembers, John and his group climbed aboard one of the Lancs and were flown back to England. They landed at Cosford, where they were processed and given a thorough medical check up. After an overnight stay on the 12th of May 1945, John Morrison took the train to his parents' house at Aberdeen. When he was shot down, his wife Margery moved up there from Darlington, and she was waiting for him. He was given a special ration card headed 'for malnutrition and expectant mothers'.

First Halifax Ops for 78

The first operations for 78 since they converted onto the Halifax took place on the night of April 29/30th 1941. Five fresher crews were detailed for a raid on the docks at Ostend. Led by S/L Snow, the attack was carried out from 14,000 feet. Conditions over the target area were very good. It was a clear night with no cloud and a bright moon. The main aiming point was the Bassin-de-Chasse. Snow's bombs started fires in the main dock area. F/L Knox was not able to attack as the bomb-load hung up. Despite five runs over the target, still the bombs would not release. Eventually, having tried all the way home, the bombs were jettisoned in the sea 30 miles off Filey on the Yorkshire Coast. Sgt Bedford and his crew also attacked the basin area. During the run-up to the target the navigation log was accidentally dropped from the camera hatch. The last crew, flown by Sgt Hedge, also managed to bomb the primary. The navigator, Sgt Hewitson, observed their 8 bomb bursts on the canal entrance and Docks 10, 11 and 12. W7663, flown by F/O Shattock, failed to return. This aircraft, the first to be lost by 78 since their conversion onto the Halifax, had crashed not far from the target, all of the crew were killed. They now lie in the Town Cemetery at Dunkirk.

Operation Millennium

On the morning of May 30th 1942, a WAAF corporal of 76 Squadron stood in front of a large blackboard. In her left hand she held a sheet of paper from which she copied, her right hand was chalking the Battle Order for the night's operations. This was a list of aircraft captains, and the identification letter of the aircraft that they would fly. It also contained other assorted information relevant to the impending raid.

Over at Croft, an identical exercise was being carried out at 78, and for that matter, practically every other squadron in Bomber Command. Just before this work had commenced, the Snowdrops began to seal the camp. All public phone boxes were chained and padlocked. No one was allowed to leave the station. Guards were put on all known exits, including holes in the fences and hedges. Later in the day, at briefing, the inhabitants of Goosepool would find out that this was not to be just another operation, but the first in a series of raids that would change the face of Bomber Command forever.

To appreciate the events that would unfold as this special day continued, one must go back to the night of Palm Sunday, March 28/29th 1942. On this date, 234 aircraft of Bomber Command attacked Lubeck, a shipbuilding town some 35 miles northeast of Hamburg. There were many useful targets in Lubeck, including the Dragerworke, which produced oxygen equipment for German U-boats. This raid was the first real success for Bomber Command, as with a full moon, good visibility, plus a lack of heavy defences, everything was in the bomber's favour. The raid was carried out in three waves, which were led by experienced crews. Many attacks were carried out from low level, some as low as 2,000 feet. The Gee sets were out of range for bombing, but they were used for navigation during part of the bomber's outbound flight, and on the way back. On their return to their bases, the 191 crews taking part reported the raid to be a huge success, as did the aerial photographs. Even the Germans recorded that the town had suffered greatly from the attack, and that 11,812 buildings were seriously damaged, or had suffered slight damage. Reports stated that 3,070 were residential, whilst 261 were agricultural, commercial or industrial. Public buildings also came under attack, with 70 being reported as being badly damaged or destroyed. Over 400 tons of bombs rained down on Lubeck, many fell on the aiming point, which was the Altstadt. This was the old part of the town, which had narrow streets and many wooden houses. The flames had little trouble in spreading from one side of the narrow street to the other, quickly swamping the fire fighting crews. Harris had planned this, and to gain the effect, he ensured that 66 percent of the bombs dropped that night were incendiaries. This resulted in 109 acres of the town being destroyed. In human terms, the death toll reached over the 300 mark, with 136 seriously wounded, a further 648 receiving wounds of a less serious nature.

This number of dead, however, was less than the 367 French people killed during the attack by Bomber Command on the Renault factory in Paris during the night of March 3/4th 1942. In this factory at Boulogne-Billancourt, on the western side of the city centre, the French were producing an estimated 18,000 trucks per year for the Germans, and it was considered to be a legitimate target. Unfortunately the Parisians were blasé about air raid sirens, as the allied bombers frequently plied their way across France, en-route to Germany. They often took little heed of the air-raid warnings. Bomber Command was acutely conscious of the risk of hurting French civilians, and ordered the raid to be carried out from very low level, thus reducing the chances of bombs going astray.

Three of 76 Squadron's Halifaxes took part in this raid. Led by S/L Burdett in MP-X R9487 were F/S Lambeth's crew in MP-R R9447 and that of Sgt Kenny Clack in MP-O L9620. The weather was fairly good, visibility being estimated at 4 to 5 miles, and the 8/10ths-cloud base was well above 8,000 feet. A slight ground haze was encountered over the target area, but this was not thick enough to obscure the target. For each aircraft, the run up to the target was straightforward, with only a small amount of inaccurate light flak. Searchlight activity was negligible. For Goosepool's part, F/S Lambeth and his crew attacked first at 20:45. They bombed from a height of 3,000 feet. Their bombs fell accurately on the target and fires were started. Following close behind was S/L Burdett and crew, they bombed from the same height one minute later. Two bomb bursts were seen in the target area on the north bank of the Seine. Burdett's crew also reported seeing a large number of flares in the Croissy district, and later over the target area. The third aircraft, MP-O, flown by Kenny Clack, attacked the target at 21:02 from 3,400 feet. Numerous brightly-lit flares were seen in the target area. Their bombs were accurately placed, but the results were obscured by smoke. In Paris itself, the blackout was good. Approximately 8 miles to the south of the target, a reddish glow was seen from a fire that suddenly appeared in a wood. This was believed to be a decoy fire and was ignored. This raid saw the largest number of bombers sent to a single target thus far in the war. 235 aircraft took part, consisting of 89 Wellingtons, 48 Hampdens, 29 Stirlings, 26 Manchesters, 23 Whitleys and 20 Halifaxes. The main raid, consisting of 3 waves, lasted for 110 minutes. The average timing between each bomb load was only 30 seconds, another record.

Also new was the use of a large number of flares, and the employment of the most experienced crews to open the proceedings. This tactic would become SOP[58] for the Pathfinders, after their formation later in the year. Over 450 tons of bombs were dropped, another record, which destroyed 40% of the factory. Production was affected for several months, estimated at the loss of over 2,500 trucks. One 311 Squadron Wellington crew was lost when their aircraft crashed near Creil.

[58] Standard Operating Procedure

Another Wellington, from 158 Squadron, that had suffered engine trouble after taking off from Pocklington, crashed on the airfield after turning back, injuring 2 crewmembers. A 35 Squadron Halifax crash-landed at Oakington, after being hit by flak, fortunately without injury to the crew. Finally a 218 Squadron Stirling, out of Marham, having successfully carried out its attack, landed safely back at base, only to have a hung-up bomb fall off the aircraft and explode. All on board were injured. Two of the crew showed great courage when they went back into the blazing aircraft to rescue two other trapped crewmen. Sadly, despite their heroic efforts, the two trapped crewmen died later of their injuries.

The very successful raid on Lubeck and another on Rostock spurred Harris on to attempt greater things. He was in haste to show that Bomber Command was a major asset to the war effort. For some time, the Admiralty, and to a lesser extent the British Army, were plotting to acquire his aircraft for their own needs. The Navy wanted them to bolster Coastal Command in an attempt to combat the U-boat menace. The Army, on the other hand, saw the bombers as air support for their push across North Africa, Operation Torch, and beyond.

Harris hatched a bigger and better plan to follow hot on the heels of Lubeck and Rostock. His idea to send 1,000 bombers to a single target was warmly received by Winston Churchill, who also discussed it with Chief of the Air Staff, Sir Charles Portal. He too was impressed. And so the seed was sown. Initially the concept was a bit of a gamble, as up to that point, Bomber Command only had about 400 fully trained crews to carry out its work. This was something of a short fall to say the least. However, doing his sums, he realised that he did have a large number of aircraft in the command's training units. He also hoped to muster aircraft from each group's Heavy Conversion Units. Cajoled by Churchill, Coastal Command, under Sir Philip Joubert, offered 250 of their bombers.[59] The less experienced aircrews could, it was argued, be captained by their instructors, who were usually first and second tour men having a so-called rest from Ops.

Flying Training Command offered 50 aircraft, which dwindled away after close inspection, as most of them were just not equipped for night operations. They eventually provided just four Wellingtons. This operation provided many firsts for Harris and his planners, as the logistics of flying 1,000 bombers over one target in as short a time as possible was worked out. The bomber stream was invented, and as it was developed, it was realised that by keeping the aircraft in a narrow corridor one could quickly swamp the enemy defences. Instead of going their own merry way, all the bomber crews would fly the same speed and course to the target, one behind the other in a semi orderly queue, hence the name - bomber stream.

This way, the aircraft would not be divided and scattered about over enemy territory, waiting to be picked off by radar vectored German night fighters. They operated in an air defence system, which was part of the Kammhuber line, so named after the major who had conceived it. Stretching from a point about 90 miles southeast of Paris all the way up to the Danish border, this line had begun to take its toll of allied bombers. Each German night fighter pilot operated in his own square area of sky, called a box, and was controlled by a ground radar operator. There was a limit to the number of bomber interceptions the pilot could carry out before time and the need to refuel overtook him. By keeping the bomber stream in a narrow corridor of sky, only a few overworked boxes would be employed and quickly swamped. The remainder would simply circle their own bit of real estate, awaiting the bombers that would never materialise.

Harris accepted the risk of collision, and his planners minimised the problem by giving each aircraft a slot time and height to fly, just like the modern airliner of today. Many new innovations produced for the 1,000-bomber raids would work for the command during the rest of the war, and pave the way for the crowded skies of today. Up to this time, it was normal for a force of two or three hundred bombers to have the luxury of two or more hours to pass over a target. The total time for the whole of Millennium was kept to an hour and a half. The impact on the defences over the target was not lost on Harris and his advisors. Once the attack was initiated, the huge force would condemn the fire fighters below to total inadequacy. To this end, it was planned to get as many incendiaries onto the target as possible, and use high explosive bombs to rip the buildings open, letting the fires in.

It was decided that the more experienced crews would find the target, hopefully accurately identify it beyond all reasonable doubt, and mark it for the remainder of the stream and their less seasoned followers. On a clear night, Cologne was just about the easiest place in Germany to find, as the Rhine passed straight through its centre. Although Harris intended to pick his night for the attack based on perfect weather, he gave orders that the raid leaders were to be equipped with Gee, to ensure accurate navigation and foolproof target identification.

As the planning continued, someone in the Admiralty realised that if this raid was successful, Harris would prove beyond doubt the worth of Bomber Command. This would secure its future, with the possible acquisition of hundreds of extra aircraft that would be otherwise destined for Coastal Command. To this end, following an instruction from their masters in the Admiralty, the offer of the 250 Coastal Command aircraft was withdrawn.

Harris and his team went into overdrive to cover this shortfall. No stone was unturned. They took another look at the training units. It was hoped initially to use crews who were fairly advanced in their training programs. This was reviewed, as it was realised that the total number of reasonably experienced aircraft and crews available for the operation fell far short of the magic 1,000. The operational squadrons took another look at their spare aircraft, and what they had in the way of up and coming crews. The Command's training units were milked of even less experienced trainee crews as attempts were made to intermix some of them with operationally experienced personnel.

At Middleton, secret preparations for who knows what had been going on throughout May. On the first day of the month, at 14:00 hours, P/O Moorhouse flew Halifax MP-E X1013 from Middleton to Croft. This aircraft had been borrowed from 78 for the Tirpitz raid. Although only a very short flight, this was deemed to be good experience for this fresher captain and his crew. An identical exercise had been given to P/O Anderson, who was also a fresher. He had returned Halifax MP-K W1006 to Croft three hours earlier.

---

[59] Most of their crews were Ex-Bomber Command anyway

May 3rd saw 9 aircraft complete their air-tests, including two others that carried out an air-firing program. New aircraft to bolster 76's numbers continued to arrive from the factories, including W7672, which arrived during the afternoon. In 76's operations room, a new face appeared in the form of P/O Long, the squadron's new Navigation Officer, who had been posted in on April 22nd. The same day, seven crews, plus one fresher crew (Flown by Sgt Anderson) were briefed for an attack on the dock area of Hamburg. Just before take off, Ops for the fresher crew were cancelled. Six of the seven aircraft dispatched bombed the target. Halifax MP-H R9451 did not return. This aircraft, flown by Sgt L N Williams, had taken off at 22:55, only to crash at Ottensen, 15 miles southwest of Hamburg. The engineer, Sgt Fox and the observer, Sgt Leaman baled out and became POWs; the remaining members of the crew were killed. Sgt Williams was buried in Hamburg Cemetery, whilst the remainder, Sgts Owens, Jackson and Jones, have no known graves.

Also on the same night, 78 lost one of its Halifaxes on a raid to the same target. This aircraft was flown by one of the squadron's stalwarts, S/L Snow. Flying Halifax R9391, he and his crew crashed in the North Sea. Six of the crew are buried in cemeteries at Sage or Kiel, whilst the rear gunner, Sgt Edwards, has no known grave. The next day saw three new crews posted in to join 76, these were classified as 'Under Training'. Each crew consisted of pilot, observer, bomb aimer, WOP/AG and tail gunner.

During the morning, instructions were received from the squadron CO, W/C Young, that these crews were to be kept intact, and that no crewmember could operate with another crew. Middleton and Croft were receiving more and more new aircrew personnel. No sooner had the three crews previously mentioned settled in to their billets, than six new air gunners arrived at the guardroom. Four of them had come from 7 AACU, whilst the other two were posted in from 1484 TT & GT Flight. At 12:35 on May 6th, in an attempt to gather as many serviceable aircraft as possible, P/O Dobson took off for Tain in MP-U. He was carrying Sgt Bingham and his crew, who were to ferry back to Middleton, Halifax W1018, MP-M. This aircraft had been left in Scotland on 30th April for repairs, after the last raid on the Tirpitz. Dobson in MP-U landed back at Middleton two hours and fourteen minutes later, at 14:50. As the repaired aircraft was not ready, Sgt Bingham was not able to depart Tain until 16:25. He landed safely back at Middleton at 18:45. On the same day, a 30 minute air-test was carried out on a recently repaired Halifax, whilst a cross-country training flight was undertaken by P/O Moorhouse and his crew.

All stops were pulled out to have as many crews trained and aircraft serviceable as possible. By the end of the day, it was reported that 7 Mk II Halifaxes belonging to 76 were operationally serviceable. That night, one of 78's Halifaxes was detailed for a raid on Limoges. Flown by F/O Bedford, this aircraft returned safely after what was described as a very successful attack. Their route had them cross the French coast at St Aubin-Surmer. On the way home two hours later, they dropped Nickels whilst flying over Verdone. The next day the air-tests continued, including one on MP-G W1016. Michael Renaut in MP-L W7660 was also detailed to carry out a 40 minute air-test, whilst also taking part in a fighter affiliation exercise. Meanwhile that evening, the training of P/O Moorhouse continued with a local solo night flying exercise lasting one hour thirty minutes. By the end of the day, eight of 76 Squadron's Halifax Mk IIs had been returned as operationally serviceable. On the 8th, the preparations were stepped up as 6 hours 55 minutes flying time was employed whilst completing no less than 10 air-tests. That night, 8 of 76's aircraft were detailed for an attack on the Heinkel aircraft factory at Warnemunde, including P/O Moorhouse. Six aircraft bombed the primary, whilst one flown by F/S Kenny Clack developed engine trouble and had to return early. Somehow he managed to land safely at Dalton on two engines. Sadly, P/O HB Moorhouse and his crew were killed when their Halifax MP-F R9456 crashed near Rostock during this raid. By the end of the day, 8 Halifax Mk IIs and a similar number of crews were reported as being operationally serviceable, despite the absence of S/L Packe who was to go on 12 days leave. Whilst he was away, F/L Warner was to assume temporary command of 76's B Flight. The next morning F/S Anderson carried out a 5-hour search to locate a dinghy, which had been seen by a returning bomber low on fuel that could not loiter. Despite an intensive search of the North Sea, the dinghy was not found. Postings in of extra aircrew were continuing with the arrival of air gunner F/S Salway from 158 Squadron. Also received the same day was Halifax MP-F W1104, a replacement for P/O Moorhouse's missing Halifax. And so the preparations for the 1,000-bomber raid continued, without any one on the station really knowing what was afoot.

On the 10th, a further 7 air-tests were carried out during the afternoon. This was complemented by 2 night flying tests flown by P/O McIntosh and Sgt Johnny Harwood. The final tally for 76 that day was 8 serviceable Halifaxes and 9 long-range crews. The next day the number of available aircraft went up to 10, but the available crews fell to 8, as three captains were on leave and one was sick. The 12th saw the return of the sick captain and the arrival of another Halifax, taking the final total of serviceable aircraft to 11. On the 14th, news came through that S/L Iveson was to receive the DFC and Kenny Clack the DFM. At the same time 76's Squadron Engineering Officer, F/L Gardiner, was posted out to the Middle East. He was replaced by F/O Patterson.

During the second half of the month, formation-flying practice was carried out by up to eight aircraft at a time. Still the build up continued. May had been a terrible month for weather, most days suffered from poor visibility and excessive amounts of rain. Much to-ing and fro-ing amongst aircrew was taking place. F/S Borsberry was screened on the 16th and departed to Marsden Moor as a flying instructor. At the same time, two new flight engineers were posted in from 1652 Conversion Flight, and two pilots, P/O Raymond and Sgt Nicholson, left to attend a BAT course at Driffield. Another air gunner, F/S Cooper, came as F/S Hall went to 24 OTU at Honeybourne.

By the 17th, the number of aircraft had risen to 13 but long-range operational crews were the problem, as only 9 were available at this time. Mannheim was the target on the 19th. Seven aircraft took off but three returned with mechanical problems. A fourth failed to return. This aircraft had been flown by fresher Sgt Anderson and his crew. Carrying Christopher Cheshire's old squadron markings, MP-L W7660 had been shot down by Oblt Wilhelm Herget of II /NJG4. It crashed near Marche-en-Famenne, Luxembourg, 28 miles S/S/W of Liege, Belgium. Fortunately the crew baled out and became POWs. The other three crews landed safely back at Middleton.

Despite lousy weather during the whole of the month, the air-tests and training continued. On the 20th, S/L Packe returned from leave, just in time to see, or rather not to see, F/S Tackley and his crew divert to Leeming. Middleton's weather had suddenly manifested itself across his windscreen, blotting out the landscape, thus preventing him from landing (amazing the difference 15 miles can make). He would have to wait until the 22nd to find the weather to ferry it back to Middleton. On the 22nd eight Halifaxes of 78 Squadron were briefed to attack St Nazaire, none were able to locate the target and all returned safely to Croft, having jettisoned their bombs in the sea. The return to Goosepool of F/S Tackley in MP-N was countered by the unserviceability of MP-C, as it was damaged in a taxiing accident with P/O Perry at the controls. On the 25th, just 4 days before Millennium, 14 air-tests were ordered, of which 8 had to be cancelled due to unserviceability. On the same day a brand new Halifax II, MP-L W1144, was delivered by a beautiful blond slip of a girl in immaculate white overalls. She was part of the ATA,[60] and had brought the Halifax up from the English Electric Company at Warton. Just as the pilots and groundcrew of 76 were licking their lips at the new aircraft (and the girl no doubt), they were informed that they were not to get too excited as the new Halifax had landed on the wrong airfield. It was actually earmarked for 78 Squadron at Croft, where it ended up on the 27th.

By the 28th, just two days before the impending 'Big Show', 76's tally of Halifaxes had grown to eighteen Mk IIs and one Mk 1, the latter belonging to the squadron's conversion flight. Meanwhile, the number of available operational crews had grown to 22. Crews on leave were suddenly recalled, including two fully operational ones who were duly summoned to report back to Middleton by 09:00 hours that morning. Surprisingly, on the night before the 1,000 raid, operations against the Gnome & Rhone works in Paris were ordered. Seven 76 Squadron aircraft took off, but only six returned. MP-G W1065, flown by P/O J D Anderson, was hit by flak over the target area. Anderson and his crew were all killed, they rest in Viroflay New Communal Cemetery, 9 miles southwest of the Eiffel Tower. At the end of the same day, 76 Squadron reported that seventeen of their operational Mk Is, plus five Mk IIs, plus another Mk I belonging to the Conversion Flight, were serviceable. If required, the number of available crews was shown as 21, including 2 from the Conversion Flight. Eventually, following a supreme effort by everyone in Bomber Command and its training units, the grand total of available aircraft and was expected to reach 1,052.

Hamburg, Germany's second largest city to Berlin, had been Harris's first choice of targets, but due to troublesome weather predictions, Cologne would now become the recipient of the world's first 1,000-bomber raid. It is difficult to imagine today's RAF being able to provide even a hundred aircraft for anything, let alone 1,000. As the day progressed the usual ritual of 'Guess the target' continued as the aircraft were bombed up. At Croft, Norman Thompson was struggling with a

Instrument mechanic checks compass prior to operations   Photo: IWM CH. 6661

[60] Air Transport Auxiliary

leaking coolant radiator on a Merlin. Having removed the offending item, he realised that its matrix had ingested tiny pieces of flak during a previous raid. Although the Halifax itself had not suffered actual flak damage, the radiator (which was just about the most flak susceptible component on the aeroplane) was holed, causing a slightly weeping coolant leak. A higher than normal temperature had been indicated on the offending engine's temp gauge, this had been reported by the crew and thus appeared on the aircraft's snags list that morning. Norman and his oppos had been working flat out for days. There was some kind of flap on, although no one really knew what it was all about. It seemed that there were not enough hours in the day, as whatever was afoot demanded that all squadron aircraft were to be on 'top line'. He and the other 78 ground personnel worked for as long as it took, sometimes well into the night. On more than one occasion, the engineering officer personally brought them hot Cocoa around midnight.

At Middleton, Norman Frankish and his oppos at 76 were similarly tasked. The airfield was bustling with activity, day and night. Even the usual lame ducks and squadron crates that no one wanted to fly were required for something, God knew what. Everything that was capable of flight was pressed into service. Struggling with 32 tiny 4 BA nuts on a Merlin's header tank was not Norman's favourite pastime. Whilst standing on a servicing gantry out on the airfield in all weathers, it was common to drop these nuts, especially when one's fingers were blue with cold. How come, if one drops something like a 4 BA nut, gravity never ensures that it will be found directly below one, thus necessitating a trip to the stores and the wrath of one's Chiefy.[61]

The morning of May 30/31st dawned fair with slight showers. The Halifaxes of 76 Squadron carried out five air-tests. Meanwhile, a high flying Spitfire had been despatched, to check on the weather over Germany, relative to an operation on Hamburg/Cologne. Having checked the report brought back by the Spitfire's pilot, Harris held a morning conference with his advisors (better known to the folks at Bomber Command HQ as morning prayers). They informed Harris that, with a lot of good luck, they could probably muster the expected total of 1,052 aircraft for the night's raid, (later amended to 1,047). During the morning, confirmation that Operation Millennium would take place that night simultaneously rattled down the teleprinters of all Bomber Command Groups. The target was confirmed as Cologne, the required fuel and bomb loads were indicated. The Groups Planning Teams having checked the serviceability state of all of the squadrons in their group then simultaneously contacted the commander of each station involved in the night's operation by teleprinter. At Middleton, the teleprinter clicked once, and sprang into life. The operator sat down at the keyboard and watched as it began to print out a document that was headed-

Station Operation Order 244. - MOST SECRET

Period. Hours of Darkness May 30/31st 1942.

Intensity. 21 A/C of 76 Squadron.

Target. Primary: - Cologne X

Alt. Essen B LR Any built up area in the Ruhr.

Route. Spalding - Southwold - Ouddorp - Target - Euskirchen - Noordland - Southwold - Spalding - Base.

Timings.

Base (Set Course)	23:40 hours.	
Spalding	00:23 hours.	
Southwold	00:49 hours.	
Ouddorp	01:16 hours.	
Time on Target	01:55 hours.	
Time off target	02:05 hours.	
Euskirchen	02:11 hours.	
Noordland	03:05 hours	
Southwold	03:44 hours.	
Spalding	04:17 hours.	
Base	05:10 hours.	

Average height.

3,000 feet to Spalding.

5,000 feet to Southwold.

12,000 feet to Ouddorp.

14,000 feet to Target.

10,000 feet to Noordland.

2,000 feet to Southwold.

3,000 feet to Base.

IAS.   Out :   160 mph   **Home :** 150 mph.

Bomb Load.   12 SBC 30% (30-lb) 70% (4-lb). Distribution setting 0.1 Seconds.
3 (1,000-lb) GP Bombs fused TD 025. [62]

---

[61] Flight Sergeant I/C of an aircraft's groundcrew
[62] GP = General Purpose bomb   TD = Time Delay in seconds

No.1 and 3 Groups were to attack target A. No.4 Group and all other aircraft operating from its stations, would attack target X, along with Army Co-operation Command and 92 Group. Target Y was to be attacked by 5 Group, and all other aircraft operating from its stations, in conjunction with 91 Group aircraft. Bombing height was to be between 14,500 - 15,000 feet. It was ordered that after bombing, all aircraft were to increase speed and lose height down to 1,000 feet. When over the sea, height had to be regained to 5,000 feet by the time they reached the English coast. The order continued with a directive that no recco flares, or photoflashes,[63] were to be dropped, and that no coloured identification flares were to be used. The time on target was of the utmost importance, and every endeavour was to be made to identify and bomb the target in the period ordered. If an aircraft was late on arrival an attack was still to be carried out but it was imperative that every aircraft turned for home at 02:40 hours wherever they might be, whether they had dropped their bombs or not.

Aircraft of 2 Group were to carry out intruder attacks on enemy night fighter airfields around the bomber stream's path. Fighter Command were also to provide cover for returning bombers as far as possible out to sea from the East Coast of Britain. Note 4 reported that selected crews from 1,3,4 and 5 Groups would attack the target, just before 02:25 hours, to photograph the results of the attack, and make a visual reconnaissance. Aircraft of 1 and 3 Groups were to commence the attack with all available TRs between 00:55 – 01:00 hours. This was to be followed by the heavies of 4 and 5 Group between 01:55 – 02:25 hours. The remaining aircraft were to bomb between 01:10 – 02:10 hours.

The Total number of aircraft dispatched by each Group was to be as follows.

1 Group - 150 A/C made up of Wellingtons.
3 Group - 235 A/C, made up of 155 Wellingtons and 80 Stirlings.
4 Group - 156 A/C, made up of 135 Halifaxes, 9 Wellingtons and 9 Whitleys.
5 Group - 156 A/C made up of 33 Hampdens, 45 Manchesters, and 79 Lancasters.

This made a total of 697 aircraft from the operational groups. The Operational Training Unit groups provided a further 355.

On the morning of the raid, the total number of aircraft available on paper was shown as 1052.[64] By the time of the raid, for a variety of reasons, this number was reduced to 1,047. At Croft, Station Operation Order 245 stated the same as Middleton's, with two exceptions. The number of Halifaxes to be detailed by 78 Squadron was 22, one more than 76. The other difference, as far as 78 Squadron was concerned, was in the timings. Their first aircraft would take off from Croft five minutes earlier than 76 from Middleton. Their timings were calculated thus: -

Base (Set Course)-------------------------------2335 hours.
Spalding-------------------------------------0018 hours.
Southwold -----------------------------------0044 hours.
Ouddorp-------------------------------------0112 hours.
Time on Target------------------------------0155 hours.
Time off Target ----------------------------0205 hours.
Euskirchen-----------------------------------0212 hours.
Noordland------------------------------------0306 hours.
Southwold -----------------------------------0342 hours.
Spalding-------------------------------------0416 hours.
Base---0508 hours.

Around the country, all Bomber Command stations were sealed, phone boxes on the airfields were chained up, and all exits from the camps guarded against anyone leaving. Anyone on the camps wishing to leave, civilian or military personnel alike, were unable to do so until the time the bombs began to fall. Although some aircraft went sick leading up to take off time, Bomber Command was still able to amass 1,047 serviceable bombers of all types. This final total was made up of

156 Wellingtons from 1 Group
134 Wellingtons and 88 Stirlings from 3 Group
9 Wellingtons, 131 Halifaxes and 7 Whitleys from 4 Group
46 Manchesters, 34 Hampdens and 73 Lancasters from 5 Group
236 Wellingtons and 21 Whitleys from 91 (OTU) Group
63 Wellingtons and 45 Hampdens from 92 (OTU) Group
4 Wellingtons from Flying Training Command.

The total number of aircraft types equalled 602 Wellingtons, 131 Halifaxes, 88 Stirlings, 79 Hampdens, 73 Lancasters, 46 Manchesters and 28 Whitleys. Collectively, they were to drop a total of 1,455 tons of bombs, one third HE, the remainder incendiaries.

Meanwhile, at Goosepool, The total number of serviceable 76 squadron aircraft available for the nights raid was then teleprinted back to Group. This would then be sent to HQ Bomber Command.

The young WAAF in the squadron office had completed her work, despite many interruptions. Everyone wanted to know if they were 'On' for tonight. The target, however, would remain a mystery until briefing. As the groundcrew prepared the aircraft, the aircrew looked for any suggestion of the target. One of the biggest give-aways was the fuel load. One could often hazard an educated guess as to the location of the evening's venue by the amount of petrol being put into the fuel tanks. Due to the weight penalty, more fuel meant fewer bombs and so the fuel load was calculated as close to the minimum requirement as possible, plus an extra 120 gallons or so for the wife and kids. This would, it was hoped, get one home if

[63] A brightly burning flare dropped by the attacking bomber after release, used to illuminate the target and allow the crew to photograph the results of their attack
[64] On Station order 244 this number was incorrectly calculated as 1053

stronger than forecast winds were encountered, or one's nav was a bit off. As both Normans worked, they were subconsciously aware of the sound of passing tractors towing bomb trolleys as they made their way to the dispersals. These trolleys were strung together end to end, three or four at a time, and were nicknamed bomb trains. Often driven by WAFFs, they were used to tow bombs from the dump out to the arming sheds. The sheds had open doors at each end to allow the trolleys to be driven in (and out). The tractors were then detached and driven off to allow the bombs to be fused by the armourers. Once the fusing process was complete, the bomb trains were towed to the waiting aircraft. Having reached the appropriate bomber, the trolleys were detached from the tractor. This would allow the armourers to manoeuver the trolleys one by one, by hand, under the aircraft. The precarious job of winching the bombs into the cavernous bomb bay would then commence. The pilots and crews visited the aircraft during the day, checking that all was well and that any outstanding snags had been sorted. Air-tests were carried out as required, with further adjustments being made by the groundcrews if needed, but not after the bombs were on board.

Bombs arrive from the fusing shed   Photo: IWM

Bombs being winched up into Halifax bomb bay and SBC's containing incendiaries being winched into the wing bomb bays, note winch on inside of aircraft in photograph on next page; Photo: IWM 6625

Winch on inside of aircraft located above bomb bay - pulling bombs up into Halifax bomb bay.   Photo: IWM 6682

As far as the groundcrews were concerned, the aircraft belonged to them. The aircrews only borrowed 'their' aeroplanes, and they were expected to bring them back in one piece. If an aircraft went missing it hit the groundcrew badly, especially if the crew lasted for a while, and they got to know them. Norman Frankish had the distinction of looking after both Christopher and Leonard Cheshire's aircraft whilst stationed at Middleton. It hit him and his oppos very badly when Christopher was shot down. Each aircraft was looked after by a team consisting of engine fitter, airframe fitter[65] armourer, electrician, radio mechanic, and on occasion an instrument basher.

Briefing was called for 17:00, where the CO announced that the target was Cologne. Next came the intelligence officer, followed by the heads of each separate department - navigation, wireless, gunnery, bomb aiming - finishing with the meteorological officer. After the main briefing, each crewmember went to their own offices to receive any special instructions relative to them. For example, the navigators would go to the navigation office and pick up all necessary maps, sextants, met reports, and any other equipment required by them for the operation. Then it was off to the locker room for everyone to collect their flying kit. At the due time, the transport arrived to take them over to the dispersals. Throwing their parachutes onto the back of the busses or canvas-covered trucks, they clambered aboard and set off for their aircraft. The crews were at the aircraft about an hour before take off, to carry out their checks and to prepare the bomber for the night's operation. About 20 minutes before the first aircraft was due to take off, a Very pistol heralded the time to start engines. One by one, in the proper sequence, the Merlins were fired up and thoroughly checked, along with the associated hydraulic, pneumatic and electrical systems that they powered. It was standard practice for the radio operators to test their equipment, unwittingly announcing to the German listening stations that a large raid was imminent. The German operators manning these stations knew the frequencies used by the various RAF bomber squadrons, and were aware that Middleton and Croft, amongst many other stations, were operating that night.

With the bombers fully checked and cleared as serviceable, when zero hour was reached, a Very pistol was fired, and the first aircraft began to taxi towards Croft's runway 27. In preparation for setting course at 23:35, S/L Kirkpatrick in EY-N became airborne from Croft at 23:06. He was followed by F/L Woodroffe in EY-L at 23:07, and F/O Bickerdike in EY-T at 23:10. P/O Wittingham flying EY-P was the 6th Halifax to take off from Croft at 23:20. This was about the time that Wing Commander David Young, in the first 76 Halifax, was turning onto Middleton's main runway. Seconds later, Middleton thundered to the sound of 20 Merlins, as, with hardly a minute between them, the first Halifaxes of 76 Squadron took off. Young in MP-Y was first off at 23:21, S/L Hank Iveson in MP-E at 23:22, F/S Thomas in MP-O at 23:23, F/L Michael Renaut in MP-A at 23:24, and P/O Philp in MP-F at 23:25. It took only five minutes for the next wave to congregate at the runway's holding point and they too kept up the snappy timing; P/O Perry in MP-C at 23:30, F/S Stell in MP-D at 23:31, Sgt Aston in MP-H at 23:33, F/L Warner in MP-M at 23:34, and Sgt Bingham MP-U at 23:36.

[65] Better known as riggers

Without further ado came Sgt Harwood in MP-S at 23:37, P/O McIntosh in MP-R at 23:38, F/S Kenny Clack in MP-Q at 23:39, P/O Kofoed in MP-U at 23:40. Practically all of the station was out to see the spectacle, certainly the groundcrew were working overtime. A twenty-one aircraft take-off had never been seen at Middleton, and with great credit to all on the station there were no non-starters. At 23:43, after only a three-minute breather, P/O Anderson in MP-T continued the flow. Next came Sgt Alcock in MP-W, who took off at 23:45, followed by F/S Tackley in MP-N at 23:46,

Towards the rear were Sgt West in MP-Z at 23:49, P/O Norfolkin in MP-B at 23:50, the penultimate crew off were in MP-K, flown by P/O Dobson, at 23:51. The last Halifax was logged out at 23:53, this was MP-L, flown by S/L Jock Calder. It had taken only 32 minutes to get all 21 aircraft airborne, an average of 90 seconds between each aircraft. No mean feat as the maximum number of 76 Squadron aircraft detailed for a raid up to this point in the war was around the 14 mark. At Croft they had despatched 22 Halifaxes, at an average time between them of 144 seconds (2.4 minutes). This too was an amazing effort and was to herald the shape of things to come.

Wing Commander David Young and his crew set course for Spalding. This Norfolk town, 15 miles northeast of Peterborough, was chosen for its proximity to the Wash, which lay just 9 miles away. This huge expanse of water with its unmistakable shape is just about as good as it gets as far as navigational landmarks go. Now settled down in the cruise at 3,000 feet, and with Middleton receding behind him, Young was feeling a little understaffed. Whereas a Halifax captain would normally have the usual crew of six or seven to accompany him, Young in fact had only four, F/S Garland, Sgt Dickson, Sgt Spriggs and P/O Higgins. There were many temporary crew changes taking place that night, as the more experienced members of the Command were used to bolster the operationally uninitiated, and make up the numbers. Not far behind Young's Halifax was R9457, A for Apple, which was flown by Michael Renaut. It was 130 miles down to Spalding, and at an indicated speed of 160 mph, Michael had calculated that it would take them approximately 48 minutes. He re-checked his course on the magnetic compass, 160°. They reached Spalding at 00:23, some six minutes early. Re-calculating their ground speed at 182 mph, the observer explained that they had a slight tailwind component. Overhead Spalding, A for Apple was turned onto its next compass heading, 118°. Next stop, Southwold, just nine miles south of Lowestoft. Again this coastal town was chosen for its prominent features. Less than a mile to the south of Southwold is the river Blyth, which is a natural inlet, leading from the sea at Walberswick to the sailor's haven of Blythburgh. Throughout the war, the navigators of Bomber Command would often utilise this easily identifiable visual reference point.

The 82 miles from Spalding were covered in 26 minutes. Young climbed to the required 5,000 feet en-route. Although their air speed indicator had been fairly steady on 160 mph, their ground speed had actually been 189. This would help their fuel consumption. The Halifax's most economical outbound cruise speed was 158 mph. This returned about 1.05 air miles per gallon of fuel. Over 160 mph, whilst fully loaded and with the superchargers in high gear, this fell off drastically. Even a 10 mph increase in speed would cause the air-miles per gallon to slip down the graph curve to .9 galls per air mile. After this, fuel economy plummeted to a disproportionate figure, so a tailwind, however slight, was much appreciated. Thundering out to sea, Young began to climb. They had 104 miles of sea to cross before reaching the Dutch Coast at Ouddorp. The course now was 111°. Thanks to a very strong northwesterly wind, their ground speed had risen to 231 mph. Twenty-seven minutes after leaving the English coast, they arrived overhead Ouddorp, at the briefed height of 12,000 feet. Yet again a new course and height was required for the final run-in to the target. Cologne lay 144 miles to the southeast, bearing 116°, ground-speed 221 mph, time to target 39 minutes. Young began a gentle climb to the bombing height of 14,000 feet. All aircraft bombed in bright moonlight, from a height of 14,000 feet. There was no cloud, and the visibility was described as excellent. All of 76's and 78's crews reported that, by the time they arrived at the target, a huge conflagration was laid out below them. The crew of Sgt Dennis's aircraft, W1014 of 78 Squadron, reported seeing two aircraft collide and one shot down over the target area. Sgt Dennis had 3 of his High Explosive bombs hang up in the bomb bay, along with three 30-lb and 9-lb incendiaries. On the return these were jettisoned, just after leaving the Dutch coast.

Sgt Lunan's crew, also from 78, saw another aircraft shot down over Cologne. Also on the way home, they reported seeing a bright light in the sea about 54 miles due west of the Dutch coast. During the take-off run of 78's L9264, flown by S/L James, a cockpit hatch blew open, and all attempts to close it failed. Despite the intense cold and wind buffet, he elected to continue with the operation. Despite his resolve, he had to jettison his bombs and turn back when the port outer began to overheat and became U/S. He landed safely back at Croft at 03:27, after 4 very cold hours in the air.

On their return to Croft at 05:00, P/O Bunclark's crew reported to the De-briefing Officer that on their arrival over Cologne, they had easily identified the target by the bends in the river. It was however, impossible to distinguish their bomb bursts, such was the intensity of the fires and the smoke. At 02:05, whilst at their bombing height of 14,000 feet, they saw a bomber explode over the target area. Wing Commander Seymour Lucas also utilised the river and bridges to identify his position. His bombs dropped from 14,500 feet and landed S/E of the marshalling yards. His bursts were seen, but they were quickly swallowed up by the fires started by the bombs of other aircraft. At 03:58, whilst at 12,000 feet on the way home, his aircraft began to ice up and the instruments became U/S. Thirty minutes later he gave the order to abandon the aircraft, after which he carried out a belly landing at Wittering, 9 miles N/W of Peterborough. Sadly, one of his crewmembers Sgt Webb was injured and died on the way to hospital. The only aircraft to be lost by Middleton or Croft on this raid was Halifax W1013, flown by P/O Foers of 78 Squadron. It collided with Hampden GL-P3 P5321 belonging to 14 OTU, based at Cottesmore, 9 miles N/W of Stamford. S/L Falconer DFC[66] the pilot, was the only member of the 4-man crew of the Hampden to survive. He had emerged from a rain cloud only to find 78's Halifax right in front of him, displaying its navigation lights. A collision was inevitable. Both aircraft crashed near March, Cambridgeshire, about 13 miles east of Peterborough. When 78's Halifax crashed, Sgts Bolton and Caie were killed; P/O Foers, Sgt Warner and F/S Gamble were injured. Only the navigator, Sgt Curtiss was uninjured. Despite severe injuries, Foers recovered, only to be killed later

[66] S/L D.B. Falconer had survived a serious crash whilst flying with 49 Squadron at Scampton a year earlier. Having been awarded the DFC and AFC, and now with the rank of Wing Commander, he was to lose his life on the 30th December 1944. As the C.O. of 156 Squadron flying Lancaster GT-N (PB621) out of Upwood, he was on his 55th trip when hit by flak, again on a raid to Cologne.

whilst on a raid to Krefeld on 2nd October 1942. He is buried along with 5 members of his crew in Rheinberg War Cemetery.

Owing to the icing conditions at 10,000 feet, the Halifaxes of 76 Squadron climbed rapidly to 15,000 feet, and then proceeded to the target at this altitude. The average temperature was minus 20° C. The opposition encountered, both over the Dutch Coast and the heavily defended en-route anti aircraft belt, was intense. However, by the time both 76 and 78 arrived over the target area itself, the searchlights and flak were practically non-existent, having been virtually inundated by the intensity of the raid. On arrival at the target area, which was clearly identified despite some slight cloud, the visibility was perfect, although dense smoke was rising up from the already burning city to a height of about 2,000 feet. This prevented accurate pinpointing of the actual aiming point. Although searchlights in the target area were not in evidence, the ones located in neighbouring districts were still active. Although there were no fighters to be seen, S/L Jock Calder was hit by heavy flak, fortunately without serious damage or injury.

Owing to the intensity of the fires already burning, it was difficult to observe individual bomb-bursts or the sticks of incendiaries as they hit. However, what could be seen was that the bombs dropped by the squadron certainly did add to the general conflagration, and enlarged the areas of destruction. On the return journey, the glow from the fires could be clearly seen from over 100 miles away. All of 76 Squadron's aircraft completed the operation with the exception of two. F/S Kenny Clack had to turn back due to low oil pressure in his port outer. Sgt Bingham had a similar problem. All 76 Squadron aircraft returned safely to Middleton, having dropped a total of 61 x 1,000-lb high explosive bombs, 488 x 30-lb and 16,380 x 4-lb incendiaries. This equates to 62.75 tons, each aircraft carrying an average of 6,496-lbs (2.9 tons).

On the ground, the Germans had to fight 2,500 separate fires. Cologne was a modern city, with less wooden buildings than most. This, and its wider streets, helped to reduce the spread of fire to some extent. However, 3,300 buildings were destroyed, and a further 2,090 badly damaged. Like most large cities, Cologne had many residential buildings, a large proportion of which were flats and apartments. The total number of dwelling units destroyed came to over 13,000, with 6,360 seriously damaged and 22,270 slightly damaged. Also totally destroyed were 14 public, 7 official administration, 4 university, and 10 postal and railway buildings. Also destroyed were 17 churches, 9 hospitals, 16 schools, 2 newspaper offices, 4 hotels, 6 department stores, 7 banks, 2 cinemas and 10 buildings of historical interest. The crews would have been pleased to learn that most of the 58 military personnel killed were from flak units. The city fire fighters and other emergency services were hampered by the loss of 17 water mains. Also cut were 32 mains electricity cables and 12 main telephone routes. Prior to this raid, Cologne had a population of 700,000 inhabitants. After the raid, it was reported that up to 486 had been killed and 5,027 injured. 45,132 were bombed out, and as many as 150,000 people decided to vacate the city to find somewhere safer to live. Up to this point, the highest number of aircraft lost during a single night's operations by Bomber Command had been 37. This had been during raids to Berlin, Cologne, Mannheim and other targets on 7/8th November 1941. The 1,000-bomber raid on Cologne created a new record with 41 aircraft (3.9%) being lost; 29 Wellingtons, 4 Manchesters, 3 Halifaxes, 2 Stirlings, 1 Hampden, 1 Lancaster and 1 Whitley.

76 and 78 - June 1942

June 1st saw the RAF undertake a second 1,000-bomber raid, or to be exact a 956 bomber raid, this time to Essen. The plan was similar to the one carried out on Hamburg, and employed 545 Wellingtons, 77 Stirlings, 127 Halifaxes, 74 Lancasters, 33 Manchesters, 29 Whitleys and 71 Hampdens. 21 of these aircraft belonged to 76, whilst 78 sent 20. Thirty-four aircraft were lost, including 3 Halifaxes from 78 and 1 from 76.

Sgt West of 76 was homebound from Essen with his crew in MP-J W1064 when the starboard inner began to vibrate. Soon after, it seized completely. Just when it seemed things could not get worse, they did. The Halifax was attacked by a night fighter, flown by Oblt Heinrich Prinz Zu Sayn - Wittgenstein, of III. /NJG2. MP-J crashed at 01:45, between Grez-Doiceau and Bossut, Belgium. Two members of the crew, Sgt West and J R Thompson, were killed, the remainder baled out. The engineer, Sgt W J Norfolk and the wireless operator, Sgt P Wright managed to evade capture, whilst the rear gunner, P/O W B Milligan RNZAF and the navigator, Sgt J A Oldfield were captured, and became POWs.

P/O J S Lawson RCAF was flying with his crew in 78 Squadron's Halifax R9364, when they found themselves receiving the unwanted attention of the German flak gunners over the Dutch Coast. Whilst taking avoiding action, Lawson discovered one of the less desirable traits of the early Halifaxes, rudder overbalance.[67] The Halifax entered a flat spin after the rudders locked over, which caused the bomber to crash into the sea. The Halifax broke in two, and by a miracle, F/S T B Miller GM RCAF and P/O P J Jones were thrown clear. Although badly injured, they managed to inflate the dinghy and clamber aboard. Having drifted for days, they eventually became POWs after being rescued by the Germans. The remainder of the crew were killed on impact.

The second 78 Squadron Halifax to be lost that night was EY-F W1143, flown by P/O H G Clothier RNZAF. This aircraft had been borrowed by 10 Squadron at Leeming. Having taken off from Leeming, this aircraft crashed in the waters of the Haringvliet, off Hellevoetsluis, 16 miles SW of Rotterdam. Only Clothier's body was found. He is buried in Crooswijk General Cemetery. His crew are commemorated on the Runnymede Memorial.

---

[67] On early marks of the Halifax, the triangular shaped rudders had a tendency to lock fully over to one side or the other if the rudder pedals were used too vigorously. This could cause the aircraft to spin, a fatal manoeuvre if at low altitude.

The third and final 78 Squadron Halifax to be lost, W7698, was flown by S/L G D Layland. Having left Croft at 22:55, this aircraft collided with a German night fighter 31 miles northwest of Essen, whilst over Bocholt. Having struck the enemy aircraft, the Halifax, which was travelling in a northeasterly direction, managed to fly on for a further 10 miles before crashing. The Halifax eventually came down 5 miles over the Dutch border at Winterswijk, Holland. S/L Layland, the navigator P/O L G Geddes RCAF, and the wireless operator Sgt C G Pugsley, survived to become POWs. The remainder of the crew, Sgt J Lyons, Sgt W Brooks and Sgt J Strang were killed. They are buried in the Canadian War Cemetery at Groesbeek, 5 miles S/S/E of the centre of Nijmegen.

Apart from the 34 aircraft lost on the main raid on Essen, one Mosquito had been shot down whilst attacking Cologne, and 3 Blenheims were lost on intruder raids to Venlo airfield, Holland. The breakdown of Bomber Command's losses on the Essen raid worked out at 9 Halifaxes, 16 Wellingtons, 4 Lancasters, 2 Stirlings, 1 Manchester, 1 Hampden, and 1 Whitley. 4 Group in particular had lost many Halifax crews. These included 3 from 78 at Croft, 3 from 10 Squadron at Leeming (including the one that flew EY-F W1143, which had been borrowed for the occasion from 78), 1 from 76 at Middleton, 1 from 102 Squadron at Dalton, 1 from 405 at Pocklington, and 2 from 460 at Breighton.

Although the weather was reasonable, many of the crews experienced great difficulty in locating the target, despite the large numbers of flares dropped by the raid leaders in 3 Group's Wellingtons. The south of the city received the most damage but this was reported by the Germans as being surprisingly light. They stated that only 11 houses were destroyed and 184damaged. Casualties on the ground were recorded as 15 people killed, with the injured totalling 91. During the raid a POW camp was also burned out. Once again the old problems with navigation and target identification reared their ugly heads, as bombs fell on at least 11 other towns in the Ruhr. Oberhousen in particular received much attention from the wayward bombers; 83 of its citizens were killed. Duisburg was also mis-identified. Here a further 52 people were reported as being killed. Mulheim lost 15. Of the 20 aircraft detailed at Croft for this raid, 17 claimed to have attacked the primary. After encountering large numbers of enemy fighters, one crew abandoned the operation and jettisoned their bombs in the sea, owing to the rear turret being jammed. The fate of the final two has already been described.

The following night, 7 of Croft's Halifaxes were again despatched for Essen. On their return, 6 reported having bombed the primary, whilst one had abandoned the op, again due to a jammed turret. It too jettisoned its bombs 'safe' in the sea. All of 78's Halifaxes returned safe. Unfortunately, back at Middleton, 76, who were on operations to Bremen, were not so lucky. They lost F/S Stell and his crew in MP-A R9457. This aircraft was shot down by Hauptmann Helmut Lent of II /NJG2, and crashed near St-Maartensvlotbrug, on the coast of the Dutch island of De-Koog, 50 miles north of Amsterdam. Five of the crew, including F/S Stell were killed, whilst the second pilot Sgt D H Nelson and the navigator Sgt R C Cockburn baled out and became POWs. F/S Stell and the front gunner Sgt C R Metcalfe have no known graves; the engineer Sgt W Archer, wireless operator Sgt D P Brooks and tail gunner Sgt R Greenwood lie in Bergen General Cemetery. Pilot Officer Philp and his crew took off from Middleton at 23:14 in Halifax MP-F W1104 never to return. It is presumed that this aircraft was lost somewhere over the North Sea. The bodies of P/O J A Philp and the tail gunner Sgt W Watson were never found. The bodies of engineer Sgt J Battersby and wireless operator Sgt R S Mulhauser RCAF were washed ashore, and rest in Germany's Sage War Cemetery. The navigator, Sgt F E Ormerod and front gunner, Sgt J H Harte came ashore on the Island of Vlieland, where they are buried in the General Cemetery. Sgt Mulhauser was actually an American from Huntington Woods, Michigan.

Whilst taking off from Goosepool at 23:03, Sgt Bingham, flying MP-U W1035 ran over a Glim lamp. Bingham elected to continue with the operation and successfully bombed the primary, Bremen. On arrival back at Middleton, he ordered his crew to take up their crash positions behind the main spar, and began his final approach. All was well until the Halifax touched down. The port undercarriage leg collapsed, causing considerable damage to the aircraft. After the aircraft cart-wheeled to a stop, and even before the dust had settled, the uninjured crew scrambled for the hatches and put as much distance between them and the aircraft as possible.

June 3rd saw 2 Halifaxes of 78 Squadron attack Bremen, whilst on the 5th a further 10 were again detailed for Ops to Essen. Whilst climbing away from Croft the port inner of P/O H E Bedford's Halifax burst into flames. Showing great flying skill, Bedford managed to retain control of the stricken bomber and began a wide circuit of the airfield at 150 feet. The crew jettisoned the bombs, flares and incendiaries 'safe' before turning onto final approach. As they did so, the port wing dropped, and after only 4 minutes in the air the Halifax crashed and burst into flames. P/O Bedford and 2 other crewmembers were killed, the other 4 were injured. Out of the 4 aircraft sent to Essen by 76, one flown by P/O McIntosh turned back with engine trouble, the remaining 3 bombed the target and returned safely.

1516 BAT Flight were politely informed on the 4th that they were required to vacate their offices in No.2 hangar, in anticipation of 78's return to Goosepool from Croft. Accommodation at Middleton was at a premium at the best of times during the war, and 1516 found themselves relegated to a tented HQ. At the time, 1516 were in the process of changing over to the new alcoholised fuel, and were draining the tanks of all their aircraft and refilling with the new fuel. This was completed by the 7th. That afternoon, five of 76's Halifaxes took part in an unsuccessful sea search for a Spitfire, which was reported to have come down in the sea.

The 8th saw Essen on the agenda once again, as 6 aircraft from both 76 and 78 at Croft successfully bombed the primary. Middleton's Base Commander Tommy Trail tagged along with Michael Renaut's crew as a gash bomb-aimer in MP-L. Their route was: Base – Flamborough Head – Katwijk – Essen. The return trip was via Brussels – 050° 57' North, 025° 50' East (9 miles south of Beachy Head) – Orfordness – Spalding – Base. The total bomb-load carried by 76's Halifaxes was 18 x 1,000-lb GP bombs, plus 4840 x 4-lb and 144 x 30-lb incendiaries. The target itself was the residential area to the southeast of the Krupps Works. The weather conditions were classed as being good, due to there being no cloud and fine visibility. The target itself was clearly identified by the Krupps Works and Duisburg docks, by the light of the flares. All bombing took place between 01:12 and 01:27.

Back to Goosepool

Two days later on June 10th a raid involving 9 of Croft's Halifaxes was cancelled just before take-off. These aircraft joined the remainder of 78's aircraft as they began the move back to RAF Middleton St George. Also moving out was Croft's Conversion Flight, which departed to Dalton, near Topcliffe.

Having moved back to Middleton, Norman Thompson and the rest of 78's groundcrew also found out that there was no room at the inn. Before going over to Croft, they had the comforts of the centrally heated H-Blocks, now they, were temporarily relegated to a tented camp on the playing field opposite the Sergeants' Mess, sandwiched between the guardroom and the Station HQ building.

On the morning of the 16th, P/O Perry of 76 Squadron took up one of their Halifaxes for an air test. This aircraft was MP-A BB199. Perry had along with him a crew of 6. During the flight, the port inner engine caught fire. The flames from the engine reached the petrol tanks and the fire quickly spread along the entire wing. It was not possible to feather the propeller on the burning engine as no hydraulic feathering pumps were fitted. In order to save his crew, at 11:05, P/O Perry attempted to crash-land the Halifax in a field. As the aircraft was about to touch down it sank, and ploughed through some tall trees. Sgt Hoskins the tail gunner was fatally injured when the trees ripped his turret from the fuselage. Perry himself was also slightly injured in the ensuing crash.

During the evening of the 19/20th Ops to Emden were carried out by 78. F/S Crow had taken off from Middleton at 23:43 along with his crew in BB200. Nothing further was heard from this aircraft. It is thought that the Halifax may have crashed into the sea somewhere off the S/W coast of Denmark. The body of the engineer Sgt R K Frankland was washed ashore, and now lies in Kiel's War Cemetery. The sea also gave up the body of the navigator Sgt R W Morgan. He is buried 85 miles away, in the Fourfelt Cemetery at Esbjerg, on the outskirts of the Danish coastal town of Jerne. F/S M M Crow and the rest of the crew have no known graves. They are commemorated on the Runnymede Memorial.

Emden was the target for 76 on the night of June 20/21st. P/O Norfolk and his crew were hit by flak whilst flying at 15,000 feet. They were then attacked by a night fighter,[68] and the Halifax crashed near Ulrum, 13 miles NW of Groningenin, Holland. The captain, P/O H Norfolk and the wireless operator did not survive the crash; the remainder of the crew however, managed to bale out. As the bomber plummeted to earth, the tail gunner Sgt Salway quickly scrambled to the escape hatch. Once there he realised that he did not have his parachute. His friend Sgt Smith, the front gunner, told Salway to hang onto his back so they could jump together. Sadly, as Sgt Smith's parachute opened, the jolt caused Salway to lose his grip, and he fell to his death. His body was found at Houwerzijl, just over a mile away from Ulrum. The rest of the crew, including Sgt Smith, survived to become POWs. This also included Sgt Painter, who had survived the crash landing of Halifax BB 199, flown by P/O Perry on the 16th.

On June 24th , Norman Frankish was servicing a 76 Squadron Halifax out on the flights. It was 11:18, and his thoughts were about how long it would be before he could stop for lunch. Whilst he worked, he became aware of the sounds of two approaching aircraft. The next thing he heard was a loud bang. Looking up he saw two aircraft falling to earth. One of them was a 76 Squadron Halifax, the other an Airspeed Oxford from 1516 BAT Flight. Both aircraft had been flying quite low, in and out of the cloud base, and had collided head-on over the airfield after the Oxford suddenly broke cloud and found the Halifax in its path. The Oxford, serial number V4140, had been practising a SBA.[69] Its two pilots would have had their heads down inside the cockpit, concentrating on the instrument panel. This would account for them not seeing the Halifax until it was too late. In fact, the Oxford's pilots tried to dive under the Halifax at the last moment, but the tail unit struck the bomber. The Oxford disintegrated and fell in small pieces onto the airfield. The Halifax, W7661, spun in from about 2,000 feet, and crashed just inside the airfield's western perimeter. It hit just a few yards from a parked aircraft that was being worked on by 76 groundcrew. They had beaten a hasty retreat after the sound of the collision, as bits began to rain down close by. Sgt Bingham and his crew in the Halifax, along with the two occupants of the twin engined Oxford, Instructor Sgt F R Mason and pupil Sgt Sealey, died of multiple injuries and burns. Two Queen Mary's arrived the next day from 83 MU to remove the Cat E wreckage of both aircraft.

This accident was to herald the start of several more that took place during the next few days. The very next day, Halifax MP-D R9482 began to take off from Middleton for an air test when it crashed almost immediately. It was suspected that one, or even two, port engines had failed during the takeoff run. The aircraft, having reached about 100 feet, stalled and spun into the ground, where it burst into flames. The pilot, Sgt Aston, along with Sgt Smith, Sgt Barnett, P/O Cole, and Sgt Richardson died. The rear gunner, P/O Higgins DFM was injured and taken to the Darlington Memorial Hospital but died later. The mid-upper gunner, Sgt Richardson had also survived the crash of BB199 back on the 16th whilst flying with P/O Perry. Later that day, around 20:00, a 76 conversion flight Halifax, MP-K R9378, was being prepared for a raid on Bremen. As the groundcrew fussed over the aircraft, some of the incendiaries that formed its bomb load fell out of the bomb bay and onto the tarmac. They ignited, and the aircraft burst into flames. Despite the valiant efforts of the fire crew, the Halifax completely burned out.

The 25th also saw Sgt J E Meyer RCAF and his crew take-off for Bremen in 76 Halifax II MP-G W7747. Nothing is known of this aircraft's fate, it was lost without trace. Mayer and his crew are commemorated on the Runnymede Memorial. Seventeen of 78's aircraft were detailed for operations to Bremen on the same night. One was a non-starter, 13 aircraft bombed targets in Bremen (simply labelled D and X in the squadron's operational record book). One aircraft failed to return. This Halifax was W1067, flown by F/O J A Whittingham. Shot down by Unteroffizier Heinz Vinke of II /NJG2, this aircraft crashed into the Ijssselmere, just off the Dutch Coast. F/O Whittingham is buried in the Hemelumer-Oldeferd

[68] Possibly Oblt Egmont Prinz Zur Luppe
[69] Simulated Beam Approach

General Cemetery, whilst Sgt Dronfield's body was never found. He is commemorated on the Runnymede Memorial. The rest of the crew became POWs. Sadly, the rear gunner Sgt R A Brown died in captivity on 22nd April 1945, just a few days before the end of the war. His grave has since been lost.

The next morning, just after starting work on the south side of the airfield, Norman Thompson was removing the cowling from an engine when a tractor pulled up along side the Halifax he was working on. The driver told Norman that he had to tow a Halifax from the perry track near the end of the runway to its dispersal. The aircraft had landed during the early hours, after completing its sortie to Bremen. He asked Norman if he would mind sitting in the cockpit and working the brakes. Norman jumped down from the servicing gantry and jumped onto the tractor. As they travelled to the bottom of the airfield he wondered why the crew had left it close to the end of the runway and had not taxied it to its proper dispersal. Perhaps it had run out of fuel. Once at the aircraft the driver hitched up the tractor to the tail of the Halifax whilst Norman climbed up into the cockpit. To Norman, when being towed, it always seemed strange to be sitting in a Halifax travelling backwards, but that was the way it had to be done. The tractor driver pulled the Halifax to a very remote part of the perry track, well away from all of the other parked aircraft. By now Norman was wondering what was going on. Once the aircraft stopped. The driver unhitched the tractor and Norman applied the parking brake. To be able to hear any instructions from the tractor driver, Norman, who had been sitting in the pilot's seat, had slid the cockpit side window open. Norman was sat operating the controls, pretending to be bombing the Ruhr, when the driver pulled up along side. 'You had better get out of there' he shouted up to Norman with a funny look on his face. 'There's a live cookie hung up in the bomb bay, the crew left it at the end of the runway last night and walked back, rather than risk taxiing it'. With that the driver departed as fast as he could in a cloud of exhaust smoke. Norman was out of the aircraft in a flash, he remembers overtaking the tractor as he put as much distance between himself and the Halifax as possible. He was only too pleased that whilst he played at dropping bombs on Germany; he hadn't got as far as pressing the bomb release switch.

Bremen B was the target for 78 on the night of the 27th, when only 7 out of the 11 aircraft detailed managed to bomb. The remainder had the usual mechanical problems. Sgt Dennis attacked the primary from 15,000 feet, but 10/10ths cloud-cover prevented the results being observed. During the homeward journey, they developed engine trouble and began to lose height. By the time they were 40 miles from the East Coast of England, they were down to within 200 feet of the sea. They sent off a SOS transmission, and by a miracle they managed to coax the two remaining engines to get them up to 1,000 feet. They limped on, and crossed the coast near Hull. Turning north and flying up the coast they landed safely at Catfoss airfield, still on 2 engines. On the 28th, Halifax MP-N W7665 crashed at Middleton whilst carrying out a simulated 3 engined approach. All of the crew were injured, including the pilot, F/S S Tackley, who died the following day whilst being treated in Darlington's Memorial Hospital. The loss of 4 aircraft in 4 days to non-operational flights was, to say the least, bad for 76's moral. The final operation for June went to 78 Squadron on the 29th, when Bremen D was attacked. All 5 Halifaxes detailed managed to bomb the primary, although no results were observed due to 8/10ths-cloud cover. All aircraft returned to Middleton safely.

A small section of the Reichswald Forest war cemetery   Photo: author

76 and 78 - July 1942

On July1st 1942, Field Marshal Erwin Rommel launched a strong armoured attack on the Alamein line and the British 8th army commanded by General Richie. This had been preceded by a new German North African offensive that had begun on June 15th. By the 21st, Tobruk, under the allied Commander in Chief General Auchinlech, had surrendered. This was not a new battle but one that had played seesaws for two years or more. The Africa Corps, along with their allies the Italians, had struck eastwards from Libya and sought control of the strategic port of Tobruk. Their eventual aim was to capture Egypt and the Suez Canal. From there would come the next onslaught, to reach out for the Persian Gulf and its oil. The British Eighth Army made a tactical retreat to Alamein and began forming a strong line of defence ready for Rommel's arrival. Fortunately, counter attacks by the allied forces prevented Rommel from breaking through. The Allied Commanders realised that he who had air superiority had the upper hand, and so with this in mind they plotted to turn the tide. In response to events taking place in North Africa, back at Middleton St George, 76 had received orders to prepare 16 aircraft and crews for a 16-day detachment to Palestine. Norman Frankish remembers that they took the groundcrew with them in the aircraft. At Leeming, 10 Squadron were also preparing to join the party and they too swung into action.

The squadron's experience against German ships at Brest and other ports such as Kiel would stand them in good stead against the Italian fleet. Norman also recalls that the aircraft were being fitted out for their flight south. Long-range fuel tanks were fitted to the aircraft. They were then flown to observe the fuel consumption of each aircraft before their eventual departure. Sand filters were added to the engine air intakes. Spare engines were loaded into the aircraft with other spares and tools. On the 2nd, 78 Squadron detailed 6 aircraft to bomb Bremen D. Many large fires were started as the bombs fell across the target area, all aircraft returned safe. On the 8th, a Halifax became a non-starter when one of its wheels went off the peri-track and the aircraft became bogged down. This reduced the squadron's strength to 5, but the target, which was the submarine base at Wilhelmshaven, was successfully attacked. All aircraft returned safely, including one that had to land at Driffield on 3 engines.

On the 9th, Wing Commander J B Tait DSO DFC assumed Command of 78 Squadron, whilst W/C A H S Lucas was posted to Driffield. 76 Squadron crews were summoned to a briefing, where it was announced that the target was the Italian fleet, which was concentrated in the eastern Mediterranean. They were to take off the next morning at 06:00 for Gibraltar; the detachment was expected to last 7 days. As it was to be such a short detachment, they were warned to take only a steel helmet, a spongebag, and their lightweight khaki drill. They were instructed to leave their rooms just as they were, and not to touch any of their personal belongings as they would be back within the week. Security was very rigid, phone lines were cut, and letters home were opened and censored. They were also asked not to write any letters for the first seven days once they got to where they were going. Many of the crew illegally had their wives and sweethearts secreted in accommodation in Darlington, Stockton, and other surrounding areas close to the airfield. During the war, RAF rules stated that no wives were to be allowed to live within 12 miles of any airfield, a rule strongly, but not always successfully, enforced.

Next morning was the 10th, and the first wave of aircraft, complete with a full complement of groundcrew, began departing Goosepool for the first leg to Gibraltar at 03:50. First off was P/O Bill Kofoed NZAF and his crew, followed by F/S Granger, S/L Hank Iveson,[70] F/S Thomas, F/O Bickerdike, Wickham, P/O Raymond and finally F/L Bryan. Next day, 8 other crews were detailed to follow in their footsteps. Some of the crews were in their aircraft and about to take off when, at the last moment, this order was cancelled. On the 13th Duisburg D was the target for 78, all returned safe.

On the 14th, eight more of 76's aircraft traced the steps of the first wave. They were flown by the boss, W/C David Young, along with S/L Warner, F/O Knox, P/O Kenny Clack, F/S Brown, F/L Michael Renaut, F/S Alcock and P/O McIntosh RAAF. With the departure of these 16 aircraft, 76, under the command of S/L Calder DFC, was left with 1 serviceable aircraft. There were no crews available, as all the fully qualified captains had departed for Gibraltar. The remaining aircrew members of the squadron were grouped together under the command of P/O D Anderson.

Michael Renaut had become airborne from Middleton at exactly 06:00, along with his crew of 6, and with 4 fitters travelling as passengers. They set course for their first turning point, Blackpool. They then turned south, past the Welsh Coast, and then began their long flight over the Atlantic. Braking land at St David's Point on the Pembrokeshire Coast, they then changed course to the south. To their left and in the distance they could vaguely maintain a view of southern England, until the rear gunners eventually lost sight of Penzance.

Just over 500 miles later, they made landfall at Cape Finisterre, on the northwestern coast of Spain. From here they flew south just off the Spanish Coast. When they had left Middleton at six a.m. it was chilly, but by now the temperature inside the cockpit was becoming rather warmer. Bit by bit they began to shed their layers of heavy flying clothing. This started with the Sidcot flying suit, a bit further south the woollen pullovers were also discarded. Next came Portugal. By Lisbon, the sun was beating through the Perspex and it became very uncomfortable. Their battledress tops, shirts and trousers were the last to go. Having reached the Strait of Gibraltar they turned east, and Michael made his final approach into Gib clad only in his underwear. The 1,673-mile flight had taken them just over 8 hours and 45 minutes. At Gibraltar, the 1,200-yard runway perched between the rock and the sea looked very short. By keeping the revs up and flying a powered approach in the very bumpy conditions caused by the airflow around the rock, and with judicious use of the brakes, they stopped without getting their feet wet. 10 Squadron's Halifaxes, under the command of W/C Seymour Price, were already there. It turned out that Rommel was carrying out a sudden counter-attack against British troops and 76 had arrived at an inappropriate moment; however, after some doubt and a short delay they did in fact depart for the Canal Zone.

---

[70] The leader of the first wave of 8 aircraft

During September, their so-called temporary detachment saw them amalgamated into 462 Squadron of the Royal Australian Airforce. I hope the reader will forgive me, but it is not within the scope of this book to cover the Middle East detachment's glorious exploits, as they are covered admirably in other publications. Suffice it to say that this 16-day soiree to warmer climes in fact lasted much longer than that. Norman Frankish remembers that a small number of these aircraft did return to Middleton, but this was about a month after their departure. When they landed they unloaded crate after crate of bananas. The balance, however, remained in the Middle East and did not return to Middleton. The squadron had a very hard time whilst in the Canal Zone. They were sent there during a very fluid period, when Rommel was making his counter attack against the 4th British Army. On their arrival at the destination airfield,[71] 76 did not get a very rousing reception, and were left to their own devices. The conditions were atrocious. The semi-constant wind ensured that sand (the nasty gritty type) got into everywhere. One airman asked some one to pass the jam during one typical lunchtime break; his oppo waved his hand over a huge swarm of flies gathered on the table, thus revealing the jam pot.

F/L Michael Renaut completed his 35th trip whilst operating from Fayid, an airfield near Cairo. He was then screened from operations, as this was the end of his first tour. He was posted to 2 Middle East Training School at LG 224, better known as Aqir. Here he worked as an instructor, joining David Young, its commander. Later Michael returned to England on the Mauritania during April of 1943. After a short spell of leave, he was posted as a flying instructor to Marsden Moor which was, and still is, located on the Wetherby to York road. G/C Cheshire was the Station Commander, and he told Michael that his old friend David Young was now the Station Commander at Rufforth and wanted him there. Rufforth is an airfield just 4 miles from Marsden Moor along the B1224 road, and only four miles west of the centre of York. The next day Michael arrived there to begin training crews from 4 Group. He was appointed Deputy Flight Commander under S/L Hank Iveson, who also had recently returned from the Middle East. Soon after for the Middle East detachment, the wheel turned full circle as Hank Iveson and Kenny Clack rejoined 76 at Holme-on-Spalding-Moor, after the squadron moved there from Linton on June 16th 1943.

Hank Iveson

Douglas Iveson was born in Hull on November 21st 1917. Educated locally he became an office boy for a cement manufacturer. He joined the RAF Volunteer Reserve in May 1939 and learned to fly during weekends. Because he was six foot three and sported a huge handlebar moustache, he was christened 'Hank', after the famous cartoon character of the time. When war broke out, the newly commissioned Pilot Officer Iveson was posted on an instructor's course at the RAF's Central Flying School.

In 1941 he was again posted, this time to 77 Squadron, to fly Whitleys. During his first Whitley flight as captain, one of his engines failed and the aircraft ended up in the bomb dump, where the bomb-load exploded, but not before Iveson vacated the aircraft. He was very lucky to survive.

Having joined 76 at Goosepool, he served with the squadron until he was sent to the Middle East in July 1942. Having returned from the Middle East in November 1943, he commanded 76 Squadron at Holm-On-Spalding Moor, where he carried out a full tour of operations before being screened. After a spell as a Chief Flying Instructor, he was sent on a public relations tour of America.

After the end of hostilities, he commanded 51 Squadron, which was flying Avro York and Short Stirling transport aircraft. After that he went to 1639 Heavy Transport conversion unit as a Chief Flying Instructor on Douglas DC3 Dakotas. Then there were more staff appointments and a winter trials command in Canada. In 1947, he commanded the staging post set up in Moscow for the all-important four-power conference. On his return from Russia he was given a permanent commission before taking up yet another post, this time with the Empire Navigation School. Whilst serving there he commanded the navigation research and development squadron. Toronto, Canada became his new home in 1949 when he attended the RCAF Staff College. The following year he moved south to the Headquarters of the Second Airforce of the American Strategic Air Command. This was followed by a conversion onto the B47 Stratojet in Florida. He eventually returned to the UK, where he took up a staff position with Bomber Command, and was chief flying instructor at 232 OCU.

Flying a Handley Page Victor at an average speed of 655mph, Iveson set a new world's record of 2 hours and 44 seconds on October 14th 1958, whilst flying between London and Malta. His next post was as Station Commander of the V bomber base at Waddington in Lincolnshire, where he remained until 1960. He was then posted to Singapore during 1961 as an intelligence officer with the Far East Air Force Command. His last appointment began in 1964 when he joined Headquarters Signals Command. After 25 years of service he finally retired in 1967, having been awarded the DFC (twice), and the DSO He was also mentioned in despatches and later received a Queen's Commendation.

Squadron leader Douglas (Hank) Iveson DSO DFC
Photo: IWM CH.14798

Hank Iveson went on to serve as Secretary and Director of the Sheffield and Rotherham Chamber of Commerce until 1982, when he moved to Filey. His last official position was as head of the 76 Squadron Association. Group Captain Douglas (Hank) Iveson died on Thursday 8th December 1994 in St Catherine's Hospice in Scarborough, age 77. Margaret, his wife of 53 years had died just two months earlier. They had met whist she served as a nurse at RAF Brize Norton during 1940. They left two daughters, and a son, Group Captain Robert Iveson, who carried on the Iveson flying tradition. He won the Air Force Cross whilst flying a Harrier during the Falklands war, and went on to command 617, formerly the famous Dam Buster Squadron.

Kenny Clack

Squadron Leader, Kenny Clack DFM flew his last operation on the night of March 30/31st 1944. Now on his second tour with 76 Squadron, he was flying Halifax MP-X LW696 to Nuremberg.[72] He had taken off at 22:10 from Holm-On-Spalding Moor, and while outbound to the target he was shot down by a night fighter. His Halifax crashed at Daubhausen, and all on board were killed. They are buried at Hannover War Cemetery. Lost with Kenny that night was his bomb-aimer F/O D C Nowell DFM. He, too, was a second tour man, who also had served with 76 at Middleton during 1942. Kenny Clack had earned the DFM during his first tour with 76 at Middleton.

Meanwhile, back at Goosepool, on July 15th 1942, 76 were trying to rebuild the squadron the best way that they could. Sgt Butt and his crew were able to carry out a navigation test only by borrowing an aircraft from 78. Butt was one of the only two medium captains on the squadron. This number was reduced to one when, on the 18th, he departed for a BAT course at Driffield. On the night of July 19/20th 78 despatched 9 Halifaxes to Vegesack, near Bremen.[73] One of these was borrowed from 76, complete with crew. This aircraft developed a problem with its TR1335 radio transmitter and returned early, having jettisoned its bomb load in the sea at approximately 20° east (about 35 miles off the East Coast). The Halifax was seen crossing the airfield at 3,000 feet, flying an erratic course whilst steadily losing height. Soon after, 5 of the crew baled out. Later, word arrived that the captain, F/S Belous RCAF, and the engineer, Sgt Hebron, had been killed when the aircraft crashed at Yarm. Yarm Ambulance Service had rushed to the scene and was later praised for the professional help that they provided. On the 21st, seven of 78's aircraft attacked Duisburg D. During the day, 76 received Halifax BB195 when it was ferried in from 12 MU. Their total number of operational captains had reached 2, one fresher and one screened, although there were no serviceable aircraft. Two nights later, 6 of 78's aircraft were again sent to Duisburg D. During the day two more Halifaxes, 76 for the use of, arrived at Middleton, one from English Electric at Preston and one from 8 MU. Just for good measure, 78 went back yet again to Duisburg D, on the 25th. These three raids had been lucky for the squadron, as all aircraft had returned safe.

A Conversion Flight Halifax belonging to 76 was also among the strong contingent of bombers sent to Hamburg on the night of the 26/27th. Sgt Butt in R9485 was at 18,000 feet over the target when the aircraft was set on fire by flak. The Halifax was immediately turned to the southwest and the crew elected to attempt a forced landing. During the last few moments of flight, Sgt Butt flew the stricken bomber through some trees, and in so doing removed the wings (and fuel). It is some testimony to his flying skills that 4 of the crew survived to become POWs, including Sgt Butt himself. The same night, 78's commander, W/Cdr Willie Tait, was leading the squadron, as they, too attacked Hamburg D. The visibility was good, as from his bombing height of 16,000 feet the docks were clearly identified. Sgt Marshall the second pilot saw their HE bombs burst accurately in the target area, and their scattered incendiaries caused extensive fires over a wide area. There was, coincidentally, a second Tait flying that night, in the form of Sgt Tait, commander of another of 78's Halifaxes, R9454. Unlike his namesake, his operation was not going to plan, as half way across the North Sea, his Halifax developed a nasty Glycol leak in the port outer engine.[74] Turning back to base, the bombs were jettisoned in the sea at 54° 34' North - 05° 03' East (70 miles due east of Redcar). They had been carrying Nickels and these were brought back to Middleton. Flying Officer Mitchener and his crew also took off for Hamburg that night. 78 Squadron's records simply state, 'This aircraft was airborne at 22:53 hours. Since then nothing has been heard of either aircraft or crew.' It must therefore be presumed 'Missing'. It was very difficult for the squadrons to gain information as to the whereabouts of their aircraft at any one time. They either came home or in due course information of their demise would filter through from the Germans. No such information was received concerning this aircraft. It was lost without trace. The crew of W1184 are commemorated on the Runnymede Memorial.

Meanwhile, in Suffolk, 419 Squadron at Mildenhall was operating its Wellingtons IIIs against Hamburg on the night of the 28/29th. One aircraft in particular, VR-H X3488, had been flown by Wing Commander John Fulton RCAF. It is presumed that this aircraft crashed into the North Sea. Wing Commander Fulton was a Canadian from Kamloops British Columbia serving with the RAF. John Fulton would leave a legacy of leadership and proficiency to be rekindled at Middleton some months hence.

The following night, 78 sent their Halifaxes to Saarbrucken. Having taken off from Middleton at 23:10, F/S Dennis and his crew were attacked several times by a night fighter whilst over the Belgian coast. Time after time their adversary came in for the kill. F/S Dewhurst the Halifax's tail gunner identified it as a Ju88. He returned fire and on the last pass he hit the fighter and it fell to earth. By now F/S Dennis was unable to maintain height. They soldiered on but eventually gravity won and they had to ditch off Calais. Such was the severity of the fighter attack that it was with some amazement that the crew found themselves uninjured. They quickly vacated the sinking Halifax and took to the dinghy. They drifted for over 14 hours, expecting a German vessel to turn up at any moment. Eventually a boat did hove into view on the horizon. Their hearts sank as they saw it was heading straight for them. Eventually it arrived and hauled the Halifax's crew aboard. The

---

[72] The disastrous Nuremberg raid
[73] The target was the Vulkan U-boat yard
[74] Merlin engines were water-cooled. Glycol (antifreeze) was mixed with the water. Some pilots feared a Glycol fire more than one involving petrol.

boat's crew turned out to be surprisingly friendly and immediately broke out the Rum. The Coxswain pointed the bow of the RAF Air Sea rescue launch in the general direction of west, and headed back to Dover.

By the 31st, 76 had 3 operational crews and the same number of serviceable aircraft. The closing entry for July goes to 76 and the crew of P/O Ronnie Waite in particular. They were on operations to Dusseldorf on the night of the 31st in MP-B BB195. For Ronnie, this was only his second trip as a fresher captain, having only qualified on the 22nd. Having carried out their attack on the target they headed for home. When over southern Holland they were attacked simultaneously by a Ju88 and a Messerschmitt Bf110. The Halifax's crew, completely outgunned and outmanoeuvered, stood very little chance. A pitched battle ensued, and despite operating under a hail of fire the Halifax crew acquitted themselves very well. The Ju88 came off worst when the Halifax's tail gunner, P/O Glasgow, shot it down. It had been flown by one of Germany's greatest Luftwaffe aces, Hauptmann Herbert Boensch, whose tally of allied planes shot down had reached 30. The Bf110 broke off the attack and disappeared. As they continued home it was realised that the mid-upper gunner, Sgt McAuley, had been fatally wounded, the navigator and P/O Glasgow in the tail turret were also wounded. The Halifax had also been badly mauled in the attack, all instrumentation was shot to hell. It was doubtful that the aircraft would reach the UK, let alone Middleton.

The nav told Waite their only option was to set their course by the pole star. Fortunately, for a while anyway, they were able to limp on, losing height all the way. By the skin of their teeth, they reached the British Coast, south at Orfordness, by which time they were committed to abandoning the aircraft. The six surviving airmen baled out, leaving the body of Sgt McAuley on the doomed aircraft, which crashed at Fristling Farm, near Stock on the B1007, 2 miles west of the Hanningfield reservoir, and just 3 miles south of Cheltenham. Safely on the ground, albeit widely dispersed, the airmen headed independently for the nearest village pub, where they toasted their survival with a pint of wartime beer. Featured in the Daily Mail, the crew's feat of bravery was hailed throughout the land. Unfortunately their senior officers dismissed their claims as a sham. They felt that it was highly unlikely that the Ju88 and Messerschmitt would have been operating together.

During December 1994, Dutch workers digging the foundations for a new office block found the remains of a German aircraft. The remains of its three-man crew were still inside. Dutch Historian Hans Onderwater was able to trace the plane's military records. They confirmed that it had been a Ju88, which had been shot down whilst patrolling with a Bf110 on the night of the July 31st 1942. At the time of the discovery in 1994, Ronnie Waite, by then an 82-year-old retired optician, was highly delighted that the top brass had been proven wrong. He admitted that at first he was really upset that the senior officers had not believed him, although they still put the story out for propaganda purposes. After the passing of time however he came to accept it. The tail gunner Sam Glasgow was even more annoyed, he was at the business end of the Halifax and during the attack had the best seat in the house during the attack. He was in no doubt as to who or what was firing at them, but still the brass would not budge. The Senior Officers had believed British intelligence reports, which stated that German night fighters never flew in pairs. It was accepted at the time that British Bombers had only a one in five chance of surviving an attack by a single night fighter. To double up was considered to be a complete waste of resources. One possibility is that the Ju88 had been flying with the Messerschmitt because it had been testing experimental airborne interception radar, which was under development at the time.

Sgt McAuley is buried in St Oswalds Roman Catholic Churchyard in Longton, Lancashire. The crew of the Ju88, Haptmann Herbert Boensch, F/W Otto Botcher and F/W August Willie, paid the ultimate price for their attack on BB195.

76 and 78 - August 1942

Bochum was the target for 78 on August 5th when Sgt Stevens and 3 of his crew were forced to abandon W1180 over Odilienberg, Holland. They became POWs, but no details are available as to why Sgts Clark, Gall (RAAF) and Gilbert (RCAF) did not bale out. All three are buried in the Jonkerbos War Cemetery, Nijmegen, Holland. Of the 5 aircraft detailed, one was a non-starter and two returned early, one with a petrol leak, the other with an undercarriage that would not retract and a U/S port outer boost gauge. The remaining crews found Bochum covered in a ground haze, which prevented accurate observation of the bombing. Goosepool's crews must have been the only ones to bomb the target, as the official report on this operation states that out of the 8 aircraft sent by Bomber Command that night, only 3 actually bombed Bochum.

78 also sent two aircraft Nickeling to the Paris area. The weather was good, and with the Parisians' usual half hearted attempt at the blackout, the crews had little problem in finding the place. Also on August 5th, Goosepool heralded the arrival of Squadron Leader Leonard Cheshire DSO DFC, older brother of Christopher Cheshire, who as you have read, was shot down during August 1941. Leonard Cheshire took command of the remaining contingent of 76 Squadron. He had been asked to whip the squadron back into an effective bomber force. Meanwhile, on a raid to Duisburg on the night of August

Wing commander Leonard Cheshire, centre, with 76 squadron football team. Norman Frankish, back row 4th from right
Photo: Norman Frankish

6/7th, Halifax EY-P W1237 of 78 Squadron was shot down by Hauptmann Heinrich Prinz Zu Sayn-Wittgenstein of I /NJG1. This attack took place at 04:15, and the Halifax came down in the sea, 6 miles west of the Hook of Holland. The only body to come ashore was that of the rear gunner Sgt J Hoare, who is buried in the General Cemetery. Whilst the German pilot was a Prince, the bomber's pilot, F/O J M J A d'Ursel Chevalier of the Order Leopold, and Croix de Guerre, was the son of a Belgian Count.

Lost with him that night were his crew of F/Ss Luck and Johnston RCAF, and Sgts Cole, Scott, Cantwell and Hoare RAF. With the exception of Sgt Hoare, they are all are commemorated on the Runnymede Memorial. 78's luck was well and truly out on the 9th, when a raid on Osnabruck became somewhat of a fiasco. 7 aircraft had been detailed for the raid but only two actually got to the target and bombed. Four aircraft had taken off, when the fifth had one of its engines cut out on the take-off run. It blocked the runway thus preventing the two remaining aircraft from taking-off. Now down to four aircraft, the airborne contingent of the squadron soon had this number reduced to three as another Halifax returned early with an over-heating port outer. Three became two as the Grim Reaper partook of another. 76 had loaned this aircraft, MP-B W1106, to 78 for this raid, from which it never returned. It is presumed that its captain Sgt W A Wilson and his crew were lost over the sea, from which only 3 bodies were eventually recovered. Sgt Wilson and the remainder of the crew are commemorated on the Runnymede Memorial.

Cheshire was not one to sit on the ground for long. The 11th saw him on a raid to the huge chemical works in the industrial town of Mainz. He had the habit of bringing back superb photographs of many of his targets, and would insist on circling the target area whilst some members of his crew took snaps of the effects of the bombing. Whilst most crews were happy to bomb and head for home as quickly as possible, he would often be seen orbiting the target area, acquiring photographic evidence for Group HQ. Cheshire was well loved by all at Middleton. Norman Frankish remembers that he was a wonderful man, kind, considerate and very caring. From AC2 to high-ranking officers, he had no demarcation in this regard. One Flight Sergeant, in charge of discipline, would have everyone on constant parades. Even if one had a break at lunchtime, everyone had to assemble, and there would be a parade before everyone resumed work. Cheshire, always the humanitarian, put a stop to it all, and allowed everyone to get on with the war in peace.

78 also went to Mainz that night and bad luck struck again. Out of the 7 crews detailed, one returned early having used up much of its precious fuel avoiding German intruders on the way out over the UK. The crew had little choice but to jettison their bombs and come home. W/O W E Lunan and his crew became coned in the target area and were severely damaged by flak, wrecking both port engines and injuring most of the crew. They were then attacked by a night fighter, after which the Halifax crashed at Wommelgem, 5 miles from Antwerp. W/O Lunen and Sgt F A Scotland were killed. With the exception of the second gunner F/S A E Fay RCAF, the remainder of the crew became POWs. Fay managed to get back to the UK, and returned to Canada where he retrained as a pilot and won his wings in October 1943.

Sgt E G Monk's crew crashed at Igstadt, 3 miles east of Wiesbaden. The tail and second gunners, Sgt J A Mitchell RCAF and Sgt J Peart respectively, escaped in January 1945 and managed to join up with the Soviet army. They arrived back in the UK on the last day of March.

F/S J Fleetwood-May and his crew were not so lucky. They are presumed lost over the sea. Only one body, that of P/O J F Myrick RCAF, was recovered from the waves. He is buried at Esbjerg, Denmark. They had been given a third class fix when the crew had given their position as very close to the Dutch Coast. After that nothing further was heard. The fourth aircraft to be lost was flown by F/O D A Kingston and his crew. They crashed at Mean, Belgium. Kingston, and all but two of this crew were killed.

It was also on August 11th that a seed planted by the new Deputy Director of Bomber Operations at the Air Ministry, Group Captain Sidney Bufton (who, you will remember, was the first Commanding Officer of the newly reformed 76 Squadron at Linton), came to fruition. Acting on the findings of the Butt report, the practice of employing the most experienced crews from each Group to correctly find, and light up, the targets, had in recent months, allowed the less experienced bomber crews to be best utilised. At first, Harris was opposed to Bufton's suggestion that a dedicated elite target finding squadron be formed. Bufton argued that something had to be done in the light of the Butt report findings, and he won an ally in the form of Sir Charles Portal, who was all for the idea. Portal pushed Harris, who eventually, and grudgingly, went along with things. Initially, the Commanders of 1, 3, 4 and 5 Groups were allowed to choose one squadron each from their Group. Now formally called the Pathfinder Force (PFF), the unit consisted of No. 7 Squadron operating Stirlings, 35 with Halifaxes, 83 with Lancasters, 156 with Wellingtons, and later 109 Squadron with Mosquitoes. They were based at airfields in Cambridgeshire and Huntingdonshire. Their communication channels were direct from Bomber Command, via 3 Group HQ. Once the idea of the PFF was established, Harris relented a little. Its leader he chose himself. Having returned from Sweden after his exploits evading capture earlier in the year, when he was shot down whilst attacking the Tirpitz, 31 year old Australian Don Bennett was given the job. Unlike the normal crews, who did a tour of 30 Ops before being screened, the Pathfinders had to complete 60. In recognition of this, they were each allowed to be promoted up an acting rank. Bennett arrived as a Wing Commander but was immediately upgraded to Acting Group Captain. Within 4 months the initial 4 squadrons would increase to 6, and become a Group in their own right, 8 Group, under the command of their new Air Officer Commanding, Air Commodore D T Bennett.

The first few raids were a learning curve. The first one was to the U-boat construction yards at Flensburg on the night of August 17/18th 1942. This was not a success. The next, to Frankfurt on the 27/28th, was only slightly better. During the third attempt, the Henschel Fieseler aircraft factories at Kassel were attacked. The PFF were getting better, and much damage was carried out by the 300 bombers employed. However, 10% of their number failed to return.

Bennett looked into introducing bigger and better marking methods. At first they utilised a standard 250-lb bomb casing, filled, not with High Explosives, but, for the first time, with an incendiary filling. This filling consisted of Benzol, rubber and phosphorus. By the night of September 5/6th they were becoming a much more coherent entity. For the first time, during a raid on Bremen, they employed their new tactics, which would over time become honed into a basic procedure used regularly by the PFF throughout the war. Having first found and correctly identified the target, the first group of aircraft, called 'Illuminators', would mark the target area by creating lanes of white flares. Now the target area was defined, the target itself was identified by the next group of aircraft, 'Visual markers', who dropped coloured flares to mark the actual aiming point. The final group of PFF aircraft, the 'Backers up', quickly followed the Visual markers and dropped incendiaries on to the coloured flares. Now the show could commence. With the target clearly identified and marked, it only remained for the main force to begin dropping their HE bombs and/or incendiaries on top of the incendiaries dropped by the backers up.

By the night of September 10/11th, for a raid on Dusseldorf, Bennett's boys had a new toy. With the success of the 250-lb incendiary bomb (called Red Blob), someone had the idea of making it a bit bigger, a lot bigger in fact. This resulted in the use of a standard 4,000-lb 'Cookie' casing, filled with the same incendiary filling as Red Blob. Used as target markers for the first time, they were christened 'Pink Pansies' by the aircrews, due to the huge pink flash that came off the thing when it exploded. Also new for this raid were red flares, dropped on the west side of the town. They were complemented by green flares dropped on the east. The bombers flew between the reds and the greens and bombed the Pink Pansies. The only problem with Red Blobs and Pink Pansies, was that once the fires took hold they ceased to be seen amongst the growing conflagration below. However, the use of controlled markers reduced the chances of the bombers aiming at decoy fires, started by the Germans in open fields away from the main target area. New words also became commonplace amongst bomber crews, 'Sampson' and 'Shaker' for example. Shaker was the original code word used when selected PFF crews dropped their markers on the target using Gee, and other experienced crews then visually marked the aiming point with incendiaries. Sampson was the code word for the technique of marking a cloud-covered target. When using this technique, both dropped their markers 'blind' using Gee fixes. The PFF modified their marking techniques into 3 main groups. Visual ground marking had 'Newhaven' as its code word, whilst 'Parramatta' identified blind ground marking. This left blind skymarking - 'Wanganui', used for the first time by S/L H E Bufton during a raid on Dusseldorf, on New Years Eve 1942. The origin of one of the chosen code words was the name of Bennett's hometown in Australia, Parramatta. Newhaven was the home of his personal WAAF assistant, CPL Ralph, whilst another member of his staff, S/L Ashworth hailed from Wanganui, New Zealand.

It takes but a few seconds at most for an aircraft to spin into the ground from 1,000 feet, the aircraft barely completing one rotation. This height is deemed the minimum for a safe evacuation and deployment of one's parachute. Slim is the chance for a bomber crew member to realise his plight, grab his parachute pack, clip it onto the harness, struggle to the escape hatch, release it, jump, and have his chute open before the gyrating aircraft hits the ground. I hasten to add that in a spin, one would usually be pinned against the inside of the fuselage by severe G-forces, rather like a fairground ride. One would be unable to go anywhere. Such were the circumstances surrounding one training flight undertaken by a 76 Squadron Halifax from Middleton on August 19th. The crew of MP-M V9992, flown by F/S Gillies, were returning from an air firing exercise that had taken place out to sea. They were near Thirsk on the way back to Goosepool, flying at 1,000 feet when the aircraft was seen to enter a spin and crash, there were no survivors. They were yet another crew to succumb to rudder lock-over on the Merlin powered Halifax.

78's next raid from Middleton was on the 20th, when two crews were briefed to drop Nickels in the Lyon area. The river Loire was used to get within 15 miles of Lyon where the Nickels were dropped from 15,000 feet. No flak was in evidence and both crews reported that the French blackout was very poor. After a series of cancellations and stand-downs, 78's last raid during August came on the night of the 28/29th, when Saarbrucken was the target. Out of the five aircraft detailed, one returned early as the crew could not get it to climb above 10,000 feet. The bomb load was jettisoned and the crew returned safely. Of the remaining four aircraft, three reached the target and carried out a successful attack, after which the Teesside weather persuaded two of the crews to land at Pocklington and the third at Breighton. The fourth Halifax was never seen again. It had crashed between Overijse and Tombeek, 10 miles southeast of Brussels. Sgt J A Marshall and his crew died, they are buried in Overijse Churchyard.

On the 24th Group Captain W N McKechnie arrived at Middleton to replace Group Captain Traill as Goosepools Station Commander. Tommy Traill was to be posted to H.Q. 333 Group with effect 25.8.42. Tommy trail had been the airfield's very first Station Commander and was well liked by all. His friendly and fare attitude was extended towards everyone, from the newest AC1 to the highest ranking officer.

On August 31st, Sgt A I Moir of 76 Squadron was attempting to take off on a training flight from Pocklington in MP-O BB196. Having just become airborne, the port outer engine lost power and thick smoke poured from the exhaust manifold. Sgt Moir slammed the throttles fully open, but the Halifax would not climb. Struggling to maintain three hundred feet, as the aircraft would not climb higher, he eventually crash-landed 15 minutes later at Catfoss, an airfield twenty miles to the east. Catfoss was a Coastal Training Unit, and was equipped with 5 Avro Ansons and 12 Bristol Blenheims. This equipment status was about to be reduced by one, as, when the Halifax touched down, the undercarriage collapsed and it slid into Blenheim Z7302, wrecking both aircraft. [75]

76 and 78 - September 1942

On September 1st 78 detailed 6 crews for a raid on Saarbrucken. The target was easily identified by the bend in the river, which showed up well in the bright moonlight. All were able to accurately bomb the target and return safe. Many large fires were started, one particularly large explosion was seen and on their departure the fires had grown into large masses of flames, which could be seen 80 miles away during the return trip. 76 had 6 serviceable aircraft but only 4 available crews, therefore they sent 4 Halifax's to the same target. Only 3 came home. P/O H G Sherwood flying MP-D W1244 was killed when his aircraft crashed into De Blankaat nature reserve, 2 km south of Woumen, some 14 km north of Ypres, Belgium. He held his stricken aircraft long enough for his crew to escape and become POWs but he was unable to get out in time.

78 sent a further 6 aircraft to attack Karlsruhe the next night, with similar results. Again all crews returned safe. 76, now with only 5 serviceable aircraft available were able to provide 4 but had to rely on sending the squadron and flight commanders along to make up the numbers.

The weather was not so good the following night and 76 briefed a single crew to carry out a single aircraft operation. This was later cancelled. This did not prevent 78 sending a lone fresher crew to attack Emden by bombing on ETA through 9/10ths cloud. One bomb hung up but the crew were able to jettison it in the sea on the way home and land at Topcliffe as Goosepool's weather had not hung out the welcome mat. It didn't want to play the next night either as 5 of 78's crews returned from Bremen, only to receive the BFX signal on the way home diverting them to RAF Waterbeach and Docking in the south. There had been 8 crews briefed for this raid but one had become U/S just prior to takeoff. A second returned early with engine trouble whilst a third returned early with a coolant leak. 76 had been asked for a maximum effort and 6 aircraft were made available. Only five crews were available and they were briefed, (Sgt Richardson had been deemed qualified for operations the previous night). Four of 76's aircraft were to carry only incendiaries and nickels whilst the 5th aircraft, MP-G, was to be loaded with HE bombs. Later this aircraft and one of the incendiary aircraft were scrubbed. The remaining aircraft bombed the target and also diverted to Waterbeach and Docking on the way home.

---

[75] Later in the war, Sgt Moir was commissioned and won the DFC. He became an instructor but was killed in a training accident at Marsden Moor on May 25th 1943. He is buried at Harrogate's Stonefall Cemetery.

On September 6th, Sgt Moir and his crew, this time with the Station Commander Group Captain McKechnie along as second dickey, were taking part in a three aircraft Op to Duisburg. They were one of three crews sent there by 76. Moir had a very difficult flight home, as the bomb-doors would not close properly. This caused quite a bit of drag and the Halifax wanted to drop its port wing, but he held it all the way home and they managed to reach Middleton. On his first operational sortie, Bill Richardson had a close encounter of the Third Reich kind. His aircraft was attacked and hit by a fighter on the way to the target. He continued on and eventually dropped his bombs on the target after which his aircraft was coned and hit several times by flak. In an attempt to break free of the defences he turned 90° to his course but strong winds and the layout of the defences took them back and not away into open country. Richardson soon realised what was happening and immediately turned west and battered his way out, despite being hit several times more. He managed to resist the temptation to lose height and headed for home. This was quite a feat for such an inexperienced captain. He and his crew made it back to Goosepool safely after their extreme baptism of fire. S/L Leonard Cheshire flew the third aircraft and compared with the other two 76 crews had a relatively uneventful trip.

78 sent 6 aircraft on this raid, whilst a singleton flown by Sgt E A Williams departed to nickel Paris. One of the Duisburg aircraft returned early with mechanical problems but the remainder bombed the docks causing many large fires. Meanwhile Paris had been found easily by the nickeling aircraft due to the poor blackout over the city and the river Seine. All returned safe.

The next day was the 7th and 1516 BAT Flight moved over to Croft. On the 8th Frankfurt was the target for 9 of 78's Halifax's whilst 76 contributed 6, its entire available strength. The Pathfinders were unable to accurately locate Frankfurt and only about 6 aircraft dropped their bombs on Frankfurt where one person was killed. The majority of the bombs fell 15 miles to the southwest in or around Russelsheim. Owing to the very poor visibility P/O R Atkinson's crew attacked the alternate target, Mainz, having been hit by flak whilst on the way to the target. Having turned for home Atkinson had great difficulty controlling the aircraft but was able to reach the UK. As the aircraft was low on fuel his intention was to land at the first available airfield but as each time the Halifax was slowed it became almost impossible to control. With the height down to 5,000 feet the crew abandoned whilst flying over Northamptonshire, all landed safely.

After taking off at 19:59, W/O C G Dennis and his crew were attacked by a Me.110 night fighter on the way to the target. The tail gunner, F/S W Dewhurst, was killed. With the tail unit extensively damaged and a full bomb-load still on board W/O Dennis turned for home and made an emergency landing at Tangmere at 01:42. Most of the remaining aircraft attacked the alternative with varying levels of success. Sgt Williams turned back as he was finding it extremely difficult to control his aircraft. He was able to make base after jettisoning his bomb-load on the way home.

F/L P H Tippetts-Aylmer DFC and his crew took off from base at 19:35 after which they were shot down by a night fighter. This Halifax crashed at 22:40 near Sclayn, 12 km E/N/E of Namur, Belgium. F/L Tippetts-Aylmer was killed, along with his tail gunner P/O E W Gibbs and mid-upper gunner /S G R Yeates RCAF. The Flight engineer Sgt J Hodge, and the navigator Sgt T Brandon RCAF became POWs, whilst the bomb-aimer Sgt J A Winterbottom and the wireless operator Sgt R Brown both evaded capture by way of Spain and Gibraltar and were back in England by mid October.

Meanwhile, 5 out of the 6 crews dispatched by 76 found the target and successfully bombed. Bursts could be seen all around the target area and the glow of fires were seen reflecting off the cloud. Moir was the first to take-off at 19:57, he bombed at 23:36 and was home by 02:40. P/O Atkinson's aircraft was the last one to reach base, arriving at 03:51.

A total of 249 aircraft took part in this raid, 5 Wellingtons and 2 Halifaxes were lost, both were from Goosepool.

Sgt J. E. Nicholson

It was not just fighters, flack and the weather that worked to bring about the demise of unwary airmen. To this list we should add the Gremlins. They are the invisible workers of the Grim Reaper and they can and do get into everything. Something as innocuous as a photoflash sitting quietly in the bomb bay could attract their attention and spell disaster for unsuspecting airmen. On the night of September 8/9th 1942, 76 Squadron Halifax A-Apple W1228 had departed Middleton at 17:58 for an operation to Frankfurt. Whilst en route to the target, F/S J E Nicholson and his crew were just 20 minutes and 41 miles from base, near to the little village of Holtby, 4.6 miles east of York. A split second, later the Halifax disintegrated as the bomb-load exploded. Such was the severity of the explosion that the wreckage of the aircraft was distributed over a very wide area. All crewmembers were killed. Not two nights before, a 115 Squadron Wellington III, BJ724 KO-P out of Marham, had also exploded in exactly the same circumstances. Out of the crew of 5, only the pilot, F/S Lanceley RCAF, and the rear gunner, Sgt Hands survived the crash, which took place near Blofield, 6 miles east of Norwich. Sadly, F/S Lanceley died of his injuries two days later.

The Captain of the Goosepool Halifax was F/S John Eric Nicholson from Manchester. His crew consisted of:
F/S A N Thompson - Second Pilot
P/O A Robson - Navigator/Bomb Aimer
Sgt L V Harvey - Wireless Operator
Sgt R L Stevens - Mid upper Gunner
Sgt J T Murray - Flight Engineer
Sgt G R Rundle - Tail Gunner

An inquiry suggested that the photoflash had detonated in the bomb bay, which in turn ignited the fuel lines that ran across the fuselage floor directly above it. The aircraft's fuel and bomb-load (including incendiaries) would have quickly followed. The photoflash was a large pyrotechnic device dropped by an aircraft. It would ignite and illuminate the target, allowing the crew to take their bombing photographs.

As Nicholson's Halifax had only flown a distance of 41 miles from Middleton, it would have still been in the climb when the accident occurred. The aircraft's altitude when the photoflash ignited can only be guessed at, but probably this would have been several thousand feet. As the resultant explosion took place at only about 500 feet, it is possible that due to the aircraft's close proximity to York and its surrounding habitation, F/S Nicholson may have been trying to descend for an emergency landing at nearby Pocklington. This would have been in preference to taking the risk of abandoning the aircraft, which in the dark could have fallen on surrounding housing. One of the mysteries surrounding this accident is why the remainder of the crew did not bale out. The author has no wish to postulate about the actual circumstances of this tragedy, as the possibilities are endless. I leave the reader to draw his or her own conclusion as to the events that may or may not have taken place that night. However, the reader needs to be aware that, due to the design of the Halifax, all but two of the crew were grouped together in the front section of the aircraft, leaving only the mid-upper and tail gunners isolated at the rear.

As the nose went down, the burning fuel sloshing around in the fuselage behind the crew could have run forward into the nose section. It is possible that the crew would have been overwhelmed by the flames, and had little chance to don their parachutes and leave by the nose hatch. Due to the intense heat from the fire, the intercom cables running to the rear of the aircraft would have been instantly severed, thus removing any possibility of the two gunners in the tail section hearing the abandon order. Even the abandon signal lights placed in both the mid-upper and tail turrets would probably have suffered the same fate. Possibly, by the time the two gunners realised what was happening, it was too late, and the bomb-load would have exploded.

F/S Nicholson is buried in the Churchyard at Barmby Moor, near Pocklington. He is not alone. He rests not only with his flight engineer, Sgt Murray and tail gunner, Sgt Rundle, but with the many other aircrew members who share this hallowed place.

The Life of a Bomber Pilot

Before joining up, F/S Nicholson attended Manchester University. His thesis, entitled 'The Educational needs of the Senior Schoolboy - 1940', still exists in the University. As with many wartime airmen, F/S Nicholson's operational life was relatively short. His first Op was to Le Havre on April 10th 1942, acting as a second pilot to P/O Kofoed in Halifax W1036 MP-Y. This was his first taste of life as a bomber pilot with 76 Squadron. His next second dickie trip was on the 22nd, again with Kofoed, this time to attack the Tirpitz. On May 6th he flew with S/L Packe to Stuttgart, followed by an operation to Cologne on the 30th with Kofoed. His last trip as second pilot was on June 1st, again with Kofoed, the target that night being the Krupps Works at Essen. His first operation as captain came on the evening of the July 26/27th, when he and his crew, flying MP-A W1228,[76] attacked Hamburg at 01:30 from a height of 12,000 feet. Their bombs were seen to drop in the dock area starting a large fire around the target. With the exception of the second pilot P/O A C Campbell, this was the same crew that would perish with him at Holtby. He continued operations with a raid to Saarbrucken on the 29th and Dusseldorf on the 31st.

During this raid he and his crew were unable to bomb the primary target due to all four engines developing abnormal cooling temperatures. The aircraft would not climb above 12,000 feet, so a large built up area was bombed instead. This was later identified as Kampen. Flak was encountered just after bomb release, which continued until the Halifax was well clear of the target. They returned safely to Goosepool at 04:20. Sgt Nicholson's only Op during August was back to Saarbrucken on the 28th. Sgt Nicholson and his crew were substitutes for P/O Waite's crew, who were minus their engineer. His route to the target was Base - Spalding - Orfordness - Furness - Target. An enemy night fighter was encountered over the Belgian coast, but it did not engage. F/S Thompson dropped their five 1,000-lb GP bombs right on the target. After this, Sgt Moir, in one of the other three 76 Squadron Halifaxes also taking part, reported seeing large fires burning in the centre of the target. These fires were the product of Nicholson's accurate bombing. September began with a raid to Karlsruhe on the 2nd, followed two days later with another to Bremen. It was at this point that Sergeant Nicholson became Flight Sergeant Nicholson, just in time for his last operation, from which he would not return.

On the night of September 16/17th 1942, 76 Squadron carried out their last raid from Middleton St George. They made up part of a force of 369 aircraft to attack Essen, which was considered to be a very difficult target. The raid included aircraft from the training groups, including 10 OTU from Abingdon, flying Whitleys; 11 OTU from Bassingbourn and Steeple Morden, flying Wellingtons; 12 OTU from Chipping Warden; 15 OTU from Harwell; 21 OTU from Edgehill; 22 OTU from Stratford; 23 OTU from Pershore; 25 OTU from Finningley; 26 OTU from Wing; and 27 OTU from Litchfield.

10 OTU lost Whitley VP4931, which was flown by W/O L A Death RNZAF. Their SOS was last heard on the W/T at 01:28. The crew survived and became POWs. This was the last Whitley to be lost during bomber operations over Germany during WW II, although 10 OTU were to lose many more when the type was relegated to coastal and anti submarine duties. Losses from these training units, due in part to inexperience, were not well received by Bomber Command, and this raid was the last time they were asked to support main bomber force operations. From a losses point of view, September 16th 1942 was a very bad night, as 10% of the attacking force did not return. Those lost included 21 Wellingtons, 9 Lancasters, 5 Stirlings, 3 Halifaxes and 1 Whitley, 39 aircraft in total. Bombing was scattered but it was considered to be the most successful raid on Essen thus far.

---

[76] This aircraft was to be used exclusively by the crew for all but one of their operations

View of pasture where Halifax crashed   Photo: Author

View of farmhouse and damage caused by explosion when aircraft crashed.
Farmer with part of propellor ploughed up after the war   Photo: Author

Resting place of John Nicholson, his flight engineer, Sgt Murray and tail
gunner Sgt Rundle, who lie in Barmby Moor cemetery near Pocklington along
with many other wartime airmen   Photo: Author

At Essen, on that fateful night, over 30 very large fires were started, and 80 or more medium ones were also observed. Amongst the many smaller targets that were hit were eight large industrial and six transportation complexes. One of the most important targets in Essen to receive the attention of the RAF was the Krupps factory. It was hit by 15 high explosive bombs. A bomber, laden with incendiaries, was shot down over the target area, this too fell onto the factory adding to the destruction. There was not enough left of it to be identified. Its crew joined the ranks of the lost. No trace of them has ever been found. Many houses were damaged, and in the Essen area, 47 people were killed and 92 injured. Some crews attacked their alternates of Bochum and Wuppertal. A large lorry garage at Herne was badly damaged by a huge fire started by a single bomber. Another crew devastated Cochem, a small town 90 miles south of Essen. Its single bomb load destroyed 4 houses and killed 15 people.

One of 76 Squadrons Halifaxes had sustained flak damage during this raid. Halfway home from the target the crew realised that the aircraft would not reach Middleton and so they diverted to Waterbeach. Here it was decided that the badly shot up Halifax was going nowhere until it received some extensive TLC. And so it came to pass that Norman Thompson, an electrician, an instrument technician, two airframe fitters and two mechanics were detached to RAF Waterbeach where they would repair the aircraft and thus allow it to be flown back to base. Packing up their tools and spares they promptly set off for Waterbeach.

At 36 minutes past midnight on September 16th 1942, Oberleutnant Herbert Rauh of II /NJG4 slid his nightfighter in behind MP-C R9365 and fired his cannon into the Halifax. The stricken bomber fell to Earth, and became the last 76 Squadron (and wartime RAF) aircraft to be lost whilst stationed at Middleton St George. This aircraft crashed at Rubrouck in France, and took with it the lives of all on board. P/O A C (Lex) Campbell RAAF, Sgt S G White, Sgt S A Witchell, F/S M J Standley RAAF, F/S W N Geddie, Sgt J R Runnicles and Sgt A Moffatt.

September 17th 1942 dawned bright. This was a very special day for Goosepool, a day touched with much sadness. Goosepool was bidding farewell to both 76 and 78 Squadrons, who were departing for their new home at Linton-on-Ouse. Throughout the day the airfield was being stripped of all the remnants and paraphernalia of the past 18 months. Way was being made for the arrival of the Canadian squadrons, which 4 Group had been collecting for quite some time. Both 76 and 78 Squadrons had provided an introduction to Bomber Command for the people of Teesside. Many friendships and loves had been kindled, many had been tragically taken away in the twinkling of eye. There were many tears and thoughts for the airman who awoke in the morning to fasten their shoelaces, and who did not live long enough to untie them at the end of the day.

Meanwhile at Waterbeach, their task completed, Norman Thompson and his oppos asked for a pilot to fly the now-repaired Halifax back to Middleton. When the pilot eventually arrived, he asked Norman how he and his colleagues were getting back to Middleton. 'No idea', they replied. 'Jump in', said the pilot, and so they all returned to Middleton in style, only to find that they had been deserted. The squadron had gone. When the two squadrons had moved to Linton-on-Ouse, they had left 6 lame ducks behind at Middleton. Norman and the other returning tradesmen were ordered to remain behind and repair these unserviceable aircraft before rejoining the squadron at Linton.

When they requested spares for these aircraft, they were told to cannibalise the worst Halifax for the parts they needed. During the war, a donor aircraft such as this was usually called a 'Christmas tree' by the groundcrew. Once the aircraft were repaired they were airtested, and flown off to Linton, leaving only the Christmas tree standing forlornly in No.2 hangar. Having ordered the spares to replace those pinched from the cannibalised Halifax, they sat back and relaxed to await their arrival.

Norman and his oppos were the only non Care and Maintenance staff at Goosepool, and for the next few days they lived like lords. With only a small contingent of station personnel to cater for, the cookhouse became a top class kitchen. Norman recalls, 'We had some excellent meals prepared for us, it was like dining out every day at a top class restaurant.' Eventually the spares arrived, and the job of getting the beat-up old wreck of an aeroplane airborne again began. And a wreck it was, it should have been scrapped long ago. The undercarriage would not retract, and most panels were bent and badly fitting. They managed to patch it up, and had to bash the cowlings on with a hammer, to make them fit. Eventually the old Halifax was ready for flight testing, well, as ready as it was ever going to be. A signal was passed down to the squadron at Linton, requesting them to send up their craziest pilot. He duly arrived (no names, no pack-drill) along with an engineer and wireless operator. The Halifax was brought out of the hangar and a pre-flight check carried out. The pilot and engineer climbed aboard, did their checks and ran up the engines. Being satisfied that all was well, one by one they shut them down again. Moments later they jumped down from the plane. The pilot announced with a grin that all was ok. He instructed Norman and his oppos to prepare the aircraft for flight. He intended to take the Halifax up for a test hop after lunch, before clearing it for its trip to Linton. Having given the groundcrew their final instructions the pilot and crew went off to the mess for lunch.

On their return, the crew were told that the pre-flight had been completed and she was ready to go. With the Form 700 duly completed, the pilot turned to the battered Halifax and said, 'Ok my lovely, lets see what you've got.' With that, he brought the fingers of his right hand up to his mouth and transferred an implanted kiss onto the lowest prop blade of the port outer Merlin. He and the crew then climbed aboard. Again Norman and his oppos went through the engine starting sequence as the Halifax was brought to life. With a wave from his open window the pilot released the brakes and promptly began to taxi the bomber around the end of hangar two. Even more promptly, he struck the sliding hangar door gantry with the port wing, putting a huge dent in the leading edge, close to the tip. The Halifax was going nowhere. Once again the pilot shut down the engines, applied the parking-brake and leapt out of the aircraft, this time to observe the damage. Having given the offending wing the once-over, he reported with a shrug of the shoulders and yet another grin, 'No problem, it'll be ok.'

Norman Thompson, (left) with oppo who hailed from Darlington but Norman doesn't remember his name

Photo: Norman Thompson

Inspecting the huge dent in the wing, Norman and the rest of the groundcrew gave each other a knowing look, shook their heads and pulled the hapless aircraft away from the hangar. Once the Halifax was clear, the engines were re-started and the jovial pilot taxied away. They watched with bated breath as the Halifax reached the end of the runway and was run up. The pilot appeared to be taking great care in doing his pre-flight checks. Also with great care he lined up on the runway and took off, much to the relief of all on the ground, and with even greater care he carried out a wide circuit, screamed over the airfield at zero feet, beat up the control tower, with inches to spare, and promptly flew away.

Everyone on the ground waited for the return of the Halifax, as they wanted to clear the snags list before knocking off time. There were often snags to fix after any test flight even for the best of aircraft, and this old kite was a total heap. After about an hour they began to get a bit worried. Where was the old tub, had it crashed somewhere? Were Norman and his oppos for the high jump? The pilot had seemed such a nice man, a bit young to end his days in that old crate. Eventually, word came through that the Halifax had already arrived at Linton-on-Ouse. Having flown around the Darlington area for a bit, the pilot had deemed that the old bus was not too bad, he would dispense with landing back at Middleton. He felt that with a good slice of luck the aircraft would probably just about make it to Linton, despite not being able to raise the undercarriage that is.

Having completed the task of getting all the lame ducks away, Norman and his oppos followed suit, and departed by road to Linton, thus ending 76's exploits at Goosepool. With their departure, the airfield said goodbye to the only two RAF squadrons to serve at Goosepool during WW II. The way was now clear for the arrival of the Colonials.

78 Losses - 1941 and 1942

May 3/4 1941, Whitley Mk V Z6483 EY, Ops - Cologne. Took off MSG 20:45, crashed 06:30.

This was the first aircraft to be lost from Goosepool. After suffering from W/T failure and a shortage of fuel; this aircraft was abandoned on the way home and crashed near Leominster, Herefordshire. All survived.

Sgt L Hatcher
Sgt Chandos
Sgt H B Buttell
Sgt T K Moodie
Sgt T Hall

May 8/9 1941, Whitley Mk V, T4147 EY-D,   Ops - Breman. Took off MSG 22:25

Crashed at Heisfeldefeld, 2.5 km north of the centre of Leer Germany, some 91 km W/N/W of the target. All perished and are buried at Oldenburg, in the Sage War Cemetery.

Sgt L Thorpe	K
P/O R W Wallis-Stolzle	K
Sgt P J Lewis	K
Sgt H E Bailey	K
Sgt P W Emmett	K

May16/17 1941, Whitley Mk V, Z6493 EY-V, Ops - Cologne. Took off MSG 22:43 – crashed 02:34.

This aircraft crashed between Helenaveen and Maasbree, Holland, 9 km west of Venlo, having been shot down by Uffz Pross, 3./NJG1. All rest in Jonkerbos War Cemetery, Nijmegen.

P/O J A Garrould	K
Sgt R S Kaymer	K
F/S R J Garlish	K
Sgt E Oakes	K
F/S A P Smith	K

May 28/29 1941, Whitley Mk V, Z6484 EY-E, Ops - Kiel. Took off MSG 23:55.

Cause of loss unknown. This crew are buried at Soltau, in the Becklingen War Cemetery.

Sgt A T Copley	K
Sgt W B Smith RCAF	K
Sgt A Cooke	K
Sgt A Gregory	K
Sgt D R Stickland	K

June 8/9 1941, Whitley Mk V, Z6571 EY-, Ops - Dortmund. Take off MSG 23:00.

On the way home from this raid, and whilst flying back up the country towards Goosepool, this aircraft crashed, whilst descending through cloud, prior to landing at base. The Whitley crashed 4 miles N/W of Masham Yorkshire, in a small wooded valley, near the small hamlet of Ellingstring. There were no survivors.

Sgt D R Simm	K
Sgt J S Tomkinson	K
P/O A V Snelling	K
Sgt J B Stevenson	K
F/S G Billing	K

June 16/17 1941, Whitley Mk V, Z6492 EY-K, Ops - Cologne. Take off MSG 22:32.

Sadly, no details concerning the loss of this crew are available, only that they were all killed, and are commemorated on the Runnymede memorial.

P/O D S Lake	K
Sgt H T Ivory	K
Sgt R C Rae	K
Sgt H Bailey	K

June 18/19 1941, Whitley Mk V, Z6560 EY-, Ops - Bremen. Take off MSG 23:03.

Lost without trace, this crew are also commemorated on the Runnymede Memorial.

F/S V H Marks	K
Sgt J G Wooley	K
Sgt W P Herman	K
Sgt J H Harris	K

June 18/19 1941, Whitley MkV, Z6661 EY-, Ops - Bremen. Take off MSG 23:00.

This aircraft crashed at Lorup, 80 km W/S/W of the target area. All on board were killed, and are buried in the Reichswald Forest War Cemetery, near Kleve, Germany.

P/O T C Richard	K
F/S H R George	K
Sgt C F Cook	K
F/S R C Berwick	K

June 29/30 1941, Whitley Mk V, Z6664 EY-, Ops - Bremen. Took off MSG 22:43.

This crew were presumed lost over the sea. Only the body of the tail gunner, F/S Hird, was recovered from the water, the remainder of the crew were lost without trace, and are commemorated on the Runnymede Memorial.

Sgt R S Green	K
Sgt E R Ingram	K
Sgt K I Jones	K
Sgt A W Adams	K
F/S L Hird	K

July 2/3 1941, Whitley Mk V, Z6558 EY-, Ops - Duisburg. Took off MSG 23:24, crashed 01:03.

Shot down by Lt Reinhold Knacke, 11./NJG1, this aircraft crashed at Itteren, 5 km north of Maastricht, Holland. None of the crew survived. They are buried in Jonkerbos War Cemetery.

Sgt A Jepson	K
P/O G M Kennedy	K
Sgt G A Avory	K
Sgt J F Hollingworth	K

July 8/9 1941, Whitley Mk V, T4209 EY-W, Ops - Hamm. Took off MSG 23:00, ditched 04:29.

Hit by flak over enemy territory, this aircraft managed to get within 9 miles of the English Coast before having to ditch. The navigator, Sgt Hafferden, swam to shore and raised the alarm. Sadly, the remainder of the crew were never found, and are commemorated on the Runnymede Memorial.

Sgt W M McQuitty RAAF	K
P/O E A Scott	K
Sgt J F Hafferden	
Sgt D J Clow	K
Sgt W Forster	K

July 8/9 1941, Whitley Mk V, Z6555 EY-, Ops - Hamm. Took off MSG 23:03, crashed 02:51.

This aircraft crashed in the North Sea, only the body of the wireless operator, Sgt Noddle, was recovered. The remainder are commemorated on the Runnymede Memorial.

Sgt O W McLean RAAF	K
Sgt C MacMartin RCAF	K
P/O H H Mountain	K
Sgt K Noddle	K
Sgt L Byrne	K

July 8/9 1941, Whitley Mk V, Z6625 EY-L, Ops - Hamm. Took off MSG 22:57, crashed 04:05.

Despite having had one of its engines fail whilst returning over the North Sea, this aircraft managed to reach the vicinity of Bircham Newton airfield, 14 miles northeast of Kings Lynn, Norfolk. Whilst trying to land there the Whitley collided with a haystack at Shernborne and crashed. No injuries were reported.

P/O Wright
Sgt Jones
F/S R Jopling
Sgt R Boucher
Sgt A D Wills

July 29 1942, Whitley Mk V, Z6838 EY-, Training. Took off MSG.

Flown by Sgt Turnbull RCAF this aircraft took off From Goosepool and crashed almost immediately due to jammed ailerons. No injuries reported.

August 6/7 1941, Whitley Mk V, T4158 EY-, Ops - Frankfurt. Took off MSG, ditched.

Having ditched 12 km north of Dunkirk, this crew were picked up by High Speed Launch 145 out of Dover. The crew were plucked from under the noses of the German coastal gun batteries, which were bombarding the area with heavy gunfire.

P/O Atchison
Sgt Harwood
Sgt McMullen
Sgt Elliott
Sgt J Bell

August 8/9 1941, Whitley Mk V, Z6655 EY-, Ops - Kiel. Took off from MSG 22:19, ditched.

This aircraft was badly damaged by flak over the target area and was ditched 78 miles northeast of Blyth, Northumberland. The crew were later rescued.

Sgt J W Bell
Sgt Pindon
Sgt Buttell
Sgt R Boucher
Sgt Porter

August 16/17 1941, Whitley Mk V, Z6577 EY-F, Ops - Cologne. Took off MSG 22:52, crashed 02:47.

All of the crew were killed when this aircraft crashed at Ohe en Laak, 3 km northeast of Maaseik, which is 30km N/N/E of Maastricht, Holland. All are buried in Jonkerbos War Cemetery.

Sgt T A Sherman RCAF	K
Sgt G L Olsen RCAF	K
F/S R Jopling	K
Sgt D A Wilson	K
Sgt D F Hawks	K

August 16/17 1941, Whitley Mk V, Z6754 EY-, Ops - Cologne. Took off MSG 23:05, crashed 03:50.

Crashed at Buggenum, 5 km N/N/E of Roermond, Holland, some 16 kms northeast of the crash site of Sgt Sherman's aircraft. All on board lost their lives and rest with Sgt Sherman's crew in Jonkerbos War Cemetery.

Sgt J H Malet-Warden	K
Sgt J C Bearmore	K
Sgt A J Millard-Tucker	K
Sgt G H Buchanan RCAF	K

August 16/17 1941, Whitley Mk V, Z6823 EY-B, Ops - Cologne. Took off MSG 22:56, crashed 03:15.

This aircraft crashed at Velddriel, 29 km N/N/E of Tilburg, Holland. The e second pilot, P/O J L Asprey RAAF, rests in Jonkerbos War Cemetery, whilst the 1st wireless operator, Sgt A D Wills, is buried in the Woensel General Cemetery, Eindhoven. The remainder of the crew became POWs.

F/L J A Cant	POW
P/O J L Asprey RAAF	K
Sgt W E Kerr	POW
Sgt AD Wills	K
Sgt J Geary	POW

August 24/25 1941, Whitley Mk V, Z6466 EY-A, Ops - Dusseldorf. Took off MSG 20:09.

Crashed near Wavre, 23 km southeast of the centre of Brussels, Belgium, all of the crew were killed are buried in the town's Communal Cemetery.

Sgt W G Rogers	K
Sgt E C Findon	K
Sgt J Hadfield	K
Sgt W D Edge	K
Sgt B Douglas	K

August 24/25 1941, Whitley Mk V, Z6742 EY-, Ops - Dusseldorf. Took off MSG 20:17, crashed 02:27.

Crashed near Mistley Essex, after being abandoned. Sgt Sinclaire RCAF, who was flying the aircraft at the time, died when the aircraft crashed, his body was found in the wreckage. He is buried in Ipswich Cemetery.

P/O Fransden	
Sgt D A Sinclair RCAF	K
Sgt Becker	
Sgt Young	
Sgt Gale.	

August 27/28 1941, Whitley Mk V, Z6508 EY-, Ops - Mannheim. Took off MSG 01:35.

This aircraft came down in the sea off the French Coast near Dunkirk, there were no survivors. Only the body of the Observer, Sgt Harper, was recovered, the remainder of the crew are commemorated on the Runnymede Memorial.

P/O K W Davies	K
Sgt S E Rowed RCAF	K
Sgt G T Harper	K
Sgt J W Bills	K
Sgt P Gennon RNZAF	K

August 27/28 1941, Whitley Mk V, Z6872 EY-, Ops - Mannheim. Took off MSG 20:02, crash-landed 00:45

This aircraft crash-landed on its returned to base, after being hit by flak whilst attacking the alternative target, Bruges.

Sgt H A Woodhatch	Inj
Sgt Childs	Inj
Sgt Olley	Inj
Sgt Davidson	Inj

September 6/7 1941, Whitley Mk V, Z6864 EY-, Ops - Huls. Took off MSG 20:25, crash-landed 03:15.

This aircraft was attacked on the way home by a German intruder, and crash-landed a few hundred yards southeast of the small village of Markington, 7 miles southwest of Dishforth airfield, North Yorkshire. No injuries were reported.

Sgt Jones RAAF
Sgt Jones
Sgt Miller
Sgt Vere
Sgt Rouse

September 6/7 1941, Whitley Mk V, Z6881 EY-, Ops - Huls. Took off MSG 20:37, 01:25.

Shot down on the way home by Oblt Helmut Lent, 4./NJG1, this aircraft crashed at Bergum, 13 km east of Leeuwarden, Holland, just 38 km from the Dutch Coast. All were buried in Bergum's Tietjerksteradeel Protestant Churchyard.

P/O F B Thorp	K
Sgt C V Matheson	K
Sgt D V Logan RAAF	K
Sgt G Carman RNZAF	K
Sgt C J Storer	K

September 29/30 1941, Whitley Mk V, Z9126 EY-, Ops - Stettin. Took off MSG 21:39.

This aircraft was last heard calling for help on the W/T whilst on the way home. Radio cross bearings plotted the Whitley's position as being near to the North Frisian island of Sylt, 71 km W/N/W of Flensburg. The crew were lost without trace, and are commemorated on the Runnymede Memorial.

Sgt R W Bird	K
Sgt I McCarthy	K
Sgt H B Buttell	K
F/S B Ward	K
Sgt R R Vosper	K

October 10/11 1941, Whitley Mk V, Z6825 EY-, Ops - Essen. MSG.

After aborting its take-off, this aircraft caught fire on the runway after it was struck by another Whitley, which was trying to become airborne,

P/O Fransden	
Sgt Dennis	
Sgt Bowden	
Sgt Young	
Sgt Taylor	Inj

October 10/11 1941, Whitley Mk V, Z9127 EY-, Ops - Essen. MSG

During its take-off run this aircraft collided with Whitley Z6825, as detailed above, and burst into flames. Again, only one member of the crew was slightly injured.

P/O Leyland	
Sgt Dench	Inj
P/O Geddes	
Sgt Donnaldson	
Sgt Vere	

October 14/15 1941, Whitley Mk V, Z9213 EY-, Ops - Nuremberg. Took off MSG 22:52, crashed 06:15.

Low on fuel, this aircraft was abandoned on the way home and crashed near Hythe, Kent, all landed safely.

P/O D S King RCAF
P/O Pruden
Sgt Jupp
Sgt Lyndon
Sgt Campbell

October 16 1941, Whitley Mk V, Z6646 EY-, Training. Took off from Croft, crashed 20:10.

After taking off from Croft for a night training exercise, this aircraft belonging to 78 at MSG suffered a loss of power in one of its engines. Whilst trying to execute a gentle wide left-hand circuit back to Croft it crashed at Stillington, near Sedgfield, Co Durham. All but the Canadian tail gunner, Sgt Kidd, suffered burns.

P/O B O Smith	Inj
Sgt Whitehorn	Inj
Sgt Duffort	Inj
Sgt Kidd RCAF	

November 1/2 1941, Whitley Mk V, Z9152, Ops - Kiel. Took off Croft 17:32.

At 01:16 this aircraft was last heard on W/T by the wireless operators of RAF Linton-on-Ouse, as the crew were in contact with RAF Burcham Newton on W/T. This aircraft was presumed lost over the North Sea. The crew are commemorated on the Runnymede Memorial.

S/L J Mercer	K
Sgt R F Duggan	K
F/L J R Campbell	K
Sgt T P Woodhouse	K
F/S V/G Wright	K

November 7/8 1941, Whitley Mk V, Z6948 EY-F, Ops - Berlin. Took off Croft 22:31, crashed 06:30.

This aircraft crashed between Oudemirdum and Nijemirdum, 10 km west of Lemmer on the Dutch Coast, after being shot down by Oblt Ludwig Becker, 4./NJG1. The aircraft's captain, Sgt Bell, rests in Lemmer General Cemetery, whist the remainder of the crew are buried in Nijemirdum General Cemetery.

Sgt J W Bell	K
P/O G M McCombe	K
Sgt G T Webb	K
Sgt D Cameron	K
Sgt R Boucher.	K

November 7/8 1941, Whitley Mk V, Z9151 EY-, Ops - Berlin. Took off Croft 22:27.

Nothing is known regarding the loss of this aircraft, only that the captain, Sgt E J Sargent, was killed. He rests in Berlin's 1939-1945 War Cemetery. The remainder of the crew baled out and became POWs.

Sgt E J Sargent	K
Sgt E W Penn	POW
P/O J V Saunders RCAF	POW
Sgt T Hall	POW
Sgt T Paterson	POW
Sgt E G Freeman	POW

December 17/18 1941, Whitley Mk V, Z9129 EY-, Ops - Le Havre. Took off Croft 16:43, ditched 18:50.

This aircraft was ditched in the Solent, off Spithead, after its starboard engine caught fire at 6,500 feet on the way to the target. All were rescued.

P/O H G Bedford
Sgt Howell
P/O Ponds
Sgt Oliver
Sgt Parks

December 18/19 1941, Whitley Mk V, Z9277 EY-, Ops - Brest. Took off Croft 15:53, crashed 21:53.

Not being able to receive a response from Middleton's W/T for a homer bearing, the crew had little choice but to let down through the cloud to ascertain their position. In so doing, they crashed into high ground in the Yorkshire Dales, at Simon's Seat, (1591 feet), near Appltreewick , 14 miles W/N/W of Harrogate, Yorkshire. No injuries reported.

P/O J F Beadle
Sgt Cox
P/O Franklin
Sgt White
Sgt Gale
Sgt Kendall

December 18/19 1941, Whitley Mk V, Z9308 EY-, Ops - Brest. Took off Croft 16:07, crash-landed 16:30.

The starboard engine failed, just after take-off, causing the aircraft to crash-land, close to Croft airfield at Keanly Sides Farm, near Hurworth, Co Durham. No one was injured.

Sgt J A Atwell
Sgt Martin
Sgt Howitson
Sgt Turpin
Sgt Johnston

December 27/28 1941, Whitley Mk V, Z9276 EY-, Ops - Dusseldorf. Took off Croft 17:40, crashed 18:45.

This aircraft suffered severe icing, which blocked the engine air intakes, causing the engines to over-heat. The captain attempted to carry out an emergency landing at Driffield, Yorkshire but before this could be done the aircraft collided with overhead high-tension cables, and crashed at Foxholes, 10 miles north of Driffield. The aircraft burst into flames on impact, 3 of the crew were injured.

P/O Shattock
Sgt Wado
Sgt Lee
Sgt Newman
Sgt Lyndon

1942

January 2/3 1942, Whitley Mk V, Z6656 EY-, Ops St - Nazaire. Took off Croft 16:22, crashed 02:05.

Crashed on high ground on the way home, at Woogill Moor in the Yorkshire Dales, (1,500 feet AMSL). The aircraft had been descending through cloud at the time, in preparation for a landing at Croft.

Sgt A J Attwell RCAF	Inj
Sgt E C Smith	Inj
F/O K Blyth	Inj
Sgt J D Johnson RCAF	Inj
Sgt V E Shirley	Inj

January 28/29 1942, Whitley Mk V, Z9305 EY-, Ops - Rotterdam. Took off Croft 17:20, crashed 19:05.

Crashed into the sea, 1 hour and 45 minutes after leaving Middleton, whilst outbound to the target. The aircraft came down near the Cork lightship, off Harwich, Suffolk, after shot down by British trawlers. F/S Campbell's body was one of only two recovered from the sea. His remains were immediately committed back to the sea. He, along with the other three crew members whose bodies were never found, is commemorated on the Runnymede Memorial.

Sgt A N Williams RAAF	K
P/O D L Williams	K
F/S D R Campbell RCAF	K
Sgt D Curnick	K
Sgt R W Dobson	K

This crew ditched, 20 miles south of Bournemouth on the way home. They strayed off track whilst on the way home, due to the aircraft's radio equipment becoming U/S. The crew were rescued and treated in the Haslar Royal Navy Hospital.

Sgt J C Stevens	Inj
P/O Atkinson	Inj
Sgt R Shipley	Inj
F/S Rogers	Inj
P/O Turner	Inj

March 13/14 1942, Whitley Mk V, Z9214 EY-, Ops - Boulogne. Took off Croft 18:08.

This crew were lost without trace and are commemorated on the Runnymede Memorial.

Sgt H D McColl	K
P/O D R Hockaday	K
Sgt R D Ash	K
Sgt P W Bland	K
Sgt A Macleod	K

March 13/14 1942, Whitley Mk V, Z9389 EY-, Ops - Boulogne. Took off Croft 18:09, crashed 00:40.

Having returned to base, this aircraft crashed during its fifth attempt to land. The second WOP/AG, Sgt Davies, died from his injuries. This was the last Whitley to be lost by 78 during operations.

P/O C F Ferris	K
Sgt R C Bell	K
Sgt N T Gander	K
Sgt J I Davies	Inj
Sgt M M Henshall	Inj

April 23 1942, Halifax Mk 11, R9427 EY-, Ferry Flight. Took off Croft, crashed 11:44.

This aircraft, flown by P/O H E Bedford, was being delivered to 405 squadron, Pocklington, Yorkshire, where it crashed whilst trying to land. A strong crosswind was a contributory factor in this accident. No injuries were reported.

April 29/30 1942, Halifax Mk 11, W7663 EY-, Ops - Ostend. Took off Croft 21:03.

The crew rest in Dunkirk Town Cemetery. This was the first 78 Halifax to be lost on operations.

F/O R M Shattock	K
Sgt D H McDonald	K
Sgt T J Naish	K
P/O J B Brown RCAF	K
Sgt R W Watson	K
Sgt C R Campbell	K
Sgt S K Springham	K

May 3/4 1942, Halifax Mk 11, R9391 EY-, Ops - Hamburg. Took off Croft 23:05.

Crashed in the North Sea, circumstances relating to the aircraft's loss are unknown. With the exception of the tail gunner, Sgt Edwards, who has no known grave, the crew are buried in cemeteries at Kiel and Sage.

S/L A J Snow	K
Sgt E C Smith	K
Sgt F R Mills	K
F/O E C Hebblethwaite	K
P/O J R Kennedy RCAF	K
Sgt T P Davies	K
Sgt G M Edwards	K

May 3/4 42, Halifax Mk 11, W7662 EY-, Ops - Hamburg. Took off Croft 22:54.

Crashed Luneburg Heath, with the exception of the rear gunner, P/O Hanna, the crew are buried in Hamburg's Ohlsdorf Cemetery.

P/O A W Hedge RAAF	K
Sgt D W Drew	K
Sgt F R Hipwell	K
Sgt J Hewitson	K
Sgt J A Lloyd	K
P/O G W Copeland RAAF	K
P/O J E Hanna	POW

May 20 1942, Halifax Mk 11, W1103 EY-, Air Test. Took off Croft. Crashed 11:05.

S/L G D Leyland was carrying out an air test when it crashed, 2 miles north of Croft, on final approach. One crewmember slightly injured.

S/L G L Leyland

May 27 1942, Halifax Mk 11, W1090 EY-, Air Test. Took off Croft 08:40.

Flown by Sgt W Dench, collided with another Halifax immediately after take off. The second aircraft was later repaired. No injuries.

Sgt W Dench

May 30/31 1942, Halifax Mk 11, W1013 EY-, Ops - Cologne. Took off Croft 23:28, crashed 04:05.

Crashed at March, Cambridgeshire, after colliding with a Hampden, of 14 OTU, on the way home from the 1,000 bomber raid. The Halifax's captain, P/O Foers was badly injured in the crash, but was eventually able to return to operations. Sadly, he lost his life whilst flying with 78 on a raid to Krefeld, on the night of the 2/3rd of October 1942, whist the squadron were operating out of Linton-on-Ouse.

P/O G C Foers	Inj
Sgt Curtiss	
Sgt A H Warner	Inj
Sgt G Bolton	K
F/S A W Gamble	Inj
Sgt A Caie	K

June 1/2 1942, Halifax Mk 11, R9364 EY-, Ops - Essen. Took off Croft 23:03.

Due to rudder lock-over, his aircraft entered a flat spin after being attacked by flak near to the Dutch Coast. The fuselage broke into two as the Halifax hit the sea. Miraculously, F/S Miller and the tail gunner, P/O Jones, were thrown clear. Although both were quite badly injured, the two survivors were able to enter the dinghy. After being adrift for four days, they were picked up by the Germans.

P/O J S Lawson MiD, RCAF	K
Sgt R McGlen	K
F/S T B Miller GM, RCAF	POW
Sgt D E West	K
Sgt W Thompson	K
P/O P J Jones	POW

June 1/2 1942, Halifax Mk 11, W1143 EY-F, Ops - Essen. Took off Leeming.

Crashed in the waters of the Haringvllet, between the Dutch coastal town of Hellevoetsluis, and the island of Overflakkee. Sgt Forbes was the only survivor. Only the body of the captain, P/O Clothier was recovered, he is buried Crooswijk General Cemetery. The remainder are commemorated on the Runnymede Memorial. This aircraft had been borrowed by 10 squadron at Leeming.

P/O H G Clothier RNZAF	K
Sgt W R Forbes	POW
F/O J R Ganderton RNZAF	K
F/S J S Clapham	K
Sgt J Simpson	K
Sgt A O Mireau RCAF	K
F/S T A Morris	K

June1/2 1942, Halifax Mk 11, W7698 EY-, Ops - Essen. Took off Croft 22:55.

This aircraft collided at 14,000 feet, with a German night fighter over Bocholt, Germany. Although the Halifax was damaged, it was able to continue on for another 16 km, before crashing Wintersijk, Holland. Three crewmembers were killed, they are buried in the Canadian War Cemetery at Groesbeek, Holland. S/L Leyland had suffered several crashes whilst with 78, the first of which took place on the 10th of October 1941, when his Whitley was in collision with another on the runway at Middleton. This was 78's last loss whilst based at Croft.

S/L G D Leyland	POW
Sgt J E Lyons	K
P/O L G Geddes RCAF	POW
Sgt C G Pugsley	POW
Sgt W Brooks	K
Sgt J Strang	K

June 5/6. 1942, Halifax Mk 11, W7669 EY-. Ops – Essen. Took-off Croft 23:21.

As the Halifax took off and began to climb away from the runway the port inner caught fire. P/O Bedford flew a wide circuit of the airfield at around 150 feet.. As he turned onto final approach in preparation for a landing the port wing stalled and the aircraft crashed and caught fire.

P/O Bedford	K
Sgt V G Mussselwhite	K
Sgt J O'Rourke	K
Sgt W L Turner	Inj
P/O Alder	Inj
Sgt Phillips	Inj
Sgt Mellor	Inj

June 19/20 1942, Halifax Mk 11, BB200, EY-, Ops - Emden. Took off MSG 23:43.

This aircraft crashed in the North Sea, S/W of Denmark. Only the bodies of two crewmembers were washed ashore. The remainder are commemorated on the Runnymede Memorial. Sgt Morgan was buried on the 5th of September in Esbjerg Cemetery, Sgt Frankland is buried in Kiel War Cemetery. This was the squadron's first operational loss having returned to Middleton from Croft.

F/S M M Crow	K
Sgt D Smith BEM	K
Sgt R K Frankland	K
Sgt R W Morgan	K
Sgt E K Davies	K
Sgt L H Seal	K
Sgt J R Williams	K

June 25/26 1942, Halifax Mk 11, W1067 EY-, Ops - Bremen. Took off MSG 23:00, crashed 00:42

Crashed in the waters of the Ijsselmeer, Holland, after being shot down by Uffz Heinz Vinke, 11./NJG2. Sgt Dronfield's body could not be found. He is commemorated on the Runnymede Memorial. The body of the aircraft's captain F/O Whittingham rests in Hemelumar- Oldeferd General Cemetery, in the small Dutch town of Koudum.

F/O J A Whittingham	K
Sgt A G Springthorpe	POW
P/O G Gibson	POW
Sgt D B Donaldson	POW
Sgt H Dronfield	K
Sgt R A Brown	POW

June 29/30 1942, Halifax Mk 11, W1062 EY-, Ops - Bremen. Took off MSG 23:45.

This aircraft crash-landed at Docking airfield, Norfolk, after being badly damaged by a Ju 88 night fighter. The Halifax caught fire, and the tail gunner, Sgt Summerfield, received injuries, from which he later died. The fighter was damaged during the attack and was last seen diving towards the ground with its starboard engine ablaze.

F/L Woodroffe	
Sgt David	Inj
F/S L Geddes RCAF	Inj
P/O LeBeau	Inj
F/S V Fulton RCAF	Inj
Sgt E C Summerfield	Inj

July 26/27 1942, Halifax Mk 11, W1184 EY-, Ops - Hamburg. Took off MSG 22:53.

Lost without trace. All are commemorated on the Runnymede Memorial.

F/O C Mitchener	K
Sgt E A Tweedale	K
Sgt W J Taylor	K
Sgt W K Daniel	K
Sgt D Horgan	K
Sgt G A Bissonnette RCAF	K
Sgt L G Dowling	K

July 29/30 1942, Halifax Mk 11, W1059 EY-L, Ops - Saarbrucken. Took off MSG 23:10.

Attacked several times by a night fighter off the Belgian Coast, the enemy fighter was claimed as destroyed. The Halifax was badly damaged and had to be ditched off Calais. The crew were adrift for 14 hours before they were rescued by an Air Sea Rescue Launch.

F/S C G Dennis	
Sgt Griffiths	
Sgt P P Smith	
Sgt Newman	
Sgt Keikibelt	
Sgt R Gray	
F/S W Dewhurst	

August 5/6. 1942, Halifax Mk 11, W1180 EY-. Ops – Bochum. Took-off MSG 21:55.

This aircraft crashed at Saint Odilienberg, 5 km south of Roermond, Holland. The three airmen that died are buried in Nijmegen and Jonkerbos War Cemetery.

Sgt J C Stevens	POW
Sgt A Greenacre	POW
P/O R Shipley	POW
Sgt D Willoughby	POW
Sgt J W Clark	K
Sgt H M Gall RAAF	K
Sgt J R Gilbert RCAF	K

August 6/7 1942, Halifax Mk 11, W1237 EY-P, Ops - Duisburg. Took off MSG 00:49, crashed 04:15.

Shot down by Hauptman Prinz zu Sayn-Wittgenstein, 1./NJG1, whilst on the way home, crashed in the sea 10 km off the Hook of Holland. Only the body of the tail gunner,

Sgt Hoare, was recovered, the remainder of the crew are commemorated on the Runnymede Memorial.

F/O J M J A d'Ursel Chevalier	K
Of the Order Leopold,	
and Croixe de Guerre	
(Belgium)	
F/S W E Luck	K
Sgt W J Cole	K
F/S A G Johnstone RCAF	K
Sgt G W Scott	K
Sgt G J Cantwell	K
Sgt J G Hoare	K

August 11/12 1942, Halifax Mk 11, W1061 EY-, Ops - Mainz. Took off MSG 21:37, crashed 03:10.

Badly damaged by flak in the target area, after being coned by searchlights. Several crewmembers were injured and both port engines were put out of action. The aircraft came down at Wommelgem, 5 km east of Antwerp. The two airmen that died are buried in Schoonselhof Cemetery. Having successfully evaded, he mid-upper gunner, gunner, Sgt Fay, returned to Canada and carried out a flying course, gaining his wings during October 1943.

Wo2 W E Lunan RCAF	K
Sgt J R Dickinson	POW
Sgt F A Scotland	K
F/S L C Jupp RCAF	POW
Sgt J K Howes RCAF	POW
F/S A E Fay RCAF	Evd
Sgt J H Wyatt	POW

August 11/12 1942, Halifax Mk 11, W1233 EY-, Ops - Mainz. Took off MSG 21:39.

Presumed lost over the sea. With the exception of P/O Myrick RCAF, all were lost without trace, and are commemorated on the Runnymede Memorial. P/O Myrick RCAF was buried on February 27th 1945, in the Fourfelt Cemetery, near Esbjerg, Denmark.

F/S J Fleetwood-May	K
F/S F N Thomasson	K
Sgt L Kelly	K
F/S G H Higgins RAAF	K
P/O J F Myrick RCAF	K
Sgt M J Hisley	K
Sgt J O Harrison	K

August 11/12 1942, Halifax Mk 11, EY-, Ops - Mainz. Took off MSG 21:42.

Crashed at Igstadt, 5 km east of Wiesbaden. The mid upper gunner, Sgt Peart, has no known grave, Whilst the tail gunner, Sgt Mitchell RCAF is buried in Durnbach War cemetery.

Sgt E G Monk	POW
Sgt D F Lemon	POW
P/O E H Bodman	POW
Sgt H Corbishley RCAF	POW
Sgt D Kimber	POW
Sgt J Peart	K
Sgt J A Mitchell RCAF	K

August 11/12 1942, Halifax Mk 11, W1245 EY-B, Ops - Mainz. Took off MSG 21:45.

Crashed near Mean, 33 km southwest of Liege. Those killed are buried in Mean Communal Cemetery.

F/O D A Kingston	K
Sgt P McCann	K
P/O G W Macallister	K
Sgt J Stewart	POW
Sgt I B Griffiths	K
Sgt E F Burrell	K
Sgt R G Kendall RCAF	POW

August 28/29 1942, Halifax Mk 11, W7809 EY-, Ops - Saarbrucken. Took off MSG 19:41.

Crashed between Overijsse and Tombeek, 17 km southeast of Brussels. The crew are buried in Overijse Churchyard.

Sgt J A Marshall RAAF	K
Sgt G E Dunn	K
W/O T M Manning	K
Sgt J P Martin	K
Sgt T H Miller	K
Sgt S Ross RCAF	K
Sgt J G Mellor	K

September 8/9 1942, Halifax Mk 1l, W1252 EY-, Ops - Frankfurt. Took off MSG 20:06.

Damaged by flak, When speed was reduced for an emergency landing, the Halifax became uncontrollable. The crew baled out at 5,000 feet over Abthorpe, 10 miles southwest of Northampton. No injuries were reported.

F/O R E Atkinson	
Sgt C C Crofton	
P/O W Harris	
Sgt A E Thomas	
Sgt C E O'Keefe RAAF	
Sgt F Lister	
Sgt G McBride	

September 8/9 1942, Halifax Mk 11 EY-C, Ops - Frankfurt. Took off MSG 19:35, crashed 22:40.

Crashed near Sclayn, 11 km E/N/E of Lamur, Belgium, after being shot down by a night fighter. The three that died are buried in Haverlee War Cemetery, 24 km east of Brussels. The two who evaded reached Spain on September 24th, and returned to the UK on October 19th 1942. Their expeditious escape had been made possible by Comete.

F/L P H Tippetts-Aylmer DFC	K
Sgt E T Hodge	POW
Sgt T S Brandon RCAF	POW
Sgt J A Winterbottom	Evd
Sgt R Brown	Evd
F/S G R Yeates RCAF	K
P/O E W Gibbs	K

September 10/11 1942, Halifax Mk 11, DT491 EY-, Ops - Dusseldorf. Took off MSG 20:14.

Crashed near the target area, The crew were initially buried in the town's Nordfriedhof, later they were exhumed and buried in the Reichswald Forest War Cemetery, near Kleve. This was the last 78 squadron crew to be lost from Middleton-St-George.

P/O C J Stevenson	K
Sgt R J Roy	K
Sgt B B Warren	K
Sgt A E Arnold RNZAF	K
Sgt W Hodgson	K

| Sgt W C Hiscock | K |
| F/S J H Woodford RAAF | K |

Total number of aircraft lost whilst at MSG/Croft 68.
Operational 63, non-operational 5.
Total number of aircraft lost from MSG Operational 43, non-operational 1.
Total number of aircraft lost whilst at Croft Operational 20, non-operational 4.
Total aircrew killed 203 (plus 2 that were injured but died later), POW's 36, Inj 36 (two died later), Evd 2.

76 Losses - 1941 and 1942

June 15 1941, Halifax Mk 1, L9514 MP-, Training. Took off and crashed at MSG.

This aircraft, flown by P/O A E Lewin, was landing on the crosswind runway when it swung to the right, causing the starboard wheel to leave the runway. The starboard undercarriage collapsed after the wheel dug into soft ground. The aircraft was a write-off. No injuries were recorded.

June 23/24 1941, Halifax Mk 1, L9492 MP-, Ops - Kiel. Took off MSG 23:09, crashed 02:32.

Shot down by Oblt Reinhold Eckardt, 11. /NJG1, this aircraft crashed at Eilendorf, 24 km southwest of the centre of Hamburg. All but one of the crew were killed, and rest in Becklingen War Cemetery, Soltau, Germany. This was the first Halifax to be lost on operations.

P/O W K Stobbs	K
Sgt A Turner	K
Sgt J L Cullum	K
F/S G H Barnard	K
Sgt J S Lopton	POW
Sgt R S Adair	K

July 21 1941, Halifax Mk 1, L9533 MP-, Training. Crashed MSG 12:45.

This aircraft was returning to Goosepool after completing a fighter affiliation exercise with a Hawker Hurricane. The fighter followed the Halifax back to Middleton and flew across the Halifax's path as it approached to land. The bomber's pilot took evasive action and the Halifax crashed, killing all on board.

P/O L R Blackwell	K
Sgt K N Hudgell	K
Sgt A J Grenyer	K
Sgt J W Boggis	K
Sgt A J Howes	K

July 24 1941, Halifax Mk 1, L9494 MP-, Ops - La Pallice. Took off Stanton Harcourt 10:05.

This aircraft ditched off La Rochelle, France, after being hit by flak, and later by fire from a Bf 109. The crew were picked up by a French Fishing vessel but the ditching had been seen by a German patrol boat and the Halifax's crew were transferred to the German craft. This was the first successful ditching of a Halifax.

S/L W R Williams	POW
P/O J G Ireton	POW
Sgt A H Turner	POW

Sgt L J Butler	POW
Sgt N Kershaw	POW
Sgt S Jones	POW
Sgt J R Wedderburn	POW

July 24 1941, Halifax Mk 1, L9517 MP-, Ops - La Pallice. Took off Stanton Harcourt 10:57.

Crashed into the sea off La Rochelle, after being shot down by flak. Only four bodies were recovered from the sea. They were taken to local cemeteries for burial. Sergeants Ford-Hutchinson, Rice and Summers are commemorated on the Runnymede Memorial.

P/O J F McKenna	K
Sgt R F Ford-Hutchinson	K
Sgt G Summers	K
Sgt V A Davis	K
Sgt J M Pilbeam	K
Sgt L T Rice	K
F/S R W Hill	K

July 24 1941, Halifax Mk 1, L9529 MP, Ops - La Pallice. Took off Stanton Harcourt 10:34.

It is likely that this aircraft was shot down by fighters near L'Aiguillon-sur-Mer, 20 km N/N/E of the target area. Three of the crew were buried in the town's Communal Cemetery.

F/L A E Lewin	K
Sgt W H Gourley RAAF	K
F/S C H Horner	K
Sgt B Phillips	POW
Sgt P J Vickery	K
Sgt W A Finlayson	POW
F/O N W McLeod	POW

August 5/6 1941, Halifax Mk 1, L9516 MP-, Ops - Karlsruhe. Took off MSG.

Possibly crashed near Glabeek, 42 km east of Brussels, Belgium. Sgt Brown is buried in Durnbach War Cemetery, Germany. The Australian rear gunner, F/L Leigh, was shot by the German Gestapo, after taking part in the mass breakout from Segen POW camp, as depicted in the film 'The Great Escape'.

Sgt T A Byrne	POW
Sgt C B Flockhart	POW
Sgt J H Pitt	POW
Sgt L A Thompson	POW
Sgt G W Taylor	POW
Sgt R Brown	K
F/L T B Leigh	POW

August 12/13 1941, Halifax Mk 1, L9562 MP-, Ops - Berlin. Took off MSG 21:29, crashed 05:25.

Crashed and burst into flames, after stalling on final approach to Middleton, due to possible damage by flak or fighters.

Sgt J McHale	K
Sgt R J McInnes RCAF	K
Sgt C Austin	K
Sgt S C Mayes	K
Sgt E P Hogan	K
Sgt L E Brown RCAF	K
F/S J G West DFM	K

August 12/13 1941, Halifax Mk1, L9531 MP-R, Ops - Berlin. Took off MSG 21:34.

Crashed near Wittstedt, 15 km S/S/E of Bremerhaven. Everyone was able to abandon the aircraft but five of the crew landed in an area of swamp and drowned. They were buried in Becklingen War Cemetery. The other two became POWs. Only Sgt Kenworthy survived the war however. The tail Gunner, F/S Bone, died, when allied ground attack aircraft shot up the POW column he was marching in, on April the 19th 1945. He rests in Berlin's 1939-1945 War Cemetery.

Sgt C E Whitfield	K
Sgt J J Berry	K
Sgt K R Kenworthy	POW
P/O V D Durham	K
Sgt A Critchlow	K
Sgt N F Brotherton	K
F/S W A Bone	POW

August 12/13 1941, Halifax Mk 1, L9530 MP-L, Ops - Berlin. Took off MSG 21:35.

Shot down near Parnewinkel, 14 km S/S/E of Bremerhaven. Sgt Niven and F/S Woods are buried in Becklingen War Cemetery.

F/L C C Cheshire	POW
Sgt P H Horrox	POW
Sgt R C Wash	POW
F/S G J Smalley	POW
Sgt E C Gurmin	POW
Sgt A T Viven	K
F/S W Woods	K

August 29/30 1941, Halifax Mk 1, L9518 MP-, Ops - Frankfurt. Took off MSG 21:13, crashed 04:15.

Having dallied in the target area this aircraft became low on fuel and crashed near Pocklington airfield, Yorkshire on the way home. The aircraft was abandoned at 2,000 feet, but S/L Bickford and the tail gunner, Sgt Duckmanton, baled out too low and were killed.

S/L R Bickford DFC	K
P/O Jones	
Cpl Randall	
F/S J Flannigan	
Sgt Reilly	
Sgt G W Duckmanton	K

September 13/14 1941, Halifax Mk 1, L9567 MP-, Ops - Brest. Crashed 02:55.

After only 73 minutes airborne, this aircraft crashed on the outward journey, near Water End, Renhold, 5 miles northeast of Bedford. The crew baled out and landed safely.

P/O R E Hutchin	
Sgt Wood	
Sgt Crow	
Sgt Browne	
F/S J Flannigan	
Sgt Littlehales	
Sgt Wallace.	

October 12/13 1941, Halifax Mk 1, L9561 MP-H, Ops - Bremen. Took off MSG 19:45, crashed 21:49.

Crashed near Wons, 10 km south of Harlingen, on the Dutch Coast, after being shot down by Lt. Leopold Fellerer, 4./NJG1. The captain, F/S Muttart remained at the controls long enough for his crew to bale out, but was not able to escape himself. He is buried in Harlingen General Cemetery.

F/S E B Muttart RCAF	K
P/O N F Trayler	POW
Sgt D Cotsell	POW
Sgt L A Roberts	POW
Sgt R W Alexander	POW
Sgt W H Hunt	POW
Sgt G H Patterson	POW
Sgt J W Duffield	POW

October 31/November 1 1941, Halifax Mk 1, L9602 MP-N, Ops - Dunkirk. Took off MSG 19:17.

Lost without trace, all are commemorated on the Runnymede Memorial.

F/S C S O'Brien RCAF	K
P/O N F McLean RNZAF	K
Sgt C W Wood	K
Sgt J R Johnson RCAF	K
F/S J Flannigan	K
P/O F C Brooks RCAF	K
Sgt J Mycock	K

November 30 1941, Halifax Mk 1, L9604 MP-W, Ops - Hamburg. Took off MSG 17:18, crashed 23:35.

Crashed after returning to Middleton, no injuries reported.

Sgt G R Herbert	
Sgt J H Bingham	
Sgt Street	
Sgt M H Roberts RCAF	
Sgt J B Fanning	
Sgt Fulton	
Sgt M C Glover.	

December 30 1941, Halifax Mk 1l, L9615 MP-X, Ops - Brest. Took off MSG 11:22.

Crashed into the sea off the French Coast, after being hit by flak. The crew were lost without trace, and are commemorated on the Runnymede Memorial. This was the first Halifax 11 to be lost by 76 squadron.

P/O D S King RCAF	K
Sgt W R Gates RCAF	K
Sgt P D Randall	K
Sgt S M Wilson RAAF	K
Sgt L Blair	K
Sgt H J Tosco	K
Sgt F Eaton	

1942

January 15. 1942, Halifax Mk 1, L9578 MP-C. Training.

Undercarriage collapsed whilst carrying out a landing at base.

Sgt J B Stark

January 17. 1942, Halifax Mk 1, L9611 MP-J. Training. Took-off MSG 11:00.

Crashed on take-off. No injuries.

Sgt F W Anderson.

January 29/30 1942, Halifax Mk 1, L9581 MP-Q, Ops - Tirpitz. Took off Lossiemouth 02:17, ditched 10:05.

Due to severe icing and W/T failure, this aircraft ditched 4 miles off Aberdeen, Scotland, after the port inner lost power. The icing had caused the crew hardship for many hours. No injuries were reported.

Sgt J W (Johnny) Harwood
Sgt Patey
Sgt Young
Sgt Smardon
Sgt Scott
Sgt Roche
Sgt Petch

February 6 1942, Halifax Mk1, L9570 MP-E, Training. Took off MSG, crash-landed 15:15.

This aircraft was written off when the undercarriage collapsed whilst landing at Tain, Scotland. No injuries.

Sgt H J Lambeth,

March 30/31 1942, Halifax Mk 11, R9453 MP-K, Ops - Tirpitz. Took off Tain 18:30.

This aircraft was last heard on the W/T at 02:15. It was believed that this Halifax crashed into the sea some 16 miles to the south of Sumburgh Head, in the Shetland Islands. Only S/L Burdett's body was recovered from the sea. The remainder of the crew are commemorated on the Runnymede Memorial.

S/L A P Burdett	K
Sgt D C Martin	K
F/S W J Cadger RCAF	K
P/O N F Bowsher RCAF	K
F/S L W Fletcher RCAF	K
Sgt S Davis	K
Sgt L W Hanson RAAF	K

April 10/11 1942, Halifax Mk 11, R9484 MP-G, Ops - Essen. Took off MSG 21:02

Crashed at Oer-Erkenschwick, 5 km N/E of Recklinghausen, 26-km northeast of the target area. There were no survivors. The crew rest in the Reichwald Forest War Cemetery.

F/S H J Lambeth	K
Sgt R Kitchen	K
Sgt W D George	K
P/O J R Connolly	K
Sgt M C Swain	K
Sgt S F Parker	K
Sgt C N Reynolds RAAF	K

April 12/13 1942, Halifax 11, R9452 MP-L, Ops - Essen. Took off MSG 21:59, crashed 00:30.

This aircraft veered off the runway on takeoff and struck a dispersal platform, damaging the propellers and undercarriage. The Halifax suffered severe vibration, caused by the damaged propellers. Fuel and bombs were jettisoned, after which the aircraft was pointed towards the coast and the crew ordered to bale out. The Halifax crashed after a total of 2 hours and 30 minutes in the air, at Hunmanby, 2 miles S/S/W of Filey, Yorkshire.

F/S J N Hobbs RCAF	
Sgt Butler	Inj
Sgt H D Jones	
F/S Rooney	
Sgt W H Charlesworth	
Sgt Roberts	
Sgt R Davidson	

April 12/13 1942, Halifax Mk 11, R9487 MP-X, Ops - Essen. Took off MSG 22:00.

Crashed at Buer, 5 km N/N/W of Gelsenkirchen, after being hit by flak. Although initially buried at Gelsenkirchen, the 6 crewmembers that died were exhumed, and reburied in the Reichswald Forest War Cemetery.

Sgt K F (Keith) Loyd-Jones RAAF	K
P/O W Culmsee	K
P/O R Fairclough	POW
F/S R W Hawksworth MiD	K
Sgt H E Hothersall	K
Sgt P L Wheeldon	K
Sgt W A Moule RCAF	K

April 27/28 1942, Halifax Mk 11, W1017 MP-T, Ops - Dunkirk. Took off MSG 22:05.

This aircraft came under attack by heavy flak whilst over the target area. Whilst taking evasive action, the aircraft became uncontrollable and crashed. Possibly another case of rudder lock-over.

Sgt P C Morris	K
Sgt G A Simpson	K
P/O W A Trickett RAAF	POW
Sgt J Potts	K
P/O W A Shiells	POW
Sgt J W Brown	POW
F/S G Sanderson	K

May 3 /4 1942, Halifax Mk 11, R9451 MP-H, Ops – Hamburg. Took off MSG 22:55

This aircraft crashed at Ottensen, 3 kms S/S/W of Buxtehude. Sgt Williams rests in Hamburg cemetery; the remainder of those who died have no known graves.

Sgt J B Williams	K
Sgt C R Fox	POW
Sgt N H Learman	POW
Sgt H E Owens	K
Sgt B B Jackson	K
Sgt A W Jones	K

May 8/9 1942, Halifax Mk 11, R9456 MP-F, Ops - Warnemunde. Took off MSG 22:00.

Crashed near Rostock. The crew are buried in Berlin's 1939-1945 War Cemetery.

P/O H B Moorhouse	K
Sgt D R Neve	K
F/O W L Long	K
Sgt J J O'Reilly	K
Sgt T P Smith	K
Sgt R Davison	K

May 19/20. 1942 Halifax Mk 1, W7660 MP-L. Ops – Manheim. Took-off MSG 22:35.

Crashed at 01:09 near Marche-en-Famenne, 22 km N/N/W of St Hubert, Belgium after being shot down by Oblt Wilhelm Herget of 11./ NJG4.

F/S F W Anderson	POW
Sgt E K Southward	POW
Sgt C Ilian	POW
Sgt R H Baird RCAF	POW
Sgt J B Gowers	POW
Sgt A E Redding	POW
F/S R A La Franchise RCAF	POW

May 29/30. 1942. Halifax Mk 11, W1065 MP-G. Ops – Gennevilliers. Took-off MSG 23:56.

Crashed in the target area after being hit by flak. The crew rest in Viroflay New Communal Cemetery.

P/O J D Anderson	K
Sgt W Brown	K
P/O N H Bowack	K
Sgt T R Marshall	K
F/S D A Minere	K
Sgt J Nicol	K
Sgt M S Corker	K

June 1/2 1942, Halifax Mk 11, W1064 MP-J, Ops - Essen. Took off MSG 23:06, crashed 01:45.

Starboard inner began to vibrate on the way home, soon after it seized up. It was then set upon by Oblt Heinrich Prinz zu Sayn-Wittgenstein, 111./NJG2, and shot down near Grez-Doiceau, 25-km southeast of Brussels. Sgt's West and Thompson are buried in Heverlee War Cemetery.

Sgt T R West	K
Sgt W J Norfolk	Evd
Sgt J A Oldfield	POW
Sgt J R Wright	Evd
Sgt J R Thompson	K
P/O W B Mulligan RNZAF	POW

June 3/4 1942, Halifax Mk 11, R9457 MP-A, Ops - Bremen. Took off MSG 23:16.

Shot down by Hptm Helmut Lent, 11./NJG2. Crashed at St-Maartensvlotbrug, 6 km west of Shargen, and 48 km N/N/W of Amsterdam.

F/S J W Stell	K
Sgt D H Nelson	POW
Sgt W Archer	K
Sgt R C Cockburn	POW
Sgt D P Brooks	K
Sgt C R Metcalfe	K
Sgt R Greenwood	K

June 3/4 1942, Halifax Mk 11, W1035 MP-U, Ops - Bremen. Took off MSG 23:03, crash-landed 05:00.

Ran over a Glim lamp during the take off roll, which burst the port tyre. Sgt Bingham elected to continue with the operation, which was completed with out further mishap. The aircraft returned safely to Goosepool, only to have its port undercarriage collapse whilst landing. The aircraft was deemed a write-off, the crew however were unhurt.

Sgt J H Bingham	
Sgt G Thom RCAF	
Sgt M C Glover	
F/S M H Roberts RCAF	
Sgt J B Fanning	
Sgt R G Warkcup	
Sgt R N Bircher	

June 3/4 1942, Halifax Mk 11, W1104 MP-F, Ops - Bremen. Took off MSG 23:14.

This aircraft was presumed lost over the North Sea. The captain P/O Philp and tail gunner Sgt Watson are commemorated on the Runnymede Memorial. Sgt Mulhauser, from Michigan USA and Sgt Battersby rest in Germany's Sage War Cemetery. Sgt Ormerod and Sgt Harte are buried in the General Cemetery on the Dutch Island of Vlieland.

P/O J A Philp	K
Sgt J Battersby	K
Sgt F E Ormerod	K
Sgt R S Mulhauser RCAF	K
Sgt J H Harte	K
Sgt W Watson	K

June 16. 1942, Halifax Mk 11, BB199 MP-A, Air Test. Took off MSG 11:05

The port inner caught fire during the flight and the flames soon spread to the wing. As the engine was not fitted with feathering pumps, it was not possible to feather the propeller. Before the airfield could be reached, the aircraft crashed, after ploughing through tall trees, which tore off the rear turret. The tail gunner, Sgt Hoskins, was badly injured, and died later. He was laid to rest in Darlington's West Cemetery.

P/O R L Perry	Inj
Sgt H Coats	
F/S R Scott	
Sgt R W Painter	
P/O R M Craine	
Sgt L D Richardson	
Sgt B F Hoskins	inj

June 20/21. 1942, Halifax Mk 11, W1114 MP-F. Ops – Emden. Took-off MSG 23:28.

This aircraft was first hit by flak and then shot down at 01:43 by a night fighter. It crashed near Ulrum, 20-km northwest of Groningen, Holland. Sgt Salway was unable to get to his parachute and clung onto Sgt Smith. When Sgt smith's chute opened Sgt Salway lost his grip and fell to his death near Houwerzijl, 3 km S/S/E of Ulrum. The 3 airmen that died are buried in Ulrum General Cemetery.

P/O H Norfolk	K
Sgt H D Jones	POW
P/O E A White RCAF	POW
Sgt R W Painter	POW
Sgt W H Charlsworth	K
Sgt D S Smith	POW
F/S E Salway	K

June 24 1942, Halifax Mk 11, W7661 MP-, Training. Crashed MSG 11:18.

Collided with an BAT Flight Airspeed Oxford overhead the airfield at 2,000 feet. The two men in the Oxford (V4140), Sgt's Mason and Sealey, died, along with the entire crew of the Halifax. The wreckage of both aircraft fell onto the south side of the airfield.

Halifax Crew

Sgt J H Bingham	K
Sgt M C Glover	K
F/S M H Roberts RCAF	K
Sgt J B Fanning	K
Sgt R G Warkcup	K
Sgt R H Bircher	K

Oxford Crew

Sgt Mason	
Sgt Sealey	

June 25 1942, Halifax Mk 11, R9378 MP-K, Ground Accident. Caught fire. MSG 20:00.

This aircraft belonged to 76's Halifax Conversion Flight. It was being made ready for the night's operation to Bremen, when an incendiary container fell out of the bomb bay, and ignited. The aircraft caught fire and was destroyed.

June 25 1942, Halifax Mk 11, R9482 MP-D, Air Test. Took off MSG 15:30.

Having just become airborne, this aircraft suffered a loss of power to one or both of its port engines. Having attained a height of around 100 feet, it stalled, and burst into flames as it hit the ground. P/O Higgins DFM was taken to Darlington's Memorial Hospital but died later.

Sgt A Aston	K
Sgt H R Smith	K
Sgt C D Barnett	K
P/O W J Cole	K
Sgt L D Richardson	K
P/O H R Higgins DFM	inj

June 25/26 1942, Halifax Mk 11, W7747 MP-G, Ops - Bremen. Took off MSG 23:36.

Lost without trace. The crew are commemorated on the Runnymede Memorial.

Sgt J E Meyer RCAF	K
Sgt J S Almond	K
Sgt J McCameron	K
Sgt W C Francoeur RCAF	K
Sgt A C Gasson	K
Sgt W J Mills	K
Sgt A Wearmouth	K

June 28 1942, Halifax Mk 11, W7665 MP-N, Training. Crashed MSG 15:45.

This crew was practicing three-engined approaches when the aircraft crashed on landing. F/S Tackley died whilst being treated in Darlington's memorial Hospital.

F/S S Tackley	Inj,
Sgt H W Owen	Inj
Sgt Wilson	Inj
Sgt Morgan	Inj
AC1 Robertson	Inj

June 19/20 1942, Halifax Mk 11, W7670 MP-B, Ops - Vegesack. Took off MSG, crashed 01:45.

Returned early due to technical problems. Over-flew the airfield at 3,000 feet, flying an erratic course and steadily loosing height. Soon after, 5 of the crew baled out. The aircraft crashed near Yarm, 3 miles east of the airfield. The captain, F/S W L Belous RCAF, and the engineer, Sgt F Hebron, were killed.

F/S W L Belous RCAF	K
Sgt F Hebron	K

July 26/27 1942, Halifax Mk11, R9485 MP-H, Ops - Hamburg. Took off MSG 23:03.

Crash-landed at Buxtehude, 21 km southwest of Hamburg, after being hit by flak whilst flying at 18,000 feet. During the crash, the aircraft passed between a row of trees, which removed the wings. The three crewmembers who were killed are buried in Becklingen War Cemetery.

Sgt E J Butt	POW
Sgt P Barr	K
P/O A S Hawkins	K
Sgt R G Woollard	POW
Sgt C M Muir	POW
Sgt D L Osborne	K
Sgt E C Sudbury	POW

July 31/August 1. 1842, Halifax Mk 11, BB195 MP-B. Ops – Dusseldorf. Took-off MSG 23:26.

Badly damaged by a night fighter flown by Hptm Herbert Boensch of NJG2 whilst on the way home over Holland. Sgt McAuley was fatally wounded in the encounter. The tail gunner, Sgt Glasgow managed to shoot down the JU88. Hptm Boensch and his two crewmen, Fw Otto Botcher and Fw August Willie were killed. P/O Waite and his crew abandoned the aircraft once they had reached the UK. It came down near Frisling Hall Farm, near Stock, 6 miles S/S/W of Chelmsford. Sgt McAuley rests in St Oswalds Roman Catholic Churchyard at Longton, Lancashire.

P/O W R Waite	
Sgt H S Greenwood	
Sgt G R Poole RCAF	Inj
Sgt J F Miller RCAF	Inj
Sgt W N Geddie	
Sgt J A McAuley	K
P/O S N Glasgow	

August 9/10 1942, Halifax Mk 11, W1106 MP-B, Ops - Osnabruck. Took off MSG 00:07.

Borrowed by 78, this aircraft was presumed lost over the sea. Three bodies were recovered from the water in different areas. Sgt Howard is buried Esbjerg Cemetery, Denmark, F/S Ironmonger rests in Bergen op Zoom War Cemetery, Holland, and F/S Porter RCAF lies in Sage War Cemetery, Germany. The other four crewmembers are commemorated on the Runnymede Memorial.

Sgt W A Wilson	K
Sgt C M Howard	K
Sgt G A Palmer	K
F/S E J Ironmonger	K
F/S D J Navin RCAF	K
F/S A C Porter RCAF	K
Sgt G D Humphreys	K

August 18. 1942, Halifax Mk 11, V9992 MP-M. Training. Crashed 18:43.

Spun into the ground from 1,000 feet whilst returning to base after completing an air firing exercise.

F/S J Gillies	K
Sgt J A Triscott	K
Sgt A Collins	K
F/S J H Sydes	K
Sgt C C Lee RCAF	K
Sgt W C Bacon	K
Sgt S Dowling	K

August 31 1942, Halifax Mk 11, BB196 MP-O, Training. Took off Pocklington 14:20.

As the aircraft became airborne, the port outer engine faltered. Despite the application of full power, because the aircraft had not reached its 3-engine safety speed, it would not climb above 300 feet. It managed to reach Catfoss airfield, where it crash-landed. During its progress across the airfield, the aircraft's undercarriage collapsed, and the bomber slid into Blenheim Z7302, belonging to 13 OTU. Both aircraft were written off. Sgt Mouir was later commissioned, and won the DFC. He was killed during 1943, whilst instructing at Marsden Moor.

Sgt A I Moir

September 1/2 1942, Halifax Mk 11, WI244 MP-D, Ops - Saabrucken. Took off MSG 23:10, crashed 03:30.

This aircraft crashed into De Blankaart, a nature reserve, 2 km south of Woumen, and some 14-km north of Ypres, Belgium. P/O Sherwood remained at the controls long enough for his crew to escape, but was unable to get out in time. He was initially buried locally, but was re-located later, to the Canadian War Cemetery at Adegem, 45-km northeast of the crash site, and 18 km east of Bruges.

P/O H G Sherwood	K
Sgt LN Park	POW
Sgt C H Smith	POW
Sgt D W Coverly	POW
Sgt E J Kingston	POW
Sgt H Fowler	POW
Sgt H F Turvey	POW

September 8/9 1942, Halifax Mk 11, W1228 MP-A, - Ops Frankfurt. Took off MSG 19:58, crashed 20:18.

Having been airborne for only 18 minutes, this aircraft exploded over the small Yorkshire village of Holtby, 4.5 miles east of York. The wreckage of the Halifax landed in a field only 50 yards from the village itself. The aircraft had been on fire for a short time before the explosion, which had been caused by the photoflash igniting in the bomb bay.

Sgt J E Nicholson	K
Sgt J T Murray	K
P/O A Robson	K
F/S A N Thompson	K
Sgt L G Harvey	K
Sgt R L Stevens	K
Sgt C R Rundle	K

Sept 16/17 1942, Halifax Mk 11, R9365 MP-C, Ops - Essen. Took off MSG 20:35, crashed 00:36.

Shot down by Oblt Hubert Rauh, 11./NJG4, this aircraft crashed at Rubrouck, 36 km E/S/E of Calais. All are buried in Longuenesse Souvenir Cemetery, 2.5-km southwest of St Omer, France. This was the last 76 squadron aircraft to be lost whilst the unit was stationed at Middleton - St - George.

F/O A C Campbell RAAF	K
Sgt S G White	K
Sgt S A Witchell	K
F/S M J Standley RAAF	K
F/S W N Geddie	K
Sgt J R Runnicles	K
Sgt A Moffatt	K

Total of aircraft lost by 76 whilst serving at Middleton St George, Operational 37, non-operational 12.
Total Aircrew Killed 162, plus 3 injured aircrew who died of their injuries later. POW's 62, Injured 11, Evaders 2.

Royal Canadian Airforce Station
Middleton St George

Welcome the Canadian Geese

For some time Bomber Command had been forming squadrons made up of personnel from the Commonwealth and other countries. These included Australians, Canadians, New Zealanders, Poles and to a much lesser extent, the French. The Canadian people not only provided the manpower, but also paid for much of the Royal Canadian Airforce's expenses during WW II. The Commonwealth Air Training Plan (CATP) employed 100,000 personnel, based at some 97 Flying Schools, and 184 ancillary units. At its peak, it employed as many as 10,000 aircraft. By the end of the war, 131,553 aircrew had been trained in Canada. This number of aircrew trained consisted of 41,110 RAF, 72,835 RCAF, 9,606 Australian and 7,000 New Zealanders.

419's crest depicts a moose charging. "MOOSA ASWAYITA"
means "Beware of the moose in Cree Indian language.
Photo: Courtesy of Alan Austin
Copyright MOD/reproduced with permission of Her Majesty's Stationery Office.

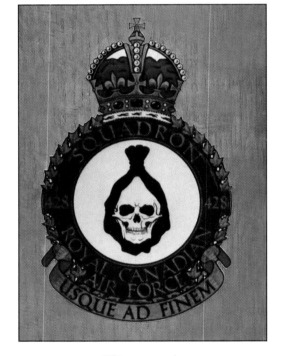

428's crest reads -
"USQUE AD FINEM"
which translates into "To the very end"
Photo: Courtesy of Alan Austin
Copyright MOD/reproduced with permission
of Her Majesty's Stationery Office.

420's crest PUGNAMUS FINITUM
"We fight to the finish"
Photo: Courtesy of Alan Austin
Copyright MOD/reproduced with permission of Her Majesty's Stationery Office.

419 Squadron

First formed on December 15th 1941 at Mildenhall, Suffolk, 419 were the third Royal Canadian Airforce Squadron to be formed abroad. Its CO Wing Commander John (Moose) Fulton DSO DFC AFC came from Kamloops, British Columbia. W/C Fulton and his crew in Wellington VR-H X3488 had been lost on the night of July 28/29th 1942 during a raid on Hamburg. The last transmission received from their wireless operator, F/S N G Arthur simply stated, 'Fighters – wounded - 500.' Seven QDM's plotted the Wellington's position as being ten miles west of the Friesian Islands. Arthur's body was

Wing Commander John "Moose" Fulton DFC AFC RCAF
Photo: IWM CH.5396

later recovered from the sea and buried in Kiel War Cemetery. The second pilot F/S E Monroe and navigator P/O W G Campbell were also recovered, they rest in Kiviberg Cemetery, Sweden. W/C Fulton, the tail gunner F/S H J Dell, and the front gunner Sgt H Bryden were never found and are commemorated on the Runnymede Memorial. F/S Dell had just completed his tour but decided to volunteer for one more sortie, just to help out.

W/C Fulton's post as Squadron Commander was temporarily filled by Squadron Leader D L Wolfe, one of the squadron's Flight Commanders. Wing Commander A P Walsh RCAF arrived at Mildenhall on August 5th, to take over command of the squadron. Five days later, on the 10th, an advanced party of 25 squadron personnel left Mildenhall for Shippea railway station, some 5 miles to the N/N/E of Mildenhall. From here they took the train to Leeming Bar, North Yorkshire. Next day, the squadron's motor transport section worked diligently to load 25 railway goods vans which were parked in the sidings at Shippea. By dark the task was completed. Next day a party of 200 squadron personnel, commanded by F/L D S McCann, were driven to Shippea and loaded aboard a special train, made up of 30 carriages. At approximately 11:30 hours, the train departed for Leeming Bar station. Meanwhile, 17 aircraft transported an

Wing Commander AP Walsh DFC AFC RCAF, extreme right, talking to his crew
Photo: courtesy of Canadian forces

additional 150 men by air. These aircraft landed at Leeming's Satellite airfield, Skipton-on-Swale. The special train arrived at Leeming Bar at 21:40, and all personnel were transported to Skipton, where they were fed and bedded down for the night.

On the 13th the unloading of equipment and general organisation occupied all of the day, and the aircraft, (Wellington IIs), were flown from Skipton to Leeming, where they landed on the one and only serviceable runway. Next day the rear party, made up of 30 squadron personnel, arrived from Mildenhall to complete 419's move to Leeming. Five days later on the

18th, 419 and their aircraft found themselves on the move again. This time they were on detachment to Topcliffe, 9 miles to the S/E of Leeming, and just a short distance from Thirsk. The whole squadron made the move, with the exception of the Maintenance Section, which remained at Leeming.

The aircraft continued operations from Leeming during August including one on the night of the 28/29th to Saarbrucken, from which Sgt Zaparynuk and his crew failed to return. Shot down by a night fighter near the French town of Givet, there was only one survivor, the observer, Sgt W H Ledford RCAF, who evaded capture. Returning to England on November 2nd 1942. Sgt Ledford received the DFM for his exploits and resumed operations. He was eventually killed on August 22/23rd 1943 whilst flying with 434 Squadron during a raid on Leverkusen. The Halifax V, flown by Sgt R S Harrison RCAF that he was flying in was shot down by a night fighter and crashed with no survivors near Tongeren, Belgium.

September 1942

From Topcliffe, the squadron continued with operations on September 1st, with another raid to Saarbrucken. The next day, 419 was stunned when the Squadron Commander W/C Walsh DFC AFC and his crew failed to return from a 4 aircraft raid on Karlsruhe. There were no survivors when their Wellington III, VR-R X3711 was shot down by a night fighter over Dinant, Belgium. W/C Walsh was on the last operation of his first tour. Next day his duties as 419's commander were temporarily taken over by S/L J D Pattison. He carried out his duties until the 8th, when Squadron Leader M M Fleming arrived to take command of the squadron. On September 27th, 419 would begin to move yet again when F/L Ashford led an advance party of squadron personnel, this time to Croft. The main party travelled over by road from Topcliffe on the 30th. The rear part arrived the next day, thus completing the squadron's move to Croft.

Wing commander MM Fleming DSO DFC RCAF
Photo: courtesy of the Canadian forces

October 1942

The 419's strength on their arrival at Croft on the 1st of October 1942 was: -

RCAF Officers (Aircrew)	25
" (Groundcrew)	3
RCAF Airmen (Aircrew)	77
" (Groundcrew)	207
RAF Officers (Aircrew)	5
" (Groundcrew)	0
RAF Airmen (Aircrew)	19
" (Groundcrew)	134

No time was wasted, as the very next day, 419 were off on their first Op from Croft. They despatched nine Wellingtons to Krefeld. Two returned early. Sgt Goddard and crew in X1623 had a problem with a hydraulic oil pipe, which rendered the rear turret U/S. F/S Powell in BJ729 had an engine overheat, this prevented the aircraft gaining height. Powell decided to jettison his bomb load of 810 x 4-lb incendiaries and return to base. The remainder of the aircraft, which were led by P/O Hastey, returned safely.

F/S S V Stow in VR-C BK269 failed to return. The Wellington had been shot down by a German night fighter flown by Oberleutnant Hans Dieter Frank of I NJG/1. The aircraft had come down at Oosterens in Holland, only the bomb aimer Sgt N Nelan RCAF survived. He had baled out and whilst landing he fractured his ankle. Unable to evade capture, he became a POW. The remainder of the crew are buried in Uden War Cemetery, Holland. Three nights later Aachen was the target, again nine Wellingtons were detailed, two aircraft failed to return. On approach to the French coast, Sgt Wakeman, the pilot of Wellington BJ604, was informed by his tail gunner F/S Streeting that his turret had jammed and could not be released. Wakeman had already been informed by the observer P/O Bell that the Gee set was U/S. When about five miles north of Le Crotoy he decided to drop his load of incendiaries and return to base.

Sgt Frederick and his crew encountered severe icing conditions at the turning point, which iced up the rear turret and caused the aircraft to fall out of control for over 2,000 feet. The bomb load was jettisoned in the sea and the Wellington turned for Croft. Sgt Heinze encountered severe electrical storms whilst over southern England. This put the intercom and W/T equipment out of action so the aircraft returned to base. Sgt Crewe had taken off from Croft with his crew in VR-V Z1623, after which nothing further was heard. They were lost without trace and are commemorated on the Runnymede Memorial. F/S Powell RCAF, who had suffered the overheating engine three nights earlier, crashed at Maastricht in Holland, four hours after leaving Croft. All on board were killed. They are now buried in Jonkerbos War Cemetery. The remainder of 419's Wellingtons returned safely.

The following night, six aircraft were sent from Croft to attack Osnabruck, all returned safely. On 9th October, F/L Harrison assumed the duties of 419 Squadron's adjutant. Next day VR-Y flown by Sgt Scobie crashed in the vicinity of the airfield. The Wellington had been on a training flight when it caught fire whilst overhead Croft. Sgt Colvin RCAF the wireless operator and the tail gunner Sgt Hicks RCAF were killed, the other four crew members were injured. Sgt Scobie, P/O Campbell the second pilot, and Sgt D'Aperng the bomb aimer were dangerously injured, Sgt Lloyd the observer was seriously injured. Sgt Scobie died from his injuries at 12:40 the next day. The funerals of the three dead airmen took place at Darlington's West Cemetery at 14:00 hours on the 13th. Sgt Aperng was to die on operations later.

That night, 10 Wellingtons from Croft attacked Kiel. Sgt Wakeman and his crew crashed into the sea off Brockeswalde, Germany. All of the crew were killed. They are buried in Becklingen War Cemetery. Another aircraft failed to return on the next operation from Croft. This was on the 15th, when 10 Wellingtons of 419 attacked Cologne. Sgt Jolly RCAF and his crew crashed near Monchengladbach where their aircraft burst into flames. All on board the Wellington were killed. In view of the loss of his son, the father of Sgt Jolly, who was himself a Flight Lieutenant, visited the squadron. On the same day, 419's engineering officer F/O Scott welcomed his understudy F/L Bartlett, who would be shortly taking his place.

420 Squadron

Formed at Waddington on December 19th 1941 under 5 Group, 420 (Snowy Owl) Squadron was the fourth RCAF squadron to be formed overseas. They had flown Hampdens from their formation up to August 1942. They had then converted onto Wellingtons and during October of 42 the squadron had moved to the brand new airfield of Skipton-on-Swale, North Yorkshire.

On Thursday October 1st 1942, a bus containing ENSA personnel was returning to Skipton at night from an ENSA show at Leeming, when it ran into the back of a parked lorry in the dark. The blackout required that all vehicle lamps were shielded to almost a pinprick of light to guard against being seen by enemy aircraft. The light was so dim that the parked vehicle had not been seen. Despite this, the RAF driver would eventually be brought to book in a civil court for the accident. He was fined £1 for reckless driving and also had to pay £7 and 15 shillings court costs, in those days a considerable amount of money. Aircraftsman Reid of Skipton's Station Headquarters, who had been a waiter in the Sergeants' Mess, was killed. Sgt Gagan, also belonging to 420 Squadron, was seriously injured in the crash and was taken to Catterick Military Hospital. Four other 420 Squadron Sergeants who were less seriously injured were taken back to Leeming's SSQ. The next day, Sgt Boniface was placed on the dangerously injured list as a result of his injuries sustained in the previous night's bus crash. Later in the day, Sgt Loftus of the station's Orderly Room was also admitted to hospital as a result of the MT accident.

On Saturday October 3rd, preparations were made for operations. Seven aircraft and crews flew across to Leeming whilst the ground personnel were transported by road. Later the operation was cancelled and the aircraft were left at Leeming whilst the personnel returned to Skipton by road. Ninety-five ground and forty-five aircrew personnel proceeded to Leeming the next morning to prepare for operations. Again the operation was cancelled and everyone returned to Skipton.

During the afternoon a Wellington III arrived bringing the number of 420 Squadron aircraft to 18. On Monday 5th, the ground and aircrews were again bussed and trucked over to Leeming. Nine aircraft were prepared for the night's raid but due to a change of bomb load only three were ready in time. One returned early with intercom problems and the other two successfully attacked the target and returned safely.

On Friday October 9th, Wing Commander Bradshaw, 420's Squadron Commander, accompanied the Adjutant and section heads by road to Middleton St George. The reason for the trip was to allow them to look over the airfield, which would become their new home on the 15th. In preparation for the move, an advance party of squadron personnel departed by road for Middleton on the 12th.

Next day ten Wellingtons belonging to 420 took off for a raid. One aircraft collided with another aircraft returning from the target and had the top portion of its tail cut off. However it was able to return to base and land safely, whilst the other aircraft had to make a forced landing at Docking, where it overshot the runway. Two members of its crew suffered broken legs and had to be taken to hospital, the remainder of the crew were unhurt. A third Wellington, flown by F/S Croft RCAF, crashed at Leeming whilst trying to land in very marginal weather conditions. As it overshot and attempted a climbing turn, the aircraft lost power and crashed onto a house. All five on board were killed. They were buried on the 17th at Ripon Cemetery. On the same day 1516 BAT Flight left croft and returned to Goosepool. At the time they had 7 Oxfords; V4103, V4124, V4126/7/8, DF 289 and DF 448.

On Wednesday the 14th, preparations for the move to Middleton were well under way, their equipment being loaded at Topcliffe railway station. Next morning the big move began in earnest. The main party of squadron personnel departed by train for Middleton at 11:30. The air party took off at 11:15, whilst the road transport left Skipton at 15:00.

Goosepool once again reverberated to the sounds of aero engines, when the circuit was filled with 420's Wellingtons led by W/C D A R Bradshaw, after their short trip from Skipton, some 19 miles to the south. On arrival at Middleton, seven of 420'sWellingtons were immediately readied for a raid on Cologne. Taking off a few minutes before 19:00 hours, all aircraft returned safely to base, with the exception of F/S White RCAF and his crew in PT-B X3808. They became the first 420 Squadron aircraft to be lost from Middleton St George. They were lost without trace and are commemorated on the Runnymede Memorial. Two days later, on Saturday the 17th, the rear party, with F/L Goff in charge, arrived at Middleton from Skipton to complete the squadron's move.

Meanwhile, on October 21st, W/C Waterhouse was welcomed to Croft, whilst three days later, five of 419's Wellingtons were despatched on a daylight raid to Krefeld. All returned safe having turned back due to unfavourable weather conditions. On Thursday the 22nd, 420 made preparations for a daylight Moleing raid on Emden. A reconnaissance aircraft sent to check the cloud cover reported that the weather over the Dutch Coast was clear, and so the operation was cancelled. Moleing operations were normally carried out during the hours of daylight, using thick cloud cover to hide in.

Next day, Moleing operations to Krefeld were planned by both 419 and 420, this time they were to send five Wellingtons each. With the exception of one of 420's aircraft, which bombed the target, all of the aircraft were forced to turn back due to clear weather over the target. This aircraft eventually returned safe and landed at Waddington. Meanwhile, Croft entertained G/C Cameron RCAF, who had paid an informal visit to the airfield. The remainder of the month for 419 and 420 was fairly uneventful.

The last day of October saw both squadrons undertake another daylight Moleing raid. Three of 419's crews, flying over and burrowing through total cloud cover, made their way to attack Emden. Bombing was carried out on ETA through 10/10ths-cloud cover, a classic Moleing operation during this period. Three of 420's crews were also briefed for this Op but only two took off after the third suffered intercom failure. All aircraft returned safely.

427 Squadron formation - November 1942

On the first of November, due to the absence of a proper church, a voluntary church parade was held by 420 as an experiment in Middleton's NAFFI. Three of 420's aircraft were bombed up for a daylight raid, but they were not required. The weather continued to be foggy over the next few days, which prevented any operations. After the bad weather caused a series of stand-downs, 419 and 420 sent three Wellingtons apiece on the same cloud cover daylight operations, when both squadrons formed part of a 14 Wellington and 5 Lancaster force to bomb Essen, Osnabruck and Wilhelmshaven. 420's pilot Officer J Hudson did not attack Wilhelmshaven as briefed. The town was seen below cloud at 6/8,000 feet but the aircraft

was hit by flak. Hudson took cover in the cloud and turned away from the target and attempted to bomb a cargo ship from about 1,200 feet, after which he and his crew returned to Goosepool.

P/O Burt was also unable to bomb Wilhelmshaven. Having mistaken an eastern lake for one further to the south, he and his crew tried to turn north to reach the primary. Before this could be done, the alternate target appeared on their track and this was bombed. An inlet was seen, with a jetty containing three large barges about 100 feet long. These were bombed, although no results were seen. Despite the directional gyro becoming U/S, Burt and his crew were able to find their way home, where they landed at 16:35. The story for the remainder of Middleton's crews was similar. In all, only six out of the 19 aircraft were able to bomb Wilhelmshaven and Osnabruck through cloud with any real success. All 19 aircraft returned safe. Meanwhile on the same day, 420 welcomed its new Adj, F/L G N Goff.

419 ceased to be operational on Saturday November 7th, and preparations were made for the dispersal of the squadron prior to their conversion onto the Halifax. On the same day, Wing Commander Waterhouse, who had been on a short attachment with the squadron, returned to 102 Squadron at Pocklington. Also, S/L A P Dart, 419's B Flight Commander, was posted to 20 OTU for instructor duties. A third member of the Squadron to leave was P/O Parnham, posted to 196 Squadron, which had been formed at Driffield on the 7th. Twelve of 419's crews were attached to 1659 Conversion unit at Leeming and Topcliffe, for training on Halifaxes.

Wing Commander Waterhouse RCAF
Photo: courtesy of the Canadian forces

134

A small nucleus of 419's crews remained behind at Croft to form a brand new RCAF unit, 427 Squadron. New squadrons were now urgently required for the build up of 6 Group. The very successful method of cloning a new unit out of a small number of experienced personnel drawn from an existing squadron, was by now standard practice.

The next day, preparations were underway for 419's next move, this time to Middleton St George. Also on the 8th, 420 detailed 10 crews for a successful gardening sortie to the Friesian Islands. One Wellington flown by Sgt Lawson was slightly damaged by flak. This aircraft had run into the defences off Borkum, where the light flak was intense. The defences could not be evaded, and although the run-in was initiated at 3,000 feet, the aircraft had to dive to 50 feet before it could escape. The wireless operator had received a small wound to his right leg during the attack, and the aircraft sustained damage to its intercom and flaps. The aircraft was unable to sew its vegetables and both mines were brought back. All aircraft returned safe.

On the 9th, 419's Squadron Adjutant, F/L W G Harrison, led an advanced party, which began the move to Middleton. The afternoon saw the arrival of S/L D W S Clark who was to assume the duties of Flight Commander.

Goosepool's fuel farm, taken from the roof of hangar 4, looking west
Photo: via Geoff Hill

420 had offered 15 aircraft for the night's raid on Hamburg. Ultimately only 11 got off, and only two bombed the objective. Sgt W S Beale and his crew in PT-B Z1679 crashed in the sea off Pellworm Island in the northern Friesians. Only the body of one crewmember, Sgt C Collard, was recovered from the sea. P/O W J (Jock) Maitland's crew in PT-K suffered oxygen failure and were only able to reach a point some 27 miles off Bridlington. Having taken off at 17:54, he and his crew returned to Middleton, having flown 2 hours and nineteen minutes.

S/L L K Smith had to abandon the operation, as on reaching 7,000 feet his hearing deteriorated. Despite changing helmets with the bomb-aimer he was still unable to distinguish anything said by the crew. The bombs were jettisoned from 7,000 feet after which the aircraft was turned for home. Later, as the aircraft reduced height, S/L Smith's hearing gradually returned. Sgt Thomas's crew returned early when all the petrol in one wing was used up, owing to the incorrect positioning of the fuel cocks, which caused one wing to drop on the way home. S/L Jacobs's crew encountered 10/10ths cloud and were engulfed for the whole trip. The aircraft was heavily attacked by flak and holed in several places. Jacobs dropped from 14,000 feet to 6,000 before shaking off the defences. Unable to see anything, Jacobs decided to abort the mission and return to base. Next day, 420 switched to night gardening operations and sent five Wellingtons, all of which returned safely and diverted to Swinderby in Lincolnshire. On Armistice Day, the remaining 419 aircrew not attached to 1659 HCU or 427 Squadron moved over to Middleton. 420 were still hard at it, and sent another five aircraft that night on gardening operations. The weather prevented accurate navigation and no mines were dropped. All returned unharmed to Goosepool.

The following morning, 419's Engineering Officer F/O Scott and the Dental Officer Captain Stewart reported to Middleton. The Electrical Engineer P/O Tupling would follow them on the 16th. Meanwhile, 420's Hockey team played 424 Squadron at Durham Ice rink and won 4-0. This 'chocked up' the second victory for the squadron. On the 13th, the first three Halifaxes arrived at Middleton and were received by 419. On the 16th and 17th, 420 continued gardening operations without loss. Two more Halifaxes arrived for 419 on the 18th along with W/C Fleming DFC, who had returned from 1659 Heavy Conversion Unit at Leeming.

Halifax Mk II Operating Data

The Halifax Mk II was a heavy bomber fitted with four Merlin XX or 22 engines and Rotol fully feathering propellers. The Halifax Mk V was similar to the Mk II but was fitted with a Dowty instead of a Messier hydraulic undercarriage system.

There were twelve self-sealing fuel tanks fitted to this mark of Halifax. They were arranged in six pairs, and consisted of:

Two 247 Imperial gallon inboard tanks (No 1), Two 100 gall wing nose tanks, (No 2), Two 188 gall centre tanks (No 3), Two 161 gall outboard tanks (No 4), Two 122 gall outer engine tanks (No 5) and Two 123 gall outer engine tanks No 6).

Tanks No 5 and 6 were plumbed together, and could be classed as one tank .On early aircraft the No 6 tanks were not fitted. In addition to this normal tanking arrangement, three self-sealing 230-gall long-range ferry tanks could be fitted inside the bomb bay. If even longer range was required, two 80-gallon tanks could be fitted in the fuselage centre section at the crew rest position.

Walk around

Before entering the aircraft, checks were carried out to ensure that the engine, cockpit, and most importantly, the pitot covers had been removed. This was followed by a search for oil, fuel and coolant leaks. Next on the list was to check that all engine cowlings were secure and that the huge tyres had no cuts. Whilst looking at the tyres the pilot checked that the 1 inch wide yellow line that was painted across the bead of the tyres and the wheel hub were aligned, and had not crept out of line during the previous landing.

Whilst in the vicinity of the undercarriage he next checked the Oleo legs for even compression*. After this, his attentions were drawn to the undercarriage accumulator pressure gauge, which was checked to see that the pressure reading was above the minimum 150-psi mark.** He also checked that the Accumulator pressure gauge for the undercarriage doors read higher than the minimum 350 psi.

With the external checks completed, the pilot walked to the side door and entered the Halifax. This oval shaped opening was located on the lower port side of the fuselage, between the wing trailing edge and the tailplane. He would be happy to see that the crewmembers that had already boarded were busy stowing all loose equipment. A check that all control locks were removed and stowed was followed by a quick look at the Ground/Flight switch. This was located on the starboard side of the fuselage at the engineer's station. The large round 6-inch diameter rotary switch was checked to see that it had been set at "Ground". This was necessary as the Trolley-Acc was plugged in ready for engine starting***.

Halifax flight engineer standing at his panel behind the pilot   Photo: IWM CH.5399

Once in his seat the pilot began his cockpit checks. At the same time the engineer disengaged the undercarriage up-locks, which were positioned above the rest seats and behind the rear wing spar. He then ensured that the clips were secured in their stowage.

Whilst there he opened the adjacent nitrogen fire protection valve, which purged the flammable oxygen, trapped in the airspace above the 100-octane petrol in the fuel tanks, and replaced it with inert nitrogen. On some aircraft, an automatic nitrogen fire protection system was fitted. As fuel was used, this system automatically replaced the potentially explosive fuel/air mixture in the top of the tanks with nitrogen.

Next came the hydraulic system checks, whilst at the rest station the engineer checked that with the flaps up, the port and starboard flap accumulator pressure gauges read 500-lb, psi. Underneath the flap accumulators was the flap isolating cocks control, which he unscrewed. Bomb doors accumulator pressure was checked next to see if with the bomb doors closed the gage read 500-lb psi. Moving to the aft face of the rear spar, he checked that all of the fuel tank cross-feed cocks were turned off.

Clambering over the rear and front spars the engineer positioned himself by his control panel, which was located on the left-hand side of the cockpit behind the pilot and facing forward. Once there he checked the eight fuel tank contents gauges.

Halifax pilot. Note temporary dual controls fitted to right hand side of cockpit   Photo: IWM CH.5398

*Oleo leg-hydraulic suspension strut
**PSI- Pounds Per Square Inch pressure reading
***Trolley-Acc. Mobile accumulators (Batteries) for the engines electric starter motors, this saved weight in the aircraft

Meanwhile the pilot was carrying out his pre-engine starting checks.

Flaps and landing lamp --Retracted.

Undercarriage lever down, flaps and bomb doors lever -------------------------Neutral.

Brake pressure, brakes --On.

Flying controls --------------------------------Check for free movement and full travel.

Oxygen capacity and flow --Check.

Visual call light system---Test.

It was now time to start the engines.

The lever of the number one engine's master engine cock was moved to the up position. At the same time, the engineer was asked to turn on fuel tanks 1 and 3. Next, he moved the throttle levers on the top of the central throttle control box forward, and set them to about 1/2 inch open. His hand dropped to the bottom of the box to the single two-position lever (Marked S and M) that controlled the superchargers, he selected "M". Moving up a few inches to the centre of the throttle box, he checked that the 4 propeller control levers were pushed fully up into the "Fine" position.

"Carb-air intake" he enquired, "Set to Cold, Skip," answered the engineer, whose job it was to operate this control, placed on the port side of the fuselage, next to his control panel. This was just about the least used control in the aircraft, as due to the fitment of gapped ice guards in front of the carburettor air intakes, Carb icing was rare. If ice was allowed to form however, this would reduce the air to the carburettors and cause an over rich fuel/air mixture, called a "Rich cut". This could occur, stopping the engine, or engines. Warm air was available from a duct around the exhaust manifold to remove, or prevent, ice forming, when the control was set in the hot position. There was, and still is, a down side, to warm air, as it reduces air density, (and thus causes a drop in rpm).

"Radiator shutters to Shut", the pilot continued, "already done skip". The engineer was responsible for the hydraulic radiator shutters, which when shut - reduced the cooling air that passed through each engine's coolant radiator and allowed the Merlin to warm up quicker. Once the engines were running the shutters were adjusted to give the optimum engine coolant temperature.

Along with the Carb air and radiator shutters, the engineer, who spent a large amount of his time standing behind the pilot, had controls for a variety of other functions. These included the engine's starting magnetos, starter buttons, fuel transfer pump switches, fire extinguishers and oil dilution switches. He also had the majority of the engine pressure, temperature and fuel contents gauges and electrical system controls.

Shouting out of the window the pilot instructed the ground crew to prime No.1 engine. The selector cock and priming pumps were located at the rear of each undercarriage faring and served both engines on that side. A ground crewman turned on the cock and operated the hand-priming pump, until the suction and delivery pipes were primed. This was indicated by a sudden increase in resistance on the pump handle as the pressure in the system built up. Both appropriate magnetos were then switched on and the pilot instructed the engineer to switch on the starter magneto. He pressed the starter button for No 1 engine. As the engine began to turn, the ground crewmember continued to prime the induction system.

As the air temperature on this particular day was only about 10 degrees, the priming handle in the engine nacelle had to be operated for about 7 strokes, to ensure that the engine would start.

After the Merlin spluttered into life it had to be helped along by the ground crewman who continued to operate the priming handle until the carburettor picked up, and was able to sustain the engine. Once this was achieved, the engineer was told to switch off the engine's starter magneto. The ground crewman would then turn off that particular engine's priming cock and screw down its priming handle. This ritual was repeated for each engine, after all four engines were running satisfactorily, the Ground/Flight switch was turned to Flight and the ground starter plug was removed.

Each throttle was gradually opened to 1,200 rpm and the engines warmed up. Whilst the engine temperature gauges were rising, The D.R. compass switches were turned on. Next the hydraulic system was tested by lowering and raising the flaps. After this, the brake pressure was checked, along with the Pesco vacuum pumps* and the aircraft's intercom.

The pilot and the engineer continued with the after start up checks. Each engine would in turn receive it's own set of checks.

Revs to 1,500, check magnetos for rpm drop, this entailed switching off each magneto in turn whilst watching the rev counter for that engine, (max drop 150-rpm). Open each engine up to + 4 lb./sq.in. boost, and check operation of two-speed supercharger. RPM should fall, and boost rise momentarily when the S ratio is engaged. After these checks were completed, the control lever was returned to M ratio. As the boost check on each engine was taking place, the propellers constant speed units was also checked for correct operation. Rpm was checked on each engine and the lever was brought fully down, when completed, the lever was returned to the fully up (fine pitch) position. To check take-off boost, the throttles were momentarily opened fully, if all was well the boost gauge should have read +14 lb./sq.in. At the same time, the engine's rpm was checked. The throttles were then pulled back to +9 lb./sq.in. to test slow running (Tick-over), and each magneto tested again, the rev drop was not to exceed 150 rpm.

The aircraft was now ready to taxi out onto the perry track. The brake pressure gauge was required to read 90 psi and the supply pressure 250-300 psi. The D.R. compass was switched to 'Normal'.

At the runway the final pre-take off checks were carried out.

*Required to drive the Gyro instruments on the instrument panel, (artificial horizon, turn and slip indicator, direction indicator (D.I.) etc)

Autopilot controls --------------------------------Main switch OFF
Trim tabs------------------------------Rudder and aileron controls
Propellers----------------------------------Speed controls up (fine)
Fuel -------------------------------Engineer to check cock settings
Flaps ----------------------------0-35 degrees down (as required)
Superchargers ---M ratio.
Radiators --SHUT.
Air intake --COLD.
Boost control cut-out ----------------------------Correct position.

Clutch IN.   Full and free movement
NEUTRAL.   Elevator 1/2 division tail heavy.
(INCREASE REVS).

Crew at stations, all hatches closed.

For take-off the throttles had to be opened slowly at first, then fully as the aircraft accelerated. There was a tendency to swing to port, but this was checked initially by the throttles, and as aerodynamic speed was reached, by the rudders. Sometimes a dab of differential brake saved the day.

The elevators were heavy at first, but when sufficient speed was attained the tail was easily raised by the pilot's firm pull on the control column.

At weights of around 50,000-lb. the Halifax flew itself off the ground, but at 60,000-lb, 100 mph I.A.S. was required, along with a firm pull to unstick. After lift-off, the indicated safety speed was 140 mph, (130 actual).

Climbing

Fully loaded the initial speed for maximum rate of climb was 140 (150 mph I.A.S.)
After the undercarriage was retracted and the flaps had been raised, the engineer engaged the undercarriage mechanical up-locks and closed the flaps isolating cocks.

General Flying

In a high-speed dive the aircraft became tail heavy and required forward trimming. The trim tabs on the elevators, ailerons and rudders were powerful, the elevators especially. As the undercarriage and or flaps were raised a slight nose down trim change was experienced.

With the advent of the larger square fins (Mod 814), the rudders were somewhat heavy in operation; on the other hand, the tendency to lock over during sideslip manoeuvres had been removed. Prior to Mod 814 the smaller, triangulated fins were lighter on the feet, much lighter in fact than the elevators and ailerons. Care was required to prevent excessive sideslipping, and the resultant possibility of rudder lock-over. The secret in a turn was to use the elevator early and prevent the nose from dropping, and thus negate the need for the application of top rudder. Many Halifaxes were lost due to this rudder overbalancing. A large sideslip or skid would stall the fins and cause the rudders to lock-over. In this event the Halifax could enter a spiral dive, with, if ones height was insufficient, little chance to recover.

Actions for recovery were included in the pilot's notes for the Mk II and V Halifaxes. They required that:-

a; the nose was to be lowered to gain at least 150 (160) I.A.S., although care was required against acquiring excessive speed.
b; Throttle back all engines.
c; Centralise the rudders.

Excessive use of the ailerons opposite to the direction of the rudders was to be avoided, as this would increase the sideslip.

At speeds below 140 mph I.A.S. the aircraft was much more pleasant to fly if 30-40 degrees of flap were used.

Stalling

The stall in the Halifax was straightforward and quite gentle, with no pre-stall buffet or warning. There was no tendency to drop a wing. Pushing the control column forward allowed the pilot to recover quite easily.

The stall speed was determined by the weight of the aircraft and was also dependent on the position of the undercarriage and flaps.

At a weight of 45,000 lb., the stall with U/C and flap down was 78-mph (84) I.A.S. and at 55,000 lb., 86-mph (92).

At a weight of 45,000 lb., the stall with U/C and flap up was at a speed of 95 (102) I.A.S. and at 55,000, 105 (113).

Landing

Just as they did during take-off, the pilot and the flight engineer had to work closely together during the landing phase. The pilot would check with his engineer: -

Radiator shutters- 'Closed'.
Carburettor air-intake heat control- set to 'Cold'.
Undercarriage up-locks- disengaged and clips secured.

Fuel tanks in use- contents checked.
Total fuel and all up weight - calculated
Flaps isolating cocks- 'Open'.

Speed was then reduced to 140 (145) mph IAS, providing the flap limitation speed of 150 (160) mph* was not exceeded the flaps could be utilised to assist in this regard.

*The speed below which the flaps could be safely lowered without causing airframe damage or severe control problems

Pre landing checklist

Brakes- 90 lb./sq.in. (Supply 250-300 LB./sq.in.).

Undercarriage- Down (check- down and locked Lights).

Propellers- R.P.M. increased to 2,850 (approx).   Superchargers- M ratio.

Flaps- fully down (80 degrees) or less in high winds.

If the all up weight of the aircraft was 55,000 lbs. the recommended speeds for the approach were; engine assisted 105-mph I.A.S. and glide approach 115-mph I.A.S.

During an overshoot in normal trim and with undercarriage and flaps down the Halifax became nose heavy when the throttles were fully opened. Once safely airborne again the flaps were raised to 40-degrees before the undercarriage was raised.

After landing checks.

As the aircraft was turning off the runway the radiator shutters were opened to provide as much cold air to the Merlin's coolant radiators. The flaps were raised to prevent damage to their underside by stones and other FOD** thrown up by the propellers.

As the air pressure required for braking was derived from a compressor on one of the inner engines, the brake supply gauge was checked to see if sufficient pressure was available to reach one's dispersal. If so, the two inner engines could be stopped, and to save fuel, the aircraft could be taxied in using only the two outer engines. Once at dispersal the aircraft was parked into wind with the tail-wheel central.

Selecting the master cocks to "off" stopped the engines; this also operated the slow-running cut-outs. Once the engines had stopped the Magneto switches were turned off, as were all tank cocks. The switches for the undercarriage position indicator, fuel contents gauges and the pitot heater was also switched off. Next came the Ground/Flight switch, which was turned to Ground. The D.R. Compass and T.R.9.F. radio equipment were the last items to be switched off.

Halifax pilot's view from left hand window   Photo: IWM CH.6595

**FOD- Foreign Object Damage. A relatively modern term but amounting to the same

The next day, several more officers and aircrew returned to Goosepool, having also completed their Halifax conversion courses at Topcliffe. It was here that existing squadron aircrew did their conversion onto the Halifax, whilst new crews destined for 419 completed theirs at Leeming. As the crews arrived back from Leeming, a party of 50 ground personnel was leaving Middleton for Marston Moor to attend a short Halifax conversion course; they were to return later in the month. 1659 HCU had been formed at Leeming on October 6th. This unit was instigated as part of the Empire Air Training Scheme, responsible for training RCAF crews in preparation to the formation of 6 Group.

6 Group RCAF initiated its own conversion training program and formed 61 Training Base Headquarters at Topcliffe.

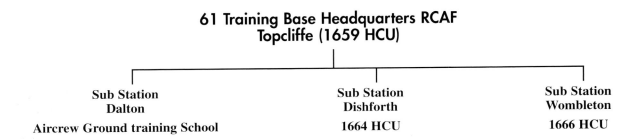

1659 HCU initially absorbed 408 Squadron's conversion flight, which had formed on September 20th. 408 (Goose) Squadron had been based at Leeming since September 14th. However, due to the poor state of the runways it was attached to 1652 HCU at Marston Moor for conversion onto the Halifax.

The 20th saw 420 send nine Wellingtons to bomb Turin. The aircraft had earlier departed to Harwell, which was to be their advance base for the operation. Twenty groundcrew had also been sent to Harwell to assist in the night's operation. The target was found by PFF flares and by pinpointing the rivers Rip and Po located to the Northeast. The target itself was very lightly defended. Wing Commander D A Bradshaw attacked from 16,000 feet, in clear moonlight, and reported an uneventful trip with excellent navigation. Next day the aircraft returned from Harwell greatly thrilled after their first trip over the Alps. Next day 420 sent 10 more aircraft to Harwell, two of which transported a groundcrew servicing party for the night's raid on Stuttgart. All returned safe with the exception of one Wellington, which crash-landed on its return to Harwell due to heavy flak damage. The co-pilot, an officer from 427 Squadron, had received a small flak wound to the leg. All aircraft returned from Harwell the next day, with the exception of the crash landed aircraft, which was damaged beyond repair. The squadron was to carry out three more gardening operations during November from which all crews would return safely.

During the month, 419 continued to build up as more and more aircrew arrived from Leeming. On the 25th, 420 sent two aircraft back to the Friesians for yet another gardening operation from which both returned safe. The next day, despite a visit by the AOC Air Vice Marshall Roddy Carr and AVM Brooks RCAF, 420 returned once again to the Nectarine[77] area for more of their favourite pastime, gardening. Out of the seven Wellingtons that had taken off, only three were able to sew their vegetables in the appropriate patch. The other four brought theirs back due to very bad weather conditions. The good old Teesside weather was up to its usual tricks and Dishforth was as close to home as they could get. On the 28th, having been repaired, Leeming's runways were deemed serviceable once again. This allowed 405 (Vancouver) Squadron's conversion flight to arrive from Topcliffe, where they were also embodied into 1659. Meanwhile, back at Middleton St George, at 11:30 on the 30th Halifax DT 540 crash-landed on the airfield during a training flight, sustaining damage to the propellers and undercarriage. This became 419's first Halifax prang, fortunately without injury to F/S Frederick and his crew. As November 1942 drew to a close, 419 Squadron's strength was recorded as: -

Aircraft - 5 Halifax Mk IIs

Aircrew officers   RAF 6, RCAF 17,
Aircrew airmen   RAF 32, RCAF 83.
Groundcrew officers RAF 1, RCAF 4.
Groundcrew airmen   RAF 163, WAAF 35, and RCAF 333.

December 1942

During December, more and more aircrew arrived at 419. A certain amount of night flying training was carried out as the squadron continued to become more familiar with their new mount. Mannheim was the venue for 420 on the 6th. After a couple of minelaying trips during the two days between, the squadron departed again for Turin, via Harwell, on the 9th. Canadian Group Captain Dwight Ross arrived at Goosepool on the 10th, to assume command of the station.

On most occasions throughout the month, Teesside's weather had necessitated almost constant diversions. The closest anyone could get to base was Dishforth. On the 12th 1516 BAT Flight departed Goosepool for Hampstead Heath. On the 15th, Middleton welcomed yet another unit to its fold. 1535 BAT Flight was formed in Hangar 1 on this date, the aircraft were to arrive later in the month.

[77] Codeword for the Friesian Islands

Mines being loaded onto Wellingtons prior to gardening operation. Note parachute pack on end of mine   Photo: IWM CH.6232

Due to bad weather, by the 18th, 420 had only been able to carry out 3 gardening trips. When again the next day dawned with dubious weather, there was no alternative but to celebrate the squadron's first anniversary. Duisburg on the 20th required 420 to brief 13 crews, of which only 10 successfully bombed the target. One aircraft returned when an engine caught fire. Another returned when the navigator became unconscious at 18,000 feet. Although he had sufficient oxygen, the navigator was apparently physically unable to remain conscious. This was rather unusual, as he had completed 23 operations under similar conditions. After returning to base he was immediately admitted to SSQ for a thorough examination. He was found to have pneumonia. The third aircraft to return early also suffered oxygen problems. This aircraft, flown by Sgt W A Horborenko, had reached a point only 10 miles east of Flamborough Head when the navigator F/O D C Porter caught his foot on the oxygen hose, which then became disconnected from the economiser. The problem could not be rectified and the crew had to return early.

Goosepool took its turn to become a diversion airfield when 10 Lancasters dropped in after running short on petrol. On the 22nd, six of 420's Wellington and one Recco aircraft carried out an operation on Emden. Four successfully attacked the primary target whilst one attacked Pilsum, 10 miles N/E of Emden. The 6th aircraft suffered temporary loss of control when its ailerons jammed. All returned safe. The 23rd saw the steady arrival of 8 Oxfords for 1535, which had been flown in by ATA pilots from 23 MU, based at Aldergrove, near Belfast,

Although no operations were carried out during December, 419 Squadron was able to amass a total of 177 hours 35 minutes of flying training. With the exception of skeleton crews, after 44 consecutive days of Ops or standbys, 420 were given a stand-down to enjoy the Christmas festivities. A Christmas Eve dance was held in the Sergeants' Mess, and the usual Christmas Day festivities took place in the Airmen's Mess, lunch being traditionally served to the airmen by the officers and NCO's. Boxing Day dawned a real pea souper, thus putting paid to a planned operation for 420. Even the birds were walking. The airfield enjoyed a general holiday. A dance held in the Officers' Mess that night was followed by further festivities on New Years Eve in both the Officers' and Sergeants' Messes. Sunday the 27th dawned with 420 'On' for a gardening Op. Later a cancellation came through. De-bombing commenced, but again the squadron was warned, this time for a late take-off at 04:00 the following morning. The hapless armourers did an about turn, and commenced to bomb the aircraft up again. At 02:45, when all the preparations were complete, the operation was finally cancelled.

Thursday December 29th was a day of great note for 420, when the squadron celebrated its first wedding. Both Flying Officer Porter and his bride were from 420. The wedding took place in the little church at Middleton One Row, which was built in 800 AD. The station orchestra offered their services and a very impressive ceremony was held.

Flying training had continued throughout December without major incident. By year's end, 419 Squadron's strength had risen to 594 personnel and 18 Halifaxes on charge. As for 420, their year ended with W/C Bradshaw departing the squadron for privileged leave. Taking the helm was S/L D S Jacobs who assumed command in his absence.

CHAPTER SEVEN
Goosepool War Diaries 1943

January 1943 – Formation of No. 6 Group
Royal Canadian Air Force.
February - 1943.
March - 1943
April – 1943.
Farewell to 420.
May – 1943.
420 losses.
June – 1943.
July – 1943.
Reap the Whirlwind.
August 1943.
Peenemunde.
September – 1943.
October – 1943.
The Ghost Squadron.
November - 1943.
The Battle of Berlin
December – 1943.
431 and 434 – Tholthorpe to Croft.

Goosepool War Diaries 1943

January 1943 - Formation of 6 Group RCAF

Friday the first of January 1943 heralded the formation of 6 Group RCAF. The RAF had been collecting RCAF squadrons and crews for some time, most of them in 4 Group. Their Headquarters were at Allerton Park near Knaresborough (affectionately known by its Canadian occupants as Castle Dismal), it was formerly the home of Lord Mowbray. The financing of 6 Group RCAF came from the Canadian Government. With the exception of RAF and other non-RCAF personnel, this included Airmen's pay. The Canadians also met fuel, food, and armaments, along with operational and training costs. The RCAF provided most of the aircrew, although for quite some time the flight engineers were supplied by the RAF, as were the support and administration personnel.

The Canadians also financed the manufacture of their own version of the Avro Lancaster. Built by the Victory Aircraft Company of Canada, they were classified as the Mk X. During December 1941 an order for Canadian built Lancasters was announced. The first drawings arrived from England in January 1942. The first East to West Atlantic ferry crossing by a Lancaster took place on August 25th, flown by Clyde Pangborn. This aircraft, a Mk 1 (R5727) was to be used as a master tool and pattern standard for the construction of the Canadian built Lancasters. The factory used to build the Canadian Lancasters was The National Steel Car Corporation's plant at Malton, Ontario. Later, due to management problems, the Canadian Government took over the operation on November 5th 1942 and it became a Crown Company, renamed 'Victory Aircraft'. The first off the production line, KB700, which was to become the RCAF's flagship, first flew on August 1st 1943, just 16 months after the arrival of the initial drawings from the UK. She was flown by Ernest Taylor, and his crew. She was christened the 'Ruhr Express' during a formal naming ceremony on August 6th, by Mrs Power, the wife of the Hon C G Power, who was the Canadian Minister for National Defence for Air. After her electrical fit and 'first aircraft off the production line' flight-testing program, she was flown across the Atlantic by the RAF's 45 Group. Her pilot for the trip was S/L R J Lane. He and his crew were between tours. The Ruhr Express arrived in England on September 15th 1943, after a flight of 9 hours and 30 minutes. She was initially operated at the end of October by 405 Squadron, by then an 8

KB700 The Ruhr Express arrives in England from its transatlantic delivery flight   Photo: courtesy of the Canadian Forces

Group Pathfinder squadron, based at Gransden Lodge, Bedfordshire. KB700 only carried out two operational sorties with 405. During the first she had to return early when one engine failed. During her second trip she successfully bombed Berlin and returned safely. After this she was withdrawn from Ops for a while. As you will read later, the Ruhr Express was destined to be used predominantly by 419 Squadron at Middleton after this unit converted to the type in early 1944.

The first of January 1943 was also the date that 419 became operational at Middleton St George. The new Station Commander, Group Captain D Ross, carried out an inspection of the squadron's hangar and Station Headquarters. Over at Croft, the Camp Commandant S/L D S McCann was carrying out similar tasks.

For 420 there were no Ops that day, but they did stand by for a daylight raid on the next. It turned out that they were not required for this Moleing operation due to insufficient cloud cover. A night operation was ordered, but this too was cancelled. They did, however, have to stand-by to assist on the 3rd, in the event that 427 were unable to get their required schedule of aircraft over from Croft for bombing up. In the event they were not required as no Ops were called.

Monday the 4th saw Air Chief Marshall Sir Ludlow Hewitt visit the airfield on a tour of inspection. He was accompanied by the AOC, Air Vice Marshall Brooks, who also interviewed two NCOs for commissioning. Two days later, with no Ops called, 420 did carry out extensive training. One Sgt Pilot, whose name I will not divulge was put on a charge.

The Charge sheet (Form 252) read -

Sgt X is charged with negligently flying His Majesty's aircraft in such a manner as to cause his aircraft to strike a tree, resulting in damage to this said aircraft.

Secondly, negligently flying His Majesty's aircraft at a height of seventy feet in such a manner as to cause danger and bodily injury to members of crew of said aircraft.

Having been found guilty of both charges, the offending NCO was sentenced to receive a severe reprimand, and to take rank and precedence as if his promotion to the rank of Sgt bore the date 5/3/42.

On the 8th, six of 419's Halifaxes were prepared for operations. The crews were briefed but the scrubbed order was received just before take-off. 420 were not so lucky. They had already taken off by the time the cancellation was received. Precious fuel had to be dumped before a landing was possible. F/S Lundeen's wireless operator in BJ699 did not hear the recall signal, due to faulty W/T equipment, and this aircraft continued with the operation. However, after four hours of flying he was forced to bring his mines back due to low cloud and heavy weather. Because of their efforts, he and his crew were awarded a sortie.

The first aircraft to be lost by 6 Group RCAF since its formation occurred on the same day. Wellington III BJ604 ZL-A was transiting to Croft, where it was earmarked for use by 427 Squadron. The weather was bad and the crew were unable to find the airfield. They did however find Middleton and at about 12:25 attempted to land on runway 01. The flarepath was only identified at the last moment as the Wellington was on final approach. This caused the pilot, Sgt Harwood, to land well down the runway, leaving insufficient distance within which to stop. The Wellington overshot and ended up slewed around 90 degrees to the runway direction, with its starboard wing overhanging the Darlington to Redcar railway line. The

Wellington after overshooting runway 01 which ended up with its wing protruding onto the Darlington to Redcar railway line
Photo: PRO AIR 28/543

Second view of Wellington on railway line Photo: PRO AIR 28/543

Although this was a 427 squadron Wellington it still bears 419s identification letters   Photo: PRO

crew were slightly injured but were still able to vacate the Wellington at a high rate of knots, as they thought that a train might come along at any minute. Less than two minutes later a fish train approached from the Eaglescliffe direction. The wing was ripped from the bomber and carried off down the track by the speeding railway engine. Fuel from the ruptured wing tanks enveloped the locomotive and was ignited by its firebox. This spread back to the aircraft, which also caught fire. The engine driver immediately applied the brakes, but despite his quick actions it took over 100 yards for the train to stop. Meanwhile the fireman, who was trying to escape from the blazing engine, panicked, and jumped from the footplate with fatal results. The station fire crew were quickly on the scene with their foam truck and put out the blazing fuel. The Wellington's crew were taken to the SSQ with cuts and abrasions and were released later.

Next day was the 9th, and five of 419's Halifaxes proceeded from Middleton on a large gardening operation to the Nectarine area. They would form part of a 121 strong gardening party consisting of 78 Halifaxes, 41 Wellingtons and 2 Stirlings. The force was broken up into three, with 419 being part of the Friesian Island detail. The other two dropped their mines in the German Bite and Siverthorn (the Kattegat area). 4 Halifaxes would not return. This operation, the squadron's first on Halifaxes, was led by S/L Clark, flying Halifax II DT 619. He was the first to take off at 16:30. His crew that evening were Sgt R Williams - navigator, F/O I Duncan - bomb aimer, Sgt F Jackson - wireless operator, Sgt V Lee - engineer, Sgt J Thompson - mid-upper and F S J Brunet - tail gunner. They carried two 1,500-lb mines. The visibility over the target that night was excellent. The vegetables were planted successfully but their parachutes were not observed by the crew. Sgt Barker and his crew in W7857 had left Middleton two minutes behind Clark, nothing further was heard from this aircraft. The bodies of the navigator - F/S Dunn RCAF and the bomb aimer - F/S Hugli RCAF were washed up and now lie in Sage War Cemetery. The wireless operator - Sgt Watson RCAF is buried in Sweden's Kviberg Cemetery. The pilot - Sgt Barker RCAF, flight engineer - Sgt Sackville-Golden, mid-upper gunner - Sgt Cameron RCAF, and tail gunner - F/S Murphy RCAF were never found. They are commemorated on the Runnymede Memorial.

The next to take off was S/L Kenney in DT 617. He found the target using the Dutch Island of Schiermonnikoog as a pinpoint. The bomb aimer Sgt Doolan dropped both mines, which were seen to enter the water by the tail gunner, Sgt Batkin. P/O Frederick's crew in DT 639 also found the target. They used Simonsand Island as their pinpoint. They, too, planted their mines successfully in the correct 'Patch' and, for some unknown reason, landed back at Croft rather than at base. Having dropped his mines, F/O Porter encountered two flak ships just off Wierrum. Fire was exchanged between the Halifax and the ships. The aircraft escaped unscathed but Sgt Taylor the tail gunner was convinced that both ships had sustained damage during the action. All remaining aircraft returned safely.

Also taking part in an all NCO-crewed gardening operation that night was 420 Squadron. They sent nine aircraft, seven of which were successful. Out of the other two, Sgt Sanderson brought his mines back as Terschelling Island (code-word Mussels) could not be pinpointed. Wellington X3926, flown by F/S Townsend, had the starboard engine cut just after takeoff, the aircraft had to be flown on one engine. Loaded with fuel and 3,000 -lbs of mines, it would not maintain height however. Initially, fuel was dumped in an attempt to reduce weight, but this took time. With only 300 gallons jettisoned[78] and the aircraft down to 1,500 feet, the mines had to go. They fell close to the Seamer/Hilton Road near Stokesley, 450 yards E/S/E of the junction with the Hutton Rudby Road.

On January 15th, utilising heavy cloud cover, 420 took part in a daylight raid to Norden, on the German Coast, some 45 miles to the west of Bremerhaven. Only one aircraft was successful in reaching and bombing the target. This was Wellington X3800 flown by F/S W W Kennedy and his crew. Having taken off from Middleton at 12:14, they found their first pinpoint at the Friesian Island of Juist. From there they set course 035° west of Norden then on to the town itself. The cloudbase was about 1,000 feet and the visibility was good. Once over the target area they descended to 600 feet and

[78] 2,100lbs (approx)

dropped their four 1,000-lb GP bombs at 14:27 hours. Three of their bombs were seen to explode in the centre of the built up area, just to the N/W of the main road leading to the town from the southeast. After that it was back into the cloud base and away back to Middleton, where they landed at 17:16.

F/S J S Thompson's crew in BK330 landed back at base with their four 1,000-lb bombs, 49 minutes after takeoff. They had experienced engine trouble and the furthest they could get was 54° 22'N - 1° 05'W (61 miles due east of Scarborough). Before landing, they brought the weight of the aircraft down by jettisoning 400 gallons of petrol (approx. 2,800-lbs.). The crew of BK331, flown by Sgt Horborenco, had a narrow escape when they encountered a semi-circle of six flak ships. They had unknowingly flown into a position roughly in the centre of the formation of ships before the gunners opened up on the Wellington. Trapped in daylight between the sea and the 1,000-foot cloudbase, the four 1,000 GP bombs were immediately jettisoned 'fused' and the aircraft violently manoeuvred in an attempt to escape the situation. The Wellington stalled and fell towards the sea, only recovering when at a height of around 20 feet. During its descent, the aircraft was hit by the flak just above the door behind the co-pilot. They returned to Middleton safely.

P/O J B Purt's crew found the cloud cover ranging from 1,800 to 3,000 feet, with large gaps in the lower cloud. Purt decided to adhere to orders and he too brought his bombs back. The Wellingtons flown by Sgts Sanderson and Lawson were recalled by W/T, as the cloud-base was well broken with large clear patches. Down to 800 feet on the way home, Lawson's bomb-aimer, F/S Evans, spotted a U-boat with its conning tower awash. Turning back for an attack they entered low cloud and lost it. Despite a five-minute search of the area the submarine was not found.

Wing Commander Fleming led six of 419's aircraft on a raid to Lorient later that night. This raid involved 122 aircraft from different squadrons. Although mining operations had been carried out by 6 Group, Lorient marked their first actual bombing operation. The main target during this, the first of 8 area attacks on the port, was the U-boat base. Flying in DT 689, Fleming's bomb load consisted of five 1,000-lb GP bombs and some incendiaries. Identifying the target from landmarks south of the town, he successfully carried out the attack. His bomb bursts were clearly observed and the incendiaries seen to start many fires. By the time they left the target the flames had taken a good hold. On the way home the glow could be clearly seen 50 miles away. P/O Sherk and his crew in DT516 carried out the 'recco' of the target, having dropped his bombs through the smoke and haze caused by previous bomb bursts. F/O Porter had to turn DT 616 around and jettison the bombs 'safe' when the port outer failed on the way to the target. He and his crew landed safely back at Middleton, two hours earlier than the main force.

Four of 420's Wellingtons had also undertaken operations to Lorient that night, led by F/L Cook. Each aircraft carried 9 cans of SBC[79] (90 x 4-lb) incendiaries. All successfully attacked the target and landed safely at Tangmere. On the 18th, 419 stood down whilst Wing Commander Fleming undertook a visit to 6 Group HQ at Allerton park. During the night of the 21/22nd, they sent 10 aircraft on another gardening sortie to the Nectarine area. All observers used the Islands of Juist, Borkum and Nordernay as Nav aids. The flak ships north of Nordernay paid the Halifaxes special attention, fortunately without major damage to any of them. All aircraft arrived safely back at Middleton.

Over at 420, things were somewhat different. Three Wellingtons took off for the same objective. The aircraft operating that night were to be flown by Sgt Lawson, Sgt Sanderson and Sgt Gergley. Sgt Lawson and his crew found the Friesians partly obscured by cloud, with the visibility only about 3 miles. Sea mist was also encountered up to about 700 feet. Using the west end of Juist as a visual fix, they began a 14-mile run-up to the release point. The navigator F/S Tucker turned on 'Mandrel'[80] and asked Lawson to steer 346 degrees and maintain 200 mph. Just short of the release point the bomb aimer, F/S Evans, lying in the nose, opened the bomb doors. A loud roar ensued, the slipstream's smooth flow being disrupted as it was deflected by the hanging bomb doors and the rear bomb bay bulkhead. As the aiming point came up, Evans pressed the tit and with a double click, the mines left the bomb bay. Sgt Emond in the tail of the Wellington saw both parachutes open successfully, and despite the haze he even saw the mines enter the water. Now some 3,000 -lb lighter, the aircraft was allowed to climb. Lawson told F/S Raspin in the front turret and Emond in the rear to keep a good look out for aggressive German night fighters. Sgt McKinnon, manning the radio, sent off the operation successful signal.

Taking off one minute after Lawson was Sgt Sanderson in BK235. Using Juist, Borkum and Norsemen as pinpoints, he and his crew steered 339°, also at 700 feet. Their speed was more like the norm, 160-mph. After a run-in of 19 miles, both parachutes were seen to open by F/S Dorland in the tail. It was rare for the mines to be seen actually entering the water, but where else would they go? Arriving back at Middleton at 22.24 after 5 hours and fifteen minutes airborne, they were the first ones back. Although Lawson had taken off just before Sanderson he was not back yet. Nor were Sgt Gergley and his crew. Having taxied in and shut down, Sanderson and the rest of the crew completed their final checks and vacated the aircraft. As they waited for their transport a well-earned fag was enjoyed by all. Twenty minutes later, they were being dropped off at the Hangars when the sound of an approaching aircraft was heard. A black shape touched down on the flarepath and rumbled down the runway, decelerating as it went. In the dark, Sanderson presumed it was a 420 Squadron Wellington by the sound of its engines. 419's Halifaxes, with their four engines, sounded much different to the Wellington's two Bristol Pegasus radials. He had no idea who the crew of the returning Wellington were. They entered Hangar 1 and walked down the left-hand side to the door of the de-briefing room. Sanderson's crew entered the room. Each collected a hot cup of tea and sat down at the table where a WAAF Officer was waiting. When the de-briefing was well underway, the crew who had just landed entered the room. Sanderson saw that it was Lawson's. When both crews finished their de-briefing, they left for an early breakfast and bed.

The third Wellington, PT-R, had left Middleton at 17:10, after which nothing had been heard. By morning, R for Robert was posted missing. This aircraft had been flown by Sgt Gergley, with P/O Kendle, Sgt Walsh, Sgt Hollingshead, Sgt Olson and Sgt Dunphy. They were to be the very first all RCAF crew to be reported missing since the formation of 6 Group.

---

[79] Special Bomb Container, normally used for carrying large numbers of small incendiary bombs, including 4lb and 30lb types
[80] Radio counter-measures to disrupt German radio transmissions

Their fate is unknown. It is probable that they still lie beneath the cold waters of the North Sea. All are commemorated on the Runnymede Memorial.

The Pathfinders provided the son et lumiere over the U-boat pens at Lorient on the 23rd. 419 swelled the ranks of a much larger force visiting the Kriegs Marine's submarine base. Not only the docks, but the whole area was lit by the flares dropped by the PFF. Only 3/10ths cloud covered the target and this offered no protection for the U-boat pens. Many bursts and incendiary fires were seen straddling the target, especially to the west of the built up areas around the aiming point. The raid was a huge success, all of 419's aircraft returned to Middleton tired but happy. Earlier that day four of 420's aircraft had taken part in a daylight cloud-cover raid on Wilhelmshaven. Although the primary was not actually attacked, all six Wellingtons sent by 6 Group, including the 4 from 420, managed to find something to bomb, and returned safely.

The series of raids on Lorient continued on the 26th, when ten of 420's Wellingtons were detailed. Nine Wellingtons of 427 at Croft also visited Lorient. Sgt Hartney's aircraft returned early and landed at Harwell due to engine trouble. The weather during the day was cold and misty. Due to lack of fuel, the returning aircraft landed at various locations, including Croft, Dishforth, Exeter, Sealand, Upavon and Wing.

At about 23:32, whilst on the way home, 427's P/O Taylor in ZL-Z X3348 emerged from the bottom of the cloud base only to find high ground below and ahead. He immediately pulled back on the control column and hit the throttles in an attempt to climb away. Seconds later the Wellington struck the ground. It decelerated violently and quickly came to a halt. The bomb-aimer, P/O Mortimer had been in the front turret at the time of the crash, which crushed around him. The navigator had also been thrown into the bomb-aimer's compartment by the impact, followed by the second pilot who fell on top of him. The wireless operator, too, had been thrown forward by the deceleration, and ended up against the pilot's instrument panel. Fortunately the Wellington did not catch fire, and despite their unorthodox arrival, the crew were able to quickly scramble out of the aircraft. Once clear, they began to take stock of the situation. Suddenly they were aware of someone groaning. The sounds came from the front turret, and fearing the worst, they quickly re-entered the aircraft, where they found Mortimer trapped in the turret. The framework had been crushed in-over, trapping him. He was pretty badly cut about, including one fairly severe cut along his head. He also suffered a sprained ankle and knee, and was pretty badly bruised. After half an hour of pulling and pushing, the injured bomb aimer was released from the mangled turret and carried out of the aircraft. The navigator P/O Martin set off down the mountain to get help. He soon returned, having located a farmhouse in the valley. Mortimer was then carried down to the farmhouse by the rest of the crew where they all spent a comfortable night. Mortimer was admitted to Buxton Hospital with slight injuries, and with the exception of the bomb-aimer and second pilot, the remainder of the crew were able to return by train to Croft the next day. The Wellington had come down on Blackden Edge, 2 miles north of Edale, 1,562 feet up in the High Peak region of Derbyshire, half way between Stockport and Sheffield. They had skidded to a halt on a tiny plateau, just a few yards long on the only piece of semi flat ground for miles around. For the crew this had been a most miraculous escape, for if they had come down anywhere else, their injuries would have been much greater, probably fatal.

Next morning, word was received from the town of Kamloops, British Columbia, that it wished to adopt 419 Squadron as a gesture of commemoration of its native son, the late W/C John (Moose) Fulton DFC AFC, the squadron's first CO. An immediate affirmation was sent back to Canada and 419 awaited the outcome. Seven new aircrew from 1659 Conversion Unit reported to 419 for duty the next day, whilst on the 29th, they sent 12 Halifaxes back to Lorient. Five turned back due to bad weather and Gremlins in the engine department. This time Mother Nature was having an off day, she provided 10/10ths cloud up to 22,000 feet, along with lightning and very poor visibility. Gee was the salvation for five of 419's Halifaxes, as it allowed the target to be bombed through the thick cloud cover. Later, due to the atrocious weather and engine failures, a further seven gave the job up as a waste of time. Those that did manage to bomb knew they were in the right place by the red clouds below. The predicted[81] flak burst above the cloud as it searched for the bombers, the German gunners getting no feedback as to the effect of their labours. Some of the crews were painfully aware of the opposition, including F/L Cranswick, who ended up belly landing at base with his wheels retracted at 00:09, after a very eventful night. Fortunately no one on board was injured.

420 had sent 8 Wellingtons on this operation and a further 4 on gardening. On their return all crews had the same to say at debriefing. Although the weather was clear on takeoff, heavy cumulous cloud was encountered along the route. This caused terrific rain and electrical storms, and for a good proportion of the trip, heavy icing. Wellington DF626 crashed on the way home whilst landing at RAF Exeter. The bomb load had been jettisoned shortly before the impact. Four out of the six crewmembers were killed, including the captain Sgt D R Sanderson. A second aircraft, DF615 flown by P/O E J Stanton, was lost without trace.

By the end of January, 419 had seventeen Halifax Mk IIs on charge. Personnel numbered 25 RCAF and 11 RAF aircrew officers, 112 RCAF and 57 RAF NCO airmen.
Groundcrew numbers consisted of 3 RCAF officers and 1 RAF officer, 241 other ranks (RCAF) and 152 other ranks (RAF). WAAFs numbered 44.

420 had 41 RCAF aircrew and 4 groundcrew officers, 57 other non-commissioned aircrew, and 216 groundcrew. RAF officers totalled 12 aircrew and 1 groundcrew, with 35 non-commissioned aircrew and 114 groundcrew. The squadron also had 2 RAAF aircrew officers and 1 non-commissioned aircrew member.

February 1943

F/L A P Cranswick left Middleton on February 1st, and was posted to 35 Squadron at Graveley for Pathfinder duties. He had a very successful career with Don Bennett's boys, where he was considered to be one of the foremost bomber pilots

[81] Radar controlled

of the war. It was on a raid to Villeneuve on July 4th 1944 where, as Primary Visual marker of the Pathfinder force, he lost his life. Still with 35 Squadron, S/L A P Cranswick DSO DFC, set off from Graveley on operations at 23:16, flying Lancaster TL-J ND846. At the time he had flown over 100 sorties. Ironically the target was Villeneuve-St-Georges, 15 Km S/E of Paris. Having just released its target markers, the Lancaster was hit by flak at 8,000 feet. Moments later the aircraft exploded, throwing one of the crew, F/S Horner, clear. He was the only crewmember to survive the long drop to Earth and become a POW. S/L Cranswick, along with 7 out of his 8-man crew, rest in Clichy New Communal Cemetery, situated in the northern suburbs of Paris.

The first operation in February came on the 2nd and was a mining trip for 419 to the Kattegat gardening area, from which all returned safe.

All members of the Snowy Owl Squadron had their eyes and ears on the operations room. As the morning progressed, the tension got worse, until word was received that they had been stood-down. Great whoops of joy emanated from the flights, as everyone realised that no operations were to be called for that night. This allowed the preparations for 420's first anniversary bash to proceed. The sale of tickets was then completed and everything was ready. A wonderful lunch had been organized, which was augmented by the contents of many food parcels. The Baths Hall in Gladstone Street, Darlington, had been booked for some time as a venue for the evening's event. The water had been drained from the pool and a trestled wooden dance floor erected over the top. A 12 piece Dance band was provided and the whole event was deemed a huge success. Complimentary tickets were issued to the Station Commander and his section heads, also present was 420's former Adjutant, S/L N A Mitchell, who had been posted to Leeming as Squadron Leader Admin.

Next day there were a few hangovers, but 420 got back to the war and prepared 6 aircraft for a night raid on Hamburg. Bad weather was predicted and the crews were not surprised when they all had to turn back. A huge Cu-Nim packed front, containing ice and electrical storms, blocked their path. In some places it went up to 23,000 feet, and it was impossible to climb above it. Out of the eleven Halifaxes sent by 419, six turned back due to the weather, and Halifax T-Tare failed to return. As VR-T crossed the French Coast, the navigator Sgt Garnettt informed the pilot Sgt Mackenzie that they would be five minutes late crossing the coast. As they had plenty of height, Mackenzie stuffed the nose down and traded height for speed in an attempt to make up the lost ground. At some point after crossing the coast the intercom went U/S, and the rear gunner Sgt F/S Milton could not be raised. To make things worse, at 21,000 feet and just 25 minutes from the target, the Halifax was attacked by a night-fighter. Mackenzie must have received some warning that the fighter was closing for the kill as he began to corkscrew.[82] However the Halifax was raked from stem to stern by cannon shells and Mackenzie was killed. The engines and controls had been badly damaged and the bomb bay had also been hit, igniting the incendiaries. The engineer Sgt Duthie grabbed a fire extinguisher in an attempt to quell the blaze. He was fighting a losing battle, and with the pilot dead, Garnettt, using the call light, gave the order to abandon the aircraft. Having continued to return fire with the fighter, Milton, on seeing the abandon signal on the call light, opened the turret doors, grabbed his chute, clipped it on and after turning his turret sideways, leaned backwards and dropped out. In the fuselage, the remainder of the crew also prepared to bale out. Garnettt moved to the hatch in the nose and saw that Duthie was still at his station, as was the wireless operator Sgt Hill. No one was in the rear of the aircraft and so the condition of the mid-upper Sgt Connett was unknown. First out of the front hatch was the bomb aimer Sgt Marquand who had been injured in the ear. He was followed immediately by Garnett. As they began departing the aircraft, the fighter opened up on the crippled bomber for a second time. It was possibly during his second attack that Duthie and Hill perished, whilst waiting in the queue for the hatch. They, along with Connett, did not survive. It will never be known whether Connett, the mid-upper, was killed during the first or second attack, or as a result of being injured and unable to leave the aircraft. On landing, Garnettt, Marquand and Milton released their parachutes and took stock of their position in preparation for escape and evasion. Unfortunately the Germans had other plans and they were soon captured. The three were to spend the rest of the war as POWs.

For the remainder of 419's crews, the weather caused many turn backs. Iced up guns and control surfaces were amongst the main problems, along with ice blocked pitot tubes, making the pilot's and navigator's airspeed indicators U/S. Ice-blocked or restricted engine radiator intakes were another casualty which caused many engines to overheat. Having to feather an engine (or engines) on a heavy icebound and fully laden bomber was courting disaster even if the bomb load was jettisoned. With the above in mind, imagine trying to coax that lot over 23,000 feet high Cu-Nims that stretched across your path, whilst being shot at by predicted flak.

Next evening was the 4th, and five of 419's Halifaxes took off for the long trek to Turin. Sgt Blakewell's crew suffered a Glycol leak in one of the engines and had to jettison their bomb-load whilst over France to lighten the load. On the way home, a second engine became U/S and the Halifax had to divert to Middle Wallop where it landed safely. F/O Snider's crew fared little better. They had a complete hydraulic failure half an hour after take-off. The flaps would not retract and the undercarriage doors would not close. Their speed was greatly reduced due to the extra drag. Two out of their three 1,000-lb GP bombs were jettisoned, the third hung up. Also dumped were the 450 x 4-lb incendiaries, which were dropped from 3,000 feet. Snider managed to land back at Middleton after a hectic one hour and eight minutes airborne. W/C Fleming in DT689 reached the target and bombed on the PFF markers. The visibility was good and Sgt McLean the bomb-aimer saw their bursts close to a fire that was already burning. The flak was very accurate and on leaving the target area they were shadowed by an enemy aircraft. Fleming took evasive action and managed to lose the fighter. S/L Clark had a similar sortie, minus the fighter, and like the other four aircraft, returned safely back to Goosepool.

The Snowy Owls had a different venue, Lorient. Out of the 12 aircraft dispatched, one returned early, the remainder successfully dropped their incendiaries on the target and also returned safely. After an unsuccessful gardening trip by both squadrons the previous day, they joined forces again on Sunday the 7th for a return trip to the docks at Lorient. 420's Sgt Rosser, like most that night, had trouble keeping his Wellington straight on take-off, due to the strong crosswind.

---

82 Probably from the call light button operated by the rear gunner

He did manage to get off with some difficulty, but not before he blew a tyre. One 420 aircraft returned with a sick navigator, but the remainder, including Sgt Rosser, successfully bombed the target. One was hit by flak and had to land at RAF Exeter whilst another landed at Pershore. On his return Sgt Rosser, complete with that blown tyre, crash-landed at base, without too much damage being inflicted on the aircraft, and with no injuries to the crew. For 419, the raid had few surprises, and despite F/S Bell's crew having to come home on only two engines, all got back without too much drama. Mining operations continued for 420 two night's later when 3 Wellingtons were sent to the Nectarine area. Two nights later they sent 3 more back to the same target and a further 6 to garden in the Jellyfish area (Brest).

Mayor Lewis of Ottawa, Ontario paid a visit to the station on the 11th and interviewed personnel who hailed from there. He was accompanied by Mr Mooney, the Governmental Industrial Relations Representative from Montreal, and S/L Butler from 6 Group HQ.

Later that night, 420 sent 3 Wellingtons back to the Nectarines and a further 6 to the Jellyfish area, all returned safe. With their gardening duties completed for a while, 420 rejoined 419 on Saturday the 13th to take another bash at Lorient. 419 had little trouble but 420 lost P/O L G Gibson's crew when they crashed in the target area in Wellington BK330; there were no survivors. One of 427's aircraft, BJ778, crashed due to bad Viz, 12 miles southeast of the airfield on Black Intake Moor, near Chop Gate in the Cleveland Hills. All on board were killed, including the pilot, Sgt O P Adlam. He and his navigator P/O Dunn were buried in Thornaby Cemetery on the 15th. The remainder of the crew were buried in their own home towns. February continued with both of Goosepool's squadrons carrying out a raid on Cologne on Valentine's night. Heavy cloud cover made it difficult for the 90 Halifaxes, 85 Wellington and 68 Stirlings taking part in this operation. The PFF used H2S[83] to drop their sky-markers but due to the overcast, the raid was not a huge success.

Two nights later both squadrons took part in the last of a series of raids on Lorient, during which 1,675 aircraft had dropped 4,000 tons of bombs during 8 raids for the cost of 24 aircraft and 185 aircrew killed, 14 from Middleton. With perfect visibility, the crews had little trouble hitting the target in the bright moonlight. The bomb-aimers were able to clearly see the aiming point and the accurately placed PFF markers.

Crews continued to report to Middleton throughout the month from 1659 HCU. The Station Commander called a parade of all personnel at 08:00 hours on the 18th to carry out gas mask drill. That night 419 sent 3 aircraft to bomb the U-boat base at Wilhelmshaven. This number was reduced to 2 when one of the Halifaxes returned with an oil leak on its port outer. A further 8 crews went on mining operations to the Nectarine. This gardening Op saw the loss of F/S Levasseur and his crew in VR-B DT639. They were lost without trace and are commemorated on the Runnymede Memorial. It is possible that this aircraft was encountered by a fighter, as were two other 419 crews. F/S R G Goddard's Halifax was attacked by a Me110 in the drop area. Having warned his captain to take evasive action, the tail gunner F/S Gaunt fired a long burst into the fighter, which then dropped its nose and disappeared below. This aircraft was claimed as a 'probable' and was later confirmed. The next crew to gain the attention of a night fighter was that of W/O G A McMillan. At 1,500 feet, in the gardening area, the tail gunner Sgt H G Bess saw the fighter slipping in behind them. Before the enemy aircraft could open fire, Bess got there first and the fighter quickly broke away, never to return.

The next evening Wilhelmshaven was again attacked, by 338 aircraft, Goosepool contributing 11 aircraft from each of its squadrons. There was 10/10ths cloud over the target area and the force bombed onto the PFF skymarkers. F/S R Taylor's crew belonging to 428 squadron had a very shaky trip. Their Wellington carried one 4,000-lb Cookie. At 19,000 feet and having just completed the bomb run the aircraft was hit by flak. On the way home a fighter had a go at them, and in the confusion the tail gunner Sgt G J Beresford baled out for some unknown reason, leaving the remainder of the crew to return to Goosepool without him. After this raid Sgt Taylor was recommended for the DFM.

During the morning of the 24th, a raid to Cologne was detailed for eleven crews from each of Goosepool's squadrons. Just before takeoff the target was changed to Wilhelmshaven and the crews were re-briefed in the crewroom. This operation was an all 6 Group affair. Only one Wellington, from 424 squadron based at Topcliffe, was lost, when it crashed and burst into flames on its return to base. The captain, F/S Banks, and 2 of his crew were killed, the remaining 3 crewmembers were injured.

Sgt Bell and his crew returned to Middleton with their Halifax looking more like a colander than an aircraft. They had received the unwanted attentions of a night fighter and their aircraft had sustained two large holes in its fuselage, fortunately without injury to the crew. Only two of Middleton's crews ventured out the following night when 419 detailed a gardening trip. This turned out to be a bit of a non-event, when one of the two Halifaxes returned with a U/S tail turret and stoppages in all 4 guns. The other one hit a tree on take off. This aircraft, flown by Sgt P S Harrison, managed to become airborne but not without receiving damage to the wing leading edge, propeller tips and engine radiator cowlings. Shortly after, the port outer cut and the heavy laden Halifax began to lose height. The only answer was to get rid of the mines and this was done near Scorton, 10 miles to the southwest of the airfield. After reducing the weight, the Halifax became much more controllable and Harrison was able to carry out a successful landing back at base on three engines.

On the 26th, G/C Ross bade farewell to S/L D G Mawer, Senior Ops and Intelligence Officer, who was one of the most long standing members of Goosepool's fraternity, having been posted in during March 1941. He was to be replaced by S/L Brown MBE.

That night both squadrons detailed crews for a raid on Cologne. This involved 427 aircraft of Bomber Command made up of 145 Lancasters, 106 Halifaxes, 126 Wellingtons, 46 Stirlings and 4 Mosquitoes. This was the largest operation on the city since the 1,000-bomber raid. German records state that most of the bombs fell on the southwest side of the city but it was estimated that only one quarter of the bombers actually hit Cologne.

---

[83] Downward pointing radar system with aits rotating scanner mounted under the fuselage. A screen was located on the navigators table, on which a radar picture of the ground below the aircraft was shown. It was capable of showing coastlines and prominent ground features, even though the aircraft may have been above cloud.

Middleton's crews had no such problems and attacked the primary. Sgt P J Cozen's sortie in Wellington X3800 was typical of that of 420's other 11 crews. Although there was haze over the target they had little problem in locating the green TI marker flares. At exactly 21:30 hours, from 17,500 feet, they unloaded their bomb load consisting of 2 X 500-lb TD, 1 X 500-lb bomb, and 4 SBF containers, each holding 90 X 4-lb incendiaries, and also 2 more containing 8 X 30-lb incendiaries. Having observed a fair concentration of fires starting, the crew left the target area and headed for home. 419's crews reported very good fires, which were well concentrated, many in the centre of the aiming point.

F/O Weadon and his crew were nearing the Dutch Coast, when in the inky blackness, they got a bit too close to another aircraft. Their trailing aerial snagged on the other bomber and was confiscated, fortunately without too much damage being done to their Halifax. When 75 miles from the target on the outbound leg, P/O Sherk's crew suffered the loss of their port outer. They were still 30 minutes from the target, but elected to continue with the operation even though they could not attain the correct bombing height. By the time they reached the target, they were down to 9,000 feet, and risked the chance of being hit by bombs dropped by their higher flying comrades. They gritted their teeth and continued with the job of dropping their bombs on target. On his return to base, Sherk was to receive an immediate DFC for his part in this operation. Wellington BK468, flown by Sgt H A Hansen, had left Goosepool at 18:41, after which nothing further was heard. It later transpired that this aircraft had crashed near Monchengladbach with the loss of all on board. A 419 Halifax, VR-P DT615, went missing the following night. This aircraft had dropped one of its mines close to Simon Island, and had re-positioned for the dropping of the other when it developed engine trouble. The crew, flown by Sgt Gray, had not been aware that they had taken a small, but not insignificant, flak hit in the fuel system. This affected the port inner, which, on the Mk II Halifax, powered the Messier hydraulic system. This provided the power for the operation of the undercarriage, flaps, radiator shutters, landing lamps and the bomb doors. The latter were still open and could not be closed, causing excessive drag, which, with the much reduced engine power, meant that ditching was inevitable. Once on the water, the crew quickly vacated the aircraft and took to the dinghy. A sea search was instigated next morning, and after 22 hours afloat the crew were finally rescued by the Royal Navy. For the tail gunner, Sgt R Harling, this was his second ditching. Quite surprising really, as this had been only the second successful ditching by a 419 aircraft.

Another of 419's Halifaxes, DT619, was attacked by a flak ship and then by an enemy fighter. Sgt G I Dunbar the tail gunner and Sgt A D Grogan the engineer were killed. The navigator, Sgt A A Mellin was also seriously wounded, sustaining compound fractures to both bones in his lower leg. To allow other members of the crew to fight the fires in the fuselage, Mellin dragged himself up from the nose, under the instrument panel and up to the engineer's panel behind the pilot, a distance of some 12 feet. Once there, and despite his wounds, he took over the duties of the dead flight engineer until after the fires were put out and he was relieved by another crewmember. Despite considerable pain and loss of blood, Sgt Mellin then crawled back down to his table and insisted on continuing with his navigation duties. He assisted the pilot, Sgt McIntosh, to reach Coltishall and would only move back to the rest position just prior to landing. Despite the fact that the mines were still on board, Sgt McIntosh managed to crash-land the Halifax at Coltishall without further injury to the remaining crewmembers. For his efforts during this operation, Sgt Mellin was to receive the CGM on April 30th. 420's Operational Record Book for that night is typically brief. 'Eight aircraft carried out gardening, all aircraft laid vegetables in required area and returned safely.' What can an author, 60 years on, do with that?

The final Op for 419 and 420 was to the U-boat base at St Nazaire on the 28th. Heavy flak and searchlights greeted the crews, but fortunately the only Halifax to take a slight hit was that of Sgt Jackson when a round went through the wing between the inner engine and the fuselage. At this time, the rapid Canadianisation policy was making things most difficult for some squadrons. 420's adjutant recorded that finding accommodation for everyone was proving problematic. He went on to say that what would happen during the next few weeks was something not to be looked forward to. It was expected that 420 would have to double up with the RAF and RCAF for some time in the technical branches, as these could not be changed overnight.

At the end of February 1943, 420's nominal roll showed: -

RCAF officers - aircrew 40 and groundcrew 3, RCAF other ranks - aircrew 61 and groundcrew 240. RAF officers - aircrew 9 and groundcrew nil, RAF airmen - aircrew 33 and groundcrew 82.
RAAF officers - aircrew 2, RAAF airmen - aircrew 1.
WAAF airwomen - 32.

March 1943

The first day of March cost 419 another crew. Twelve Halifaxes had been detailed for a raid on Berlin. Two returned with engine trouble and one, flown by P/O Herriot DFM, was presumed lost over the North Sea. It is most likely this aircraft was shot down by Hauptmann Helmut Lent, IV /NJG1. On March 3rd, the body of the engineer, Sgt Cherkinsky RCAF, was found on the island of Schiermonnikoog, in the West Frisian Islands and was buried two days later in Vredenhof Cemetery. Sgt Gray the wireless operator lies in Kiel War Cemetery. The remainder of the crew have no known graves.

Sometime after take off, S/L D H Kenney's bomb doors had come open, and despite all efforts of the engineer Sgt G M Goodman they could not be closed. The drag was tremendous and DT607 had only managed to climb to 3,000 feet in 50 minutes. The Halifax was turned around and after one hour and fifty-four minutes airborne landed back at base. Also on the 1st, 420 lost Wellington PT-C whilst on a training flight. Flown by F/S Townsend RCAF, this aircraft crashed at 14:50 whilst northeast of Leeming airfield when part of the fabric covering came off one of its wings. This caused the Wellington to roll inverted and crash into the ground, killing all the crew. The port wing had separated from the aircraft at about 1,800 feet and was found one and a half miles from the main wreckage at Yafforth. The loss of this crew was taken very badly.

On March 5th the squadron adjutant wrote, '*No crew has been missed more than this one, and the tragedy of it all was that most of them had nearly completed their tour of operations.*'

On the 3rd, a representative from 419 attended the funerals at Coltishall of Sgts Dunbar and Grogan, killed on February 27th. The same day, Sgt Gray and his crew returned to the squadron after their dinghy ordeal in the North Sea. That night, eight of 419's Halifaxes and 6 Wellingtons of 420 attacked Hamburg. The gunners of VR-L had a very fruitful night. The Halifax was engaged by an Me110 night fighter, which the mid-upper P/O Wagner shot down in flames. This aircraft was claimed as destroyed when it was seen to crash and burn. Soon after, a Ju88 also fancied his chances, this too was dispatched by Wagner and the tail gunner Sgt Weeks.

Two days later, ten 419 crews were detailed for a raid to Essen. One, flown by Sgt Bakewell, failed to return from this raid. Hit by flak over the target and finished off by a fighter, this aircraft crashed at Elst, half way between Arnhem and Nijmegan. Sgt Bakewell, the navigator F/S Scowen, bomb-aimer F/S Marvel, wireless operator Sgt Bennett, engineer Sgt A C Turner, mid-upper gunner Sgt W J Clark baled out and became POWs. The rear gunner F/S Couper did not survive. The Snowy Owls lost P/O Grayham and his crew during this raid. No details are available as to what happened to them, only that the crew were buried in the Hauptfriedhof at Dortmund. Their aircraft, HE280 PT-V, was the first Wellington Mk X to be lost by 420.

Sadly, earlier that day, one of the station's vehicles struck and killed Mrs. Sanderson of West End, Hurworth Village, who had been riding her bicycle at the time. The Padre, F/L Taylor RCAF and F/O Kelly RAF represented the Airforce at the subsequent funeral, where officers of both Middleton and Croft provided floral tributes. Durham Constabulary praised the courageous conduct of Sgt Malyon of the Station Fire Section on the 6th. He had stopped a runaway horse in Blackwellgate, Darlington on February 20th, averting what might have been a serious accident resulting in injury or death to people in the street.

A gardening trip on the 8th employed 5 of 420's Wellingtons, whilst 419 sent 10 Halifaxes to swell the ranks of a 335 aircraft raid on Nuremburg. Due to the distance involved, Oboe could not be used and the crews had to rely on H2S, the Mk 1 eyeball, and the city's proximity to the Regnitz River. The bombing results proved to be scattered due to haze and the fact that the Pathfinders dropped their markers 5 miles apart. Half the bombs fell outside the city's boundaries. However, 600 buildings were destroyed and a further 1,400 damaged. Amongst these were the Siemans and MAN motor factories and railway yards. By daylight the next day, all of 419's and 420's aircraft were safely tucked up at Middleton.

The next night, nine 419 crews were detailed to attack Munich. Three aircraft returned early including the one flown by P/O W J Boyce. This raid was followed by an investiture, which was carried out at briefing the next day by 419's squadron commander, W/C Fleming. The recipients (who shall remain anonymous) of the medals for the most highly derogatory order of the irremovable finger were the captain, P/O W J Boyce, and wireless operator, Sgt B E Chambers of one of the squadron's aircraft, (I lied about the anonymous bit). The award was given after their efforts the previous night. Whilst the aircraft was ready to taxi out to the runway for the evening's raid, the wireless operator realised that he had left some of his kit behind. The crew were unaware that he had left the aircraft to go and get it. He returned to find that Boyce had taken off without him. After takeoff, Boyce had carried out an intercom check. When he got to the bit where he asked the wireless operator to check in, there was a stony silence. He then asked the nav, sitting at his table in the nose, to pop his head around the corner and poke the wireless operator and tell him to plug his helmet in. Imagine the look of horror on the pilot's face when he was told that the W/OP was not aboard. Having told control of the situation, he was ordered to dump the bomb load out to sea and jettison fuel to below the safety weight for a landing back at Middleton.

For the Germans on the ground at Munich, the raid itself had been fairly typical. During the raid, the local flak gunners had fired 2,314 rounds of 105mm ammo, 8,328 rounds of 88mm and 3,592 rounds of 20mm, a total of 14,234 rounds in total. There had also been 7 night fighters involved in the protection of the city. For the population of Munich, the down side was that 291 buildings had been destroyed, 660 severely damaged and 2,134 damaged to a lesser extent. Amongst these were the cathedral, 4 churches, 11 hospitals and many public and cultural buildings. Also destroyed were 22 retail and 3 wholesale buildings. The most seriously damaged industrial complex was the BMW aero engine assembly plant, which was put out of action for 6 weeks. Over 141 small workshops were destroyed, along with the local Flak Brigade Headquarters. 294 military buildings were damaged. Amongst the total of 208 people killed were 2 Nazi Party officials who were on duty, 10 German soldiers and a Hitler Youth boy who was gaining valuable experience whilst assisting a flak battery to shoot down British bombers. A further 425 were injured. Bomber Command, on the other hand, lost 5 Lancasters, 2 Halifaxes and 1 Stirling.

A raid to Stuttgart by 419 on the 11th also reduced the Luftwaffe's inventory of captured British aircraft by one. Halifax VR-N DT689, flown by S/L Clark, was attacked by a twin-engined aircraft, thought to be a Wellington. Unfortunately for the Germans, the RAF had not operated any Wellingtons that night and Middleton's crews knew it. Clark's rear gunner, Sgt Brunet, claimed the captured enemy aircraft as a probable, as it was seen to go down in flames.

On the night of the 11/12th German bombers attacked to the north and northeast of Goosepool. Four enemy aircraft were shot down, one crashing just five miles away. The Station Medical Officer proceeded to the scene of the crash where two German airmen were rounded up before being taken to hospital.

The same day, the station's soccer team played against Middlesbrough Police team. A large crowd attended the match, after which the airmen were the guests of honour at tea, which took place at the Steelworks' Social Club. After an hour or so they departed for a new venue, having been invited to attend a dance in a hall at Middlesbrough fire station. Music was provided by the band of the National Fire Service who played until about 22:00. The 'Boys' band had been playing at the Empire Theatre earlier that evening, and they came over to continue the music for a further hour and a quarter. During the dance, the famous BBC star Miss Beryl Orde arrived, and put on a 10-minute act. During the dance, a raffle raised £5, which was added to money collected during the football match, the proceeds of which went to the RAF Benevolent Fund. Middlesbrough's Chief Constable, MR A E Edwards worked very hard to ensure that the 38 airmen enjoyed themselves. After the party was over, tea and biscuits were provided for the airmen before they set off back to Middleton. The night had been a huge success, everyone's behaviour had been exemplary. The good people of Middlesbrough had made the Canadian boys feel perfectly at home, and formed cordial and lasting relationships between both parties.

On March 12/13th, Essen was attacked by a force of 457 Bomber Command aircraft. Just to the west of the city centre lay the giant Krupps factory. The Germans recorded that over 500 houses were destroyed, and that nearly 200 people were killed, 64 men, 45 women, 19 children, 4 soldiers, 61 foreign workers and 5 POWs. The Krupps works had been heavily bombed on the night of March 5/6th, but this later raid was reported to have been 30% more devastating. The bomber force lost 5% of its aircraft, 7 Halifaxes, 2 Stirlings, 8 Lancasters and 6 Wellingtons. One of these was from 420. Flown by G H Cook, HE690 was hit by flak and crashed at Brielle, 14 miles west of Rotterdam, and just 4.6 miles from the Dutch coast. The wireless operator Sgt A R Dawson was killed instantly when the flak shell ripped through the geodetic structure and fabric covering and exploded in the fuselage. The remainder of the crew survived to become POWs. Two of the squadron's Wellingtons had returned early and the remaining 7 went on to bomb the target and return safe.

The next night saw the loss of another 420 Wellington crew when 9 of their number set out to join 17 Lancasters and 42 other Wellingtons on a mining operation. The gardening patch that night was between Lorient (mining code word Artichokes) and the Kattegat area. One 9 Squadron Lancaster from Waddington was lost without trace. Another belonging to 57 Squadron at Scampton was hit by a fighter and crashed whilst attempting to land at base. 427 lost Wellington HE278 when it lost power and crashed just after taking off from Croft. Fortunately its crew flown by Sgt W H Schmitt were uninjured. The final loss of the night was suffered by 420, when Sgt C H Tidy and his crew in BK296 were lost without trace.

A second local air raid took place on the night of the 14/15th, in the same location as the one on the 11th. In response to these raids, the Station Commander ordered a practice sounding of the airfield's air raid sirens. When the 'warning red' was received for the second raid, most on the airfield personnel did not know what the sirens were for, and ignored them. This prompted an awareness program and air raid practices.

The station soccer team played Summerson's athletic team in the Darlington Hospital Cup semi-final ties. Middleton's team was soon 1-0 down and during the first half, Summerson's scored another goal. During the second half, Middleton started fighting back and managed to finish the game with a score of 3-3.

On Tuesday March 16th, one of 420's Wellingtons was flown out of Middleton, having completed a full tour of operations. Next day, F/L Cook and F/L Anderson, who were former deputy A and B Flight commanders, revisited their old squadron to take a last look at what was left of the old 420 gang, as the whole squadron was in the process of 'turning over'. They remarked that it was very hard to recognize the new aircrew lads who were now on the squadron's strength.

Fifteen Snowy Owl crews were briefed on the 26th for a raid on Duisburg D. Four freshman crews were included in this operation but these were cancelled just before take-off and only 11 Wellingtons actually took off. One, flown by Sgt J T Clary, returned early, due to electrical failure in the rear turret, which caused the heating system and gun sight to fail. Another flown by F/S W Horborenco diverted to RAF Docking with engine trouble on the way out. One of 419's Halifaxes, JB862 flown by Sgt J A Morris, suffered a failure to its port inner during take-off, but it was able to land safely back at base after jettisoning the bomb load in the sea. Although there was 10/10ths-cloud cover, the Viz at 19,000 feet above Duisburg was good. The PFF's red and green A and B flares were on time, but the release point flares were late, as was the bombing. There was some flak and searchlights on the way in but there was not much in evidence on the run to the target. Having taken off at 18:58, Sgt J Kennedy and his crew in MS479 attacked at 21:42 from 17,000 feet, whilst steering 190° Magnetic at a speed of 160 mph. As the PFF flares were late, they bombed on ETA from the Greentrack flares, as did the crews of F/S J S Thompson, Sgt L M Horahan and Sgt G Perks. They had previously circled over the target area for 10 minutes whilst waiting for the release point flares. Some crews had circled for over 30 minutes as they waited for the markers to go down, leaving themselves wide open to the flak. In desperation some crews even bombed on flak concentrations. The red and green markers when they did go down were widely scattered, resulting in poor bombing. For example, Halifaxes flown by 419's P/O L P Ainsworth and F/S R G Goddard bombed on the TI flares, as did Sgt B F McSorley's crew. Having made two circuits whilst waiting for the release point flares, F/L J D Snider bombed on ETA. Although 455 Bomber Command aircraft took part, the raid itself was not a success. Five of the Oboe Mosquitoes had to turn back with technical problems and a sixth flown by F/L L J Ackland was last heard at 22:30 calling for help, in the region of the North Forland. Both F/L Ackland DFC and his navigator W/O F S Strouts DFC RCAF were lost without trace and are commemorated on the Runnymede Memorial. This was the first Oboe Mosquito to be lost on operations. The aircraft itself, DK318, had completed 153.25 flying hours.

This raid, in comparison with the others in this series of attacks on the Ruhr, was a failure. The lack of the 6 Mosquitoes and 10/10ths cloud cover resulted in a scattered attack. Only 15 houses were destroyed and a further 70 damaged. Not a good result considering the raid had employed 455 heavy bombers. Six aircraft, including the ditched Mosquito, were lost, and 25 aircrew were killed. This was more than the Germans had lost on the ground. Their recorded fatalities during the raid totalled 11, with a further 16 injured.

On the night of March 27/28th, eleven of 419's Halifaxes undertook Ops to Berlin. One turned back with engine trouble, nine successfully bombed the target and one failed to return. Whilst S/W of Bremen at 17,000 feet, VR-E flown by Sgt C E Porter was hit in an engine by flak on the way to the target. He continued on to the target, which was successfully bombed. Unfortunately, whilst on the way back across enemy territory, the Halifax was attacked by a fighter whilst north of Hamburg and shot down. Whilst his crew baled out and survived to become POWs, F/O Porter remained at the controls to allow them to escape. F/O Porter was killed and now lies in Hamburg's Ohlsdorf War Cemetery. Another aircraft engaged in the attack entered into a spin whilst evading flak over the target, and the captain gave the order to abandon the aircraft. The bomb-aimer, Sgt Douglas, complied with this instruction and departed the Halifax tout de suit. Immediately afterwards the captain managed to regain control of the aircraft and cancelled the order to abandon. With the exception of Sgt Douglas, now a POW, the remainder of the crew returned safely to Middleton.

The Berlin raid itself was later classed as a failure. Although the actual aiming point had been the city centre, the Germans had thought that the target had been a secret Luftwaffe technical stores depot located in a wood 11 miles to the southwest at Teltow. This was due to creep-back from the 2 groups of PFF markers, which were themselves dropped short to the southwest of the city centre. Such was the belief that the site was the true target that the Gestapo interrogated everyone in nearby houses to find out who had flashed light signals to this special force of bombers.[84] The Luftwaffe also suffered scattered bombing to their base at Tempelhoff airfield in the city itself, and at the training base at Staaken, causing a further 70 casualties. The scattered bombing accounted for only 16 houses being destroyed, despite 396 aircraft having been employed. Photos showed no bombing within 5 miles of the city centre. Most bombs were scattered and fell far short, between 7 and 17 miles southwest of the correct aiming point. Casualties on the ground consisted of 102 killed and 260 injured. They included the 80 German solders killed and 63 injured when a military train returning from the Russian front was hit by 2 stray bombs in the Anhalter railway station. One factor in the Berliner's favour was that 25% of the bombs dropped were duds and did not go off. 2 Stirlings, 4 Halifaxes and 3 Lancasters of Bomber Command were lost.

On a raid on St Nazaire the following night, 419 lost another crew when VR-O, flown by Sgt Becket RCAF, was shot down near Nantes, France. They all rest in the War Cemetery of Escoublac-La-Baule. 420 sent 15 Wellingtons on this one, but 4 returned early due to a variety of technical reasons. The next night, 420 took part in a diversionary raid on Bochum in the Ruhr, whilst the main force attacked Berlin. They encountered heavy icing and some atrocious flying weather and so 4 of their aircraft had to turn back. The last 420 Wellington III to go missing did so during this raid. Sgt R L Brandow and his crew in X3814 crashed at Metzkausen, 8 miles northeast of Dusseldorf, all on board were killed. The bomb aimer Sgt H C Sleep (RCAF) was from Detroit, Michigan. The squadron lost a second Wellington, a Mk X, when P/O B A Grant's crew in MS484 was shot down by a night fighter and crashed near Wanroij, 12 miles south of Nijmegan. Only the bomb aimer F/S A G Skiggs (RAF) survived to become a POW.

The Bochum raid itself was a flop. The main force consisted of 149 Wellingtons, with 8 Mosquitoes providing the marking. The night was overcast and moonless and the marker aircraft were not able to stick to their timetable and there were long gaps in the sky marking. Only 4 buildings in the Bochum area were destroyed, with another 45 being damaged. Again the losses in the air exceeded those on the ground. The number of Germans killed totalled 28, whilst the number of aircrew lost when 8 Wellingtons failed to return reached 59. Along with the two Snowy Owl crews lost during this raid, 64 Base also had to add a 427 crew from Croft. Flown by Sgt D F McFadden, the crew of HE744 were lost without trace. This was the squadron's first Wellington X to go missing. At the same time 8 of 419's Halifaxes were heading for the German capital as part of the main force. Four turned back due to severe icing. After jettisoning their bombs the crew of P/O Ainsworth's Halifax encountered heavy icing whilst between 8,000 and 10,000 feet. As a result of the gusty conditions experienced on their return to Middleton, Ainsworth had to over-shoot. During the go-around the Halifax crashed. Fortunately no injuries were recorded. The other four crews attacked the target and returned safely to base. The raid was another failure, the markers fell too far to the south. Most of the main force arrived late and dropped their bombs in open country some 6 miles to the southeast. A few however, did manage to hit the city, and 148 buildings were destroyed, with 140 killed. Bomber Command, on the other hand, lost 6.4% of the aircraft dispatched that night, 11 Lancasters, 7 Halifaxes and 3 Stirlings. This equated to 100 aircrew killed, 11 POWs, 7 injured and 1 evaded capture. Another crew belonging to 408 Squadron at Leeming, flown by Sgt R H Bachelor, were temporarily put out of circulation. Hit by flak in the port engines and fuel tanks, the crew were unable to reach England with the fuel remaining. They elected to head for neutral Sweden where the aircraft crashed near Blindburg. The crew survived and was initially interned until April when they were returned to England.

During March, Topcliffe had seen the arrival of 7 Group's 1659 Heavy Conversion Unit. Many newly converted crews, versed in the intricacies of the Halifax III and Lancaster Xs, were destined to wend their way to Middleton from 1659 over the next few years. 1659 were to remain at Topcliffe until they were disbanded in September 1945.

April 1943

April 2nd saw 420 carry out a 3 aircraft raid on Lorient Z from which they all returned safe. On the night of April 3/4th, five of 419's Halifaxes were briefed for a raid on Essen. P/O Boyd and his crew were lost when they were shot down by Hauptmann Herbert Lutje of III /NJG1. The Halifax crashed at Duur, Holland. All are buried in the local cemetery. Another aircraft was attacked by a night fighter and badly damaged. Despite three members of the crew being wounded in the encounter, the pilot managed to get the aircraft safely back and was able to land at Coltishall. Crews continued to arrive at Middleton from 1659 HCU, and on the 4th, Kiel was attacked by three of 419's aircraft and a further 13 belonging to 420. All returned safe. At 10:30 the next day, 420's commander W/C Bradshaw and five of the squadron's most experienced crews set off by road for the Heavy Conversion Unit at Topcliffe. They were to be the first of 420's crews to convert onto the Halifax, and because of this, no Ops were called that day.

During a seven aircraft raid to Duisburg D on the 8th, Sgt Morris and crew from 419 were lost in VR-Q BB372. They crashed near Bochum, and with the exception of Sgt Turner, who survived to become a POW, the crew, whose average age was 23, were initially buried in Krefeld. Despite being in the middle of their Halifax conversion program, the Snowy Owls

---

[84] A story still considered by the Germans to be true today

also contributed 6 Wellington crews. They, too, lost a crew during this raid. Flown by P/O W A Walkinshaw, a second tour man, this aircraft, MS479, crashed at Essen-Borbeck with no survivors.

Over at Dalton 428 squadron lost an aircraft during the Duisburg raid. They also lost a tail gunner when flak sliced his turret off the back of the aircraft.

This 428 squadron Wellington was hit by flak in the tail, which removed the rear turret. The gunner inside fell to his death. Notice the fabric covered geodetic construction of the Wellington   Photo: IWM CH.9867

Rear view of damaged 428 Wellington   Photo: IWM CH.9866

The next day W/C D A R Bradshaw assumed command of RAF Station Middleton St George during the leave of Group Captain Ross. As thirteen of 419's aircraft were prepared for Ops to Duisburg on the 10th, Wing Commander Fleming set off by road up the old A1 (now the A167) to a small mining village just south of the City of Durham, called Ferryhill. Having taken the salute at a march past of 25 airmen and 25 airwomen, he give a speech as part of 'Wings for Victory' week. During the proceedings, donations were collected from the large crowd to go towards the war effort.

During that night's raid to Frankfurt, 420's P/O Jackson and crew flying Wellington HE422 lost their bearings on the way home and found themselves low on fuel. Jackson selected the autopilot and ordered the crew to bale out. The crew managed to parachute to safety on land just before the aircraft flew out to sea; but their skipper fell into the water and drowned. The remainder of the crew were surprised to find that they had landed in Wales, near Tenby on the Pembrokeshire coast. P/O Jackson's body was recovered by Air Sea Rescue launch and he was later buried in St Mary's (Carew) Churchyard. The squadron's record book states, and I quote, *'The crew were found 50 miles from where the aircraft crashed and burned, which only goes to prove that flying an aircraft might not be so difficult.'*

Photo taken at 6 group headquarters after being screened. Squadron Leader Laurence MacKinnon DSO DFC, left,
Wing Commander Dan McIntosh DSO DFC middle and Flying Officer Harry Spence, right   Photo: courtesy of the Canadian Forces

Earlier that day, 420 welcomed a new commander in the form of W/C (Mac) McIntosh DFC The squadron also bade farewell to its Adjutant. F/L G N Goff who relinquished his post to become second dickie to the Station Commander. He was replaced by F/L (Dave) Small. At the same time S/L Lark assumed command of 419. This was followed on the 12th with a visit to the station by F/L Nichols of 6 Group Headquarters, to discuss the compilation of the Historical Diary. Next day F/O J Tyler and his crew arrived at Middleton from 1659 HCU and reported to 419 for flying duties.

The following night was April 14th, and 419 sent thirteen Halifaxes to Stuttgart. 462 Bomber Command aircraft approached the target from the northeast and almost immediately creepback developed. This was a trait that Bomber Command was never able to completely eliminate and would dog them throughout the war. This raid was typical of the reluctance amongst some crews to get right to the centre of the target area. Quite understandably most crews just wanted to get in and out of heavily defended targets as quickly as possible. Even the Pathfinders were not immune to creepback and had been known to re-mark the earliest markers in the run-up to the target. During this raid however, some good came out of the creepback. Laying on the approach to the main target was the town of Bad Canstatt. Its many industrial buildings and huge railway repair workshops took a beating, as did Munster and Muhlhousen. Few bombs actually hit the centre of Stuttgart, but some of the ones that did destroyed an air raid shelter killing 257 French and 143 Russian POWs.

All of 419's aircraft returned safely to Middleton with the exception of Sgt Green and his crew, who, having developed engine failure and shortage of fuel, had to land at Downham Market. 420 were not so lucky. They detailed 11 aircraft for this raid, but by the next morning only 9 would return. HE550, Squadron Leader F V Taylor's Wellington, was shot down by a Ju88 whilst at 12,000 feet on the way home. This aircraft came down at Misnel-St-Laurrent, 3.5 miles E/S/E of Saint Quentin, France. S/L Taylor and the navigator F/O G C Crowther evaded capture. The wireless operator Sgt H N McKinnon was captured and became a POW. The bomb aimer F/O S Brown and the tail gunner P/O J A Simpson were killed.

Also shot down by a night fighter on the way home was the crew of HE863 flown by Sgt P J Cozens. All on board were killed when the Wellington crashed at Rocquigny, 32 miles N/N/E of Reims, France.

And still more crews were arriving from 1659, two more arrived at 419 on the 15th, captained by F/O Elliot and Sgt Westerman.

Next day the squadron sent 15 Halifaxes to the Skoda armament works at Pilsen, Czechoslovakia, as part of a 327 aircraft raid. Although there was a full moon this raid was not a great success. The PFF markers were only intended as a guide to the bombing, and the crews were ordered to visually identify the target. The outcome was that an asylum building some 7 miles away was incorrectly identified as the Skoda works and bombed by mistake. The Skoda plant was not hit and some crews brought back bombing photos showing that the bombs were only within 3 miles of the correct target. The only consolation for the crews was that a large German barracks was situated near to the Asylum and 200 soldiers were killed when it was hit. All of Middleton's crews returned safe, having covered the 1,800 mile round trip, two thirds of which was over heavily defended real estate. On their return to base some crews gave contradictory reports. F/O Vaillancourt stated that he had seen a huge explosion, which sent smoke billowing up to 15,000 feet. F/O Weedon saw his bombs hit a plant building and other bomb loads fall into a seething cauldron of fire. On the same night, 420's run of bad luck continued. They lost Sgt L M Horahan and his crew in HE682, who were taking part in a 271 aircraft raid on Mannheim. Having taken off from Goosepool at 21:14 they were shot down whilst outbound by Oberfeldwebel Rahner of 1./NJG4. The crew were killed when the Wellington exploded near Froid-Lieu, 5 miles southeast of Beauraing, Belgium. Mannheim itself was badly hit, and although only 130 buildings were destroyed, over 3,000 were badly damaged. Over 6,954 people were bombed out.

Farewell to 420

On the 17th, 420 stood down, amid much excitement. The squadron had been selected to go to North West Africa as part of 331 Wing, along with 424 and 425 Squadrons. Each section was busy selecting their best men and fitting them to their position in the squadron's establishment. No RAF groundcrew would be going with the squadron, and the work began to replace them with RCAF personnel from other squadrons. The sorting, labelling and crating of equipment began. All personnel had to be issued with tropical kit and firearms and receive medical and dental attention. The next day a nominal roll was prepared of all personnel selected for the African trip according to the squadron's establishment. This was somewhat difficult due to the secret nature of the move. All was completed however, by 02:30 the following morning, and rushed by dispatch rider to G/C Dunlap, CO of RAF Leeming. Also on the 18th, F/L A B Crawford replaced 419's F/L W G Harrison as Squadron Adjutant when he left for Dishforth to take up post as Administrative Officer. P/O Garton, the Squadron Gunnery Leader, also left as he had been posted to 429 Squadron. Eight Snowy Owl Wellingtons departed for 427 Squadron at Croft the next day to participate in operations. The raid was scrubbed however, and the crews returned to Middleton by road transport. The aircraft however, remained at Croft as the squadron was re-equipping with Wellington Xs. If they were required for Ops, the crews would have been driven over to Croft to depart from there. Meanwhile 420's Equipment Section were securing supplies and putting them into crates made by the Maintenance Section. On the 20th, W/C McIntosh spoke to all of 420's personnel about security relating to the big move.

During a 339 aircraft operation to Stettin that night, P/O T Jackson's crew, flying in 419's VR-B, were shot down by a night fighter whilst flying at 16,000 feet, some 30 miles N/W of Stettin. With the exception of the engineer Sgt Watkins DFM, all survived. Stettin was more than 600 miles from Middleton, but despite the extended range, this raid was very successful. Approximately 100 acres of the centre of the city was devastated. Many industrial buildings were located near to the centre and 13 of these were destroyed along with 380 houses. A large chemical plant was hit and all production was halted.

The next day, most of the new RCAF groundcrew arrived at 420, and the sorting and shifting of personnel continued. Meanwhile F/L McCarthy DFC arrived to take over command of B Flight. Over the next few days 419 bade farewell to more of its sons. On Good Friday the 23rd, S/L J D Pattison arrived at Middleton to assume command of 419's B Flight. He was replacing S/L Clark, who was being posted to 1659 HCU. Clark was followed to 1659 on the 25th by F/S Goddard, who had been screened from Ops, having completed 24 operational sorties. Also that day 420's Engineering Officer had completed all weighing and packing as far as he could go.

Duisburg was the Op for 420 on the 26th. The crews were transported to Croft and briefing was carried out there. One crash-landed away from base due to a crippled engine. A second landed away to check flak damage, whilst a third landed away with a technical problem. Sgt Newburg and his crew in PT-P HE693 failed to return. They had been shot down by a fighter near Heikant, 10 km N/N/W of Breda, Holland. All on board were killed. The same night, 427 had loaned one of their Wellingtons to 420 for this raid. Flown by Sgt Hall, this aircraft crashed half way between Middleton and Croft whilst returning to base around 06:20. All on board were injured. The second pilot Sgt C D Alder RCAF died soon after. This was to be the last aircraft lost by 420 whilst stationed at 64 base. 419 also took part in the Duisburg raid, their contribution being thirteen aircraft, all returned safe.

Next day W/C McIntosh visited Dishforth to inspect 420's new Mk X Wellingtons, in anticipation of them being ferried over to Middleton.

Over the next two nights Bomber Command would undertake two major mining operations, the first on the night of the 27/28th to the Biscay and Brittany ports and the Frisian Islands involved 160 aircraft, 46 Lancasters, 31 Wellingtons, 25 Stirlings and 58 Halifaxes, of which 10 came from 419 at Goosepool. Three of these were destined to return early. Only 1 Lancaster was lost.

On the night of the 28/29th, 419 carried out an 8 aircraft gardening operation to the Skaggerak area (code word Polyanthus), north of Denmark, as part of a 207 aircraft operation. The other mining patches that night was various areas around Heligoland and in the River Elbe, One 419 Halifax, VR-Q JB923 flown by Sgt Smallwood RCAF, failed to return. The aircraft and all on board were lost without trace. All are commemorated on the Runnymede Memorial, including the tail gunner F/S R R Gourde RCAF, an American from Longview, Washington. Despite a diversionary raid on Wilhelmshaven by 6 Mosquitoes, which dropped flares to divert attention away from the minelayers, 22 Aircraft were lost during this operation. This was to be the largest number of aircraft lost during a mining operation in WWII. These losses were due to the excessive low cloud encountered over the Danish and German coasts. This caused the crews to fly low in order to establish their positions before sowing their vegetables. In so doing they came into the clutches of the flak gunners.

Earlier in the day, the ranks of 420 were swelled with the arrival of several new crews from 426 Squadron at Dishforth to bring up the unit's establishment. On the last day of April, Sgt A A Mellin received the award of Conspicuous Gallantry Medal for his conduct during the attack by a German night fighter on the night of February 27th. On the 30th, despite the fact that it rained all day, the funeral of Sgt C D Alder took place in Darlington's West Cemetery, with his crew acting as pallbearers. Sgt Alder had only been posted in to the squadron on 12th April. It was a gloomy day and it was made much worse when the news broke that 420's aircrew establishment had been cut to 20. The squadron felt that it was like a monkey wrench being thrown into the works. Kits had to be returned and men posted.

420's strength on April 30th 1943 was 1 Wellington Mk III, 4 Mk Xs, and 5 Wellington Mk Xs (Tropical). The number of RCAF officers serving with 420 totalled 52 aircrew and 3 groundcrew;
RAF Officers - aircrew 12 and groundcrew 0;
RAAF officers - aircrew 2 and groundcrew 0;
RCAF NCOs - aircrew 66 and groundcrew personnel of various ranks 347;
RAF NCOs - aircrew 28 and groundcrew personnel of various ranks 74;
RAAF NCOs - aircrew 3 and groundcrew 0.

419 commenced May 1943 with 21 Halifax Mk IIs.

May 1943

Due to the squadron's requirement to re-equip with Halifaxes, on the 1st of May, 427 began their move from RCAF Croft to RCAF Leeming. On the same day, 420 were also taken off Ops, to allow them to continue bringing their Mk X Wellingtons over from Dishforth. They had acquired 3 thus far and were expecting a steady flow over the next few days to complete their requirement of 20 aircraft. During the day final instructions were received that all equipment had to be on the move the following morning. A dispatch rider left Middleton for Sunderland Quay at 20:00 hours to notify the Embarkation Officer of the number of crates being shipped. Meanwhile, W/C McIntosh departed from Darlington Railway Station to attend a conference in London relating to the squadron's role whilst overseas. On the 2nd, S/L Clark was posted to 1659 HCU, whilst at 09:00 hours the final truck load of 420's crates drove out of the gates for the Fighting Cocks railway sidings in Middleton St George village. The task of moving so much equipment was immense, but by the late afternoon, 23 railway wagons had been loaded.

The best effort so far for 419 came on the 4th when they launched 18 Halifaxes in 18 minutes for a 596 aircraft raid on Dortmund. This was the largest raid so far on a single target, and the first major attack on the city. The number of casualties on the ground amounted to 693 killed (a new record) and 1,075 injured. A nearby decoy site cost many bombs, but the marking was fairly accurate, although over half of the main force only managed to bomb within 3 miles of the AP.[85] During the raid, 1,218 buildings were destroyed and a further 2,141 seriously damaged. Among the industrial complexes badly damaged were the Dortmunder Union Steel Factories. One of 419's aircraft returned early due to flak damage and two more failed to return. VR-A W7817, flown by F/O Vaillancourt RCAF, was shot down by a night fighter and crashed near Zwolle, in Holland. With the exception of the rear gunner Sgt Stanley, the crew baled out and became POWs. The second Halifax, VR-Y DT794, was flown by F/O Elliot RCAF. It crashed in the centre of Dortmund; all on board were killed.

Croft received 5 Halifax Mk Vs on the 5th in anticipation of the arrival of 1664 HCU, who would be arriving to take up residence during the next few days. The 5th also saw the departure of the remainder of 427 Squadron for their new home at RCAF Leeming.

During this period, Croft was in the process of being built up from a single squadron station to the normal two-squadron station, a task that would not be fully completed until the end of the year. Many buildings were to be constructed before Croft would fulfill this requirement. Another tooth in the cog was Eryholme railway junction, situated on the boundary of the airfield. This junction had fallen into disuse over the years, and it was proposed during May to have it brought into service as a railway station for Croft's personnel.

May 1943 continued with half of 420's personnel being sent on embarkation leave on May 7th. Croft was visited the same day by Sir Philip Joubert de Lafertem, Inspector General. The next day, S/L McCann, Croft's Camp Commandant, was posted overseas with 331 Wing.

420 were presented with their squadron crest by (Black Mike) McEwan on Tuesday the 9th, with Middleton's Station Commander G/C Ross and a large representation of 420 being present at the ceremony. Their crest depicted a Snowy Owl with its wings elevated and adorsed. The squadron's motto, in Latin, read, 'Pugnamus finitum' (We fight to the finish). The Snowy Owl is indigenous to Canada and, appropriately enough for a wartime bomber squadron, hunts at night.

On the 10th, the formation of 6 Group's 1664 heavy conversion unit, under the command of W/C D W S Clark, took place at Croft, a place they were destined to remain until December 7th 1943. Later that day, F/Ls A R Dawson and R P Bales arrived at 1664 from 1659 to take post as Engineering Officers. This was a busy day with many new arrivals. One new face was S/L D H Kenney, who had been posted to Croft from 419 to become a flight commander. Arriving with him was S/L R H G Boosey from 408, who was to become the other flight commander. This brought 1664's strength up to 7 officers, 26 NCOs and 132 other ranks. Croft's station strength on 10th May was 771.

1664 would convert many a crew onto Halifax Vs and Lancaster 1s. During the same day, the balance of 420's groundcrew were allowed to go on embarkation leave. The replacements for the RAF tradesmen were still arriving from other stations, but by the end of the day, the squadron's establishment was deemed complete.

On the night of the 12/13th, 419 sent 10 Halifaxes to Duisburg. Two turned back due to severe icing, whilst two more failed to return. They were VR-X JB791 flown by W/O McMillan, and VR-C JB861 flown by F/S Palmer. Soon after leaving the target, VR-X was flying at 20,000 feet when it was hit by flak. Some of the crew abandoned the aircraft, which crashed at Bedburg-Hau, 46 km northwest of Duisburg. Five survived to become POWs, W/O McMillan was killed. Sgt Alison was found critically injured and died soon after being admitted to hospital. F/S Palmer and his crew were shot down by a night fighter and crashed near Zuidland on Putten, 20 km southwest of Rotterdam. Bad luck for 419 continued the next night when the crews of Sgt Buckwell and Sgt Adams failed to return from a raid on Bochum. Sgt Buckwell's crew in VR-Z JD113 were on their way home at 18,000 feet when they were shot down by Hauptmann Herbert Lutje, III./NJG1. Four of

[85] Aiming point

157

the crew, including Buckwell, did not survive, the other three managed to save themselves and became POWs. Those that died were buried in Dalan Protestant Churchyard. Sgt Adams and his crew were killed when their Halifax crashed near Monchengladbach. They were initially buried in Monchengladbach's Stadtfrienhof on May 18th. They now rest in the Rheinberg War Cemetery. The thirteen remaining aircraft returned safely to Middleton. On the 13th, Croft welcomed its new temporary Camp Commandant, in the form of F/L H F Francis.

With a view to leaving Middleton at 00:20 hours the next morning, 420's overseas movement personnel, consisting of 4 officers and 307 airmen, were inspected by W/C McIntosh at 21:30 on Monday May 15th. McIntosh gave a brief talk and wished the assembled group all the very best of luck in their new venture overseas. Having completed the farewell proceedings, the whole party was handed over to S/L Joe McCarthy, who was acting as Officer I/C the movement. He was accompanied by F/L Dave Dell, who was to assume the post of Adjutant and second in command. Later, the airfield's MT section transported the party to Dinsdale railway station, where G/C Ross and other members of Middleton St George wished them good luck as the train pulled out at 00:20. The Women's Division was also there and added lipstick and blushes to many an airman's face.

The train arrived at Liverpool at 07:45, and by 09:30 embarkation aboard the SS Samaria was complete. Quarters were allocated in troop decks B2, 3, and 4, just below the main deck. Whilst the 4 officers shared a cabin, the senior NCOs were quartered together in a lounge on the quarterdeck, where bunks had been built for them. The troop decks accommodated approximately 140 men. They slept in hammocks or on mattresses. Kitchens were provided for the troop decks, Messes for the officers and senior NCOs. Due to the large number of men aboard, 2 sittings had to be arranged to serve the officers and NCOs. The food itself was considered excellent in all respects. Rifles, sten guns, and webbing were stowed away. Once standing orders were passed around and read to the men, guards and troop deck details were organized, and life belts and lights issued. Emergency rations, water purification tablets, soap and mosquito cream were also passed around, and then it was deemed that all were ready for the voyage.

Prior to sailing, several HQ officers arrived to inspect the ship. They included Air Marshall Edwards, Commander in Chief, RCAF HQ Overseas and Air Commodore Waite. At 20:30 the ship set sale for Greenock, Scotland. It arrived at the River Clyde at 12:00 on the 17th and awaited the arrival of the rest of the convoy. On May 19th the convoy was fully formed, and set sail at 17:50 for Algiers. At 16:00 hours each day, the alert would be sounded, and soon everyone was reaching their lifeboat station in record time. For those not on duty during the first few days, the time aboard was spent lazing about playing cards, or reading or writing letters. As they headed south, the weather improved and sunbathing became another option, along with watching the other ships in the convoy. It was, in the main, a rather uneventful trip, apart from the day they were visited by German aircraft that dropped a few bombs, fortunately without hitting anything vital. Destroyers protected the convoy, and occasionally they could be seen dropping depth charges on some unseen U-boat. The sea was mostly calm throughout the trip and only one day produced stormy weather. Up to then, the men had been wearing their usual battledress attire, but this soon changed to tropical clothing. By the evening of the 25th they were passing Tangiers, and they docked at 10:00 hours, two days later, at Algiers.

420 went on to contribute greatly towards the allied effort in North Africa, but we, alas, must return to cooler climes.

420 losses

October 15/16 1942, Wellington Mk III, X3808 PT-B, Ops - Cologne. Took off MSG 18:52.

Lost without trace. The crew are commemorated on the Runnymede Memorial.

F/S L E White RCAF	K	Pilot
F/S G R Bing RCAF	K	Navigator
P/O F W Buck RCAF	K	Bomb aimer
Sgt D B Smyth RCAF	K	Wireless operator
F/S J M Joynt RCAF	K	Air Gunner

November 9/10 1942, Wellington Mk III, Z1679 PT- B, Ops - Hamburg. Took off MSG 17:53.

This aircraft crashed into the sea off the island of Pellworm, North Frisian Islands. Sgt Collard's body was recovered and buried on the island. After the war his remains were taken to Hamburg's Ohldorf Cemetery. The rest of the crew have no known graves.

Sgt W S Beadle RCAF	K
Sgt A J Smith RCAF	K
Sgt C S Snider RCAF	K
Sgt C Collard RCAF	K
Sgt J D McDonald RCAF	K

January 21/22 1943, Wellington Mk III, BJ966 PT-R, Ops - Gardening. Took off MSG 17:10.

Lost without trace during a mining operation to the Frisian Islands. All are commemorated on the Runnymede Memorial. This was Bomber Command's first all Canadian crew to be lost.

Sgt S J Gergley RCAF	K	Pilot
P/O E G Kendle RCAF	K	Nav
Sgt R H Welsh RCAF	K	B/A
Sgt C W Hollingshead RCAF	K	W/O
Sgt A G Olson RCAF	K	A/G
Sgt C A Dunphy RCAF	K	A/G

January 29/30 1943, Wellington Mk III, DF615 PT-, Ops - Lorient. Took off MSG 16:26.

Lost without trace, the crew are all commemorated on the Runnymede Memorial.

P/O E J Stanton	K
P/O W D Marks RCAF	K
P/O F Noon	K
Sgt W G Goode	K
Sgt J C Desrosiers RCAF	K

January 29/30 1943, Wellington Mk III, DF626 PT-, Ops - Lorient. Took off MSG 16:32, crashed 23:10.

Unable to maintain height due to engine trouble the crew jettisoned the bomb load just prior to crashing at Exeter.

With the exception of F/S Sealy, whose body was claimed by his family, and buried in Somerset, the crew members who died were laid to rest in Exeter Higher Cemetery.

Sgt D R Sanderson RCAF	K
F/S C M Downton RCAF	K
F/S H H Sealy RCAF	K
Sgt Sgt P G Beauchamp RCAF	Inj
Sgt J D Bittner RCAF	K
Sgt H R Ernst RCAF	K

February 13/14 1943, Wellington Mk III, BK330 PT-K, Ops - Lorient. Took off MSG 18:19.

Crashed in the target area. The crew are buried in Guide Communal Cemetery.

P/O L G Gibson RCAF	K
P/O F R Chapman	K
Sgt B W Somerford	K
Sgt T V Hughes	K
Sgt D A MacDonald RCAF	K

February 26/27 1943, Wellington Mk III, BK468 PT-, Ops - Cologne. Took off MSG 18:41.

Crashed near Monchengladbach, where they were buried. After the war they were reburied in Rheinberg War Cemetery.

Sgt H A Hansen RCAF	K
F/S R M Jupe RCAF	K
F/S B M Chaamney RCAF	K
F/S P H Mitchell RCAF	K
Sgt L E Kellaway RCAF	K

March 1 1943, Wellington Mk III, Z1724 PT-C, Training. Took off MSG, crashed 14:50.

The fabric wing covering on this aircraft, which was flying straight and level at the time, became partially detached, causing the port wing to detach from the aircraft, at an estimated height of about 1,500 feet. The aircraft crashed near RAF Leeming, killing all of the crew.

F/S P E Townsend RCAF	(Pilot)	K
F/S J Wreakes	(Navigator)	K
P/O S Spector RCAF	(Bomb Aimer)	K
P/O E M Hollowell	(WOP/AG)	K
P/O K J Brown	(WOP/AG	K

March 5/6 1943, Wellington Mk X, HE280, Ops - Essen. Took off MSG.

No details of the loss are available, the crew were initially buried in Dortmund's Hauptfriedhof. Later they were buried in the Reichswald Forest War Cemetery. This was the first Mk X to be lost by the squadron

P/O R Graham RCAF	(pilot)	K
P/O W G Lee	(second pilot)	K
P/O J K MacDonald RCAF	(navigator)	K
P/O D E Bennett RCAF	(Bomb aimer)	K
Sgt H T Lawson RCAF	(WOP/AG)	K
F/S D G Culver RCAF	(WOP/AG)	K

March 12/13 1943, Wellington Mk X, HE690 PT-, Ops - Essen. Took off MSG

Crashed at Brielle, 23 km west of Rotterdam, after being hit by flak, which killed Sgt Dawson. The wireless operator. He is buried in Crooswijk General Cemetery, Rotterdam.

Sgt G H Cooke RCAF	(P)	POW
Sgt J Morris	(N)	POW
Sgt R G Mercer	(B/A)	POW
Sgt A R Dawson	(W/O)	K
Sgt T S McKinnon RCAF	(A/G)	POW

March 13/14 1942, Wellington Mk III, BK296 PT-, Ops - Gardening. Took off MSG 00:03.

Lost without trace. All are commemorated on the Runnymede Memorial.

Sgt C H Tidy RCAF	(P)	K
P/O J D MacFarlane RCAF	(N)	K
Sgt G R Hall RCAF	(B/A)	K
Sgt H Reddy	(W/O)	K
Sgt J A Corbett RCAF	(A/G)	K

March 29/30 1943, Wellington Mk X, MS484 PT-, Ops - Bochum. Took off MSG 19:33, crashed 23:15.

Crashed near Wanroij, 19 km south of Nijmegen, Holland, after being shot down by a night fighter. The wireless operator Sgt Dyson lies in Eindhoven General Cemetery. The bodies of the pilot P/O Grant, the Navigator Sgt Bradshaw, and the air gunner Sgt Barron, are buried in the Canadian War Cemetery at Groesbeek.

P/O B A Grant RCAF	K
Sgt S V Bradshaw RCAF	K
F/S A G Skiggs	POW
Sgt R Dyson	K
Sgt P E Barron RCAF	K

March 29/30 1943, Wellington Mk III, X3814 PT-, Ops - Borchum. Took off MSG 19:33.

This aircraft was the last Wellington Mk III to be lost by 420. It crashed at Metzkausen, 13 km northeast of Dusseldorf, and 29 km southwest of the target. They are now buried in the Reichwald Forest War Cemetery, having been moved from their original graves in Dusseldorf's NordFredhof.

Sgt R L Brandow RCAF	(P)	K
Sgt C W Cockaday RCAF	(N)	K
Sgt H C Sleep RCAF	(B/A)	K
Sgt L G Jones	(W/O)	K
Sgt J M Greer RCAF	(A/G)	K

April 8/9 1943, Wellington Mk X, MS479 PT-, Ops - Duisburg. Took off MSG 21:15.

Crashed at Essen-Borbeck, 5 km northwest of the centre of Essen. Having been originally buried in Nordfriedhof in Dusseldorf, the crew were moved after the war to the Reichwald Forest War Cemetery.

P/O W A Wilkinshaw RCAF	K
P/O K W MacDonald RCAF	K
F/S D F Evans RCAF	K
F/S F Bemi RCAF	K
F/S R G Rispin RCAF	K

April 14/15 1943, Wellington Mk X, He550 PT-G, Ops - Stuttgart. Took off MSG 21:12.

Shot down at 12,000 feet whilst on the way home by a Ju 88 night fighter. Crashed at Mesnil-St.-Laurent, 5 km E/S/E of St-Quentin. F/O Brown and P/O Simpson are buried in Mesnil-St.-Laaaaurent Churchyard.

S/L F V Taylor RCAF	Evd
F/O G C Crowther RCAF	Evd
F/O S Brown RCAF	K
Sgt H N McKinnon	POW
P/O J A Simpson RCAF	K

April 14/15 1943, Wellimgton Mk X, HE863 PT-, Ops - Stuttgart. Took off MSG 21:09.

Shot down by a night fighter on the way back from the target. Crashed at Rocquigne, 46 km northeast of Laon, France. All rest in Rocquigne Communal Cemetery.Sgt P

J Cozens RCAF	K
F/S W G Blight RCAF	K
Sgt S G Giffin RCAF	K
Sgt J Paplowski RCAF	K
Sgt L Dutton RCAF	K

April 16/17 1943, Wellington Mk X, HE682 PT-T, Ops - Mannheim. Took off - MSG 21:14.

Shot down by Ofw Rahner, 1./NJG4 and exploded near Froid-Lieu, , Belgium, 42 km S/S/E of Numur. The bomb aimer, Sgt Plank, is buried in Sohier Communal Cemetery, 2 km south of the crash site. The three remaining crewmen lost their lives are buried in Haverlee War Cemetery.

Sgt L M Horahan RCAF	K
Sgt J E Isaacs RCAF	K
Sgt L K Plank RCAF	K
Sgt H S Radford	K
Sgt K T Allan RCAF	K

April 26/27 1943, Wellington Mk X, HE693 PT-P, Ops - Duisburg. Took off MSG 00:34, Crashed 03:39.

Shot down by a night fighter, crashed at Heikant, S/S/E of Breda, Holland. All are buried in Bergen op Zoom War Cemetery.

Sgt E L Newburg RCAF	K
Sgt F J Duffy RCAF	K
Sgt R Mucklow RCAF	K
Sgt O K Glascock RCAF	K
Sgt K B Cooke	K

April 26/27 1943, Wellington Mk X, HE771 ZL-, Ops - Duisburg. Took off Croft, crashed 06:20.

Borrowed from 427 squadron at Croft, this aircraft crashed on return to base, The second pilot, Sgt Alder, who was 25 years old at the time of his death, is buried in Darlington's West Cemetery. This was the last 420 squadron operation whilst based at Middleton St George

Sgt G E Hall	Inj
Sgt C D Alder RCAF	K
Sgt J P Bishop RCAF	Inj
Sgt G W Bedford RCAF	Inj
Sgt E A Shaul	Inj
Sgt L D Annis RCAF	Inj

Aircraft lost by 420 squadron RCAF whilst based at Middleton-St-George (Oct 1942 to May 1943), Operational - 18, non-operational - 1.   Aircrew killed – 85, Injured – 6, POWs – 6, Evaders – 2.

These figures do not reflect the loss of tail Gunner, Sgt G J Beriesford RCAF, who abandoned Wellington Mk 111, DF637, over the target area, (Wilhelmshaven), on the 19/20th of February 1943, leaving the remainder of the crew to land at Coltishall.

Back at Goosepool, on the 16th, three of 419's Halifaxes took part in a night flying exercise involving local searchlight units. There were few operations for the majority of Bomber Command that night, as the night sky over Germany was mainly reserved for the famous 617 Squadron Dam Buster raid that took place that night. Meanwhile, over at Croft, G/C N S MacGregor DFC assumed command of the Station.

May was turning out to be disastrous for 419, when, on the 23rd, Sgt Green and his crew, flying in Halifax JB862, were shot down during operations to Dortmund. They were initially damaged by flak, soon after, the starboard engine failed. The Halifax was finished off by a night fighter, and came down near Monchengladbach, killing all the crew. This raid turned out to be the fourth operation in a row in which a pair of Halifaxes were lost by 419.

Fortunately the second Halifax to meet its demise that night did so without taking its crew with it. Desperately short of fuel, F/O Weedon almost got BB348 back to Middleton. The airfield was in sight as the fuel starved engines spluttered and stopped. With only two miles to touchdown the Halifax crash-landed at Dinsdale, fortunately without injuring the crew.

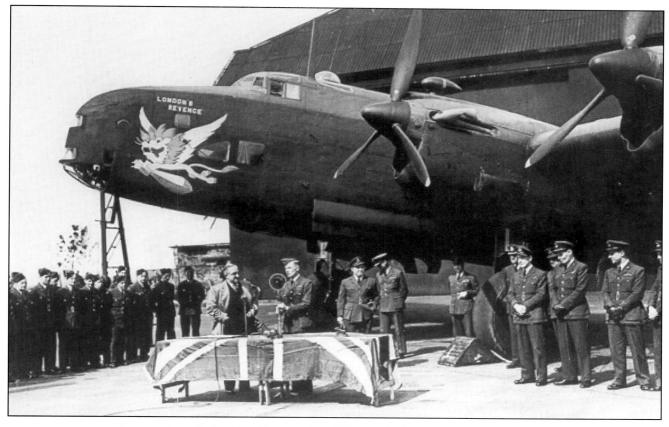

The presentation by MGM to Lion Squadron Middleton-St-George   Photo: IFox Movietone News

Meanwhile at Leeming on the afternoon of the 25th, the MGM Film Company formally adopted 427 Squadron. All squadron personnel were gathered outside their hangar. Amongst those present were Mr Eckman, the Managing Director of the MGM Film Company in Great Britain, G/C Slemon from 6 Group HQ, W/C Carscallen, Leeming's station Commander, and W/C Burnside, CO of 427. During a speech by Mr. Eckman, 427 were welcomed to the ranks of MGM as the Lion Squadron, and W/C Burnside was presented with a bronze lion to mark the occasion. A draw took place to determine which pilot got Lana Turner's name to paint on his aircraft. The whole ceremony was photographed by the London News Agency reporters and Fox Movitone news.

Eleven of 419's Halifaxes attacked Essen on the 27th, all returned to Middleton, with the exception of F/O McIntosh, who, having been hit in the port and starboard inners, managed to reach the safety of Coltishall's runway. With only two days of May remaining, 419 suffered yet another double loss, this time during an operation to Wuppertal. Whilst on the way home, the crew of Sgt Winegarden's aircraft were shot down by a night fighter and crashed in the Barrage de la Gileppe, 6 km to the S/W of Eupen and 25 miles east of Liege, Belgium. P/O Hubbs, and Sgts Mingay and Ward (all RCAF) baled out and evaded capture with the help of local people. They were, however, eventually captured and became POWs during January 1944. Sgt Hall the second pilot also baled out but his body was found at Jalhay. Winegarden and the two gunners, Sgts L R Lamoure and R M Ricketts, did not survive. Oberleutnant Rudolf Altendorf, I. /NJG4, shot down the second Halifax, JB805, flown by Sgt P S Johnson. This aircraft crashed at Peronnes-lez-Bincche, 14km E/S/E of Mons, Belgium, killing all the crew.

Next day, the Wings for Victory parade took place in Darlington. Amongst the high-ranking officers who attended the march-past were Brigadier General G H Gilmore and Middleton's G/C Ross. Darlington was represented by the Town Clerk, Mr H Hopkins and Mrs Jackson the Mayoress. The total number of aircraft lost by 419 during May 1943 reached 10. Out of the 70 men who made up the crews, 45 had been killed, 18 became POWs and seven were uninjured. By now, 419 had 20 Mk II Halifaxes and had taken part in 84 sorties.

June 1943

On June 1st, 1535 BAT flight, which had formed at Goosepool on December 15th 1942, departed for their new home at Dalton. Also on the same day, 1664 at Croft welcomed its first intake of 6 crews from 428 for conversion onto the Halifax.

After 18 days of being the only squadron at Middleton, 419 prepared to receive another squadron into their fold. On Thursday June 3rd, Goosepool welcomed an advanced party of personnel from 428 Squadron, who had travelled by road from RCAF Station Dalton. Along with 419, the new squadron would remain at Middleton for the duration of the war, a period of exactly two years. 428's thirteen Wellingtons arrived at Goosepool the next day. The aircraft and crews were as follows.

Group photograph of 428 squadron at Dalton 1943, just prior to leaving for Middleton-St-George   Photo: IWM via Geoff Hill

'A' Flight aircraft and crews

D (HE981)
Capt F/L Weeks
    F/O Robertson, P/O Stewart
    Sgt Goodfellow, F/O Ward
Groundcrew - Cpl Farnworth, LAC Bye.

F (HE571)
Capt Sgt Sheridan
    Sgt Murphy, Sgt Lifman
    Sgt Cogger, Sgt Marks
Groundcrew - Cpl Cook, LAC Vicary.

J (HE322)
Capt P/O Ross
    Sgt Webber, Sgt Chliszczyk
    Sgt Winter, Sgt Bridges
Groundcrew - Cpl Forde, AC1 McGreggor.

L (HE239)
Capt Sgt Baker
    P/O Bovard, Sgt Lewis
    Sgt Holms, Sgt Klein
Groundcrew - Cpl Angus, LAC Elder.

K (LN402)
Capt F/O Barrett
    P/O Bentley, Sgt Goundrey
    Sgt Coe, Sgt Hamilton.

G (HE703)
Capt P/O Eaton
    P/O Whitham, P/O Elmore
    Sgt Weigh, Sgt McKenzie.

B Flight aircraft and crews

W (HE917)
Capt S/L Bowden
    Sgt Rowe, P/O Gritten, Sgt Reynolds, Sgt McLean.
Groundcrew - AC1 Smyth, LAC Beaton.

O (HE738)
Capt F/L Morgan
    F/O Ditchburn, Sgt O'Leary, Sgt Gillis, Sgt Nelmes
Groundcrew - LAC Oates, LAC Watt

S (HE319)
Capt P/O Sylvester
    Sgt Forde, Sgt Kelly C, Sgt Rose, F/S Smith E
Groundcrew - AC1 Sparks, LAC Burn

V (HE367)
Capt W/O Harrison
    Sgt Bush, Sgt Brock, Sgt Freeman, Sgt North
Groundcrew - AC1 Ketchum, AC1 Litt.

X (HE505)
Capt Sgt Mitchell
    Sgt Brown, Sgt Lunny, Sgt Lott, Sgt Hamer
Groundcrew - LAC Eckersley, AC1 Jackson

T (HE174)
Capt P/O Lambert
    Sgt Peacock, P/O Coutts, Sgt Mailman, Sgt Viau.

R (HE750)
Sgt Lachman
    Sgt Jette, Sgt Askew, Sgt Marchand
Groundcrew - LAC Jones, LAC Howie

P
Capt P/O McDonnald
    P/O Balkam, Sgt Goudry, Sgt Lythgoe, Sgt Kirkham.

Although 428 had begun to re-equip with the Halifax Mk V on the 5th, their crews and Wellington aircraft were offered for operations until the crews were ready to go to the conversion units. On the 6th, a mustering parade was held for 428, with the Squadron Adjutant, F/L Maidens taking charge. During the parade, the squadron's first Halifax Mk V joined Middleton's circuit and landed. Although 428's aircraft had been detailed for Ops over the next few days, each time the raid was subsequently cancelled.

After Middleton, and thus Croft, transferred from 4 to 6 Group, it was decided to consider upgrading Croft to sub-station status. By June 7th, the decision had been made, and Air Ministry authority S71521/C Est 2A to the establishment WAR/BC/185A was promulgated. Seven days later, Croft welcomed the arrival of its new Station Commander, G/C N S MacGregor DFC. Seven days after that, on the 18th, he assumed command, as Croft became a Sub-station in its own right. With Middleton becoming 64 RCAF Base, Croft became 64 RCAF Base sub-station. The next day, Croft's partly completed Admin site was taken over, allowing SHQ, which had been housed in the Technical Site, to move in. F/L Francis became Acting S/L Francis. He then relinquished his job as Camp Commandant and moved in as well, to become Croft's Station Admin Officer. All that was needed now was an Adjutant. This position would be filled on July 6th by F/L D Sigler. The month also saw the completion of the new Squadron Site, situated to the north of the Control Tower. The Link Trainer, Photography and Bombing Teacher sections were also situated on this site.

Croft's SHQ Staff at this time totaled 24, and consisted of the following personnel.

Commanding Officer	G/C N S MacGregor DFC	Armament Officer	F/L I C Nelson
Senior Admin Officer	S/L H F Francis	Meteorological	F/O F Buckley
Station Adjutant	F/L D Singler	Meteorological	F/O K C Crossley
Flying Control	F/O F P Moyer	Meteorological	P/O J Hodkinson
Operations Officer	F/O D Williams	Signals Officer	F/L C Cramp
Engineering Officer	S/L R C Scott	Equipment Officer	F/L H P J McCurry
Engineering Officer	F/O F Candlish	Station Padre	S/L E Lautenslager
Engineering Officer	F/L J B Dickey	Medical Officer	F/L C B Church
Flying Control	F/L W H Dotesio	Electrical Engineer	P/O W L Taite
Flying Control	F/O F J Maher	Dental Officer	Capt A Gardiner
OC 1499 A A Flight	F/L A J Wilkins	OC I/C W.A.A.F	S/O J I Boyd
Catering Officer	F/O S McGann	Administrative	S/O M A Fuller

Meanwhile, at Goosepool, the build up of 428's personnel continued, as on June 8th, when 39 additional ground staff were posted in. On the 10th, the 7 Wellingtons sent over to Croft for the night's operation returned, as again the raid had been cancelled.

During June, 419 carried out raids on various targets. The first Op was on the 11th when 17 crews were briefed to go to Dusseldorf. Due to mechanical problems, one was a non-starter; one returned with engine trouble, and four more returned due to severe icing conditions. VR-A JD143 flown by F/O W J Boyce was shot down by flak and crashed at Uedemar Bruch, 21 miles southeast of Nijmegan. F/O Broyce, his second pilot W/O H A Tripp, and the wireless operator Sgt D E Chambers, were killed, the remainder of the crew became POWs. On June 11th several of 6 Group's squadrons were briefed for operations to Dusseldorf. During this raid, 419 lost one of their 17 Halifaxes when it crashed at Uedem. One of 428's Wellingtons crashed whilst taking off. It had been carrying a 4,000-lb Cookie, which went off on impact. Four of the crew were killed outright. The pilot, Sgt Lachman, was flung out of the aircraft and was found 30 yards away. He was still strapped into his seat, seriously injured. Members of the SSQ treated him the best they could, before transferring him to the RAF General Hospital at Northallerton.

428's F/O Barrett, in Wellington HF571, was some 56 miles short of the Dutch Coast, at a height of 15,000 feet, when engine trouble forced him to turn back. Having left Middleton at 23:04, P/O W D Ross and his crew arrived at Dusseldorf at 01:38. The visibility was fair, with 6/10ths-cloud cover up to 10,000 feet and only a little haze. At 17,500 feet, Ross turned onto a heading of 030° and began the bomb-run, their indicated airspeed was 140 mph. Once the bombs had left the Wellington, he turned for home. Below, there were intensive fires burning in the target area. The trip home was fairly uneventful, but Middleton's weather was not very hospitable, and, like several crews that night, they had to land a whole six miles away at Croft. Similar reports were filed by the crews of P/O D R McDonald, Sgt A L Mitchell, P/O J M Lambert and P/O V T Sylvester, who also landed at Croft.

The raid itself caused more damage to Dusseldorf than any other raid during the war, with 130 acres of the city claimed as destroyed. Most of the 326 Lancasters, 202 Halifaxes, 143 Wellingtons, 99 Stirlings and 13 Mosquitoes bombed the markers dropped by the PFF. One of the Oboe Mosquitoes dropped its markers 14 miles to the north, and caused part of the main force to bomb open country. However, the majority bombed the correct markers. A large part of the city centre was destroyed and 42 industrial sites were put out of action. 140,000 people were made homeless and the death toll reached 1,292. On top of all this, 20 military sites were hit, 8 ships were sunk and the local Government Headquarters was destroyed.

During this operation, 419's VR-S, flown by P/O R A Bell, dropped a 2,000 HC bomb, bang on the correct PFF target markers. The people of Dusseldorf would never know that the bomb had been dropped with the inscription 'From Anne' chalked on its casing. Earlier, a letter had been sent to HQ 6 Group from the CAS - RCAF in conjunction with the Dominion of Canada's National War Loan Drive. This letter was from a Dutch child residing in Canada. She had contributed 500 Canadian dollars, sent to the CAS personally, with the request that a bomb be dropped by an RCAF aircraft on Germany, marked 'From Anne'. Approval for this event had been given, and the War Loan authorities wanted to take it public. They asked that the bomb to be dropped was either a 500-lb or a 1,000-lb HC bomb, and marked 'From Anne'.

The bomb was to be dropped sometime after Tuesday May 25th 1943 on an appropriate target in Germany. It was suggested that 419 Squadron be selected to undertake this mission, and the Station Commander was requested to forward pictures and necessary descriptions to HQ 6 Group as soon as possible after the raid had been completed.

Next day 428 acquired 4 more Halifax Vs, bringing their total number of aircraft on charge to 5. Meanwhile F/L B N Jost was posted in from 1659 OCU to become 419's 'A' Flight Commander. He would be replacing S/L C E Harris, who was posted to 434 Squadron along with F/O J W Tyler. That night, the squadron sent 14 aircraft on operations to Bochum. Four aircraft returned early, and Sgt B D Kirkham's crew in DT616 were shot down by a Me110 and became POWs. During this raid, Sgt W H Barnes, the tail gunner in DT 689, shot down a Ju88 after it tried to attack the Halifax on the return journey, whilst 60 miles from the Dutch Coast. P/O R Harling, another of 419's gunners, also had success that night, he too dispatched a Ju88 over the target area.

The funerals of three out of the four Wellington crewmen killed whilst taking off for the Dusseldorf raid three days earlier, took place on the 14th at Darlington's West Cemetery. 428's Commanding Officer, with an attending party of 12 officers and sergeants, 18 sergeant pallbearers, 4 sergeants acting as mourners, and a party of 25 airmen, represented the squadron. 428's Halifaxes had been arriving at a steady rate, as were more groundcrew personnel. On the 16th, four of them were attached to 419 for operational duties, and by the 18th they had 9 Halifax Mk Vs serviceable out of the 14 now on charge.

At Croft on the 19th, RCAF Station HQ moved into its new quarters on the Admin site. During the same day, motor transport through Middleton St George village was severely affected when a Cole's crane overturned outside the Fighting Cocks pub. The driver had taken the bend too fast. Fortunately no one was hurt but it proved extremely difficult to right the vehicle before nightfall.

That night, 14 Halifaxes belonging to 419, along with a further 276 aircraft of 3, 4 and 6 Groups, attacked the Schneider armaments factory and the Breuil Steelworks at Le Creusot. Due to lingering smoke from the marker flares, most crews only managed to bomb within 3 miles of the target, only about one fifth managed to hit the factories. Many bombs fell on nearby French residential areas. Two Halifaxes were lost. Fortunately all of 419's Halifaxes returned safe, including 4 aircraft and crews borrowed from 428. They were flown by Sgt K D Fry, F/S L F Williamson, F/S C R Pearce and Sgt M Chepil. The latter lost his port outer some 60 miles short of the target, and although this was his first Halifax sortie, he decided to press on. Arriving late over the target, he and his crew found that there was a considerable amount of smoke covering the target. Fortunately there were no searchlights and only light flak. Without the port outer and the hydraulic pump that it turned, Chepil and his crew had to manually lower the bomb doors before dropping their bombs. They successfully attacked the target and managed to make it back to Tangmere where they landed without further incident. Later during the following month, Chepil was awarded the DFM for his efforts in carrying out this sortie.

Pearce's crew managed to reach the target, but had to do three runs before they could accurately locate the correct AP. The flare over the target was practically out but they managed to bomb a bright glow showing through the smoke. Low on fuel on the way home, they managed to divert to Elsham Wold. Despite the compass being 30° out and the autopilot U/S, Williamson's crew reached the target area and bombed from 8,000 feet. A decoy target had been illuminated by the Germans some 5 miles northeast of the real target, but this failed to fool anyone. Short of fuel, Williams also diverted on the way home.

Next day, the airfield hosted a visit by 405 Squadron Air Training Corps (ATC), who were given an aircraft recognition lecture by F/L J M Forman, 419's Gunnery Leader. At the time, there were many hundreds of ATC squadrons throughout the country. These units trained and groomed air minded youngsters who were just a little too young to join the RAF. Darlington had two ATC squadrons. The young Air Cadets belonging to 405 were based in wooden huts behind the Empire Cinema,[86] on Poplar Road car park, just off Russell Street. The second squadron had its HQ in a large house on Haughton Road. The author became a cadet in 405 at the end of the 50s, at the tender age of 14. The cadets normally remained with their squadrons until age 17, when they usually joined the RAF. Like the author, many cadets went on to enjoy careers in military or civilian aviation and then return to command ATC squadrons. 405 Squadron remains in operation today. They spent many years in the old wooden huts on the car park. During the late 60s, due to building work, 405 had to relocate to former wartime building on the TA site on Neasham Road, Darlington. Here they remained until the late 80s, when they moved just a few yards to their present location within the new TA Centre building. Today, 405 are still turning out fine young air-minded lads to carry on the traditions of the Corps.

On the morning of June 21st, the faint sounds of a heavy-laden aircraft were heard approaching Middleton. At first, everyone strained their eyes to identify what seemed to be a very strange flying object. Eventually the dot became larger. It was only then realised that the one dot had now become two. Consternation replaced inquisitiveness when the excessive closeness of the aircraft to each other became apparent. As both aircraft neared the airfield, all was revealed. It was a Whitley, towing a large Horsa Glider. This was the first time anyone on the airfield had seen such a thing. The pair joined the circuit for No.2 runway, (19/01). Whilst down-wind, the glider pilot released the cable joining the Horsa to the Whitley. Completing half a circuit, the glider pilot lined up parallel with 19 and landed on the grass down the side of the runway. The Whitley continued to circle, the cable still trailing. The tug completed another circuit and landed safely on the main runway (24/06). The Glider was being used to deliver a replacement Merlin, which was required for another squadron's aircraft that had landed at Middleton two nights before, due to engine trouble of its own, the Whitley/Glider were unable to take-off until the next day. The following morning, everyone came out of the woodwork to see their first Tug/Glider take-off. All went well, with the wags in flying control noting the take-off times as, Glider 10:00 hours and the Whitley, 10:01.

86 Now Wilkinson's Supermarket

That night, 15 of 419's Halifaxes attacked Krefeld. Three of the crews taking part had been some of the 8 sent over from 428 to gain operational experience. One of these failed to return. Flown by Sgt C R Pearce DFM RNZAF, this aircraft, W1271, crashed at De Posthorn, near Rucphen, 4 miles east of Roosendaal, Holland. All on board were killed. The two remaining 428 aircraft, flown by Sgt K Q Fry and Sgt L F Williamson, returned safely to base. Fry's crew managed to successfully bomb the target. On the way home they were able to see the glow of the fires from the Dutch coast, a distance of over 100 miles. Williamson's crew returned early. They had reached a point some 50 miles east of Lowestoft, when it was realised that the aircraft's intercom was U/S.

The following day, 419 sent 10 crews, of which 2 were from 428, on a gardening operation to the Friesian Islands. A further 3 carried out operations as part of a 557 aircraft raid on Mulheim. At Mulheim, the markers went down well and the bombing was very accurate. During the raid the PFF and the bombers moved slightly to the northern part of the town. This cut off all roads and communications with nearby Oberhousen, which itself suffered much damage to its eastern areas. As a consequence of this raid, 64% of Mulheim was destroyed. 578 people were killed and a further 1,174 injured. 1,135 houses were destroyed and 12,637 were damaged. A large proportion of the town's industrial capacity was also damaged. Against this was the loss of 6.3% of the bomber force, which consisted of 8 Lancasters, 12 Halifaxes, 11 Stirlings and 4 Wellingtons. 427 Squadron at Leeming lost 4 crews. Of the 28 men that made up these crews, only 2 survived to become POWs. All of Middleton's crews returned safely.

View from the roof of hangar 1 during 1943   Photo: via Geoff Hill

View from the roof of hangar 1 during 2003   Photo: Author

View from the roof of hangar 2 during 1943   *Photo: via Geoff Hill*

View from the roof of hangar 2 during 2003   *Photo: Author*

Two nights later, on the 24th, 16 Moose crews were added to the 630 that bombed the Elberfeld district of Wuppertal. Just after take-off, P/O A V Reilander's Halifax suffered a failure to the starboard inner. Having dumped his bombs in the sea some 63 miles off Redcar, he brought the Halifax safely back to base. The attack itself destroyed 94% of the Elberfeld district, which is situated in the southwest sector of Wuppertal. An earlier raid during May had taken place on the Barmen district, which is located in the northeastern sector of the town. Over 3,000 houses and 171 industrial buildings were destroyed and a further 2,500 houses and 53 industrial buildings damaged. The toll on the ground was put at 1,800 killed and 2,400 injured. The crews, flown by F/O Fanson, P/O Heintz, Second Lt Furey USAAF, Sgt Chapman and Sgt Blackmore, all described similar events over Wuppertal. The weather had been good. There was no cloud below 18,000 feet and the red TIs[87] had been well covered by their bombs. They all had the same bomb-loads, consisting of 2 X 1,000-lb, 48 X 30-lb, and 630 X 4-lb incendiaries.

Amongst the 34 Bomber Command aircraft lost that night, 2 were from 419. JD147, flown by F/L Jost DFC, was shot down by a night fighter, flown by Ober Feldwebel Reinhard Kollak of III./ NJG4. It crashed near Herten, 1.25 miles S/W of Roermond, Holland. Four of the crew survived, but F/L Jost, his wireless operator F/O R O Goodwin, and the flight engineer Sgt J B Johnson were killed. The second Halifax lost was that of Sgt G V Neale. Having been shot at by a FW 190, the crew of this aircraft, JD214, sent an SOS over the target area. This was followed by another, sent whilst on the

[87] Target indicators

166

way home over Holland. The second message indicated that no further transmissions would follow. Shortly after, the aircraft forced-landed at Wageningen, 10 miles west of Arnhem. The crew survived and were captured by the Germans. Sgt R Whitfield and his crew flying JD258 belonged to 428 Squadron, but were gaining operational experience by flying with 419. They were all killed when their Halifax was shot down by Hauptmann Hans-Dieter Frank and crashed at Acht, in the northwest suburbs of Eindhoven.

428's P/O Reilander had taken off from Goosepool, and had reached a point some 17 miles due east of Whitby, when the revs of the starboard engine began to drop off. The oil pressure fell and the engine was making very unhappy noises, before failing all together. The engine was feathered and Reilander ordered that the bomb-load be jettisoned. He then returned to Middleton where a safe landing was carried out. The next night, 419 sent 13 Halifaxes on operations to bomb Gelsenkirchen, including 3 from 428. This was the first concerted raid on the town since 1941, when its oil plants had received a fair bit of attention. It had been hit accidentally many times after that, by bombs dropped during raids on other nearby Ruhr targets.

By the 26th, all of 428's crews had completed their experience trips with 419, and had returned to their own squadron for operations. By this time, a total of 13 crews belonging to 428 had completed their conversion onto the Halifax. Meanwhile, at Croft, S/L Francis was dispatched to London on the 28th. He had been told not to return without acquiring a decent piano for the station. That evening, 419 briefed 11 crews for operations to Cologne, from which P/O H W Fowler and his crew did not return. Their mount that night was Halifax JD215. This aircraft was shot down by Major Gunter Radusch of I./NJG1. Their Halifax came down at Waalre, 3.4 miles south of Eindhoven, with the loss of all on board. Next day was a stand-down, and as the weather was not too good for flying, some of 419's crews enjoyed the facilities of the nearby River Tees, whilst partaking practice dinghy drill.

July 1943

On July 1st, a communication from Mrs W M Fulton informed 419 that the City of Kamloops, British Columbia, had adopted the Squadron. Mrs. Fulton was the mother of the squadron's first CO, the late W/C John (Moose) Fulton DFC AFC. Kamloops was Moose Fulton's hometown, and from that moment 419 had officially become 'The Moose Squadron'. Its personnel were to become better known as the Moosemen. The letter, dated April 22nd and written by Mrs Winifred M Fulton to wing Commander Fleming read: -

I beg to inform you that the city of Kamloops has now organized a special committee to take care of comforts and cheer for the officers and men of the 'Moose' squadron. This squadron, as well as HMCS 'Kamloops' of the RCN, has been officially adopted by the city, and the citizens felt that there should be an official body organized to look after them. A supply of official letterheads is in the course of being printed, and I hope soon to send one to you that you may know the names of the officers of the committee, which will be printed thereon. The committee will be known as the Kamloops Civilian Auxiliary to the HMCS 'Kamloops' and 419 B 'Moose' squadron RCAF Overseas. In the meantime, as secretary to the committee, I have been asked to communicate with you to ask if there is any way in particular that you know of how we could serve the squadron. We propose to send regular supplies of smokes, with chocolate bars or other sweets and gums, as well as any knitted articles that would be needed from time to time. We may also include subscriptions to Canadian magazines and forward new books occasionally. We would like to know the number of men and officers serving with your squadron and, if possible, the proportion of flying and ground personnel.

On the same day, 428 sent 15 airmen to represent the squadron at the Dominion Day celebrations which were taking place at Ripon, North Yorkshire. The Day began with a church service followed by a parade.

The number of crews arriving at the Moose Squadron from 1659 and 1664 increased during July. 419 and 428 took part in a 653 aircraft operation on Cologne on the 3rd. This raid saw the Germans carry out new tactics against the bombers, code name 'Wild Sau'.[88] This employed Jagdgeschwader 300,[89] who worked in conjunction with the flak gunners. The idea was to have the flak explode at a certain height, above which the German fighters could roam freely. They would pick off the bombers illuminated by the glow of fires on the ground, or perhaps the light from searchlights or target indicators. This was new to the bomber crews, and some reported that they had been fired upon by other bombers whilst over the target area. The penny was slow to drop at first, as the crews were not accustomed to meeting up with fighters over the target area. 12 bombers were shot down over the target area during this raid, both the flak gunners and the night fighter pilots claimed that they had done so.

As to who actually shot what down, no one could actually prove one way or the other, and so both agencies had to be content with shared victories. 419 lost P/O A H Bell and his crew from this raid, they were on their 29th trip. Shot down by Oberfeldwebel Reinhard Kollak of 7./NJG4, Halifax JD159 crashed at Muizen, on the southeastern outskirts of Mechelen, 14 miles S/S/E of Antwerp. Out of the 8-man crew, 5 survived and became POWs. P/O Bell, the second pilot Sgt J A Anderson, the eighth crewman (who was on his first operational trip), and the engineer Sgt W B Taylor, were killed. Out of the 10 Halifaxes sent by 428, all returned safe. Only one aircraft, flown by Second Lt K R Knapp USAAF, failed to taxi back to dispersal in the normal manner. His Halifax made a spectacular arrival on the airfield, crash-landing, fortunately without injury to his crew.

[88] Wild Boar
[89] Fighter Squadron 300

Between the 4th and 8th of July, the Teesside weather put paid to operations. The squadrons made good use of the stand-downs. Meanwhile, 428's Bombing Leader, P/O C Maddin, was promoted to the rank of Acting Flight Lieutenant. On the 8th, there was an ENSA show in the NAFFI and all the camp turned out to enjoy the entertainment.

Gelsenkirchen was the next target for Middleton's crews. It was visited on July 9th by 11 aircraft sent by each of Goosepool's squadrons. Unfortunately, out of 6 Oboe carrying Mosquitoes, 5 had trouble with their sets and a 6th incorrectly dropped its sky markers some 10 miles north of the correct aiming point. The strange result was that somehow the bombers unloaded over Bochum and Wattenscheid, some 6 miles southeast of Gelsenkirchen, and 16 miles southeast of the incorrect makers. However, some bombs did fall on the southern districts of Gelsenkirchen and the synthetic oil plant at Scholven.

428 suffered the loss of their first Halifax V since converting onto type. Hit by flak, S/L Bowen DFC and Bar, the squadron's 'B' Flight Commander, flying DK229, remained at the controls to allow his crew time to bale out. He was unable to leave the aircraft in time and was killed. The Halifax crashed near Cologne. S/L Bowen, who had completed one tour of operations, was nearing the end of his second. The squadron mourned the loss of this fine officer and his presence was sorely missed by all. The remainder of the crew landed safely and were quickly captured.

The next day, 419 had a stand-down, which allowed 'B' Flight to trounce their groundcrew at softball. The Canadians at Goosepool introduced softball to the folk of Darlington. The main venue for this new found sport was a church hall (now no longer there), just opposite the junction of Yarm Road and Hundens Lane. On the twelfth, 428 celebrated, along with Acting Wing Commander D W Smith, Acting Squadron Leader W R Suggitt and Second Lt K R Knapp of the US Forces, who were to be the recipients of the DFC. Also decorated was F/S B A Nicholls, who by now had been promoted to Pilot Officer and who was to receive the DFM.

View from the roof of hangar 2 towards hangars 4 and 5 during 1943   Photo: via Geoff Hill

Second Lt B J Furey was on detachment to 419 from the US Army Air Force. He and his crew were lost on the night of the 13th whilst undertaking operations to Aachen. Shot down by a night fighter near Venlo, Holland, 6 of the crew, including Furey, jumped out and became POWs. The tail gunner, Sgt W C Batkin RAF, was killed. During the same raid, the crew of VR-E, F/L Keddie's Halifax, was approached by a single engined fighter whilst at 20,000 feet. The enemy aircraft, which had a white light in its nose, moved in slowly from astern. The Halifax's tail gunner, F/O R J Wagner, gave the fighter a long burst of fire from 900 yards, followed by two more as it got closer. The enemy aircraft burst into flames and dropped several thousand feet before entering cloud. A few moments later an explosion was seen through the cloud as the aircraft hit the ground. Wagner claimed the fighter as destroyed. The combat had been seen by the Halifax's mid-upper gunner, Sgt G A Hurst and the engineer, Sgt E R Kirkham.

The 13th was also to bring bad tidings for 428 during the Aachen raid. They were to lose no less than three aircraft. Taking off from Middleton at 23:45, F/L D S Morgan and his crew were attacked by a night fighter near Tilburg whilst out-bound, some 18 miles northwest of Eindhoven. The aircraft, DK257, flew on but eventually crashed at 02:00 near Genderren, 13 miles north of Tilburg.

Again the number 13 showed itself. It is unlikely that the mid-upper and tail gunner saw the fighter's first pass, as neither got out. Both are commemorated on the Runnymede Memorial. One of the crew, P/O J P O'Leary, managed to evade capture, while Morgan and the remainder of the crew became POWs.

F/L W G Weeks and his crew, who were flying NA-D, now lie in Belgium's Florennes Communal Cemetery, having been shot down by a night fighter at Mesnil-St-Blaise, 5 miles S/S/W of Dinant, Belgium. The third loss was that of P/O W D Ross, who was hit by flak whilst leaving the target area. The aircraft was later abandoned at 02:30 near Marche-en-Famenne, Belgium, 50 miles southwest of Aachen. All on board managed to bale out. Ross and three of the crew became POWs whilst the navigator Sgt D J Webb and the tail gunner Sgt E A Bridge evaded capture. Both P/O Ross and F/L Weeks were on their second tour, whilst F/L Morgan was on his 16th operation. Two other 428 aircraft had scrapes with fighters, one of which was seen to be hit by fire from one of the bombers before flying away.

On the 19th, five new aircrews arrived at Middleton, 428 Squadron for the use of. This raised the squadron's number of crews to 21. Two days later, 13 new ground-crew personnel arrived. They had been posted in from the Personnel Dispatch Centre at Bournemouth, having just arrived there from Canada. After a series of stand-downs and cancellations during 10 days of mainly good weather, rumours began to abound that Bomber Command was up to something. Throughout the country, the Command had most of its squadrons kicking their heels. It seemed as if Harris was saving his force for something big. During the morning of the 24th, eleven Moose crews and fourteen belonging to 428 were warned of an impending raid that would take place that night. When the curtain was drawn back from the briefing map all was revealed. 'Ok Fellas, hear it is, Hamburg.' The city of Hamburg was the target for a force of 791 aircraft of Bomber Command. Hamburg, Germany's second largest city after Berlin, sported Europe's biggest port. Harris had sent orders to the commander of each bomber Group during late May, instructing them to begin planning a series of 4 heavy raids on the city that would take place over 10 nights. Hamburg had seen small to medium size attacks on no less than 98 occasions thus far in the war, but now it was time to step up the ante.

Bomber Command had a magic card up its sleeve for this operation, and it was called 'Window'. Two-centimeters-wide by 27-centimeters-long black paper strips, backed with thin aluminium foil, were dropped by the millions. Window, dropped in large enough quantities, had the effect of swamping the German radar and cloaking the bombers in false echoes. Although used for the first time during this raid, Window had actually been available since April 1942, but it was feared that once the cat was out of the bag, the Germans would use their own version against British defence radar. The Germans relied heavily on radar to combat the bombers. Their night fighter interceptions relied on the giant, ground based Wurzburg radar stations to position the fighters in the same bit of sky as the bombers. After that, the smaller Lichtenstein radar sets, fitted in the night fighter's nose, allowed the pilot to close in on the bomber once it got within a reasonable range. Windows disrupted all of these systems, and for good measure the flak gun laying radar also.

The crews took off around 22:00. Their course took them just to the north of Whitby and on over the North Sea. Their landfall on the enemy coast was near Cuxhaven, only 60 miles from Hamburg. The direct track from Middleton to Cuxhaven was 410 statute miles, and saved the crews from flying over more enemy-held territory than was absolutely necessary. Hamburg was beyond the range of Oboe, however, the distinctive coast line, the River Elbe and Hamburg's huge dock basin, were just what the doctor ordered as far as H2S was concerned. The approach routes and aiming points were designed to take into account the inevitable creepback. This would ensure that the bombs would fall right across the required residential areas, which were located on the northern bank of the Elbe. The shipyards and Hamburg's huge port, situated on the southern bank, were not part of the main targeting strategy. The objective was to disrupt the city's production capabilities by hitting its workers. The weather was clear with light winds, and the markers were dropped fairly accurately, close to the city centre. Despite the fact that less than half of the crews bombed within 3 miles of the city centre, the bombing itself was concentrated and developed well, with 2,284 tons of bombs being dropped over a 50 minute period. The creepback extended back from the city centre some 6 miles, but still remained within the confines of the city. The districts of Emsbuttle and Hoheluft were severely damaged, along with Altona, situated on the northern bank of the Elbe, some 2.75 miles west of the city centre. Over 1,500 people were killed. The Hagenbeck Zoo, which is located 5 miles northwest of the city centre, saw 140 animals killed when stray bombs exploded. The raid was to be followed up by daylight raids, which would be carried out by the Americans. The targets were to be industrial and naval, but when they got there, the smoke and haze from the Bomber Command raid prevented the operation from being carried out successfully. The B17s were withdrawn, and after the Hamburg raids would no longer follow any further Bomber Command operations, due to the problems caused by smoke. During the RAF raid of the 24/25th, twelve aircraft were lost. This low 1.5% figure was clearly attributed to the first ever use of Window. Those that were lost consisted of 1 Wellington, 4 Halifaxes, 4 Lancasters and 3 Stirlings, none were from Goosepool.

Essen was the target the following night, and 10 Moose crews and 12 from 428 were detailed to join a force of 705 Bomber Command aircraft. The flak was intense, and the crews had to negotiate between two rows of searchlights during their bombing run, each row containing up to 40 lights. The raid was successful, with the eastern part of the city receiving particular attention. This area contained much of Essen's industrial buildings, of which over 50 were destroyed. The Krupps works took the brunt of the attack, its most damaging of the war. Doktor Gustav Krupp had a stroke the next morning and never recovered. Window was used again, but the losses of the force compared to the previous night's raid doubled to 3.7%.

Having just dropped their bombs from 17,000 feet, the crew of 419's A-Able JD256, flown by W/O L Chapman, entered a Cu-Nim thundercloud. Moments later, something unseen collided with the Halifax's tailplane and the controls were wrenched from the pilot's hands and ended up jammed in the forward right hand position. The aircraft rolled inverted and dived for the ground. With his controls immovable, Chapman was unable to recover control. Having given the order to abandon, he loosened his seat straps and, as the aircraft was inverted, dropped out of the top hatch above his head. As pilot, Chapman was the only one wearing a seat type parachute pack. The rest of crew, who did not have their chutes clipped on, were unable to get out in time and were killed. So little time was there to escape, that Chapman had only swung a few times on his chute before he landed in a suburb of Essen, and was soon captured. Having only joined the squadron that afternoon, the second pilot F/O S W Handforth was killed along with the rest of the crew. Coincidentally, F/O Handforth had been Chapman's flying instructor during his training in Canada. He was along for the ride with his former pupil to gain operational experience.

Whilst crossing the French Coast at 14,000 feet on the way home, Sgt L Northcliffe, the tail gunner in F/S R Stewart's Halifax, saw an approaching Fw 190. The German pilot closed in at the same level as the bomber, and at 400 yards, switched on a small yellow light. Northcliffe fired a burst at the fighter, which immediately broke off. A few moments later, the 190 tried again. Before the pilot could fire, it exploded, as Northcliffe pumped 400 rounds into it. Small burning pieces of the fighter fell from the area behind the bomber and disappeared into the cloud below. The 190 was claimed as destroyed.

This was confirmed by the mid-upper Sgt A D Garland, who had, for some reason, swapped turrets with Northcliffe.

There were no losses from 428, however, only 9 aircraft reached the target, as there were three that had to return early due to technical problems. Later that day, F/O E Smith was posted to 419 from 6 Group to take up his post as Squadron Armaments Officer. F/O Smith had been with the Moosemen in a former life when he held the position of W/O in charge of the armoury. During the day, 2 Moose aircraft took part in a sea search in an attempt to find a downed crew, unfortunately without success.

Reap the Whirlwind.

The second operation of the 4 planned for Hamburg took place on the night of July 27/28th. This time, 787 aircraft took part, of which the Moosemen contributed 14, whilst 428, led by W/C D W Smith, donated 15. For a third time, Window was used to confound the defences. The markers used H2S to pinpoint the target, which once again was planned to be the centre of the city. However, the markers actually landed 2 miles east of the desired spot, but they were well concentrated and accurate bombing began. The 2,326 tons of bombs dropped contained the usual mix of incendiaries and HE bombs. In similar ratio to the loads used during the raid on Hamburg 3 days earlier, this was fairly typical of the type of loads dropped during most raids on German cities. Hamburg was enjoying a very warm dry summer, and, as events would prove, this situation conspired to create a terrible phenomenon for the population of the city. The day had been a roaster, and by 6pm the temperature still hovered around the 30-degree mark. The average humidity at this time of year should have been around 50%, but on this particular day it was only about 30%. Also, the bulk of Hamburg's firefighters were still busy dampening down fires in the western sectors of the city, including Altona, that persisted from the raid that took place on the 24/25th. This second raid saw 600 bombers unload in the built up areas on the eastern side of the city centre, in the districts of Hammerbrook, Hamm and Borgfelde. This was an area measuring only 2 miles by 1. Although only 2 miles from the still smoldering Altona, the Hammerbrook district could not be easily reached by the firefighters, as the rubble filled streets inhibited their vehicles from reaching that part of the city. Although some could negotiate around their own particular area, they, too, soon found the roads impassable as the new bombing collapsed buildings into the streets. As the raid progressed, the various fires in Hammerbrook, just 900 yards from the city centre, began amalgamating, and soon they became one large conflagration. To satisfy its insatiable appetite for oxygen, the fire drew in huge amounts of air, and became capable of sucking in everyone and everything in its path. Of the 40,000 people who perished during this raid, many suffocated or died of carbon monoxide poisoning when the air was sucked out of their underground shelters. The bombs continued to fall, enlarging the firestorm and progressing it towards the east. It was still fully developed two and a half hours after the bombers had departed. Slowly, the hurricane force winds began to abate when there was nothing left to burn.

In keeping with Harris's directives, the main area of devastation was residential. This included 16,000 apartment buildings, which were all destroyed. The 729 bombers that actually attacked Hamburg that night dropped 2,326 tons of bombs. After this raid, 1,200,000 of Hamburg's residents, nearly 66% of the entire population, left the city to find somewhere safer to live. Despite the continued use of Window, 17 aircraft were lost, most to night fighters. The Moosemen however, were not among the squadrons losing aircraft that night, nor was 428. Hamburg was still smouldering two nights later, when Bomber Command paid its third visit. The Moosemen detailed 16 aircraft for this raid whilst 428 sent 17. This time 777 bombers approached from the north, with the intention of bombing the so far untouched northern and northeastern areas of the city.

The PFF had actually overshot the intended aiming point, and had dropped their markers further east than intended. This brought about the destruction of the Barmbek and Wandsbek districts, Barmbek is located 3.2 miles N/N/E of the city centre whilst Wandsbek lies 3.2 miles to the N/E. In Wandsbek itself, the basement of a large department store was being used as an air raid shelter. When the building was hit, debris covered the exits, preventing some 370 people inside from escaping. Unfortunately, there was a coke store close by, which was burning. Carbon monoxide fumes seeped into the shelter and everyone died. The inevitable creepback saw the next port of call as being just north of Hamburg's centre. The districts of Uhlenhorst and Winterhude, lying 2 miles and 3.3 miles north of the city centre respectively, were also devastated. After three major raids in 6 days, Hamburg's fire fighters had little left to offer and were completely overwhelmed. 2,318 tons of bombs were dropped on the city during this third raid, some by the 16 participating Moose crews. Sgt F B Alan and his crew, flying VR-P, did not manage to reach Hamburg, his port inner went sick over the North Sea on the way to the target and they had to return early. On the return journey, most of the remaining Moose crews reported seeing Hamburg's fires burning from over 160 miles away. On their return to base, the good old Teesside weather was waiting to greet the crews, and several aircraft had to divert a whole six miles to the west, and land at Croft where the Viz was better. Not among the returning bombers was 428's NA-Q, flown by Sgt D H Bates. Shot down by a night fighter, this Halifax exploded in the vicinity of Luneburg. Only one member of the crew, Sgt P Demcoe, survived to become a POW.

Earlier that day, W/C Fleming, S/L McMurdy the A Flight Commander, F/L Parnel the Navigation Leader, F/L Rice the Signals Leader, F/L Shields the Bombing Leader and F/L Kinyon the Gunnery Leader had been invited to Blyth, 11 miles north of Tyneside on the Northumberland coast. They were guests of the Royal Navy, and were taken on several practice dives in a submarine. More crews were continuing to arrive at the Moose Squadron from 1659 OCU at Topcliffe.

The last raid for 419 during July was quite small in comparison to the Hamburg sorties, but this operation marked the end of the Battle of the Ruhr. Their target was the small town of Remscheide, which is located 18 miles E/S/E of Dusseldorf, and also some 18 miles to the south of the Ruhr. Oboe was used to mark the target, and the small force of 273 aircraft bombed very accurately. By the conclusion of the raid, 3,115 houses and 107 industrial buildings were destroyed. The town was heavily involved in war work and would never fully recover. Although 26 people had been killed by stray bombs since the war began, this raid was Remscheide's first. Over 83 percent of the town was destroyed by the 871 tons of bombs dropped that night. 1,120 of its inhabitants were killed during this operation and a further 6,700 injured. Bomber Command lost 17 aircraft.

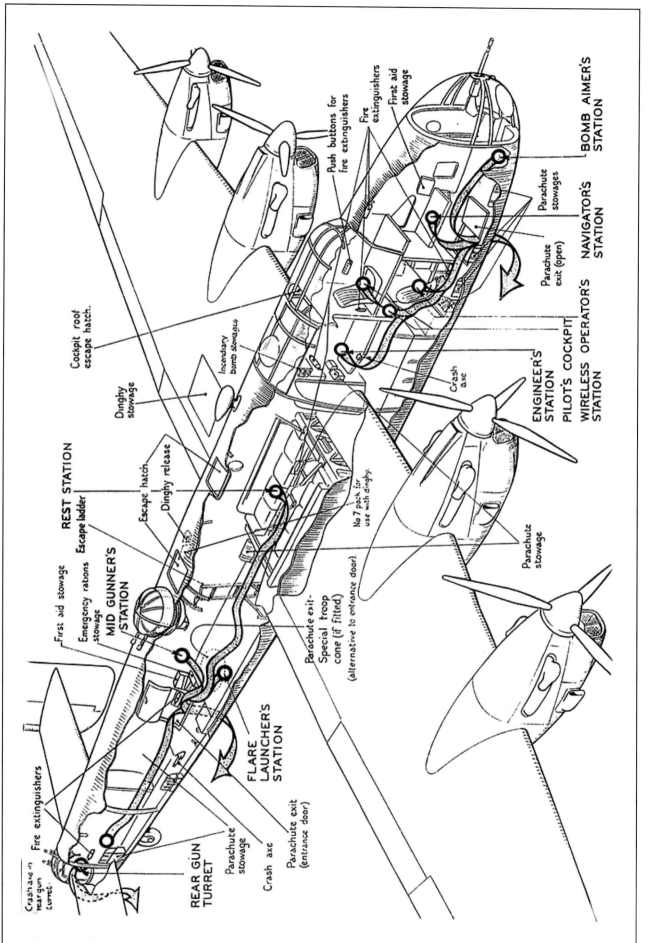

BOMB AIMER'S STATION

Fire extinguishers

First aid stowage

Push buttons for fire extinguishers

Parachute stowages

Parachute exit (open)

NAVIGATOR'S STATION

Cockpit roof escape hatch.

Dinghy stowage

Incendiary bomb stowages

Crash axe

ENGINEER'S STATION

PILOT'S COCKPIT

WIRELESS OPERATOR'S STATION

REST STATION

Escape ladder

Escape hatch

Dinghy release

No 7 pack for use with dinghy.

Parachute stowage

First aid stowage

Emergency rations stowage

MID GUNNER'S STATION

FLARE LAUNCHER'S STATION

Parachute exit - Special troop cone (if fitted) (alternative to entrance door)

REAR GUN TURRET

Fire extinguishers

Crash axe in rear gun turret.

Parachute stowage

Crash axe

Parachute exit (entrance door)

Halifax exit routes   *Photo: © Crown copyright/MOD Reproduced with the permission of the controller of Her Majesty's Stationery Office*

171

The Moosemen had few problems. Three out of the five aircraft were flown by rookie crews, captained by Sgt Allan, Sgt Batterton and F/O Hewitt. The searchlights were out in force during the leg between Dusseldorf and Cologne, but very little flak was experienced. All returned safe. For their part, 428 dispatched 12 of their aircraft, all returned safe. The approach of an electrical storm, just prior to take-off time, cancelled an operation detailed for the 31st. By now, 428 had increased its crew status to 27 and the number of aircraft on charge to 21 Halifaxes and 1 Wellington.

For Croft, July had seen the taking over of the new Communal Site from the Ministry of Works Directorate. The new 22 bed medical quarters were taken over on July 16th. Although the Officers' Mess had moved over on June 27th, the Airmen's Mess was not be taken over until July 25th. The Communal site was located on the eastern side of the camp, adjacent to the west bank of the main North/South LNER railway line. The site not only included the Messes, but also a NAAFI and gymnasium (also used as a cinema and theatre). A squash court and the Station Commander's quarters were also situated on the site. During his stay at Croft during late 41 early 42, Norman Thompson and the remainder of the airfield's population had complained bitterly about the problems with the water supply. This had not gone away, and in spite of the continuous efforts of the Clerk of Works (pushed on by the Station Admin Officer) to fix the problem, the water problem remained acute. A three-inch water pipe, fed from the Richmond area, was totally inadequate for such a large and expanding community, especially when the phantom airlock reared its ugly head. Most of the ablutions buildings had to have their water turned off to allow cooking to take place.

Saturday July 31st saw a house-warming party take place in Croft's new Officers' Mess. Many dignitaries were invited, including Air Commodore B F Johnson, G/C Ross from Middleton, G/C J L Plant, Leeming's Station Commander, G/C Simpson from Topcliffe, and His Worship the Mayor of Darlington and entourage.

August 1943

The first day of August heralded the first page of a brand new Operational Records Book (ORB Form 540). It had been agreed that, from this date, Croft would have its own ORB. Up to this point, memoranda relative to the day to day events at Croft were sent to Middleton, to be included in its Operational Records Book.

The first page of the ORB described the situation at Croft on August the 1st 1943. It recorded that, at that time, there was one T2 type hangar in use and another under construction. A third hangar, a B1 type, was to be built for Cat AC Aircraft. The airfield was referred to by the locals as 'Dalton', and covered a site of approximately 2 square miles. There were 36 hard-standings located around the perimeter track, and about 800 service structures and 13 dispersed sites. The airfield was located at 54° 28' North and 1° 34' West. At 180 feet above sea level Croft was the highest of 6 Group's airfields.

Croft had 3 runways. The North/South runway was 1,400 yards long. The East/West runway was 2000 yards, and the third, which ran northwest/southeast, was 1,400 yards. The Station's strength had grown from 950 during June to 1,460 by August the 1st.

Sadly, on the 6th, Leading Aircraftsman R A McMaster was killed whilst riding his bike down the hill near the Comet pub in Croft village. Riding without lights during the late evening, McMaster struck a pedestrian in the dark and was thrown to the ground, fracturing his skull. The station ambulance was called but McMaster died later without regaining consciousness. LAC McMaster was buried in the military plot of Darlington's West Cemetery on August 9th. August's weather had been atrocious, rain and more rain. Work by GPO telephone engineers to link the PBX and the new station HQ building was constantly hampered by heavy rain. On the last day of August, one of 1664's Halifax was able to land at noon only after the firing of many pyrotechnics from the ground to aid the pilot to find the airfield in the gloom. Other aircraft aborted their cross-country training flights due to the very poor weather. Also during the day, Halifax D became completely bogged down in the mud at the side of the peri-track.

During the early part of August 1943, experiments were carried out on the artificial horizons which were fitted to 419's Halifaxes. W/C Fleming headed an investigation team, which was trying to establish the cause of some malfunctions which were occurring with these instruments. Many were failing to re-erect quickly enough for safety after toppling. At the same time, experiments were being carried out on arming the mid-under gunner's position on the squadron's Halifaxes. As events later in the month would testify, the interest in mid-under guns on the Halifax would not always bear fruit.

On the 2nd, Hamburg was yet again the target for sixteen Moose and fifteen 428 squadron aircraft. This was the 4th and final raid during Harris's series of attacks on the city. The weather conditions over the target were very bad. There were 4 separate fronts over the North Sea and a particularly bad one over Hamburg itself. Only ten crews reached the target. 5 Moose Halifaxes got as far as the enemy coast but had to turn back due to severe icing, turbulence and thunderstorms. The pilot of the sixth aircraft, Sgt J S Sobin, saw lightning ahead, but as it was at a lower level, he elected to continue, and maintained his present course and height. With the target less than five minutes away and the Halifax about to reach its last turning point, Sobin saw a huge Cu-Nim dead ahead, blocking their path. The aircraft was already icing up and he was not happy about the prospects of what the huge cloud held for them. P/O Sibalis the navigator suggested that they continued as they were only 60 seconds to bombs release. Sobin thought better of it, and with the cloud filling the windscreen, he announced that he was going to jettison the bombs and fly out of the cloud. The words had barely left his mouth when there was a blinding flash and the Halifax was struck by lightning. At that, all electrical power was lost and the engines stopped. There was a terrible stench of burning insulation permeating through the cockpit. The wireless operator Sgt J W Farrow (RAF) reported that the radio had exploded. The aircraft by now was in a steep dive, and all control was lost. The Halifax fell until it reached 5,000 feet, when the angle of dive lessened somewhat. Farrow, who had been pinned to the floor by the G forces, was then able to move up to the cockpit. Whilst getting there, he saw a large hole which had been punched in the fuselage on the starboard side. Sabalis and the bomb-aimer, Sgt J M Mahoney, had already jumped.

Farrow left by the rear hatch at about 600 feet, and his chute was barely deployed when he hit the boggy ground. Sgt Sobin, his engineer Sgt R E Horswill, the second gunner Sgt J Sedeskie and the tail gunner Sgt D J McCarty did not have time to get out and they were killed.

428 suffered the loss of two of their aircraft. The first belonged to P/O V T Sylvester and his crew, flying NA-U EB212. This aircraft was lost over the North Sea. Only the bodies of F/O H G Funkhouser, who was acting as second pilot, and Sgt Lunn the mid-upper gunner, were found. The remainder of the crew were lost without trace.

The second of 428's Halifaxes to go missing that night was flown by Sgt Chepil DFM. This aircraft and its 8-man crew was lost without trace, all are commemorated on the Runnymede Memorial. F/O FL Rogers was the 8th man on board, gaining experience as the second pilot. The raid itself was a total failure, as no PFF marking was possible. The crews that made it that far, who were not either struck by lightning or iced up, elected to find other targets of opportunity. Bombs were scattered over a wide area of northern Germany, and one town in particular received more that its fair share. The little town of Elmshorn is located 20 miles to the northwest of Hamburg, and during the storm, one of its houses caught fire when struck by lightning. Without further ado, the town became the center of attraction for many of the bombers, which began to attack the town through a hole in the clouds, Elmshorn had become a haven for many who had fled Hamburg after the previous 3 raids. By the time the bombers departed, 254 houses had been destroyed, during which 57 people lost their lives. Out of the 740 aircraft taking part in this raid, 30 were lost, at the cost of the lives of 130 aircrew. The first raid had seen Window reduce the percentage losses to 1.5%. The Germans seemed to waste no time in adapting to the use of Window, as during the second raid the losses increased to 2.2%. They rose again during the third to 3.6%, and finally, 4.1% during the fourth and last of the series. Obviously the atrocious weather during this last raid distorted the figures, however, at least 10 aircraft were shot down by fighters, whilst 5 more are confirmed to have been shot down by flak (probably radar assisted). The fate of many more is unknown, and it is possible that some of these were also shot down by fighters or flak. For its part, the weather claimed at least four, either struck by lightning or victims of iced up airframes and engine air intakes.

On the 4th, F/L P G Weedon was promoted to the rank of Acting Squadron Leader and put in charge of 419's 'B' Flight. At the same time, W/C Fleming assumed temporary command of Goosepool whilst Group Captain Ross went on leave. In

Hamburg after the bombing   Photo: courtesy IWM C.3917

turn, S/L McMurdy, 419's 'A' Flight Commander, filled Fleming's shoes and took over temporary command of the Moose Squadron. During the afternoon, the squadron received another new face; in the form of P/O Treasure, who was posted in as the new Electrical Engineering Officer. P/O Turner, who, as you will remember, was the engineer of Sgt Bakewells's crew, shot down over Essen on 5th March, had by now returned to Middleton, having safely evaded capture. He gave a most entertaining and instructional lecture to the crews on his exploits whilst escaping back to the UK. Between the 4th and 9th, there was a lull in operational flying, mainly due to bad weather.

Sixteen of 419's aircraft were detailed on the 9th for Ops to Mannheim. They were joined by fifteen of 428's Halifaxes. One Moose aircraft, VR-J, burst a tyre whilst taxiing out to the runway and its operation had to be scrubbed. Another returned early with intercom failure, and F/O Ludlow's crew, flying their 12th Op, failed to return. Their Halifax crashed at Ludwigshafen with the loss of all on board. The remaining Moose crews landed safely back at Middleton, although one aircraft was badly holed by flak. VR-L had also been hit, the port undercarriage leg had been badly damaged and a tyre burst. The airfield held their breath as the Halifax turned onto final approach. Everyone was expecting to see the weakened undercarriage collapse and the huge bomber come to grief. However, the pilot, P/O Hamilton, pulled off a masterly landing, and the undercart held.

One of 428's crews, flown by Sgt B R Harrison, had a narrow escape when their aircraft was struck by flak, slightly injuring two members of the crew. All of 428's crews returned safely, including S/L W R Suggit, 428's 'A' Flight Commander, who was now able to celebrate the end of his second tour. Also screened were Second Lt Knapp USAAF and three members of his crew, having also just finished their first tour.

The next night, the Moosemen and 428 went to Nuremberg, as part of a 653 aircraft raid. All sixteen of 419's Halifaxes, and the 14 sent by 428, bombed the target and returned safely to the UK, but several of them had suffered flak damage. One belonging to 419 was badly holed by flak and the port outer caught fire. The pilot, F/O Ludlow, managed to fly back on three engines and land safely.

Having some luck in the undercarriage department, and gaining much fame in the Mess the previous night, P/O Hamilton conducted a repeat performance, when VR-L was again hit in the undercarriage. This time the hydraulics were damaged, and the crew (and all on the ground) had some anxious minutes whilst the engineer attempted to lower the wheels by way of the emergency hand pump. He was successful and once again they landed safely.

On the 12th, both squadrons dispatched a total of 28 crews as part of a 504 aircraft raid on Milan, covering a total distance of 1,500 miles. All fifteen Moose crews returned safely, as did W/C D W Smith and the thirteen 428 aircraft that he led. However, due to the distance, all the aircraft involved were unable to land at Middleton because of a shortage of petrol. All were diverted to airfields in the south. On the same night, Turin was the target for a separate force of 152 aircraft. A few days earlier, on the 8th, Bomber Command had sent several squadrons belonging to 1, 5 and 8 Groups to bomb Milan, Genoa and Turin. A series of raids throughout August was part of a Bomber Command plan to attack various Italian cities, in the hopes that the Italians would throw in the towel and give the war up as a bad job.

Home safe after a tough one   Photo: courtesy IWM CH.6642

Next day 419 bad farewell to F/O McIntosh who had completed his current tour of operations. He left to become the Flight Commander of 1691 Bombing and Gunnery Flight, gaining the acting rank of Flight Lieutenant.

On August the 14th, the Moosemen were the recipients of a gift of 2,000 cigarettes from the Toronto Hydroelectric Club. The same number of cigarettes were also received from the Calgary Brewing and Malting Company. In addition, 419 were given several copies of McLean's Magazine and newspapers from Kamloops and Calgary. That afternoon, W/C Fleming returned to resume command of the Moosemen as G/C Ross had returned from leave. 428's Adjutant, F/L D F Maidens, after much badgering, was promised a seat in W/C Smith's Halifax for a 'Bullseye' exercise. All was set for that evening, but later Smith had to break the bad news to him that the exercise was cancelled due to bad weather. Milan was to be attacked again that night, and also on the night of the 15/16th, although due to bad weather at base, Middleton's crews were not involved. The next day, the defenders of Milan enjoyed a rest whilst Turin took another battering.

Peenemunde

Peenemunde on the Baltic Coast was the home of the German rocket research establishment. Here, a group of German rocket scientists headed by Werner Von Braun were undertaking development work on V2 ballistic missiles. On the night of August 17th/18th, 596 of Bomber Command's aircraft were dispatched to Peenemunde. This air fleet was made up of 324 Lancasters, 218 Halifaxes and 54 Stirlings. 419's contribution was to be 17 Halifaxes, 428 sent 3 less. For their part, 428 were charged with destroying special equipment used chiefly in radio-location. This operation was to employ the newly conceived 'Master Bomber' tactics. 8 Group had developed this method of attack, which had been practiced earlier in the month during a raid on Turin. In principle, the Master Bomber system employed a Controller, or Master of Ceremonies, who flew over the target area and observed the developing situation. As a raid got under-way, circumstances could change due to a variety of reasons. It was his job to direct and re-direct the bomber force, and ensure that the target was correctly attacked and that all the bombs fell in the right place.

Group Captain J H Searby of 83 Squadron had been the Master Bomber on the Turin raid, and, employing the skills learned there, he was to be the Commander at Peenemunde. This operation was to be one of the rare precision bombing raids carried out by large numbers of Bomber Command aircraft at this time of the war. It would be possible (and successful) only by the advent of the recently formed PFF and the Master Bomber technique. There were to be three main aiming points. The most important was the accommodation sites for the scientists and the workers. They would be the hardest to replace at short notice by the Germans. To this end, their living quarters would become the focus for the early part of the raid, utilizing as much as possible the element of surprise. The next most important target was the rocket factory. Production of the rockets had to be curtailed at all costs. Every rocket destroyed meant one less to fall on England. Finally, the experimental station would be targeted. After the first wave of bombers went in, it was realised that the markers had been dropped about a mile and a half south of the correct aiming point. This error caused the first bombs to fall onto wooden buildings housing over 500 slave workers, a large proportion of whom were Poles. The Master Bomber quickly redirected the Pathfinder force to the German workers housing estate. Over 1,800 tons of bombs fell on Peenemunde and 180 Germans were killed. The operation put back production of the V2 rockets to an extent that it never reached its intended capability. As far as the experimental work being carried out at Peenemunde, this was retarded by about two months.

To ensure the success of the operation, a full moon period had been chosen. This allowed the navigators to find Peenemunde and the targets more easily. The attack was carried out by three waves of aircraft. A spoof raid by Mosquitoes to Berlin would, it was hoped, ensure that most of the German night fighters would be employed elsewhere. This ploy was

PR photograph of labour camp south of Peenemunde, housing forced labour and POWs.
This site was misidentified as German workers accommodation   Photo: IWM C.3750

only partly successful. By the time Goosepool's aircraft arrived over the target area during the third wave, some of the fighters arrived and losses began. 5 Group lost 17 out of a total of 109 aircraft (14.5%). The Canadian squadrons in 6 Group lost proportionately more, 12 aircraft out of 57 (19.7%).

A total of forty bombers were lost during this operation. Some of the bombers were shot down by German night fighter pilots whilst on the way home, flying below them and employing for the first time, 'Schrage Musik' aircraft.[90] These fighters were equipped with upward firing guns fitted behind the cockpit, which allowed them to slip in underneath the bomber, where they couldn't be seen by either the tail or mid-upper gunners. Interestingly, out of the three Halifaxes lost by 419 during the Peenemunde raid, all had employed mid-under gunners, who, it would have been thought, would have had a better chance to see the Schrage Musik fighters below them.

[90] Schrage Musik - German for Jazz Music. Actually, Jazz music itself was banned as western decadence in Germany during the war, by Hitler.

At the time 419 was equipped with the Mk II Halifax). On Halifaxes employing a mid-under gunner, the gunner sat on a bicycle seat with a 50 caliber Browning machine gun poking out into the slipstream. This modification caused a draft down the fuselage and made the aircraft much colder for the crew, even up in the nose.

During this raid, 6 Group used Lancasters for the first time. 426 Squadron at Leeming dispatched 9 Mk IIs to Peenemunde, led by the Squadron Commander W/C L Crooks DSO DFC, who was an Englishman. Two Lancasters belonging to 426 were lost on the way home from Peenemunde, including the one flown by W/C Crooks.

Goosepool lost six crews during this raid, three from each squadron. F/L G W Fanson and his crew in NA-V took off at 21:09, after which nothing further was heard. They had crashed in the Baltic. Eventually, six bodies were recovered from the sea. Sgt R A Lewis's body was never found. The second 428 crew to be lost was that of Sgt J F Sheridan, flying in NA-F. They also crashed in the Baltic. They all rest in Berlin's 1939-1945 War Cemetery. Sgt W W Blackmore and his navigator Sgt F S Williams were killed when NA-I crashed near Barth-Velgast, 45 miles W/N/W of Peenemunde. The remaining 5 crewmembers survived and became POWs. F/L Fanson and Sgt Blackmore had both completed 19 operations, Sgt Sheridan 13. Most aircraft on their return had to divert, the majority of which landed at Bassingbourne.

Out of the three aircraft lost by 419, the first, VR-D, flown by F/O S M Heard, also crashed in the Baltic. There were 8 souls on board, as Sgt D M Macpherson had joined the crew to gain operational experience as second pilot. All were killed when the aircraft came down in the sea off Stralsund-Gross, 30 miles W/N/W of the target area. Only 4 bodies were recovered from the sea, the remaining 4 have no known graves. The Baltic was to also claim the crew of F/S S T Pekin, flying in VR-C. Only two bodies were ever recovered from the sea. The sixth and final Goosepool aircraft to be lost that night was VR-N, flown by Sgt Batterton. He and his crew almost reached home. Two radio fixes were obtained, the second only 20 miles from the English coast. The last W/T call was heard at 04:26 by the D/F station at Hull. They put the aircraft's bearing as 064° from Happisburg on the Norfolk coast. An intensive air-sea search was immediately instigated, without result. At the time, a heavy sea was running, and it was surmised that the loss of VR-N was due to an unsuccessful ditching attempt. All are commemorated on the Runnymede Memorial.

Meanwhile, the artificial horizon problem on 419's Halifaxes had not gone away. This prompted a visit on the 18th by W/C Smith of Bomber Command, S/L Ferndale of HQ 6 Group and a Mr. Howard of the Royal Aircraft Establishment. They had arrived to check the difficulties relating to the artificial horizons. On the same day, 419 received word that they were to have priority for the fitment of H2S.

Although aircrew members were frequently being submitted for medals, groundcrew members could also become the recipients of awards. During the day, W/C Fleming forwarded the recommendation that F/S Hall - Armourer, F/S Brackenbury - Fitter IIe, and Sgt Olsen - Fitter IIe were to be Mentioned in Dispatches.

The next night saw the last of the attacks on Italian cities, when Turin was attacked by a force of 154 aircraft. 419's part in this operation was scrubbed during briefing. The thirteen crews left the briefing room and took the rest of the night off. On the 22nd, fifteen of 419's crews and sixteen from 428 were warned for an attack on the I B Farben factory at Leverkusen, situated in the northern outskirts of Cologne.

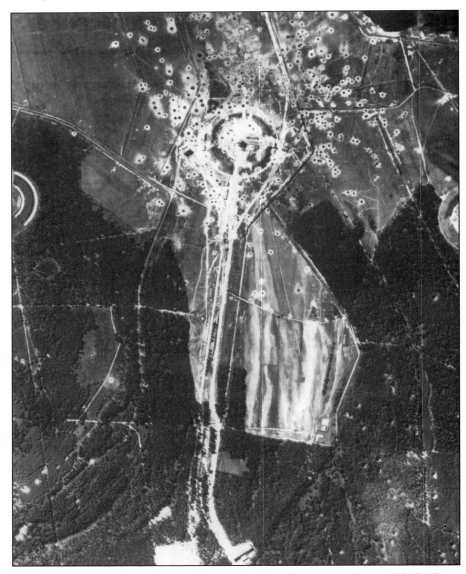

One of Peenemunde's rocket launch sites taken by a photo reconnaisance (PR) Spitfire, the morning after the raid   Photo: PRO AIR20/9193

176

The partial failure of the Oboe signals and thick cloud cover removed any chance of the raid being successful. Only 4 bombs fell on Leverkusen itself, the remainder were scattered by the 462 aircraft taking part over a wide area. Dusseldorf, 20 miles N/N/W of Leverkusen got most of them. Solingen, 10 miles to the N/N/E, also had its share; here 40 people were killed, and a further 65 injured. Only the acid plant in IG Farben's factory received slight damage, injuring 5 German workers and killing 1 foreign worker. All of Middleton's crews returned safe.

During the day, Sgt Matherall undertook an air-test with his crew in VR-W. Matherall returned to Middleton and settled on the approach for a landing. As the aircraft touched down, it did so rather heavily, and the starboard undercarriage was smashed. The throttles were immediately slammed open and an over-shoot initiated. The Halifax was taken on another circuit whilst the hapless crew decided what to do. None of the crew fancied jumping out, and so it was decided that a belly landing would be their best option. Matherall lined the bomber up with the main runway and gently lowered it onto the ground. He held the right wing up with aileron until the airspeed got too low. It eventually dropped, and began scraping along the ground. Matherall had done a good job in holding the wing off and there was no fire. The aircraft slowed, rotated around the grounded wing and came to a screeching halt in a cloud of dust. None of the crew had been injured and they were all able to depart the aircraft safely.

To follow on the heels of the Hamburg successes, Harris turned his attention to more of the same for the Berliners. He started with 3 raids, which were to take place between August 23rd and September 3rd. They would be followed by many more which would take place over the next few months. 32 of the aircraft taking part in a 727 aircraft raid on Berlin during the night of August 23/24th, came from Middleton. Track markers were dropped by PFF Mosquitoes to ensure that the bomber stream kept to the desired routes. The PFF went on to try and mark the center of the city, but at this stage H2S was not accurate enough and the markers went down over the southern outskirts of the city.

The planned routes were designed to have the crews turn and approach the aiming point from the southeast of the city. However, the main force arrived late and many crews took a short cut across the southwestern corner to make up time. Due to creep-back, many bombs fell on the thinly populated southern outskirts of Berlin, in open country, or on villages around the southern periphery of the city.

This raid employed a Master Bomber, in the form of W/C J E 'Johnny' Fauquire, who was, at the time, the CO of 405 Squadron RCAF. After the bombing began, Fauquire attempted to redirect some of the force to more central locations in the city. The number of buildings destroyed, both residential and industrial, totalled 2,611. The district of Lichterfelde, 7.5 miles southwest of the city center, was one of the most devastated residential areas, as was Lankwitz. From an industrial point of view, the nearby districts of Mariendorf, Marionfelde and Tempelhof took the brunt. Understandably, the defences in the German capital were particularly horrendous. Some crews managed to hit closer to the city center, particularly in the Wilhelmstrasse area. For the Berliners, this was the worst raid so far, despite the scattered nature of the bombing. Many chose not to go the shelters, and this resulted in 854 people being killed. Flown by F/S H A Read, NA-H was attacked by a night fighter whilst outbound. Four crewmembers baled out and became POWs. The remainder, including Sgt C E Crampton, who had become stuck in the forward escape hatch, remained in the aircraft. Crampton was killed when the aircraft crashed at Annelov, in neutral Sweden, 125 miles N/N/W of Peenemunde. Read and F/O J J McQuade survived and were interned.

For Bomber Command, it was evident that the Germans had, to some extent, overcome the initial advantages of Window. The losses during this raid totaled 56 aircraft, 7.9%. The first 3 raids on Berlin were not by any means as successful as the ones on Hamburg. Losses would turn out to be high. The 3 raids equated to 1,669 separate sorties, during which 125 aircraft were lost.

During the next day, 428's RDF Section had moved from its cramped workshop housed in the side of 1 hangar, and joined 419's RDF section in their Nissan hut behind the control tower. By the 27th, the experiments on the artificial horizons had achieved much, and during the day an experimental version had arrived from the RAE.[91] W/C Fleming had the instrument fitted to a squadron aircraft and carried out a series of tests on the new AH to his satisfaction.

That night, 32 of Middleton's crews were detailed for a raid on Nuremberg, from which all but one returned safely. One of 428's aircraft, flown by Sgt A L Mitchell, was shot down by a night fighter. Five members of the crew, including Mitchell and F/O J A McGleish, who went along as second pilot, were killed, the other three became POWs. That night saw 6 pilots from new crews tagging along with 428's more experienced pilots, in the hope that they would be able to gain valuable operational experience. On the outbound section of the trip was the town of Heilbronn, and the PFF were given the job of testing their H2S equipment by dropping one of their 1,000-lb bombs on the town whilst approaching Nuremberg. This experiment proved successful, as 28 out of the 47 Pathfinder aircraft managed to locate this small target and release their bombs. Although the bombs came down close to the industrial sector of the town, only one house was destroyed, without inflicting any casualties. The weather over Nuremberg itself was clear, but the crews found it particularly dark. Although some bombs fell on the southeastern and eastern sectors of the city, many fell in open ground. At the time, Nuremberg was not a good H2S target, and this resulted in the PFF having great difficulty in marking.

The Master Bomber was unable to get any real coherence into the proceedings, as for some reason only about 25% of the bomber crews were able to hear him. On their 4th operation, the crew of VR-G, flown by F/O M T Brown, had bad luck, when, only 20 miles from the target, their aircraft lost an engine. They elected to continue with the operation, and despite losing height steadily, managed to bomb from 9,000 feet, suffering only slight flak damage. They then began the long haul home on three. Fortunately they reached base, and for his part in the evening's proceedings, Brown was awarded an

[91] Royal Aircraft Establishment

immediate DFC. Out of the 33 aircraft lost during this raid, none were from Goosepool. One of 428's crews however, had tangled with a Ju88, but good co-ordination by the crew prevented serious damage being inflicted on the Halifax. The tail gunner Sgt A McKenzie and the mid-upper Sgt Shimwell eventually shot the fighter down in flames.

For Middleton's crews, their penultimate raid during August took them to Monchengladbach on the 30th. They were part of a force of 660 aircraft attacking the city, which lies some 10 miles beyond the eastern edge of the Belgian-German border. The centre of Monchengladbach was to be attacked first, and then the bombers' attention was shifted, some 2 minutes later, 1.8 miles to the south, to the small town of Rheydt, which at the time lay close to the city's southern suburbs. Oboe was used by the PFF to mark the first phase of the operation and was described as 'spot on'. The markers then went on to highlight Rheydt.

Although all Moose crews returned safely to base, this raid was not without drama for some of its crews. F/O D D Laidlaw and crew in VR-R had an encounter with a night fighter whilst at 18,000 feet, which sprayed their Halifax with cannon fire. The aircraft suffered damage to its bomb bay where a fire was instigated. Further fires were started in the batteries half way down the fuselage. Further damage was inflicted on the hydraulics, and the Gee, IFF and radio sets. With flames spreading back along the fuselage it was time for some quick action, and the engineer, Sgt J N Ashton RAF, wasted no time. Grabbing an extinguisher he doused the fires in the fuselage. Although he was without oxygen, he quickly located another extinguisher and raised the floor inspection panel leading to the bomb bay. Flames blew back towards his face but he continued to spray the fires through the opening until they were extinguished. His prompt action allowed the badly damaged aircraft to return to Goosepool, where it was landed with great skill and without further drama. For his quick action in saving the aircraft, Sgt Ashton received an immediate DFM. Another Moose aircraft, VR-T (T-Tare) flown by F/O J A Westland, was the recipient of cannon fire from a Ju88. The tail gunner, Tec/Sergeant B Blount (USAAF), returned the compliment with 2 bursts of fire into the fuselage of the enemy fighter and it burst into flames. The Ju88 fell like a stone to the ground, where it was seen to explode. Westland flew the badly damaged Halifax back to base and landed safely.

The Luftwaffe was to lose another aircraft from its itinerary that night, when the crew of X-Xray, flown by Sgt H L Bullis, was attacked twice during a short space of time, possibly by the same FW 190. The Halifax sustained extensive damage to its port outer engine and aileron, flaps, bomb bay and rudders. The fighter had come up close for the kill and ended up paying the price. The Halifax's rear gunner, Sgt M Potter, couldn't miss. He poured all he had into the 190 at short range, and watched it fall until it dug itself a fiery grave. Back at Middleton, Bullis attempted to land the badly damaged bomber whilst those on watch held their breath. When the Halifax slowed for its landing it developed the flying characteristics of a tramcar. Using all his skill, and with the crew sitting silently at the rest position, Bullis carried out a textbook landing. The aircraft rolled to a stop in one piece, albeit close to the runway's end, much to the satisfaction of all concerned. The Bomber force itself lost 4 Wellingtons, 6 Stirlings, 7 Lancasters and 8 Halifaxes. None were from Goosepool, although Laidlaw's aircraft, JD381 was, on closer technical inspection, deemed beyond economical repair and struck off charge on September the 10th.

On the 31st, W/C Fleming approved the design of 419's squadron crest, which had been submitted by the Chester Herald. The design consisted of a Moose in natural colours, depicted in a charging pose. The motto on the crest was in Cree language and stated 'Moosa Aswayita' (Beware of the Moose). The crest was then dispatched to be approved and registered by the appropriate authorities.

That night, Berlin was the target for a force of 622 Bomber Command aircraft. Goosepool's contribution was 30 Halifaxes; 3 from 419 and 2 from 428 would not return. The total number of aircraft lost during this raid was 47, equating to 7.6% of the main force. Two thirds were lost to fighters over or near to Berlin. The Germans used a new tactic - fighter flares. They were dropped to identify the bombers' routes to and from the target. All three of 419's aircraft that failed to return were lost to fighters.

F/L D J Corcoran, and his crew in Halifax JD331, had left Middleton at 19:46 hours. They were bypassing Hannover when the aircraft was surrounded by fighter flares. At the same time, another Halifax was seen below them by the mid-upper Sgt W E Greenside and the tail gunner F/O D E Larlee. The Monica receiver made its usual peeping sound, but a fighter managed to attack K-King before the gunners knew it was there. The Halifax received many hits from the fighter's cannon, one hit the tail turret missing Larlee by inches. The intercom was also hit and put out of action. The port wing and its engines were on fire. The fighter came in, cannon blazing, for another attack, this time from the port quarter-down position. Larlee returned fire but could not see the fighter, only the gun flashes. By now the incendiaries in the bomb bay were also ablaze, but as the hydraulics were now U/S, the doors could not be opened to jettison them. The whole aircraft was in flames and so Corcoran signaled on the call light for the crew to bale out. He held the aircraft level to allow the crew time to abandon. He remembers undoing his harness but little else after that. When he recovered consciousness his parachute was open and he was floating to earth. His earphones had been ripped from his helmet as they were still plugged in to the aircraft and his head and shoulders hurt and were badly bruised. His rip chord D ring had not been pulled and it is believed that the aircraft exploded as he left his seat, throwing him out of the aircraft with force enough to open his chute. F/O Larlee turned his turret sideways with the dead-mans handle and was sucked from the turret, but his left leg was trapped. He tried to get his leg free, but was only able to do so at about 2,000 feet, and at the cost of leaving his flying boot behind in the aircraft. He landed in the garden of a farmhouse and was soon captured by shotgun wielding farmers who had been watching his descent. He had little chance of escape, as he had torn some of the ligaments in his leg and had also sprained his knee. W/O A G MacKenzie, the navigator, had done one full tour and was taking part in the 10th trip of his second tour. During the attack, he had been wounded by flak in both legs but was able to jump. As he prepared to jump, he had seen F/S Harris the bomb-aimer waiting his turn to jump, and was surprised when he learned that Harris was not one of those that survived. The mid-upper, Sgt Greensides became unconscious when his oxygen tube was severed during the attack. When he came to, he found himself unhurt and near to the wreckage of the aircraft, and being spoken to by some German soldiers. How he got there he didn't know, but presumed that he was still on board the aircraft when it came down, and was somehow thrown clear when it hit. The Halifax crashed in the Hillentrup area, 20 miles E/N/E of Bielfeld, some 37 miles S/W of Hannover. Corcoren, who was on his 12th operation, and 3 of his crew survived to become POWs. Sgt D W Sweet the engineer, F/St Harris the bomb aimer and W/O H d'Aperng the wireless operator were killed. Sweet was standing in for the crew's regular engineer, Sgt J C Allen.

Sgt. W D Cameron and crew had taken off in VR-P JD270, 12 minutes after Corcoran's crew. They made their way to Berlin and had bombed the target. They were about to leave the city, and had just flown over the outer ring of searchlights when a single engined fighter collided with them. The 109 or 190 (no one knew) fell to earth, and was seen to crash by the tail gunner St R E Boos. The fighter had struck the Halifax's port wing, and the wireless operator, Sgt L H Duggan RAF, who had been dropping Window at the time, was knocked off his feet. To the crew, it seemed as if the Hally had lost its momentum as the two aircraft met. It had then dropped from beneath their feet before regaining flying speed. Bits were being shed from the port wing and the whole aircraft was vibrating badly. Soon after, the port outer caught fire, and despite the efforts of the engineer, Sgt J T Mullany, RAF, the prop could not be fully feathered and continued to windmill. The controls were locked solid and the bomber went into a dive. Cameron told Mullany to help him on the controls as he tried to pull the aircraft's nose up. Despite their combined strength nothing could be done to un-jam the controls. With the situation hopeless and their height reducing quickly, Cameron gave the order to abandon. Duggan met the mid-upper Sgt B W Scharf and Sgt Boos at the rear door and jumped first. They were the only 3 members of the crew to escape. Cameron, who was on his 18th sortie, Mullany, the navigator Sgt G E Birtch and the bomb-aimer Sgt V J Wintzer, did not get out.

A third Moose Halifax, VR-N, flown by F/O R Stewart, was shot down by a night fighter whilst flying at 18,000 feet on the way home. The aircraft came down near the Black Forest. The navigator P/O S E James, engineer Sgt H R Tenny, wireless op Sgt A Embley and second gunner St L Northcliffe, baled out and were captured. F/S Stewart, the bomb aimer Sgt D A Cleveland, and the tail gunner Sgt D H Garland, died in the crash and have no known graves.

The majority of the Moose crews returned unscathed. The odd one had slight flak damage, but F/O B E Betcher's crew brought back a veritable basket case. Their Halifax had holes in the fuselage, wing, rudder and the engine casing of the starboard inner. Of the two aircraft lost by 428, the first, NA-K, flown by Sgt B R Harrison, crashed at Holzdorf, killing all the crew. The second Halifax, NA-X, flown by Sgt J D Este, was hit by flak on the way home. The port inner was knocked out and a petrol tank was set on fire. Soon the flames had spread and reached inside the fuselage. Sgt Burdoff, who was slightly wounded by shrapnel, picked up an extinguisher and tried to put out the fire. The blaze had too good a hold and he eventually had to bale out and become a POW, along with 3 other members of the crew. Este, the mid-upper Sgt. S E Towle and the tail gunner Sgt R W Briggs – Jude were killed when the Halifax crashed near Oberhaching. All three are commemorated on the Runnymede Memorial.

The raid itself was not a success. The defences were daunting to say the least and cloud covered much of Berlin. Problems with the H2S caused the markers to be dropped south of the intended city centre target. The defences encouraged the main bomber force to drop their bombs even further away from the centre on the most southern markers, and the creep-back zone stretched for over 30 miles. Given the large number of bombers involved, Berlin itself got off relatively lightly. Although 2,784 people were bombed out, only 68 were killed and 109 injured. Only 7 industrial buildings were damaged, none were actually destroyed. Amongst those damaged was the headquarters of the city's inland canal and harbour system.

Berlin's Gauleiter, Goebels, decided after this raid to evacuate all children and anyone not employed in war work from the city. They were sent to safer areas further to the east.

September 1943

On September 2nd, a brand new Halifax was delivered to the Moose Squadron from the MU. It joined another to be used by 419, which had arrived the previous day. Later, 4 of their crews were detailed for the squadron's first mining trip in over 10 weeks. All returned safely from the gardening patch which was in the Friesian Islands. 428's 'A' and 'B' Flights also contributed 2 aircraft each, this gave the squadron the opportunity to initiate four brand new crews into operational life, albeit gardening.

The next day was September the 3rd. During the day, one of 419's wireless operators, Sgt K I Deane, was killed in a railway accident at Thornaby whilst on leave. Sgt Deane had served with 419 virtually since the squadron was formed, and had completed 24 operations. Meanwhile, a third new Halifax was received by the Moosemen during the afternoon. 428 were not to be left out either. P/O Eaton ferried two crews down to Leeming to pick up two Mk II Halifaxes, NA-F JD386, and NA-V JB968. P/O Eaton's Halifax, along with the two new ones, arrived at Goosepool just in time for the crews to join in the dance being held in the Sergeants' Mess that night. The occasion was the anniversary of four years at war with Germany.

Earlier that day, Wing Commander Fleming bade farewell to 3 members of his crew. F/O A P Smith, his wireless op, was being posted to 429 Squadron as Signals Leader. His bomb aimer, Sgt O D McLean, and gunner Sgt G F Clark also went to 429 for operational duties. Also departing Goosepool was Major Kent of the USAAF, who was ceasing his attachment with 419 and rejoining his own unit after gaining valuable night flying control experience and instruction in general bombing tactics. The USAAF returned the compliment the next day, and found an opening for F/L W M Keddie who had completed his operational tour with the Moosemen. During the afternoon, 4 more new Halifaxes arrived, both squadrons receiving two each. Also, three new pilots were posted in to 428, F/O M C Walley, F/O R H Sherback and Sgt J H Sinclair.

On the 5th, yet another Halifax arrived for use by 428. They also received another crew who had arrived from 1664 at Croft, captained by P/O E N Bell. Mannheim was the target for both squadrons that night. Whilst the aircraft were being marshaled, 419's VR-A was struck by NA-U, one of 428's aircraft. Both aircraft were removed from the battle-order with corresponding wing-tip damage. After departure, VR-R returned early with electrical problems. This aircraft was followed soon after by VR-T which had returned early with its intercom system U/S. 428 also had two early returns, but unlike the Moosemen, their remaining 13 aircraft were able to bomb the target and return safely. VR-V, flown by Sgt F B Allan, was hit by flak and broke up over the target, only the bomb aimer P/O J R Harris survived. Sgt Allan RAAF, who was on his 13th Op, was flying a very cosmopolitan crew. Sgt H Nuttall the engineer, Sgt A R Slaney the wireless op, Sgt J H Kilpatrick the second Gunner and Sgt H J Hudson the tail gunner were all RAF. The 2 remaining crewmembers, P/O J R Harris the navigator, and P/O R W Burk the bomb aimer, were both Canadian.

The second of 419's Halifaxes to be lost was VR-S, flown by F/O J A Studer RCAF, who originally came from New York. He shared his American heritage with the bomb aimer P/O H A Danniger. Both had joined the RCAF at the beginning of hostilities. There were no survivors from this aircraft, which had crashed on the north bank of the Rhine at Hattenheim, 9 miles W/S/W of Wiesbaden.

This 605 aircraft raid was a double affair and encompassed both Mannheim and Ludwigshaven. The PFF were told to drop their markers on the eastern side of Mannheim, which is itself only 1.5 miles east of Ludwigshaven. This took into account creep-back, which for once would be used as an asset, and would allow the bombers as they approached from the west to flatten Ludwigshaven. As it happened, this ploy worked very well and both the markers and the bombers kept creep-back to a minimum. Both towns were badly damaged and the whole affair was deemed a huge success. The Hamburg raid had sounded the warning bell for the Germans, and many of the larger German towns and cities had begun to disperse non-essential personnel away from the ever-increasing might of Bomber Command. To this end, many of the inhabitants of these two towns had fled. This was reflected in the relatively low losses that took place during this raid. There were 1,993 reported individual fires of which 3 were large fire areas. Although 1,080 houses, 6 military and 4 industrial buildings, including the huge IG Farben works, were destroyed in Ludwigshaven, the casualties reported there tolled only 127 killed and 568 injured. Ten of the dead were German flak gunners. 13 Lancasters, 13 Halifaxes and 8 Stirlings were lost, 34 aircraft, 5.6% of the aircraft dispatched. Despite the huge tonnage of bombs dropped, the cost to Bomber Command was 170 men killed, 43 more fatalities than were suffered on the ground in Ludwigshaven. A further 2 were injured, 65 became POWs, and 9 more evaded capture.

Next day, the funeral of Sgt Deane, killed at Thornaby station 3 days earlier, was carried out at Harrogate's Stonefall Cemetery. He was laid to rest in the RCAF plot, with the remainder of his crew and other representatives from 419 in attendance.

That evening, Munich was the target for sixteen Moose and fourteen 428 crews. Thick cloud over the target area prevented any chance of accuracy. The only option was to bomb on a timed run, initiated from the Ammersee, a large lake situated some 20 miles to the southwest of the target. This resulted in a scattered attack, which caused some damage to the southern and western parts of Munich. Despite fairly aggressive fighter activity, all Moose aircraft returned safely, but they had to divert to Tangmere and Ford in the South, due to low fuel and the usual dubious weather in the Northeast. 428 had two early returns, one with low oil pressure and another with a sick pilot. W/O Harrison's Halifax was shot up by an enemy fighter during the return trip and had to land at Dunsfold, fortunately without injury to the crew. Sgt W M Brown and his crew reached Strasbourg but had to turn back due to engine trouble. The aircraft flew for 170 miles before crash-landing at Le Vertus, 17 miles W/S/W of Chalons-sur-Marne, France. Sgt Brown was killed in the crash, but the remainder of his crew survived to become POWs.

Next day, due to the absence of the diverted aircraft, a stand-down was ordered for both squadrons. 428's Adj, F/L Maidens, departed for SHQ to become Goosepool's Station Adjutant. A new Adj, F/L H E Davies, arrived to take his place. On the 8th, W/C (Merv) Fleming celebrated his first anniversary as Commanding Officer of 419, whilst 'A' Flight acquired a new Deputy Commander in the form of F/L Dyer.

A raid on Berlin had been planned for that night but was cancelled during briefing. 428's S/L Suggit took the opportunity to nip off down to Dunsfold in the Station 'Hack'.[92] This trip was to allow him to inspect one of the squadron's aircraft, which had landed there with battle damage sustained during the Munich raid. The new Gyro gun sight was becoming more prevalent throughout the squadrons, and to that end, 419 sent Aircraftman S W Skolney to Melksham, near Bath, to learn the finer points of the new device.

Also on the 8th came news of Italy's unconditional surrender. Bomber Command's heavy raids on Italian cities had pushed them over the edge and they had thrown in the towel. Despite the surrender of Italy, the Germans stubbornly refused to budge.

Poor weather allowed 428's crews to learn the jobs of their fellow crewmen, which would allow them to take over their duties if either one sustained injury during an operation. They began with F/L Davies providing the squadron's bomb aimers with instructions on how to fly the aircraft, in the event of their pilot becoming incapacitated. The lectures continued with the engineers being taught bomb aiming. The same day, the engineering section moved into the Station HQ building, which it was hoped would allow them to be in closer touch with the other sections.

Meanwhile, over at Croft, 1664's Halifaxes underwent a change from T/R9 R/T radio transmitters to the new T1196 variety. This, it was hoped, would enable pilots to contact base from 50 miles away. Also at Croft, the continuation of heavy rain caused the flooding of the airfield's defensive gun posts. Croft's Airfield Controller gave the WAAF driver of the NAFFI van a good telling off for failing to stop after receiving a red Aldis lamp signal on the perimeter track. Evidently, her reply was, 'Oh, I didn't know you meant me to stop, I thought you just wanted a cup of tea.'

---

92 In Middleton's case this was a twin engined Airspeed Oxford

On Sunday the 12th, it poured down again. This was compounded with fog to make it a very unpleasant day indeed. There was some consolation however, as Middleton's Station Padre reported a larger then normal attendance at church. Croft had a bit of excitement during the day when a Halifax Mk II, HR910, belonging to 405 Squadron, made a hasty landing minus an engine. The starboard inner had fallen off the aircraft during flight, due to severe vibration, before its prop could be feathered. Over the next few days, this aircraft was carefully scrutinized by representatives of Handley Page and Rolls Royce to find out why. The fog and rain continued throughout the next day and hampered the sprucing up operation which was being carried out in preparation for the impending visit by 'Butch' Harris, C-in C Bomber Command. The incessant rain had caused most of the sections to become flooded, and caused a terrible mess.

On the 14th, S/L P H (Hairless Phil) Weedon, 419's 'B' Flight Commander was screened, along with his nav, F/O P (Paddy) Campbell and P/O M Wigsworth, who had all completed their tour. During the day, poor weather caused the cancellation of the visit by Bomber Harris. For some time, 428's F/L Smith had been carrying out experiments on the use of dinghy radios, in conjunction with the Marconi R1155, as an emergency radio in the aircraft.

Croft's friendly bobby, Constable Benson, turned up in the Adj's office at Croft, complete with a sheepish looking airman and four freshly deceased chickens. It was thought that the airman would have a great deal of explaining to do to the Magistrate, as a large number of feathers found in his billet were identified as not emanating from his bolster.

The next day, being September the 15th, saw the annual Battle of Britain parade commence at 08:30, after which Middleton prepared for the night's operation This was to be a moonlight milk-run to the Dunlop rubber factory at Montlucon in central France. Included with the 14 aircraft sent by 419 and the 16 provided by 428, were 5 American B17 Flying Fortresses, which formed part of a 364 aircraft raid. Flak was practically non existent and none of the crews had any real problems. As winter was approaching, this was the last raid during 1943 that would see the Pathfinders employ the Master Bomber method of attack. Although the PFF continued to mark targets as usual, it would be the following spring before the Master Bomber technique would be resumed.

On this occasion, the Master Bomber was W/C D F Dean, and the attack went very well. Every building was hit and a large fire engulfed the factory after a huge explosion was seen at around 23:41. The crew of W/C Morrison's Halifax observed that this sent up a huge cloud of black smoke, which rose from the factory, all the way up to, and beyond, the bombing height of the aircraft. S/L McMurdey was just about ready to leave the target area when his Halifax shook as 3 holes suddenly appeared in the starboard wing. Luckily, although they were in the vicinity of the petrol tanks, there was no fire and he and his crew, along with the remainder of 419's Halifaxes, returned safe. It was with some shock however, that word arrived that 428's Commanding Officer W/C Smith had not returned from the night's operation. He had led the 16 crews sent by the squadron to Montlucon. He and his crew were flying in NA-N LK913, and were approaching the target when they were hit from above by incendiaries dropped from another bomber. Although the aircraft was badly damaged, Smith managed to fly on, but only for a while. Eventually the Halifax came down near Cerilly, 20 miles N/N/E of the target area, fortunately everyone got out ok. With Smith was P/O E N Bell, who had tagged along as second pilot. To compound things even further, also on board had been the squadron's Gunnery Leader F/L Forman, who was also the Acting Flight Commander. The squadron's Navigation Leader, F/L E B Mason, was also with them, as was Sgt C Hayworth, the Engineer Leader. Other members of the crew were P/O H Dereniuk bomb-aimer, Sgt R O Malins wireless op, W/O Nelmus mid-upper and F/L J M Forman tail gunner.

Over at Croft, 1664 suffered its first fatal crash when the hatch cover of Halifax EB198 came off and struck the aircraft's rudder. The crew baled out leaving the pilot F/O H A Poulter at the controls. Sadly he was not able to leave the aircraft in time and was killed.

Croft's guardians, 4294 AA (Anti-Aircraft) Flight, departed the airfield during the day, and were replaced by 2753 AA Flight, under the command of F/O G Roberts.

The next night, 419 detailed 14 aircraft to attack the railway marshalling yards and the western entrance to the Mont Cenis railway tunnel at Modane in the

Canadian Ice Hockey team members wait at Feethams bus station at Darlington for the bus to Durham ice rink. The bus station was called the Lead Yard until the 60s when the present bus station was built on the other side of the road. The bus stop sign reads "Aycliffe-Ferryhill-Durham". The Tudor style pub at the end of the road (the Boot & Shoe) was still going strong in 2003   Photo: via Geoff Hill

The Dolphin Centre recreational building has now replaced the old metal clad cafe. The bus stop however remains   Photo: Author

French Alps. They were accompanied by 15 aircraft sent by 428. This target was located about half way between Grenoble in France and Turin, Italy. Damaging the strategic rail infrastructure between occupied France and Italy would cause the Germans great difficulties, especially at this time of the war. Goosepool's crews joined the 170 Halifaxes, 43 Lancasters and 127 Stirlings of 3, 4, 6, and 8 Groups for this attack. Also employed were 5 American B17s. Unfortunately the target was situated in a steep valley and was hard to identify amongst the Alps. This caused the markers great difficulty, and the resultant bombing was not accurate. One Stirling went missing that night, along with two Halifaxes.

One of the Halifaxes lost was flown by F/L Quaile, 419's Deputy 'B' Flight Commander. He, the wireless op F/S T J Bright and the tail gunner F/L Kenyon, who was the squadron's Gunnery Leader, were the only RAF crewmembers on board, the remainder being all RCAF. Quail was on his 26th sortie, Kenyon was on his 44th. Kenyon was one of the original members of 419, having joined the unit in March 1942. Their loss had occurred during the early part of the return journey. As they returned to base, they were aware of the close proximity of other bombers around them. Several times the Monica tail warning system alerted them of approaching aircraft. By the time they were approaching the French coast they had become somewhat blasé. When Monica flashed again soon after, Quaile did not take much heed and did not take any evasive action. The Monica signals intensified and the bomb-aimer, P/O T G Graham was suspicious of the indications and asked if anybody could see the approaching aircraft. F/L B L (Bobo) Kenyon in the tail turret, who had been staring out into the night, replied that nothing could be seen and that everyone should keep their eyes peeled. Within seconds, a Ju88 opened up hitting the port wing and its engines. As the enemy fire was received Kenyon shouted into the intercom, 'Corkscrew starboard, 'Go.' Although he was still unable to see the fighter in the inky blackness of the night, he immediately brought his guns to bare on the port quarter down position on what he believed to be the root of the tracer.

Kenyon thought that there could possibly be two attackers, as another burst of fire was directed at the port wing, which then caught fire. Kenyon was convinced that he had got the fighter and this was later confirmed by F/O Wally, a crewmember of another squadron aircraft who was flying close by. He reported that he had seen the first fighter go down and explode as it hit the ground. Quaile ordered the crew to open the hatches and prepare to bale out. As the navigator, P/P L E Aspinall tried to jettison the nose hatch cover, it became jammed in the opening by the force of the slipstream. He was joined by the wireless operator F/S T J Bright, who unsuccessfully kicked at the offending hatch cover in an attempt to dislodge it. P/O Graham reached the hatch and employed his large stature to aid the efforts of the other two. He jumped on the hatch with all his weight and was rewarded when the hatch cover departed the aircraft. The only problem was that he went with it. He was totally unprepared for such an immediate response to his actions and had not had time to unplug the intercom leads from his helmet. He landed at Vimontiers, 18 miles E/N/E of Falaise, on the bank of a small river. Graham had sprained his left leg and spent the next few days nursing a sore neck brought about by the unplugged intercom lead. The remainder of the crew got out ok.

As it happened, Quaile also had an interesting departure from the aircraft. In his haste to vacate his seat he caught the D ring of his parachute on the throttle levers and deployed his chute in the fuselage. Gathering up the contents of his chute he made for the escape hatch, where he promptly got stuck. The slipstream had other ideas and sucked the canopy of the chute out of the hatch, dragging Quaile out with it. As he left the hatch he injured his hand and one of his shoulders when they were struck on the opening. He reached the ground safely where he landed in a tree, but he was soon captured, along with Kenyon, Aspinall, and the second pilot, Sgt E E Bowden. Graham began walking, and after a day or so met a local Frenchman who sheltered him and eventually put him in touch with the underground. Later he was sent to Paris and eventually reached the Spanish border. He was able to return to England during October.

The engineer, Sgt L F Martin, lost one of his boots whilst baling out but managed to land unharmed in a tree near Fervaques, 7 miles N/N/E of where Graham had landed. Coming to rest some 30 feet from the ground, Martin sought a way to vacate his lofty perch. Having dangled there for quite some time, he eventually achieved his wish, and fell from the tree after pulling at the risers of his chute. He was unceremoniously deposited on the ground in an instant. He regained consciousness and amazingly found himself otherwise uninjured. Having buried his chute, he set off walking across a field. Soon he retraced his steps, followed by an angry bull which took exception to his presence. Martin eventually reached Gibraltar with the assistance of the French underground. Having landed without incident, the second gunner F/O H R Smith was also assisted by the French, he too evaded capture and reached England in December. Quaile, Aspinall, Kenyon and the second pilot Sgt E E Bowden were captured and sent to a POW camp where they remained until the end of the war. Meanwhile, the remainder of the squadron's aircraft returned safe, but were diverted due to bad weather at base.

Over at 428, S/L Suggitt took command of the squadron after the loss of W/C Smith. Despite heavy rain, all 15 of their aircraft managed to take off. All reached the target and bombed successfully, with the exception one aircraft which had to return early due to heavy icing. This crew, along with all but one of 428's aircraft, diverted to the USAAF base at Molesworth, with the exception of one Halifax that landed at Dunsfold, short of fuel. Next day it was still raining, and with F/L Kenyon missing, the vacancy of Moose Squadron Gunnery Leader was filled by F/O R J Wagner. Later, word came through to 428 that Sgt Webb, lost during the raid on Aachen on July 7th was safe, and had returned to the UK having evaded capture. Meanwhile no time was lost replacing S-Sugar and a replacement was ordered. Her successor, a brand new Mk II Halifax, would be with the squadron by the 20th.

No operations were called for that night as the aircraft were still welded to the ground at Molesworth due to Teesside's bad weather. By the 18th, the weather had relented sufficiently to allow all but one of the diverted aircraft to return to base. The lame duck belonged to 428, and had to remain behind with a cracked propeller. That day the Station Commander, Group Captain Ross, departed the airfield for some well-earned leave, leaving W/C Fleming in charge of Goosepool. His post as 419's boss was temporarily filled by the squadron's 'A' Flight Commander, S/L G A McMurdy. Recalled from leave, F/L H F Davis took command of 428's 'B' Flight, a post he would fill for only 5 days. Meanwhile, Sgt Oakley became the flight's Engineer Leader.

At Last! On the same day, Mr G P Robinson of the Air Ministry Works Department, London, arrived at Croft to sort out the water supply problem. Croft's potential water supply was 60,000 gallons per day, but due to a breakdown at Catterick, this was not happening. Croft's daily requirement was 45,000 gallons, but they were only being supplied with 40,000. The problem was the 3-inch supply pipe. Mr Robinson was on the ball and ordered not one but two 6 inch pipes to be installed. If he had known, Norman Thompson would have been *so* happy.

Manpower at Croft was a major problem. People were being poached for other airfields, leaving a constant shortage of help. For example, the Electrical Officer was desperate for 6 more men. He was promised that 6 more men would be posted in to his section. In actual fact, 4 of his existing men were posted out. The Station Engineering Officer was desperate and in need of at least 5 Electricians II and 5 Electricians II WAAF. In fact, there was not a single electrician on SHQ staff. The atrocious September weather caused frequent failures of the airfield's telephone system. In addition to the miles of GPO telephone lines, over 10 miles of D8 temporary cable had to be pressed into service to feed the 19 field-telephones strewn around the airfield. Another problem was the night prowling of airmen on the WAAF site. This problem was partially thwarted by the liberal use of barbed wire.

Despite it only being September, due to the persistent chilly wet weather, it was decided to issue solid fuel to all of Croft's personnel. One of Croft's ORB entries for the 20th reads, 'The MT section is still without its sorely needed hard standing. Vehicles are mired in a bog of mud, such as can be seen only at Croft, Minsk and Pinsk, and the Pripet Marshes.' Also, during night flying training, all of the airfield lights failed, the reason, you guessed it – Damp. On the other hand, the excess of water on the airfield was countered by more problems with the water supply - there wasn't any! The system was up to its old tricks, with 1, 2 and 6 sites completely devoid of H2O. Cpl X took the crash tender for a practice spin around Croft's peri-track. The vehicle was well named, as it turned over whilst he avoided a parked aircraft, and crashed onto its side. Cpl X was extricated, and taken to SSQ with a severely gashed leg. Fortunately he was not seriously injured, and having spent a short time in hospital, was pronounced fit enough to be placed on a charge and attend the subsequent Court of Inquiry. After this event, the remainder of the MT section had to endure a thorough drubbing down on the question of careful driving. The good news was that a liberty bus was to be laid on, which would operate between the aerodrome and Croft railway station. The bus would leave base at 16:00 hours each night for the station, and be waiting there to meet the folk off the 23:25 from Darlington; cost of a return ticket, sixpence. The next day, the new Fusing Huts, Detonator Sheds, Rubber Stores and WAAFs Dining Room were handed over by the Air Ministry Works department.

After a period of stand-downs at Middleton, Ops were called on the 22nd. Although 16 Moose crews took off, VR-H returned early due to the failure of its oxygen system. The remainder reached the target and along with 16 Halifaxes belonging to 428 became part of a 711 aircraft force attacking Hannover. This was the first major raid on the city for 2 years. Unfortunately, due to stronger than forecast winds, Hannover's city centre was not hit, and the bombing started some 2 miles S/S/E of the desired A/P and stretched back about 5 miles. The Moosemen successfully bombed the target and turned for home. Hannover had been well plastered, and on the way back the tail gunners could see the fires burning from over 200 miles away.

Along with the 711 Bomber Command aircraft taking part were five B17 Flying Fortresses of the USAF. This was their first night bombing operation of the war. That night, Bomber Command lost 3.6% of its total bomber force, some 26 aircraft, including 2 Wellingtons, 5 Stirlings and 7 Lancs. Also missing were 12 Halifaxes, including two from Goosepool. Scant information is available about their fate, other than that they were both from 428. The first, NA-H had left Middleton at 18:28, flown by F/O H E McCrae, after which nothing further was heard. All were lost without trace and are remembered on the Runnymede Memorial. The second aircraft, NA-K, took-off 3 minutes later. Only Sgt E G Bartram the tail gunner survived to become a POW. The bodies of the remaining crewmembers, captained by F/O K W Jones, were recovered and rest in Becklingen War Cemetery.

On the 23rd, it was Mannheim's turn to receive the attentions of 419 and 428. Their contribution to the 628 aircraft involved in this raid totalled 31. This was reduced to 29 when one of 428's aircraft failed to start and another returned early with its starboard outer U/S. The A/P was the northern part of the town, and to a large extent this was where the majority of the bombs fell. Some creep-back developed towards the end of the raid and extended across the Rhine into the northern part of Ludwigshaven and beyond into open country. As it happened, this accidental divergence from the intended target caused the A G Farben factory to be badly damaged. In Mannheim, 25,000 people were made homeless. Amongst the buildings damaged were 927 houses, 11 schools, a church, 6 public buildings and 20 industrial sites. The creep-back took in the small towns of Oppau and Frankenthal. The latter was completely destroyed and 38 people lost their lives. Ludwigshaven suffered 47 dead and 260 injured with a further 8,000 being bombed out. Mannheim itself had 102 dead and 418 injured.

Having taken off at 19:23, F/S C R Newton's crew found the weather clear all the way to the target. There was a large concentration of searchlights on their track over the enemy coast. On reaching the target they found many more, concentrated in cones. The flak barrage surrounding the target was bursting up to 20,000 feet, as were many red and white rockets. Sticks of incendiaries laid by the PFF, could be seen in several places along their track on the way in. At 22:17, despite an unserviceable bombsight, Newton's crew were able to hit the green TI's from their bombing height of 17,000 feet. From their lofty perch, many large fires could be seen to the southeast of the target area, also there were good concentrations of fires in the centre of the target. Heavy smoke was rising to 15,000 feet or more. Meanwhile P/O Ford's crew saw the target identified by red, yellow and green TI's. As they bombed a descending green TI, they could see two lines of flarepath fires running parallel from northwest to southeast, with green markers between the lines. Fires were spreading along these lines towards the northeast. W/O E B Edwards crew reported seeing many scattered fires, caused by numerous cases of jettisoned incendiary loads. Many seemed to be burning miles away from the target area. Sgt Sherback, flying NA-O, saw green TI's being dropped some 15 miles northwest of the target, and presumed that a change of aiming point had been ordered. To assist the fighters, three searchlights were laid horizontally to indicate the direction of the bombers run in. Soon after, about 50 fighter flares were dropped from about 21,000 feet, right up to the target. Sherback's crew also reported seeing a large number of jettisoned bomb loads bursting, and considerable tracer activity. Most crews could see Bomber Command's spoof attack taking place on Darmstadt, some 27 miles to the N/N/W.

By the time the crews returned to Middleton, it was realised that 2 aircraft were missing from each squadron. Sgt J Kelley and his crew in VR-F had departed Middleton at 19:02, nothing further was heard from their Halifax, JD457. What is known is that all on board were killed and are buried in the Rheinberg War Cemetery. The second Moose aircraft to be lost was flown by Sgt R T Griffiths, again the circumstances of its demise are unknown. The crew, whose average age was just 20, are buried in the Reichswald Forest War Cemetery. The navigator, Sgt R Dempster, at 23 was the oldest member of the crew. It is most likely that both crews were lost to fighters. The crew of VR-E had more luck, they had a short engagement with a FW 190 but their tail gunner Sgt J H Lynk persuaded the enemy fighter pilot that it was in his best interests to back off. The 190 disappeared and no further problems were encountered. 428 lost NA-Q flown by F/L Davis, the squadron's new 'B' Flight Commander of only 6 days. This aircraft was hit by flak and a night fighter and crashed near Geinsheim. Three members of the crew, including Davis, became POWs, the remainder were killed. The situation leading to the loss of a forth aircraft, NA-B, flown by P/O W A Hadden and his crew, is unknown. They are all buried in Rheinberg War Cemetery. The squadron nearly lost a third aircraft that night when P/O Eaton's Halifax was badly shot up over the target area. On his return to Middleton, Eaton reported that they had been attacked by either a fighter or, possibly, another Halifax. The starboard inner engine fairing was completely shot away. He and his crew were however able to get what was left of the bomber back to Goosepool. Despite having a cannon shell through the starboard tyre, Eaton was able to carry off a safe landing, and received a 'Good show' from his Flight Commander.

Next day, no time was wasted in appointing a new 'B' Flight Commander and F/L McLeish quickly filled the shoes of F/L Davis. The next raid was on the 27th, when Hannover was again the target. The seaweed and corns brigade[93] got the forecast wrong, and the crews found out the hard way. Severe icing conditions were encountered, and Halifax VR-C returned early with its Airspeed Indicator U/S, the pitot head being iced up. The same reason caused the early return of VR-R, and of VR-N, which also came back early having suffered severe ice accretion. The crew of VR-L had a most interesting night. They were struck by lightning, and also had the ASI[94] ice up. On top of that, the Gee box caught fire, and the DR compass went completely U/S. They had to jettison the bomb-load 'live' whilst over enemy territory and turn for home. VR-E had hydraulic and radio trouble, whilst VR-P was holed by flak.

Twelve of 419's aircraft managed to find the target and carry out the attack. By the time the Moosemen reached Hannover, flak was not the only bright lights in the sky. A fully formed thunderstorm was underway. In a large bomber stream, one was aware that one could be in close proximity to other aircraft. The constant buffeting by the slipstream of the chap in front was commonplace, and was to some extent taken for granted. When nearby flak bursts or lightning lit the sky, a view of the actual closeness of the surrounding aircraft could be, to say the least, disconcerting. To see another 4 engined bomber, flying 20 feet below with its mid-upper turret almost touching the nose of one's aircraft, did nothing for those that feared a collision. The nose could itself be rearing up and down from the prop-wash effects of the aircraft in front. Crews could on occasion also find themselves hemmed in from each side, with nowhere to go, sometimes with their wings overlapping those of another aircraft. During the war, many did collide, especially over the target area, despite the crew's desperate attempts to keep a good lookout.

During this raid, 38 aircraft were lost from the original force of 678. These included 17 Halifaxes, 10 Lancasters, 10 Stirlings, 1 Wellington and an American B17. This represented a loss rate of 5.6%.

The incorrectly forecast winds caused those that got there to miss the target in the city centre and to bomb an area about five miles to the north. Although some did hit the northern part of the city, the majority fell on open ground and on small villages to the north of Hannover. Although many fighters were active on the routes in and out and over the target itself, the Moosemen had little aggravation from them. Attacking in pairs, the fighters were operating with other aircraft that dropped fighter flares. The only recorded hit to a Moose aircraft came as Sgt Bullis and his crew were carrying out their bomb-run. They were hit by a single cannon shell in the port tailplane. For some reason the 2 fighters did not persist and no further damage was inflicted. Sgt Bullis and his crew were able to return safely.

Goosepool's squadrons were having a bad run of luck during September, with five aircraft being lost by 419 and six by 428. The latter suffered no less than 5 more aircraft lost during the Hannover raid. Up to now, the squadron had made good use of its flock of Mk V Halifaxes, but amongst the aircraft operating that night was their first Mk II, NA-R JB968. This aircraft was initially delivered to 408 on the April 3rd. It served with them until being passed on to 429 Squadron, who eventually handed it over to 428 on the September 3rd. Flown by F/O R H Sherback, NA-R was to become the first Mk II Halifax lost by 428. Details of the circumstances leading to the demise of this aircraft are not known, only that the crew, who were all killed, are buried in Hannover's War Cemetery.

The second of 428's aircraft to be lost was NA-T, flown by Sgt J E Farmer and crew. This aircraft crashed at Oosterhof, Holland, having been shot down by flak. Only the navigator, Sgt D A Griffin, survived to become a POW. The remainder of the crew, including Sgt Farmer, now rest in Epe General Cemetery, alongside the crew of a 69 Squadron Wellington, which crashed in the same area on April 7th 1945. F/O M G Whalley's crew, flying in NA-V, were shot down by a night fighter in the Hannover area. Only Whalley and the bomb-aimer F/O W B Higgins escaped to became POWs. P/O M Kogan in NA-O turned back 2 hours and 56 minutes after take off, having encountered heavy icing. On their return to the UK, and on reaching Hull, the port inner failed, followed by the air-speed indicator and starboard inner. This put paid to the undercarriage hydraulic system and so the order to bale out was given. Kogan's crew of six vacated the aircraft. Soon after, he spotted the flarepath of Ludford Magna airfield, 16 miles inland from the Lincolnshire Coast. Kogan headed for the runway where he carried out a successful belly landing, from which he was able to walk away uninjured.

[93] Weather Forecasters
[94] Air Speed Indicator

Ludford Magna airfield, 6 miles east of Market Raisen, had only been opened 3 months earlier. It was destined to have only one permanent lodger for the duration of the war, 101 Squadron, flying Lancaster 1s and IIIs. The final loss for 428 came when Sgt Wilson's crew in NA-U overshot Framlingham airfield in Suffolk. The Halifax crashed at Parham House Farm, 5 miles W/S/W of Saxmundham, Suffolk. Wilson was injured, as was his bomb aimer P/O B W Roughton. The tail gunner Sgt E P Wainwright was uninjured, sadly the remainder of the crew were killed. This Halifax, built by Fairy Aviation, had only arrived at 428 on August 10th. The usual Darlington weather prevailed and so on their return 11 Moose aircraft diverted to Bassingbourne whilst one found its way to Linton. The only aircraft to get anywhere near to home landed at Thornaby.

The last operation during September 43 came on the night of the 29th, when Bochum was the target. Twelve of 419's Halifaxes took part in this raid, along with 9 from 428. This was Goosepool's first raid on the Ruhr for over 2 months. Four of 419's crews were also briefed to carry out gardening operations in the Baltic. Just before take-off, the gardening Op was cancelled, and so only the Bochum sortie was carried out. One aircraft, VR-P, returned early as the boost caps on the port inner had burst and the ASI was U/S. By briefing time, it was not clear what level of cloud would be encountered over the target area, and so both sky markers and ground markers were loaded onto the PFF aircraft. As it turned out, the early cloud had cleared by the time the main force got there. Both types of markers were used to good effect during the raid. The marking was spot-on and the bombs emulated the position of the markers. Huge orange fires were seen to encircle the markers. The flak was not as intense as usual, this warned the crews that night fighters must have been in attendance. The usual intense searchlight activity was in evidence however, working in groups of 4, plus a blue tinged master light. F/S Doubassoff and crew nearly ran into a Halifax that suddenly came from nowhere and flew across their path at 90 degrees. F/S F H Palmer's aircraft was coned over Hengelo, Holland and was then in receipt of every available flak shell for miles around. The wireless operator and navigator acted quickly, ripping open bundles of the appropriate type of Window, and began to dump them overboard. This did the trick and soon the Halifax broke from the clutches of the defences and managed to get away. By now precious time had been lost, and so it was decided to dump the bomb-load and head for home. To continue on to the target would mean arriving after the last markers had been dropped. VR-G, flown by P/O J R Saymons failed to return from this operation. He and his crew were lost without trace.

October 1943

On the night of October 3rd, sixteen of 419's Halifaxes were detailed for Ops to the town of Kassel, close to the Eider dam. All returned safely to base, but VR-F, flown by F/S D T Cook was fired upon by an unknown aircraft whilst northwest of Lincoln. The tail gunner Sgt D W Robertson saw tracer being fired at them from their port quarter at about 400 yards range. He was unable to report the attack as he discovered that his intercom was U/S, and by the time he went for the call light the attacker had disappeared. Fortunately Cook had also seen the tracer on the starboard side, and had initiated an evasive diving turn to port and extinguished the Halifax's nav lights. Although the attack had only lasted 5 seconds, the Halifax was hit in the elevator, and on returning to Middleton, Cook wrestled with the controls in an attempt to land the damaged aircraft. He did manage to carry out a landing of sorts, but on finals, F-Freddie hit hard. By the time it came to a halt, the aircraft's port wing had been torn off and the fuselage was broken in three places. Fortunately the crew were not seriously injured, although the engineer, Sgt Simpson broke his lower left arm, whilst the bomb-aimer F/S H H Campbell suffered a twisted knee.

428 had contributed 13 of their crews, one of which returned early. Sgt K A McArthur's crew in NA-S failed to come home, they had been hit by flak and had crashed at Sehlen, 32 miles southwest of Kassel. McArthur and his bomb aimer P/O T J Elliot were killed, whilst the remainder were captured by the Germans and became POWs.

W/O F B Edwards, who was halfway through his second tour, had taken along P/O R P Goldstein as a second dickey, who was hoping to gain valuable operational experience. Goldstein had only just reported to 428 three days earlier, having been posted in from 1659 HCU at Topcliffe. As an ex-instructor, he had amassed 2,400 flying hours before arriving at 428. Sadly he, Edwards, and all but two of the crew were killed when NA-G crashed at Hofgeismar, 13 miles N/N/E of Kassel.

The final loss for 428 that evening was NA-E, flown by F/S C R Newton and his crew. They had been badly shot up by a Fw190, but were able to limp home and land safely at the old Battle of Britain airfield at Tangmere, Sussex. So badly shot up was this aircraft that it was later declared as beyond economical repair and scrapped. Amazingly, none of the crew were injured in the attack.

The routeing out to the target was excellent and the PFF did an excellent job in starting the show. They had dropped their markers each side of the target and everyone was bombing the greens. A spoof attack on Hannover, 73 miles away, by 10 Mosquitoes helped to confuse the German fighter controllers. Red track markers and white fighter flares dropped by enemy aircraft were seen by most crews between the target and Hannover. With the exception of F/S C R Newton's crew, who bombed at 21:58, nine out of the ten Ghost crews that reached the target were in and out within 15 minutes of each other, beginning with F/O Lord's at 21:15 and ending with Sgt E O'Conner's at 21:30.

Newton's crew had good reason to be late. They were running in to bomb when they came in for some unwanted attention from a Fw190. Before their bomb doors could be closed one of them was shot away. The port tail fin was badly damaged, along with the port inner, which became U/S. With the failure of the port inner, the hydraulic system went on strike and also became totally unserviceable. Just to round things off, the starboard outer's coolant radiator matrix picked up some shrapnel and began to leak Glycol. Sgt H P Gough in the mid-upper position and Sgt J M Jacobs in the tail turret took revenge and saw strikes hitting the 190's tailplane. After the bombs were dropped, a 190 came in from port. Jacobs fired at the fighter, whose pilot suddenly remembered that he had business elsewhere and promptly scarpered. As they left the target area, the smoke from the fires was climbing up to 12,000 feet. Newton was able to return to England and land safely at Tangmere.

F/O Murphy's crew in NA-C managed to reach the target and bomb, despite the Halifax's electrical system becoming U/S. Someone fired a huge red rocket at them as they passed over Texel. They also returned to the UK and landed safely at Tangmere. Three aircraft were seen dropping their bombs on the phony white track markers. However, even though the raid had just started, and only 15 to 20 bombers had unloaded, the incendiaries were taking a firm hold.

As it turned out, the H2S blind marker overshot the correct aiming point by quite a large margin. Due to the haze, the visual markers were unable to correct the situation and the western suburbs and outlying areas took the brunt of the bombing. The town supported the Fiesler and Henschel aircraft factories, and both of these were badly damaged by incendiaries, along with other important industrial buildings. The Wolfshanger district, 1 mile to the northeast of the city centre, also took a beating. A large ammo dump at Ihringshousen, one and a half miles further north, was hit by stray bombs, which started a huge fire. This attracted many more moths, and by the time they left, 84 of its buildings were destroyed.

Next day, 419 sent sixteen aircraft to Frankfurt, whilst 428 detailed 10, two of which aborted due to engine failures, whilst a third returned early. Two of 419's Halifaxes, flown by Sgt Fare and F/O Hamilton, did not return. The first, VR-D, had been flown by Sgt A R Fare RAF, the only survivor was the bomb aimer Sgt W L Renner. The aircraft was on the return leg, having successfully bombed the target. It was hit without warning by cannon fire from a night fighter of 1./NJG4, flown by Hauptmann Wilhelm Herget. As the fighter struck there was a large explosion. None of the crew were injured and there was no fire. The engines were operating normally but the skipper reported to the crew that he was unable to maintain control. The aircraft began to quickly lose height and Fare gave the order to abandon. The crew scrambled for their parachute packs. The last thing Sgt Renner remembered was reaching for his. He must have blacked out, and when he regained consciousness he was surprised to find his chute had deployed and he was about to land. He came down at Cour-sur-Heure, about a mile and a half south of the aircraft, which crashed at Ham-sur-Heure, 6 miles southwest of Charleroi, Belgium. Once safely on the ground, he took stock of his situation and realised that he had suffered two broken ribs. These injuries had occurred before he landed, and his only assumption was that there must have been another explosion which had been thrown him out of the aircraft. Local people reported that the aircraft had been on fire as it fell, and that he was the only survivor. Three members of his crew were found inside the wreckage, whilst the other three were thrown out on impact. Only Renner and the tail gunner were RCAF, the remainder of the crew were RAF. The six who died were taken to the communal cemetery at Gosselies, 4 miles north of Charleroi, and just 10 miles north of the crash site.

Renner was found by a priest, who was accompanied by a doctor. They had been looking for the downed airman, and having been treated by the doctor for his injuries, Renner was sheltered by the priest. Three weeks later Renner was moved from the priest's house and taken to another in Laneffe by the Belgium Organization. Soon after, he was moved again, this time to Fairoul. Here he was to remain for 8 months until July 30th 1944, when, after the D-Day invasion, German troops began to retreat from the area. Four days later, having had to relocate to a hiding place in nearby woods, Renner was liberated by the advancing Americans.

Sgt T A Reay, wireless operator on Halifax VR-L (L-Love), woke up in a hospital bed. He was surprised to find himself in a German POW camp and had no idea how he got there. His last recollection was of Goosepool. It transpired that he had been a member of the crew of the second of 419's aircraft to go missing that night during the Frankfurt raid. He remembered nothing of the night's proceedings, not even the briefing back at Middleton.

F/O Bill Hamilton (second from left) and his crew, shot down on the night of October 4/5 1943 by a night fighter.
He, along with F/O Jack Dale (third from left), Sgt EH Griffin and F/S A Bortolussi were killed. Flying Officer EL Riley (6th from the
left) and Sgts J McEwan and TA Reay survived to become prisoners of war   *Photo: via Geoff Hill*

419's F/O W H Hamilton in VR-L was on his 15th trip and was about 60 miles W/S/W of the target outbound when his aircraft was hit by a fighter. The port inner caught fire and soon the flames began to spread. The burning engine was feathered and the order to bale out was given. The Halifax came down at Sohren, 57 miles W/S/W of the target area. Reay, the navigator F/O E L Riley and the engineer Sgt J McEwan baled out and became POWs. Hamilton, the bomb-aimer F/O J R Dale, the second gunner Sgt E H Griffiths and the tail gunner F/S Bortolussi were killed.

Of 428's seven remaining Halifaxes, one failed to return. F/S J Harkins and his crew, flying NA-W, were shot down by a night fighter whilst outbound. The Halifax came down on the eastern bank of the Our River at Ubereisenback, 112 miles to the west of Frankfurt. All managed to jump out and land safely. Harkins and the tail gunner, Sgt N W Lee, managed to evade capture, whilst the rest spent the remainder of the war as POWs.

This, the first concerted raid on Frankfurt thus far in the war, employed 406 aircraft; 4 Mosquitoes, 170 Halifaxes, 162 Lancasters, 60 Stirlings and 3 B17s. Losses totaled 5 Hallys, 3 Lancs 1 Stirling and 1 B17. This would be the last time that American aircraft accompanied RAF Bomber Command on night-bombing operations. Over the next few weeks however, individual B17s continued to carry out occasional bombing sorties. Total cloud cover persisted all the way from England until about 50 miles from the target, when the predicted forecast provided the crews with clear weather over Frankfurt. The main bombing took place in the eastern part of the city. Although landlocked, Frankfurt has the river Main, which meanders east to west through the southern part of the city. This strategic inland waterway provided vital transportation for war materials. Its important dock areas and many of its large barges were badly damaged during this raid. In the city centre, several important buildings were damaged, including the new Rathaus, which had its roof destroyed. The city's records state that a direct hit on the air raid shelter of an orphanage in a former Jewish hospital killed 90 children, 14 nuns and other members of staff. This raid had a very marked impression on the people of Frankfurt and resulted in the mass exodus of many of its residents. Over the next few days, the railway station was overrun with people trying to evacuate the city.

428's S/L Suggitt was promoted to Wing Commander on October 6th. The next day, P/Os Westell and Douglass were allowed to bypass their next natural promotion to Flying Officers, and were promoted directly to the rank of Flight Lieutenants. They then took up the posts of 428's Navigation and Gunnery Leaders respectively.

Meanwhile, after one year and one month in the post, the Moose Squadron's 'Boss', Wing Commander Mervin 'Merv' Fleming, relinquished command. He was handing over to W/C G A McMurdy, who had been the squadron's 'A' Flight Commander for quite some time. Fleming, who had commanded 419 since September 8th 1942, departed for 6 Group HQ on October 8th, to take up his new position as Senior Operations Officer. He had been the third Moose Squadron officer to be awarded the DSO for his high degree of leadership, outstanding skill, courage and devotion to duty whilst on operations.

A trip to Hannover that evening for 12 Moose aircraft went without loss. They were part of a force of 504 aircraft, which included 26 Wellingtons supplied by 432 RCAF and 300 Polish squadrons. This was to be the last Bomber Command raid for the long serving Wellington, and appropriately, to mark the event, there were no losses amongst the 'Wimpies'. Unfortunately however, 14 Lancs and 13 Hallys failed to return. A spoof attack on Bremen failed to fool the German controller, who quickly called his fighters away from Bremen to fly the 63 miles towards the real target, Hannover. Over the target, the weather was clear and the PFF put their markers down on the correct aiming point, just to the east and west of the city centre. As the first TI landed on the eastern side, one of the first crews to hit them was that of F/L Dyer of the Moose Squadron. Sgt K P White and crew in VR-W, were disturbed during the critical part of their bombing run by a warning from their tail gunner, who reported sighting a 109 climbing up a searchlight beam towards them. White turned towards the approaching fighter and stuffed the nose down. Heading steeply towards the attacking 109, White managed to thwart the attack, and the fighter pilot lost the plot and disappeared. By the time White's crew recovered, they found themselves at a reduced altitude to the briefed one. They also found themselves on the wrong heading for the correct bomb-run and decided to drop their load from an angle some 30 degrees to that of the briefed heading. As they departed the target area, fighter flares were seen dropping behind them from about 20,000 feet. Despite seeing an estimated 100 searchlights over the target area, White's crew managed to complete the sortie without further incident.

The heavy flak barrages were set to explode at 22,000 feet, whilst the light flak failed to reach the Moosemen's operating height. During the raid, creep-back was limited to about 2 miles. This raid was considered to be Hannover's worst of the war, and resulted in severe damage to the city centre and most other parts. Only the western areas escaped serious damage. As the bombs began to go down during the early stages of the raid, their effect was felt on the electricity and telephone systems, which were quickly put out of action. Also badly affected was the water supply for the firefighters, as many of the city's water mains were cut. Two main conflagrations developed, one in the city centre and another just to the south of it. Despite the efforts of officials, who herded people from these areas to less affected districts, 1,200 were killed and 3,345 were injured. Between 6 to 8,000 people had to be treated for eye injuries due to the smoke and heat. Destroyed buildings totalled 3932, whilst a further 30,000 were damaged. Amongst the industrial buildings badly affected were the Continental Tyre and Rubber factory and the Hanomag Machine Works. All Moose aircraft returned safely from this raid but due to bad weather at base had to divert.

The Ghost Squadron

The Moose Squadron were not the only Goosepool unit to take part in the Hannover raid. They were joined by thirteen Halifaxes of the 'Ghost Squadron', who also returned safely. Teesside's weather however, didn't help the proceedings, and forced the returning crews to divert to Manston in Kent. During the day, confirmation had been received that, from October 8th 1943, 428 Squadron RCAF would henceforth be officially known as the 'Ghost Squadron'. The name had been chosen due to the state of the squadron after the very high losses sustained during recent months. During September for example, 419 had lost 6 Halifaxes on operations, whilst 428 lost 11. As stated, during the raid on Hannover on the 27/28th, they lost 5 in one night. These losses were almost double those of 419 during September.

On the 10th, 419's Medical Officer gave the aircrew a lecture on Tropical Medicine. The purpose of the lecture was to give instructions and advice as to the procedures to be followed in the event of them landing in any tropical or sub-tropical countries. During the afternoon, an escape and evasion exercise was organized for the Moose Squadron's 'A' Flight. The evaders were taken in covered vans to unknown locations at distances between 4 and 10 miles from Middleton. They were dropped off singly without their passes and with only 1 shilling[95] in their pockets for expenses. It must be remembered however, that 1 shilling could buy much more than 5 pence does today. Even in the 50s, I remember, three pennies would buy a large bag of chips, and with the remaining nine pennies a young child could have a field-day at the local sweet shop.

Their task was to evade capture by the Home Guard, civil and service police and Auxiliary Army Units. The exercise was a huge success and everyone entered into the spirit of things, especially the two-aircrew members who undetected, managed to sneak back into camp and cheekily enter the Station Intelligence Officer's office through an open window. During the day, S/L Bartlett reported in to assume command of 428's 'B' Flight. At the same time, F/Os Watkins and Brown arrived for duty from Croft.

Next day saw W/C McMurdy begin his first day at work as Moose Commander. During the same day, the squadron bade farewell to another of its oldest aircrew members, F/L W G Rice, who was being repatriated to Canada. 'Pop' Rice had flown with 419 as a wireless operator since being posted in on September 15th 1942. He had held the post of Squadron Signals Leader since June of 43. He had been affectionately known as Pop due to his gray hair and paternal demeanor. Later that day, 419 saw the arrival of aircraft fitted with new and secret equipment.[96] Two crews were screened to begin special training on this equipment. So secret was it at the time that no detailed title was given to it in the Squadron's Operational Record Book.

On the 12th, the Moosemen began their fifth Victory Loan campaign, with a self-imposed target of 30,000 Canadian dollars. It was noted that, owing to the enthusiasm of all Section and Flight Commanders, 25,150 dollars was raised on the first day of the drive, a record for any squadron for a one-day sale of the bonds. The largest donation was for 500 dollars, as opposed to the normal 50 and 100-dollar donations. On the 20th, the poor weather continued, which allowed 7 of 428's pilots and engineers to visit the Rotol Airscrew factory on Norton Road, Stockton.[97] Here, they made propellers, from the basic materials to the completed article.

After a long period of stand-downs due to bad weather, it was the 22nd before operations were resumed. On this occasion, Kassel was the target for 32 of Goosepool's Halifaxes. Due to inaccurate met forecasts, the aircraft had encountered icing conditions by the time they reached York. Three Moose Halifaxes returned early, as did the same number of Ghost aircraft, examples of which were VR-B with its port outer U/S, VR-F with its port inner U/S, and VR-N, due to severe icing conditions. The remaining crews pressed on to the target, but out of these, one from each squadron was lost. After only 11 days as 419's Squadron Commander, W/C/ McMurdy and his crew in VR-A failed to return. Ten minutes late over the target, due to a U/S airspeed indicator caused by an iced up pitot tube, the Halifax was illuminated by a searchlight during its bomb run, but McMurdy gave it the slip by turning sharply to port. Two minutes later, a warning was called by the tail gunner F/S P W Peterkin, 'Fighters up, fighters at 3, 6 and 9 o'clock high.' McMurdy initiated a corkscrew and the fighters on both beams flew by harmlessly. The one in the 6 o'clock position below and behind the Halifax must have stayed put. After the evasive action was over and McMurdy began to regain height, the fighter opened fire, hitting the port inner on A-Able. F/S P W Peterkin shouted 'Fire', to which McMurdy inquired, 'Which engine?' Having been told it was the port inner, he immediately feathered the affected engine. He ordered the crew to stand by to abandon the aircraft and within a few seconds gave the bale-out command. First to jump was the navigator P/O W C Coleman, followed by the bomb-aimer F/L R K Shields and the wireless operator Sgt R J Woods. Like so many airman in similar circumstances, F/L Shields probably knocked himself out whilst leaving the aircraft, as he woke to find himself choking. He was falling and grabbed at the parachute's D-ring but it was already deployed. As he floated to earth he realised that he wasn't that far from the target area, as the raid was still on and he could hear the bombs exploding. Along with Coleman and Woods, he was captured and became a POW. This had been his 20th and last operation with the Moose Squadron, and his loss was deeply regretted by the folks back at Goosepool. He was considered to be one of the best Bombing Leaders of 6 Group, having been with 419 since September 1942. The aircraft crashed at Lauenforde, 25 miles N/N/W of Kassel. McMurdy must have remained at the controls to hold the aircraft steady in an attempt to allow the remainder of his crew to escape. When the wreckage was searched, the bodies of McMurdy, F/S A B Wilson the second pilot, Sgt T Rawlings the engineer, W/O2[98] F Yackison the mid-under gunner and F/S Peterkin were inside. They all rest together in Hannover War Cemetery. F/S Peterkin was an American and hailed from Yarmouth Port, Massachusetts.

---

[95] 12 old pennies = 5 new pence
[96] G-H blind-bombing system
[97] This factory returned to its peacetime role as Hill's Joinery after the war
[98] Warrant Officer 2nd Class

The Ghost Squadron saw NA-I take off at 17:17. Having been hit by flak and fighters, Sgt E J Sykes and his crew had to make an emergency landing at Snetterton airfield, Norfolk. During the attack, the mid-upper gunner, Sgt P Stuart was badly injured, whilst Sgt T F Clemenhagen in the tail turret was killed. Fighter attacks also claimed the life of Sgt P D Emms, the rear gunner in P/O Ford's crew, whilst also injuring Sgts Yule and Proctor, the latter seriously.

Over the target, the marking was carried out 'Blind' by way of H2S. Initially the TIs overshot, but 8 out of 9 visual markers found the centre of Kassel. The main force bombed the city with great accuracy, although a decoy fire drew a small number of bombers away from the main target. Kassel received the most devastating attack on a German city, second only to the firestorm attack on Hamburg during July of 43. Here, too, there was a firestorm, not quite as widespread as Hamburg's, but as far as raids were concerned, its like would not be exceeded for another 9 months. After the raid, 63% of Kassel's living accommodation was unusable. Up to 120,000 people had to leave their homes. Kassel had many flats and apartments, and 4,349 blocks of flats were destroyed. They contained 26,782 separate family living units. A further 26,463 living units were damaged in the attack. The fire service was overwhelmed and found themselves tackling over 3,600 separate fires. 78 public buildings were destroyed or badly damaged, along with 11 hospitals, 38 schools, 25 churches, 16 police, military and Gestapo buildings. In addition, 155 industrial buildings were destroyed. Kassel hosted 3 Henschel aircraft factories that were employed in the construction of V1 flying bombs. These factories were seriously damaged and put the German flying bomb programme back many months. Kassel's railway system was another victim of the bombing. As for the casualties, by the end of the following month the number of dead recovered totalled 5,599, out of these, 1,817 were unidentifiable. 3,587 people were also injured. A further 3,300 were missing. After several days of ceaseless toil, 459 people were pulled alive from the rubble of their homes and shelters. The smoke and heat had been so intense that a further 8,084 had to be treated for heat and smoke injuries to their eyes. The raid itself had employed 569 aircraft, 247 Halifaxes and 322 Lancasters. At 7.6% of the main force, the loss of 25 Halifaxes and 18 Lancasters was badly received back at Bomber Command. The raid had cost 43 aircraft lost, 243 aircrew killed, 7 injured and 75 POWs.

Wing Commander WP (Bill) Pleasance DFC (seated on the right), talking to his engineer, P/O MD McGill from Homewood, Manatoba, during debriefing

Photo: courtesy of the Canadian Forces

Two days later, Wing Commander W P (Bill) Pleasance arrived at Middleton from 431 Squadron, based at Tholthorpe in North Yorkshire, to assume command of 419 after the loss of W/C McMurdy. Meanwhile, no flying could be carried out thanks to the quirks of the weather, which continued up to and beyond the end of October. On the last day, the records showed that, to date, the Moose Squadron had carried out 1,000 sorties, at a cost 41 aircraft lost. The number of aircrew lost was shown as 293, of which 77 were confirmed as deceased and 83 as prisoners. The fate of the remainder was not known. On the 26th, 428 bade farewell to W/C Suggitt, who was being posted to 617 Dam Busters Squadron.[99] His place was being filled by S/L French, who reported for duty that afternoon along with his crew. Suggitt carried out his last briefing the following day, when 16 of 428's aircraft were detailed for operations. The aircraft were marshalled in readiness, but at 16:05, word came through that the Op was scrubbed. The poor weather continued, and a further operation planned for the 30th and briefed by S/L French, was again scrubbed at the last moment. The last day of October was a Sunday, the church parade being carried out by Middleton's Chaplain, S/L Crees.

November 1943

November 1st saw the crew of Wing Commander Pleasance report in from 431 during the day. That evening he travelled over to the small seaside town of Redcar, where he addressed a 'Wings for Victory' gathering for the Borough of Redcar. During the proceedings, he presented a plaque to Redcar Borough on behalf of the Air Ministry. In return, the citizens of Redcar presented him with two logbooks to be kept by the squadron. Each of these logbooks depicted the operations that a particular aircraft had carried out and the crews that flew them. The local funds gathered by the people of Redcar during the 'Wings for Victory' campaign had 'bought' the two Halifaxes. It was agreed that the logbooks would be returned to the Borough after the cessation of hostilities. The same day the No. 5 Ice Hocky Season opened at Durham ice rink. Goosepool got off to a good start when they beat East Moor 9 – 0. No.1 line included P/O M Schmidt and LAC Bauer, formally of the Boston Bruins. If they continued to play like this, the team felt that they would have no problem in taking the Overseas Championships. Due to the continuation of inclement weather, the next day, two crews of 419's B Flight visited the Royal Ordnance Factory at Aycliffe.[100] They escaped the station parade, which was inspected by the Station Commander G/C Ross prior to a route march and march-past. Later, the Station Security Officer, F/L Phillips addressed the aircrew personnel of 419 on the subject of 'Prisoner of War interrogation'.

99 Squadron Leader Suggitt died of his injuries, after his 617 squadron Lancaster crashed on high ground on February 13th 1944. He had just taken off from Ford Airfield, Sussex, following a raid on the Antheor Viaduct. His crew were killed in the crash but S/L Suggitt died later in Chichester hospital
100 Now the town of Newton Aycliffe

On the 3rd, Dusseldorf was the target for Goosepool's Halifaxes. All Moose aircraft returned safely to Goosepool with the exception of VR-K, which landed at Leeming due to an error by the crew. Flown by F/S White, this crew were gaining quite a reputation for landing away after operations. This had occurred 5 times out of 9, albeit mostly from circumstances beyond their control.

428 lost NA-E, flown by F/O R G Eaton, when it crashed south of Kyme, 7 miles northeast of Sleaford, Lincolnshire. All eight crewmembers were killed. The tail gunner, P/O A E MacKenzie was just 18 years old, the youngest RCAF aircrew member to be killed during 1943. Eaton was on his 16th Op.

It was during this raid, carried out by a force of 589 aircraft, that 38 Mk II Lancasters, 13 from 3 Group and 25 from 6 Group, made the first large-scale test of the G-H blind-bombing system. This took place at the same time as the main raid and was directed against the Mannesmann tubular steel works situated on the northern outskirts of Dusseldorf. It was not an auspicious start to the G-H bombing system, as the equipment on 16 of the aircraft failed to operate. Five aircraft had to return early whilst 2 more were lost. The remaining 15 aircraft managed to accurately bomb the target and several assembly halls were destroyed.

On the 4th, Captain Stewart, 419's Dental Officer, departed for 4 Group HQ at Birmingham. He was one of 419's original members, having reported for duty two days before the squadron actually formed. He was considered to be a very likeable person and a staunch supporter of the Moose Squadron and was sadly missed by his many friends.

On the 11th, both squadrons sent five each of their most experienced crews all the way to Cannes on the French Rivera, nearly 600 miles away. The target was the railway marshalling yards on the coastal line to Italy. All returned safely to Middleton from what had been described as a milk run. The target was missed, and unfortunately, some of the bombs fell on a working class suburb and 39 French people were killed. F/L M A Hewitt's crew in VR-P found Cannes cloud-free and bathed in the light of a full moon. The target was identified visually by the two islands off its southern tip and the marshalling yards, which were visible long before the TIs were dropped. The PFF were ten minutes early and actual recognition of the target itself was impossible, due to the fact that there were too many red and green TIs. The typical bomb-load in each aircraft consisted of 4 x 1,000-lb GP bombs, 8 X 30-lb and 180 4-lb incendiaries, which were dropped right on the TIs. The only opposition noted was two light guns firing out to sea. These were accompanied by two feeble searchlights, their intensity only managing to increase after the aircraft had left the target. Similar observations were reported by the crews flown by F/S G H Marjoram in VR-N and F/L H L Shackleton in VR-Q. All crews returned tired but safe.

The next night the station armourers held a very successful party in the Imperial Hotel, Darlington. The chair was taken by F/S Hall, who was the Senior Armament NCO. The guest of honour was W/C Pleasance, who gave a speech, along with F/L Pedley the Station Armaments Officer. These were suitably replied to by 419's Armament Officer, F/O Smith. The armourers supplied their own entertainment and the whole affair developed into a very enjoyable evening. The Moosemen had operated for some weeks without a Bombing Leader due to the loss of F/L Shields, eventually, on November 13th, the post was filled by F/O Haseldine.

Two days later, the RCAF travelling trade-test board arrived at the Moose Squadron to begin the trade testing of 419's ground-crew personnel. Their ultimate findings were, to be frank, somewhat disappointing. First to be tested were the engine mechanics. Their knowledge of aero-engines was observed to be generally below average. This included the Merlin, the engine currently being used by the squadron. The main weakness was in special knowledge of the engine ancilliaries, such as pumps, generators etc. Next to be tested were the airframe mechanics. They were also found lacking in their knowledge of airframes and their accessories. Also noted was a particular weakness towards the finer points of hydraulic systems, controls and trouble-shooting. No less criticised were the armourers (Guns). Three were tested and all failed their trade test. Their weaknesses turned out to be their knowledge of VGOs, turret operation and maintenance of small arms. Their counterparts, armourers (Bombs) fared slightly better. Out of the 5 that were tested, 2 failed, due to being unfamiliar with storage groups, regulations, fusing, pyrotechnics and workshop practices. The last trade to be tested were the electricians. The majority of the squadron electricians were not recommended for a trade-test at this time. P/O Treasure, the Squadron Electrical Engineer Officer, realised that the electricians stood little chance of passing the trade-test and did not recommend that they should try. He had been acutely conscious of their shortcomings and had initiated a series of training lectures. The response to these lectures had not been encouraging and had been met with little enthusiasm. After the electricians realised that they were not considered good enough to be put forward for their trade test, the lectures suddenly began to increase in popularity. S/L Bales, the Squadron Engineering Officer, had instigated lectures for the engine and airframe mechanics a short time before the trade test board was due to arrive. They had been organized for a Tuesday and Thursday, operations permitting. Although too late to have much effect this time, it was hoped that they would result in a more favourable showing in subsequent trade-tests.

During the 16th, a sea search was called for after a Flying Fortress raid on Norway. 419 was requested to have 17 aircraft standing by, with 429 offering a further 12 for a 13:00 take-off. During briefing, this number was reduced to 10. At 12:30, this was again cut to 3 crews, and by 13:00 take-off was postponed until 15:30, when they eventually took off. The aircraft returned after dark and all reported seeing a light in approximately the same position. During the day, word came through that the Moosemen's former commander, W/C Fleming had been awarded the DSO for his excellent work whilst commanding 419. Next day, one Moose Halifax took off to continue the sea-search, but returned without result. In relation to this, W/C Pleasance, assisted by S/L Brown and F/L D G Hall, took the opportunity to lecture all Moose aircrews on the subject of Air-Sea Rescue and the advantages of being up to date with ditching procedure.

The Battle of Berlin - 18th November 43 – 31st March 44

Butch Harris was about to begin his all out assault on Berlin, which would see 16 major raids on the 'Big City'. The first began on November 18th, employing 440 Bomber Command aircraft. There would also be a further 16 raids on other German cities. To this end, on the night of the 18th, sixteen Moose and fifteen Ghost crews were detailed for a raid on Mannheim and Ludwigshaven, this was later increased to 18. This turned out to be the last major raid on Mannheim for 15 months, as the adjacent towns of Mannheim and Ludwigshaven had received more that their fair share of bombs thus far in the war. Amongst the industrial targets hit that night was the Daimler-Benz car factory. Only 10% of the giant plant was still capable of production after the bombers had departed. Also hit was the military airfield at Sandhofen, along with 4 military barracks. 7,500 people were bombed out, but by now, as with other large industrial based towns, many had left for safer areas and only 21 were killed and 154 injured. 248 Halifaxes, 33 Lancasters and 114 Stirlings of 3, 4, 6, and 8 Group took part in what was, in essence, a diversionary raid, aimed at giving the Berlin crews a better chance of survival.

When 419 reached the target it was cloud covered, which caused the bombing to be scattered. F/S Sedgwick was on his 3rd trip, he and his crew reached the target 20 minutes late. Although they had by-passed several flak-infested areas, it appeared that they had managed to reach Mannheim without attracting the attentions of the flak gunners or fighters. Having completed their bombing run they turned for home. Their aircraft was about 15 minutes from the target when the engineer Sgt E K Canny looked at his fuel gauges and quickly changed tanks. Ten minutes later the starboard outer began to splutter and then stop. This was followed shortly after by the starboard inner, the port inner and finally the port outer. None of the crew were aware of any encounter with flak nor had any hits been felt, but one or more of the tanks must have been holed somehow. The Halifax was obviously suffering from fuel starvation, and so with all engines stopped and the aircraft descending steeply, Sedgwick gave the order to bale-out. The navigator F/O E R Hoe and Sgt J Pappas the bomb-aimer, who were in the nose, tried to jettison the hatch cover, but it stuck in the opening against the slipstream and wouldn't budge. They were still trying to free it by the time the Halifax had dropped to 4,000 feet. They decided to give it up as a bad job and struggle uphill for the rear hatch, from which they eventually jumped. They were the last out. Sgt Canny, Sgt W K Dingley the wireless operator, Sgt N McVickar the mid-under gunner and Sgt D M Johnson the tail gunner had already baled out of the rear hatch. The whole time Hoe and Pappas had been wrestling with the hatch cover, Sedgwick had been holding the aircraft steady to give them a chance to escape. In doing so he left himself insufficient time to save himself, and he was killed when L-Love crashed. His body was found by the Germans. He now rests in Rheinberg War Cemetery. After the war, when F/O Hoe was able to give his report, he stated that he saw the aircraft explode some 10 to 15 seconds after he had jumped. He was in no doubt that Sgt Sedgwick had given his life to save the two crewmembers in the nose. He also stated that, in his opinion, Sedgwick should be awarded a posthumous award for his sacrifice.

The Moose Squadron was to lose a second Halifax during this raid. VR-K flown by F/O E D Fogg took off from Goosepool at 16:47; next morning K-King had not returned. The circumstances relating to the crew's demise are unknown. The only information available is that their average age was just 22. P/O M P Stronach and his crew could not bomb the primary, as they were unable to see any TIs. They elected to attack an area about 20 miles northeast of Mannheim. Here there was only 2/10ths cloud and some haze, but they still had to bomb by ETA. On the way back they saw Mannheim ablaze. It had been very difficult to make any accurate observation due to the astrodome Perspex freezing up. This was proving to be a regular annoyance.

F/S J A Parker's crew managed to bomb Mannheim and found it clear of cloud but very hazy. They bombed on the red and green TIs and the falling incendiaries. To them the attack seemed scattered, although 6 small fires soon began to join up and take a good hold. Their bomb-load was typical of those of the other Moose Halifaxes, and consisted of 1 X 1,000-lb HC, 32 X 30-lb LC, and 810 X 4-lb incendiaries. They found the flak over the TA heavier than briefed and had one of their cans of incendiaries hang up on them. F/S R G Herbert's crew were also able to bomb the target, but later reported that the attack did not appear to be particularly successful. Having taken off at 16:48, F/O H T Brown's crew found themselves way off course and close to the Frankfurt-Darmstadt area. The time was 20:42, and being 40 miles to the north of the target area and unable to reach the target in time, they decided to turn for home. Nine minutes later, and still in the Frankfurt area, they happened across a searchlight concentration and deposited their bomb-load thereon. VR-F, flown by Sgt W L Hunter, suffered a U/S Gee set 2 hours after take off. It was realised that this had put them way off course and unable to reach the target within the allocated time. The furthest point they reached was St-Omer in France. Hunter decided to turn back. Meanwhile, they were hit by intense predicted flak, which put a large dent in their tailplane. They made it back to Middleton, having jettisoned their bomb-load 25 miles W/S/W of Southend.

P/O J G Hamilton's crew in VR-H had a similar evening. Having taken off from Middleton at 17:04, and having only reached a point south of Cleethorpes, a call on the R/T was heard informing them to abandon the mission. They were only at 6,500 feet, and some confusion arose regarding the call signs 'Fairman' and 'Kremlin'. The R/T was actually talking to one of 428's aircraft, which was in difficulty. Hamilton heard what he considered to be his call sign, and believed the order to land was for his aircraft, especially as when he called for permission to jettison his bomb-load he was given the OK. This he duly did, and landed back at Goosepool 1 hour and 8 minutes after taking off.

The stronger than forecast winds continued to cause problems for the Moosemen. F/S H C Eyjolfson's crew in VR-J were off-track for some reason, it was assumed that the wind had changed. Their indicated airspeed was down to 150 mph. They elected to bomb an unknown built-up area on ETA. The wireless operator, Sgt Jones was praised for not only doing his own job, but also attending to the engineer, who twice became unconscious due to oxygen starvation.

The only casualty for the Ghost Squadron was Sgt Perehinski, a gunner in F/O Wadkins's crew, who was wounded. Wadkins managed to land at Woodbridge, the nearest port of call he could find.

On the 19th, twelve Moose aircraft were detailed for a raid on the town of Leverkusen, situated on the northeastern outskirts of Cologne. They were joined by 11 crews belonging to 419. This number would have been greater, but several of their aircraft were unable to return in time from their diverted bases. After take-off, VR-M and VR-T returned early with gun stoppage problems that could not be cleared. The 10 remaining aircraft continued on to the target, but could not find the markers and had to bomb on ETA. Bomber Command's force that night was small in comparison to recent raids, only 266 aircraft taking part. Failures in the Oboe equipment meant that it could not be used to good effect. Due to the unfavourable weather conditions, the PFF were unable to provide accurate target marking and the bombing was scattered. Over 27 other towns located to the north of Cologne received hits, whereas Leverkirchen itself recorded only one HE bomb falling on the town. There was a suspicion that the Germans had dropped bogus markers over a 50 mile area, whilst markers known to have come from PFF aircraft were seen up to 30 miles away from the target.

The atrocious weather did provide one consolation however. It kept most of the German night fighters on the ground, resulting in a very small loss rate for the bombers. Only 1 Stirling and 4 Halifaxes were lost during the raid (1.9%). Whilst returning over the straights of Dover, F/O R L Boe's tail gunner, Sgt H A Salkeld, saw another Halifax below and to port. Beneath the other aircraft he saw a Ju88. He instructed Boe to 'corkscrew port' and immediately rattled off 50 rounds at the intruder, which promptly disappeared. The British anti-aircraft gunners were obviously spooked by intruders, as when the crew of VR-R reached England, they were coned by searchlights. They had a few apprehensive moments, within which they managed to correctly identify themselves to the twitchy gunners by firing off the colours of the day.

Fortunately all of Middleton's crews returned unscathed, although some had to divert to Ford and Woolfox Lodge. The Ghost Squadron lost NA-T during this operation when it was hit by flak near to the target. Its pilot, Sgt K Hawthorn, managed to get the damaged Halifax back to the UK, but as it approached the Kent Coast it was realised that it would have to be abandoned. Hawthorn gave the order, and the crew, minus the mid-upper gunner Sgt J A McEwan, baled out. He was still inside the bomber when it crashed into a cemetery in Canterbury, and he has no known grave. A second 419 Halifax went missing during this raid. F/S H C Shepherd and his crew took off from Middleton at 16:06, and were homebound when they were hit by predicted flak near Bonn. Although the aircraft was badly damaged, Shepherd used all his skill to steer it away from danger and was able to reach Holland. The aircraft was becoming unflyable and so he had no choice but to give the abandon order. Everyone got out ok. Shepherd and four of the crew were captured and became POWs. The remaining three managed to evade capture.

Back at Middleton two days later, 419 carried out experiments on the mid-under gunner's blister. The gunner sat so far back in the fuselage that he did not enjoy the cabin heating provided for most of the forward crew. During very cold conditions, his oxygen mask tended to freeze up. Another area of the aircraft to suffer the same problems was the astro-dome on the top of the fuselage. Experiments were carried out to see if some kind of appliance could be fitted to change the airflow in the new type astro-dome.

On the 22nd, Berlin was the target for 17 Moose and 17 Ghost crews. This was their first involvement in the Battle of Berlin. The Command was sending its biggest force yet to the Big City, some 764 aircraft. This was made up of 469 Lancasters, 234 Halifaxes, 50 Stirlings and 11 Mosquitoes. Once again Berlin was completely cloud covered, but this did not prevent this raid becoming the most devastating attack on Berlin during the war. Both the marking and bombing was extremely accurate, resulting in a huge swathe of destruction, stretching from the city centre and westwards across the residential areas of the Tiergarten, 3 miles to the W/S/W, and Charlottenberg, 4.6 miles to the west.

In the city centre, the church of Kaiser-Wilhelm, situated on the main Kurfustendam, was badly damaged by a direct hit by just one bomb, which struck the tip of the church spire. The bomb took the upper part of the spire off, just like the top of an egg, it then fell into the church and exploded without disturbing the walls of the spire. Meanwhile, the adjoining church building was completely destroyed. Today, visitors to Berlin can see the spire, which was left black and charred just as it was after the raid. Now called the Kaiser Wilhelm Memorial, it stands next to a new and futuristic glass church built after the war.

The church was built by Franz Schwechten, in the Neo-romanesque style, on Kurfurstendamm (meaning road of Princes), Berlin's longest boulevard. Construction of the church, which was in honour of Emperor William the First, began in 1891, and was completed by 1895. After the war, it was decided to build a new church on the site, but the Berliners wanted to keep the old one in memory of those killed and injured in the city during the war. They had long since christened the remains of the old church 'Hollow Tooth', a name that lingers on to the present day. In 1961, the architect Emil Eiermann combined the old with the new, and built a new church side by side with the remains of the old one.

The new complex combines an octagonal church, a vestry and a 63m high bell tower. The bells toll every hour, and play a song written by Prince Louise Ferdinand.

The church itself has a great deal of glass in its construction. I worked in Berlin during the early 70s, and whilst there I took the opportunity to visit the church whilst walking in the sunshine down the Ku'damm. As I entered, I found that the pale red and blue light permeating into the interior provided a very reverend and calming ambiance. Outside, the blackened overbearing remains of the old church stood as a stark reminder of darker days.

Kaiser Willhelm memorial church, dedicated to all who lost their lives in Berlin in WWII. The light coloured structure at the very top of the spire is the copper lining as the outer stone was damaged by the bomb. The stone was stripped away after the war to prevent masonry falling onto the street. To the right can be seen the new glass church

Photo: by kind permission of Mongolo

Charlottenberg Castle was one of the other historic losses of the night, along with Berlin Zoo and a good part of the famous Unter-den-Linden. The Ministry of Weapons and Munitions and the Waffen SS Administrative College were also destroyed. At Spandau, the barracks of the Imperial Guard was another victim of the bombing, as were 5 factories belonging to the Siemans Electrical Group. That night, the management of the Alkett tank factory were questioning their recent move from the Ruhr as they found their works in tatters. The weather had been dry of late, and many firestorm areas developed. 2,000 people were killed, 500 when bombs made a hit on their shelter in the Wilmersdorf district, 1.3 miles southwest of the Tiergarten. Another shelter, located next to the Neukoln gasworks, received a direct hit from a stray bomber, killing 105 people in a huge explosion. This was some 2 miles southeast of Tempelhof airfield, over 5 miles southeast of the city centre. 3,000 houses and 23 industrial sites were destroyed and several thousand more were damaged. The number of those bombed out exceeded 175,000. After the raid 50,000 German soldiers (3 Army divisions) were diverted in to Berlin to assist in the aftermath. Next day, a German pilot reported seeing smoke from the still burning fires whilst flying at 19,000 feet. Due to the bad weather at their bases, many fighters were unable to take-off, and bomber losses sustained during this raid were comparatively light. In total, 26 aircraft were lost, 11 Lancasters, 5 Stirlings and 10 Halifaxes.

One of these was 419's VR-F, flown by Sgt W L Hunter on his 4th operation. Having taken off from Middleton at 16:33, this aircraft was shot down by a night fighter. It crashed two and half-hours later near Diever, 11 miles northwest of Hoogeveen, Holland. All on board were killed. The average age of the crew was just 20. The youngest member of the crew was the engineer, Sgt W B Jones, who, at 18, was also one of the youngest Canadian airmen killed during 1943. The tail gunner, F/S J A Lesage had been with 419 for 9 months and was on his 26th Op. He was not part of the normal crew, and was only standing-in as the regular tail gunner was sick.

VR-R had R/T trouble and made an early return, as did VR-T, having suffered severe icing. VR-Y returned early due to a faulty intercom system and with its tail guns U/S. This trio was joined soon after by VR-W, due to a petrol filler cap being left off one of its tanks.

One of the Ghost Squadron's aircraft, flown by F/O 'Suds' Sutherland, was hit by flak, fortunately without injury to the crew. They were able to return safely. Less fortunate was the crew of NA-D, flown by 428's Sgt J M Jacob. This aircraft came down at Scherenbostel, 10 miles north of the center of Hannover, with the loss of all on board. The remaining aircraft bombed successfully and returned safely to base.

The missing petrol cap was a groundcrew problem, but turn-backs had been few and far between up to this point. After this raid, an investigation into the sudden increase of turn-backs was initiated by W/C Pleasance. He and his section heads carried out searching questioning of crews in an attempt to get to the bottom of the growing problem. After the inquiry, certain recommendations were made with the expectation that it would reduce the number of turn-backs. Amongst these were that all guns were to be tested on the dispersal point, prior to marshalling for a raid, and the practice of testing the guns over the sea whilst en-route was to be discontinued.

For the Short Stirlings, this was their last bombing operation over Germany. With increasing numbers of Hallys and Lancs coming into service, the type was being withdrawn from front line bombing missions over the Fatherland.

The next day was a stand-down and this was put to good use. Aircrew from both squadrons were lectured by G/C Saerby DSO DFC of the PFF on 'Pathfinder Techniques'. During his talk he also highlighted some of the difficulties which had been confronted by the Pathfinder Force. Over at 428, its Flight Commanders and Section Leaders held a conference with the squadron CO to decide on a crest, motto and name for the squadron. On the 24th, a lecture on PFF techniques was given by Group Captain Enersham. Some of 428's NCOs were late for the start, and so the Station Commander, G/C Ross ordered a parade of all aircrew to take place at 08:30 the following morning. Next morning it was very cold and damp, but still the parade was held. Everyone was sent along the perimeter track on the double to warm up.

Frankfurt on the 25th was the venue for 32 crews, an equal number being sent by each squadron. There were no turn-backs. The raid itself was disappointing. Cloud covered the target and the bombing was scattered. Out of the 262 aircraft taking part, only about 100 managed to hit the city. Although there were no planned diversionary raids at first, the German fighter controller was unsure whether the target was Mannheim or Frankfurt. Soon he correctly stuck his money on Frankfurt and advised the fighters accordingly. The flak was also restricted to 15,000 feet. Having bombed the target, all Moose crews returned safely, but for some of them the operation was not without incident. VR-T's crew caught site of a fighter who was moving in for the kill, but managed to shake it off before its pilot could attack.

VR-E, flown by W/O J R Morrison, was attacked by two Ju88s working together as a team, as it left the target area. Quick action by the bomber's tail gunner Sgt J H Lynk ensured that the skipper could take evasive action. As Morrison began corkscrewing, Lynk opened up on one of the fighters as it closed to between 50 to 100 yards. His tracer was seen to enter the cockpit area of the Ju88, which then went out of control and went into a dive. A second attack followed shortly after, and when Lynk opened up, only one of his guns fired, the other three had suffered stoppages. His call to Morrison had come in time, and again his skipper began to corkscrew. Morrison's evasive action again saved the Halifax from destruction as the fighter's rounds passed safely by. The fighter was shaken off but 35 minutes later they were attacked again. It is not clear if it was the same Ju88, but this time Lynk suffered a stoppage in the fourth gun. He could only sit-back and instruct his skipper to take evasive action again. For a third time Morrison corkscrewed; the Halifax took on the appearance of a sitting duck, but as the fighter made a single pass, for some reason the pilot did not fire. The Ju88 continued on its way and disappeared into the cloud. A further attack ensued ten minutes later. It began with fighter flares being dropped above the Halifax, after which a Ju88 came in for another non-firing pass and was gone.

The crew of VR-Y were on the way into the target area. The first that the tail gunner, Sgt O R Lee knew of the impending danger was when he saw tracer from a fighter dead astern. There had been no warning from the aircraft's Monica system, but Lee's eagle eye and quick response saved the day. He shouted instructions into the intercom for the pilot, Sgt G M Scade to break to starboard. After Scade had complied, Lee asked him to resume course as the tracer had stopped. Scade however, dropped the nose and allowed the right turn to develop into a spiral dive. By the time he recovered from the dive, the Halifax had lost 10,000 feet, and only then did they resume course.

One hour and ten minutes later, whilst on the way home, the Monica squeaked, warning the gunners of an aircraft on their tail. A fighter hove into view with its navigation lights burning. Again Lee gave a warning to the skipper, who began corkscrewing. The fighter pilot was experienced and decided not to play the bomber's game. He remained about 600 yards off the Halifax's starboard quarter whilst Scade carried out his evasive actions. Eventually the enemy pilot closed in to about 400 yards in preparation for the kill. Once again, Lee's evasive warnings resounded in his skipper's earphones. At the same time, he aimed a 125 round burst at the enemy aircraft, which at the same time opened up on the bomber. The fighter's rounds raked the Halifax. Most of the Perspex nose blister was blown away, and the bomb-aimer's seat was hit and Sgt J A Barlow was thrown back onto the step leading up to the cockpit. With the nose open to the elements, all the navigator's maps and charts were sucked out. It was impossible for the navigator, Sgt W R Dickinson RAF and Sgt Barlow to remain in their positions in the nose. The 200-mph freezing gale would have inflicted them with frostbite within minutes. They both quickly made their way back to the rest position at the main spar and took stock of the position. The instrument panel provided Scade with some small protection from the icy blast, but he still had his work cut out to maintain control. Along with the damage to the nose blister, he also had to contend with the other damage caused during the attack.

The rounds from the fighter had also removed the starboard undercarriage door and holed the port rudder, starboard wing and starboard inner's cowling. He elected to jettison the bomb-load and headed VR-Y for home. All the time, the fighter was sitting off at 600 yards, in his favorite position. Lee never took his eyes off the fighter, his fingers twitching on his gun triggers. He was ready for another attack, which he knew would only be a matter of time. Dickinson, sheltering from the blast on the floor behind the main spar, removed his glove and began searching in his trusty Nav bag for anything that he could use to get the stricken bomber home. Soon his hand brushed on something paper. Pulling the battered article out, he found that it was an old discarded navigation map. He set to work using what he had and gave Scade a preliminary course to steer. Still the fighter sat off their port quarter, like a leech that could not be shaken off.

As the bomber headed West, Scade periodically asked Lee if the fighter was still there, each time the answer was in the affirmative. Scade's reply was equally repetitive. 'Keep an eye on the bastard, and let me know straight away if he does anything.' The skipper realised that he had no need to worry about Lee or the rest of his crew being on the ball, they had as much to lose as he did. However, it helped him alleviate that nagging feeling brought about by the thought of the fighter just sitting there waiting his moment. Eventually the Halifax crossed the coast and flew out to sea. Having reached a position about 30 miles out, Scade received a call came from Lee. 'I've lost him skip, he's disappeared.' Seconds melted into minutes, all the time the crew expecting the fighter's tracer to come curving in at them, to deliver the final blow. Eventually, after what has seemed an eternity, the realization that the fighter must have given up on them slowly dawned. The fighter could have become low on fuel, or its pilot could have been vectored onto another plot. Either way, it did not return. But return VR-Y did, with its crew safely on board. Later, for displaying unusual skill and devotion to duty in spite of great personal discomfort, Scade and Dickinson would each receive the DFC. All of 419's aircraft returned safely, some to base, whilst others diverted to Marsden Moor, Wymswold and Dunsfold.

The Ghosts had a less happy ending to the night. F/S Pattinson's crew returned early, having been attacked by a fighter. Fortunately none of the crew were injured. S/L J R Beggs, the squadron's 'A' Flight Commander, and his crew failed to return. They had come under attack by a night fighter whilst at 19,000 feet over Frankfurt. During its first pass, the fighter hit the bomber's starboard inner, setting it on fire. The next pass killed Sgt P J Barske the bomb-aimer, and set the starboard outer on fire. The remainder of the crew were able to jump out and spent the remainder of the war as POWs. Sgt McMaster actually belonged to P/O Armour's crew. He had been flying as navigator with Beggs's crew, as their Nav, F/O Elliot, was in hospital with the flu.

Earlier that day W/C D W S Clark DFC assumed command of Croft. He would become the station's temporary commander for 8 days, until the arrival of G/C D Edwards on December 3rd.

The next night, nine Moose crews were detailed for a raid on Stuttgart. During the day, that number was increased by 4 as some of the aircraft diverted the previous night returned to Middleton. As the aircraft were taxiing out, VR-H had to return to dispersal, as one of its coolant radiators had sprung a leak. Another Halifax, VR-J, was already on its way back to dispersal with brake failure. VR-V returned early, as its mid-under gunner Sgt Fox had taken ill. Later he was admitted to SSQ with a severe case of flu. 428 had detailed 11 crews to take part in the evening's proceedings, but P/O Armour's aircraft remained behind, reducing this number to 10.

A total of 607 aircraft were prepared for war that night. The main target was Berlin, with Stuttgart as the diversionary. The force set the same course until they neared Frankfurt. Then the bomber stream split into two. 443 Lancasters and 7 Mosquitoes set course to Berlin some 263 miles to the northeast. The 157 Halifaxes and 21 Lancasters of the diversionary force turned S/S/E to fly the 93 miles to Stuttgart. The 14 Moose crews operating that night took part in the diversion raid. The German controllers got it wrong, and in the early stages convinced themselves that Frankfurt was the main target. They concentrated their main fighter force in the Frankfurt area. It is with some irony that this was the case, as they had their pick of the full 607 strong force. There were rich pickings for all, and several bombers were shot down as they passed Frankfurt.

By the time the main force reached Berlin they were well scattered. The markers missed the city centre and dropped their TIs about 7 miles to the northwest. Such was the size of Berlin that this meant that the bombs still fell within the city's boundaries. Tegal, 6 miles northwest of the city centre, saw some small amount of bombing. Siemensstadt, 6 miles to the W/N/W, with its many electrical factories, came in for some heavy bombing. Creep-back saw some bombs fall in the Reinickendorf district. This industrial area provided an unexpected windfall for Bomber Command. Some creep-back extended as far back as the city centre. Berlin Zoo was accidentally hit, and although many of the animals had been evacuated to safer parts of Germany, several wild animals were liberated by the bombing. These included jaguars, leopards and panthers, which were hunted down and shot. The flak over Berlin was as murderous as ever, but with most of the fighters elsewhere, it was less of a problem. However, the Berlin raid was to cost 28 Lancasters lost, with a further 14 crashing in England. Meanwhile, the diversion raid on Stuttgart had finished and the crews were on their way home. The bombing had been scattered and the crews had to contend with the fact that they had drawn off part of the fighter force from the Berlin crews. VR-Q had to land at Bradwell Bay, short of petrol. Six Halifaxes were lost over enemy territory (3.4%), one was from the Moose Squadron.

The crew of VR-N, flown by F/S S E Clark, had never reached the target. No real details of their fate were ever learned. It is thought that their aircraft fell near Sankt Ingbert, 6 miles northeast of Saarbrucken. They were all killed. We do know something about them though, their average age was just 20.

Fate dealt an even more cruel blow to the Ghost Squadron. F/S R M Buck and his crew were returning to Middleton, and came within 2 miles of home when their aircraft, JN966, was in collision with a Lancaster Mk III, ED417, which was one of several 103 Squadron aircraft diverted to Middleton and Croft that night. Both aircraft crashed 2 miles northeast of the airfield near Urlay Nook. The only survivor out of both crews was Sgt S T Bowyer, the mid-upper gunner from the 103 Squadron aircraft, which was based at Elsham Wolds. This aircraft was flown by F/O R W Brevitt. F/S Buck had received permission to land, and was down to about 200 feet on finals when he was hit by F/O Brevitt's Lancaster. Brevitt, who did not have permission, had also tried to land. The 103 Squadron aircraft was one of 5 lost that night. The only one to land without injury to its crew had diverted to Croft, where the badly damaged Lancaster was found to be beyond economical repair. It was eventually struck off charge on December 17th.

Ironically, it would eventually find itself a few yards from Urlay Nook, the resting-place of its sister ship that had collided with 428's Halifax. Urlay Nook was the place where crashed and written off aircraft went to die. There were two sites in England where these aircraft were taken during and after the war. One was at Cowley, Birmingham, called No.1 site, which took crashed and written off aircraft that ended up south of a line crossing the country. No.2 site was the Nuffield site at Urlay Nook, near Eaglescliffe, which took care of aircraft north of the line. Urlay Nook, which was built and organized by the Nuffield organization,[101] had its own railway siding, and like No.1 site, had teams of people who stripped every useful component off the aircraft, leaving only the aluminium to be smelted down in its furnaces. The ingots were then sent back to be reformed into aluminium from which more aircraft would be made. The ferric components (steel), like undercarriage

---

101 Named after Lord Nuffield the industrialist

oleo legs and the like, were dumped in local quarries to rot. Even enemy aircraft went through the process, they weren't fussy. Today we would call it re-cycling. When the war was over, thousands of surplus aircraft were 're-cycled' at these two sites. Some were brand new and had just been rolled out of the factory, but had come too late for the war.

Once Urlay Nook had completed its work at the end of the 40s, half of it was used as a Royal Naval Stores Base. During the late 70s, it was parted down the middle, with the naval base on one side and the remaining unwanted strip-down pads on the other. Today this section is still fenced off and used as a nature reserve. Nothing remains of the aircraft. Most of the buildings used at the time have been pulled down, only the odd brick hut can be seen. However, from the air, on final approach to Teesside Airport, if one's careful, one can still see the layout of the strip-down pads, all lying like a pack of cards in a game of patience.

They tell me that after the war, it was heartbreaking to see fields of Lancasters, Whitleys, Stirlings, Wellingtons, Halifaxes, and even Spitfires, along with many other types of unwanted aircraft, just waiting for the scrap man. Fortunes were made between 1945 and the early 50s, when these beautiful aircraft came under the hands of the Philistines. They would turn up and lower the undercarriage so the aircraft would sink onto the ground. Usually one of its wings would rise to the sky whilst the other fell to the ground as it tipped over. A bulldozer would then use this wing as a ramp and climb on top, its weight breaking the back of the once proud aircraft. It would then be cut up, and mobile smelters would reduce the aluminium scrap to a more manageable size, ready for transportation. Today, our museums are without a single Whitley or Stirling. Both were the backbone of the Allied struggle against German tyranny. The only example of a Halifax is at Elvington, near York. It had to be remanufactured as a one-off by dedicated and very skillful people, using bits found all over the UK and Europe. Fortunately, the wings were similar to those found on the Handley Page Hastings post war transport aircraft. This allowed the Halifax, named 'Friday the 13th', to be completed.

On August the 31st 1977, the author, as a young RAF Flying Officer, had the unenviable task of recovering the only large bits of Stirling Bomber left in Britain. A request had been received from Ken Hunter, the curator of the RAF Museum at Hendon. Could we recover the remains of Stirling LK488 from the top of Mickle Fell, near Barnard Castle? This lonely place is slap on the border between Co Durham and Cumbria. Located 2,300 feet above sea level, its inhospitable terrain had protected the Stirling from recovery for over 30 years. LK 488 was made by The Austin Motor Company at Longbridge and delivered to No. 6 MU on January 22nd 1944. It was one of a batch of 42 Stirlings serialised LK-479-LK-521. It reached Wratting Comon during June 1944 having been stored at 6 MU since its delivery from Longbridge.

The aircraft had crashed in the early hours of October 19th 1944 after taking off from Wratting Common, Cambridgeshire, with a fresher crew on board, six from the Royal New Zealand Air Force and one from the RAF, (The pilot). This was the crew's final triangular cross-country training flight before being posted to an operational squadron and was supposed to take them to York, Hexham and back to base. Having passed York, the crew became lost in low cloud. The captain climbed, and whilst trying to maintaining the correct course for Hexam, crashed, just 30 feet short of the summit of Mickle Fell about midnight. Sadly, Mickle Fell is the highest peak in the area, another 30 feet and the crew could well have made it. One wing was torn off during the initial impact, after which the aircraft summersault over the summit. There was only a small fire as the Stirling was by now low on fuel.

The sole survivor was Sgt Alan Small RNZAF, the tail gunner. He had sustained severe injuries as his turret broke free during the first impact and somersaulted over the summit onto the other side. Amongst the horrific injuries he sustained were two broken legs, and some ribs, along with skull damage and several other fractured bones and lacerations. He proceeded to crawl around the crash site in the glow of the small fires, checking on his fellow crewmen, none were alive. A light caught his eye in the valley below and he set off in the dark towards it, crawling in great pain as he went. Eventually, many hours later, despite having to cross the fast flowing and rocky River Tees, he reached Burkdale Farmhouse. Knocking on the door he raised the farmer from his sleep, he then collapsed at the door. He was taken to the RAF Hospital at Northallerton and was able to recover. At the time of the recovery of LK488, Sgt Small was alive and well in his native New Zealand.

Personnel from No.60 MU removed the bodies and as removal would have been impossible at the time, due to the height and remoteness of the crash site, the aircraft was broken into smaller pieces.

After the war, each time an aircraft went missing, the wrecked Stirling would be spotted and misidentified as the one they were looking for. Because of this, the RAF returned to the site and broke the aircraft up into even smaller parts and the mighty Hercules engines were rolled into natural sump holes and shell craters.

It was the author's job to head the team to recover these parts, as it was hoped to undertake a rebuild of the aircraft, up to display standards anyway. To make a long story a bit shorter, we managed, with the aid of local Air Cadets from Darlington and Stockton, and two 33 squadron RAF Puma HC1 helicopters from the JATE team at Odiham. The Helicopters were based at RAF Catterick during the operation, one was a spare, whilst F/L Holloway in Puma XW213CK carried out the recovery work.

Previously, since the 6th of December 1976 and over the winter and spring months of 1977, we trekked the two and a half miles up above the snowline each weekend to the summit of Mickle Fell. The area is a restricted danger area use by the British Army for munitions training, often of the heavy caliber type. Local Air Cadets from 405 and 266 squadrons and RAF volunteers formed the main nucleus of the recovery team. As most of the cadets were still attending school during the week this left only long weekends for the work to be carried out. This involved camping on the summit from Friday until Sunday, often in snow, very strong winds or rain. Navigation from the valley floor to the summit was usually undertaken in cloud (thick fog) and one could not see more than a foot or two ahead. This on occasion required the use of a hand held compass, as no visual navigation clues were available. Once there we made camp and began to manhandle the sometimes large and heavy pieces of wreckage onto the only flat bit of ground available. For the best part we encountered atrocious weather. Several times we reached a point half way up when thigh deep snow prevented us from going any further and we had to turn back. However, preparation work was completed in July of 1975. When the lift operation began on the 31st of August the wreckage was again manhandled, this time into cargo nets, which were slung under the Pumas and flown to a site located two miles away on the Brough road. Here, two Queen Marys[102] supplied by RAF Stafford, were parked. The hovering Pumas then carefully lowered several loads of Stirling components onto the Queen Marys trailers. The Puma flew many trips over the two days. For the most of the time the weather was unkind and low cloud forced the operation to be halted on more than one occasion. However most of LK488's remains were recovered before the weather really closed in and curtailed the operation. Some of the loads recovered included two wing and two main fuselage/tail sections, along with the 4 Hercules engines and many other smaller sections of the aircraft. They eventually found their way to the RAF Museum at Hendon, via RAF Catterick. During the 80s, the parts were moved to the large airship hangers at Cardington near Bedford for storage. Today, somewhat late, an organization has been formed to attempt a rebuild, incorporating parts recovered from abroad. How much simpler it would have been at the time for the powers that be to have saved a couple of each aircraft types from the scrap man. Oh for foresight, or even better, a time machine.

Due to bad weather, the remainder of November 1943 saw no further operations for either squadron. Colds and flu abounded, there was mud and water everywhere. The groundcrews however, were busy carrying out overdue servicing on several aircraft. These included VR-J, which had its port outer changed, whilst VR-R and VR-W each had an engine block replaced due to over-heating.

*The author assists air cadets from 405 and 266 squadrons to move wreckage to the helicopter
pick up site. Ably assisted by the wife: shown on the right hand side of the picture,
who came along for the helicopter ride*   Photo: Author

---

102 Long trailers constructed tubular steel designed for the transportation of aircraft. The wings were removed and stacked each side of the fuselage.

December 1943

On December 1st, 14 Moose and 13 Ghost crews were detailed for another bash at the Big City. Everything was prepared, but when only 15 minutes from take off time, their departure was postponed until 23:30 hours. Due to bad weather, the squadrons had only carried out 7 operations during November, and again it would have the last word, for at 22:45 and 23:40 respectively, operations for both squadrons were scrubbed. The next night saw a change of target when 14 Moose crews were briefed for Leipzig. The briefing was undertaken by S/L Dyer, as W/C Pleasance had been hospitalised. S/L Dyer's first attempt at briefing the squadron was well received by the crews, who offered compliments on his concise delivery and full coverage of the operation. 428 had prepared 13 aircraft for the same raid. This time, things progressed a little further, and at the appropriate hour, the aircraft were marshalled and given clearance to take off. However, the first of 419's Halifaxes were hardly airborne when again the scrubbed signal for both squadrons was received.

Earlier that day, those navigators not detailed for the evening's raid were given training on Gee, whilst at the same time the wireless operators received a lecture by the Signals Leader, F/L Brown, on the intricacies of the H2S radar equipment. In keeping with this, a great deal of time was also spent in the W/T Training Section, setting up demonstration tables. Not to be outdone, those air gunners not warned for that night's Op carried out training in skeet shooting and aircraft recognition. Later that day they also gained experience on the spotlight trainer and air firing.

On the 3rd, both squadrons attempted to have another go at Leipzig. Again crews were briefed for a 23:30 take-off. The cloud was 2,000 feet thick with its base at 5,000 feet. Moderate airframe icing was encountered on the way to the target. VR-D, flown by F/S Parker, had to return early as his port undercarriage leg would not fully retract. Soon after, another aircraft flown, by F/O Byford, was forced to return prematurely when heavy icing jammed the rear turret.

A similar fate befell P/O Hamilton's crew when ice began to block the engine coolant radiators, causing the Merlins to overheat. One engine had to be feathered as it was in immediate danger of catching fire. Whilst still about 20 minutes from the target, P/O Metheral's Halifax also suffered overheating and the engineer had to feather the starboard inner. As the aircraft was then unable to maintain height, the temptation to jettison something was irresistible, however, showing great determination, he and his crew pressed on to the target with their full bomb-load. By the time they reached Leipzig, they were on their own and down to 13,000 feet. The other 526 aircraft in the stream had already bombed and turned for home. They were to be the last aircraft to land back at Goosepool, and arrived back an hour after the first returning Halifax. For his devotion to duty, P/O Metheral, who was one of 428's most experienced captains, was put forward for an immediate DFC. 428's only other noteworthy event that night was when Sgt Gay's crew landed at Mildenhall with a duff engine.

The only Moose aircraft to take hits had been VR-Q, flown by F/S McLeod. Q-Queen had suffered flak damage to one of its wings, an engine cowling was also damaged along with the oil tank. The aircraft was able to make it back however, and the crew landed without further incident at Wratting Common All 26 of Middleton's crews returned safely from this raid, which turned out to be the most successful against Leipzig during the war. The PFF dropped their markers in the usual Wanganui fashion and the bombs followed suit. One of the noteworthy buildings to be badly hit was the pre-war World Fair Exhibition site. This had been pressed into service and used as factories, turning out materials for the German war effort. A Junkers aircraft factory was housed in the largest of the exhibition buildings, and it, like the other surrounding buildings which made up the complex, was severely disrupted. The planned route out to Leipzig was a direct one, direct to Berlin that is. The idea was to head for Berlin and then turn for Leipzig at the last moment, thus keeping the fighter controllers guessing. This ruse worked well, especially as a decoy raid on Berlin was being carried out by a small force of RAF Mosquitoes. Some of the fighters were in the outbound bomber stream, and although some successes were scored against the bombers, they were soon diverted to Berlin once the Mosquitoes began to bomb. By then the stream had turned towards Leipzig, where few fighters presented themselves to the bomber crews. The big problems came on the southern return leg, when many of the bombers strayed into the defended areas surrounding Frankfurt. Out of the 24 aircraft lost during the Leipzig raid, over half were lost there.

During this raid, 619 out of Woodhall Spa in Lincolnshire had been one of the squadrons taking part. One of their aircraft carried a VIP in the form of Ed Murrow, the famous American wartime news broadcaster and celebrity. Quite a brave thing for a civilian newsman to do, considering that only the night before, two reporters who went along on a raid to Berlin had failed to return. Both men had flown in Lancasters belonging to 460 (Australian) Squadron, based at Binbrook, Lincolnshire.

Out of the 25 aircraft it sent to Berlin the previous night, 460 lost five. One, flown by P/O J H English RAAF, carried Mr. N Stockton, a reporter for the Sydney Sun. Their Lancaster exploded when hit by a fighter. Although 3 of the crew baled out and became POWs, P/O English, 3 of his crew and 40 year old Mr. Stockton were killed. They are all buried in Berlin's 1939-1945 War Cemetery. The second reporter was aboard another 406 Lancaster, flown by F/O A R Mitchell RAAF. Captain J M Grieg, a Norwegian war correspondent for the Daily Mail, and all of the crew were killed when the aircraft crashed near Doberitz. Although 4 of the crew are buried in the Berlin 1939-1945 War Cemetery, Cpt Grieg and the other 3 members of the crew have no known graves.

Due to the inclement weather and various other considerations, the Leipzig raid would be the last for some 17 days. The time was not wasted however, and much training was carried out by both squadrons. Navigators underwent a considerable amount of Gee training and instruction on air navigation. The signals section had their own training programme, and took the time off to hone their procedures in signals and operations. Meanwhile, 18 gunners set off for the ground ranges at Sutton Bank[103] for a turret firing detail. Some of the crews headed off for Thornaby swimming baths to carry out wet dingy drill. Crew navigation lectures were commenced and these were followed by security lectures. Over at the armament

---

[103] East of Thirsk in North Yorkshire, Sutton Bank in the Cleveland Hills is today the home of a Gliding Club

section, practice bombing up was carried out with the new 4-lb incendiary cluster projectile.

On Monday the 6th, it was decided by the Moosemen to organize a POW cigarette fund. The idea was to send cigarettes to ex-419 personnel who had become POWs. It was hoped that 500 fags[104] could be sent to each prisoner at 3-month intervals.

As a further 18 gunners departed for Sutton Bank, the engineers were treated to a lengthy discussion relating to the intricacies of the Merlin XXII engine. On the same day, some considerable amusement was caused in the Armament Section by the arrival of an Acceptance and Inspection Sheets for the Armament Officer's signature, in regard to the inspection of the station 2-seater Tiger Moth light aircraft. This had given rise to the rumour that it was intended to arm elementary training aircraft with hand grenades for the opening of the second front. It may be added that the Intelligence Section went on to quickly squash this rumour.

A football match between the Armaments Section and the Station I & R Electrical Section resulted in the Leckies (electricians) winning 11 to 1. It was noted that the only casualty during the match was the armourers goal-keeper, who suffered a strained back from having to pick the ball out of the back of the net so often.

Word came through that, as from this date, the airfield would be unfit for flying until at least December 14th, as I quote 428's records book as stating, 'The runways are undergoing repairs by the "Wonders and Blunders" boys.'

Training continued, with a special talk being given to the gunners by S/L Dyer, the main subject being 'Gunner co-operation with the pilot.' Meanwhile, F/L Hall, the Moose Squadron's Engineering Leader departed to attend the Initial Engineer Leader's Course. By the 8th, it was the beginning of the full-moon period, and so 8 crews were sent on leave. They joined a further 9 crews already on leave. Special navigation training was initiated for the bomb-aimers during the morning, whilst in the afternoon, pilots, navigators and bomb-aimers were shown a special film on H2S equipment. At the same time a special crew arrived from Topcliffe to carry out tail modifications to all Moose Halifaxes.

431 and 434 - Tholthorpe to Croft

At 09:00 hours the same day, preparations were underway at Tholthorpe, 12 miles N/N/E of York, for the departure by road of an advance party of 431 Squadron RCAF personnel, under the command of W/C W F M Newson DFC. They would be leaving for their new home at Croft. Led by F/L Valentine, the party consisted of 3 Officers, 8 Senior NCOs and 28 other ranks. Next day, a 40-strong convoy of lorries left Tholthorpe for Croft, carrying all the squadron's heavy equipment. The main rail party, under the command of the Adjutant, F/L Walker, was paraded at 08:20 in preparation for their departure. All personnel, both air and groundcrew, were marched the 3 miles to Raskelf Railway Station for the trip to Croft. The train departed at 09:20, and by 11:15 the party, having arrived at and marched from Cowton Railway Station, reached Croft. An air party, consisting of 13 aircraft led by S/L Higgins, the 'A' Flight Commander, departed Tholthorpe for Croft. 431 had been at Tholthorpe since July 15th 1943, having previously operated out of Burn, Yorkshire.

On the 11th, 434 also left Tholthorpe, in similar circumstances to 431. The air party, consisting of 16 aircraft under the command of W/C C E Harris, departed for Croft after playing the 'How close to the control tower can I fly without hitting it' game. On arrival, the squadron recorded that Croft was even more widely dispersed than Tholthorpe, and in some respects not so far advanced. Also, it was noted that contractor's workmen were everywhere, and wet sticky mud was much in evidence. The next day, Croft's Station Commander, G/C Edwards AFC held a conference with both Squadron Commanders and their Adjutants to sort out any problems arising. Two days later the bombs arrived at Croft Railway Station.

The following morning individual crew navigation training continued at Goosepool and engineers were given special training in Astro Navigation. During the next couple of days, crews from both squadrons took off for Topcliffe to continue their radar training. This was necessary as Middleton's runways were in an unsatisfactory state and were still undergoing repairs by the contractors. By the 10th, the writing was on the wall that the Moosemen would shortly be converting onto Lancasters. Both squadron air and groundcrew expressed their reservations about the difficulties involved in changing over without an actual conversion course. These concerns were tempered the next day with the arrival of the Airborne Lifeboat Demonstration Unit and great interest was shown by the crews.

Due to the work being carried out on Middleton's runways, the Ghosts sent five of their newest crews over to Croft on the 11th to take part in operations. Unfortunately their efforts were in vain and the operation was scrubbed at 01:00. The crews were returning to Goosepool when the truck they were travelling in swerved to avoid other traffic. Several aircrew members were thrown off and received cuts and scratches although none were hurt too badly.

On December 12th, two Canadian built Lancaster Xs landed at Middleton. One was none other than The Ruhr Express, KB 700. At the controls was 419's very own F/S Parker, who had been attached to 405 Squadron for eight days whilst he gained instruction on the Lancaster. Both aircraft had been provided for 419's conversion on to type, and all sections wasted no time in showing a great interest in the new arrivals. Soon after, the three crews dispatched to complete their radar training returned from Topcliffe.

A grand party was thrown in the Officers' Mess by 428 on the evening of the 13th to celebrate the promotion of Flying Officers Lord, Watkins and Murphy to the rank of Acting Flight Lieutenant. Not to be outdone, P/O Brown also celebrated his promotion to temporary Flying Officer.

By the 14th, the conversion of Goosepool's squadrons to the new Bomber Command Servicing Unit had been completed. All that remained to be done was the actual posting of the various bodies to HQ Wing, I & R and the Servicing Echelons.

104 English slang for cigarettes

KB700, the RCAF flagship, complete with dual controls. Note the mid-under gun position   Photo: courtesy of the Canadian Forces

Although the groundcrews were attached to squadrons, for the purpose of pay and administration they now belonged to a designated service echelon. Meanwhile, not much stirred as Goosepool's inhabitants continued to endure the fog and mist, not to mention the mud and water.

That evening a meeting was held by members of 419 who had been on the squadron's strength during the period when Moose Fulton had been in command. At the meeting it was decided to form a 'Moose Club', eligibility for membership being confined to those who had, at any time, served with 419. It was agreed that a dinner would be held a month hence, on January 12th. This date was chosen, as it was the 2nd anniversary of the squadron's first operational flight. A committee was formed to handle the details of the dinner. It was also decided that only those personnel who had been on the squadron's strength at that date should be invited, together with some special guests. It was anticipated that, during the meeting, a constitution of the club would be drawn up, and officers elected during the course of the dinner.

And still the stand-downs continued. crew and gee training went on however, along with dinghy drill at Thornaby baths and turret firing at Sutton Bank. On the 16th, a demonstration was given to all of 419's aircrew on the new incendiary clusters; this took place on open ground behind the bomb dump. And still the foul December weather grounded everything, it seemed to go on and on.

The Vale of York and its airfields was, as usual, the only area to suffer. Linton-on-Ouse, 9 miles northwest of York and only 32 miles to the south of Middleton, was clear as usual. Both of Linton's squadrons operating to Berlin that night would however, between them lose 6 aircraft. During the morning of the 18th, Teesside's weather finally relented, and 27 of Goosepool's crews were detailed for a raid on Leverkusen. However, this was later scrubbed during briefing. Next day, two crews were detailed to carry out air-tests. VR-R, flown by S/L J G Stewart, was carrying out a practice three-engined approach. There was a tricky crosswind, and as Stewart tried to overshoot, the Halifax bounced and the crosswind took it and it crash-landed away from the runway. The undercarriage was carried away as it hit the ground and the aircraft received category E damage. Fortunately the crew were unhurt. Also during the day, the Ghost's Flight Engineering Leader P/O Oakley took a jump in promotion and became acting Flight lieutenant.   Finally, on the 20th, both of Goosepool's squadrons briefed 14 crews each for a trip to Frankfurt, whilst at Croft 431 and 434 put up 11 and 15 respectively. Due to the bad weather, this was the first raid for Croft's new squadrons since arriving.

Despite two early returns by Moose aircraft, the remainder reached the target and bombed successfully. The 650 strong bomber force was plotted by the Germans as it left the English Coast and all the way to Frankfurt. A diversionary raid to Mannheim failed to have any effect in drawing the fighters away until after the main attack. However, it did allow the returning bombers a quieter ride home. The PFF unexpectedly found 8/10ths-cloud cover over the target and were unable to carry out their originally planned ground marking technique. Dummy TIs and a decoy fire some 5 miles southeast of the target claimed some of Frankfurt's bombs, but the inevitable creep-back alleviated the problem somewhat. At the time, it was thought that the raid was a bit of a flop. Most of 419's returning crews stated that the marking was not particularly good. However, 466 houses were destroyed and a further 1,948 badly damaged. Frankfurt itself came in for some effective bombing, as did its southern district of Sachsenhousen, located to the south of the river Main. Creep-back ensured that the district of Offenbach on the city's eastern outskirts was badly effected. Some bombs even fell on Mainz, some 17 miles to the west of Frankfurt, and all points along the waterfront in between. In all, Frankfurt saw 23,000 people bombed out, whilst surprisingly only 64 lost their lives, although later, a further 111 were found to be missing or still buried by rubble. Damage to the industrial sections of the city was light, however the city's hospital, library and cathedral were hit, along with 69 schools. Someone had a go at a train, which had stopped some 6 miles south of Frankfurt. Thirteen people were killed when a 4,000-lb Cookie hit it.

Out of the 650 aircraft taking part, 41 were lost (6.3%). Although all Moose Squadron aircraft returned safely to base, the Ghost's bad luck continued. Of the two Halifaxes to be lost by 428 that night, the first, NA-P EB252, flown by P/O W J Armour DFC RAAF, had left Middleton at 16:00 hours. No information relating to the cause of its loss is known. Only the navigator, F/O J D Elliot survived. The remainder of the 8-man crew are buried in Rheinberg War Cemetery. Joe Armour is described as one of the best types ever from 'Down Under' and was sorely missed by the entire squadron. Johnny Elliot was not the crew's regular navigator. He had been in hospital on 24/25th November, when his normal crew, flown by S/L Beggs, was shot down during the Frankfurt raid. His place had been taken on that raid by Armour's Nav, F/S McMaster, who failed to return.

Left to right, back row: F/O Ken Mosher, RCAF; Sgt J Slater, RAF; Sgt T Dagnall, RAF; Sgt G Kensall RAF; Front row: Sgt G Jessimen RCAF; F/Sgt J Keighan RCAF POW; W/02 EL Tycoles RCAF   Photo: by kind permission of Elmer's brother, Fred Tycoles

Flight Sergeant J L Keighan's crew in NA-B LK928 took off from Middleton at 16:14, and crashed at Glees, 25 km northwest of Koblenz, some 68 miles northwest of the target area. Only Flight Sergeants Keighhan and Elmer L Tycoles RCAF survived the crash and became POWs. They were taken to Reserve Lager Maria Loast. Sadly, Flight Sergeant Tycoles died on the December 24th, whilst in captivity. Those that died were initially buried at Glees on December 27th. They now rest in the Rheinberg War Cemetery. This had been a mixed crew, 4 being RCAF and 3 RAF.

Croft, or more particularly 434, lost Halifax Mk V, IP-N LK970, flown by P/O A W G Austin and crew. Fortunately all survived to become POWs. Sadly, W/O W R Ferrier, flying IP-L LK686 on the second trip of his second tour, was killed, along with the rest of his crew, when they crashed into the sea off the Dutch Coast. Only two bodies were recovered.

On the 21st, flying was cancelled, due to heavy rain and strong winds. The riggers however, listened intently whilst Sgt Richardson of the Air Ministry completed a series of lectures on the Lancaster Xs airframe. Meanwhile, Sgt Kane, who was I/C 419's Squadron Stores, returned from RAF Wyton after studying their system of stores procedures for Lancaster spares. As the Moosemen readied themselves for the arrival of their new mount, further preparations were underway. Engineering publications for the Lancaster X and its Merlin engines were arriving in increasing numbers.

On the 22nd, aircraft from both of Middleton's squadrons departed for a Bullseye exercise. Along for the ride were 8 officers from the local searchlight and ack-ack groups. Unfortunately the exercise had to be cut short, due to enemy intruders who were seen hanging about. Next morning the crews were warned of a raid to take place that evening. By noon it had been cancelled. At Goosepool, Christmas Eve was marked with a stand-down during the afternoon. The lads over at Croft were not so lucky. 431 was detailed for a 12 aircraft gardening sortie, and had to ask Middleton for a loan of some special slings to load up their mines, as they were short of them. All returned safe.

During the day, Croft put on a party in the Y Club[105] for about 50 children, some local kids and evacuees. The party, organized by the Y Club representative, Mr Kirk Bell, started at 15:00, and after their sandwiches and cake, the kids were entertained with several Mickey Mouse Films. A fully decorated Christmas tree had been set up in the corner. Father Christmas duly arrived to distribute a gift of toys and sweets to each child. There was nothing special organized for Christmas Eve, but to quote Croft's ORB, 'After a merry start to the evening in the various Messes, most departed the camp for the bright lights of Darlington and the Croft Spa Hotel. Christmas Day saw the usual festivities, with the traditional Christmas Dinner being served in the Airmen's Mess at 12:30 by the officers. They had their turn when their Christmas Dinner was served in the Officers' Mess at 14:30. When they had completed their fare, they served the Mess staff with their Christmas Dinner.

Group Captain Ross, in white chef's attire, leads Goosepool's officers to airmen's mess to serve the traditional Christmas lunch. December 1943. Note Halifax Mk II on airfield   Photo: PRO

[105] YMCA Club

W/C Newson of 431, and several other officers from the squadron, visited the station hospital, to distribute cigarettes and chocolates to the patients. Christmas Dinner, Sergeants' Mess style, was served at 18:00 hours, with the remainder of the evening being enjoyed as only members of a Sergeants' Mess know how.

Christmas 1943 was a most enjoyable event, but 428 were warned of a raid on the morning of Boxing Day. Fortunately, the Telex chattered 15 minutes later, and much to everyone's satisfaction, Ops were scrubbed. No operations were called until the 27th, when 8 crews from each of Middleton's squadrons were warned for a gardening trip This was later scrubbed. During this period, many radar (H2S) training flights were carried out by both squadrons. Over at Croft, 431's commander, W/C Newson, took pen to paper on the 27th to thank His Worship, Bruce Whiteside, the Mayor of Simcoe, Ontario, for the kindness shown by the people of the town in adopting the squadron.

Meanwhile, it had been found that the extremely damp weather was having an adverse effect on the Moosemen's flying clothing. Their locker room was damp, and therefore so was the clothing. To alleviate the problem, drastic measures were called for. An improvised drying system had to be developed. Next door was the bomb-aimers' instruction room, and this was pressed into service when operations were imminent. The Moosemen's flying clothing was hung on lines and a heater van was backed up to the window. A hose was passed through the window, and the heat turned on until both room and clothing were dry.

 On the 29/30th, Berlin was the venue for 17 of 419's Halifaxes, led by W/C French. A further 16 were sent by 428, 13 by 431, and 14 by 434. The latter squadron nearly lost one of its aircraft whilst it was at its dispersal when a can of incendiaries fell off its bomb racks. Having been warned of the situation by the groundcrew, the pilot, Sgt W McQueen was on the ball and quickly started two of the engines, which allowed him to taxi the aircraft out of harms way. His quick thinking certainly saved the aircraft from serious damage, and prevented any possible injury to his crew. In the end, all 14 of 434's aircraft were able to take off. 419's VR-B, flown by P/O D T Cook and crew, returned early with its port inner U/S and the associated hydraulic problems that went with it.

The raid itself was carried out by 712 aircraft, 20 of which were lost, 11 Lancs and 9 Hallys. One of these was VR-Y, flown by F/S R L Thompson. Having taken off from Goosepool at 16:48, and on reaching the general vicinity of Berlin, the port outer lost power and eventually burst into flames. The flames began to spread along the port wing, and soon the inner engine was engulfed also. Thompson gave the order to jump; his crew did not need a second telling. Although Y-Yoke was to become the Moosemen's only operational loss during December 1943, its crew survived to become POWs. All remaining Moose aircraft managed to return to base, with the exception of the two that diverted to Coltishall. The Ghost Squadron contingent reported a good trip and all returned safely.

431 lost 13 good men when two of their aircraft failed to return. The first was SE-A LK659 flown by F/O J N Nelson. Little is known of its demise, only that it must have been shot down in the target area, as all 7 members of the crew now rest in Berlin's 1939-1945 War Cemetery. The second aircraft, LK701, flown by F/O G E Bishop and crew, had only one survivor, Sgt N Boffin, when it crashed near Hannover.

Two of 434's Halifaxes had close calls. With his engineer Sgt Bostock dead and most of his crew injured, P/O R A Pratt somehow managed to wrestle his badly damaged aircraft back to land at Woodbridge. F/L BP (Barney) Keenan's aircraft was hit by 4 accurate heavy flak bursts over Hannover. The petrol tanks were hit, as were the hydraulic system and the radios. Barney managed to set the damaged aircraft down on its wheels at Croft, after stalling the aircraft and shaking the undercarriage down prior to turning onto final approach.

The raid itself had a long approach route via the south of the Ruhr and on to Leipzig. A diversionary route by Mosquitoes confused the German controllers and bad weather on the outbound route determined that fighter opposition over the target was minimal. Berlin was cloud covered and sky markers were required. The east of the city received the most of the bombs and 10,000 people were bombed out.182 people were killed and 600 injured.

On the last day of the year, 14 crews from each squadron were warned for a raid on Frankfurt, which was scrubbed one hour before take-off. The crews were out of their kit post-haste, and wasted no time in preparing for the New Year's festivities. The New Year Party organized for the Officers Mess had been cancelled when word of the night's operation had been received. Fortunately, this was quickly resurrected, in plenty of time for it to take place. A good time was had by all and they prepared to toast-in 1944. All Canadian members of Goosepool's Officers' Mess (and for that matter, the whole of 6 Group) raised their glasses and drank to the toast, 'That hoped and wished that the next New Year's Eve party would be celebrated back in God's country – Canada.'

CHAPTER EIGHT

Goosepool War Diaries 1944.
January – 1944.
February – 1944.
Relegated.
March – 1944.
April – 1944.
May – 1944.
June - 1944.
Walter Poynter.
Andrew Mynarski.
July – 1944.
August – 1944.
The Road to Goosepool.
September – 1944.
October – 1944.
November – 1944.
December – 1944.

Goosepool War Diaries 1944

January 1944

January 1944 began for 419 when they sent 12 of their Halifaxes gardening to Brest on the night of the 4/5th. They were joined by 6 Ghost aircraft. It had been four months since 419 had last done any mining trips. Only ten Moose aircraft managed to carry out the operation to the Cinnamon Area, which was in the area of La Rochelle. They utilised the northern tip of the Isle d'Oleron for a radar fix, which allowed them to pinpoint the patch of garden they were looking for. All aircraft returned safely, without major encounters with flak or fighters. This included the two that were unable to reach the target. VR-P however, crash-landed at Glatton when it ran out of petrol. Fortunately none of the crew were injured. 428 tried out a new tactic during this operation, when the mines were dropped from 15,000 feet and cameras were used. The results were extremely good, with four from HQ 6 Group congratulated on the good show they put up.

For Middleton's crews, it was a matter of checking over the flights each evening to see if one was on the battle order for the next day. If one's name was posted on the board, it meant that one was available for operations. If one was not on the battle order, there would be training, either flying or lectures, or, if one was really lucky, it could mean a day off. If flying training was the order of the day, one would either do practice bombing, a cross-country navigation exercise or fighter affiliation. Fighter Affil usually meant simulated attacks by a Spitfire or Hurricane. This gave the bomber crew plenty of practice at corkscrewing.

Two nights later, both squadrons went gardening again, 419 to Brest (Jellyfish) and 428 to St Nazaire (Beech). The crew of VR-O, flown by F/S McIvor, had an encounter with a Me109 whilst running in to the drop point. Sharp use of the Mk 1 eyeball by the Halifax's tail gunner, Sgt Dujay, ensured that his skipper had a running commentary on the fighter's whereabouts. Canny corkscrewing by McIvor kept the fighter at bay. Dujay fired a burst towards the fighter from 400 yards, after which all 4 guns jammed. The fighter was again sighted by the vigilant gunner, just after the bomb run, and again evasive action followed Dujay's prompt warning. This time, the fighter did not return for a third helping and was shaken off. Some crews suffered the loss of their H2S and Gee equipment. The flak gunners popped at several of Goosepool's aircraft but the raid was deemed a success, and all returned safe. This included 428's F/O Brown and crew, who also managed to shake off a fighter attack.

On the 7th, 17 air gunners belonging to 419 set off for the ranges at Sutton Bank to carry out firing practice, whilst on the 12th they welcomed a new 'B' Flight Commander in the form of S/L Humber. The Moosemen filled the time with various training tasks. These included lectures on Lancaster systems and equipment for the pilots and the engineers.

Both of Goosepool's squadrons were then stood down for two weeks, mainly due to bad weather and the moon period.

The Vane Arms at Stockton was the venue on the 13th, when the inaugural dinner of the newly formed Moose Club was held. The evening was voted a huge success by the 115 original members of the squadron who had served under the leadership of the late W/C 'Moose' Fulton.

Strensall range near York was frequently used by many of 4 and 6 Group squadrons for bombing practice. 419 availed themselves of the range's facilities by sending two crews on the 15th to carry out bombing practice. On the 19th, the squadron's air gunners threw a dinner party in Darlington's Imperial Hotel.

Operations to Berlin on the 20/21st renewed Goosepool's efforts to smash the Fatherland. The Moosemen sent 15 Halifaxes to join the 15 offered by the Ghost Squadron, to bolster a force of 769 other Bomber Command aircraft also visiting the German capital that night. The deployment of a small diversion force, and the tactic of bringing the main force in from the north, failed to fool the German defences. The controllers employed their night fighters to good effect very early on. As the bombers turned for home they were still harassed by the fighters, back to and beyond the enemy coast. 428 had actually dispatched 16 aircraft, but icing and a little inexperience caused the fresher crew flown by F/S Gouthrean to return early. One Ghost aircraft that did not return was NA-P, flown by F/S F F Reain and crew. They had been shot down by flak. Sgt W R Wynveen, the mid-upper, was captured and became a POW. The remainder of Reain's crew managed to evade capture. The wireless operator, Sgt W T Banner, managed to reach neutral Switzerland.

Berlin was completely covered in cloud, therefore the bombers dropped their cargo onto skymarkers dropped by the pathfinders. H2S was used by the crews to confirm that the intended target, which was the eastern sector of the city, was indeed attacked. The PFF markers were well spread out along a line crossing the bombers path. Most crews chose to bomb the centre marker in the line to ensure sufficient saturation of the target.

Having taken off from Middleton, the crew of VR-M, one of 419's Hallys, struggled to gain height. After fifty-five minutes in the air, the crew were in the process of discussing why the thing was only at 5,000 feet when a loud bang was heard. After a thorough check of the airframe, it was discovered that the undercarriage had not fully retracted. The resultant drag was the main cause of the aircraft's poor climb rate. The pilot, F/S Hopkins cycled the undercarriage lever, down then up, but still the wheels would not fully retract. By the time they reached the Dutch coast they had barely reached 13,000 feet and could climb no higher. It was decided that if they were to continue with the operation it would be prudent to lose some weight. The most expendable weighty commodities were the incendiaries, nestling in the wing bays. These were duly jettisoned in the sea, allowing the Halifax to climb to the desired height of 20,000 feet. Berlin was reached without further ado and the bombs released. Having left the target area, the aircraft routed via a turning point near Leipzig. Just after turning onto a new heading, a fighter cut across their bows. The rear gunner, Sgt McCagey, then saw a fighter, possibly the same one, and shouted into the intercom, 'Corkscrew Starboard.' Hopkins immediately took evasive action, during which the starboard outer, which has earlier been giving cause for concern, caught fire. As yet, the fighter had not attacked the bomber and so was not to blame for the engine's demise. Although the prop was feathered and the fire put out, the flames must have been seen for miles. Soon after the engine fire was extinguished, a JU88 moved in from below and raked the bomber from stem to stern. The tail gunner gave the fighter a good burst of fire as it passed through the sights of his gun. Another attack began, and again the Hally took evasive action. Whilst this was taking place, the starboard inner, which had also been overheating, caught fire. There were also fires in the bomb bay and fuselage. During the attack, Hopkins was hit in the shoulder and leg. The undercarriage controls had also been hit and it was impossible to stop the wheels from lowering. This caused an inordinate amount of drag. Every bit of power was coaxed out of the remaining engines, but the Halifax was very difficult to handle, and could not maintain height. Hopkins gave the order to abandon the aircraft. All on board survived the bale-out and spent the remaining years of the war as POWs. Although the crew survived their encounter with the JU88, one crewmember, F/S MacKenzie, was to lose his life at the hands of the allies, just 29 days before V/E day. The column of prisoners he was marching in was strafed by Hawker Typhoons on the April 19th 1945, near Gresse, 30 miles E/S/E of Hamburg, and he was killed.

A second Halifax, VR-X, flown by P/O Bullis, lost the use of its H2S and Fishpond whilst over the Dutch Coast. The navigator W/O Towers reverted to old-fashioned eyeball and compass navigation with a little help from the Goon Box. When the aircraft reached the final turning point, some 60 miles N/W of Berlin, Towers was pleased to see the route markers dropped by the PFF glowing beneath the aircraft. With only twenty minutes to go to the target, F/S Potter saw a Me109 appear from a cloud directly astern and below the aircraft. His lips had no time to move before the fighter opened fire, killing the engineer F/S Fergusen, and injuring P/O Bullis, W/O Towers, and the bomb-aimer Tech Sgt Boisvert (USAAF). Potter was on the ball and blasted the fighter, which was seen to descend into the clouds on fire.

Potter had changed his helmet three times between the rally point south of Heligoland and the time the fighter attacked them. Ice accumulation on the mouthpiece of his oxygen mask had caused communications between the gunner and the rest of the crew to be periodically lost. The instrument panel had been shattered in the attack, as had the windscreen. The tailplane had also received hits, damaging the elevators and rudders. To make things worse, a fire started in the bomb bay and the bombs had to be jettisoned.

As they were now down to 6,000 feet, Bullis turned the aircraft around and headed west. Although he ordered the crew to prepare for a possible bale-out, he managed to hold the bomber under control. With many of his vital instruments shot to hell, he had great difficulty in holding his course, although he was able to gain a little height. In fact they were able to reach 18,000 feet when some 25 miles S/E of Hamburg. Whilst approaching Lauenburg, they were hit by predicted flak. Both port engines were set on fire and the mid-upper, Sgt Sanderson, was injured.

Bullis gave the order to abandon the aircraft. Boisvert, Towers, the wireless operator, Sgt Bonathan, and Potter baled out. Sanderson was badly injured and unable to get out, and so Bullis decided to ride the Halifax down and save the gunner. By now the port wing was well ablaze. Before Bullis could descend for a landing, the wing folded, and came off. With no possible chance to help Sanderson, Bullis, despite the injuries to his hip, reached the escape hatch and jumped. Sadly Sanderson died in the crash. The remaining five members of the crew became POWs.

Wing Commander Pleasance and his crew found themselves low on fuel on their return. This situation was made 100% no better when the port outer gave up on them. By the skin of their teeth, the Halifax's crew reached Woodbridge with only 30 gallons remaining. During the raid, the wireless operator of P/O Cook's aircraft heard what was thought to be an enemy radio operator transmitting a fake message. He was inviting the bomber stream to return to base at 16,000 feet, below the upper height limits of the flak. It was not thought that anyone fell for this one.

Three of 428's aircraft, I-Item, B-Beer and Y-York, flown by S/L C S Bartlett, S/L W A G McLeish and F/O Woolverton respectively, were badly damaged when they were attacked by fighters. Fortunately no one in any of the three crews were hurt, all three aircraft made it back.

The following night a carpet of layer cloud covered Magdeburg. The flak defences and fighter opposition was described as 'Fanatical'. Several aircraft were seen to be shot down by fighters, who had dispensed with their telltale tracer rounds. These aircraft simply exploded for no apparent reason. This new tactic made it harder for the tail gunners to spot the attacking fighters.

One of 419's Halifaxes, flown by F/S McNary, was hit by flak whilst near Wilhelmshaven. The port engine was damaged and caught fire. Although the fire was extinguished, this engine drove the vacuum pumps that operated the artificial horizon and other gyro driven instruments on the pilot's panel. Although the aircraft was turned for home, the crew's adventure was not over yet. Whilst the Halifax was departing the Friesian Islands on the way home, it was attacked by a rocket armed enemy night fighter. The Halifax's tail gunner, Sgt Sangster managed to see the fighter off and the aircraft returned safely.

F/S Hawkes and his crew in JD420 were approaching Bremen on the return journey when they were hit by predicted flak that burst close by. The nose section of the Halifax took some hits, injuring the navigator, F/S Fletcher in the stomach. The bomb aimer, F/O Hovison was also hit in the shoulder. The radio operator, W/O McDevitt, who was also in the nose, had escaped injury and went to Fletcher's aid. He quickly checked the unconscious navigator and pronounced to the skipper that he was dead. The port outer had failed and Hawks, who had been hit in the right arm, asked the engineer, Sgt Board, to feather the prop. The port inner was overheating, the 'temps' were off the clock and this engine, too, had to be feathered before it caught fire. When it was realised that the radio had been destroyed, it became obvious that the crew had to abandon the aircraft. The remaining crew baled out and became POWs. They included the mid-upper, Sgt Bowman, and the tail gunner W/O Barnes, who had only 4 more trips to do before being screened.

S/L Hamber and his crew had a close call when their Halifax was caught by predicted flak. Battered for several minutes, they returned to Goosepool to count the 85 holes punched in the aircraft. The crew counted themselves very lucky, many of the holes were in the fuel tanks, which fortunately were of the rubber self-sealing variety. The remainder of 419's bombers were diverted to Cambridgeshire on their return, with some landing at Wratting Common and the American bases of Lakenheath and Mildenhall. For P/O Metheral and crew, this would be their last raid for a while. They became the 19th crew to finish their tour and be screened since 419 had begun to operate the Halifax about a year before. Along with P/O Metheral, his crew, consisting of P/Os Chiswell, Marrit, and Mercier, F/Ss Kelsall and Edwards, and Sgt Pollard would depart for a well-earned rest.

Having taken off from Middleton at 19:41, nothing further was heard from F/L Hermitage and his crew in JD466. Later it transpired that they had reached the target area, but no details are available as to why this aircraft crashed at Borne, 18 km S/S/W of Magdeburg. The crew were only on their second operation, sadly all were killed.

Of the Ghost Squadron's 10 aircraft taking part, one was a non-starter, whilst another returned early due to a sick bomb-aimer. F/S R E Terry's crew in NA-L was shot down over the target area by a night fighter. With the exception of Sgt S J Smith, the crew survived to become POWs. Sgt Smith the mid-upper was badly injured, and died two days later whilst being treated in a local hospital. He now rests in Berlin's 1939-1945 War Cemetery.

Having taken off from Middleton at 19:30, W/C French in NA-D bombed the primary from 19,000 feet at 23:02. He found the target partially covered with about 3/10ths cloud, which was estimated to be at about 5,000 feet. The first set of TIs were wrongly placed, but these were soon corrected. Zero hour had been 23:00, and just a little after that, two lines of incendiaries were seen burning, one to the southwest and another to the S/S/W of the AP. When leaving the target, French's crew were able to see a great deal of tracer fire covering the area. They was surprised at this, as they had seen little tracer whilst over the target itself. On the way home, the tail gunner was able to see Magdeburg burning through the clouds when they were 100 miles away.

The main problem for the 648 bombers who were operating that night was the development of the German night fighter tactics, code-named Tame Boar. The German fighter controllers had realised that Bomber Command's planners were using more and more spoof and diversionary tactics. Often, the intended target would only be revealed after the bomber stream had flown a series of dogleg courses.

One example of this took place on the previous night's raid to Berlin. The track of the bomber force had taken a wide swing to the north, before suddenly turning south onto a short final approach to the target. This allowed the Germans little time to accumulate a tangible force of fighters to combat the raid. This sort of tactics caused the Germans to employ much of its fighter force covering large areas of sky to cover all eventualities. This obviously depleted the effects that the fighters had on the bomber stream. For the bombers however, too much wandering about the sky meant using up lots of extra fuel, so compromises were inevitable, and these limited the effect of the spoofs.

Another problem was that it increased the time that the bombers were over enemy territory, which also increased the chances of being shot down. The German's answer to the spoofs and diversions was to meet the bomber streams as early as possible and mingle with them as they tracked towards the targets. The German listening posts tuned into the frequencies of the British bombers during the day of a raid, and could tell there was something brewing. As the air-tests were carried out, and later, when the formations assembled prior to departing for the continent, the ears of the Luftwaffe were wagging.

During the Magdeburg raid, the controllers had sent the night fighters out to sea, to mingle with the bombers as they approached the enemy coast. Then, when the bomber stream began to carry out their dogleg spoofs and diversions, they were already intermingled with the fighters. During the raid, Magdeburg was not immediately identified as the target. This did not really matter, as the fighters had already enjoyed many successes within the bomber stream, long before it reached German territory.

Due to stronger than forecast winds, some of the main bomber stream reached the target area ahead of the time that the PFF was supposed to mark the target. Rather than hang about to be shot down, the early birds decided to attack without waiting for the Pathfinders. The bombing was not accurate, and the fires they started, coupled with some very effective enemy decoy fires, meant that most of the bombs fell outside the city. Losses that night totalled 57 aircraft, 35 Halifaxes and 22 Lancasters, 8.8% of the 648 aircraft sent.

There was some excitement at Middleton on the 25th when word came through that one of the Ghost Squadron's Halifaxes was in a little spot of trouble. F/S Vallse was carrying out an air-test, when it was realised that his wheels would not lock down. Everyone came out of the woodwork to watch him crash-land the bomber on the grass alongside the main runway. When the dust settled, he and his crew clambered out, none the worse for wear. Amazingly the aircraft was not badly damaged, thanks to Vallse's flying skills, and after a wipe down with an oily rag (well almost), the Halifax was able to fly again.

For the next week, either bad weather or stand-downs gave Middleton's crews a respite from operations. This time was put to good use, and routine flying training was carried out on the squadron's Halifaxes. Several of 419's pilots were also converting onto Lancasters. F/L Hall, the Squadron Engineering Leader was also running parallel lectures for the groundcrews, relating to the Lanc's electrical and fuel systems.

For the aircrews, there was dinghy drill in one of the local baths, usually Darlington or Thornaby. This entailed climbing the 16 feet tall diving board, wearing ones flying clothing, Mae West and parachute harness. The 16-foot drop simulated the approximate speed at which one would hit the water if descending by parachute. Once in the water, it was a matter of removing one's harness, and inflating the Mae West. After that, one headed for the dinghy, which, if I remember correctly, always seemed to inflate upside down. There were straps around the perimeter and bottom of the dinghy, and these were pulled towards one, whilst pushing the bottom of the dinghy away with the feet or knees, hopefully inverting the dinghy so one could climb aboard. This was anything but fun in the sea during a gale, and only slightly easier in the baths. Sometimes it took several goes to get the blessed thing the right way up.

A force of 515 Lancasters revisited Berlin on the night of the 27/28th. Middleton's Halifax crews were absent from this raid. It is interesting to note however, how the tactics of both the Germans and Bomber Command were being modified as they attempted to thwart each other. Apart from the huge force of Lancasters, which carried out the main assault on the German capital, other types of aircraft assisted in extensive diversionary operations. A force of 80 Wellingtons and Stirlings planted vegetables along the Dutch coast, whilst 21 Halifaxes did the same further north, near Heligoland (code word Eglantine). They were dispatched to draw the fighters away from the main force, and this they did with great effect.

Some of the German aircraft were sent over 75 miles out to sea, after the successes of the earlier raids. Again, they hoped to mingle with the bombers as they crossed the North Sea on their way eastwards to the Dutch coast. This time the diversionary tactics worked well. The Halifaxes sent to Heligoland attracted over half of the night fighters away from the main bomber stream. At the same time, 18 Mosquitoes dropped bogus fighter flares, whilst in another area, 12 more flew Serrate patrols. Other aircraft were employed in electronic counter measure sorties, to confuse the German fighter pilots and their controllers. Altogether these 140 diversionary aircraft ensured that the intensity of the night fighter force was much less than of late. However, 33 Lancasters and 1 Stirling were lost. Although cloud covered the target, and sky markers had to be employed, the raid itself was deemed a success, although many bombs fell in the southern part of the city. 567 people were killed and a further 20,000 were bombed out. 50 industrial buildings were damaged and several vital factories producing war materials were badly damaged.

The following night, the preparations were even more elaborate. To begin with, 5 hours prior to the main operation, 63 Stirlings, supported by 4 Pathfinder Halifaxes[106], went gardening in Kiel Bay. An hour later, 6 Mosquitoes bombed Berlin, whilst 18 more attacked the night fighter bases at Venlo on the Dutch/German border, Deelen, 15 miles N/W of Cologne, and Leeuwarden in Northern Holland. Four Mosquitoes carried out a diversionary raid on Hannover, and 6 more undertook Serrate[107] patrols whilst the main raid was taking place.

To augment the diversionary tactics carried out by these units, the main bomber force of 677 aircraft approached Berlin from a route that took them via Northern Denmark. This was too far north for most of the fighters, who did not have the pre-warning, or the fuel, to reach such a northern latitude in time. The fighter controller did guess the bomber's intentions however, and was able to concentrate a large number of fighters over the target. Many of the 46 aircraft lost that night fell in the target area.

For a refreshing change, for the bombers at least, there was only partial cloud cover. Bomber Command claimed that this raid was the most concentrated attack of the period. The main concentrations of bombing were to the southern and western areas of the city centre. Also hit were 77 areas outside the city. 180,000 people were bombed out. There were many huge explosions, showing that the bombers had found their mark. The new Reichs Chancellery was amongst the many buildings hit, along with 4 theatres, 5 embassies, 6 hospitals, the State Patent Office and the French Cathedral. Although the Germans described the casualties as considerable, the recording system for the city was in disarray, and therefore no accurate figures of casualties are available. Returning crews stated at de-briefing that they had observed the glow of the burning city from as far away as 250 miles.

That night, Bomber Command lost 6.8% of the total force dispatched. These consisted of 20 Lancasters and 26 Halifaxes. Halifax VR-O JP119, flown by F/S Palmer of 419, was one of the 14 Goosepool Halifaxes detailed to take part in this raid. His was amongst the 46 aircraft lost that night when it was shot down near Zuhlen, 47 miles N/W of Berlin. All on board were killed.

Throughout January, the number of groundcrew personnel posted in to Goosepool had reached 200. They were required for the Station Servicing Wing, and 419's Echelon. For this reason, 419's groundcrew were reduced to about 240.

---

[106] This was the first time the PFF assisted a minelaying operation
[107] Radio jamming counter measures

February 1944

Flight Sergeant McLeod carried out his first Lancaster solo flight on February 1st. His mount was KB700. On the 3rd, the Ghosts detailed 11 crews for a gardening trip to Radishes (Kiel), from which all returned. They were off again the next day, this time to La Rochelle. Again, a good trip without incidents was reported by the returning crews.

419 flew KB700 down to 20 MU on the 5th for an overhaul. A store was set up at Middleton on the 8th to cater for the large numbers of Lancaster spares, which had begun to arrive. Later that night, the Ghosts sent six aircraft on a gardening operation to Oslo (Onions). All the aircraft reached the target, but one returned with its mines, due to electrical failure. Two more, one of which was damaged by flak, returned on three engines.

The next day, 428 bade farewell to S/L C S (Chris) Bartlett, O/C 'B' Flight, who was to assume the rank of Acting Wing Commander and depart for Croft, where he was to take up post as C/O of 434. He was a very popular officer, and was sorely missed by all on the squadron. He was replaced by F/L F R McGugan, who was promoted to Acting Squadron Leader. F/L C E Murphy was moved up to become deputy 'B' Flight Commander. He took this post from F/L F G Lord, who was to become 'A' Flight Commander.

On the 11th eight Ghost crews were detailed for another mining operation, this time to Brest. All crews reached the target, mined and returned safe.

NA-C had been received from Leeming, or rather had been dumped on 428. This Halifax was clapped out, and was no sooner at Middleton then it was deemed unserviceable, taken off flying duties and scrapped. 428's engineering officer was not well chuffed to have been palmed off with this lump of unwanted flying junk.

Six aircraft belonging to 419 were sent on a gardening mission to Borkum in the Friesian Islands on the night of the 12th. VR-R, flown by F/L Laidlaw and his crew, was lost without trace. One of the crew, Sgt Ashton, had been awarded an immediate DFM on September 28th 1943, after his prompt actions helped save the aircraft he was flying in during a raid on Monchengladbach. The other 5 aircraft returned safely. The same night, a Halifax was lost in the Cheviot Hills, north of Newcastle, and it was thought at the time that this might have been VR-R. Aircraft were dispatched from Middleton the next day to search for the missing Halifax, but the weather closed in and the search had to be abandoned. Two cars of personnel were sent from Middleton to the area in the hopes of finding the crash site, but their search was unsuccessful due to low cloud. It later transpired that the aircraft was not VR-R, whose fate is currently unknown. All members of the crew are commemorated on the Runnymede Memorial.

Berlin was the target for 891 Bomber Command aircraft on the night of February 15th/16th. 419 contributed 15 Halifaxes, the Ghosts 16. This was the largest bomber force sent to Berlin thus far. It consisted of 561 Lancasters, 314 Halifaxes and 16 Mosquitoes. The number of sorties for the night including diversionary aircraft totalled 1,070. 26 Lancasters and 17 Halifaxes were lost.

The German controllers plotted the bombers soon after they left the English Coast, and decided that the long trek to Denmark was not worth it and ordered the fighters to head for Berlin. A diversionary raid by 24 Lancasters of 8 Group to Frankfurt-on-Oder was uninterrupted by fighters, they weren't falling for that one. During this raid, 147 buildings were damaged and 59 people were killed or injured. Oboe equipped Mosquitoes were out in force, they attacked 5 night fighter bases in Holland. Berlin was covered in cloud for most of the raid but this did not prevent 2,642 tons of bombs falling on targets in the centre and southwestern districts of the city. Over 1,000 houses and 526 temporary wooden barracks were destroyed. Many civilians had fled the city after the battle of Berlin had started. On this occasion the number of dead and wounded was disproportionate to the huge damage inflicted on buildings and industrial premises. Despite the huge size of the city, only 196 civilians, 34 service personnel, 9 air raid workers, 80 foreign workers and 1 POW were killed. A further 260 civilians were buried alive. It is unclear how many of these, if any were dug out alive. This raid was the penultimate Battle of Berlin raid of the series.

The fighters were ordered to remain clear and to leave the city for the flak gunners. This order however, was not complied with by all of the fighter pilots. Several bombers were attacked by the fighters whilst over the target area. The flak was described unanimously by returning crews as intense.

Halifax VR-B, flown by P/O Parker, was lost in the Baltic. All on board were killed. F/S Donald's body was recovered from the sea on the 17th, whilst the tide brought in Sgt H T Raine to Mommark on the 21st. He is buried in Abenra Cemetery, whilst F/S Donald and F/S Fornier lie in Magleby Churchyard on the island of Langeland, their resting-places some 28 miles apart, separated by the cold waters of the Baltic. The remainder of the crew have no known graves.

The remaining aircraft were diverted to Bury-St-Edmunds, where they became guests of the USAAF. Most crews had by now realised that it was better to 'accidentally' divert to an American base, rather than an RAF one. It wasn't for the fact that the RAF's food was often austere, and in meagre supply, you understand. Nor was it that the American's 'Have as much as you can eat' policy had anything to do with it. It certainly wasn't because the Americans did not suffer from rationing, or that they had ice cream and other wonderful things like that, which were unavailable in a war-torn and rationed England. The superb American hospitality received by the crews did not play any part what-so-ever in their decision to divert to an American base. Not much it didn't!

The American's tendency not to stock spare parts for British aircraft often meant a protracted stay at these USAAF bases. This forced the RAF and Commonwealth crews to have to patiently wait for the RAF groundcrews to arrive and repair their shot up aircraft. Meanwhile they had to endure the luxuries and opulence of life on the American bases.

Back at Goosepool, because most of its aircraft were diverted, 419 were asked to make their two remaining aircraft available for another large raid on Berlin. This was finally scrubbed, due to the weather. The next day, the two available aircraft were again requested for Berlin, only to be scrubbed again. On the third day, it was more of the same, as the raid was scrubbed due to bad weather over the target.

During the late afternoon, the aircraft diverted to Bury-St-Edmunds were able to find a break in the weather and return to Middleton, minus VR-W, which had magneto trouble. When 419's diverted crews finally returned to Goosepool, they asked that a letter be sent to the C/O of Bury-St-Edmunds air base, thanking all concerned for the exceptional treatment and hospitality they had received during their stay.

Fifteen of 419's aircraft and 14 from 428 were detailed to visit Leipzig on February 19/20th. This raid employed 823 aircraft of Bomber Command, consisting of 561 Lancasters, 255 Halifaxes and 7 Mosquitoes. This raid was to have a devastating effect on Bomber Command. They were to lose 78 aircraft, 44 Lancasters and 34 Halifaxes. These losses amounted to 9.5% of the total bomber force. So bad were the effects of this raid, that Harris permanently withdrew all Halifax Mk II and V aircraft (Merlin water-cooled) from further operations. A gardening diversion to Kiel Bay by 45 Stirlings and 4 Pathfinder Halifaxes encouraged the fighter controller to send part of his night fighter force to intercept them. Night fighter airfields were attacked by 16 Oboe carrying Mosquitoes, whilst a diversionary raid to Berlin employed 15 more, losing one of their number in the process. 12 Serrate patrols completed the diversionary tactics for the night.

The main bomber force was met at the Dutch Coast by the majority of the fighters. Once the main force had been identified, the fighters sent north to Kiel were recalled. The fighters hounded the bomber force all the way to the target. Stronger than forecast winds caused Middleton's bombers to gain between 30 and 45 minutes en-route to the target. This caused them (and most of the other crews), to arrive ahead of the Pathfinders. Whilst they circled waiting for the PFF, 20 aircraft were shot down by flak, and 4 more were lost in collisions. The target was cloud covered and the PFF had to use sky markers. Once the raid got underway, the bombing was concentrated but it soon became scattered.

Despite having to take evasive action to avoid two separate fighter attacks, VR-A LW327 had reached the last turning point, which was Stendal, 85 miles N/N/E of the target. F/L Lucas, like most of the other captains, realised he was early and flew a series of doglegs to waste time. Suddenly there were several fighter flares surrounding his aircraft. Seconds later they were hit by cannon fire and the port wing tanks burst into flames. Sgt Dehoux the tail gunner and Sgt Newbery the mid-under gunner were dead. A fire was raging behind the pilot near the engineer's position. Sgt Herriot the engineer tried to put the fire out, but was unable to do so. Lucas gave the order to bale out and the aircraft was quickly abandoned. The navigator, F/O Davis, baled out with the remaining 5 crewmembers, but for some unknown reason he was killed. It is possible that his parachute may not have opened. Lucas landed at Gorzke, 4 miles S/W of Brandenburg. Herriot reported that he walked around for 2 days trying to get someone to capture him. A second Moose aircraft, VR-V JD114 disappeared without trace, its crew, who were flown by F/S Macleod, are commemorated on the Runnymede Memorial.

The Ghosts suffered 2 early returns and the loss of F/O A W Woolverton and his crew. They had crashed off the coast of Andijk, in the cold waters of the Ijsselmeer, all on board perished.

F/O W V Blake's crew, who had taken-off at 23:43, suffered no less than 11 sightings or attacks by fighters, one of which was at 01:37 and occurred before they had even reached the enemy coast. The second came whilst near Grenengen some 30 minutes later. In both cases, no damage was inflicted on the Halifax. On reaching Celle at 03:02, predicted flak shot off half of the starboard rudder and cut the intercom to W/O J T Houston in the rear turret. The mid-upper and tail turrets were put out of action and both suffered damage to their oxygen systems. The port tyre was punctured and the undercarriage also received damage. Numerous holes were also punched in the fuselage skin. This was followed immediately by an attack by a Fw190, but no damage was inflicted. Two minutes later, they were attacked again by an unseen enemy aircraft that blew a 1-foot diameter hole in the starboard side of the fuselage, and caused further damage to the oxygen and intercom systems. At 03:30, they were attacked by another fighter, but suffered no further damage. Blake pressed on and the bomb-aimer F/O W D Watt managed to bomb.

Although the aircraft had received considerable damage, the navigator F/O N A Bell was able to provide a course for home and the aircraft was able to return to base. During the attacks, the tail gunner W/O Houston was wounded in the shoulder. Despite damage to his oxygen and intercom systems, he continued to give his captain evasive action directions by way of light signals. On their return to Middleton, both Blake and Houston were recommended for a decoration. Blake received word on February 29th that he was to be awarded the DFC, Houston's came on March 10th.

After less than two hours airborne, F/S S Side, on his way out in NA-N, had reached 20,000 feet and was still over the sea, his position some 35 miles short of Texel. His Halifax was unable to climb through cloud due to carburettor icing (which caused the carbs to supply an excessively rich mixture to the engines). He instructed his bomb-aimer F/O A H Murphy to jettison the bomb-load, after which he turned for home. On his return, he and his crew reported that many other aircraft had also encountered carb icing, they had seen at least 16 other aircraft that had also threw the towel in and turned for home.

W/O M G Forsberg's crew also arrived at Leipzig early, and had to fly east of the last leg and return via a reciprocal course to waste time. They also diverted 8 miles whilst out to sea, and again near their turning point at Oldeburg, and still they arrived early. Having left Goosepool at 23:11, they eventually bombed at 04:05 from 23,000 feet. Noting the indicated airspeed as 150 mph and checking their course as 219° magnetic, the bomb-aimer F/O M E Talmage pressed the tit and watched his bombs fall towards the 10/10ths cloud cover, which was estimated to have its tops at 9,000 feet. Over the target, they had found an exceptional amount of sky-markers, which were mixed with exploding flak. Due to the thickness of the cloud, no one was able to record the results of the bombing.

Such is the way of aerial warfare, that P/O N F Brown's crew estimated the tops of the cloud cover as being 15,000 feet. Having bombed the sky-markers from 22,000 feet, their tail gunner, Sgt T Hawthorn, was able to clearly see the glow of the burning target as they left for home.

F/S G W Lillico's crew were late on target, due to having to swan about wasting time in order to avoid arriving early. They thought they had done a good job at that and had corrected their time error, when they were delayed by two encounters with searchlight batteries and four more with fighters. After all their efforts they eventually reached the target late but were able to bomb using H2S to confirm the position of the sky-markers, which were the correct green with red stars.

This raid was to be the last Halifax bombing operation over Germany for 419 squadron. In light of the directive issued by Bomber Command that Halifax Mk IIs and Mk Vs would no longer be sent to targets in Germany, it was heard that they were to be classified as second line aircraft. As second line Halifax squadrons they were still allowed to attack Maritime targets and those not in Germany.

Relegated

Five Ghost crews flew to Graveley on the 21st, to ferry back Halifaxes transferred from 35 Pathfinder Squadron. Also during the day, the issue of the ribbon for the Canadian Volunteer Service Medal and Maple Leaf Clasp started on the squadron. That night, ten of 428's crews took part in a gardening operation to the La Rochelle area.

Next day, twelve more were warned for a mining operation. Unfortunately the take-off times were changed several times and eventually set very early. This resulted in the take-off time being due before the mines could be delivered to Goosepool. In the end, only five crews actually managed to have something to drop and were able to take-off.

With Bomber Command's directive, 419's role became one of marking gardening patches for the minelayers. This did not prevent losses however. F/O Warren and his crew in VR-G were detailed for mining Op to Kiel Bay on the night of February 25/26th. Having taken off from Middleton at 20:03, nothing further was heard from this aircraft. It was lost without trace; its crew are commemorated on the Runnymede Memorial. 428 sent nine crews the same night to drop marker flares for 3 Group Stirlings in the Koge area. They also went gardening in the Kiel area. P/O Kruss lost an engine close to the target due to flak and could not maintain height, there was no option but to turn back and return to base.

For several days, 419 had been trying to collect the Ruhr Express from 20 MU, where she had been overhauled. The weather had prevented the aircraft from returning to Middleton. On the 29th, a further attempt was tried but once again Darlington's weather had other ideas. Meanwhile Middleton's Station Commander was posted out to H.Q. No. 64 base. His post was taken by G/C Gordon, who had arrived from Tholthorpe.

By the end of February 1944, the number of Halifax IIs on charge with 419 had dropped to 13, the number of aircrew totalled 185.

March 1944

At the time, Bomber Command had a thing about enemy aircraft and aircraft component factories. On March 2/3rd, 419 and 428 sent 10 and 16 aircraft respectively to carry out a low-level raid on the old Potez aircraft factory at Meulan/Les Mureaux, N/W of Paris. Due to some scattered to broken cloud over the target area, and the fact that the Pathfinders were six minutes late, some of the bomb aimers had to do dummy runs. This of course left the French workers in little doubt as to the intended target and gave them time to head for the shelters before the bombing commenced. Fortunately there were no fighters. The attack was carried out from 6,000 feet. The marking was very accurate, and fell right amongst the factory buildings. The bombs followed suit and the whole operation was a milk run. W/C Pleasance observed that the red TIs could be clearly seen nestling in between the buildings. Four of the bombers brought back excellent bombing photographs, the factory and the Seine bathed in the light of the photoflashes. A similar report was filed by 428's commander, W/C French. Trips like this presented the greatest challenge for the bomber crews, although all of Goosepool's crews returned safely.

The next two nights saw both squadrons back on gardening duties, the first to the Geronne estuary and Giroude River (Bordeaux, code word Deodar) in southern France, the second to Brest. All aircraft returned safely. Much to the annoyance of 428's groundcrew, on the first raid, one of their aircraft, NA-U, became sick at the last moment. What was galling was that they had worked tirelessly all day, without meals or rest, to get two engines serviceable (including radiator changes). They had the job completed, and the kite at the marshalling point just 10 minutes before take-off time, then at the last moment another engine developed a mag drop and she couldn't go.

The operation to Brest was straightforward enough, with all crews returning safely. The only fly in the ointment was the usual Teesside weather, which covered the base with heavy snow and strong winds. Leeming on the other-hand, a whole 15 miles away, threw out the welcome mat and tucked the boys in for the night.

With three months to D-Day, Bomber Command were detailing targets designed to cause as much disruption for the Germans as possible. A Transportation Plan had been formulated, which it was hoped would prevent the reinforcement of enemy troops and equipment prior to and after D-Day. If the railway network could be severely disrupted, the Germans would have no alternative but to take to the roads. This would have the effect of delaying the re-deployment of troops and armour. The trains could move large numbers of tanks, troops and their equipment quickly to where they were needed most, regardless of the weather and road conditions. At the same time, the use of motor transport would cause a large logistical problem. Huge numbers of lorries were required. Coal and water for the railway engines were in plentiful supply, petrol was not. The Germans were already beginning to suffer fuel supply problems after the allies had targeted Axis oil fields and synthetic oil installations. After the lead up to D-Day, this situation was to get much worse.

To this end, on Friday March 6th, Goosepool briefed 27 crews to bomb the railway marshalling yards at Trappes, a suburb of Paris. Each aircraft carried 12,000-lbs of high explosives, (5.3 tons), a record for Middleton's aircraft at that time.

Now it was time again for the crews to attack precision targets such as marshalling yards, many of which were inside the boundaries of towns and cities. Bad enough if they were German towns, but during the run-up to D-Day, the majority were in occupied France. There were many different ways employed to warn the French civilians of an impending raid. Wherever possible, the French underground were informed of an impending raid and given the opportunity to spread the word. The bombers were often briefed to circle the area a few times giving everyone time to get to the shelters. This did not always work, and many French civilians were killed. The use of the newer Mk XIV bombsite increased bombing accuracy to a level undreamed of at the beginning of the bombing campaign. This had re-kindled the possibilities of precision bombing.

The Trappes raid began with good marking. Target indicators were dropped in the centre of the tracks, this led to a concentrated attack. The rails were easily visible in the light of the flares and photoflashes. Every single section of rail was cut, some in several places. Some fires were started in the target area, and the yard's electrical system and control tower was put out of action. The western exit of the complex took the brunt, and was deemed impassable by the end of the attack. The yards were put out of action for over a month. On their return the aircraft had to be diverted to Linton, with all crews remarking about the lack of flak and fighter opposition. Good aiming point photos were brought back by the crews of S/L Dyer, S/L Hamber, P/O Scade and F/S Krants, showing that the raid had been a huge success. All returned safely, but yet again, Middleton's welcome carpet had been whisked away by the weather. Only three managed to return to base, Linton was the closest the others could divert to.

This was the first of 18 raids on railway installations ultimately carried out by Middleton's aircraft. The next one came the following night, this time at Le Mans. Many crews arrived at the appropriate time, only to find broken cloud over the target area. Missing altogether were the Pathfinders. They did arrive eventually, some 12 minutes late, and began to mark the target. The cloud cover prevented the successes of the previous night, but some crews were able to bomb, although the results were hard to assess. In strict accordance with orders, rather than risk bombing French civilians, two crews brought their bombs home, as they were unable to see the markers with any degree of certainty. Again, flak and fighters were conspicuous by their absence.

On the 9th, G/C Gordon, who had been the new Station Commander of only 9 days, was admitted to Goosepool's SSQ with pneumonia. From here he was taken to the RAF Hospital at Northallerton, as he was seriously ill.

To date, March was looking like a record month. By the 10th, 428 had flown 69 sorties. Next day Middleton received a consignment of Perspex mid-under blisters, which had been shipped over from Croft. During the morning British Oxygen was phoned at Billingham, regarding moisture in the aircraft's oxygen. On Sunday March 12th, the attendance at the station church was not as good as normal, despite a very good address given by Padre Crees. The new Padre, F/L Coleman RCAF, was in attendance and read the lesson. That night, a special party was laid on for 428's groundcrew, who had excelled themselves in recent times and had ensured the maximum number of kites were serviceable for each raid. Meals and rests had been missed on several occasions to ensure that the maximum effort was achieved, over and above their normal high level of efficiency. The night's huge success was ensured by W/O Cauthier, who spent a great deal of time and effort in its preparation. He acted as Master of Ceremonies, whilst W/C French took the chair. French extended to the groundcrew the hearty thanks of the aircrew for their efforts, and the aircrew gave a toast to them. After the event it was decided that the party had done a great deal towards bringing all the sections together and should become an annual event.

Middleton's crews continued through March with more gardening raids and a revisit to Le Mans on Monday the 13th. This raid was a huge success and all returned safely. All except the crew of F/O Barclay that is. The short runway at Middleton, 19/01, was in use that night, and VR-Q was a bit reluctant to lift its 5-ton bomb load. As Barclay tried to coax the laden bomber off the deck, she ran out of runway and struck a concrete pillbox. Various bits departed the aircraft, including the tail wheel, mid-under blister, part of its bomb doors and the fin off one of the 1,000-lb bombs. The Halifax also sustained damage to its main undercarriage and its rudders. Somehow she got airborne, but it was decided not to continue with the operation and the bomb load was jettisoned in the designated area off Whitby. Returning to Middleton, Barclay attempted a crash landing, which resulted in the Halifax hitting an M/T vehicle and injuring the driver as it slid across the perimeter track. The crew escaped without injury.

On the 15th the Overseas Ice Hockey finals were played at Liverpool. Middleton won the game 9 – 5 against Welsbourn. The scorer's for Goosepool were Schmidt, who scored 2 goals, Toby Greer who also scored 2. Bauer, Plave, Fairservice, Smith and Vicary all scored 1 goal each.

That night, The marshalling yards at Amiens were the target for 14 Ghost and 11 Moose Halifaxes. A new searchlight belt was discovered during this operation and was duly plotted. Thick cloud prevented the observation of results but the operation was deemed to be successful.

The next day they went back and did it again. This raid was also very successful, and culminated in a huge explosion as an ammo train went up. Again all crews returned safe.

For some time, aircrew had been complaining about microphone failures. Mikes fitted inside the oxygen masks suffered condensation problems, which, apart from causing rust, had also caused several mike failures when the water got into the electrics. The matter was well known to Bomber Command, and on the 16th, word came through that 428's suggestion to fit thin rubber over the mike could be tried. When asked for the rubber, Bomber Command came back with the answer, 'Find some yourself.'

Next day, the Ghosts received 6 target tokens for the raid on Meulan-Les-Mureaux, which had taken place on March 2/3rd, and 11 more for the Trappes raid on the 6/7th.

In keeping with 419's conversion onto the Lancaster, flight engineers and bomb aimers were given time in the link trainer, so that if the pilot was incapacitated they could act as emergency second pilots. Arrangements were made on the 16th to remove three 419 Moose crews at a time from Halifax operations and train them to fly Lancasters. At the same time, F/L D C Hall, the Flight Engineer Leader, who had recently returned from Avro, gave each set of crews a three day course on the Lancaster's systems.

Gardening and marshalling yards continued to be the targets throughout March. On the 18/19th, ten Moose crews took part in a gardening operation to Heligoland (Rosemary). Four of the crews mined as normal, the other six acted as high level PFF markers for the raid. 428 contributed sixteen crews for the same operation, seven of which also acted as high level markers. Enemy action was slight, but VR-J had to return with its starboard inner U/S. The remainder returned safe.

On the 19th G/C Gordon was posted out to take up post with Overseas H.Q. He was replaced the same day by G/C F A Simpson, who had arrived from No.61 Base.

On the 21st, Middleton's crews were briefed for operations. All aircraft were marshalled and five actually took-off before the mission scrubbed signal was received. Group transmitted the wrong cancellation call sign to these aircraft. The mistake was only realised when the aircraft had been airborne for an hour and the correct call sign transmitted. By now, the crews (including 428's W/C French) were well on their way, and were not well chuffed when they eventually got the call to turn around and fly home.

On the night of the 22/23rd a mine-laying sortie to Kiel Bay cost 419 another Halifax. VR-W, flown by P/O Peck RCAF, had its port outer catch fire at 15,000 feet over the Danish Coast on its way to the target. The fire was extinguished and the prop feathered. P/O Peck RCAF, elected to continue with the sortie. After successfully planting their vegetables, the crew turned for base. They were 20 miles short of the halfway point on the way home when the port inner also caught fire. The engineer put out the fire and feathered the prop. With two engines out on the same wing, Peck was unable to maintain flying speed without lowering the nose slightly. The Halifax travelled on for a while, losing height as she went. Eventually, they were down to 5,000 feet, and it was realised that the aircraft was going nowhere. At 23:56, the wireless operator sent off an SOS, followed by a position report. They were within 50 miles of the English Coast when the ditching order came. Just 10 minutes after transmitting the SOS, they were safely in the water, having inflated the dinghy. Some time later the crew of a Lockheed Hudson out of Thornaby reached the position sent by the Halifax's wireless operator. They began to circle the area, looking for the dinghy, firing off Star Shells as they searched. Back in the dinghy, the Halifax crew saw the Star shells exploding in the distance, loaded the Very pistol and fired it into the air. The Hudson crew saw the flare from the dinghy and headed towards it. They located the downed crew and their Halifax, which was still floating near by. They began to circle the dinghy, dropping flame floats as they went. At the same time, the wireless operator in the Hudson transmitted back that they had located the aircraft and that its crew and had marked the exact location with flame floats. Once the dinghy was encircled by flame floats, the Hudson departed. At 03:30, a trawler hove into view, having been guided to the dinghy by the flame floats. The Halifax crew were duly rescued and safely returned to Middleton, but not before the trawler sank VR-W with its guns.

The Ghosts had briefed nineteen crews for this one. One was a non-starter, and F/L Kegan had to bring his Halifax back early with H2S failure. The remainder, led by W/C French, completed their gardening stint and returned safe.

Next day, the work to fit H2S to the Ruhr Express was completed. It had been thought that the Lancaster X's oversized bomb doors might have affected the efficiency of the H2S. After air trials, this was found not to be the case. The range in fact turned out to be very good.

That night, 428 sent eighteen aircraft to the marshalling yards at Laon, 25 miles N/W of Reims. The main operation was carried out by a total of 143 aircraft from 3, 4, 6 and 8 Groups. The weather was clear, but the PFF arrived late, and caused 428's aircraft to make a considerable number of dummy runs on the target. The marking was also considered to be slightly inaccurate, and therefore the operation was not really a success. The Master Bomber stopped the raid after only 72 of the aircraft had bombed. Half of the bombs dropped had hit the yards and several railway tracks were cut. The area around the station was hit and 83 houses were damaged. Fortunately, most of the people who lived by the station were in the habit of vacating their homes and moving to safer parts of the town after dark. Despite these measures, 7 civilians were killed and 9 more injured. The cut tracks were repaired the next day.

Interspersed with the gardening Ops were more visits to marshalling yards. Amongst the other railway-orientated venues attended by Goosepool's crews during the latter part of March was Aulnoye, 40 miles east of Cambrai, which was attacked on the 25/26th. VR-L, flown by P/O H C Eyjolfson, lost power in its port outer just after take-off at 18:28. He elected to proceed on track to the English Channel, where the port inner also lost power. The aircraft was headed for RAF Ford, Sussex, but overshot the runway and crashed into a ploughed field at 21:05 whilst trying to make an emergency landing. VR-L was written off and all members of the crew were slightly injured.

The following night, after using Snow-Go and blade ploughs on the runways and taxiways, an attack was carried out on the yards at Courtrai, Belgium, 16 miles N/N/E of Lille. W/C French led the sixteen Halifaxes of 428, whilst the Moose Squadron detailed thirteen. All returned safely after a very successful operation.

That day, 419 saw two of its crews graduate from F/L Hall's Lancaster course, having completed their ground training and soloing of the Lancaster. This paved the way for two more crews to begin their training on the Lancaster X. During the day, photographs were taken both inside and outside of the H2S installation fitted to the Ruhr Express. They were to be used for future fitment of H2S to the Mk X Lancaster.

During a raid on the 29/30th on the yards at Vaires, on the outskirts of Paris, 419 lost VR-A HR912 VR-F flown by W/O Greenidge RCAF. It is thought that this aircraft may have carried out an unsuccessful ditching in the English Channel. All on board were lost without trace and are commemorated on the Runnymede Memorial.

The last raid during March was to Heligoland on the 30/31st. The moon was very bright, and although several fighters were seen, no attacks were made, all returned safely.

419's aircraft strength at the end of March stood at 13 Halifax IIs and 5 Canadian built Lancaster Xs. Despite the reduction in the number of available operational aircraft, brought about by the change over to the Lancaster, March 1944 had seen 419 have its busiest month since June 1942. They carried out a total of 171 individual sorties, dropping 617 tons of HE, incendiaries and mines.

Operations for 428 were ordered on 22 days. Of these, 6 were scrubbed and 16 carried out, with no losses and no accidents. During the month they had marshalled 292 aircraft. 62 were scrubbed, 2 were non-starters and 4 were early returns. Due to 419's conversion onto the Lancaster, 428 carried out more sorties than 419, the total being 224.

April 1944

April saw 419 gardening around the Friesian Islands on the 1st, and Texel on the 8th. 428 suffered a series of scrubs and stand-downs. Both squadrons joined forces to attack the marshalling yards at Lille on the 9th. The following night there was more of the same, this time at Ghent, Belgium. This raid was carried out by an all-Canadian force of 122 aircraft.

On the 12/13th, both the Ghost and Moose squadrons sent five aircraft each on a gardening Op to the Heligoland Bight. All returned safe and elected to divert to the USAF base at Molesworth, near Huntingdon. Here once again they had to suffer the superb hospitality (and food) of the American Air Force.

On the 13th, the Ghosts went mining near Cherbourg. Earlier that day, the diverted crews bade farewell to their hosts at Molesworth and reluctantly headed for Middleton, where they arrived during the morning, just before the weather closed in again.

The weather during April was particularly bad, and a lull in operations was taken advantage of with Lancaster conversions and ground training. Operational status for 419's Lancasters was drawing closer, and so the armourers carried out bombing up practice. This involved winching up 4,000-lb HE Cookies into the Lancaster's cavernous bomb bay. Next day they tried it again, this time with the 8,000-lb variety. The armament section was pleasantly surprised at the ease in which the Lancaster could be bombed up. 419 were to be the first unit within Bomber Command to be equipped with Lancaster Xs.

428 sent 12 aircraft to mine in the Kiel area on the night of the 17/18th. Pilot Officer G W Lillico and his crew, flying Halifax NA-U, failed to return. They were lost without trace, and are commemorated on the Runnymede Memorial.

Gardening at Fakse Bay and Mecklenburg Bay in the Baltic the next night cost 419 P/O Quinn RCAF and his crew in Halifax JN973. Sgt Petrina RCAF was washed ashore months later, near to the radar station at Kryle, on August 22nd. He was buried the same day at Nysogn. P/O Quinn's body came ashore at Hense. He was buried on the August 31st at Esbjerg. The remainder of the crew have no known graves. The loss of this aircraft may have been caused by a night fighter.

On April 20/21st, Middleton's Halifaxes attacked the marshalling yards at Lens. This raid employed a Master Bomber, which would be the norm from this time on. During this raid, the Ghost Squadron lost Halifax JP113, flown by F/L C G Ford. This aircraft was badly damaged during an attack by a night fighter, and three crewmembers baled out as ordered. Ford managed to reach the East Anglian coast, and attempted a crash-landing at Attlebridge airfield, 8 miles northwest of Norwich, Norfolk. Ford, Sgt J W Carrigan, F/O B D Ardis and P/O A Shaw were injured. P/O Shaw died later from his injuries.

428 lost another of its crews during a mining operation against French ports the same night. S/L F R McGugan's crew in NA-O were at 20,000 feet over French waters when the starboard engine overheated and caught fire. An unsuccessful attempt was made to feather the prop, but the constant speed unit had failed and it continued to windmill. The windmilling increased to such an extent that the engine speed also increased, causing it to run away. This in turn caused the fire to increase. Meanwhile, height was lost, and the captain ordered the crew to abandon. All crewmembers baled out with the exception of S/L McGugan. The navigator F/O Steel was the last to leave the aircraft. As he jumped, he saw that S/L McGugan had left his seat, as though preparing to abandon. The aircraft finally crashed a mile northeast of Dielert Ladygrove Farm, near Didcot, Berkshire. S/L McGugan's body was found in the wreckage. The remainder of the crew survived the bale-out, with the exception of the bomb aimer, F/O G A England, whose body was found some miles from the crash scene. It appeared that his parachute had failed to open, its appearance was that of it bursting open on impact with the ground. Both S/L McGugan and F/O England were laid to rest in Brookwood Military Cemetery on the 27th.

At the same time, 419 was carrying out night cross-country training flights. Five aircraft taking part in this exercise found themselves approaching Hull at the same time as German target marker flares were going down for a raid on the city. The British anti-aircraft guns around Hull opening up on the German bombers persuaded the Moose crews to quickly vacate the area.

Two nights later, the marshalling yards at Laon resulted in 9 aircraft out of 181 being lost. One of these was flown by P/O Courtney of 635 Squadron. On board was the Master Bomber himself, W/C Cousens, who was killed. Another aircraft lost was 419's HX189, flown by F/O C A Thomas USAAF. The tail gunner, Sgt Knox, reported that there was an aircraft behind the Halifax. Seconds later, J-Jig was hit by cannon fire from a Ju88. Both port engines caught fire and the intercom went U/S. The order to abandon was given and the crew headed for the hatches. The Halifax crashed at Couvron-et-Aumencourt. It was thought that Sgt Knox may have been killed in the attack, or was so badly wounded that he was not able to bale out, he did not depart the aircraft. He was buried in the communal cemetery at Couvron-et-Aumencourt.

The remainder of the crew landed safely. Sgt Thompson the engineer and W/O Murphy RCAF the radio operator were captured. The navigator F/S Lindsay RCAF gave himself up to a Frenchman the next morning. He took him to the resistance, who kept him for a week. He was then moved around, finding himself in Bichancourt, 28-km from the crash site. From there he was taken to Amigny-Rouy, 9-km away, and later Bethancourt-en-Vaux, a further 13-km, from where he was liberated after D-Day by the advancing Americans. The mid-under gunner, Sgt Green, landed in the northern suburbs of Laon. There were Germans everywhere, running towards a crashed Ju88 about a hundred yards away. Sgt Green believed that the JU88 was shot down by Knox. Having hurriedly vacated his chute, Green ran off. He headed north. After covering a few kilometres he rested for a while, before starting off again. He came across the village of Chery, 9-km north of where he landed, here he obtained food. He retraced his steps and headed south, passing around the western side of Laon. On the morning of the 26th, after a 40-km journey, he arrived at Vregny, where he curled up in a hayloft. Having rested, Green moved on, reaching Conde-sur-Aisne at around 7pm, a distance of 7-km. He bumped into an old man, who took him to see his son who had connections with the local resistance.

The bomb aimer F/O J A Neal RCAF had carried his chute and Mae West for about a mile before burying them. He then moved on until about 3 in the morning, when he rested in a haystack. As dawn broke, he saw to his consternation that the haystack was about half a mile from the airfield at Convron. He was found by two Frenchmen, who took him to another hideout where he was given food and cigarettes. After dark, he bade farewell to the Frenchmen and set off once again. Travelling south he passed several villages, including Crepy-en-Laonnois, 3-km south of the crash site. Having walked another 4-km, Neal reached Bucy. Wishing to put as much distance between himself and the crash site, he passed quickly. He came across a barn, just to the north of Suzy, some 8-km further on, where he sheltered. Eventually, the owner turned up and offered Neal food and a change of clothing. The farmer then gave him directions on how to find the nearest resistance group. He stayed with the group for about two and a half weeks. On D-Day, he was taken 31-km northwest, to a farm at Ugny-le-Gay. Here he met up with the crew's navigator, F/S Lindsay and other downed airmen, including two Americans. Ultimately Thomas, Lindsay, Neal and Murphy evaded capture, and were repatriated back to England after D-Day, when the area they were in was overrun by advancing American troops.

During a gardening detail against the Baltic ports on the 23/24th, the Ghosts lost their last Halifax crew whilst on operations. This was Halifax Mk II, NA-Z LW285, flown by F/O W V Blake DFC. Their aircraft was attacked by a Ju88 whilst at 13,000 feet. Fire from the night fighter wounded the engineer Sgt T Jerry. Such was the damage to the Halifax that Blake immediately set course for neutral Sweden. Later, having reached Sweden, the bomber became uncontrollable, and was abandoned from 9,000 feet. With the exception of F/O Blake, who remained at the controls to save his crew, everyone baled out and were interned by the Swedish. The aircraft crashed about 500 yards from the shore in approximately 15 feet of water. F/O Blake is commemorated on the Runnymede Memorial.

A raid on the marshalling yards at Villeneuve-St-Georges, to the southeast of Paris, on the night of the 26/27th, was 419's last all Halifax operation. P/O Marjoram, who was one of the squadron's most experienced captains, stated that the PFF dropped the markers on the wrong side of the Seine. Another problem for the attacking crews was the fact that the Master Bomber's radio instructions were practically unintelligible. This may have been down to jamming. F/O Barclay was not happy with the marking of the target and decided to bring his bombs back, rather than risk killing innocent French people. All of Goosepool's Halifaxes returned safe, including the 14 aircraft sent by 428.

The following night saw 419's first operation using Lancasters. They now had 8 operational Lancs, and these were sent, along with 5 of the remaining Halifaxes, to attack the marshalling yards at Montzen, 37-km S/S/E of Berlin, close to Lake Kallinchen. This all RCAF raid, employed 144 aircraft. 14 Halifaxes and 1 Lancaster were lost. One of the Halifaxes was VR-R JN954, flown by P/O McIvor RCAF, another of 419's more experienced captains. This aircraft was shot down by a night fighter and crashed at Heer in the southeast suburbs of Maastricht. All on board were killed. This was the last Halifax to be lost by 419.

One of the Lancasters lost that night was from 405 RCAF Squadron. Flown by P/O R A Booth, Croix de Guerre, this aircraft was also the mount of S/L E W Blenkinsop DFC, Croix De Guerre (Belgium), who was acting as Deputy Master Bomber. He and his crew were shot down by a night fighter over Belgium. S/L Blenkinsop was blown from the bomber, and after landing near Webberkom, he joined with a group of Belgian resistance fighters. He was eventually captured in December 1944, and rather than being sent to a POW camp, the Germans took him to a forced labour camp near Hamburg. Later he was taken to the infamous Belsen concentration camp where he died of heart failure on January 23rd 1945.

During this raid, 419 saw two of its Lancasters return, each with a 1,000-lb bomb hung up in the bomb bay. A third returned early with an unconscious mid-upper gunner, Sgt J D Turner. Having just crossed the English Coast and whilst at around 17,000 feet, the gunner had become ill. The captain, F/L J D Virtue, brought the Lancaster down to 12,000 feet and ordered the crew to revive him. They were unable to bring him round and it was decided to abandon the operation and return to base. Back at Middleton he was immediately taken to the SSQ where it was discovered that he was suffering from a collapsed right lung.

428 had also been busy that night. Fifteen crews had been detailed for operations, seven bombed Aulnoye, and eight dropped mines. The gardening detail planted their vegetables on four separate targets, Cherbourg, Le Havre, St Malo and Morlaix. All returned safe.

On the 29th, the Ghosts returned to the same French ports as they had mined on the 27th. Having planted their crop successfully, all eight crews returned safely to Goosepool. The next day they went back again, and for good measure added St Nazaire to the list, all sixteen aircraft returned safe.

On the last day of April, there were no Ops for 419. Coincidentally, this date had earlier been set for the squadron's first official party since its formation almost two and a half years ago. On the menu was 200-lbs of moose meat and venison, donated by the Kamloops Civilian Auxiliary. The night was augmented by top-notch entertainment, and the attendance of none other than AVM Black Mike McEwan himself. Also present at the party were several former Moosemen who had been posted to other stations throughout 6 Group.

It was with some sadness that the squadron bade farewell to their 'B' Flight Commander S/L O C Hamber, who, along with his crew, was being posted to Linton-on-Ouse to take command of 426 (Thunderbird) Squadron. He was to be replaced by Flight Lieutenant J G Stewart, who would shortly become Squadron Leader J G Stewart.

The end of April saw 419's complement of Halifaxes held on charge down to one, whilst over the month the number of Lancasters rose to 15. Most crews had by now completed their conversion onto the Lanc. The groundcrew did sterling work in maintaining the Halifaxes, at the same time as they were navigating the Lancaster learning curve.

Their task when operations were called was to ensure that the Lancasters were in tip-top condition. The engines were run-up and checked for maggy drops, and taken up to full power whilst the Ts and Ps were checked. Meanwhile the radio, radar and instrument bods would visit each aircraft to check all was well. The photographic section would do their bit and ensure that the cameras were serviceable and loaded with film. The oil truck and fuel bowser would visit each aircraft and top up the tanks.

Thousands of rounds of ammo were loaded in the front and mid-upper turrets, and into canisters located in the fuselage behind the bomb bay. These canisters fed the rear turret by way of aluminium ammo tracks, which ran down the fuselage. On the mid-upper turret, the ammo was in canisters, located on its base. The front turret had a similar arrangement. If the ammo was required for a night operation, the tracer rounds were of a different type to day tracer. There glow was less intensive, as not to spoil the night vision of the gunners. They were loaded in a combination where every 20th round was a tracer. When a raid was changed from day to night, or visa versa, this would cause a right flap for the armourers, who had to prepare and change 1,000s of rounds of ammo for up to 24 Lancasters.

As if this was not enough, there was the bomb-load, which was driven to the arming sheds and then on to aircraft by tractors, each pulling 3 or 4 bomb dollies. Each dolly could hold about 4,000-lbs of bombs. Once at the aircraft, the dollies were manhandled under the Lancaster's cavernous bomb bay. Each bomb was raised up by a winch. If it was a night trip, there were other jobs for the armourers, including the loading of the photoflash. This was a magnesium flare, which would give off a light of several million candlepower, and illuminate the target for the bomber's camera.

Also prior to a raid, a truck containing the various types of Window would arrive at each aircraft. Up to 20 cartons of Window could be loaded for a big raid, each carton providing several bundles to be dispensed out of a special chute. Different types of Window were dropped in different areas, to confuse the various types of German radar. The Wurtzburg, Freya and Lichtenstein radar's operated on dissimilar wavelengths, and required strips of Window cut to different lengths. Sometimes, different types of Window were dropped together. To finish off, brown paper packs of Nickels could, on occasion, be added to the bomber's ample load.

Ron Cassells remembers. *The navs would draw the appropriate charts for the trip, including a Mercator for plotting, a Gee chart, and any topographical maps that might be required. They would also draw their nav log. They would check that they had all their Nav kit, including their protractor, calculator and several sharpened chinograph and lead pencils. All would be placed carefully in a large fabric 'Nav' bag about 18 inches square.*

At the general briefing, all crewmembers sat together at a table. First, there was a few remarks by the C/O, who would announce the target, and the time of H-hour. He would also give the headings, heights and times for each crew to bomb. The Intelligence Officer took the stage next, and addressed the crews on the route and its heavily defended areas. Next he announced the German colours of the day, and the times they would change, and to what. This allowed the crews to fire off appropriately coloured flares, to bamboozle the Germans into thinking that they were Luftwaffe aircraft. The friendly colours came next, and how they would change over each 8-hour period. The British colours of the day were supposed to be fired to convince the Admiralty and British Ack Ack gunners not to shoot them down. It has to be said that this was not always successful. The Intelligence Officer would continue by giving a description of the target area, and the objective of the raid. Next he gave the total number of aircraft employed, and informed the crews of any other Bomber Command or American 8th Airforce raids taking place at the same time. He would conclude by stating where the Mandrel aircraft would be flying whilst they jammed the German air defence, and where 'Window' was being dropped to thwart the German radar. The Signals Officer came next. He recited the Gee settings, and anything else relevant to the aircraft's radio and radar equipment. He was followed by the Engineering Officer, who gave fuel loads and the recommended engine settings for take-off, climbing and cruise. It was at this point that the crews found out whether they had enough fuel to reach base or would have to refuel on the way home at airfields in the South. The Bombing Leader would then give details of the bomb-load, fusing details, the sequence of dropping the bomb-load and the settings to be used on the bombsight. He would also give the colours of the TIs and what they would be at various times during the attack, and the code words to be used by the master bomber. The Met man detailed the winds in each area and their heights. He also provided a general synopsis of the expected weather on the way out, over the target, and on the way back. The last specialist was an officer from Flying control, who would give the order of take-off, and instructions relating to formation after takeoff. At this point the C/O would once again take to his feet, and having gone over the important points again and asked everyone to synchronise their watches, he would conclude the briefing by wishing everyone good luck.

With that, there would be the scraping of chairs as everyone but the navigators made their way out of the briefing room. The Navs would remain behind to plot the legs on their mercator charts, using the latest forecast winds. They also worked out the flying time from base to the target. They knew the time that they had to bomb, and allowing one-minute error per flying hour, would calculate the time to set course and reach the target at the right time to bomb. After that, everyone went off to collect their escape aids, flying clothing and parachutes etc. They were then taken out to the aircraft. Here the Nav would carry out a final check of the Compass, API,[108] Gee and the H2S.

[108] Air Position Indicator

May 1944

May the 1/2nd saw 419 undertake its first Op since converting fully onto the Lancaster. This raid, to the marshalling yards at St Ghislain, cost the Moosemen P/O J C McNary RCAF and crew in VR-C KB711. Half way across the channel it was discovered that the aircraft was ahead of time and so an orbit was initiated. They then continued towards the continent, where they found the cloud cover to be about 5/10ths at 6,000 feet, there was also a full moon. When they were approaching the target, they realised that they were slightly off course and a little late. The original markers were no longer evident, and so they did three orbits whilst waiting for the next set of markers. These were not forthcoming and so it was decided to bomb visually. After the attack McNary climbed the Lancaster in preparation to crossing the enemy coast. Far below them, and silhouetted against the cloud, was a fighter, which they soon lost sight of. He must have come up in the Lancaster's blind spot, as a few minutes later, the aircraft was raked by cannon fire. They were still over Belgium, in the vicinity of Ghent. A fire started in the cockpit and McNary gave the order to bale out. The wireless operator W/O T L Chartrand was badly wounded in the stomach, whilst the tail gunner Sgt D S Sangster, was injured in the right eye and arm. The engineer Sgt A G Hill handed McNary his chute, and went down into the bomb aimer's position, where F/S R C Long the bomb aimer was opening the floor hatch. With the hatch now open, the engineer jumped whilst Long was putting on his chute. Ultimately, only five crewmen escaped from the aircraft. McNary went to help Chartrand but perished with him when the Lancaster crashed in the grounds of the former gas works at Ghent-Rabot. This was the first Canadian built Lancaster to be lost by 419 and indeed Bomber Command. Opposition was minimal. F/L Stewart and his crew, flying VR-Y, made

Groundcrew talk ato Sgt D S Sangster RCAF, the rear gunner of Lancaster KB711 VR-C, on May 1/2 1944, prior to engine start time for a raid on St Ghislain. This aircraft departed Goosepool but failed to return from this raid. It crashed 1 km from the centre of Ghent. The pilot, P/O R A McNary and W/O J L Chartrand were killed. Sgt Sangster and the remainder of the crew became POWs. This was the first Lancaster to be lost on operations by 419   Photo: via Geoff Hill

history for 419 by carrying 14,000-lbs of bombs, the heaviest load so far. When asked about fighter opposition, Steward replied, 'I travelled in the centre of a large number of bombers, I saw nothing and felt very safe.'

Also on the 1/2nd, 428, who had shared the cramped navigation hut with 419, began the move into a new building of their own. This was much appreciated by 419's navs, who badly needed the elbow room. 428's first observations were that no provision had been made for section accommodation, or for equipment, lecture space etc. To overcome this handicap, the briefing room was used as a crew room and the crewroom used as the section room. This arrangement would do as long as the squadron could continue to use the old briefing room in the Station headquarters building.

The next day continued with the Ghosts scrounging additional furniture, hanging maps and blackboards etc. The YMCA were busy fitting a new radio, and easy chairs, along with billiard and Ping-Pong tables etc. Later that night, 10 Ghost crews took off for another successful gardening operation against French ports.

Meanwhile, the last of the Moosemen's Halifax IIs departed Goosepool on the 4/5th. Next day, 428 departed to sow mines at Brest, St Malo, and Morlaix. The area code-named 'Scallops' (Brest) was the venue for the crews of W/O D E Melcombe and W/O H Gouthreau, who dropped their vegetables from 11,000 feet at a speed of 220 mph. P/O E J Sykes and P/O H L Pattinson planted their vegetables at 'Hyacinth' (St Malo). W/O W C Gay's crew visited 'Greengages' (Morlaix), where, disappointingly, out of the two mines dropped, only one parachute was seen to open. They returned safely.

The same day word came through that 428's commander, W/C French, was to receive the DFC. This news was received with great acclaim as it was considered by all that he had certainly deserved it.

Training flights for the Moosemen started on the 6th, and saw some crewmembers changing roles. Three crews, dispatched on a cross country training flight that day, saw their bomb aimers doing the navigation, whilst the pilots charted the course. The experiment worked well and gave each crewman an insight into the difficulties likely to be experienced by his counterpart.

There was a change of target for 419 on the 7/8th. This time they attacked gun positions at St Valery-en-Caux, near Dieppe on the French Coast. The Ghost Squadron continued gardening, this time it was back to the Friesian Islands. The operation employed ten crews led by W/C French.

419 squadron Lancasters, marshalled in preparation for operations later that night
Photo: via Geoff Hill

Marshalling yards were back on the battle order for the following three nights. Ghent came first. All of 419's aircraft returned safely. Earlier in the day, after carrying out circuits and bumps, Lancaster KB716, flown by First Lt J H Hartshorn USAAF, burst a tyre on take-off. Hartshorn completed the circuit and successfully brought the aircraft in for a landing. Just after touchdown, the undercarriage leg with the flat tyre collapsed, and the aircraft swapped ends. No one was hurt except the Lancaster, which was deemed to have Cat B damage.

Meanwhile 428's photographic section was getting to grips with the new Leica and Contad cameras, which were to be used on future gardening trips. This type of camera was mounted inside the aircraft and was aimed at the PPI screen. Operated by the navigator, the camera showed the exact location of the mine whilst dropping.

A new piece of airborne equipment was added to the Ruhr Express during May. This was code named 'Boozer'. This equipment consisted of an Antenna and a receiver, which informed the crew of radar emissions from enemy aircraft. If trials proved satisfactory, this equipment would be fitted to all squadron aircraft.

Sixteen of 428's crews went back to Brest, Lorient and Morlaix on the 9/10th. All mined successfully, and despite the light flak at Brest, all aircraft returned safely to Middleton. Wing Commander French, his navigator F/O Derosenroll, WOP/AG F/O Miles, bomb-aimer F/O Greco, and engineer P/O Yule DFM were screened, having completed their tour of operations. French was posted to Headquarters 6 Group after a 48 hour leave. The remainder of his crew departed for 10 days leave. Wing Commander French had commanded 428 since October 27th 1943 and had always had the interest of the squadron at heart. The efficiency and good results of the squadron's efforts were largely due to him. He was to be replaced by S/L McLeish

The same night, 419 sent 8 Lancasters to attack gun emplacements at St Valery. In ideal weather, the attack took place from 6,000 feet. As the aircraft were only over enemy territory for 6 or 7 minutes, as expected, the opposition experienced was negligible.

After a raid to marshalling yards at Ghent on the 10/11th, P/O Holmes, in 419's KB704, overshot the end of Middleton's runway, careered over two ditches, and ended up damaged beyond repair, fortunately without injury to the crew. 428 contributed fourteen aircraft for this raid, all successfully attacked the target and returned.

Decorations continued to be put forward for members of the Moosemen, and these included DFC for W/C Pleasance, S/L Dyer, F/L Byford and P/O Scade.

After the Ghost Squadron sent six crews to bomb railway targets at Boulogne on the 11/12th, they returned to mining duties the next day, when 11 crews were detailed to revisit the Friesians and St Malo. All returned safely. Also on the 12th, the Ghosts welcomed a new 'A' Flight Commander in the form of F/L CE Murphy DFC. F/L Lord DFC was promoted to Acting Squadron Leader and moved over to command 'B' Flight.

The same night, 419 attacked marshalling yards at Louvain. The rail yards were extensively damaged and were still being repaired six months later. Out of a total of 120 aircraft taking part, two Lancasters were lost. Both of these belonged to 419.

The first, KB710, flown by P/O H I Smith RCAF, was shot down by a night fighter, with the loss of all on board. The second, flown by P/O B F Edwards RCAF, crashed whilst on the way to the target at Reninge, again all crewmembers were killed.   On the 14th, the Ghosts sent 10 crews back on yet another a mining op to St Malo, Morlain, Cherbourg and Le Havre. All reached the target, but despite spending an hour in the target area, F/O Gonyou's crew were unable to release their mines and had to return with them.

At 22:38 on the night of May 15/16th, one of 419's Lancs took off for a routine training flight. Flown by F/O J G McMaster RCAF, the aircraft descended below the minimum briefed safety height and crashed at Potter House Farm on Helmsley Moor near Wombleton, North Yorkshire. There were no survivors. There had been no engine or structural failure, but the cloud-base at the time had been put at 2/300 feet. The aircraft hit the fell-side in a slightly nose down attitude and disintegrated. One member of the crew, Sgt Alsop, was a native of Darlington.

Another was Second Lt E N Fordham of the USAAF, who was later buried in the US Military Cemetery at Cambridge.

Next day the new Nissen Hut wing of SSQ was officially opened, providing an additional 16 hospital beds.

Two days later, the Moosemen welcomed their new 'A' Flight Commander in the form of S/L D C Hagerman. He was replacing S/L Dyer, who was being screened, after completing a tour of operations. On May 17th, all operational aircrew of 419 undertook instruction in bombing up their own aircraft. Under the supervision of the station armoury, they loaded their own Lancasters with 1 x 2,000-lb HC, 1 x 1,000-lb MC and 2 x 500-lb MC Bombs. The exercise was repeated on the 19th. Although rumours abounded that crews might have to start bombing up their own aircraft, this never came to anything.

The duff weather of late abated, which allowed 428 to carry out a gardening operation on Heligoland. The squadron's armourers hit numerous snags during the allotted time to bomb-up the aircraft, and finally had to request some assistance from 419's armourers. This was forthcoming, and it has to be said, was much appreciated. The job was completed and the thirteen aircraft departed on time.

Wing Commander DC Hagerman DFC
Photo: courtesy of Canadian Forces

The night of the May 22/23rd saw 419 back in the Fatherland for a raid on Dortmund. It had been over three months since the squadron had been relegated to a second line squadron, but now the crews and their new steeds were deemed fully operational once again. 419 formed part of a force of 361 Lancasters and 14 Mosquitoes bombing Dortmund, the first large raid there in a year. The attack, which took place in the southeastern part of Dortmund, destroyed 6 industrial buildings and 852 houses. Of the major attacks on the Ruhr Valley during 1943, Dortmund was considered to have been the least effective. Of the 18 Lancasters lost on this raid, one was from 419. KB717, flown by P/O C E Patterson RCAF, was shot down by a night fighter. The Lancaster was carrying a crew of 8. The extra person carried was Sgt A P Chawanski RCAF, who was acting as mid-under gunner. All on board were killed when the Lancaster crashed just to the south of Munchengladbach.

One Moose aircraft returned early, as its navigator, F/S P S Smith, began to show all the symptoms of anoxia. He had been asked several times by the skipper, W/O D M Robson, if his oxygen tube had been plugged in. Several times he confirmed that he was connected to the supply, although he was not. Oxygen starvation plays funny tricks with the human brain, and this incident was typical of the effects of anoxia. As the navigator was deemed unable to continue with his job in a satisfactory manner, the Lancaster was turned around and flown back to Middleton. This crew failed to return from a raid on marshalling yards at Aachen two nights later. They were shot down by a night fighter, and crashed between Loon-op-Zand and Tilburg. The only survivor was the tail gunner Sgt W D Lillico RCAF, who was an American from New York.

Whilst the Moosemen attacked Dortmund, 428 planted their vegetables at St Malo and returned safely. The next day it was the turn of Cherbourg and Le Havre. Meanwhile, on the same day, word arrived that S/L McLeish was to be promoted to the rank of Acting Wing Commander. It was also noted that he was to become the recipient of the DFC. That night, the WAAFs held an Empire Day dance, at which both squadrons were well represented.

A respite from mining was on the cards for the Ghosts when, on the 24/25th, fifteen crews took-off for a bombing Op to Trouville, a coastal town on the south side of the entrance to the river Seine. All bombed the target successfully and returned to base. 428 had expected its first Lancaster X to arrive during the day, but in the end it did not do so. It did arrive the next day however, and was eagerly inspected from all angles by 428's personnel. On the same day, F/L Murphy was put up to acting Squadron Leader, a rank more fitting for the commander of 'A' Flight.

A large German military camp at Bourg-Leopold was attacked by the Moosemen on the night of the May 27/28th. The TIs were dropped by Oboe carrying aircraft in and amongst the buildings and barracks, and the attack was very accurate. An ammunition dump took a direct hit and culminated in a huge explosion lasting over 15 seconds. Amongst the Moosemen crews operating that night were those of P/O Tees and 1st Lt Hawthorn USAAF, who had close encounters with fighters. Fortunately the attacks were half hearted and the enemy pilots kept corkscrewing to avoid any concerted entanglement with the bombers.

It was back to mine laying for the Ghost Squadron that night, when Heligoland was revisited by fifteen crews. Meanwhile, ground training was underway for the squadron in anticipation of more Lancasters arriving. Earlier that day, P/O Curley became the first aircrew member at Goosepool to be screened under the new 'points' system, rather than by the original 30 Ops method. He had amassed 120 points, which allowed him to be screened.

Two days later, 428 detailed three crews for their penultimate mining trip during May. Dunkirk was the target and all three aircraft had a successful operation from which all returned.

Pre-invasion targets continued to dominate the Moosemen's attention, and on the last day of the month, 419 sent 15 crews to bomb a large coastal radio jamming station at Mont Couple, near Cap Gris Nez. The target was flattened, and all aircraft returned safely. This raid was not won easily however; severe electrical storms were encountered by the crews all the way there and back.

The Ghost Squadron contributed nine of their aircraft for the Mont Couple raid, and detailed another seven for a mining Op to Lorient and Brest. P/O Carter's crew returned early due to icing. W/O Forsberg's aircraft was about 10 feet off the deck when one of his engines cut. Despite being fully loaded, Forsberg continued with the take-off and jettisoned his bombs in the sea before returning to Middleton.

Meanwhile a Stirling from 1654 Conversion Unit crashed 3 miles west of Aycliffe, there were no survivors. The bodies were brought to Goosepool's Morgue. On the same day, one of Middleton's aircrew, who had been posted in on May 22nd, was admitted to SSQ with Flying Stress Anxiety State.

419's aircraft strength on the last day of May was shown as 20 Lancaster Xs, only 4 of which thus far were fitted with H2S. 428 celebrated another month without any loss or accident in which any personnel were injured.

June 1944

On June 1st, 428 were off to the Friesians again, from where all returned. S/L Murphy checked out in one of the Ghosts new Lancaster Xs. The groundcrew too were getting to grips with the Lanc, they were getting stuck in to ground training and lectures on the type.

Next day it was decided that Le Havre required some much needed gardening and 10 Ghost crews obliged. Each aircraft carried 4 X 1,850-lb mines, which were dropped without incident. All aircraft returned safely. On the 3rd, just to prove that they could do it again, they did it again, same target - same bomb-load. On their return there was duff weather over base and so they diverted.

On June 4th, bombing practice was carried out by some of 419's crews. The most noteworthy results were provided by F/O A J Arnold, the bomb aimer in F/O A C Rokeby's aircraft, who achieved an accuracy of 78 yards from 20,000 feet.

By now, 428 were hard at it with their new toy. During the day, whilst four crews continued their training, F/L Edwards checked W/C McLeish out on one of the Lancs. Next day it was W/O Forsberg's turn.

That night the Moosemen bombed gun batteries in the Calais area. They were part of a force of 259 aircraft that were undertaking spoof attacks on three gun emplacement targets in the Pas de Calais area and a fourth (for real) raid on a gun battery at Maisy. The three attacks at Calais were diversionary, to fool the Germans that Calais was the intended beachhead for the D-Day landings. At the same time, the boffins slipped in the Maisy attack, as it was located between Omaha and Utah beaches where the Americans would land on the 6th. 1,012 Bomber Command aircraft were busy that night, the targets, which were mostly coastal batteries included; Fontenay, Houlgate, La Pernelle, Longues, Maisy, Merville, Mont Fleury, Pont-de-Hoc, Ousterham and St-Martin-de-Varreville.

Maisy and two of the three gun positions were cloud covered and had to be bombed through cloud. The Calais target however, was clear. Takeoff time for the Moosemen was originally set for 22:30, but this was put back. Just after 01:00 hours, the first of their 14 Lancasters began to depart. When they reached Calais, they found broken cloud and drizzle, but were able to bomb the red markers from 7,200 to 7,600 feet accurately and without difficulty. They were told to disregard a row of green markers that were parallel with the coast, some of which extended into the sea. For the Moosemen, the raid was a huge success, all returned safely to Middleton. On the night of the 5th, fifteen 428 Squadron aircraft carried out a bombing operation on Merveille, from which all returned safe.

During the early morning of D-Day June 6th, 419 took part in a raid on Merville-Franceville and then in another at Longues. Both were cloud-covered and accurate bombing was impossible. The pathfinders began marking the target, but the TIs were soon lost beneath the cloud, and the only thing to bomb was the pale glow of the markers as they descended to earth Three crews had great difficulty seeing the markers and did not bomb. A similar situation occurred at the second target, Longues, and one crew brought their bombs back. All were diverted on their return.

That night, 20 of 419's Lancasters carried out a low-level attack on a railway bridge at Coutances, on the Cherbourg peninsular, each dropping 18 X 500-lb bombs. The Moosemen formed part of 1,065 aircraft raid, consisting of 589 Lancasters, 418 Halifaxes and 58 Mosquitoes. Whilst 419 attacked some very important bridges at Coutances, the remainder of the force bombed Acheres, Argentan, Caen, Chateaudun, St Lo, Lisieux and Vier. Although 10 Lancasters and 1 Halifax were lost, all of Goosepool's aircraft returned safe. The first enemy aircraft claimed shot down by the squadron since their conversion onto the Lancaster X, came during the Acheres raid One Ju88 was claimed as a definite, whilst an Me110 was claimed as a probable.

419 and 428's aircraft arrived too early to see the final results of the bombing of Coutances. The visibility was good, only a slight ground haze was visible. Some ground features could be seen, but the target was identified by the PFF's green and red markers. The crews bombed on the edge of the white TIs as briefed. During the raid, the bridges were badly damaged, the town itself was also hit and set on fire. 65% of the town's buildings were destroyed and 312 French civilians were killed.

Walter Poynter

Sgt Ted Reesor's crew arrived at Croft around the time of D-day to serve with 431 Squadron at Croft. His crew consisted of navigator F/O Walter Poynter, bomb-aimer F/O George Jones, wireless operator Sgt Donald Wooff, engineer, and Sgt Raymond (Ray) Sexton, mid-upper gunner Sgt James Pennuta and tail gunner Sgt William (Bill) Smith. By way of the magical Internet, Wally Poynter wrote to me, explaining what it was like to fly in a Halifax III at Croft from June to October 27th 1944, and in Lancaster Xs from then to Dec 4th 1944.

Right to left, front row: Wally Poynter, navigator; Bill Smith, tail gunner; Jim Pennuta, mid-upper gunner; George Jones, bomb aimer; Rear row: Don Wooff, wireless operator; Ray Sexton, engineer; Ted Reesor, pilot

Photo: Wally Poynter

'Having enlisted in Edmonton, Alberta during July 1942, I was posted to the Manning Depot at Edmonton. In December I was at ITS at the University of Alberta. January 1943 saw me posted to 2 Air Observers School for Navigation Training. By September 1943 I had graduated as a Pilot Officer (navigator) and was posted to Halifax, Nova Scotia for transit to the UK. Having arrived at Liverpool our batch of aircrew were taken by train to Bournemouth.

In December 1943 another posting arrived, which saw me at the Air Familiarization Flight at Millom, Cumberland. Here navigation training for my classmates and me continued in Ansons, flying over the West Coast of England, and out into the Irish Sea. This course was completed by February 1944 and we were then posted to 24 OTU to crew up. Here we attended classes in what to expect once operations began. We were then told to mingle with the other aircrew trades gathered there, and select with whom we wished to fly. After everyone had formed into crews we continued training as a crew, flying Whitleys. This lasted until April 1944, when our crew was posted to Wombleton, North Yorkshire, to convert to four engined Halifax bombers. With some surprise, having amassed only 17 hours night and 6 hours day flying as a crew, we were deemed to be ready for operations. In early May we were posted to 431 (Iroquois) Squadron at Croft, North Yorkshire. Our first op took place on June 21st.

The day of a bomber crew started with us checking the 'Battle Order' to see if our crew was on standby for operations. One of the first indications of an impending raid was the appearance of padlocks on the telephone boxes, preventing any calls, either in or out. About two hours before take-off, the Tannoy would spring into life and summon all crews to the briefing room. We often enjoyed summer days at the Croft Spa Hotel, and depending on the wind, we were able to hear the Tannoy, even from the bar. Although the muffled voice emanating from the Tannoy's speakers was inaudible, it usually meant that briefing was being called. The first thing we did was grab our bikes and go to the mess for a quick meal. Then it was off to our various sections, such as the Nav Section, and Bombing Section (for the bomb aimers), and so on. There we would collect any relevant info required. For my part, as a navigator, I would collect my navigation equipment and maps, which would show the flak areas and German fighter stations etc. Then we would proceed to the Main Briefing.

We navigators used the DR (dead reckoning) navigation method mostly, backed up with Gee and H2S. Gee however, was only accurate up to the coast of Europe, or just a little beyond. We were given the Met details during the main briefing and we later used them to determine the initial course to fly. Assuming we were going to bomb Berlin from Croft, the first thing I would do would be to draw our course from Croft to Berlin on my chart. This course would give me the direction (or directions if we flew doglegs) to fly. For this, I used a square flat piece of Perspex called a protractor which I laid on the line I had drawn on the chart. Lining the outside edge of the Perspex square with the grid lines on the chart, this simple bit of Perspex with a graticule of lines printed on it gave me my course to within 1 degree. A ruler, marked with both statute and nautical miles, was then placed along my course and the distance read off.

Now armed with a direction to steer (say 120 degrees) and the distance to fly (albeit with no wind), my next job was to use the given winds and calculate what they would do to the aircraft whilst we were flying our course. If, for example, I had been given a wind vector by the met officer of, say, 350 degrees at 50 nautical mph, I would put the course (called the track), wind speed and direction into my navigation computer. This was not an electronic computer as we have today, but a simple hand held circular slide rule, which corrected our course for wind-drift and spat out the correct course to steer. This was providing the Met wind vector was indeed correct (rubbish in, rubbish out). I would then plot this course on my chart and update it as to the airspeed and time flown. This would give me a theoretical position as if there was no wind at all, and was known as an air plot. I would mark it on the map and denote it thus >>>>.

If, after about 2 hours flying, we had ended up taking a fix which showed us crossing the coast sooner than planned, and, lets say, 50 miles too far to the south, I would immediately calculate the exact spot we would have been at on the air plot, and would draw a line connecting this theoretical point and our actual position. By measuring the distance we had drifted, and the direction, I could then determine that the Met direction was correct, but that the wind-speed had increased to 75 knots per hour. The thing to do next was to calculate a new course that would allow me to get back on course to the target (using my computer whirly wheel). I would always carry on the old air plot, but would start a new one from the latest fix. This way I could calculate the current wind-speed and direction as well as the average on the whole trip. We didn't want to reach the target ahead of time to bomb, and sometimes I would instruct the pilot to fly a triangular course, 45 degrees to port for 10 minutes and 90 degrees back for 10 minutes.

As soon as possible after take-off, I would obtain a position fix, by either visual means, Gee or H2S. This allowed me to check the accuracy of the forecast winds and enabled me to calculate the wind direction and its speed, and thus make course corrections. I would continue to take 'fixes' and make course corrections throughout the Op. One trick during very dark nights, when a visual fix was impossible, was to fly a zigzag pattern until we felt the turbulence from the planes ahead of us (if I was lost, so were they). I remember one crew who did this, ending up following the wrong stream.

Just southwest of Frankfurt there is a bend in the Rhine, which I often used as a landmark to fix our position. Over 30 years later, on a scheduled flight to Rhine Mien, I looked out of the window and saw this particular spot. Turning to my wife who was sitting beside me, I said, 'We will be landing in 10 minutes, we are just to the southwest of the airfield.' No sooner had I finished speaking, than the pilot came on the cabin intercom and said, 'Ladies and gentlemen, please fasten your safety belts, as we will be landing in 10 minutes.' The guy in the seat next to me looked at me in astonishment, and said, 'How the hell did you know that?' Well! I just had to tell him, didn't I? Today, navigation is a much simpler and more accurate thing. Although we used the forerunner of today's ADF (beacon bashing), the advent of VOR, ILS, Inertial navigation and GPS[109] systems have made life much simpler (and more accurate) for the navigator. Today's trainee pilots however, still have to learn the perils of DR, which is still the primary method of navigating light, and not so light aircraft.

Waiting by the aircraft were one's own groundcrew. There were at least 4 on duty during take-off for a raid, and sometimes as many as 5 or 6. Amongst them would be an airframe fitter, engine fitter, an instrument basher and an armourer. There was also the driver of the vehicle with the accumulators (batteries) to start the engines. During start-up, both chocks and brakes were used. The groundcrew would plug in the trolley-acc then signal the pilot that they were ready to start engines. After the Very pistol was fired from flying control to indicate, 'All aircraft - start engines', the pilot and engineer would begin the process of bringing the Halifax's engines to life. This was a well-rehearsed procedure, and we always began by starting the starboard outer first. This was followed religiously with the starboard inner, port inner and finally port outer.

Once all engines were running and the after start checks complete, the crew waited until it was their turn to taxi out of their dispersal onto the perimeter track which would take them to the active runway. The order of take-off was determined by the location of one's dispersal site relative to that runway. The aircraft's navigation lights would be on for taxiing and take off and would only be switched off after the English Coast was crossed on the way out. The use of landing and taxiing lights was kept to a minimum. Sometimes the pilot would flick on the lights if he was in doubt of what was ahead of him during taxiing. They were not used for take-off, as they tended to spoil one's night vision. Another problem was that they could attract any enemy intruders that might be in the area. The pilot would follow the aircraft ahead until he reached the runway in use. The Aldis light from the red and white caravan at the end of the runway would signal permission to enter the runway and line up. Once the light gave the all clear the throttles would be opened and the brakes released. Normally take-off would begin before the plane ahead had cleared the runway. Whenever I think of Croft, the first vision that crosses my mind is of 40 odd Halifaxes lined up ready for take off. The roar of 160 aero engines was something I will never forget.

With two squadrons, possibly having 40 plus aircraft to get off, time and fuel were of the essence. The petrol and bomb-load were carefully balanced in advance, depending where the aircraft was going. On some raids, the tanks were topped up just before take-off, to replace fuel used during taxiing. During a single aircraft take-off, the pilot would taxi to the runway and request permission to take off.

After take-off we would circle the drome until a predetermined time and then set course for the target. As most of the flights were night flights, we seldom saw the rest of the bomber force. The crews could often tell that they were in the bomber stream by the turbulence caused by the planes flying in front of them. During daylight raids the same procedure was followed, and all set off at the same time. During these daylight raids, the other planes could be seen but there was no effort to fly in formation.

My next thoughts are of flying with all the other squadrons as they joined the bomber stream. They were like flocks of geese gathering for the flight south. As we proceeded to the target, either towards the North Sea or down the length of England, we saw the black smoke from other airfields, showing all of the aircraft that had crashed on take-off.

The 'Navigator's Position' was located in the nose of the Halifax, underneath the pilot and forward of the wireless operator. I worked at a small table, which was located along the left-hand wall of the nose section. I sat facing to port, whilst to my left was the wireless operator facing forward. To my right was the nose Perspex and the bomb aimer's position. I had a light and two big oblong boxes; both had round green cathode ray tubes, what one would now call TV screens. One was the Gee set and the other H2S. I also had a couple of instruments, which I used to help me navigate, these were an airspeed indicator and a compass. I also had an oxygen outlet, a plug for the intercom leads of my flying helmet, and a portable oxygen bottle to walk around the aircraft with. This was just the thing when nature called, and one had to visit the Elsan toilet at the back of the plane. The pilot had a 'pee' tube, which allowed him to remain in his seat for the duration of the flight. Sometimes it was possible for him to miss the tube and the poor old wireless operator sitting directly below him would be rained upon. Often, Halifax wireless operators could be identified from the rest of the crew by the verdigris corrosion on the metal fittings of his helmet, caused by the poor aim of his skipper.

[109] Global Positioning System (Satellite Navigation)

We would often chat on the intercom until the English Coast was reached, however, after that it was strictly business. There was no chit-chat as we were all far too busy with our duties. As navigator, I would ask other members of the crew to look out for certain landmarks. As the enemy coast was approached, everyone would tighten up, and the gunners increased their vigilance for enemy fighters. As navigator, I was constantly checking our course and speed, to make sure that we dropped our bombs at the correct time.

There were three distinct systems for communications. First there was the intercom, which allowed us to communicate to each other. Next we had R/T, which only had a short range. Although it could be used to talk to other planes, R/T was used mainly by the pilot, for communicating with the control tower. The third system was the Marconi set, whose longer range was used to send and receive Morse code messages between base and the aircraft, this could also be tuned to the R/T frequency. During the raid, our radio operator Don Woof would, at predetermined times, listen in to base on the Marconi for messages. These were in code of course. The only instructions I can remember were the diversions, when one's base was closed by low cloud or fog. Unlike the Halifaxes that used the 1154/1155 radio sets, the Canadian built Lancaster Xs were fitted with American radio equipment, manufactured by Bendix.

Just after D-Day there were many raids in France, which were called to assist the advancing (or not) Allied armies. Often these raids would be cancelled whilst we were on our way, and the aircraft recalled, after the German troop positions were overrun. These recalls were not counted as an Op, as the bombs were dropped. Meanwhile the gunners, Jim Pennuta in the mid-upper position and Bill Smith in the rear turret, were watching, ready to alert our pilot Ted Reesor of any fighter activity.

Usually the bombing was scheduled with high explosives in the first wave, to open the buildings up. These were followed by incendiaries in the next. This, of course, varied with the target. One was always relieved when the target was spotted. Admittedly I deliberately tried to reach the target a few minutes early, as it seemed to me that the Germans would not start shooting until the first bombs began to fall. Their theory was that at night their tracer and bursting shells would help us find the target easier. As our aircraft approached the bomb-run, the pilot and the bomb-aimer George Jones were in constant contact on the intercom, in order to be in the right position to drop the bombs. At the last instant the pilot would turn control of the aircraft over to the bomb aimer in order for him to drop the bombs. I remember Ted saying, 'It's all yours.' Then, in a few seconds, would come, 'Bombs away', after which he would take control again. All in all it was strictly business on the intercom, which is probably why I am still alive today.

The R/T and Marconi could be tuned to the German frequency and we could listen to them giving vector instructions to the fighter pilots. We were aware that Bomber Command often sent German-speaking radio operators along with some crews to issue false instructions to the fighter pilots.[110] One night, I am sure that we heard this going on, as there was a great deal of rough language coming from the Germans. The R/T, which had several channels, had a range that varied greatly, due to atmospheric conditions, this could be anywhere from 10 to 50 miles. There was an emergency channel on both voice and Morse sets. In an emergency, the wireless operator could tune into the emergency frequency and lock down his Morse key so it would give a continuous signal. Any base that picked up our call would take a bearing on our signal, to determine where we had gone down. If two stations some distance apart were able to pick up the signal, all they had to do was to plot the bearing from each base or radio site, and by triangulation be able to determine our exact crash site.

The range for voice communications on the Marconi was as far as we wanted to use it. We did not use it over Europe however, as the Germans could home in on us if we did. We used a trailing aerial on both sets. As well as listening in to base at specific times for instructions, the wireless operator would also send back weather information to base, including the wind-speed and direction, which I would give him. This would continue even over the target area. These transmissions were short as possible and in code to avoid the possibility of the Germans plotting us.

Once 'Bombs away' was called, it was time to hi-tail it back to base without further delay, but not before we took our pictures. A camera in the bomb bay took a series of 6 pictures over a 25-second period. From these photographs, the intelligence people could see whether we hit the target (or not), and what damage, if any, was caused. I always prepared the course out of the area in advance and handed it to the pilot, so that I could have time to take a peak at the target and see what was going on. I remember one raid on Bremen on August 18th 44, when I looked out and saw the whole city on fire. I thought, 'My God, how many people are burning to death down there?' I really debated whether I could ever go again. Of course in the light of another day things looked different.

Another Op I remember vividly was to hit the German troops in the Fallase Gap. This, of course, was a daylight raid, and we were told to bomb the yellow smoke. Another check was that we were not to bomb until one minute and thirty seconds from crossing a certain point on the coast. Because of the battle smoke, everything looked like yellow smoke, and some crews forgot the one-minute order and bombed after 30 seconds, hitting our own troops.

Often, thanks to Teesside's dubious weather, a 'diversion' message would be sent in Morse and received by the wireless operator whilst we were still over the North Sea, or even whilst still over enemy territory. As the fuel/bomb-load weight was finely balanced, one did not have fuel to go all the way to Yorkshire and then have enough left to divert to the South, or the Midlands. When base decided that the weather was marginal they informed you where it was clear. There was no such thing as a blind landing, if you could not see the ground, you could not land. Hence the diversion message would be sent out as early as possible

It was my job to use radio fixes to assist in accurately ascertaining our position. There were two basic ways to obtain a radio fix. First we could obtain a bearing on our base by calling them in Morse code and requesting a fix. The radio operator would call first, and then hold down the Morse key for a few seconds until base obtained a bearing on our plane.

---

[110] ABC (code name, Airborne Cigar)

The bearing was then passed back from base to Don by Morse, and this was then plotted on my map. Then, taking into consideration my latest calculated wind-speed, I determined a new course to fly to base. Another method was to use the previously described method along with a bearing from a radio beacon derived by way of the aircraft's loop aerial placed on the top of the aircraft, this was called a loop bearing. By plotting the two bearings on my map, I could determine our exact location to be where the two bearings intersected.

Another way was to obtain two bearings from two bases, or beacons. Before take-off, we were always given the latest positions of all the radio beacons in the British Isles. There were a number of radio beacons around the UK, which were moved quite frequently so that the Germans could not use them. Using loop aerial, the wireless operator or I could take a bearing on any of these beacons. Each one had its own call sign and I had a map showing their locations. If I could get a bearing from two beacons some distance apart, I would plot the bearings from them and draw them on my map. Where the two lines crossed was our position. If one's radios were out of action, I was trained to navigate by the stars (Astro navigation). Once, during my training, I had to do this in a Whitley when flying from Lands End to Croft. Believe it or not, after about twelve astro observations we were dead on target, when we let down through the clouds. This however would only work if the sky above you was clear and you could see the stars.

One thing that Don learned was that you could avoid the queue for landing at base by tuning the longer range Marconi to Croft's RT frequency and asking for permission to land, whilst still out over the North Sea. That way the other crews, who, like good little boys were correctly using the shorter range R/T radio sets, had to be much closer to base than us before gaining permission to land. Hence for us, there was less waiting in line. This was strictly verboten however and you had to be careful not to get found out. When the weather was good???, we could see the aerodrome beacons flashing the airfield's Morse identification letters. Under normal conditions, we would pick out Croft's ident, and as we got within R/T range, call the tower and ask for permission to land. If we arrived back at the same time as the other 40 or so aircraft, we would have to join the stack. This entailed circling at a height given by air traffic, until permission was given for us to drop down one peg and replace the aircraft below us. He in turn would do the same until he reached the bottom of the stack, when a final call from the tower gave one permission to land. Sometimes we started circling at 10 or even 12,000 feet. When the weather was bad, as it often was, we would get as close to Croft as we could and let down through the clouds until we could see the ground and hopefully see our aerodrome. Middleton and Croft had separate circuits, and being only 6 miles apart the Drem lights seemed to interlock. Drem lights were placed on single poles and completely encircled the drome at a distance of 3 to 4 miles from the centre of the airfield. Sometimes we could see them before the landing and runway lights. All airfield lights were only turned on when someone had requested permission to land. Once, I can remember the lights being turned off when we were on our approach to land, because German fighters had been identified in the area. The beacon light was also only turned on at the request of an aircraft. If an aircraft was in distress, its wireless operator would tune into the emergency frequency and the nearest base would assist by turning on its beacon and lights (if no enemy aircraft were around).

Wally's crew completed their tour in Dec 1944, after which he was posted to Dalton, which was at the time a training station near Thirsk, North Yorkshire. Here, new crews were familiarized with what to expect and look out for on Ops. Naturally Wally covered the navigation aspects of this training. Just before VE day, he was moved to Dishforth on his way to Torquay for repatriation to Canada. He did not want to return to Canada, as his Lancashire lass had not yet obtained passage. On arrival in Torquay, Wally requested a posting in the UK and was sent to Basingstoke as a Briefing Officer on Transport Command. His job was with 435 and 436 Squadrons, who were flying Dakotas, which were supplying bases in Europe and the Mediterranean area. They also flew liberated prisoners of war back to the UK. During this period he also served at Biggin Hill in the same capacity. In June of 1946, Wally finally returned to Canada. During his long leaves, Wally usually went to Colne in Lancashire, a small town near Burnley. Leaves were arranged through the Lady Rider Club for overseas troops. During one such leave, on his arrival at Bournemouth, he was put up in a house owned by what turned out to be his future in-laws. Near the last day of his leave, their daughter returned home and it was love at first sight. They corresponded over the next few months and were married the following April. They actually only spent 32 hours together before they were married, but at the time of the writing of this book (2003) they were enjoying their 59th year together.

The last words I leave to Wally.

'My final thoughts of Croft are of the heavy losses we suffered. During the eight months I was at Croft, only 3 crews finished their tours. On average Bomber Command lost 3% of its aircraft per raid, and it was our view that when one does more than thirty trips, the odds were pretty slim.'

Meanwhile, back at Goosepool, attacks on enemy airfields came next on the night of June 9/10th 1944. A force of 401 aircraft of 1,4,6 and 8 Groups attacked the German airfields of Flers, Le Mans, Lavel and Renes. With the railways taking a pounding, it was considered that the Germans might use these airfields to bring in vital reinforcements and equipment. The next night, 419 sent 10 Lancasters to attack the marshalling yards at Versailles. Due to a structural fault, as W/C Pleasance took off, his aircraft lost power on two of its engines. The aircraft had barely left the ground and Pleasance was unable to make the aircraft climb. Twenty miles from the airfield the Lancaster was still only at about 200 feet and flatly refused to gain height. Somehow, the engineer P/O McGill managed to restore power to the two engines, and slowly the aircraft began to climb. Pleasance elected to continue with the operation and managed to bomb the target before returning to Goosepool. This raid closed the main Paris to Trappes rail link and damage large numbers of rolling stock. Both officers were later decorated for their coolness and dedication to duty during the emergency, W/C Pleasance receiving a bar to his DFC.

428 did their bit and 10 of their aircraft returned to Brest for a spot of gardening. Next day, they continued with gardening Ops to St Nazaire, Lorient and West Brest. F/O Gonyou blew a tyre on takeoff, but elected to continue with the operation.

Having bombed the target, he and his crew returned to Goosepool, where Gonyou carried out a perfect landing without damage to the aircraft or injury to the crew. During the same raid, P/O Sinclair carried out the last trip of his tour.

On June 11/12th, two Ghost Squadron crews carried out day H2S radar cross-countries. Four more carried out night cross countries and low level bombing exercises, during which F/O Martin suffered a loss of power in the port outer and lost control. He ordered his crew to abandon but remained behind in the Halifax himself. He forced landed the aircraft (N953) just to the west of Claxton Hall, some 7 miles from the centre of York. He suffered several severe injuries, including a fractured ankle, four fractured vertebrae, and burns. Help was forthcoming, and he was removed from the wreckage and taken to York Military hospital where he was placed on the dangerously ill list. Word was received at Middleton that he would probably not fly for at least a year. The aircraft was badly burned and a total loss. This Halifax II was to be the last non-operational Halifax to be lost by 428, and also the last Halifax II to be lost by a front line squadron.

That night, 428 had sent five crews on mining operations to West Brest, St Nazaire and Lorient, all returned safe.

Andrew Mynarski

On the night of June 12/13th, the Moosemen despatched 16 Lancasters to bomb the railway marshalling yards at Cambrai, 44-km S/S/E of Lille in France.

One of the Lancasters, VR-A KB726, was flown by F/O A (Art) De Breyne. As it crossed the French Coast, F/O G P (Pat) Brophy in the tail turret saw the probing fingers of several searchlights. Below he saw the flashes of exploding light flak. Each flak-burst was instantly replaced by the usual black dumbell shaped telltale cloud of smoke. Pat informed the skipper of the flak and its position. Hardly had the words left his mouth when he was blinded with blue light as the aircraft was illuminated by a master searchlight. Now the bomber had been found several other white beamed searchlights pounced on the Lancaster. Now coned by searchlights it was only a mater of time before the flak gunners would give the aircraft their undivided attention. Art de Breyne thought that it would also be just their luck to be passing a fighter box containing an unemployed Junkers Ju88 or Messerschmitt 110. Having warned the crew that he was going to take evasive action he corkscrewed left, hoping to shake off the lights. As quickly as the searchlights had found them they were gone. The bomber was once again enshrouded by the darkness of the night. Had De Breyne pulled it off, or was it that now their presence was known, the lights had let them go to allow a nightfighter to move in for the attack. If a night fighter pilot had seen them and was preparing to sneak in for the kill he would need a few moments to regain his night vision after the intensity of the searchlights.

De Breyne took this opportunity to begin reducing height down to their low level bombing height of 2,000 feet. As they approached the small village of Villers-Bocage still in the decent at around 5,000 feet, Brophy in the tail turret saw for an instant what he identified as a twin-engined fighter, below and astern of the Lancaster. Pat shouted a warning into the intercom, 'Bogey astern, six o'clock.' It disappeared in an instant as De Breyne began to corkscrew for a second time.

From left to right, front row: Pat Brophy; Roy Vigars; Andy Mynarski;
Back row: Jim Kelly; Art de Breyne; Jack Friday; Bob Bodie   Photo: courtesty of Canadian forces

Brophy saw the fighter again, coming up quickly from below; he continued his commentary on the intercom, informing the crew of the fighters every move. He turned his turret towards the enemy aircraft, which was by now identified as a Ju88, and opened fire. The enemy aircraft also opened fire, at exactly 13 minutes past midnight, on the 13th day of the month, whilst the crew were carrying out their 13th operation. It only took a couple of cannon rounds to set fire to both of the Lancaster's port engines and put them out of action. The petrol tank between the port engines was also set on fire. Coming out of the bottom of the corkscrew around 3,000 to 4,000 feet, De Breyne realised that the intercom was dead, and because the lighting had failed, he could not read the instrument panel. With the loss of two engines on the same side, and with a full load of bombs, he had no choice but to lose altitude. The Flight Engineer, Roy Vigars, was standing to the right of the pilot's seat. With the intercom dead, De Breyne used a hand signal to indicate to the engineer that the crew was to bale out. At the same time, he tapped out the pre-arranged letter P in Morse on the signal light button, to inform the crew that they too had to abandon the aircraft.

Unbeknown to De Breyne, other rounds had entered the fuselage between the mid-upper and tail turrets, severing and igniting the hydraulic fluid lines feeding Brophy's turret. Pat Brophy was aware that the intercom was U/S and suspected that he might soon receive the bale out signal. This would be a pre-arranged letter P (.--.), which would be flashed in Morse code on the red signal lamp in his turret. It never came. That circuit had been cut at the same time as the intercom.

Brophy was aware of the fire behind him in the fuselage, and realised that the aircraft was finished. His turret was still pointing to port after firing at the Ju88. As there was no room in the cramped turret for a parachute pack, the SOP for the rear gunner was to rotate his turret and align it with the fuselage with the guns pointing aft. Next, he was to open the turret doors behind his back, climb back into the fuselage, clip on his chute, and dive out of the door, which on the Lancaster was placed on the starboard side just forward of the tailplane. The alternative method of escape was for the gunner to open the turret doors, reach into the fuselage for his chute, clip it on, close the doors again, and having turned the turret fully to the left or right, open the doors again and fall out backwards.

Brophy pressed the foot pedal to rotate the turret to the left. Nothing happened. It was immobile, due to the loss of the hydraulic fluid. Meanwhile the flames were getting closer. It was time for plan B. Prising the doors open a little, Brophy managed to reach into the fuselage, retrieve his parachute, and clip it onto his chest. The turret had an emergency crank handle for just such a situation, which would allow the gunner to rotate the turret sideways manually and escape in the normal manner. Brophy grasped the handle and tried to rotate it. It was jammed solid, and broke off in his hand. He was now trapped in his turret, with no possible chance of escaping before the stricken Lancaster hit the ground.

W/O2 A C (Andrew) Mynarski in the mid-upper turret must have also received the flashing P signal telling him to bale out. He pulled down the folding step and dropped from the mid-upper turret onto the floor of the Lanc. He made his way aft towards the same escape hatch that Brophy would have used. He opened the hatch door and prepared to leave the aircraft. Just before he jumped he looked towards the rear of the fuselage and saw Pat Brophy through the Perspex of the turret. One look at the expression on Brophy's face told Mynarski that the tail gunner was in a fix, and that he needed help. Mynarski immediately moved away from the hatch and made his way through the barrier of flame towards the tail turret. The fuselage, aft of the hatch, is very cramped and Andrew had to climb over the Elsan toilet to reach the tailplane spar, which passes through the fuselage at this point. Mynarski had to climb over the spar to reach the trapped gunner. There was no space to stand up in and Mynarski whilst wearing bulky flying clothing and his chute, had to crawl on his hands and knees.

When he reached the turret the lower part of his clothing was on fire. Brophy realised that the situation was hopeless and shook his head at Mynarski, shouting, 'Don't try', and he tried to wave Andrew away. Mynarski took no notice, and with complete disregard to his own situation tried to smash the turret free with a fire axe. The turret moved slightly, but it would not give. Mynarski dropped the axe, and began to tear at the turret doors with his bare hands. By now he must have been in agony, his uniform trousers and chute were well alight and the situation was hopeless. Brophy realised that nothing more could be done. He shouted to Mynarski, 'Go back Andy. Get out.' Mynarski reluctantly suspected that he could do nothing to help Brophy. The adrenaline of the moment must have tapered away, to be replaced by pain and the shame at the realisation that he must leave Brophy and jump. Still he dallied, in disbelief that there wasn't something else he could do. Brophy waved him away for a second time. Mynarski nodded. The look on his face told it all. Andy was ashamed that his efforts had not been enough to save the trapped gunner. He turned around and began to negotiate the cramped confines of the tail section. There was little choice but to crawl backwards over the spar and through the blazing hydraulic fluid. As he went he looked back at Brophy constantly, with a look of despair on his face. From his vantagepoint in the rear turret, Brophy saw Mynarski reach the hatch and slowly stand up. Once on his feet, and with his clothes ablaze, he turned towards Brophy, stood to attention, and saluted. His lips moved, and although Brophy could not hear, he realised that Mynarski had said 'Good night Sir.' At that he turned and jumped from the hatch.

In actual fact, Mynarski had been the first to jump; the remainder of the crew jumped a short time later, having experienced some problems of their own. After the order to bale out was given, Sgt J W (Jack) Friday in the bomb aimer's position bent down and grabbed the handle on the escape hatch and pulled hard. The slipstream blew the hatch cover up into his face, striking him above the eye and knocking him out. He was found by Roy Vigars when he made his way down to the bomb aimer's position in preparation to baling out.

Vigars found Jack Friday lying unconscious by the hatch and turned him over. He had a huge gash over one eye. Roy realised that he had to get him safely out of the aircraft somehow and so he took the bomb aimer's parachute pack from its stowage and clipped it onto Friday's chest. Manhandling the bomb aimer over the hatch, Vigars grabbed the ripcord D-ring and dropped him out of the aircraft. The unconscious bomb aimer landed safely near Hedauville.

When the navigator F/O A R (Bob) Bodie reached the bomb-aimer's position he saw that Roy Vigars was hanging onto the internal structure of the aircraft whilst kicking at the hatch cover, which had jammed in the opening. Vigars eventually kicked it free and jumped, followed by Bodie.

W/O2 W J (Jim) Kelly in the radio operator's station was working the radio, oblivious to what was going on. When the Lanc took evasive action for the second time, he realised that something was wrong. Feeling the fighter's bullets slamming into the aircraft and smelling smoke, he removed his earphones and looked around. He could see the port wing on fire and realised that the others were making their way forward to the hatch. He clipped his chute onto his chest and went forward past Art De Breyne and down into the nose. Once there he followed Bodie out of the hatch.

While all this was going on, Art De Breyne was wrestling with the controls. With no lights to see the instruments by he had no idea what the speed of the aircraft was, nor its height. Flying completely blind, he gauged the aircraft's speed by the sound of the slipstream. He looked out over the port wing at a distant vertically pointing searchlight, which gave him some idea of the horizontal orientation of the crippled Lancaster. With both engines knocked out on the same wing, he fought to keep the port wing up by using large amounts of starboard rudder and aileron. If he had relaxed the pressure on the controls the tendency would have been for the aircraft to drop the port wing and roll to the left. This would have given the crew (and himself) no chance at all to get out. They would have been immediately pinned down by gyroscopic G-forces and unable to crawl to the hatches as the aircraft entered into a spiral dive. When De Breyne was sure that the others had gone, he gave up the fight to maintain height and equalised the isometric situation by closing the throttles on the two starboard engines. Now with the Lancaster acquiring the attributes of a huge glider, the port wing-drop tendency abated. Without engine power, the Lancaster increased its descent towards the ground, albeit in a wings level attitude. This allowed de Breyne to abandon the controls and make for the escape hatch, without the fear of the bomber rolling onto its back. As he did not normally move around the aircraft much, the pilot wore a seat type parachute pack, unlike the clip-on chest type warn by the rest of the crew. This saved him the time required to find his parachute in its stowage and clip it on. However, the pilot's clumsy seat type parachute pack restricted him from standing up fully. The square biscuit shaped pack dropped a little when the wearer stood up and rubbed against the back of his thighs, restricting his rearward leg movements. The pilot was always the last to go and often had little time if any to get out. The seat-pack did nothing to alleviate this situation. One took on the appearance of a waddling duck, whilst shuffling for the hatch in a semi bowed stance. However, De Breyne managed to reach the hatch and dive out, pulling the ripcord as he went. So low was the aircraft by this time that when his chute opened, he only had time to swing a couple of times before landing in a wheat field.

Now the only soul left on the earth-bound Lancaster was Pat Brophy, hopelessly trapped within his own Perspex, aluminium and steel clad coffin. The aircraft was descending less steeply now but he knew his fate was sealed. The tail turret sits approximately 50 feet from the bomb bay, which on this occasion held five tons of high explosive bombs. He braced himself for the final impact, whilst preying that Andy had survived. He dared to hope too that he, by some miracle, would come out of this alive. He did not have long to wait for the answer. The Lancaster suddenly hit the ground with a huge bang and ploughed its way across a field. During this wild tumultuous ride, the blazing port wing struck a tree and was surgically removed from the remainder of the aircraft, saving Pat from a fiery grave. God had indeed been listening to his prayers. As the aircraft hit the ground and slammed into the tree, it spun to port, the turret mechanism holding Brophy prisoner snapped around, and when the doors behind Brophy flew open under the centrifugal weight of his body he was pitched out of the turret. He ended up lying against a small tree about 50 feet short of the battered remains of the Lancaster. It was as though some gentle unseen hand had carefully removed him from the turret, and gently set him down, well out of harm's way. During that wild toboggan ride, Pat heard two huge explosions, but was not sure whether they were a couple of the bombs going off or the fuel tanks exploding. He lay for a while not daring to move. Bit by bit he began to check himself over, expecting to have broken something. He gingerly began to move his muscles, whilst anticipating the inevitable sudden stab of pain. He was pleasantly surprised to find that he could stand up, and that he appeared to be completely unscathed. In actual fact there was not a scratch on him. He did not get away completely scot-free however. When he removed his helmet, the trauma of the whole episode had caused a large clump of his hair to fall out. A small price to pay for surviving such a harrowing event.

With the intercom U/S, Art be Breyne had not known for sure if the gunners in the rear of the aircraft had got out. They would normally jump unseen from the rear hatch, unlike the remainder of the Lancaster's crew who were normally in sight of the pilot as they filed past him as they went down into the nose.

After landing, De Breyne lay on the ground, recovering from the ordeal of the last few minutes. Whilst he lay there, he watched other aircraft in the bomber stream as they descended to their 2,000 feet bombing height, prior to reaching the target some 25 miles away. He saw four more unidentified aircraft fall, and hoped that some of them at least were German. It turned out that during operations over Northern France that night, Bomber Command were to lose a total of 23 aircraft,[111] (12 on the Cambrai raid). All were from 4 and 6 Group. Cambrai was not the only railway installation on the target list that night. Other similar targets included Poitiers, Caen, Arras, Amiens/St-Roch and Longueau. The Cambrai attack was only partially successful, as some bombers missed the railway yards and their bombs fell in the town.

Roy Vigars landed close to a German airfield that was dispatching Me110 night fighters. He twisted his hip in the process but was ok. He found a clump of bushes where he slept until dawn. Having landed in a grain field, Jim Kelly remained seated, enjoying the calm after the cacophony of the previous few minutes. He, too, was aware of the bomber stream passing overhead. He realised that unlike himself, they would be back home in a few hours, enjoying the comforts of Goosepool. In the distance, searchlights plied the sky near Amiens as they attempted to pick up the bombers. Also, exploding bombs could be heard, and over to the left another town was burning.[112] Having composed himself, Kelly began to think about evading capture. He thought about the evasion lectures back at Middleton, and decided that the first thing to do was to clear out the contents of his pockets and bury them. He buried his parachute under a tree and then began to walk towards some trees that were highlighted by the red glow of the night sky. Kelly had been walking for a while when he heard someone coming towards him. The person was bareheaded and in the gloom did not look like a German soldier. He looked for a weapon and found a large stone. Then he realised that Lady Luck was with him, it was Bodie the navigator.

Bodie's arrival in France had been almost identical to Kelly's. Having buried his chute he, too, had set off for the trees, where he was startled by a shadowy figure, which happily turned out to be Kelly. They both set off to continue evading, and would spend the remainder of their time in France together. Initially they were hidden in a barn by a French farmer. Soon after, another Frenchman arrived. He had with him Andy Mynarski's flying helmet. He told them that at Bresle, a group of local people had seen an aviator descending from a burning aircraft with his clothes on fire. They rushed to his aid and found him alive, but he had suffered severe burns to his body. Sadly he died soon after.

[111] 6 Lancasters and 17 Halifaxes
[112] Probably Arras

Art De Breyne returned to the UK on September 13th, after the American First Army overran the village of Tracy Le Val where he had been harboured by the French. Jim Kelly and Bob Bodie had a similar experience and also returned to the UK.

Having stood up and found himself without a scratch, Pat Brophy threw his parachute and harness into the burning wreckage of the Lancaster and vacated the area. Having wandered around for a while, at about 5 am he met a young man who was delivering milk. His name was Paul Cresson, and fortunately for Pat, was a member of the French underground. Paul took Brophy to his mother's house. She spoke English, which was a great help. They hid Pat in the barn and got rid of his uniform. Pat was moved around, as at that stage of the war, after D-Day, it was safer to hang onto evaders rather than send them down the escape line. The situation was too fluid and it was not worth the risk of bumping into retreating German units. Whilst with the underground, Pat tried his hand at sabotage, working along side Paul and his brother Pierre. Pat met a variety of commonwealth airmen as they were harboured by different families. To avoid arousing the suspicions of collaborators they were moved around frequently. Eventually, Pat and a small group of evaders found themselves in Sallaumines, where they were liberated on September 1st 1944 by the advancing British army. He was flown from Vitry airfield to Reading, having spent three months evading capture. Once back in England, Pat was sent by train to London for de-briefing. Whilst there he was able to report Andy Mynarski's selfless act of heroism, and the fact that if he had not tried to save Pat he would probably have been there with him.

Roy Vigars woke up next morning and set off again, but despite being given help and some civilian clothing by a French family, he was later captured by soldiers from a flak emplacement who had spotted him. He was initially taken to the famous Amiens Prison, where Mosquitoes of the RAF had breached the walls to release captured members of the French underground during February 1944.

Having landed unconscious by the chateau, Jack Friday had been found by two French farm workers who took him to a doctor. The doctor was worried about treating the injured Friday, as the Germans often shot anyone who they suspected may have assisted allied airmen. He handed Jack over to the Germans who took him unconscious to Amiens Jail. He woke four days later in a cell with his head heavily bandaged. After he had recovered sufficiently to travel, he was taken to the railway station, where he was to join other prisoners who were being transported to a POW camp. While on the platform he was delighted to see Roy Vigars, who was also on his way to the same place, which turned out to be a brand new camp, Stalag luft 7 at Breslau on the Polish border. In January 1945, word arrived that the Russian Army was about to overrun the area and so the camp was to be evacuated. On the 18th, the majority of the camp departed and marched west. Amongst the departing inmates was Jack Friday. Roy Vigars remained behind to assist with the stretcher cases. Soon after this they were moved by truck to Stalag 344. After many forced marches, in which many of his fellow prisoners succumbed to starvation and the elements, Jack Friday ended up at Stalag luft 3A, where he was eventually liberated by the Russians.

The Germans had decided that all RAF POWs were to move to Bavaria as hostages. To this end, Roy's contingent was moved southwest to Stalag 7B at Memmingham on the Swiss border. Yet another move during March saw the prisoners arriving at Stalag 383. On April 22nd, the German Camp Commandant surrendered to a British Medical Officer who held the highest rank amongst the prisoners. At 4 o'clock in the afternoon an American Jeep arrived at the gates and that was that. The Americans later transported Roy Vigars and the others to an airfield at Frankfurt. From there they flew by Dakota, in groups of 24, to Reims in France. Here, Roy and his group were put aboard a Lancaster and flown back to Wing Airfield, Cambridgeshire. Roy's home was in Guildford and he arrived there on the 8th of May, VE day. Whilst there he was visited by Jack Friday, who had travelled up to see Roy from Bournemouth where he was waiting to be repatriated to Canada. To this day, except for the briefing at Middleton, Jack remembers nothing of the events prior to waking up in the prison cell at Amiens.

Despite the fact that Pat Brophy was the only witness, when the authorities received word of Mynarski's heroic sacrifice they recommended that he be awarded the highest award possible, the Victoria Cross.[113] Andrew Mynarski's posthumous Victoria Cross was promulgated in the London Gazette on October 8th 1946. Andrew was to be the last recipient of the Victoria Cross, the highest award for valour, during World War Two, and the only VC to be given to a Canadian airman.

During the summer of 2002 I took the pilgrimage to Andrew's resting place, in the little village of Meharicourt. In the middle of the village, which is just off the A1, roughly half way between Paris and Lille, is a small civilian cemetery. As you would imagine, it contains many graves, most of which belong to former civilian residents of the area. However, at the rear of the cemetery there is a War Graves Commission plot, containing several military graves. Andrew's well-attended headstone is there, surrounded by those of his fellow aviators. The village itself, unlike most of the modern ones that we are used to, is very quiet and austere. I imagine that its architecture has changed little since the war. If there must be a quiet, reverend, peaceful and appropriate place for heroes to rest, surely this must be it. God bless you, Andrew.

For their part, 428 had sent four crews to mine St Nazaire and Lorient that night. This they did, but Teesside's weather caused them to divert on the way home to Wellsbourne Mountford, near Stratford, Warwickshire.

Two other aircraft were lost on the Cambrai raid. The first was KB714 flown by F/O R N Wilson RCAF. This aircraft was also shot down by a night fighter and crashed at Courcelette, just 12 miles to the N/W of where Andy Mynarski had come down. All on board were killed.

The third aircraft to be lost by the Moosemen that night was KB731. F/O W M Lacey and his crew were shot down by flak and crashed near Vieux-Berquin, 18 miles N/W of Lille. The engineer Sgt B D Wilson-Law and the bomb aimer F/O R A Forbes RCAF survived and evaded capture.

---

[113] During the annual Canadian Veterans reunion which took place during 2002, I was informed by several people who were around at the time that, all things being equal, Andrew Mynarski should not have been flying with De Breyne's crew that night, and that he could have possibly survived the war. I was informed that Pat Brophy had a fight with the crew's regular mid-upper gunner the night before and that the powers that be had split them up. Andrew was asked to stand in at the last moment.

Pilot Officer
Andrew C Mynarski VC RCAF
Photo: courtesty of Canadian forces

Surrounded by other heroes   Photo: author

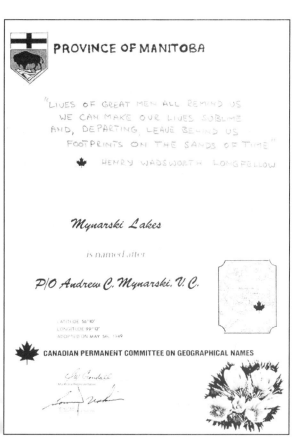

Mynarski's lakes   Photo: via Geoff Hill

Meharicourt Photo:

On the night of Wednesday the 14/15th, the Moosemen detailed 16 aircraft to carry out a raid on vital road and rail junctions at St Pol in France. Heavy cloud conditions were encountered both to and from the target and so the bombing was not considered accurate.

June 14/15th also heralded the Ghost Squadron's first Lancaster raid. Seven crews took part in operations to French marshalling yards at Cambai, Douai and St Pol. All three targets were either partially covered by cloud or haze, which caused the bombing to be scattered and inaccurate. Out of the 330 aircraft taking part, 3 Halifaxes and 1 Lancaster were shot down. The Lancaster, which carried the raid's Master Bomber, F/L J H Hewitt DFC, was shot down by a night fighter. As with the 3 Halifaxes that were also lost, there were no survivors. The loss of this 582 Squadron aircraft and its crew was a bitter blow to Bomber Command. Out of the 8-man crew, 7 of them held 4 DFCs and 3 DFMs between them. All Ghost crews returned safe.

Next day, the Ghosts briefed 6 Lancs and 6 Halifax crews to accompany the 13 to be sent by 419 on daylight operations. At the last minute, the Halifax crews were scrubbed and only the Lancs went. Although they had carried out Moleing raids previously, this was the first proper daylight raid to be carried out by either squadron. The crews had been briefed to bomb the German E Boat pens at Boulogne.

The attack was carried out from a height of 16,000 feet. Each crew had been briefed to bomb at 1-minute intervals. Due to the continuation of the very unseasonable weather, the cloud cover prevented accurate bombing and 3 of 419's crews brought their bombs back.

The formation had the luxury of a fighter escort, which probably had something to do with the fact that no enemy fighter opposition was encountered. All aircraft returned safely. This was the heaviest raid experienced by the population of Boulogne thus far in the war. Great destruction took place in the port and surrounding areas, 200 people were killed.

On the night of the 16/17th, 419 sent 16 aircraft to attack the synthetic oil plant at Sherkrade, 10 km to the N/E of Duisburg. Yet again 10/10ths cloud was found over the target area, along with heavy flak and fighter opposition. After the raid PRU photographs showed that, due to the cloud cover, the bombing was scattered.

F/L E S Smith and his crew in VR-V KB734 failed to return from this operation. Only 2 members of the crew survived, the engineer Sgt J W Trussler, who became a POW, and the bomb aimer Sgt R E Porter RCAF, who evaded capture. F/L King was the recipient of the King's Commendation for Valuable Services in the Air; this was his 10th operation.

Another 419 Lancaster, KB728, flown by P/O D Morrison RCAF, exploded during a combat with a night fighter and fell by the river at Elden, 2 miles S/W of Arnhem. There were no survivors. P/O Morrison was on his 29th trip, his penultimate before being screened from operations.

VR-G was badly holed by flak during this raid, and the navigator, F/O C E Hamilton RCAF, was slightly injured in the arm and leg. This crew were also shadowed by an enemy aircraft, which the gunners shot at. During de-briefing back at Middleton, the crew claimed this aircraft as destroyed. The crew of VR-J had to turn back on the way to the target when their tail gunner became sick.

This particular raid was carried out by 312 aircraft, belonging to 1,4,6 and 8 Groups. A night fighter beacon at Bocholt, 24 miles N/N/W of the target, had been chosen by the fighter controller as a collection point for his fighters. This must have played a large part in the demise of the 22 bombers shot down by fighters during the raid on Sherkrade. A further 10 aircraft were shot down by flak.

428 were more fortunate, their first Lancaster soiree to Happy Valley was, in comparison, fairly uneventful.

After this raid, a stand down was ordered, to allow the Moose groundcrew to carry out essential maintenance on their overworked Lancasters. The aircraft had been pushed very hard during the build up to D-Day and after the opening of the second front. Now was the time to attend to the jobs neglected due to the pressure of operations.

428 detailed 7 Lancaster and 4 Halifax crews for a gardening trip to Guernsey. Subsequently, the Lancs were scrubbed, leaving the Halifaxes to go it alone.

On the 18/19th, with the ground troops at Normandy calling the shots, a big raid was planned. 428 were to warn seven Lanc and four Halifax crews for a bombing raid, with another six detailed to mine off St Malo. Later the bombing operation was scrubbed and eventually five Halifaxes departed for the gardening operation.

419 briefed 6 Lancaster crews for bombing and 8 Halifax crews for gardening on the 19/20th. The weather for June was not very good, bad enough for Europe and the rest of the country, but throw in the Teesside weather cocktail and one had no chance.

For the next day, 428's diary reads, 'Operations laid on, but unless someone takes a hand in the weather, no deal.' 'Everyone's trying to decide what day summer was on this year.' Nothing changes. Due in part to poor weather over the continent it would be June 21st before 419 would carry out its next operation. Meanwhile, valuable air training continued to keep the Moosemen on top form. Cross country, fighter affiliation and bombing training exercises kept the aircrew busy.

Such was the fluid situation across the channel that, when Goosepool's crews were detailed at 01:00 on Wednesday the 21st for a raid on the flying bomb storage site at St Martin L' Hortier, at 11:00 it was cancelled. It was back on again at 13:40, when the squadron was told to take off at 15:45. At 15:35 it was postponed until 16:15, then postponed again until 17:15. The 15 Moose and 6 Ghost crews did manage to take off and were escorted by RAF Spitfires to the target, some 18 miles S/E of Dieppe. Just for a change, at first the weather was perfect, but by the time the bombers had reached the target they had to contend with bombing through 10/10ths cloud. Enemy opposition was considered negligible and all aircraft returned safely.

428's diary continued - 'It's mid summer's day (according to the natives), let's celebrate by putting on our sweaters.'

All of 419's gunners who were not carrying out training at the ranges at Sutton Bank were employed in the station armoury, belt filling and changing tracer in the belts from night to day ammunition. The aircrew continued their training with circuits and bumps, three engined flying, air to air firing and H2S Radar bombing exercises. Ten air gunners and the same number of engineers were detailed to carry out turret manipulation and ground firing at the Sutton Bank range. The next day the weather was 100% no better, and still too duff for operations.

On the 23/24th, sixteen of 419's Lancasters and six from 428 targeted a flying bomb site at Biendecques, 2 miles S/E of St Omer. Bombing was carried out from a height of 14,000 feet through cloud. The target the following night was another flying bomb site, this time at Bemieres, 18 km south of Lille. Six more Ghost crews took their Halifaxes on a gardening detail to French ports. Again all Moose and Ghost aircraft returned safe. Whilst the Moosemen were over France, some of their crews were carrying out night flying training at Middleton. Pilot Officer Mansfield's logbook acquired some strong words written in red ink after his attempt at a night landing. After touching down he had run off the end of Middleton's main runway and rendezvoused with the beam approach hut. Both were badly damaged, the Lancaster, VR-W, was Cat C, fortunately no one was hurt.

The fluid situation in France continued to thwart the brass in Bomber Command. On Sunday June 25th, sixteen of 419's aircraft were warned of a possible daylight mission. Later this was changed to a night Op. During the evening, this was changed yet again to an early morning raid on the 26th. This was scrubbed and 16 crews were briefed again, this time to take off at 11:00 hours. This was changed to a standby, and in the late afternoon cancelled, with a warning for an early morning take-off on the 27th.

428 were able to carry out an 8 Halifax gardening operation off three French ports, they were the only unit in the command mining that night. The weather at base was very poor and they had to divert to St Ivel, Cornwall.

After standing by till noon on the 27th, the daylight operation detailed the previous day was cancelled. Then 17 of 419's crews and 8 from 428 prepared their Lancasters for a night operation. The target was Foret Deawy and this time it took place. The crews bombed from 12,000 feet and came home. There had been only two enemy fighters seen, and only a small amount of flak encountered. During this raid, trials took place of the 'Boozer' equipment which had been fitted to The Ruhr Express. The equipment did not work properly, it was thought that this was due to an interaction between itself and other radar equipment. Whilst the Lancaster lads were at Foret Deawy, 8 of their Halifaxes were gardening off St Nazaire.

On Wednesday the 28th, the crews were getting a bit fed up of the stop start situation. After standing by all day for word of either a day or night-time bombing operation, the detail was eventually cancelled and the squadron was warned of an early morning take-off on the 29th. This did not prevent four of 428's Halifaxes from mining off Brest, however, whilst two more stood by as replacements for operations at Skipton.

Next morning 18 aircraft belonging to the Moosemen were detailed for operations and told that take-off would be 11:00 hours. The crews were briefed at 08:30, but take-off was subsequently postponed until 13:00. It was then further postponed until 16:00 hours, and then cancelled, the crews being warned of an early morning Op on the 30th and that briefing would be at 08:00. At 21:00 hours that night, the 29th, the briefing was moved forward to 02:00. At this revised briefing, the crews were told that they would take off at 05:15, this was cancelled at 05:00. The weather was still very poor but 18 Moose and 8 Ghost crews were warned for a night take-off. This was also cancelled just prior to briefing.

With the beginning of the second front, 419 thought that they would be called upon to supply a maximum effort. The number of times the squadron had actually been on operations was a great disappointment to all of its personnel. Although it was realised that the amazingly unseasonable weather had been primarily responsible for this, it had been a rather awkward situation. Since the June 6th the squadron had been briefed on 12 days and had the operations cancelled several times after having been on a stand-by basis all day. This retarded 419's training program to a marked degree, with the result that ten crews, which had reported for duty around the middle of the month, had not taken part in any operations during June. The groundcrews, and particularly the armament section, performed a marvellous job in keeping the aircraft serviceability to such an extremely high level, and in bombing and de-bombing aircraft almost daily. One snag encountered was the use of day and night tracer bullets, but that was satisfactorily ironed out by the end of the month. When daylight operations were first ordered there was a certain amount of trepidation amongst squadron personnel, but after participating in three daylight attacks, the squadron's personnel were definitely in favour of them. The number of Lancaster Xs on charge with the squadron at the end of June totalled 20. 419 had flown a total of 214 individual sorties amounting to 1,003 operational flying hours. They also flew 348 non-operational hours. The number of bombs dropped during June equalled 912.15 tons. There were also 18 encounters with enemy aircraft during the month.

July 1944

On July 1st, Goosepool's stop-start saga continued. A stand-down was ordered in the morning, this being changed at noon to a stand-by. Take off time was set for 22:30. This effort was cancelled at 19:00 hours. The lousy weather continued and even flying training was cancelled. It had rained heavily for days and days. There was a change of bomb load during the day, resulting in one load of bombs being removed from the aircraft only to be replaced by another, after which they were left in the aircraft.

Next day, fifteen of 419's aircraft were briefed for night operations, and, you guessed it, this operation was cancelled at 18:15. The day after saw more of the same, 15 briefed and 15 cancelled, one hour prior to take-off. The July 4th saw better weather conditions, which allowed both squadrons to carry out a moonlight raid on the rail yards at Villeneuve-St-Georges. Three Moose aircraft and one from the Ghost Squadron were lost during this raid.

VR-J KB718, flown by F/O Frame RCAF, was shot down by a night fighter. Frame and three members of his crew evaded capture, whilst the other three became POWs. VR-U KB723, flown by F/O C A Steepe RCAF, was hit by flak. Three crew members were killed, three evaded capture and one became a POW. KB727, flown by F/O J M Stevenson RCAF was shot down by a Ju88. Stevenson himself managed to evade capture; the remainder of the crew became POWs.

428's loss was the crew of P/O W C Gay, who had taken off at 21:43. They crashed at 00:42 near La Mailleraye-sur-Seine, 15-km W/N/W of Rouen, France. P/O Gay was killed along with his tail gunner, F/S S J Swartz. Three of the crew evaded whilst two more were captured. Their mount, Lancaster NA-Q KB756 was the first Lanc to be lost by 428. They had been classed as a very good crew and had been very popular with the squadron. The bomb aimer, P/O R M Woychuk was especially missed, as he was a very good cartoonist and had delighted the boys with his work. Woychuk had survived the crash but had become a POW. The Ghosts had taken delivery of this aircraft on 11th June; when lost, this aircraft had flown a total of 61.40 hours.

Due to the weather, more cancellations were suffered on the 5/6th, but 428 sent six Halifaxes (affectionately known as the 'Herring Fleet') to sow mines off St Nazaire and Brest. Again they were the only gardening party sent aloft by Bomber Command that night, quite an accolade considering that, on several occasions, 428 had taken the brunt of the atrocious weather over any other squadron. However, if they could handle Darlington's weather, they could cope with anything Mother Nature could throw at them. In addition, they had to travel a greater distance than anyone else to do it. On this occasion however, the return journey was a little shorter than usual, as Goosepool's weather played up yet again and they all had to divert to Poulsham on the way back. Although they didn't know it at the time, this would be the Ghost Squadron's last Halifax operation.

428 had been detailed for a gardening Op on the 7th, but this was cancelled at 13:00. Meanwhile, the squadron continued with its Lancaster training. Three crews took part in cross-country training exercises, but were unable to return to Goosepool due to duff-weather. Although only 6 miles away, Croft was clear and able to accommodate the returning aircraft. At 17.00 the weather cleared, which allowed the stranded kites to return to Middleton.

419 took off at 19:30 that night to attack enemy troop concentrations at Caen, just ahead of the allied lines. A total force of 467 bombers, belonging to 1,4,6 and 8 Groups, had been sent on this raid, in the hopes that it would assist the advance of Allied troops. The Canadian 1st and British 2nd Armies had been stalled by a series of heavily defended villages just to the north of Caen. Due to the possibility of Allied bombs falling on nearby British and Canadian troops, the initial plan was changed and the aiming point was moved back nearer to the northern edge of Caen and an adjacent area of open ground. The Master Bomber that evening was W/C S P Daniels of 35 Squadron. He ensured that the raid was carried out with great precision. The two aiming points had been well marked by Oboe Mosquitoes. Over 2,276 tons of bombs were dropped from a height of 7,000 feet, in what was a very concentrated attack in very good weather.

The northern suburbs of the city were devastated, and the raid turned out to be in the wrong place after all. Using hindsight the original decision to drop the bombs just ahead of the allied troops would have ensured greater damage to the German troops, as fewer were actually concentrated in the area bombed. The Moosemen were able to contribute only 12 serviceable aircraft for this raid, and they all returned to base without incident. Four aircraft from other squadrons were lost. The sea claimed one aircraft each from 166 and 626 Squadrons, another belonging to 550 was hit by an allied bomb and limped to Manston airfield in Kent, where it was wrecked on landing, fortunately without injury to the crew. Only one aircraft was attacked by an enemy fighter. This was a Mosquito of 105 Squadron, flown by S/L W Blessing. He ordered his navigator P/O P T Burke to bale out but was unable to do so and was killed.

Operations continued for the 419 with raids to a flying bomb site at Mont Candon on the 9/10th. On the same day, word came through that no further operations were scheduled for 428's Halifaxes, and from this date hence, all Ops would be on Lancasters. Many had completed 50-60 operational trips and the consensus was that their faithful Halifax IIs had certainly earned their retirement.

On the 12/13th, Goosepool sent both squadrons to swell the ranks of a force of 222 heavy bombers which were to attack flying bomb sites. A storage site at Thivirny, near the banks of the river Oise, some 27 miles north of Paris, was the venue for the Moose Squadron, whilst the Ghosts went to Acquet. 419 was part of another force of 234 aircraft when again Doodlebug sites were bombed on the 15/16th, this time at Bois des Jardins.

Three days later, 419 were back at Caen. 17 aircraft had taken-off at 03:30 to bomb German fortified villages, as the allies were preparing to carry out an armoured attack. Some 5,000 tons of bombs were dropped by the 942 Bomber Command aircraft taking part in this raid. Amongst the enemy units badly affected were the 21st Panzer Division and the 16th Luftwaffe Field Division.

As F/O J H Calder's bomb aimer, F/O M J Bernardi, pressed the tit to drop their bombs, his distribution panel short-circuited and caught fire. This caused one of their 1,000-lb GP USA bombs to hang up. The fire was put out by the bomb aimer without having to use the extinguisher, and the bomb was eventually jettisoned on the way home. The master bomber was heard clearly by F/L Smith and his crew, but the Germans were trying to jam his transmissions with long Morse dashes. F/L W F McKinnon's bomb aimer F/O R Lilley saw the initial red and yellow TIs go down at 05:38, and he heard the MB order that the bomb aimers should disregard the yellows and bomb the starboard red marker. Then another yellow went down and the MB ordered everyone to bomb 200 yards to the starboard of that. On their return to Middleton, P/O A M Roy's navigator, Sgt H Segal, reported that there was a great deal of smoke and dust during the attack, some of which climbed to a height of 2,000 feet, and therefore accurate damage assessment was impossible.

After a six-day break from Ops, 428 also took part in this raid. Nine crews were detailed and reported a very successful attack. All of Goosepool's aircraft returned safely to Middleton.

A second raid was detailed for later the same day, and at 22:30 both were off again, this time to bomb the synthetic oil plant at Wesseling, near Cologne. New tactics were employed during this raid. The crews flew down England, climbing to 8/9,000 feet as they went. Once they had departed the English Coast, they dropped down to low level and flew between 2/3,000 feet until about 50 miles from the target. From there they climbed to their briefed bombing height of between 12/14,000 feet. These tactics were employed to frustrate the enemy defences and that they did. Only 1 Halifax from 425 Squadron at Tholthorpe was lost out of the 194 aircraft detailed for the operation. The raid itself lasted 20 minutes and 1,000 HE Bombs fell on the target in that time. Some 20% of the plant was destroyed, as were at the controls of VR-L when it was hit by flak. F/O Hartford had just managed to rid VR-L of the uninvited attention of several searchlights when they took hits in an engine nacelle, bomb bay doors and fuselage. All returned safe. This was the first time that Middleton's crews had carried out two trips on the same day.

On the 20th, an attack on the Buzz-bomb site at Le Hay was ordered. Twelve Lancaster crews from each squadron took part in a raid carried out by 369 aircraft, which bombed 6 different V1 sites and also a V2 site at Wizernes, 2 miles southwest of St Omer. Five hours later, on the 21st, 419 were asked to supply 4 more Lancasters as part of a 52 aircraft raid on a buzz-bomb site at Anderbeck, 30 miles S/W of Magdeburg. Limited damage was inflicted on these sites, but all 16 aircraft returned safe.

On the 23rd, Kiel received its biggest attack of the war when 629 aircraft visited the city. 14 Lancasters were sent by 419, with a further 14 being sent by 428. The German controllers got it wrong and identified the approaching aircraft as a small mine-laying force. The arrival of the bomber stream was cloaked by a sizeable number of Mandrel aircraft. This confused the German night fighter controllers. Also conspiring to surprise the defences was the fact that this was the first raid on a German target for over 2 months, and it took them by surprise. The raid lasted for only 25 minutes but the port area and the U-boat yards were devastated.

The next day Stuttgart was the target for 15 crews from each squadron. Stuttgart is 630 miles one way as the Lancaster flies, and this was the first really long trip for some crews. The information from Group regarding tactics and route was late coming through, with the result that the navigators had some difficulty in preparing their flight plans for the Op. The met winds were not as forecast, which caused some crews to fly a little south of track. Fighter and flak opposition was very heavy, and a concerted flak barrage in the target area made life very difficult for the bombers. This was the first of 3 heavy raids that would take place over a 5-day period. This series of raids would cause the most serious damage of the war to the centre of Stuttgart, which was located in a series of valleys. 461 Lancasters and 153 Halifaxes took part in this raid.

Of the 17 Lancasters lost that night, the Moosemen contributed one. Flown by F/S J A Phillis on his 11th operation, KB 719 was struck amidships by a rocket projectile and burst into flames. Phillis and Sgt R G MacKinnon RCAF baled out and managed to evade capture, whilst F/S W H Devine RCAF became a POW. The remainder of the crew perished when the aircraft came down at Bassu, 40 miles S/E of Reims. After the aircraft had caught fire, Phillis gave the order to abandon the aircraft. Before the crew could begin to bale out, the Lanc went into a spin. F/S W H Devine, the navigator, managed to open the escape hatch and eventually jump, he estimated the height of the aircraft at the time to be no more than 1,000 feet.

428's NA-V KB740, flown by F/O C M Corbet, had taken off from Middleton at 21:09. At midnight, this aircraft collided with a friendly aircraft over France whilst still some distance from the target. The Lancaster suffered damage to its propellers, bomb-doors and undercarriage. The starboard inner caught fire, but the engineer was able to feather the prop and douse the fire with the engine's Graviner fire extinguisher system. Immediately after the collision, Corbet instructed the crew to don their parachutes. He delayed giving the order to bale-out until he was able to ascertain the state of the Lanc's flying capabilities. Having taken stock of the situation, he found that the aircraft was still controllable, and decided to turn for home.

Below them, for a moment they could see the other aircraft, which also had an engine on fire. From their vantagepoint, they were unable to remain in sight of the other aircraft and see whether it crashed or not. As they turned for home, it was discovered that a vital component was missing from the aircraft, Sgt J Sanduluk, the tail gunner. He had made his own incorrect assessment of the situation, and jumped out. F/O Corbet reached the Suffolk Coast and was able to crash-land the badly damaged Lancaster on Woodbridge emergency landing strip at 03:26. No injuries to the crew were reported, but the aircraft was damaged Cat E1.

Stuttgart was again the target for Goosepool's crews the following night. Again the tactics, route, and timing were very late in reaching the squadrons. By 'set course' time, the navigators had not had time to finish their flight plans. The last aircraft was airborne 20 minutes after set course time, and had to cut corners to reach the target at the required time. The aircraft were slightly overloaded, and the pilots and flight engineers had great difficulty in getting the kites off Middleton's short runway, (28/10).

VR-P, flown by F/O Bowerman, struck a fence post 50 yards beyond the end of the runway, bursting a tyre in the process. The captain elected to continue with the operation. The 10th Lancaster to take off, VR-H, was flown by F/L W F McKinnon; his sortie was recorded as the 2,500th flown by 419. Visibility over Germany was poor, and there was a wind change at a difficult stage of the route. As a result, the aircraft were scattered by the time they reached the target and also when returning to base. All returned safely to Goosepool, including VR-P with its burst tyre. The captain carried out an extremely fine landing and no further damage was caused to the aircraft.

On the 27th, after a considerable delay, 419 finally received its squadron badge. It showed a Moose charging, its motto reading 'Moose Aswayita' (Beware of the Moose) in Cree Indian language. Thirteen aircraft were detailed for a night operation, but this was cancelled at 16:00 hours, the detail being changed for a maximum effort the next morning. When the cancellation order was received, the armourers had to set to work de-bombing the 13 aircraft and bombing them up again with a different load for the following day's mission.

After several cancellations due to bad weather, the next day's operation was finally scrubbed at noon. Seventeen aircraft from each squadron were then detailed to attack Hamburg. This was to be the first heavy raid on the city since the battle of Hamburg during the summer of 1943, and employed 307 aircraft from 1,6 and 8 Groups. The harbour and western districts came off worst, but the bombing was very scattered. Over at Croft, 431 Squadron lost 5 of its Halifaxes out of the 17 it had sent on this raid. For the Moosemen, however, all their aircraft returned without drama.

W/C McLeish had led the 17 Ghost crews, of which only 16 had made it to the target. P/O T E Magill's Lancaster, NA-K KB759 never made it to the target and was lost without trace, its 8 man crew (F/O R Parsons went along as second pilot) are commemorated on the Runnymede Memorial. This was destined to be the last operation for Goosepool during July 1944. 428's S/L Lord DFC and his crew had completed their tour and were screened from Ops on the 30th. S/L Hull moved over to 'B' Flight as commander vice, whilst F/L Edwards assumed the rank of Acting Flight Commander with 'A' Flight.

On the 31st, after a lot of panic and rush, the crews were scrubbed from a night operation when the visibility reduced to practically nil and a huge downpour enveloped. By the end of July, 11 of 419's Lancasters had been fitted with H2S.

August 1944

On August 1st, both squadrons flew to within 7 minutes of the flying bomb site at Acquet. The Master Bomber turned the bombers around as a solid wall of 10/10ths-cloud cover was encountered half way over the channel, and this continued on to the target area. When the crews returned to Middleton, the weather was little better, with the cloud base being below 1,000 feet.

Over the next few days, flying bomb and V2 rocket sites occupied the lads from Goosepool. On the 3/4th and 4/5th, they attacked Bois de Cassen. One of 428's sprog crews, flown by F/O A J Carter on their first Op, showed great courage and determination after they lost an engine soon after setting course. They managed to continue on to the target and back with only 3 engines.

The summer, if you can call it that, would still not relinquish its unseasonable weather. Having been diverted to Dishforth after the second Bois de Cassen raid, the 16 Moose and 20 Ghost crews had to grope their way back to base the next morning. When they landed at Middleton they did so through mist and fog (in August?). The weather conditions were so bad that the aircraft had to be guided in by Flying Control personnel firing Very cartridges from the end of the runway. The remainder of the British Isles evidently was enjoying something of a heatwave.

Halifax "Git up them stairs" taxiing between hangars 1 & 2 at MSG   Photo: via Geoff Hill

The road to Goosepool

For many Canadian aircrew, service life began in Canada at No.2 Manning Depot at Brandon. The depot itself was based in the exhibition buildings, with a former horse barn being pressed into service as a dormitory for over 1,000 men. This was achieved by placing the 1,000 double bunks in rows of two, where the occupants lay head to head. They had about 36 inches of space between them and the bunks on either side. Between one's feet and the feet of the guy in the next row was a six-foot corridor.

Over the first few days, everyone was kitted up, and attended lectures on King's Rules and Regulations (Air). They wore the regular RCAF uniform, but were distinguished from other ranks by a white flash in their wedge caps. Their pay at the time was one dollar 20 cents per day (Canadian). Regulation haircuts were the order of the day, and some had to revisit the barber more than once until the NCO in charge was happy. Next came the needles, loads of em. One walked between two rows of Doctors and received four needles in quick succession. Some fainted, all ended up with red and swollen arms.

Drill and PT began to dominate the entrant's time, but eventually, after about 4 weeks, they moved on to Dauphin Air Station, prior to going on to Initial Training School (ITS). At Dauphin, accommodation was in H blocks, two narrow buildings, joined in the middle by a wash room, sleeping 160 men. Each contained two rows of twenty double bunks, with a coal stove placed in the middle of the building to provide heat. The wash room contained several basins and a shower room, next to which were the toilets and a urinal trough. There was also a utility room, complete with a table and ironing boards.

Duties began the next day, and consisted of peeling potatoes, washing dishes, tables and floors. Some became batmen or cleaners in the officers' quarters, or washed and polished floors. Flarepath duties were the most sought after, as they took place at night, which relieved one of PT and drill duties. If there was no night flying, one got the evening off.

The job required one to report to the storage area at 16:30 in the afternoon, to check the watering can shaped pots which were to be placed down the side of the runways for night flying, much of it in Cessna aircraft. These pots contained about 2 gallons of Kerosene and had a spout fitted with a long wick. These had to be trimmed and the pots filled, after which it was suppertime.

The airfield had no runways, but was made up of an area about a mile square covered in level packed snow. The operation was overseen by a sergeant, who rode in the truck containing the pots. Placed on the rear of the truck were two men, who placed the pots on the tailgate and lit them. The truck traveled slowly into wind and in the direction of take-off and landing. This allowed two more men walking at the rear to set the pots on each side of the runway. They had a set routine, thirty paces out for the taxiways and forty for the runway. This resulted in a runway some 240 feet wide. The whole operation of laying out both taxiways and runways took about half an hour. After that, everyone headed for the control tower to play poker or read whilst waiting for night flying to be concluded. Night flying usually began about 19:00 hours, some times only for a couple of hours, some times much longer. Providing the wind did not change direction there was little to do. If it did change, they had to rush out, collect the pots, and lay them in the correct orientation relative to the new wind direction.

Then it was off to collect the pots again. This took less time, as the truck driver would drive down each side of the runway at about 10 mph. The man on the ground would pick up the pot by its big carrying handle, swing it up to the man standing on the tailgate, where it was caught and passed to another man who extinguished the flame. What had taken 30 minutes to lay out was recovered in a third of the time.

After their stint at Dauphin it was off by train to ITS at Saskatoon or Regina. The ITS at Regina was situated in the former normal school. Some schoolrooms had been converted into barrack rooms, whilst others continued to be classrooms. There were 5 courses, each containing three flights. Each flight contained 26 airmen, who were allocated to a former classroom. The hardwood floors had to be polished daily, and one's bed made in the approved manner. Pillows had to be fluffed, and sheets folded exactly 10 inches over the blankets, which had to be smooth and tucked in, with the corners folded at a 45-degree angle. The flight with the cleanest room got a Saturday night pass. The officer carrying out the inspection always wore white gloves and passed them over the tops of doors and other surfaces in an attempt to find dust.

Time at ITS was taken up studying mathematics, navigation, meteorology, signals, armaments and aircraft recognition. After 10 weeks and a very intensive medical, the rank of Leading Aircraftsman (LAC) was bestowed upon each airman. They were allowed to sew a badge depicting a small propeller on the sleeve of their tunic. In accordance with their increase in rank, there was a pay rise of 30 cents a day.

Although all aircrew trades were required, most hoped to leave ITS as a student pilot. At a large parade, an officer holding a large piece of paper allocated each student to his forthcoming trade. Those that came top in navigation becoming navigators and so on. After that it was off to the orderly room, where each student picked up his travel warrants and proceeded to the appropriate school.

Chosen for navigator training, 19 year old Ron Cassells, a native of Warren, Manitoba, left for 7 Observer School at Portage La Prairie. Once there, work began on a 12-day cycle basis, 12 days of training and 2 days on leave. Classes started at 08:00 and went on till 12:00. After lunch, classes resumed at 13:00 and finished at 17:00. But that was not the end; most instructors gave out homework and this kept the lads busy well into the evening. There were regular tests, with failure resulting in one being washed out. Those that didn't make it became GDs (General Duties).

Ron Cassell's first flight was on April 30th 1943, and was a map reading exercise. He flew in an Avro Anson, and the first lesson to learn was that the undercarriage had to be cranked up by hand with 100 turns of the handle. As trainee aircrew, he was entitled to flying pay of 50 cents per day for every day he flew.

After 10 days, Ron completed 4 flights, during which he had received instruction in map reading, photography, and use of the drift recorder and the astro compass. Work continued with classes on the various relevant subjects, such as Morse and Astro Navigation, coupled with flying training. If one flew at night and landed before midnight, classes started at 08:00. If one landed before 03:00, classes started at 10:00. After 03:00 classes didn't start until lunch. On the nights one didn't fly, there was studying and astro shots.

Ron's course graduated on October 14th 1943, in time to be posted overseas. After a spot of leave, he was off to Halifax. Once there he was issued with overseas kit and had to undergo medical and dental examinations and pressure chamber tests.

On the morning of November 2nd, he and his contingent were marched down to the docks and boarded the Mauritania for England. The ship carried 12,500 passengers; 5,500 aircrew, 500 Americans, 500 Canadian sailors and 1,500 assorted service personnel, including nurses and airwomen. When the ship arrived at Liverpool on November 11th, Ron's contingent was marched to the railway station where they boarded trains to Bournemouth, which was a holding unit for Canadian airman. Once there, they were billeted in resort hotels and for a while life was easy. One day, they were told that they were going north, to Whitley Bay, near Newcastle, for 2 weeks' commando training. This was the Canadians first taste of northeast Britain's weather. Having left a scorching Bournemouth, it was some shock to find such a contrast with Whitley Bay's miserable weather. During their first night, Ron and his roommates burned a whole week's coal ration in an attempt to stay warm.

Once back at Bournemouth, things returned to a more civilized state, and soon they were off again to Bishops Court in County Down, Ireland. Travelling by train to Stranraer, they took a milk boat to Larne, followed by a train to Belfast. From here there was a bus to Bishop's Court, which was within 2 miles of the border with Southern Ireland.

Finding the spring-like weather much better than Whitley Bay, Ron and his fellow students were heartened, until they saw that their accommodation was a Nissen hut, that is. Bishop's Court had been a former RAF Observer's school. Ron's party was to become the first advanced flying school course. There were 64 navigators on the course, 23 Canadians and 32 Australians, all fresh from training in Canada.

In the last week of March, everyone was off again, this time to an OTU at Ossington, 6 miles N/N/W of Newark. Many of the navigators had gone to other OTUs, leaving only 18 navigators to join an equal number of Canadian pilots, bomb aimers, and wireless operators. Also posted in were 36 gunners.

They were to spend the first week in ground school with some free time. It was expected that by the end of the first week, everyone would have formed themselves into crews, and reported who was with whom to the chief flying instructor (CFI).

Ron met up with 19 year old Jack (Mac) McKenzie, a bomb aimer from Riverhurst, Saskatchewan, whom he had met at Portage La Prairie. They both went off to find a pilot, and found Cliff Clarke. Next came two gunners, Jack Watson, age 21 from Gal, Ontario, and 28 year old Bill Carr from Toronto. They too agreed to join the crew. Being stuck for a wireless operator, Ron and Mac decided to visit the wireless section and see who was there. There they found Al (Rodge) Rodgers, who was happy to come over and meet the rest of the crew. Aged 27, Rodge was from Rennie, Manitoba. Things went well during the meeting and so Al agreed to join the others.

Having reported to the CFI, Cliff's crew were immediately transferred to RAF Finningley's satellite airfield at Doncaster. Opened during January 1916, Doncaster was not as comfortable as Ossington, which had opened in January 1942. The barracks were poor, and the Mess was little better. For the next week it was back to the classroom, where they began to learn all about the Wellington which they would train on. Ron and the other navigators were introduced to the intricacies of the Gee box,[114] and warned that it was top secret and not to talk about it off the camp.

Meanwhile, Cliff and the rest of the crew were doing circuits and bumps. Soon, Cliff was ready to do his first solo in the Wellington, but once airborne, he blacked out, and Mac had to help him read the instruments and help him get the aircraft back to the airfield. They managed to land, but not without taking the boundary fence with them. Cliff was taken to hospital where he was told that his blackout was due to physical and mental strain.

With their skipper gone, Ron and the rest of the crew were taken back to Ossington. They never did see Cliff again. They reported back to the CFI, who told them that he had a pilot for them. This turned out to be Norman Noel. The crew were not too happy about having a pilot forced on them, and argued that crews teamed up on a volunteer basis. The CFI agreed and sent them off to find someone of their own. The only problem was that there were not too many pilots around at the time, and Noel was about it. After a few days, most of the crew were getting a bit bored, and so Rodge went off to talk to Noel. Having done so, he returned to the rest of the crew to inform them that Noel seemed ok. Noel was invited over to meet the rest of the crew. He was from Cape Breton Island and was 24. He had originally trained as a fighter pilot, and when he and his course had completed fighter OTU on Spitfires, they were all sent out to become bomber pilots. By bedtime he had moved his kit in, and the next day the CFI was informed that the crew had a new pilot. They remained at Ossington and began their training together. Norman Almond Noel was given a new name 'Wimp' by the rest of the crew, after J Wellington Wimpy in the Popeye films. After several training flights, Wimp's crew were ready to graduate from OTU.

Their final graduation exercise was a trip over France to drop nickels. They were a bit apprehensive about this, as the last course had lost 3 of their aircraft during the trip back from France. Returning in poor weather conditions, there was a mix up with the controllers, and it was thought that the Wellingtons were German Ju88s. A night fighter Mosquito was scrambled, and the pilot shot all three Wellingtons down. Several crewmembers were killed whilst others managed to bale out. The Mosquito's pilot did, however show great courage, and attended the funerals of the aircrew that had been killed.

---

114 Affectionately known to aircrew as the Goon box, as it was so easy to use

Wimp's graduation trip to drop leaflets on France was a fiasco. Their route was to depart Ossington and fly west at first, to the Isle of Man. Having reached there, they were to set off in an easterly direction, overfly England, drop their nickels over France and return.

All went well until they were approaching the Isle of Man, when Ron realised he had left his navigation computer on the Nav table in the briefing room back at Ossington. Without this important piece of equipment, it would be impossible to calculate the wind drift, and so they returned to base to get it. Having landed, they were not allowed to continue with the operation, and had several unpleasant interviews with high-ranking officers over the next couple of days.

Despite not completing their graduation trip, they were able to move on to the HCU at Topcliffe. They were to be billeted close to the airfield at Skipton on Swale, in a Nissen hut close to the end of the runway. It took quite a few nights to get used to the sounds of thirty plus heavy bombers skimming over their heads. As Wimp and his crew were now converting onto the Halifax II and V, they realised that they needed an engineer. Meanwhile Ron had another 'black box' to contend with. This was H2S, and training began at once. After about 3 days, Wimp returned with the news that they had an engineer. His name was Harry Stuart (Stu) Hanlin, a 24 year-old who came from Hampton, New Brunswick.

The Halifaxes at the OTU had all seen service and were pretty much clapped out. During July, the crew began to carry out cross-country navigation exercises. On their first trip, the aircraft lost an engine and they had to return early. During the second, the H2S stopped working after half an hour and again they had to return early. On the third trip, they took off and tried to climb up to 20,000 feet but were only able to struggle to 17,000, after which the plane wouldn't climb any further and actually began to lose height. Wimp and Stu managed to get the Halifax leveled out at 13,000, and they had to contend with that to complete the cross-country.

On days off, it was off to the famous Betty's Bars in York and Harrogate. During August, word came through that the crew were about to make yet another move, this time to an airfield up north called Middleton St George, where they were to join 428 Squadron. Finally, at last, they were ready for operations.

Next day was Saturday August 5th. Middleton's crews took off for a raid on a Doodlebug site at St Leu-d-Esserent. The visibility during take-off was very bad, the aircraft disappearing from sight when they were about 250 yards down the runway. On this and the two previous raids the Moosemen dropped a total of 377 tons of bombs. When F/L W J Anderson took off in VR-Q, his aircraft marked the 1,000th sortie flown by 419 during 1944. On their return from this operation, the aircraft were instructed to practice formation flying as they flew up the country; this they did, from Reading to Dishforth. Two of 419's aircraft did not participate in the formation flying. VR-I, flown by F/O B D Walker, returned to base from the target on 3 engines. Not to be out-done, F/O (Strip) Tees brought VR-B back on 2, only daring to start the troublesome third engine for the landing back at Middleton. Just to round the sortie off with a flourish, he also landed with a burst tyre, carrying out a masterly landing in the process.

After this trip, having completed their tour, 428's S/L Lord DFC and crew were screened. With the impending departure of S/L Lord, F/L Edwards assumed command of 'A' Flight, whilst S/L A C Hull took over 'B' Flight.

Next day the haze prevented flying from taking place and a stand-down was ordered, allowing the hard worked crews to have a well-earned rest.

On the 7th, Mr Turner of the Irvin Air Chute Company visited 419, and fitted two of its crews with the new back-type parachutes. This task was completed just in time to see the Moosemen contribute nineteen aircraft to swell the ranks of a force of 1,019 allied bombers that flew to the Normandy area at Caen.[115] The Ghost Squadron, for their part, provided a further 15 Lancasters. S/L McLeish was due to lead the Ghost Squadron, but was screened before take off and grounded, as he had completed his tour.

The raid itself had been planned for a daylight attack, but this was changed to the evening. The job was to assist the Canadian Army, who were about to break through the German lines at Caen. The 5 targets detailed for this raid were in front of the allied troops, and were marked by PFF aircraft, and star shells fired by allied artillery units. The weather conditions were favourable and the attack was carried out from 8 to 10,000 feet. In the end, only 600 bombers actually attacked the target, as the raid was very carefully controlled. Great effort was provided by the Master Bomber to ensure that no friendly troops were hit. Despite their close proximity to the A/P, German strong points and surrounding roads were heavily cratered.

419's F/O Walker and his crew, who had recently returned from a raid on 3 engines, were shot down during this raid. They crashed at Auberville-la-Renault, 17 miles N/E of Le Havre. None of the crew survived, all were laid to rest in the local cemetery. F/O Walker AFC was on his 12th operation. Flying with him as tail gunner was F/L M G Wilson. He was on the 10th trip of his second tour, having completed his first tour as one of the original Moosemen. He had returned to do his second tour as 419's Gunnery Leader. This was a bad blow to the squadron, as he had proved to be a very popular and capable leader within the squadron. In total, 10 Lancasters were lost during this raid, out of the 614 sent. The remainder of the force was made up of 392 Halifaxes and 13 Mosquitoes, which suffered no losses.

On the 8th, Middleton welcomed Acting Group Captain H T Miles, who had been posted in from 1659 Conversion Unit. He was to become the new Station Commander, with immediate effect. He was replacing G/C Sampson, who was being posted to 6 Group H.Q.

419 also welcomed S/L W F McKinnon as it's new 'A' Flight Commander. He was taking over from S/L J G Stewart who was departing to 1659 Conversion unit after completing his tour. Over at 428, with W/C McLeish bidding farewell to the squadron, S/L A C Hull assumed command. His place as commander of 'B' Flight was assumed by F/L G Gonyou.

---

115 9 miles inland from the Normandy beachhead

Later, 21 Lancasters from both squadrons were detailed for a daylight attack on an oil storage dump at Foret-de-Chantily, 25 miles north of Paris. In the end, only 16 from each squadron took-off. The target was plastered by the 148 Halifaxes, 49 Lancasters and 5 Mosquitoes taking part and several fires were started. The flak was moderately heavy and six Ghost aircraft were holed. No serious damage was inflicted on their aircraft however, and all crews returned safe.

The only loss during the raid was suffered by a Halifax III of 429 Squadron RCAF, based at Leeming. During its outbound flight, this aircraft, AL-H LW132, had just left Littlehampton, between Bognor-Regis and Worthing on the Sussex Coast. It had reached a point about 10 miles out to sea, and was at 15,000 feet, when it burst into flames. It fell away from the formation and was seen to break up at around 5,000 feet. One of the crew, F/S R V Harrod, was thrown clear, and landed by parachute in the sea. He sustained only slight injuries. The remainder of the crew, consisting of the captain F/L J B Hall, P/O H Glass DFM, F/O T A Jackman, P/O D Murray, P/O L B Syme and P/O W S Phillips (all RCAF) perished in the crash. Their bodies were recovered from the sea and now rest in Brookwood Military Cemetery.

At this time, the routine for the aircrews at Middleton was five weeks on duty then one week on leave.

On the night of the 9/10th, twenty Moose aircraft carried out a night attack on the V-1 site at Acquet, whilst 428 detailed seventeen of their aircraft on the same raid, to assist in the attrition of the dreaded buzz bombs.[116] Next night, the oil storage tanks at La Pallice were the target for fourteen aircraft from each of Goosepool's squadrons. Having taken off at 19:00, the crews carried out their attack from 9,500 feet, the raid was most successful and the site was extensively damaged. Only light flak was encountered and all returned safe.

The station enjoyed a stand down on the 11th, when it was visited by Their Majesties King George VI, Queen Elizabeth, and Princess Elizabeth. Members of 419's groundcrew formed the hollow square, which was drawn up, outside Hangar 3 for an investiture. 428's CO, Wing Commander Hull, commanded the station parade, whilst the remainder of both squadrons, including the aircrew, were present as spectators and to line the route of the Royal procession through the station.

The Teesside weather had no respect for the occasion, and contributed in its usual way. It started to rain just prior to the arrival of the Royal party. The assembled parade was then moved inside Hangar 3, which had been suitably adorned with flags and bunting beforehand (just in case). Wing Commander Pleasance, DFC and bar, was presented with 419's squadron crest by his Majesty. After the presentation, several members of 419 and 428 were presented with awards. Amongst the many airmen to be decorated were W/C Pleasance, W/C McLeish, S/L Lord, S/L Stewart and many others, including 1st Lt J H Hartshorn of the USAAF.

Lt J.H. Hartshorn USAAF, in hangar 3, receives the DFC from His Majesty King George VI
Photo: via Geoff Hill

Having visited the various sections on the airfield, the Royal party were invited into the Officers' Mess, where members holding the rank of Flight Lieutenant and above were assembled. After the Royal party had departed, a party was held in the Mess that evening, which was well represented by both squadrons.

The next evening, 419 detailed ten crews, and 428 eleven, to carry out an attack on Brunswick using H2S only. This experimental raid did not employ the PFF, and relied entirely on the crews bombing the target without the use of markers. The raid was designed to see if the crews could bomb accurately using only H2S. The raid was scattered, although some bombs did fall in the central and Stadpark areas. 99 people were killed. Some crews bombed towns up to 20 miles away, mistaking them for Brunswick.

All Moose aircraft returned safe. 428, however, lost NA-Z KB578, flown by F/O J A McGreggor. This aircraft, having taken off at 21:03, had been shot down by a night fighter and had crashed at 00:15 near Winsen, on the north bank of the Aller river, 8 miles N/W of Celle. F/O McGreggor and the navigator F/O C Greer were the only members of the crew to survive and become POWs. The remainder were laid to rest in Hannover War Cemetery.

The Moosemen were also requested to contribute 4 aircraft towards a second raid, which was to bomb a German troop concentration at a road junction north of Falaise, Normandy. The first of 419's Lancasters got off, but as the second taxied to the active runway, it got bogged down in the soft ground at the edge of the peri-track and the starting point. The remaining 2 Lancasters could not get past it and

116 British wartime slang for VI Flying Bombs

for them the Op was scrubbed. The single aircraft continued on to the target and returned safely to Middleton. Fortunately, after a mad scramble to prepare the aircraft, the Ghost Squadron had despatched its six aircraft contribution before the runway had been blocked. They too were able to bomb Falaise and return safely to Goosepool.

A stand-down the following day allowed both squadrons to continue with the never-ending sausage machine of training aircrew. During the day, 428's Flight Engineer Section was visited by F/L Nuggleston of 6 Aircrew School, Dalton. He had arrived to take delivery of a cut-away instructional Merlin engine, which had been prepared by the squadron's Engineering Flight.

On the 13th, Croft welcomed its new Station Commander in the form of G/C R S Turnbull DFC AFC DFM.

Falaise was revisited during daylight on the 14th. There were 7 targets for the 805 aircraft sent by Bomber Command. The bombing started well, but unfortunately, half way through the raid, some of the bombers started to bomb a large quarry which contained the Canadian 12th Field Regiment. The Canadian troops were using yellow identification flares; unfortunately the PFF were also using yellow markers, and in the confusion, over a 70 minute period, the Canadian troops were bombed, along with other adjacent allied positions.

The Master Bomber tried to stop the bombers from attacking the wrong positions but was unable to do so. Fortunately the Canadian troops were well dug in. Their slit trenches saved most of them, however 13 men were killed and 53 injured. As far as is known, this was the first time that Bomber Command had bombed friendly troops during the Normandy campaign. Many crews maintained that the troops had ignited their flares well before the bombs started to fall, The troops, however, firmly believed that the bombs fell first. Middleton's crews were not among the 25% of the bomber force that bombed short. Although it was hazy, bombing plots showed that their bombs were right on target. All 18 of 419's aircraft and the 19 sent by 428, returned safely to base.

Next day it was payback time for Bomber Command. The Moosemen and the Ghosts detailed 15 aircraft each to carry out a daylight raid on the German night fighter airfield at Sosterberg, halfway between Utrecht and Amersfoort, Holland.[117] In all, 9 enemy night fighter airfields were attacked by a strong force of 1,004 aircraft, comprising 599 Lancasters, 385 Halifaxes, 19 Mosquitoes and a lone P38 Lightning. This raid was very successful, and paved the way for a new and impending night offensive against Germany. Only 3 Lancasters were lost, none from Goosepool. As 419 began to take off for this operation, W/O2 A C Weston and crew, flying in VR-A, suffered a double engine failure. An aircraft fully loaded with bombs and fuel needs all the power it can get on take-off, and Weston had lost both his port and starboard inners. There was no time to dump fuel or reach the bomb jettison area off Whitby. Having feathered the two props, Weston gingerly dragged the underpowered Lancaster around the circuit and on to the end of the runway, where he carried out an extremely skilful landing.

428 had despatched NA-A KB748 at 09:46, after which nothing further was heard. Five members of the crew had been killed; the pilot, W/O1 A P Jakeman and the engineer, Sgt S W Wright survived when they were thrown clear as the aircraft exploded. Those who lost their lives were buried in Amersfoort General Cemetery.

On some days there was parachute drill. A Lancaster fuselage was set-up in one of the hangars and the idea was, when the order to abandon was given, to clip your parachute on to the front of your harness and head for the appropriate exit. In the Lanc, it was either the nose hatch, or the rear door placed just forward of the starboard tailplane.

As I wrote this book, I, like most of us who were not around at the time, wondered why some crewmembers managed to get out of stricken aircraft whilst others didn't. Obviously many lay dead or badly injured at their stations, hit by either flak or cannon fire from fighters. Others, on the other hand, could have been pinned down by centrifugal force and unable to reach the hatch. But perfectly able aircrew, who had no impediment whatsoever, were listed as killed. Some were reported as being seen by their fellow crewmembers, heading with them for the hatch, parachute clipped on, only to perish when the aircraft crashed.

A wartime survivor of a Stirling crew, who lives close to me, threw some light on this subject. His explanation was, to say the least, a little disturbing. During a raid on Berlin in August 1943, he had been a bomb-aimer on a Stirling. When the aircraft was hit over the city by a night fighter, the captain ordered the crew to bale-out. He clipped on his parachute and prepared to jump. Standing with him in the fuselage by the rear hatch were several members of the crew who flatly refused to jump. He was older than them, and as he stood at the open hatch, he pleaded with them to put their parachutes on and save themselves. Sadly they would not do so.

They were all young British lads, and the vision of them crying and literally screaming for their mothers as they hung onto the internal structure of the Stirling, still haunts him to this day. Here were reasonably seasoned crewmembers, perfectly unharmed, who were more scared to jump than to lose their lives. Perhaps they thought that an impending miracle would save them, and carefully place them on the ground, without them having to resort to using their parachutes, which they feared so much. The aircraft had been carrying a crew of 8, sadly there was no miracle, and only 3 survived to become POWs. The pilot also perished, however, it is possible that he refused to jump in order to try to save his crew. Those that perished in the Stirling have no known graves and are commemorated on the Runnymede Memorial.

I must be honest. Like many pilots that I have spoken to, should I ever be in the unfortunate position of being in a stricken aircraft, it would take a very hefty push indeed to make me jump. I am sure that I would have to be standing on the last remaining square inch of burning aluminium before I would take to my chute. On the other hand, with the march of technology Eigy, parachuting has become a major sport these days. However, most pilots will tell you that they would still question the sanity of anyone who would want to jump out of a perfectly serviceable aeroplane. These days, In over-crowded Britain, there would be far too many forms to fill in, should one survive the jump, only to see ones stricken aircraft

---

[117] Still in use today as a civilian airfield

fall on someone. If you survived, whilst someone on the ground was hurt by the wreckage of your aircraft, the British media would probably have your guts for garters.

Despite poor flying weather at base, operations to Stettin on the 16/17th provided good weather over the target. Between them, both squadrons sent a total of 27 Lancasters. This raid was undertaken by 461 aircraft, all of them Lancasters, from which 5 did not return. During this operation, 1,500 houses and 29 industrial complexes were destroyed. A further 1,000 houses and 26 industrial buildings were badly damaged. Five ships in the harbour were sunk and a further 8 seriously damaged. Amongst the casualties were 1,150 killed, 33 of them German soldiers. 1,654 people were injured, including 72 soldiers.

The Ghost Squadron's KB751 came down in the Baltic. The pilot, F/O W C Fairgrieves, and all but one of his 6-man crew, were lost. Sgt Toomy somehow survived and became a POW. F/O Fairgrieve's body was recovered from the waters and he now rests in the local cemetery on the Danish Island of Sejero. His companion in the next plot is F/S Dunlop of 166 Squadron, who had been placed there after he was killed during April 1944. Fairgrieve's mid-upper gunner, F/O J R Strigley, is buried in Denmark itself, at Farevejle Churchyard. The third and final body to be recovered was that of F/O H Slater, who was buried in Sweden in Varberg Church New Cemetery. The remaining 2 crewmembers were never found and are commemorated on the Runnymede Memorial.

Bremen was the target on the 18th, despite inclement weather at base. 288 aircraft took part in this, the most devastating raid on the city during the war. Visibility over Bremen was perfect, and the PFF had little problem in marking the target. The markers themselves were right on target, and these were followed by 1,100 tons of bombs. The entire centre and N/W sector of Bremen was pulverised, along with the N/W port area on the river Weser. In the harbour, 18 ships were sunk, whilst a further 61 were seriously damaged at their wharves.

Again a firestorm developed. 8,635 individual dwelling houses were burned out, whilst a further 611 were very badly damaged. So many industrial and commercial buildings were hit that no attempt at cataloguing them was undertaken, as the list would have been endless. Despite this, the published report of the devastation covered 10 pages. 1,058 bodies were recovered by the rescuers, of which 375 were unidentifiable. 300 bodies alone were recovered from the Lesmona public air-raid shelter.

The crews encountered heavy flak over the target area, although fighters were not in abundance. Some of 419's Lancasters suffered flak damage. VR-Y and X were badly damaged, with X being categorised as Cat C. During this raid, the only aircraft to be lost by Bomber Command was 428's NA-I KB743, flown by P/O C M Corbet. It was shot down in flames, and its tail gunner F/S R E Good was mortally wounded. He was later buried in Sage War Cemetery, whilst the remainder of the crew survived to become POWs. The remaining Goosepool crews returned to the UK, only to find that despite it being a beautiful August day elsewhere, they could not return to base. For the next two days, operations were dispensed with, as Teesside's weather threw everything at the airfield, high winds and rain being the most note-worthy elements. Meanwhile, on the 21st, as he had completed his tour, W/C Pleasance relinquished his command of the Moosemen and was replaced by W/C D C Hagerman DFC. W/C Pleasance was posted to HQ RCAF Overseas Headquarters.

It would be the night of the 25/26th before the weather allowed Middleton's crews to continue with the war. This raid, on the Opel motor factory at Russelsheim, was carried out by 412 Lancasters of 1, 3, 6 and 8 Groups, and took all of 10 minutes. Heavy flak and fighter opposition was encountered, and KB775, flown by F/O H D Whitwer RCAF, who was on his 11th operation, failed to return. This aircraft collided with another over the target area and entered a spin. The Lancaster broke up. Whitwer, who was not strapped in, was ejected from the aircraft and survived. The remainder of the crew, who were possibly pinned by G forces, perished.

428's Sgt R B Maxwell, on his first trip, put up a very good show. He and his crew were within 40 minutes of the target when the aircraft was struck by flak. The starboard outer was set on fire and the electrical system shattered. At the same time, the engineer Sgt R F Recabarren was seriously wounded and Maxwell himself was slightly injured. Maxwell feathered the engine and extinguished the fire. Despite his wounds and the unserviceable engine, he continued with the operation with the intention of bombing the target. This was not possible due to the damaged electrical system, but this was not realised until he had reached the target and tried to bomb. Maxwell had no alternative but to fly home on 3 engines and find assistance for his engineer. They eventually reached Thorny Island where medical help was on hand. Sadly the engineer died of his wounds soon after.

Thanks to poor visibility, the Moosemen had to divert on the way home. They were scattered about England; 1 landed at Desborough, 6 at Dunkeswell, 2 at Great Orton, 4 at Middle Wallop and 4 at Boscombe Down. It was very foggy at Boscombe, and F/O W A Milner RCAF in KB708 was not happy with his approach and decided to do a go-around. The throttles were slammed open by the engineer, but all four engines cut, due to lack of petrol. The Lancaster crashed into some trees at Winterbourne, Wiltshire, killing Milner, the bomb aimer F/O I J Kirschner RCAF, wireless operator F/S H F Anderson, and engineer Sgt J L Trotman, The navigator, F/O P E Gariepy RCAF was seriously injured, and the two gunners, Sgt L J Weston RCAF and Sgt P Wiens RCAF were slightly injured.

Next day, 419 and 428 were requested to provide 18 aircraft for a night operation, but an effort to try and get the diverted aircraft back was only partially successful. The Viz over the rest of the country was back to normal, but only two aircraft were able to land before the usual Teesside mist and smoke haze put paid to that. The remainder of the aircraft put down at Linton-on-Ouse, which was as close as they could get. With the smoky haze covering the drome, only two of 428's diverted aircraft were able to grope their way in, thus bringing their total number of aircraft available to 4. The remainder of the diverted aircraft were re-diverted to airfields where they could be bombed up for the evening's raid. The crews would have to take off from wherever they were. Eventually, the raid itself was scrubbed, and as Goosepool's weather relented a little, all but 3 of the diverted crews, L-Love, D-Dog and N-Nan, were able to return to base.

29 of Middleton's aircraft took off on the 27th for the Doodlebug site at Marguise Mimoyecques in the Pas de Calais. This was the last of the 16 Crossbow targets attacked by Goosepool's squadrons during 241 sorties. In actual fact, it was not a Doodlebug or a V1 site at all, but a 50-barrel, long-range super-gun, capable of firing one 6-inch shell every minute. Each barrel was 400 feet long, and the whole thing was set at an angle in a hillside, pointing at England, or more particularly, London. The 226 aircraft employed in this raid completely destroyed the site, removing the threat forever. VR-K lost an engine on take-off, followed 2 minutes later by another. With a full load of bombs and petrol, W/O2 L H McDonald could not maintain height, and using great skill he managed to crash-land the Lancaster some 7 miles from base in a field near Appleton Wiske, North Yorkshire. Thanks to McDonald's good airmanship, the aircraft did not catch fire when it hit the ground, and slithered to a stop without injury to the crew. No sooner had they climbed out when they were confronted by the irate farmer, who gave them the greatest rollicking of their young lives, blaming them entirely for the crash.

On the 29th, the duff weather relented a little, allowing 19 crews to be detailed by 419 for a raid on Stettin. As they were short of serviceable aircraft they borrowed 2 from 428. A bad wind-change en-route to the target caused many problems for the navs. There was a considerable amount of flack and fighter activity, especially as they flew over neutral Sweden. The Swedish gunners took exception to the RAF using their airspace for transit to Stettin, and showed their displeasure thus. Three of the aircraft lost engines over the target area. First Lt Hartshorn, flying VR-C, lost his starboard engine, as did F/O Bruins in VR-B. F/O G L Sheahan was also hit by flak, and his port outer engine was put out of action.

P/O Mansfield and his crew were flying in an aircraft borrowed from 428. An incendiary bomb dropped from an aircraft above them went through an engine nacelle, exploded inside and caught fire. This caused a flash on the port wing, similar to a flak hit. Without waiting for the order to bale out, the crew's rear gunner, Sgt B Jigursky, who was in the mid-upper turret for this trip, put on his parachute and jumped out of the aircraft, leaving the remainder of the crew wondering what they had said that had made him not want to accompany them back to Middleton. The fire was put out, and the aircraft, albeit one man and one engine short, landed safely back at Goosepool along with the other Moosemen. Jigursky, however, remained behind as a guest of the Germans.

428 had sent 17 crews, which on their return reported many fighters and lots of flak. The squadron had recently welcomed F/O L S Plunkett, who was on the 8th operation of his second tour. Sadly, he and his crew failed to return. They were presumed lost over the Baltic. The crew consisted of 4 RCAF men, including F/O Plunkett, the other three were RAF. F/O Plunkett has no known grave, whilst 3 of his crew are buried on the Danish Island of Anholt; the remainder rest in Sweden's Falkenberg Forest Cemetery.

On the 31st, eleven specialised crews from both 419 and 428 were briefed to carry out an evening attack on the Pas-de-Calais in support of allied ground forces. Take-off was planned for 16:00 hours, but this was put forward to 17:45. Eventually it was postponed to the next morning, but by then it was cancelled as the objective had already been overrun by ground troops.

Despite the weather curtailing several Ops, during the third week of August, 419 had carried out 259 sorties, a record for the squadron thus far in the war. For 419, the number of aircraft on charge by the end of August 1944 totalled 23 Lancasters. Despite being involved in changing over to the Lancaster, 428 carried out 258 sorties.

September 1944

Friday September 1st saw Middleton's new Station Commander, Group Captain H T Miles, accompany W/C Hagerman as he carried out a climbing test on one of 419's Lancasters. The purpose of the test was to ascertain the best revs and boost to be used at different heights and bomb loads.

Duff conditions returned, and it was the 6th before Middleton's weather improved sufficiently to allow operations to resume. Despite difficulties in bombing up, caused by the atrocious weather encountered by the armourers, Emden was the target for 18 of 419's aircraft and 16 of 428's. This was to be a daylight raid. In contrast to Middleton, the weather over the target was excellent, just like summer. Oh sorry, it was summer.

As things go, it wasn't a particularly large raid. The 105 aircraft of 6 and 8 groups were few in comparison to recent raids. This visit by Bomber Command to Emden was the first since June 1942. It was also destined to be the last raid on the town. The bombers were provided with an initial escort of Spitfires that would eventually hand over to American Mustangs. No details are available, other than the fact that several ships were sunk in the harbour and that the town was left a mass of flames.

Only one aircraft was lost, that of the deputy Master Bomber F/L G Wilson DSO DFC DFM of 7 Squadron. A bomber pilot of great distinction and experience, F/L Wilson was killed instantly by a single flak shell, which burst in the cockpit area. Along with him died his navigator Sgt D Jones and the bomb-aimer Sgt E R Brunsdon, who at the time was working the H2S set at the navigator's position. The remaining 5 crewmembers escaped by parachute.

The return of the duff weather meant that it was to be the 10th before the next operation was possible. A daylight attack on Le Havre in support of ground troops employed 20 aircraft from each squadron. 992 aircraft (521 Lancasters, 426 Halifaxes and 45 Mosquitoes) gave the target a real pasting. With marking by courtesy of the PFF, 8 separate German strong points were hit, and all for no loss.

Two days later on Tuesday the 12th, Dortmund was to receive the undivided attention of Goosepool's aircraft. Insufficient notice to bomb up meant that both squadrons were unable to get their full complement of aircraft into the air. In the end, both were only able to muster 14 aircraft each. Take off for the last aircraft was at 16:00, this left two and a half-hours to reach the target. This meant cutting corners and proceeding almost directly to the target with one's foot down. The routes were changed 3 times during briefing, which presented great difficulty for the navs. The weather at Middleton was fine, and surprisingly it stayed fine for the return trip. The 20 X 500-lb bombs carried by each Lancaster were to be dropped from a height between 16-19,000 feet. Many aircraft were holed by flak, with 428 receiving the lion's share. Acting Flight Lieutenant R E Curtis and his crew were just about to reach the target when their aircraft was hit by flak. His tail gunner, J J (Jimmy) Flood, was killed, and Curtis was badly wounded in the head. Curtis remained conscious and pressed on to the target and bombed before collapsing. The bomb-aimer, P/O D A McGillivray, took over the controls. It was fortunate that, for some time now, Middleton's squadrons had been training their aircrews to be able to take over the duties of other crewmembers.

McGillivray managed to get the Lanc back to the emergency landing ground at Woodbridge, and was able to land. Curtis was taken to the Ipswich and East Suffolk Hospital, where he was found to have a compound fracture of the skull and was placed on the dangerously ill list. It was later written in the Ghost Squadron's record book that the crew's outstanding efforts to get the aircraft and its injured captain back was a true example of determination, coolness and courage, of which the squadron was justly proud. Jimmy Flood had been an extremely popular member of the squadron and was greatly missed.

Next day, flying was cancelled when a breeze from the sea completely obliterated the airfield with smoke and fog.

On the 14th, fifteen crews from each squadron took off for an attack on Wilhelmshaven. An hour after set course time, the crews received the recall signal, due to the fighter escort being grounded by bad weather. On their return, 419 diverted to Linton, as the weather at Goosepool had turned duff, owing to fog and smoke rendering the airfield unserviceable again. 428 were told to land at Tholthorpe, and like 419, jettisoned their cookies in the sea. Their record book shows an entry after this raid which reads, 'The rain and fog at base is getting very depressing.'

Next day, both squadrons were warned of a raid on Kiel. 419 has its crews briefed and its aircraft serviced at Linton, due to the continuing bad flying weather at Goosepool. 428 did the same at Tholthorpe, although S/L Edwards began his trip to Kiel from Middleton. 428 started out two aircraft short. P/O Mossman's crew remained behind as their skipper had been taken ill. The second aircraft, flown by F/O Smith, had swung on take off, and had left the runway.

The old part of Kiel town and its new modern shopping centre were devastated during this raid. The port area also came under heavy attack, but the Germans claim that much of the bombing fell outside Kiel. By the time the crews returned to the UK the weather was suitable for them to land back at base.

There were no Ops the following day, which allowed F/O Gilbert to ferry F/O J Holtzer down to Tholthorpe in the squadron's Oxford. Holtzet ferried P/O Mossman's Lanc back to Middleton, as he had been admitted to Linton's sick quarters with bronchitis.

On Sunday the 17th, both squadrons detailed 18 crews for a dawn departure to attack enemy troop positions at Boulogne. The weather was perfect, and a total of 762 aircraft dropped 3,000 tons of bombs on German positions around Boulogne. All of Middleton's crews returned safe. Operation 'Market Garden', the allied army's push towards Arnhem, began on this date, with 341 other aircraft of Bomber Command carrying out two diversionary sweeps. One was to the Dutch Coast, whilst the other went into Holland, in order to draw up German fighters from the south.

The next day, a daylight operation to attack coastal guns and flak positions at Walcheren, near Domberg, Holland, was carried out by both squadrons. They were part of a total force of 74 aircraft supplied by 6 and 8 Groups. The crews reached the target only to have the Op cancelled due to total cloud cover.

Back at base, the weather degenerated very quickly, with fog and smoke blowing in on the northeasterly wind. Several of 419's aircraft tried to land but only one was able to do so. The remaining crews diverted to Leeming, two of which, VR-O and VR-Q, overshot the runway and ended up with Cat B damage. 428 managed to get 3 down at base, but the rest had to divert to Leeming and Skipton.

On the 19/20th, both squadrons prepared for another go at Domberg. 419 had 9 aircraft bombed up and despatched from Leeming, with a further 5 being despatched from Middleton. 428 sent 15 aircraft, 12 from their diversionary bases and 3 from Goosepool. Both squadrons received the recall signal after only one hour's flying time. 419 got back to Middleton first and landed. Soon after, VR-W, which had not taken part in the operation but was returning from Leeming, joined the circuit and promptly crashed whilst trying to land. Although the aircraft was damaged Cat B, the crew were uninjured. Due to 419's prang, 428 were only able to land 10 of their aircraft. The other 5 had to land at Croft and have their crews transported by road back to base.

During the day, 419 was visited by various members of the squadron who had evaded capture and had been liberated by the Americans. These included P/O Phillis, shot down on the Stuttgart raid on July 24/25th, and navigator F/O Watson from F/O Frame's crew, shot down over Villeneuve-St-George on July 4th. A few days later, F/O Frame himself returned to visit the Moosemen and pass on details of his exploits whilst evading capture.

Teesside's unique visibility problems persisted as yet again, on the 20th, both squadrons, having carried out an attack on enemy troop concentrations at Calais, could not return to base. Although Middleton was fogged in, Croft was open for 1 of the Moose aircraft to land. The remainder of both squadrons landed at Carnaby, Westcott, Oakley and Chalgrove. Next day, there was more of the same when the airfield was again rendered unserviceable by fog. During the evening, the wind shifted around and blew the fog and smoke out to sea, allowing the diverted aircraft to land. The Orb for 428 reads; 'The weather shows a faint appearance of clearing, as part of the sky was visible for a short while. One pilot claims to have seen the sun, but this was put down to operational fatigue'.

On the 22nd, 419 received a new 'A' Flight Commander, in the form of S/L W C McGuffin. He was replacing S/L Hagerman who was taking over command of the squadron. So bad was the weather that both squadrons had large numbers of personnel out on the flights, spreading cinders in the morass caused by the heavy rains of the last few days.

On the 25th, the winds and rain abated a little to allow enemy gun emplacements south of Calais to be attacked. Both of Middleton's squadrons took part, supplying 20 aircraft each. All but one Ghost aircraft returned safely to base. F/O D E Berry's Lancaster had to divert to Tangmere, having been badly holed by flak. The mid-upper gunner, P/O J F Patterson RCAF was seriously wounded in the right loin and had to be admitted to hospital in Chichester. Having seen his gunner taken care of, Berry then returned with his aircraft to Middleton. Later it was deemed as damaged Cat A. On the 26th, both squadrons went back to the same target. During a normal raid on tactical targets, smoke from the attack tended to drift over the TI's. New bombing tactics were tested during these attacks, and the TI's were dropped short of the aiming point from 10,000 feet. The bombs were dropped on an overshoot at a set time interval. This did not work too well on the first raid, but was more successful on the second.

On the morning of the 27th, 419 returned to the Ruhr Valley with 22 of its Lancasters to attack an oil installation at Bottrop. The weather over the target had deteriorated badly. The instructions from the Master Bomber were vague, and as a result of this, bombing was scattered. Duisburg was the alternative target, and received the lion's share of the bombs. Although German fighters were conspicuous by their absence, the flak was intense, and 4 of 419's aircraft were damaged. F/L J A Anderson and his crew lost 2 engines over the target area and another as they returned over the Dutch Coast. Showing great airmanship, Anderson and his engineer managed to get the Lancaster to the emergency landing strip at Woodbridge, where they touched down safely on 1 engine.

The final operation for the Moosemen and Ghosts during September took place on Thursday the 28th. Six enemy gun batteries at Cap-Gris-Nez were attacked by 38 of Goosepool's Lancasters that made up part of a 301 strong force of bombers. The attack was stopped by the MB after only 198 aircraft had bombed, as the weather was worsening. Dense low cloud was beginning to completely obscure the target. He did not want to risk hitting French civilians. All of Goosepool's crews returned safely to base. The weather, or rather bad visibility in particular, put paid to any further operations during that month.

For the Moosemen, September had been a good month. No aircrew had been lost, and taking the 2 landing accidents into consideration, the toll on its aircraft had been light. The squadron had won 3 awards during the month, with F/L R L Boe, F/O C E Siddall and P/O H C Eyjolfson receiving the DFC. The number of Lancaster Xs on charge had increased to 26, and 222 sorties were flown.

October 1944

For the Moosemen their good fortune was short lived when on October 4th, the squadron lost one of its Lancasters when they and 428 contributed 20 aircraft each for a raid on the German submarine base at Bergen, Norway. KB745, flown by F/O G R Duncan RCAF, took off at 06:15 and did not return. Word was received the following day that the Lancaster had been found by a shepherd. Mr Basil Oliver came across the wreckage of the Lancaster on a hillside at Goldscleugh, near Rothbury, 12 miles Northwest of Morpeth, Northumberland. The crew had been killed instantly.

Two days later, at 11:30, word came through from Group requesting that 419 and 428 provide 20 Lancasters each for a raid on Dortmund. Take-off time was ordered for 15:30, which gave insufficient time to bomb up the aircraft. This caused several aircraft to get away late; the last one lifted off 20 minutes after set course time. This caused many of the late crews to cut corners in an attempt to make up the time lost.

The target was reached just after dusk. The flak over the target was very heavy and several aircraft sustained damage. The bombing height was 19/20,000 feet. Munster, 30 miles to the north, was also being attacked that night, and poor PFF marking caused some confusion, with bad run-ups and some aircraft having to orbit. Fortunately all Moose aircraft returned safely. This raid saw more records for 419. As F/O P D Griffiths and his crew took off, their sortie marked the 3,000th carried out by the Moosemen. The crew of F/L C M Black also had the distinction of undertaking the 1,000th Lancaster X sortie. All 40 of Middleton's crews returned safe, but due to the Northeast's lousy weather had to divert to Wyton and Warboys.

A night raid on Bochum on the 9/10th saw the Moosemen lose another of their aircraft, KB754, flown by P/O A I Cohen on his 14th sortie. The bombs had been released and the Lanc was just past the target when the tail gunner F/S J F McQueen spotted a Ju88 on his port side quarter down. As he gave the 'Corkscrew port' warning to Cohen, the Lanc was hit. The hydraulic lines feeding his turret were severed and burst into flames. The turret and the intercom were out of action, and the flames from the port engine were streaking past the rear turret. The fuselage was well on fire and the aircraft went into a dive. An explosion blew off the turret doors and partly ejected McQueen out of the turret. He was trapped by his leg, and the flames from the burning hydraulic oil began to scorch him. In desperation he yanked at his rip chord D-ring, his chute opened with a crack and dragged him clear of the burning turret. The remainder of the crew did not survive; they now rest in the Reichswald Forest War Cemetery.

For F/L Anderson in VR-P, this was the 10th trip that he had received flak damage. They had been hit just before reaching the target, and the Lancaster had suffered extensive damage to its electrical system. Gun turrets, ammo tracks, and the H2S were put out of action. When the crew looked out, the aircraft's navigation lights were on, due probably to a short circuit. No amount of switch twiddling prevented the Lancaster from wandering around the sky lit up like a Christmas tree. It would have been quicker to hang a 'Please shoot me down' sign on the back of the defenceless aircraft, for all the night fighters to see. Just after bombs away, they were attacked by a Ju88. Anderson stuffed the nose down and headed for the sanctuary of the nearest decent sized cloud. The fighter was shaken off, although the fighter pilot's comrades had four more goes at the Lanc as it plied its way home. Each time they were attacked or shadowed, Anderson threw the Lancaster into a corkscrew, causing the fighters to lose the plot. Eventually P-Peter was able to land safely back at Goosepool without further incident. On closer inspection, VR-P had received 167 holes where holes shouldn't have been. Many had been caused by the aircraft's own ammo which had exploded when the turret feed tracks had been hit. It was amazing that none of the crew had been struck by wayward rounds.

The Ghosts had put up 15 crews for this raid. All returned safe, with the exception of F/O B B Miller's crew. Their aircraft was badly holed by flak, and the mid-upper gunner, F/S C H Kales, was killed. The wireless operator, P/O C R Olson, was badly wounded. Despite loss of blood and great pain, Olson insisted on remaining at his radio set in order to send out emergency procedures to assist Miller to land the aircraft at Woodbridge.

In an attempt to shorten the war and bring it to its inevitable conclusion, Winston Churchill and the War Cabinet decided that the Germans should be dealt an overwhelming knock out punch that would leave them in no doubt of the air power set against them. To this end, Sir Arthur Harris received a directive on October 13th 1944 detailing the format of the measures to be inflicted on Germany. It was to be called 'Operation Hurricane'. The intention was to apply, within the shortest practical period, a maximum effort on the part of Bomber Command and the American 8th Air Force against the densely populated Ruhr. After the attacks on strategic targets for the next seven months, the bombers would be employed to smash what was left of German industry. From here on in, the Ruhr Valley and areas of the Rhine were to receive the undivided attention of Bomber Command. Although Harris only received his directive the day before, the first part of Operation Hurricane began on October 14th, and was aimed at Duisburg. There had been no operations planned for the heavies over the previous 2 days, which gave the ground and aircrews time to prepare. Middleton's crews had plenty of time to prepare, as the weather at base had been unflyable since the 9th. The operation involved 1,013 aircraft, consisting of 519 Lancasters, 474 Halifaxes and 20 Mosquitoes. They were protected by a fighter screen provided by the RAF.

The Moosemen put up 18 aircraft for this raid, the Ghosts 22. The first aircraft began taking-off from Middleton at 06:00. Once the Lancasters reached the target, they found that the visibility during the first part of the attack was very poor, but improved later. High tactics were used, with the bombing heights being between 17 and 20,000 feet. The bombing was well concentrated, and although there were no German fighters to be seen, very heavy flak was encountered over the target area. Some 3,574 tons of HE bombs and 820 tons of incendiaries were dropped on Duisburg that morning. The cost to Bomber Command was 13 Lancasters and 1 Halifax. The losses were most likely taken during the early part of the raid, as later on, the defences were overwhelmed by the sheer number of bombs going down. The Americans sent 1,250 bombers to attack targets in the Cologne area, escorted by 749 fighters. They lost 5 bombers and 1 fighter.

KB800, flown by F/O A M Roy RCAF, was hit by flak, and both of its starboard engines were set on fire. F/O Roy, who was on his 20th operation, was unable to hold the stricken bomber level. It went into a spin and then exploded, throwing F/O Roy out of the aircraft. The remainder of the crew perished.

VR-V, flown by P/O Mansfield, was also hit by flak, wounding one of the gunners, Sgt G S, Morell. As soon as he could, Mansfield headed towards the emergency landing ground at Woodbridge to ensure prompt medical attention for Morell. Having seen the gunner into the ambulance, the crew took off again and returned to Goosepool. When they got back to base, VR-V was accidentally refuelled and bombed-up, the aircraft were required to go back to Duisburg later the same night.

428 lost KB780, flown by F/L W H (Bill) Janney and his crew. Bill had been the squadron's deputy 'A' Flight Commander, his crew were described as being 'Bang on'. There were no survivors, and the crew are commemorated on the Runnymede Memorial.

At 18:00 they were briefed again; by 22:00 hours both squadrons were off for a second raid on Duisburg. The aircraft climbed to height over the airfield before setting course for the target. Two of 419's aircraft returned early, one with an unserviceable airspeed indicator. Another had problems with its engines and was unable to gain altitude. Once the remainder got to Duisburg, they found that the weather and the visibility was not too good. This second raid in a single day employed a further 1,005 aircraft, that bombed Duisburg in 2 separate forces that attacked 2 hours apart. They delivered another 4,040 tons of HE bombs, along with 500 tons of incendiaries. The raid was well concentrated, on the way home, the fires were visible from over 100 miles away. With little or no flak to contend with over the target area, all Moose aircraft returned safely to Middleton. Few German records are available detailing the devastation inflicted on Duisburg.

Wilhelmshaven was attacked by 506 aircraft the next day, including 5 from 419 and 10 from 428. This was to be the port's last major raid of the war. All of Middleton's crews returned safe, diverting to Tempsford.

The remaining aircrews were taking a well-earned rest from the exertions of the previous day. On the 18th, ten of 419's aircrew were invited guests of Darlington's 'Twenty Club' for a dinner and smoker at the Imperial Hotel.

Blind bombing through cloud using sky markers   Photo: IWM CL.560

As the colder weather began to bite, 419's meagre supply of coal and coke was supplemented by the squadron's woodpile. During the morning, 419's bomb aimers received a lecture on the features of the new bombing panel which was being fitted to the Lancaster X. During the afternoon a film on Radar was shown to all aircrew personnel in the NAFFI.

Operations for the Moosemen continued on the 19th with a rather ineffectual raid on Stuttgart. P/O N A Noel's aircraft suffered an overheating engine and had great difficulty in gaining height on takeoff. He clipped a treetop just off the end of the runway. The aircraft was not damaged but an engine change was required. The aircraft landed safely, much to the relief of Ron Cassells and the rest of the crew. Middleton's weather was up to its usual tricks, all 20 aircraft had to divert again. Next day, with the absence of their aircraft, the population of Goosepool had a very quiet time of things. It would be the 31st before the airfield shed its cloak of gloom and heard the sounds of Merlins.

The Moosemen lost their 'A' Flight Commander on the 23rd when S/L McGiffin DFC went missing on a raid to Essen. McGiffin was flying the 14th sortie of his second tour. No details are available as to what befell VR-F KB776, only that all on board were killed and now rest in the Reichswald Forest Cemetery. The raid itself, which involved 1,055 aircraft, including 20 Moose and 23 Ghost crews, was the heaviest raid on the city thus far. This operation employed the greatest number of aircraft sent to any target up to that point in the war. The record number of aircraft used in this raid, 561 Lancasters, 463 Halifaxes and 31 Mosquitoes, is all the more apparent when it is realised that it did not involve the aircraft of 5 Group. More than 90% of the 4,538 tons of bombs dropped were high explosives, and included 509 4,000-lb cookies. The reason for the lack of incendiaries was due to the fact that, by now, there was little left to burn after previous attacks. As the allies advanced slowly towards Berlin, the use of more HE bombs would become the norm for targets that had earlier suffered major fire damage. During the raid, 607 buildings were destroyed and 812 were badly damaged. 622 people were killed and 569 injured. Five Lancasters and three Halifaxes were lost.

Earlier during the day, 14 of 419's screened aircrew personnel visited Newcastle, where they had a trip on a Royal Navy motor launch up to North Shields and back. Having had lunch in the naval canteen, they visited the Armstrong Whitworth factory on the banks of the Tyne. Here they were shown around the plant that built naval gun turrets and a variety of guns, including the 4, 4.5 and 6-inch versions. They were also taken around the shop where the anti-aircraft shell fuses were made. For the aircrew this was the most interesting part, although the crews stated that this had nothing to do with the fact that it was crammed with dozens of beautiful young ladies working on the production line. At this time, 419 had a large number of screened aircrew members on its books, who were lounging around the place and complaining of being bored. They were also taking up valuable accommodation space, and so these liaison visits were dreamed up. When not visiting factories involved with the war effort, they could also find themselves on coastal convoy trips or even enjoying a visit to the famous Normandy beaches.

Next day, 428 received word that S/L Edwards was to be promoted to Acting Wing Commander and was to be posted to Tholthorpe, to take command of 420 Squadron. His place as 428's 'A' Flight Commander was taken by F/L D W Lamont.

Twenty-two of 419's Lancasters revisited Essen for a daylight raid on the 25th, as part of a smaller raid, employing 771 aircraft. The target was completely cloud covered and the crews had to bomb skymarkers. Despite this, even more damage was inflicted than was the case for the previous night's raid. The number of houses destroyed was put at 1,163, and 820 people were killed. By this stage of the war, most of Essen's war industry was dispersed into smaller units and scattered around the countryside. Essen had been one of Germany's most important centres of war production. The Krupps steelworks had been badly hit during the first raid, the second more or less put paid to any further coherent production. Also decimated was the Borbeck pig-iron plant, which ceased to function after this raid. All aircraft returned safe.

The last two operations during October were to Cologne on the 28th and 30th. During the first of these two raids, 419's F/L A N Nelligan and his crew in KB712 crashed at Hurth, 5 miles S/W of Cologne, all on board were killed. This Lancaster was 419's second oldest aircraft. During these two raids, enormous damage was inflicted on the city. 2,239 blocks of flats were destroyed, as were 11 schools, 15 industrial buildings, 3 police stations, power stations, water and gas works. Also hit were railway and harbour installations on the Rhine. Also devastated were Cologne University, and the local Army Garrison HQ.

The 1,000-year-old St Gereon church was badly damaged by a single heavy bomb. After the war, it took until 1979 to restore it. A POW camp in the Heliosstrasse was destroyed, the number of inmates killed was unknown. The total number of Germans killed or missing during both raids were 1,184, whilst over 1,200 were injured.

Due to the very heavy bomb load carried, some 13,000-lbs, Goosepool's Lancasters had to forego something to get off the ground. This something was fuel, and so it was anticipated that the aircraft would have to divert on the way home. Although the divert order was given, due to better than forecast winds the fuel consumption for some was not as bad as expected. One crew did not hear the transmission and landed back at base, albeit with the gauges reading low.

And so ended October 1944, a month with few operations for Middleton's crews. With the exception of the 9 days when raids were able to take place, the weather was duff. Sometimes it rained non-stop for days. When not doing that there was low cloud and fog.

November 1944

November 1944 began with a raid on Oberhousen on the 1st. Out of the 288 aircraft taking part, Goosepool contributed 38. 419's KB767 was attacked just after bomb release. Both of the main tyres were punctured and the mid-upper turret was damaged. After leaving the target area, the captain, F/O R L Cox descended to 15,000. Some 7 minutes after the flak had struck the aircraft, a Fw190 attacked from 250 yards. Cox had no time to take evasive action. The tail gunner F/S R A Toane was wounded in the face, arms and leg. Despite his injuries, and being almost blinded by blood streaming down his face, he managed to fire 50 rounds at the fighter. The fighter's cannon shells cut the intercom, and badly damaged the fuselage, tail and the starboard elevator. The port inner was also put out of action. As this powered some of the ancillary pumps, the hydraulics and pneumatic systems were badly effected. Fortunately no one was killed.

One shell had exploded in the fuselage. The mid-upper gunner, Sgt J Wilkins, was blown from his seat, but found himself unharmed on the floor. The wireless operator, F/O L W Sitlington, was hit in the face and arm. A fire started at the radio position, but he was able to grab a fire extinguisher and put it out. The navigator, F/O S B Lindsay, was hit in the back and face by shrapnel, but despite his wounds was able to put out two fires, one in the wing root and a second at the navigator's station. Whilst fighting these fires, he burned his hands quite badly and fainted from shock. He recovered after treatment however, and was able to continue with his duties, although the DR compass and H2S was out of commission.

The fighter broke off its attack, and moments later the aircraft was again hit by flak. The Lancaster managed to cross the Belgian Coast and head out to sea. A short time later, the starboard engine stopped. With the flying controls badly damaged, twice the aircraft entered into a spiral dive. Both times Cox was able to recover at about 1,500 feet. For the crew's safety, Cox elected to return to the Belgian coast with a view to crash-landing on the beach. Having turned the Lanc around he began heading east again, the engineer Sgt F Dennis RAF, the only non-RCAF member of the crew, was able to restart the port inner. Now there was a chance of getting home, and so U-Uncle was turned about and again pointed at England. Cox managed to reach Manston in Kent and carry out a successful crash-landing. Flying Officers Lindsay and Sitlington were taken to the RAF Hospital at Halton, whilst F/S Toane was admitted to Manston's SSQ. For their part in this operation Cox, Lindsay and Sitlington received the DFC whilst Toane was awarded the DFM.

Next day, the Moosemen and Ghosts were part of a force of 992 aircraft that took part in the last major raid on Dusseldorf. The attack was mainly in the northern half of the city, where 5,000 houses were destroyed or badly damaged. Seven industrial targets were also destroyed, a further 18 were badly damaged. Amongst the properties damaged were some of the city's major steelworks. 678 people were killed and over 1,000 injured. 11 Halifaxes and 8 Lancasters were lost on this raid, one was from 428. KB782 took off at 16:16, never to be seen again. The crew, flown by F/O J Holtze RCAF, are buried in the Reichswald Forest War Cemetery.

On the night of the 4/5th, 419 and 428 joined forces with other Bomber Command squadrons to make up a force totalling 749 aircraft, which were to carry out Bochum's last major raid of the war. Severe damage was inflicted on the city centre. 980 Germans were killed and 4,000 houses were either destroyed or seriously damaged.

Taking part in this raid was VR-E, flown by F/O L A Blaney and crew. The tail gunner, F/S D H Lanctot, reported the approach of two aircraft. They turned out to be standard examples of Willie Messerschmitt's 109 and 110 fighters, which attacked almost simultaneously. They settled down, one on each quarter just below the skyline. The 110, which was on the starboard side, began its attack first from 400 yards. He was greeted with a reply from the Lancaster's tail gunner. The 110 was hit and turned away. Lanctot fired until he was hit in the face and an arm and his turret rotation system was put out of action. He made no mention of his injuries until later and continued to fire. The second fighter opened fire from 250 yards, and its pilot immediately found himself on the receiving end of 100 rounds fired from Sgt R Altham's mid-upper turret. Altham saw a blue flash as his rounds hit the 109's fuselage. The enemy pilot then demonstrated the old adage that discretion is the better part of valour by promptly breaking off. The crew then took stock of the inflicted damage. The starboard elevator had been shot away and the starboard fin and rudder took on the appearance of a lace curtain. Lanctot's injuries were not life threatening, and Blaney managed to reach Woodbridge, where the gunner's wounds were treated. For his gallant actions during this raid, Lanctot later received the DFM.

During the raid, F/O Walker's rear gunner, F/S B Ranus, in the Ghost Squadron's NA-S (S-Sugar), shot down what he described as a jet propelled enemy fighter. He later claimed it as destroyed. F/O C R Pauli in NA-N overshot on landing in a high crosswind and wrote off the aircraft. No one was injured.

Middleton's last raid before a 10 day break from operations was a daylight operation on Saturday the 6th to the Nordstern synthetic oil hydrogenation and coking plant at Gelsenkirchen, 5 miles N/E of Essen. Over 500 aircraft managed to bomb the plant before smoke and broken cloud obscured the target area. The Master Bomber gave the order, 'Second Hand', which meant that that the crews were to bomb any built up areas seen through the cloud breaks. Amongst the areas hit were Gelsenkirchen itself, along with Recklinghousen, Rollinghousen and Essen. Two marshalling yards were also bombed. F/L Anderson's bomb aimer, F/O A P McKillop, dropped his bomb-load, consisting of a 4,000-lb Cookie, six 1,000-lb and six 500-lb GP bombs on a large factory complex at Castrop Rouxel, another oil producing centre. All of Goosepool's Lancasters returned safe.

For the next 10 days, 419 enjoyed a break from operations, the longest in over 6 months. This respite allowed valuable training to continue. On November 16th, both squadrons supported troops of the American 9th Army by carrying out a precision attack on the town of Julich, south of Dusseldorf. This was one of 3 towns in an area between Aachen and the Rhine which were about to be attacked by the American 1st and 9th Armies.

The weather was mostly clear, and the 15 Moose and Ghost crews bombed as directed by the Master Bomber. With 498 aircraft attacking Julich in a 27 minute timeframe, congestion was inevitable. F/O Sheahan was packed inside a very tight swarm of about 15 aircraft, with no room to manoeuvre as they ran in for the target. All the bomb aimers appeared to press the tit at the same time, ensuring that the town was well plastered. F/O Anderson in N-Nan got a little too close to the aircraft above him. He and his crew were shocked when a lump of VR-N's wing tip departed the aircraft, courtesy of a bomb belonging to one of the aircraft above them. The Lancaster however, seemed to fly ok, and was able to return safely to Goosepool with all of the other squadron aircraft.

The other two towns, which were in a 13-mile radius of Julich, were Duran and Heinsburg. Duran was attacked by 498 Bomber Command aircraft belonging to 1, 5 and 8 Groups, Heinsburg by 182 Lancasters of 3 Group. The Moosemen were part of a force of 78 Lancasters, 413 Halifaxes and 17 Mosquitoes whose job was to disrupt communications behind the German lines. Duran's civilian population was still in the town when the bombs fell. 3,127 Germans were killed, including 217 soldiers. Heinsburg contained only 110 civilians and a small German military unit consisting of 1 officer and a small number of soldiers. 52 civilians were killed. No German records of the raid on Julich are available. Eight aircraft were lost, the Duran raid claimed 4,[118] Heinsburg 1 and Julich 3, none were from Middleton.

[118] One crash-landed at base without injury to the crew

The Americans had sent 1,239 of their heavy bombers to targets in the same area, all returned. For the American ground forces, the advance was not a great success. Due to the very wet conditions underfoot, their tanks were not able to participate in the push, and over-stretched supply lines caused a shortage of ammo for the artillery. The result for the American infantry was that their advance was protracted and cost them many troops.

The month of November continued for Middleton's squadrons with a daylight raid to Munster on the 18th, and the synthetic oil refinery at Castrop Rauxel on the 21st. The latter was completely burned out, and ceased oil production for the remainder of the war.

During the Castrop Rauxal raid, F/O Blaney's crew, flying 419's E-Easy, felt a heavy bump and heard a loud bang just after completing the bomb run. The aircraft was lifted 500 feet by the incident. There had been no explosion, so whatever they had come into contact with was probably not of German origin. After they landed back at Middleton, the crew jumped out of the aircraft and found that the bombdoors were buckled and minus some of their black paint. The conclusion was that VR-E had collided, with the tail fin, of another aircraft.

The loss of one of 419's most experienced and well-respected crews occurred during a routine training flight on the night of November 24th. VR-Y KB785 caught fire whilst over the Bradbury bombing range, 10 miles north of Middleton. The Lancaster crashed near Sedgfield, at 18:23 hours, killing all of the crew. The accident investigators concluded that for some reason, the fuel jettison socks had been deployed. Unfortunately, they had not fully extended from the trailing edge of the Lancaster's wing. Fuel had leaked into the wing, and due to the dihedral angle, had run down the inside of the wing and entered the fuselage. Once inside, it was ignited by some unknown source. Although not conclusive, one possibility put forward by the investigating officer was that one of the crew could have been smoking.

On the 27th, 35 of Goosepool's Lancasters attacked Neuss, 4 miles S/W of the centre of Dusseldorf. Although it was a moonlit night and several German night fighters were seen, none of the aircraft were attacked. On their arrival back in England, the usual northeast weather again necessitated that the aircraft divert to American bases in the South. Although none of the other squadron aircraft were hit by flak, 419's F/O Anderson and crew managed it quite easily. They landed back at their diversion airfield on 3 engines, sporting 23 large holes in their aircraft. Within the squadron it was noticed that this crew seemed to have acquired a great talent for finding flak where no one else could.

The final raid for November came on the 30th, with operations to Duisburg. All crews returned safely. 419 celebrated the fact that none of their aircrew had been lost on operations during the month. If not for the Sedgfield crash on the 27th, it would have been a completely loss free month.

December 1944

December 1944 began with a 504 aircraft raid to Hagen on the 2nd, Middleton's squadrons providing 16 aircraft each. Serious damage was inflicted on 1,658 houses, 92 industrial buildings, 21 schools, 14 culture buildings, 5 hospitals and 5 banks. Also completely destroyed was a factory making batteries for U-boats. 583 people were killed, including 100 foreign workers. 997 Germans were also injured, along with 88 foreigners. Although bombed to some extent previously, this was the first major raid on Hagen. During this operation, and the next to Karlsruhe on the 4th, the crews battled against some of the most serious weather phenomena they had experienced to date. Heavy concentrations of Cumulo-Nimbus cloud, with its associated icing conditions and high winds, caused many problems for the crews, including iced up engine intakes.

Typical of many, F/O R La Turner's crew met severe icing conditions shortly after crossing the French Coast. The aircraft began to lose height and so the order to prepare to abandon was given. The aircraft continued to descend, and when 4,000 feet was reached, La Turner gave the order to abandon. Shortly after the crew jumped out, the aircraft must have descended into warmer air, as La Turner regained some control. He then decided to land at the nearest friendly airfield. This turned out to be airfield A61, a landing strip that had been over-run by the allies. Having called them up, he was told that there were soft filled in craters at the end of the runway. In order not to detonate the bomb load by digging in, he swung off the runway before the end was reached, but in so doing the aircraft was badly damaged. La Turner was not injured and was able to leave the aircraft. He later discovered that out of his crew of six, two had not survived the jump. The body of the navigator, F/O M S Sucharov, was found by his deployed chute, but it was not clear whether it had opened on impact or during his descent. It is thought that the other member of the crew who died, Sgt M Hempseed, may have fallen through the escape hatch.

As well as bombs, many thousands of leaflets were dropped over Karlsruhe during this raid, which was carried out through complete cloud cover. Some crews diverted to airfields in the South to refuel, as their exertions in their ice-laden aircraft had cost them precious fuel. With the exception of F/O La Turner's aircraft, all from both squadrons returned safely.

On the 4th, Karlsruhe was the target for sixteen crews from both squadrons. The weather was still bad and again crews had to refuel in the south. The total number of aircraft taking part was 535. 1 Lancaster and 1 Mosquito were lost. None were from Middleton. 375 Germans were killed during this raid. The Durlacher machine-tool factory, the main Protestant church and the concert hall were among the buildings destroyed.

On the 5/6th, Soest, 27 miles east of Dortmund, was the target for 419. Weather over the target was fine and bombing was carried out from 18/20,000 feet and all 15 aircraft returned safe. The Ghosts had sent 14 of their Lancasters on this raid, only 13 returned. F/L H A Shewfelt's Lancaster, NA-E KB768, collided with a 426 Squadron Halifax, OW-N LW200, out of Linton-on-Ouse, flown by F/O A V Carter RCAF. Both aircraft came down near Rugby, Warwickshire. The bodies of the aircraft's two gunners, F/O E E Cooper, tail gunner, and F/S A G Baxter, mid-upper gunner, were recovered, as were two unidentified bodies. According to 428's ORB, the remainder of the crew had not been found at the time of writing, due to the aircraft being badly dispersed when the bomb load exploded. Whilst the bodies of the Halifax crew were identified and buried, only those of the 2 gunners in F/L Shewfelt's Lancaster were laid to rest. They, along with 6 out of 7 members of the Halifax crew are buried in Brookwood Military Cemetery. The seventh member of the Halifax crew, engineer Sgt D L Bourner RAF, rests in Dagenham (Chadwell Heath) Cemetery. The remainder of 428's crew are commemorated on the Runnymede Memorial.

Next day, Osnabruck was the target for Middleton's crews. A towering column of Cu-Nims blocked the path of the outgoing bombers, and they began to pick up ice. To make matters even worse, there was a bank of haze on the cloud tops, adding the risk of collisions to the aircrew's problems. On his return to Middleton, 419's F/O Anderson remarked that the weather during this trip had been the worst he had ever flown in. Having taken off from Goosepool, he was immediately on instruments and trying to get on top of the icing clouds. By 23,000 feet, he and his crew realised that they were flogging a dead horse, as the cloud extended from base all the way to the continent. They iced up badly, and were constantly disconcerted by the sounds of the ice, flung from the prop tips, as it hit the fuselage. Anderson flew all the way there on instruments, and having bombed on Gee fixes, turned for home. He was still dial watching all the way home when some of the instruments failed due to icing. He ordered the crew to be ready to jump, but the instruments began to work again as he descended into warmer air and prepared to join the circuit for a landing. F/L D B Hunter returned early, having lost the use of his instruments. Due to ice accretion, F/O Begg's aircraft suffered a fire in its starboard outer. When the engineer tried to feather it, the whole electrical system malfunctioned, possibly due to a short circuit. Then the port inner began to take the Mickey, followed by the starboard inner, which cut out. Eventually the problems sorted themselves out and the aircraft was able to return safely. F/L Quinn's Lancaster encountered static electricity, which broke one of the Perspex panels in the pilot's canopy and a panel in the mid-upper turret. It also tore off the trailing aerial. Blinded by the flash, Quinn lost height but was able to regain control of the aircraft and return safely. There were no less than 18 bomb hang-ups in various aircraft, caused by the ice. F/O B D Hyndman, on his 8th trip, along with his crew in B-Beer KB779, failed to return from this operation, all were lost without trace.

Mr C G White arrived at Goosepool during the day to begin an investigation into the possibilities of lengthening the runways. Under consideration was to have the East/West runway extended from 1,400 yards to 3,000, the northeast/southwest runway from 2,000 to 3,000 yards and the North/South runway from 1,400 to 2,000 yards. he was to remain at Middleton for about a week.

Ludwigshaven was the next trip for the Moosemen and the Ghosts, and this took place on the 15th. Over the previous 9 days, bad weather at base, and a series of go, no-go operations culminated in cancellation after cancellation. The almost constant bombing up and de-bombing of the aircraft put a severe strain on the armourers, but they accepted their plight and got on with the job. The target was the I G Farben chemical works. In contrast to the raids at the beginning of the month, the weather behaved itself, and the markers were clearly seen by the crews. The raid was a great success, despite intense flak opposition over the target area. Several of 419's aircraft suffered hits, but their encounters were not a patch on those of VR-J flown by 419's S/L C M Black. He and his crew had spotted an American B17 slightly above them and on the port bow. After a few moments, the fortress turned slowly to starboard and ended up ahead of the Lanc. Black climbed slightly out of the buffet of the Fort's prop-wash. At that, the B17's tail gunner and his companion in the starboard waist position opened fire, hitting the Lancaster in the nose and injuring the bomb-aimer F/S L B McKinnon in the right foot. Black flew the damaged bomber to Woodbridge, where McKinnon was admitted to the Ipswich and East Suffolk Hospital. He remained on the seriously wounded list for 6 days. 13 of the aircraft diverted on the way home, including you know who, who had increased his number of flak holes to 37. Yes! You guessed it, F/O Anderson's crew were indeed becoming celebrities amongst the German flak gunners. All remaining 419 and 428 crews diverted to Horham, as the weather at base was bad. Earlier in the day, a special discussion was held with the 6 Group Gunnery Leader regarding the fitting of Glen Martin turrets to Lancaster Xs.

The ice clouds returned for Goosepool's next operation, which was to Duisburg on the 18th. All 16 of 419's crews and the 13 from 428 bombed by cloud glow checked by Gee. No results could be measured as to the success of this raid. Yet again, Teesside's weather necessitated a diversion on the way home. Next day the weather at base was horrible, the Viz was down to 150 yards, and the planned operation was scrubbed 5 minutes before take-off time. On the 20th, conditions were no better. That morning, word came through that F/S K G Shields, one of 419's mid-upper gunners, with 7 trips to his credit, had been killed in a car accident whilst on leave in Oldham, Lancashire. His loss was felt by all on the squadron.

On the 21st /22nd, the target was the Nippes marshalling yards at Cologne. The Moosemen and the Ghosts detailed 16 crews each. Takeoff was planned for 11:00 and then cancelled. It was put back on at noon and then set back twice more. Eventually the raid did take place, but cloud cover over the target meant that the crews had to bomb sky markers and no results could be observed. In the end, only a few bombs hit the railway yards, but those that did, destroyed 40 wagons. Several railway lines were severed and a railway repair workshop was flattened, along with the city's slaughterhouse in the nearby Ehrenfeld district. None of the 67 Lancasters, 54 Halifaxes and 15 Mosquitoes taking part was lost.

On Saturday December 23rd 1944, P/O W S McMullen and his crew arrived at Middleton and reported in for duty with 428. William Stuart McMullen was to serve only 22 days with the Ghosts. As you will learn later, he was however to leave an indelible mark on the town of Darlington, not just for the duration of the war, but forever.

On Christmas Eve, 338 aircraft of 4, 6 and 8 Groups were detailed to carry out raids on German airfields, namely Lohausen and Mulheim.[119] Both of Middleton's squadrons sent 16 Lancasters each to Lohausen airfield, near Dusseldorf. The weather over the target area was good, but the airfield was heavily defended by many flak guns. 419 Squadron carried out the first 'Gaggle' attack to be employed by a Middleton squadron. In total, 6 aircraft were lost, including 419's VR-T, flown by F/O

---

[119] Now Dusseldorf and Essen civil airports

T H Cowtan RCAF, who was on his fifth operation. This aircraft, KB715, was one of the squadron's oldest Lancasters, with over 60 operations to its credit, and was only the 15th Lancaster X to come off the production line. Having taken off from Middleton at 12:06, the Lancaster was hit by flak, which knocked the starboard outer off its mountings and set fire to both inner engines. The crew jumped out and parachuted to safety, but within a few minutes, F/O R W Hale the wireless operator was ruthlessly shot and killed by German ground troops. The remainder of the crew became POWs. Due to the usual lousy weather at base, the aircraft were diverted on their return to the UK.

For the remainder of the station, the festivities on the last Christmas day of WWII were enjoyed by all. Due to the continued bad weather, 419 was unable to get its aircraft back, and the diverted crews had to spend their Christmas at Charter Hall, where they were very well received. 428's crews spent their Christmas at Wethersfield. At Goosepool, Christmas Day Teeside style was enjoyed under a blanket of fog and smoke. The groundcrews reported for work, but as there was little work to do they were allowed to go back to their billets at 11:00 and prepare for the festivities. The Ghost Squadron's Christmas Day was typical of those throughout the whole of the RAF. A delegation of sergeants visited the Officers' Mess, the visit was returned by 25 officers. At noon, Wing Commander Hull, S/L Lamont, S/L Edmonson, F/L Bowron and representatives of the various sections helped serve the airmen and WAAFs their Christmas dinner.

On Boxing Day, 419 and 428 could only offer 4 aircraft each when asked, as the weather at base prevented the return of the diverted aircraft. Much to the satisfaction of the crews concerned, this operation was eventually scrubbed, and the next morning it was scrubbed again. During the afternoon, the weather improved sufficiently to allow the diverted kites to return. The crews had been very well looked after, but were glad to be back as the messes at the diversion airfields had been over-crowded.

F/O Blaney and his crew had departed earlier for the RAF's Stonefall regional cemetery at Harrogate. They were to act as bearers at the funeral of their mid-upper gunner, Sgt Shields, killed in the car accident at Oldham.

On the 27/28th, a daylight raid to the marshalling yards at Opladen was laid on. 419 and 428 detailed 15 and 11 crews respectively. Take-off was set for 14:30. F/O F W How and his crew failed to return from this operation; their aircraft, VR-D KB338, had come down at Leverkusen-Wiesdorf, where they were all killed. It was also here that they were laid to rest. F/O How was on his 19th sortie.

428 also lost an aircraft during this raid. F/O E W Page and his crew also failed to return, they are buried in the Rheinberg War Cemetery.

Earlier that day a horrific accident took place whilst a 347 Squadron (Free French Air Force) Halifax was being prepared at Elvington, near York. It claimed the lives of no less than 13 groundcrew men and injured 5 more. A series of 5 massive explosions took place after a fire broke out in the aircraft. Most of the dead were fighting the fire when the explosions occurred. 8 of the groundcrew killed were FFAF. The number of RAF groundcrew killed totalled 5.

Next day, 17 of 419's crews, along with 12 from 428, were required for an attack on the Schloven Oil Refinery just outside Gelsenkirchen. Only 16 of 419's aircraft undertook this operation, as one had a tyre burst when it was about to take off. Over the target there was thick cloud, but the Oboe sky markers were accurately placed and the bombs followed suit from between 17/20,000 feet. Over 300 HE bombs fell within the oil plant. A total of 3,198 bombs fell in other parts of Schloven and Buer, and the surface buildings of the Hugo 1 and Hugo II coal mines were badly damaged. 93 people were killed on the ground, including 24 POWs. 1,368 people were bombed out, 1,178 through bomb damage and 190 due to unexploded bombs.

After the attack, heavy oil fires could be seen through the clouds. There had been a large amount of flak thrown up by the Ruhr defences and two of 419's aircraft were lost. VR-L KB753, flown by P/O R F Adam on his 19th Op, was hit by flak in the bomb bay and exploded. The tail gunner, W/O2 R G Rogers, was the only survivor. He was thrown out of his turret and survived to become a POW. Debris from the exploding Lancaster was scattered in the vicinity of Essen.

The second Lancaster was KB765, flown by F/O R A McVicar on his 18th sortie. This aircraft was hit by flak and cannon fire from a night fighter, after which it blew up over Gilsenkirchen-Buer. Again, the tail gunner F/S W R McLeod was the only one to get out alive. He, too, became a POW.

For Wing Commander Hagerman, flying with a brand new crew, this was the last trip of his second tour. He had to return with all his bombs and experienced great difficulty in dumping them in the sea over the jettison area. 428 were also biding farewell to one of their stalwarts. Squadron Leader G L Gonyou, the Ghost's 'B' Flight Commander, had completed his tour and was to be screened.

A raid to the Kalk-Nord railway yards (Cologne) on the 30/31st proved to be the last operation for Goosepool during 1944. 470 aircraft of 4, 6 and 8 Groups, 15 from each of Middleton's squadrons, severely damaged the Kalk rail yards and 2 passenger stations that were close by. Two ammo trains were seen to blow up during the raid. Some of the bombs fell outside the railway complex and destroyed 116 houses, 2 schools, 2 churches, 5 police or postal buildings and 3 industrial complexes.

There was an operational stand down on the 31st. Some training was carried out, but everyone was tired and felt truly grateful of the respite. Most sections quit early, to help prepare for the New Year's celebrations. All of the Canadians at Goosepool thought the same thoughts as they had done 12 months earlier, 'Here's hoping that the next year sees us all back in Canada, with the victory won and the war a series of memories, many of them happy and many of them not so happy.'

CHAPTER NINE
Goosepool War Diaries 1945
January – 1945.
William S McMullen.
February – 1945.
March – 1945.
April – 1945.
May – 1945.
419 squadron Losses – Croft 1942.
419 Losses – Middleton St George 1942.
419 Losses --Middleton St George 1943.
419 Losses – Middleton St George 1944.
419 Losses – Middleton St George 1945.
428 Losses – Middleton St George 1943.
428 Losses - Middleton St George 1944.
428 Losses – Middleton St George 1945.

Goosepool War Diaries 1945

January 1945

January 1945 was two days old when 419 and 428 carried out a night attack on Nuremberg. Lancaster KB791, flown by F/L Craton of 428, returned early when it was realised that the rear turret was U/S and only one gun in the mid-upper was serviceable. A full moon, clear sky and snow-covered ground meant that the city was easily found. The red and green target markers could be seen from some distance away and brought the crews in for a very successful raid. The city was engulfed in flames and smoke. During the raid, the mother of all explosions was seen to erupt in the middle of the conflagration. The crews counted over 30 searchlights, but these quickly went out when the illuminating flares were dropped. The old eastern half of the city centre was badly damaged. 2,000 preserved wooden medieval houses were destroyed, along with the castle, the Rathouse and practically all of the churches. The northeast and southern areas contained modern buildings, and 4,640 of these, mostly blocks of flats, were also destroyed. The death toll on the ground totalled 1,838 people, with a further 50 recorded as missing. The MAN motor transport plants and the huge Siemens factory were also located in the southern sector, they were destroyed along with 414 other industrial buildings. The only Moose aircraft to be hit was VR-S, flown by F/O Cox. It and several other aircraft were hit by allied artillery fire as they flew east over the battle zone, fortunately none of Middleton's aircraft failed to return.

For 419, the evening's raid was not entirely without loss. It was with much sadness that the squadron bade farewell to KB700. 'The Ruhr Express' had been not only its first ever Lancaster but also the flagship of the RCAF. Returning from Nuremberg with suspected hydraulic problems, KB700 was flown by F/L A G Warner. The aircraft bounced heavily on landing, and by the time the Ruhr Express stopped, it had gone off the end of the runway. It came to rest some 50 yards further on. Fortunately, the aircraft was in one piece and none of the crew was injured. Warner tried to taxi back, but it was 22 minutes to midnight and very dark. Before the peri-track could be reached, the port outer propeller struck a trench-digger and the engine burst into flames. The crew managed to scramble out of the Lancaster and into a ditch. Unbeknown to the crew, the first man to reach the aircraft did not realise that the crew had vacated the premises and searched inside for them. He got out just before the ammo and the flares began to go off. KB700 was destroyed in the ensuing fire, having completed its 49th operational sortie. The Ruhr Express had been with 419 for just over a year. Fitted with dual controls, all of the squadron's original Lancaster crews had been trained on her. Earlier during the day, Wing Commander Hull relinquished his command of 428 and departed for 4 Group HQ, to take up the post of Senior Operations Controller. He was replaced by S/L M W Gall.

Next day saw another joint effort between aircrew and armourers, when 419's bomb aimers assisted in the bombing up of 15 aircraft for a raid on the I G Farben chemical factory at Ludwigshaven. Due to bad weather, the Op was later scrubbed, and the bombs remained aboard the Lancasters until the 5th, when 14 Moose and the same number of Ghost crews were

KB700 the morning after, her crew took a last look
Photo: courtesy of Canadian Forces via Geoff Hill

Second view of KB700's demise. Note water towers protruding from behind starboard tailplane and hangar 1, visible on the extreme right, next to the burnt out port wingspar. The airport's terminal building now covers the crash site.
Photo: courtesy of Canadian Forces via Geoff Hill

Photo: courtesy of Canadian Forces

detailed for Ops to Hannover. The total force sent there that night totalled 664 aircraft from 1,4,6 and 8 groups. The raid itself was the first major raid on Hannover since October 1943, and was a complete success. Flames from the burning city could be seen from 200 miles away. 3,605 flats or apartments were destroyed and 250 people were killed.

The only noteworthy incident to befall the Moosemen during this raid was the loss of VR-A KB722, flown by P/O N D Mallen. The Lancaster was flying at 20,000 feet over Emmen, Holland, close to the German border, when, at about 21:17, it was fired at by a corkscrewing Lancaster. The rear gunner of the attacking Lanc must have thought that the aircraft behind him in the dark was a Jerry night fighter, and given his captain the order for evasive action. During the attack, A-Able's tail gunner, Sgt C Drinka, saw a trail of liquid spraying back from the starboard inner, followed shortly after by more of the same from the port inner. Soon the liquid (fuel) found the hot engines and both inners burst into flames. The engineer, Sgt P W Hall, quickly turned off the master fuel cock for both inner engines. He then pushed their feathering buttons in, just long enough to ensure that they stayed in themselves. When feathering was complete, the buttons popped back out automatically. After that, the throttles were closed, and the slow running cut out switches were moved to the idle cut-off position.

The Graviner system did its stuff and the fires soon went out. Also knocked out by the rounds from the other Lancaster were the flying instruments, some of the internal lighting and the intercom. Mallen, who was only on his second Op, got rid of the bombs from the now underpowered Lanc without delay. Initially he headed the bomber for Brussels, but then elected to head for the emergency airfield at Juvencourt. Due to fog, a landing there was impossible, and discarding the idea to head for Manston, he found a hole in the cloud and crash landed, wheels up, in a farmer's field near Guise, 15 miles N/E of Saint-Quentin. The Lancaster was badly damaged during the landing and four of the crew were injured. Both Mallen and the mid-upper, Sgt M R Poole, suffered sprained ankles, whilst the bomb aimer, F/S R S Dickinson, received cuts to his face, legs and hands; he also injured his shoulder. The engineer, Sgt Hall, had cuts around his left eye. Navigator P/O J A Miller, wireless operator W/O R B Cameron and tail gunner Sgt Drinka were transported to RAF Station Epinoy, where they were flown back to England. The four injured men were initially treated in Guise infirmary and later transferred to the American Military Hospital at St-Quentin, before they too were flown back to England. For this crew, the Hannover raid was to be their last, as they did not fly operationally with 419 again. All 14 Ghost aircraft returned safely.

For 419 and 428, an uneventful raid on the night of the 6/7th took place on the railway yards at Hanau, 10 miles E/N/E of Frankfurt-on-Main. This town was an important junction in the German railway system. Although many bombs fell on railway related areas, some also fell on the centre of the town. Over 40% of Hanau was destroyed and 90 people were killed. The nearby village of Mittelbuchen, 5 km N/N/E of Hanau centre, was also badly damaged. This raid was followed the night after by another to Munich, where the city received its last major raid of the war. 645 Lancasters and 9 Mosquitoes of 1, 3, 5,6 and 8 Groups successfully damaged the centre of the city and several industrial areas. 11 Lancasters were lost, and 4 more crashed in liberated parts of France. Goosepool's crews returned safely, and were diverted to Swinderby, just a few miles from the city of Lincoln. Also taking part in this raid was P/O William S McMullen, F/O Mutch and W/O Johnson, who were undergoing their first operational sorties as second dickies. Although he was to return safely from this particular operation, as you will read later, this would be P/O McMullen's first and last operational flight.

The reason for the diversion was - you guessed it, Teesside's dubious weather conditions. Snow had begun to fall at Goosepool, and fall and fall. On the 8th, W/C Gall gave an introductory talk to 428, after which, at 16:00, a party developed. This was interrupted when a call to help shovel snow off the runway was received. This was somewhat futile, as heavy snow was still falling and the only outcome was that everybody got wet. Next morning, it was National Snow Shovelling Day, and practically everyone was out on the airfield all day with a shovel in their hands. On the 10/11th the runways were still U/S and so there was still no operational flying. S/L Gonyou took up his post as Training Officer, his replacement as 428's 'B' Flight Commander was F/L R Swartz. During the lay-off caused by the snow, much ground training had taken place, including 'Skeet' shooting by the gunners. Next day 428's aircrew attended a lecture on the PFF, given by G/C McTavish, after which it was announced that the runways were once more open for business. During the afternoon, the diverted aircraft began

Toby Greer, outside radar repair shop. MSG 1944
Photo: via Geoff Hill

to return to the nest. Snow was still in abundance, with mounds of it piled up on either side of all main paved surfaces. At noon, some aircrews were briefed for operations, but after two postponements they were cancelled.

William S McMullen

On the evening of Saturday January the 13th 1945, Bill Gillham was playing dominoes with his sister and mother. They lived at 58a The Byway, in the Eastbourne area of Darlington. Their house was situated on what was then the eastern extremity of Darlington. Their back garden looked out onto open country. After five and a half years of war, the Gillham family were used to the familiar sounds of aircraft from nearby Middleton St George. On this evening however, something was wrong, the sound was different. Running into the garden, Bill and his sister saw a bomber surrounded by flames and lighting up the sky. The aircraft was approaching from the north, and along with the flames, they could see its navigation lights clearly. The Lancaster turned left towards them. They could see that the aircraft was descending over the outskirts of the town. Soon the burning aircraft was overhead, now at a height of no more than 600 feet and heading southeast, with its port wing ablaze. Suddenly, the huge bomber went into a very steep dive, and crashed on the other side of Lingfield Lane.

It came down about 600 yards from where Bill and his sister were standing, barely missing the houses. There was a huge explosion and the ground shook. The time was 20:49. Immediately, the glow from the blazing wreckage illuminated the dark sky, turning night into day. Bill and his sister, looking out towards the hilltop village of Sadberge, saw parachutes in the dull red glow. They both jumped the garden fence, ran across Lingfield Lane and through a field to the burning bomber. Although they lived only a few hundred yards from the crash site, by the time they got there, half the kids in the neighborhood had beaten them to it. The Lancaster had come down in a field at Lingfield Farm, crashing just a few feet from the farmhouse. Bill could see hundreds of small pieces of burning wreckage scattered over a large area. It was hard to believe that, moments before, this had been a huge bomber. The police arrived, followed soon after by the fire brigade. Bill remembers seeing a smashed turret with belts of ammunition hanging from it. Rounds were exploding everywhere, so everyone was moved back and the area cordoned off, but not before many of the kids had helped themselves to a souvenir or two. Bill didn't want to be left out, so before leaving, he grabbed a lump of aluminium, which was lying close by, which he still has to this day.

Bill Gillom in 2002, with his lump of McMullen Lancaster. It was bigger.
He keeps on sawing bits off to give to people
Photo: Author

The bomber, which belonged to 428 Squadron had taken off some three hours earlier at 17:48 in order to carry out a radar training flight. On board were the captain, Pilot Officer W S McMullen, navigator P/O W A Sage, bomb aimer F/S H H Simms, wireless operator F/S S Ratsoy, flight engineer Sgt G T Llewellin, mid-upper gunner F/S E D Dykes and tail gunner F/S J H Feeley, all RCAF. As stated earlier, Bill McMullen was fairly new to the squadron and had flown only one operational trip, as a second pilot.

At 20:35, the crew, having carried out their training exercise, were returning at a height of 10,000 feet to a position just to the west of the airfield. McMullen called for joining instructions, and was told that the visibility was 3,500 feet and that there was a thin layer of 10/10ths cloud at 1,800 feet and small amounts of other cloud at 1,000 feet. He was also told the wind direction was N/N/E at 11 mph.

McMullen turned to the engineer, Sgt Llewellin, and told him that they were going to descend, prior to landing back at Middleton. The engineer moved the throttles back until the boost gauges read 1-lb/sq inch of boost. He left the propeller pitch controls alone, their gauges still reading 1,950 RPM. This would give them a descent speed of 200 mph. Having settled down in the descent, the engineer turned to his panel and checked that all temperatures and pressures were normal. Having found everything was ok he entered the readings in his log. Soon after, F/S Ratsoy, who was sitting further back in the fuselage at his wireless operator's station, saw a heavy shower of sparks coming from the inboard exhaust stack of the port outer engine. He reported this on the intercom, and looking again, saw the engines inboard exhaust cover begin to glow red-hot. Eventually McMullen leveled out at about 2,500 feet. Initially, the sparks were mistaken by the crew for normal carbon sparks. McMullen opened the engines up to 22/2400 rpm to clear them. This action did not stop the sparking, and so he ordered the engineer to feather the port outer prop. This was done, and at the same time Llewellin turned the ICO control to the 'Engine Off' position. Looking at the rev counter, he saw no change, indicating that the prop had not feathered. He pressed the button again but still there was no change in rpm. As Llewellin had pressed the feathering button, Ratsoy saw a huge sheet of flame coming from the port outer.

From that point on, a glow spread from the front of the engine cowling as it began to burn away. After only a few seconds the cowling had completely melted away and Ratsoy could clearly see the top of the engine by the light of the fire. The prop could not be feathered, and when this became apparent, Llewellin pressed the Graviner fire extinguisher button for the port outer, but this had no effect on the fire. Standing by McMullen, he noticed that he was jockeying with the control column a little, but did not believe that he was having too much trouble in controlling the aircraft. McMullen ordered Llewellin to open up the engines to full power, in an attempt to gain height for the crew to bale out. At the same time he gave the order for everyone except the engineer to prepare to abandon the aircraft.[120] The pilot and the engineer normally worked together as a team, and McMullen needed Llewellin even more now, to keep the blazing Lancaster in the air.

[120] All crew members had experience of baling out on previous flights

By now the Lancaster was to the northeast of the airfield, heading north over Aclam, Middlesbrough. McMullen turned to port and began flying a left-hand circuit for runway 06. As the aircraft began its down-wind leg it approached the small village of Elton, some 3 miles southwest of Stockton town centre. It was at this time that the first member of the crew prepared to jump.

F/S Simms, in the bomb aimer's position, clipped on his chute, bent down and opened the belly hatch. Rather than try to dump the hatch cover out of the opening and risk it being jammed in the aperture by the slipstream, as was often the case, he threw it into the nose of the aircraft then jumped. The second man out was the mid-upper, F/S Dykes, who sprained his ankle when he landed. The remainder went out as the bomber flew west, along what is now the Hartburn to Sadberge back road. Until the building of the A66 dual carriageway, this was part of the main Stockton to Darlington road. As three crewmen jumped, the aircraft was still in cloud.

After the crew had gone, Llewellin clipped on his chute. Bill McMullan asked for more revs and boost on the three remaining engines to gain height. As they overflew Sadberge McMullen turned port, onto base leg. He then told the engineer to get out. Llewellin turned to McMullen and said, 'Are you coming Sir?' McMullen replied, 'Yes, go on, get out, I'm right behind you.' Llewellin went forward to the hatch and stood there for a moment, to see if the pilot was following him, but he was not, and with their height now down to about 600 feet, he jumped. The next thing he noticed was the fire on the ground where the Lancaster had come down. Llewellin landed safely, about 500 yards from the scene of the crash.

The 64 Base Commander, Group Captain R S Turnbull, had been standing outside the Officers' Mess at Middleton. A few minutes before the crash, he saw an orange glow light up the clouds to the west of the airfield. He took this to be an aircraft on fire, and watched it fly a large circle towards the aerodrome, and away again. He continued watching for a good two or three minutes until it broke cloud at about 1,500 feet, when the orange glow changed to the white of burning metal. The Lancaster seemed to be descending over Darlington. It appeared to be coming down under control until it reached about 5-600 feet, when it suddenly changed attitude and dived steeply towards the ground, exploding on impact.

P/O William Stuart McMullen's grave in Harrogate's Stonefall Cemetery. The card on the wreath placed there by the author reads - "To Bill McMullen, from all the grateful people of Darlington, for steering his burning Lancaster away from the town, which cost him his life". You will never be forgotten.
Photo: Author

In the light of the explosion, Turnbull could see parachutes. The Lancaster had struck the ground at a steep angle, a bit port wing low, cartwheeling the rear section of the fuselage and wings for a distance of 150 yards. Portions of the petrol tanks, which had exploded on impact, ignited haystacks and a Dutch barn in the farmyard. McMullen had been killed instantly, after which he and the pilot's seat were thrown 120 yards from the first point of impact.

He could have saved himself and jumped with the engineer, but he must have realised that below him, somewhere in the gloom of that dark night, was the blacked out town of Darlington. To bale out at that point would certainly have cost the lives of many civilians.

G/C Turnbull jumped into his car and quickly traveled the 3 miles to the crash site. The sky was lit for miles around by the flames. When he reached the aircraft, he found the wreckage and several haystacks burning intensely. He helped organize a search for the crew, who were found comparatively uninjured quite near to the crash site. J.90038 Pilot Officer William Stuart McMullen was identified by his identity discs, and having been removed from the crash site he was taken to SSQ at Middleton. Early on the morning of January 18th, he was driven to the Stonefall Regional Cemetery at Harrogate for burial. His funeral, which was conducted by S/L Clark, Middleton's Station Padre, took place during the morning. Full Service Honours were accorded, the coffin being carried by Air Force Personnel.

All members of his crew, with the exception of the injured mid-upper gunner, F/S Dykes, were in attendance. A firing party was present, and the coffin was covered with the Union Jack. The Last Post was sounded at the end. Today he still rests at Stonefall, in Grave E5, Section H.

256

An immediate inquiry into the cause of the crash began. J A Gibson was an engine fitter on 428's 'A' Flight. He was responsible for the daily inspections on the Merlin 224 engines fitted to KB793. He reported that he had carried out a complete DI[121] on the offending engine, (Rolls Royce Merlin 224, serial number V340525), in accordance with the schedule of daily inspection for this type of engine. He also reported that this engine had only minor defects reported since new, and to the best of his knowledge, was in perfect condition at the time of takeoff. In accordance with 6G/6370/Eng, dated 31st December 1944, all four engines on KB793 were checked for feathering on January 12th, the day before the flight, and found to be satisfactory.

At the time of the accident, the port outer engine, which had been installed on 21/12/44, had done only 39.52 hours; the port inner, installed on 15/12/44, had done 29.52. The starboard outer, installed on 6/8/44, had done 87.43, whilst the starboard inner, also installed on the 6/8/44, had done 87.43. The aircraft itself had flown a total of 87.48 hours. When the port outer engine was inspected, it was found that it was extensively damaged by fire. The flame traps (A cylinder block), cylinder head (left-hand side when looking from the front), most of the B cylinder head (r/h side), and the entire induction manifold were completely burned away. No.6A piston crown was burned, and there was evidence of molten metal from the piston crown beneath the valve seats. The Investigating Officer concluded that the logical sequence following the failure and burning of the 6A piston would be for particles of piston materiel to become trapped under the valve seats, which in turn would allow burning and the ultimate collapse of the flame traps. The burning particles (sparks) seen by the wireless operator, had, in fact, not been carbon at all, but particles from the piston crown. Ignition of the boosted fuel mixture in the induction system (supercharged), and burning of the induction ports would follow and a fire would rapidly develop. Once the ports had burned away, allowing the coolant fluid to escape, disintegration of the engine would quickly follow. The flexible feathering oil pipe and the Linatex fuel feed pipe were burned away. These pipes were found buried in mud at the crash site, and therefore it was deduced that they had burned in the air. Neither were protected from fire.

The burning through of the feathering oil pipe prevented the engineer from feathering the prop. This would account for the sheet of flame seen when the feathering button was pressed; the feathering pumps by then were in fact supplying high pressure oil as fuel for the fire. The Graviner fire extinguisher system seemed to have functioned normally, but its efficiency must have been reduced due to its alloy spray piping being completely fused by the heat of the fire. The examiner, F/L Frank E Lynch DFC, completed his investigation and liaised with his senior inspector, S/L Eric Newton, who summed up the inquiry by saying that the mechanical failure of the port outer engine was considered to have originated from the failure and burning of No. 6A piston. He went on to say the accident was due to the mechanical failure of the port outer engine, resulting in fire in the air and a loss of control, probably due to the effects of fire on the port wing's left hand control surfaces and its trim-tab. There was no evidence of structural failure of the airframe having occurred prior to the impact with the ground. He continued that it was possible that, if the fire had been noticed sooner, and the feathering system operated immediately, the fire might have been brought under control. From the evidence given, it was considered that the pilot and crew carried out their duties to the best of their abilities during the emergency. It is also noted that the pilot retained control of the aircraft long enough to avoid crashing into the built up area of Darlington. After this accident it was recommended that all pilots be instructed to feather the propeller immediately when any abnormal engine symptoms are noted.

The accident itself opened up a large can of worms. A letter, written by Air Commodore R E Burney for the AOC of 6 RCAF Group on March 3rd 1945, initially concurred with the findings of the Investigating Officer but added –

'This headquarters is very concerned about the 4G8 constant speed units, one of which was fitted to the engine in this report. The possibility exists that the inability to feather may have been due to the feathering boss on the CSU casting breaking away, producing the sheet of flame when the feathering button was operated. In addition, no known previous piston failures have caused an engine to fail, or have been responsible for an engine catching fire. In the past, a rigid feathering line was employed, causing five feathering bosses to fracture on two squadrons during a period of three months. Modification 37VA, the fitting of a flexible feathering line, was introduced to overcome this defect. During this time, no HaY154 CSUs[122] have failed. However, on one station, during a period of three weeks, two 4G8 CSU bosses have failed, despite modification 37VA. The inference is, therefore, that the hazard still exists with the 4G8 CSUs despite the flexible feathering line mod. A further modification for the embodiment of shot blasted 4G8 CSUs has been approved, but so far none have been received.' The shot blasting process removed all nicks and casting inconsistencies (cracks can originate from the smallest nicks and blemishes in aluminium, causing stress failures). Some CSU bosses were failing after the flexipipe mod, as they had already been stressed by the original rigid type pipe.

The ramifications of the McMullen crash went higher and higher. A letter from the Under Secretary of State on the 17th highlighted the fact that both the flexible feathering oil pipe and the Linatex fuel pipe were burned away on the McMullen aircraft. The letter went on, 'To avoid further accidents of this nature, it is requested that strong action be taken with the ministry of Aircraft Production:

(i) To replace the flexible feathering line on the Lancaster X with an approved fireproof flexible hose.

(ii) To replace the Linatex fuel pipes in the Merlin Lancaster power plants by Flexatex C7 fireproof hose, without further delay.'

The final letter on the subject reads as follows. 'It is understood that the latter of the above two modifications is being covered by Merlin Mod PP305, and it is hoped that the Air Ministry will make the AP 2140 vol. leaflet covering this mod available within the next month. It is now over two years since the decision to remove Linatex self sealing fuel pipes was made, and it is considered that the continued absence of a Vol. II leaflet covering this removal should be made the subject

121 Daily inspection
122 Constant Speed Units

of an official inquiry. The necessary C7 hose has been available for some considerable time.' This letter was signed by Harris himself.

William Stuart McMullen was born in Toronto, Ontario on September 16th 1915. He was 5 feet 6 inches tall, his religion was Unitarian and he had fair hair and blue eyes. He was a keen swimmer and baseball player, and like most air minded lads made model aeroplanes. He was educated at the Leslie Public School and went on to Riverdale High School. His last year of education was completed at the Central Technical College, which he left in 1930. He then went to work for Coca-Cola as a driver, and eventually ended up working for a gold mining company. It was while he was working there that he married his wife, Thelma, in 1937, and had a daughter, Donna Mae. Bill McMullen's greatest love was aviation, and with the outbreak of war he decided to enlist. Having decided to take flying lessons, by the time he went to the Recruitment Centre in Toronto in June 1940, he had amassed 17 hours dual and a further 7 hours as a passenger. When asked why he wanted to join the Air Force, he stated, 'There is nothing I would like better than to be in the Air Force, and see some action.' He enlisted as a pilot in the Special Reserve of the RCAF until September 16th the following year, when he was enlisted into the RCAF proper.

McMullen was posted to 4 Elementary Flying Training School at Windsor Mills, where his first rank was that of AC2, which he held until the December of 1941, when he became a Leading Aircraftsman. On April 24th 1942 he was posted to 12 EFTS[123] at Goderich. Another move on July 19th took McMullen to 16 SFTS at Hagersville. On November 6th he won his flying badge, and rose to the rank of Technical Sergeant. Another posting took place on the 21st, this time to 4 Bombing and Gunnery School at Fingal. Bill McMullen continued with his flying training, and on August 6th 1943 he was promoted to Flight Sergeant and classified as Pilot, Grp 2. Having had 14 days embarkation leave, McMullen sailed from Halifax, Nova Scotia on November 1st, and arrived at Liverpool on the 9th. Although he was initially attached to 3 PRC (RCAF), and was promoted to W/O2 on the February 6th 1944, he was later posted to 6 Advanced Flying Unit at Chipping Norton during March. Whilst there he spent some time at the Beam Approach Flight at Feltwell. Just after D-Day on June 20th, operational flying training started in earnest when he was posted to 82 OTU at Ossington, where he amassed 28 hours flying the Wellington Mk X. August 6th saw McMullen promoted again, this time to Warrant Officer 1st Class. He was not to hold this rank for very long, as 34 days later he was awarded a commission and became Pilot Officer McMullen. After 10 days annual leave, 61 Base became his home on September 20th. He was later attached to 1664 Conversion Unit at Dishforth on October 24th, flying Halifax IIs. Here he flew 10 hours dual and 34 hours solo (day), and 2 hours 20 minutes dual and 11 hours solo (night). After some ground training on the Lancaster Mk 1, he left 1664 and arrived at Middleton on November 6th 1944. He was sent over to 1666 Conversion Unit at Wombleton on the 30th. He flew both the Mk III and Mk X Lancaster. His log showed 3 hours 25 minutes dual and 9 hours 25 minutes solo by day, and 50 minutes dual and 40 minutes solo by night. His conversion onto the Lancaster complete, McMullen joined 428 Squadron on December 22nd 1944.

Pilot Officer William Stuart McMullen
Photo: courtesy of Canadian forces

McMullen reported to Squadron Leader G Gonyou, 428's officer in charge of training. On the 7th, he was sent on a check ride with F/L La Turner. It began with ground handling and takeoff, general handling when airborne, circuit procedure, and landing. F/L La Turner submitted a report to Gonyou stating that McMullen was a very good pilot and handled the aircraft very well. He had received sufficient dual instruction on the Lancaster whilst at Wombleton, and a simple circuit check was deemed sufficient to send him solo. In his estimation, Gonyers felt that McMullen was an above average pilot. At the time he had over 900 hours flying time.

After the war, Mrs. Thelma McMullen came to Darlington from Canada to receive a donation collected by the grateful people of the town. Rather than keeping the money, she donated it towards the cost of cots, which were placed in the town's Maternity Department. They were dedicated to the memory of her husband, Pilot Officer William Stuart McMullen RCAF. In recognition of his selfless act, Darlington Council decided to rename Lingfield Lane. Henceforth it would become McMullen Road. At the time, it was the closest road to the crash site, only 600 yards from the former Lingfield Farm.

[123] Elementary Flying Training School

Plaque placed in Darlington Memorial hospital to record donation from William McMullen's widow   Photo: Keith Taylor

One day in 1982, whilst an instructor with 405 Squadron, I was visited by contractors who were at the time building a new trading estate on the eastern side of Darlington. This site was on former farmland just to the east of McMullen road. They had brought with them some heavy duty plastic sacks, containing what was obviously aluminium aircraft wreckage. They had found loads of the stuff, whilst their huge mechanical diggers cleared the site for the construction of Skipper Trucks (at the time of writing, Reg Vardy's garage). This was to be a new building at the top corner of Allington Way and Lingfield Way. They explained that they had been told to contact the RAF, 'did we want it?' They had inadvertently dug up wreckage from McMullen's Lancaster. Drawings showed that the contractors were working on what had been Lingfield Farm, the crash site.

Today, many parts belonging to McMullen's Lancaster can be seen at The Northeast Aircraft Museum, which is just off the A19, near Sunderland. Here one can find a fine collection of aircraft on show, along with many interesting aviation artifacts. The Museum is situated just outside the gates of the huge Nissan car factory, north of Sunderland. On the site of the old Usworth (Sunderland) Airfield, it will provide a day out for all the family that should not be missed.

It was whilst contractors were digging the foundations for this garage complex during the early 1980s that they discovered part of the wreckage of McMullen's Lancaster. Most is now in the North East Aircraft Museum   Photo: author

The new Stockton to Darlington stretch of the A66 dual carriageway has now become the main Stockton to Darlington road. The old Stockton to Sadberge road, along which McMullen's crew baled out, is still there. Now nicknamed 'The Stockton back road' it stretches from Hartburn to Sadberge.

What about Bill Gillham? Well, he grew up and went on to become a pilot himself. Bill owns a Luscome, which he flies out of what is left of Croft. Still eating and sleeping aeroplanes, Bill also makes fine model aircraft, which he flies when not doing the real thing. If that is not enough, he is soon to trade in his Luscome, as he has now built a Minimax. This is one of the new breed of single-seater light aircraft, which he hopes will fly him through the new Millennium. Bill cut a small section off the piece of wreckage he picked up from McMullen's Lancaster all those years ago, and has given it to me.

A Memorial stone with a brief account of McMullen's last flight is situated on the corner of McMullen Road and Allington Way, just 600 yards from the crash site.

The people of Darlington salute a very brave man.

On January 14th, a double blow was dealt to the Moosemen with the loss of two Lancaster crews during an Op to the Leuna oil refinery at Merseburg. The first to take off had been KB769, flown by F/L G O Tedford. VR-I and its crew had bombed the target and were on the way home when, at 01:05, it was attacked by an unseen fighter. The Lanc burst into flames and the order to abandon was given. The navigator, F/O J Q Eddy, grabbed his chute and headed quickly for the front hatch. As he passed below the instrument panel towards the bomb aimer's position, the aircraft entered a spin and F/O Eddy was tossed around the fuselage. He found himself on the floor, and was struggling against the G forces when the front bomb aimer's Perspex bulge blew out. With great difficulty, he crawled towards the opening, and rather than mess on trying to open the floor hatch, he vacated the aircraft via this new-found portal. The remainder of the crew, who had all flown half of their tour, were less fortunate. Pinned down by G, they did not get out, Eddy was the only survivor. Once safely on the ground, he was soon captured, and became a POW.

The other crew had departed Middleton at 18:47. Their aircraft, KB799, reached the target a few minutes ahead of H minute.[124] The oil installation was itself well protected by many flak positions, and with Leipzig just next door, they found themselves virtually alone over what was a very heavily defended area. The predicted flak burst all around them as they went in for the bombing run, and all the way out again. Inevitably the Lanc was hit, and the engineer reported that the fuel tanks had been holed and that they were losing petrol at a very high rate of knots. To make things worse, the fuel transfer system had also been damaged, preventing precious fuel from being pumped to other tanks. The pilot, F/O N R Vatne, who was on the last trip of his tour, elected to head for the closest allied held real estate. It was calculated that the aircraft might have about 2 hours flying time left before the engines stopped. The engineer, Sgt B C Mitchell, suspected that the port inner's fuel line had been severed and it was decided to feather the prop. The original 2-hour estimate proved over-optimistic, and the hope of reaching allied territory was diminishing.

Eventually, with the fuel gauges reading almost empty, Vatne had to give the order to bale out. Whether the ground below contained friendly troops was not apparent until the crew landed. It didn't. They came down close to the battlefront, between Coblenz and Trier, and were soon captured. A few minutes worth of fuel had decided their fate. The mid-upper and tail gunners, P/O G J Woods and F/S R C Woods, had jumped out of the rear door whilst the navigator F/O H P Eager, bomb aimer F/O N V Hoas, wireless operator F/S F H Chatwin and Sgt Michell went out of the front hatch. At that time, the aircraft was flying straight and level and under control. Eager, Chatwin and Mitchell had passed Vatne as they wended their way to the front of the aircraft. Sadly Vatne failed to get clear of the aircraft and perished. He is buried in Rheinberg War Cemetery. All 11 of 428's aircraft returned safely. For S/L D Lamont and F/L L Kagna, this raid completed their tour, allowing them to be screened from Ops.

After what was described as an extremely successful raid on the Braunkohle-Benzin synthetic oil plant at Zeitz, 38-km S/S/W of Leipzig, during the night of the 16/17th, Middleton's crews enjoyed an 11-day respite.

Snow and bad weather caused many stand-downs and cancellations. The occasional training flight was, however, carried out during the odd break in the weather.

S/L H L Kay and his crew arrived at Middleton on Friday the 19th. F/L Kay had traveled from Croft to take over command of 428's 'A' Flight. By the 23rd, everyone was totally fed up with the weather and champing at the bit to get back to operations. Speaking in the village to the natives of Middleton St George, some aircrew were told that the current snowy conditions were amongst the worst experienced there since 1878.

Ground training continued, with lectures for the gunners on the .5 caliber Browning machine gun, and flight engineers carried on with the ground training for new Lancaster crews. Wing Commander Hagerman, having completed his second tour, was guest of honour at a 419 Squadron bash in the Officer's Mess on the 24th. He was departing Middleton for a well-earned rest. His new post was to be as commander of the Flight Engineer's School at St Athan. His successor was to be S/L M E Fergusen.

Having snowed all of the previous day, on the 28th, Stuttgart was the target for both of Goosepool's squadrons. A blizzard arrived after some of the aircraft had taken off, but it was a brief affair and fortunately it quickly passed, allowing the remainder of the aircraft to continue with their departure. The target was the important railway yards at Kornwestheim, a small town close to Stuttgart. All but one of Middleton's aircraft diverted safely to East Kirkby in Lincolnshire on the way home. Sadly, 428 lost S/L Kay and his crew in KB770. This was their first operation since S L Kay became the squadron's 'A' Flight Commander. With the exception of the navigator, F/O R L Stapleford, all on board were killed when the aircraft crashed not far from the target.

During the day, another Ghost aircraft crashed at Elton Hall near Stockton, during a training flight. P/O H L Clark and five of his crew in KB763 were killed, whilst the navigator, F/S B Crabb, was seriously injured. The aircraft had broken out of the low cloud and was completely wrecked when it hit the ground and burst into flames.

Next day, the diverted aircraft returned to Middleton, just before another heavy snowstorm arrived overnight to block its roads and runways with heavy drifts. For most of the Canadians, the landscape was almost beginning to remind them of home. A lecture on Army Support by Major Talbot on the 31st provided the aircrew with much useful information, which, as events would prove over the next few months, would stand them in good stead. For its accident free record during December, on the morning of the 30th, 419 was paraded to receive the Handley Page Efficiency Trophy. This was presented by the Chief of the Air Staff, Air Marshall R Leckie, who was accompanied by Air Vice Marshall McEwan.

---

[124] The commencement time for the raid

February 1945

On February the 1st, 428 detailed 14 crews for a night raid on Ludwigshaven. This number was reduced by one, as F/L Goldie swung on take-off, ran off the runway, and burst a tyre. The Moosemen had a logistical problem for this raid. Due to bad weather, only 6 of the 15 crews they had sent on the Stuttgart raid were able to return from their diversionary bases at Tangmere, Strubby and Oakley. Somehow, 419 managed to scrape together 9 aircraft and crews for the raid, from which all returned safely, including F/L Sheahan, who had completed his 30th trip. 428 had two of its aircraft divert on their return, whilst another, flown by F/L Googe, had to land in France.

During the raid, a night fighter was seen by one of 419's crews. The pilot, F O Bruyns, immediately began to corkscrew. An Me410 passed them by and had a go at F/L Poky Halket's Lanc, whilst they were in the middle of their bombing run. Tracer flashed by the port side of the bomber, much too close for comfort. Fortunately they were not hit. Halket stuffed T-Tare's nose down and turned to starboard, closing the bomb-doors as he went. With 300 mph on the clock he leveled out. Another fighter approached the bomber. The pilot broke off the attack at about 150 yards, unlike the Lanc's mid-upper, P/O D W Storms DFM, who fired 100 rounds into the fighter. As Halket put the bomber into a second dive to starboard, an explosion was seen by the crew. For a moment the fighter disappeared into the smoke permeating from the bombing below, and when it reappeared, it was falling to earth, ablaze. Storm was later officially credited with destroying the fighter. After that, Bruyns turned around and continued with the bomb-run, unmolested.

Bomber Command's first and last large raid on Wiesbaden took place the next night. at 20:00 hours, after six postponements. 419 contributed 15 crews for this 495 aircraft raid, and 428 twelve. Some 520 houses and 30 other buildings were destroyed, 1,000 people were killed. A further 350 were injured. The three Lancasters lost during this raid all came from Middleton. The Moosemen lost KB750, flown by P/O B W Martin, when it was hit by flak. VR-N came down near Traben-Trabach, on the Mosel River. The tail gunner, F/S W J McTaggert, was the only member of N-Nan's crew to bale out, the remainder were killed. For Martin this was his 15th operation.

The other two Lancasters came from 428. KB792, captained by F/L D E Berry AFC, exploded over the target area. Again the only survivor was the tail gunner, P/O C M Roach. This crew were on the last Op of their tour and were to be screened the next day. Having taken off at 20:17, the second Ghost aircraft, KB725, flown by F/L V M Gadkin, turned back with engine failure after crossing the English Coast. Having jettisoned the cookie, the aircraft returned to base. Whilst approaching Middleton, another engine failed, and the Lancaster overshot the main runway and crashed at 00:37 between the villages of Long Newton and Elton. Sadly, gunners P/O R A Playter and P/O J A Keating were killed, and F/L Gadkin, was injured. The remainder of the crew were badly shaken.

The Moosemen were to lose another aircraft two nights later, when they detailed 15 aircraft to attack Bonn. F/L J P Barlow and his crew in KB787 had taken off from Middleton at 17:23. The weather, both at base and en-route, was terrible and required much instrument flying. Whilst outbound over the Ardennes and still in cloud, the Lancaster collided with another, PA209, flown by F/L H D Mara DFC, from 433 Squadron based at Skipton-on-Swale. Both aircraft came down near Vielsalm in the Belgian Ardennes. With the exception of the wireless operator, P/O C T Sutter, all on board Barlow's aircraft were killed.[125] There were no survivors from the 8 man crew of the second Lancaster. Airmen from the RAF Regiment assisted in the recovery of the 14 bodies from both aircraft, and the marking of their temporary graves. P/O Sutter returned to Middleton a few days later, and after a short rest returned to operations. The PFF were late, which meant that the early birds had to bomb using Gee. Due to the height of the thick cloud, the sky markers drifted in the strong wind and the raid itself was not a success. A large number of the bombs missed their intended mark and fell to the south of the target, or in the Rhine around Beuel. All 12 Ghost crews taking part in this raid returned safe.

In anticipation of the arrival of Lancasters fitted with the new Glen Martin mid-upper turret, 419's gunners took advantage of a squadron stand-down on the 6th. This allowed them to receive a special demonstration on the Glen Martin turret itself. Next night, Middleton's crews found themselves over the Hassun area of Goch, near Nijmegan, Holland. They were part of a 464 strong force of bombers, whose job it was to soften up enemy forces in preparation for the impending attack by XXX Corps across the German border, close to the Reichswald. The cloud base was estimated at about 5,000 feet, and the aircraft were ordered to attack below this height. After 155 aircraft had bombed, the MB decided that, due to excessive smoke from the attack, the risk to Dutch civilians was too great, and he scrubbed the raid. The majority of the 27 aircraft sent by both of Goosepool's squadrons landed with their bombs still on board.

P/O R S Grant, tail gunner in VR-H, saw a Ju88 shoot down a bomber some 2,000 feet above. The fighter descended 1,000 feet and shot down another. The German pilot, who was not using tracer, must have thought that he was on a roll, and descended to have a go at H-Harry. Grant opened up from 200 yards, hitting the fighter in the port engine and wing. He saw bits flying off the fighter, which quickly broke off in a diving turn and disappeared out of range astern.

On February 13th the new 64 Base Commander, Air Commodore Dunlap CBE, visited Middleton to address the aircrews. 428's gunners spent the day learning the intricacies of the Glen Martin turret. To date the longest trip carried out by either of Middleton's squadrons had been to Munich, but on the night of the 13th, they were destined to travel further afield. For several months, President Eisenhower and Winston Churchill had talked of a series of knockout blows aimed at finishing off the Germans. Operation Thunderclap was formed and planned. It had been decided that, when the situation in Germany became critical, a series of heavy bombing attacks on Dresden, Leipzig, Chemnitz and Berlin would quickly bring the war to its ultimate conclusion. They were all vital communications and supply centres for German troops battling against the advancing Russians.

The Ivans had made great advances across Poland in the last two weeks of January and punched through Germany's eastern border. It later transpired that, along with their usual populations, these cities also contained thousands of wounded German

125 Barlow was on his 22nd trip of his second tour

troops and refugees. On February 4th, Roosevelt, Churchill and Stalin had met at Yalta, where Stalin asked for these attacks. The die had already been cast however, and the plans had already been issued. In actual fact, the Air Ministry had, at the end of January, specifically directed Harris to prepare for these raids. Churchill himself took a direct hand in the final planning of Operation Thunderclap, and actively encouraged Harris to bomb Dresden, Chemnitz, and Leipzig. Later, Churchill, despite his first hand involvement, distanced himself from the political flak caused by the bombing of Dresden. He passed the Buck down the line, and firmly onto the shoulders of his subordinate, Sir Arthur (Whipping Boy) Harris, who had to spend the post war years taking the blame for something Churchill instigated. It was strange that Harris was made to be seen as the villain at the same time as he was knighted by his country, but that's politicians for you.

The Americans were also involved in Thunderclap, and were scheduled to open the proceedings with a daylight attack on February 13th. This was to be followed later in the day by a night attack, carried out by Bomber Command. As it turned out, weather conditions over Europe prevented America's opening gambit and the job was left to Harris's bombers later that night. This was actually two separate raids, with 244 Lancasters of 5 Group carrying out the first attack using low level marking. They were able to drop 800 tons of bombs, although lingering cloud limited their accuracy. An all-Lancaster raid 3 hours later, by 1, 3, 6 and 8 Groups, found the sky clear. 8 Group carried out the pathfinder marking, and 529 Lancasters dropped over 1,800 tons of bombs. Much of the city contained wooden buildings, and large areas of the city were destroyed when a huge firestorm developed.

The number of people killed was estimated at somewhere near 50,000. Next day it would be the turn of the Americans. Along with a huge fighter escort, they sent 311 of their B17's during daylight, and unloaded 771 tons of bombs onto the still burning city. To increase the chaos, sections of their Mustang fighter escort were ordered to strafe anything that moved on the roads around Dresden. Whilst Bomber Command, and Harris in particular, were ostracised after these raids, the Americans suffered no political backlash.

The Moosemen began to dispatch their 15 Lancasters from Middleton at 20:40. When they arrived over Dresden, they found a fire burning 3 miles short of the aiming point. This was immediately identified as a decoy, along with red and green markers 4 miles northwest and 4 miles south of the aiming point. The Germans were not able to emulate exactly the colour and hue of the allied markers, and experienced crews were able to pick out the paler looking versions from the PFF variety. The Moosemen were not fooled, and their bombs were dropped on the correct markers or between them, as ordered by the MB. The latter had the effect of filling in the dark bits between the main centres of conflagration. As the crews headed home the fires from Dresden could be seen 150 miles away. Due to the extended range of the target, diversions were

Lancaster D for Daisy taxies in at MSG, after operations   Photo: via Geoff Hill

necessary. The German's were jamming the Gee system. This, and a wind change, caused navigational problems for some of 419's more inexperienced crews. Aircraft flown by F/O B A Nichols and P/O J E McGreggor, separately found themselves 40 miles south of track. Nichols's crew elected to land for fuel at the continental diversion airfield at Juvincourt-et-Darnary, 22-km southeast of Laon. McGreggor's crew dropped into Laon-Anthier for the same purpose. Whilst on the ground there, an American A-26 Invader collided with the nose of R-Robert, and the Perspex nose was smashed. As there were no repair facilities on the airfield, the Lanc had to be flown to Javencourt, where it was repaired by the RAF. Due to bad weather, McGreggor's crew did not return to Goosepool until the 19th. 428's records have little to say about this raid, only that the nine aircraft dispatched reached the target, pranged it good and proper, and returned safely.

Despite poor weather at Middleton, Operation Thunderclap continued for 5 Moosemen crews on Valentine's Day, when 499 Lancasters and 218 Halifaxes bombed Chemnitz. Four of 419's crews had landed back late from the Dresden raid and were considered too tired to be included in the night's raid. Although 7 of the 14 crews sent by 428 were taking part in their first operation, they all returned unscathed. Cloud cover thwarted the raid itself, and although some of the city was damaged, most of the bombs fell in open country. During this raid, F/O W G Cotter, tail gunner in F/O L A Blaney's Lanc, was rudely awoken by a white fighter flare which had been dropped above and behind them. The main effect of the flare's light was to illuminate a twin-engined fighter, lurking some 400 yards behind them. Having given the order to corkscrew, Cotter and the mid-upper, Sgt S E Kranyak, opened fire with about 75 rounds each, and the German aircraft disappeared. Soon after, an aircraft was seen to explode as it hit the ground. The aircraft was claimed and officially confirmed as a probable.

The weather put paid to operational flying until the 20/21st, when 14 Moose and 14 Ghost aircraft took part in Bomber Command's last large raid on Dortmund. The objective was to destroy the southern half of the city, and drop nickels whilst they were there. This was achieved, but during this raid, 14 Lancasters were lost, including KB804, flown by F/O L A Blaney. Six of the crew, including Blaney, were half-way through their tour; the bomb aimer, F/O P H Owen, was on his second tour. The aircraft was hit by flak a few minutes before their time on target. The first flak burst found the starboard wing and set it on fire whilst the second hit the bomb bay, igniting the incendiaries.

The order to bale out was given by Blaney, and Owen, in the bomb aimer's position, opened the floor hatch in the nose. Like so many aircrew during the war, he tried to discard the hatch cover out of the opening, only to see it jam due to the force of the slipstream. Listening to the stories from other aircrew who had abandoned before, many had learned to find a place inside the confines of the nose to dispose of the cover, but on this occasion it was well and truly jammed. Owen was joined by the navigator, W/O D Hanna and the engineer, Sgt T S Instone RAF, who kicked the cover free. Hanna jumped first but did not survive, it is most likely that his chute failed to open. Owen went out next and remembers nothing until he regained consciousness at about 8,000 feet, with bits of the aircraft falling around him. Instone was the last to jump out of the nose before the aircraft exploded. Meanwhile, the mid-upper, F/S L J Nozzolillo, pushed open the rear door, whilst the wireless operator, P/O A Kindret, fastened it. Nozzolillo jumped, followed by Kindret, after which the Lancaster blew up.[126]

So close to the target were they, that as the crew descended they could hear the crackling of the markers as they went down. Kindret's chute was fastened by only one hook, as he hadn't had time to fasten both. He suffered a bruised rib after wrapping his arms around the front straps of his harness.

The tail gunner, F/S Althan, had found himself trapped in his turret due to the doors behind him being jammed. Having tried to free them, he spoke to Blaney on the intercom and told him of his plight. Blaney could not help and told him to keep trying. Eventually, with the aircraft well ablaze and heading down hill steeply, Althan managed to burst the doors open with his back. His troubles were not yet over. He was trapped by his right foot, and for over half a minute he rode the blazing aircraft down, until he was able to fall free of the aircraft. F/O Blaney did not get out of the aircraft before it exploded, and, like Hanna, was killed. The remainder of the crew landed safely and became POWs.

419 had visited Duisburg 14 times thus far, and on the 21/22nd they took part in their 15th and last trip there. The raid went well for the Moosemen, and despite the Germans dropping spoof sky-markers Duisburg was left completely desolated. After this operation, there was nothing much left to bomb, and this turned out to be the last major raid on the city. Of the 14 aircraft sent by 428, all returned safe, including F/L Hay and his crew, who had been attacked by an enemy fighter. Both aircraft scored hits on each other before breaking off but no decisive damage was done.

The Ghost's day was not entirely without drama however, as earlier in the day, W/C Gall wrote KB 855 off during a training flight. The Lancaster had lost power in both port engines at 2,000 feet and was unable to maintain height. The crew were ordered to leave their stations, don their parachutes and gather in the Lancaster's rest position. Gall managed to reach Middleton and came in for a landing. The NA-F touched down ok, but skidded off the runway and was wrecked when it struck some trees. Although the crew were badly shaken, no one was injured.

On the 22nd, Middleton welcomed G/C J K MacDonald as its new station Commander. Acting Group Captain Miles moved over to Croft on the same day.

As Bomber Command progressed with the devastating raids on the industrial centres of Hitler's war machine, the Germans had to find more and more ingenious methods of diverting their production capability. By this stage of the war, underground stations, caves, sewer systems, even private houses were used as workshops to turn out some of the essential components required for the military. It was to such a site that a combined force of 25 Lancasters belonging to 419 and 428 were dispatched on the night of February 23rd. The target was Pforzheim, 16 miles S/E of Karlsruhe, and this was to be the one and only major raid on this town during the war. Middleton's crews formed part of a 380 aircraft raid on the town itself. The crews at briefing were told that a large number of houses in the town were being used as small production centres for the manufacture of precision tools and instruments.

The marking and bombing were carried out from 8,000 feet, this contributed to some extremely accurate area bombing. Some 83% of the town's built up area was destroyed when 1,825 tons of bombs fell during the 22-minute raid. 17,600 people were killed. This was the third heaviest death toll on the German continent during WWII. The predicted flak was very accurate, and as VR-M, flown by F/L M W McLaughlin, was leaving the target area, his aircraft was attacked from astern by a Ju88. As the fighter opened up from about 400 yards, the Lancaster's tail gunner, F/O J D Charbonneau, returned fire. The gunner told McLaughlin to corkscrew starboard. The fighter pilot followed the Lancaster through its evasive manoeuvering and realised at the last moment that this was a big mistake. Charbonneau gave the fighter several bursts of fire, before one by one, his guns developed stoppages, but for the fighter, the damage had been done. Too late,

126 Near Witten, southeast of Darmound

the German pilot broke away at 150 yards with sparks trailing from his aircraft. The sparks turned to fire and the fighter fell to earth and exploded as it hit the ground. Both the Lancaster's wireless operator, P/O B A Anderson, and the mid-upper, P/O E B Carlton, confirmed the kill. Charbonneau was officially credited with destroying the aircraft. Although 10 Lancasters were lost during this raid, all of Goosepool's aircraft returned safely.

The last operation for Goosepool during February 1945 was a daylight raid to Meinz in the upper Ruhr, which took place on the 27/28th. This was the city's worst raid of the war, with 5,670 buildings being destroyed when 458 aircraft dropped 1,545 tons of bombs. The bombers had an allied fighter escort, and although 1 Halifax and 1 Mosquito were lost, all of Middleton's aircraft returned safely.

The Halifax lost that night was a Mk III, RG347 ZL-G, flown by F/O R McD Scott RCAF. This aircraft belonged to 427 squadron, which you will remember was formed out of a nucleus of 419 personnel at Croft during late 1942. The loss of this aircraft was to be the last experienced by the squadron during W.W.II. This aircraft was based at Leeming, along with 429 Bison squadron. 429 had borrowed ZL-G for the raid on Meinz. Whilst taking off from Leeming, the Halifax burst a tyre whilst at high speed. The out of control aircraft crashed and all but one of the crew were killed in the ensuing explosion. Only the tail gunner: F/S J H MacKachern RCAF survived. He was immediately taken to the RAF Hospital at Northallerton. A daylight raid to support the Army at Neuss the next day was aborted after 20 minutes. After all the Moose and Ghost aircraft had become airborne, they were recalled, as the army's objective had been achieved. Rather than land heavy with their 4,000-lb Cookies on board, the crews jettisoned them in the sea before returning to base with the remainder of their bomb-load. During this period, the aircrew were kept abreast of the ever-changing situation on the continent. Each morning, lectures took place in the intelligence library for the different groups of aircrew personnel.

Lancs marshalled prior to operations at MSG   Photo: via Geoff Hill

March 1945

On March, 1st, Mannheim and its surrounding area received their last large raid of the war. Cloud cover prevented the results from being observed. Bombs spilled over into Mannheim's neighbouring town, Ludwigshaven, where 6,000 people lost their homes. By now, most Germans had fled the larger cities, and on this occasion only 5 people were killed and 17 injured. Taking off at 11:20 hours, 419 and 428 contributed 13 aircraft each to this daylight raid, which enjoyed the comforts of a fighter escort. Thick cloud cover meant that the crews had to bomb and nickel on the PFF's blue smoke without seeing the target. Gee was also used to check that the bombs were going to the right location. Although they had no fighter opposition, the flak was still very much in evidence, and several Moose aircraft received hits. F/L Osborn's aircraft, VR-P, found some flak, which disabled the port outer, on the way to the target. This aircraft carried on with the operation and returned safely to Middleton, along with the rest of Goosepool's Lancasters.

By now Cologne had found itself in the path of the battlefront, and on Friday March 2nd , with the American Army virtually knocking on the door, Bomber Command was tasked with clearing the way. Two raids were planned for that day, with the first employing 703 aircraft and the second 155 Lancasters of 3 Group. These multi aiming point raids were aimed at the western banks of the Rhine, the part of the city closest to the direction of the approaching Americans.

The weather was clear for Cologne to join the last major raid of the war club. The Moosemen and the Ghost Squadron had departed Goosepool at a very early hour and easily found the city. They had to be careful however, their target was only a few hundred yards from Cologne Cathedral, a building deliberately spared from bombing by Harris throughout the war. Their objective was to bomb the approaches to the main Rhine bridges, which included the nearby Hohenzoollern Bridge. It was hoped that these measures would prevent the Germans from moving vital troops and equipment in and out of the city. The IP was identified by reference to the Cathedral, the Rhine, and some large quarries. As the raid progressed, smoke began to obscure the target, and the MB, with the cathedral in mind, began to direct the crews relative to the upwind edge of the smoke. The flak, much of it being of the predicted variety, was as intense as ever. Several Moose aircraft took hits, but fortunately none were too serious, and all were able to return to Middleton.

The air-raid sirens had only given 2 minutes warning, and when the American arrived in the city 4 days later, they had the grim task of removing over 400 bodies from the streets. The actual number of dead is unknown, as the city's air-raid recording system had broken down by then. What is known is that 160, mostly SS soldiers, were killed when 5 bombs fell on the Krebsgasse Police station, which was the local air-raid control centre.

Chemnitz was the target on the 5/6th. After take-off, 419 had to battle against their greatest adversary, ice. Flying conditions were extremely bad, but Chemnitz was finally reached and the crews bombed the Wanganui sky markers, which were red and green stars. Out of the 14 Moose crews dispatched, one failed to return. This was KB845, flown by F/O C L Reitlo, which, probably due to ice accretion, lost control and crashed north of Aylesbury on the way home, killing all on board.

428 lost KB778, flown by F/O W Mytruk. Forced off track by ice and snow, and down to 2,100 feet, the aircraft flew into a mountain in the Ardennes and was written off. The engineer, C E Hazelby (RAF), was killed outright. The navigator, F/O W R Ashdown, and the bomb-aimer, F/O D A Wade, died of their injuries. F/O Mytruk was admitted to the hospital at Malmedy and survived. The wireless operator, P/O E, J, Snell, mid-upper F/S T J Chevrier and tail gunner F/S E L Schofield, were unhurt.

Out of the 760 aircraft taking part in this raid, 9 belonging to 6 Group crashed after take-off, some before they could even set course; the Vale of York was up to its usual tricks. For example, 420 Squadron at Tholthorpe lost two Halifaxes due to ice. The first crashed near Dishforth aerodrome, 22 minutes after leaving Tholthorpe, the second, having taken off from the same base, crashed 49 minutes later at Tadcaster, south of York. 420's sister squadron, 425, also lost a Halifax due to ice when it crashed into Little Ouseburn Church and Moat Hall, near Harrogate, 22 minutes after take-off. 426 at Linton-on-Ouse also lost two out of its three missing aircraft due to ice. One crashed at Kirkbymoorside, whilst the other broke up in flight. Some of the wreckage from this aircraft crashed into Nunthorpe Avenue, York. Amongst the dead were the crew of six, and five civilians on the ground. A further eighteen were injured. One of the engines went through the roof of a nearby school, and wrecked the kitchen.

Two days later, 419 were to lose KB797, flown by F/O B T MacNeill, during a one-off raid on Dessau. Only two of the crew survived, the remainder are commemorated on the Runnymede Memorial. Many crews complained about the protracted routing for this raid. On their return, all but one of 428's 14 aircraft diverted to Blackbush. The remaining aircraft, flown by F/L J F Hadley, landed at Juvencourt and returned the next day. For many crews, Essen was the most formidable target in the Ruhr, and had seen 28 heavy raids. Of these, the Moosemen had taken part in all but five. It had cost them 8 crews in the process, and on the night of the 11/12th March, it was payback time. Bomber Command dispatched 1,079 aircraft to deliver the final knockout blow. This was the largest number of aircraft sent to a target thus far. Cloud cover shrouded the target area, but the 4,661 tons of bombs dropped on the sky markers devastated Essen.

During six years of war, it had cost Bomber Command dearly to reach this conclusion. However, for the population of Essen the price had not been small. After this final raid on the city, most of its buildings lay in ruins. Over 7,000 people had been killed since the bombing began. Half of its pre-war population of 648,000 had fled to less precarious parts of the Fatherland. Essen would be left to lick its wounds until the arrival of American troops soon after this raid. All 15 Moose and 15 Ghost Squadron aircraft returned from Essen unscathed.

Next day an identical raid, with identical results, signalled the end of Dortmund. During this raid the record for the most bombers on target increased to 1,108, a figure that would not be exceeded by the end of the war. Another record was the total weight of bombs dropped, 4,851 tons. Most fell in the city-centre and to the south of the centre. All of Middleton's crews returned safely.

During the day, 419's 'B' Flight Commander, S/L McKinnon, bade farewell to the squadron for the short trip over to Croft, where he was to take command of 431 Squadron. He was replaced by F/L W J Watts, who was to be promoted to the rank of Squadron Leader.

On the 14/15th, 419 and 428 joined a smaller force of bombers for a one-off attack on Zweibrucken (translated into 'Two Bridges'), 27-km east of Saabrucken. The objective was to prevent the passage through the town of essential German troops and their supplies. Most of the population had evacuated, and many of those that were left managed to survive by sheltering in two large caves in the north and south of the town. Some had remained in their basement shelters where 192 perished. An unknown number of German troops were also killed during this raid.

Next day, the synthetic oil plant at Hagen was the next target on the list for the attentions of the Moose and Ghost Squadrons. The raid itself was straightforward, in as much as it took place in clear visibility, and caused severe damage to the central and eastern districts. For 419 and 428 however, the operation was not an auspicious one, as three experienced Lancaster crews were lost to night fighters.

VR-N KB814, flown by F/S C W Parish and crew, was attacked by a night-fighter over the Rhine. The aircraft crashed in the Monchengladbach area. Four out of the seven crewmembers, including F/S Parish, were killed. The remainder evaded capture. Those that died were buried one week later in the American Cemetery at Margraten, but later were laid to rest in Nederweert War Cemetery.

The second, Lancaster, VR-K KB870, flown by F/L M W McLaughlin, was attacked by a night-fighter over allied held territory, and blew up in mid air. Four of the crew, who were injured, including McLaughlin, managed to bale out, the other three were killed. Again they were initially buried at Margraten and later taken to Nederweert for final burial. Those that were injured were taken to a US hospital for treatment before being flown back to the UK.

428 lost NA-I KB846, flown by F/L J D Craton. He and the tail gunner, F/O B B Gray, were the only survivors when the Lancaster was shot down by a JU 88 over the target area. This crew were on their second tour and their loss was greatly

felt by the squadron. They were considered to be one of their best crews, and were very keen and capable. The 5 members of the crew that were killed had the same funeral arrangements as the previous two crews.

It was also during this raid that 419 were introduced to the Me262 jet fighter. VR-W, with F/O B R Lambroughton at the helm, was attacked by a 262, which approached to within 1,000 yards above and to stern of the Lanc. Having told his skipper to corkscrew, F/S A M Dennis in the rear turret opened fire at 600 yards, at exactly the same time as the fighter. The fighter's burst was short as the pilot was in too much of a hurry to break-off. A few minutes later Dennis was surprised to see two more 262s closing in on the Lanc. One was dead astern, with the other on his starboard wing and slightly above. The order to corkscrew starboard was repeated, and whilst Lambroughton took evasive action, for a second time both jets closed to 600 yards and fired. Dennis opened up on the lower of the two fighters, whilst the mid-upper F/S B K Dwyer, took on the higher one. The 262 pilots could give it, but they certainly couldn't take it. As soon as the two gunners opened fire, the fighters broke off and disappeared. The Messerschmitt pilots gave the Lanc crew time to settle down, and had another go six minutes later, with exactly the same results. The German pilots gave the Lancaster up as a bad job, and were not seen again. W-William returned undamaged to Middleton, unlike two of 419's other aircraft. VR-E had a flak damaged rudder and H2S blister, whilst VR-P returned with its blister completely shot off. The remaining Moose and Ghost aircraft returned unscathed.

During this raid a Flying Fortress flown by an RAF crew flown by F/L J G Wynne came under attack and 9 of the crew baled out over enemy territory. Four of the crew were captured and became POWs. Five were murdered near Huckenfeld on the 17th by the Germans. The town's Burgermeister at the time, Gustav Schmidt, was involved in this atrocity and was later convicted. He died in prison during 1951.

During the afternoon of March 21st, 419 detailed 6 aircraft to carry out a sea search for F/O R W Miller and his crew, missing since leaving Middleton at 01:51 hours. The aircraft were unable to locate KB786 or its crew, and eventually returned to base. F/O Miller had been on the last operation of his first tour, during an early morning raid on the Heide oil refinery at Hemmingstedt, in Schleswig Holstein. His was the only Lancaster lost during this 166 aircraft raid. The reason that he and his crew were not located in the cold waters of the North Sea was due to the fact that the aircraft had actually crashed at Odderade, 3 miles E/S/E of Hemmingstedt. P-for Peter had been shot down by a night fighter. Only the mid-upper, F/S J W Aitken, survived, when he was thrown clear as the Lancaster exploded.

Hildesheim, 12 miles southeast of Hannover, was the target for Goosepool's crews for the early morning of the 22nd. This daylight raid, which was part of Operation Plunder, left both the town itself and the railway yards badly damaged. This was the only major attack on the town during the war, with the inner part of the town taking the brunt. 3,302 blocks of flats were destroyed. This equated to 10,000 apartments. 1,645 people were killed.

The only noteworthy event was when P/O Rickert's bomb aimer pressed the tit at bomb release and nothing happened. The Lancaster had suffered a complete hang-up and the bomb-load stayed put. They had to get rid of them somewhere, and once the technical hitch had been resolved, the bombs were eventually dropped on an alternative target, the town of Wessoln, 2 km N/N/W of Heide.

428 lost KB777, which was seen flying below 5,000 feet with 2 Mustangs whilst on the way home. At that time, its feathered port inner was streaming flame. The crew were given the abandon order and 4 of the crew jumped and became POWs. The pilot, F/L J F Hadley, F/S J McKenzie and F/O D Frame, were killed.

Lanc outside the rear of hangar 2 facing north. The square building on the left with shutter doors was still in existence in 2003 as part of the fire section   Photo: via Phil Bailes

A V M McEwan arrived during a squadron stand-down the next day, to present the Moosemen with the Bristol Bombing Trophy, which they had won for their efforts during February. On Friday/Saturday the 24/25th March, a raid to Wesel softened up the town for an impending attack by allied commandos. As the smoke settled on the dazed Germans, the commandos took the town, and the final push to victory began for the allied ground-forces. An amphibious crossing of the Rhine in the Wesel area, combined with airborne landings a few hours later, took the war into a new phase. Middleton's crews were not actually involved in the raid on Wesel as they had business elsewhere. Their target was the Mathias Stinnes Benzol plant near Bottrop, from which all aircraft returned. An equally unexciting daylight raid to Hannover the next day completed Middleton's involvement in Operation Plunder. There was a small hitch for one of the Moose aircraft, when F/L Armstrong's crew lost the port outer just before reaching the target and had to feather the prop. They continued with the operation and landed safely back at Goosepool with the others.

The final operation for Goosepool's crews during March 1945 came during daylight on the 31st, and cost 419 two more crews, whilst attacking Hamburg's Blohm Voss shipyard and submarine factory. Most of Middleton's gaggle arrived 10 minutes late, after the PFF had gone home. The MB was heard over the radio, about 8 minutes before Middleton's crews bombed, saying that he, too, was going home. This did not detract from the success of the raid however, and the target was well pranged. Me262s were becoming an increasing nuisance to the bomber crews, and on this day, during a marked Luftwaffe resurgence, they were responsible for both of 419's losses. The first Lancaster to be shot down by the German jets was KB761, flown by F/L H A Metivier. The entire crew were lost without trace. The second to fall to the Messerschmitt's guns was F/O D S Bowes's KB869. This aircraft was shot down south of Hamburg and crashed near Hittfeld. F/O Bowes was killed, along with three members of his crew, the remainder became POWs. The 17 crews dispatched by 428 returned safely.

Over at Croft, F/O G P Haliburton RCAF had departed for Hamburg with his crew in KB911 WL-U at 06:25. This aircraft crashed in a southeast suburb of Hamburg at Nettelnburg, 13-km to the southeast of the city centre, after an encounter with a Me262. Haliburton was killed and has no known grave. Two other crewmen were also killed, F/O D G Rathwell RCAF

1st Lt Hartshorn sitting astride a 4,000lb cookie   Photo: via Geoff Hill

and F/S R J Green RCAF. Both are buried in Hamburg's Ohlsdorf Cemetery. Sgt J M Hanlin RCAF, F/O C K Legaarden RCAF, F/O R Deane RCAF and Sgt J A English RCAF became POWs. This was the last aircraft and crew to be lost by 434 during W.W.II.

During this raid, 8 Lancasters and 3 Halifaxes were lost out of 469. This was to be the last time during the war that Bomber Command would see losses rise to double figures during a single city raid. There had been allied fighter cover for the raid, but the last gaggle of bombers had arrived late, due, as the crews reported, to its leader wasting time on the final leg. The jets popped up out of the cloud at about 10,000 feet and quickly climbed to attack. On their return to base, five of the crews reported that they had tangled with the 262s, and due to the jet's superior speed, the gunners had experienced great difficulty in getting their rounds onto the fighters. With 7 of their aircraft lost, March 1945 had been a bad month for 419. 428 had lost 3. All had been shot down by fighters.

The introduction of the 262 as a fighter began to shorten the odds against allied aircraft. If somebody had kept Hitler out of the equation, the story for Bomber Command could have been much different. His insistence on seeing the 262 developed as a bomber wasted vital time. Had the Luftwaffe taken delivery of sufficient numbers of the fighter version earlier, it is quite possible that today we would all be walking around with swastikas on our foreheads. During early 1945, the German airforce had a field day once it began to get its hands on the fighter version of the 262. Fortunately, the type was not available in large enough numbers, although many 262 airframes were lying around in fields as engine production could not keep pace.

For Bomber Command, its fate was a self-perpetuating one. By tightening its unrelenting grip on fuel supplies and starving the Germans of the materials to produce special alloys for the 262's jet engines, it would prevail. The fighter's new-tech engines were good for only 25 flying hours, as, at the time, the German's did not have the high-temperature metals we take so much for granted today. The jet, however, was at the cutting edge of aircraft technology. If the Luftwaffe had been given a few months grace, the war would have been even more protracted, or even worse, the final outcome may have been much different.

April 1945

Easter Sunday fell on the April 1st, with a capacity attendance in the Station Chapel. The 8th Victory Loan officially opened on the 2nd, with the slogan 'Invest in the Best'. All section heads attended a conference in Victory Loan HQ during the afternoon. Over at 428, flying training ran parallel with 419, with five details of air to sea firing, three cross-countries and two bombing details. Ground school was continued, with flight engineers undertaking lectures on log snags and use of the nautical mile. During the afternoon they received lectures on prop feathering circuits and electrical faults. Air bombers were on the radar trainer and bench, whilst wireless operators studied amendments schedules and carried out Morse practice. Navigators meanwhile, improved their understanding of the intricacies of H2S. For the air gunners, general lectures on the tools of their trade continued throughout the afternoon. As for the pilots, several of them attended promotional boards in the hopes that they would receive the captaincy of their own aircraft. Next day, training continued as 428 carried out four details of fighter affiliation, more air to sea firing, and bombing practice. Three cross-countries and two air-tests kept the groundcrew fully employed during the afternoon. The lectures for the air gunners were gun harmonisation and turret manipulation. Some navigators practised dry swims, whilst some pilots utilised the link trainer for beam flying and instrument practice. Others attended lectures on VHF radio, 1196 radio equipment, Master Bomber, and air sea rescue drill procedure. Bomb-aimers spent the day on the radar trainer and blind panel drill.

Due to the small amount of un-captured German real estate left, the powers that be found less and less targets for the bombers to hit. Battle order after battle order came down the teleprinter at Middleton, only to be followed by the 'Scrubbed' message.

On the 4th, Middleton received yet another battle order, this time at midnight, this too was scrubbed at 02:30 hours. So fluid was the situation in Germany, that, at 11:00 hours, another battle order was received. This time, 419 were told that they were 'On'. At briefing it was revealed that the Leuna Synthetic oil plant at Merseburg was to be the target. Situated 26-km west of Leipzig, it would be attacked by fourteen of 419's aircraft. Takeoff was at 18:35. They were to swell the ranks of a force of 327 Lancasters and 14 Mosquitoes of 3, 6, and 8 Group. For 428, they were called early for briefing at 03:00 hours for operations, but they were cancelled at 04:00 and the crews returned to bed. At noon, operations were once again laid on for 428, and 18 crews were detailed for the same Op as 419. The target was covered with 10/10ths cloud, so bombing was carried out from between 17,000 and 19,000 feet by way of sky markers. The returning crews reported that the routes and tactics had been good, but the Oboe carrying Pathfinders were late in dropping their sky markers. The results of the bombing were not good and the bombing was scattered. Many crews complained of considerable amounts of icing.

Next morning it was the 5th and a Station Parade was held, when the Air Officer Commanding in Chief of RCAF. Overseas presented 428 Squadron with their official crest. Due to many of the boys being still in bed after the previous night's Op, the turn out was understandably somewhat limited. The crest sported a shrouded death's head, along with the inscription 'Usque Ad Finem' (To the very end).

Next day in poor weather, 428's F/L R La Turner flying Lancaster NG271 NA-Q landed after a training flight and swung off the runway. The aircraft was completely out of control and before the aircraft could depart the airfield altogether the undercarriage was retracted. None of the crew were injured but the Lancaster was written off.

Training continued throughout April. More battle orders were received (and scrubbed), with one on the 7th terminated half way through briefing. For 428, the 8th Victory Bond campaign was boosted by a pep talk given by W/C Gill.

On the 8/9th, fifteen of 419's Lancasters and 16 from 428 carried out another attack, this time on Hamburg. Using H2S and red and green flares fired by the Pathfinders to identify the target, this operation was Bomber Command's last major attack on Hamburg. All bombed the Sky markers, which were red with green stars. However, the main target for the 263 Halifaxes, 160 Lancasters and 17 Mosquitoes taking part was the shipyards, which suffered limited damage due to the bombing becoming dispersed. The yards had been paid a visit earlier in the day by American bombers, which made an accurate appraisal of, who did what to where, somewhat vague. For the Germans, apart from the damage to buildings and the dock area, they were to suffer the loss of 292 people killed on the ground. Several crews, including that of F/O Chambers, reported seeing one almighty explosion taking place at 22:38. Something very big had obviously been hit, a huge orange glow was seen through the clouds.

During this operation, MP-V KB 752 was lost. This Lancaster had been flown by 419's F/O Cram, who was on the third trip of his second tour. It later transpired that the Lancaster developed trouble when its starboard inner began to cut-out as it crossed the English Coast on the outbound leg. He and the crew elected to continue on three and a half engines, and they were able to bomb. Once clear of the target, they feathered the offending engine, and descended from their bombing height of 17,500 feet. Whilst at 2,800 feet on the way home, the starboard outer burst into flames. Although the fire was extinguished and the prop feathered, the aircraft could not maintain height, and so the order to abandon was given. Fortunately the crew were able to bale out whilst over territory occupied by the allies. Amazingly they were back in the UK within three days. On the way home, the remainder of 419 and all of 428 had to divert to RAF Wing, 10 miles N/N/E of Aylesbury, due to bad weather at base. With the exception of W/C Ferguson in VR-W (Willie), who had tyre trouble, 419 and 428 returned to base the next day at 15:30, as the Northeast's fickle weather changed its mood to become a glorious warm and clear spring day.

*419's J for Jane undergoes engine surgery. Note the combined oil and coolant radiator matrix on the exposed engine.
The slightest leak meant trouble with a capital "T" note St. George church in the background*   Photo: via Geoff Hill

Surprisingly, the weather in southern Yorkshire was less accommodating. 78 squadron based at Breighton were also on the Hamburg raid. Low cloud mixed with fog covered much of the area, causing F/L V L Jackson flying Halifax EY-D MZ361 to crash into high ground at Farberry Garth Farm, near Pocklington airfield at 01:46. This was to be the last aircraft lost by 78 whilst on operations during W.W.II. Jackson and 3 other members of his crew were injured in the crash, the remaining 3, W/O2 T W Fry RCAF, F/S J M Pougnet RCAF and Sgt M H Steel became the last members of 78 squadron to be killed on operations. Both Canadians were buried in Harrogate's Stonefall Cemetery. Sgt Steele rests in the Town Cemetery at Shoreham by Sea, Sussex.

At 19:00 hours a battle order was received for 419, detailing 16 Lancasters and one spare, to take place the next day, target - three railway yards around the suburbs of Leipzig. They were to bolster a Bomber Command force of 230 aircraft attacking the yards, which were situated in the suburbs of Wahren (Northwest), Mockau (North), and Engelsdorf (East). On the 10th, 419 took off at 13:00 and found the weather over Leipzig good. The Viz was excellent, and the bombing of the Engelsdorf and Mockau railway yards was carried out visually, onto the TIs from 18,000 feet. The attack was well concentrated, and the results proved to be very good. 428 were there also with seventeen of their Lancasters. They all returned safely to Middleton, with the exception of P/O Read who had to divert with engine trouble. A Victory dance took place on the 12th in the NAFFI. This was held for all ranks and a good time was had by all.

Friday the 13th proved very unlucky for 419's F/S C C Maclaren and his crew, consisting of Sgt G A Livingstone RCAF, F/O D W Wincott RCAF, F/O C R Loft RCAF, WO1 W Henderson RCAF, F/S E R Wightman RCAF and Sgt G J Jones RCAF. Their Lancaster, KB866, was lost without trace during an operation to the U-boat yards at Kiel. All are commemorated on the Runnymede Memorial. They will be remembered as the last 419 crew to be lost from Goosepool during W.W.II.

428, who had despatched eighteen Lancasters on this trip, also suffered losses. The first was Lancaster NA-E, flown by F/L Acres RCAF. Having successfully bombed the target, this was diverted to Church Broughton on its return to the UK. Whilst coming in to land it overshot the runway and crash-landed. Fortunately no injuries to the crew were reported. NA-K, flown by F/O Payne RCAF, was damaged by flak both on its way to Kiel and back. Over the North Sea, and with three of its engines losing power, there was no option other than to ditch. With the exception of F/S Vardy RCAF, the tail gunner, who was lost, all members of the crew managed to vacate the sinking Lancaster and enter the dinghy. The crew spent 12 days adrift in the dinghy before eventually coming ashore, where they were to become POWs. F/S Vardy is commemorated on the Runnymede Memorial. Later, two members of the crew, F/O Payne RCAF and F/O Riley RCAF were decorated for their great courage during this operation.

This raid had employed 377 Lancasters and 105 Halifaxes from N0.3, 6, and 8 Group. Although the U-boat yards were the main objective, the bombing was scattered and the bombs fell mainly on the suburb of Elmschenhagen, over 3 km from the yards. Some damage was caused nearer to the northern end of the harbour however, which included hits on an ammunition depot. On the ground, 50 people were killed. Apart from the two Lancasters lost by 419 and 428, two more belonging to 186 Squadron, who had successfully completed their attack, collided in the circuit after returning to their base at Stradishall. With the exception of three crewmembers from one of the Lancasters, all on board both aircraft were killed.

The remainder of 419's Lancasters had to divert to Wymeswold, Castle Donnington's satellite airfield in Leicestershire; they returned to Middleton the next day. More railway yards were attacked on the 16th, when Schwanrorf, 38-km north of Regensburg, some 72 km east of Nuremburg, was attacked. All aircraft returned safely after inflicting more severe damage to the German railway system. Of the 16 Lancasters detailed by 428, P/O Lisk, making his first trip, swung on take-off and burst a tyre. During the day, W/C Gall left 428 for some well earned leave and was replaced by S/L Swartz.

Next morning, word was received that a first tour now consisted of 30 trips, therefore S/L Swartz RCAF and crew, P/O Anderson RCAF with five of his crew, P/O Rose DFM, P/O Marrey, F/L Lawson RCAF, and F/O Yanko RCAF were screened. That meant that 428 needed a new commander for 'B' Flight, and some spare flight engineers to replace Rose and Marrey.

On the 18th, during an operational stand-down, W/C Ferguson personally started an intensive Victory Loan drive to sell bonds. A programme was laid on, and all crews were interviewed personally by him. The total amount of bonds sold came to 66,450 dollars by the time the 8th Victory Loan Drive was closed.

Lanc (possibly Malton Mike) takes off on 24 for a training flight, a heavily loaded Lanc would use much more runway than this. Note Goosepool's wartime control tower.   Photo: via Geoff Hill

Malton Mike prior to departure for its first operation   Photo: courtesy of Canadian forces via Geoff Hill

Also on the 18th, 419's 'A' Flight received the 300th Canadian built Lancaster, KB999 VR-M, which was christened 'Malton Mike'. It was a gift given by the builders, Victory Aircraft Ltd of Canada. Flight Lieutenants Mutch, Frail and Webb took part in a gaggle exercise to gain experience as gaggle leaders.

The same day 420 at Tholthorpe lost their last crew during W.W.II, when F/S Dunnigan RCAF and his crew flying Halifax III NP946 PT-L crashed into the sea whilst outbound on Ops to Heligoland. Four members of the crew have no known graves, whilst 3 were eventually recovered from the water and were buried in Brookwood Military Cemetery.

It would be the 22nd before 419 and 428 went to war again, this time to bomb Bremen. Malton Mike had its Maiden Flight with 419, and was flown by S/L Watts, with S/L Powell of 6 Group PRO along for the ride. They were to attack the southeast suburbs of Bremen, in preparation for an attack by British XXX Corps, which would take place two days later.

Xterminator, although clapped out, towards the end, was able to survive the war intact, bringing her crew home safely everytime
Photo: courtesy of Canadian Forces via Geoff Hill

Both 419 and 428 were part of a 767 aircraft aerial armada consisting of 651 Lancasters, 100 Halifaxes and 16 Mosquitoes. For their part, 419 and 428 provided fifteen Lancasters each. NA-L of 428 suffered engine trouble and had to return early. After 159 Lancasters had bombed the target, the Master Bomber decided to abort the attack because of cloud cover and smoke and dust caused by the initial wave of Lancasters. By the time that 419 reached the target, no instructions were heard from the Master Bomber and no markers identified the target. Therefore no bombs were dropped and all aircraft returned to base via the bomb jettison area, where partial bomb loads were unloaded.

Next day F/L Peters RCAF was taxiing VR-J KB762 around Middleton's peri-track whilst heading for 1 hangar. The undercarriage suddenly gave way and the Lancaster was damaged beyond repair. The crew managed to scramble out, fortunately without injury. 419 had writen-off its last aircraft of the war.

The German Frisian Island of Wangerooge, some 50-km N/W of Bremerhaven, was attacked on Wednesday the 25th by a force of 308 aircraft. The coastal gun batteries on the island protected the approaches to the German ports of Bremerhaven Wilhelmshaven and Bremen. A rush battle order was prepared at 10:00 for a 13:30 takeoff. Due to a very bad dose of Teesside's industrial haze, take-off was delayed by an hour. Lancaster KB 732 of 419, flown by F/L Wickham, was the first off at 14:37, followed two minutes later by F/O Chambers in KB 857. In all, fifteen Lancasters from each of Goosepool's squadrons took part. The mass takeoff was witnessed by Black Mike himself.

Having departed the English Coast at Whitby and after a flight of 382 statute miles, 347 of them over water, the crews were able to identify the German Islands of Wangerooge and near-by Spiekeroog visually in perfect weather. As they approached the target area in 'Gaggle' formation it was realised that the planners had got it wrong and that there were too many aircraft, flying too close to each other.

The crew of VR-X, (Exterminator) saw two Halifaxes on their starboard side. Moments later the two aircraft collided, and fell into the sea close to the shore. Ironically, both were from 76 squadron, now based at Holme-on-Spalding Moor. The wreckage of the two Halifaxes collided with two more as they fell. One was from 408, the other from 426. Both were from Linton-On-Ouse. The four aircraft broke up, and as they fell, bodies began to fall out, few had parachutes. Out of the 28 men in the four Halifaxes only one survived. The captain of 76 Halifax RG553 P/O G W Lawson RCAF was pinned to the underside of the aircraft's port wing by G, as it spun towards the ground. He was, however, able to push himself free, and open his chute. He landed unhurt in shallow water and became a POW.

50-km further back in the formation were 431 squadron, who had taken-off from Croft at around 15:00. They had reached a position just off the Frisian Island of Ordernay on the way out when two of their Lancasters, KB822 flown by F/O D G Baker and KB831 flown by F/L Emmet also collided. Both aircraft fell into the sea. There were no survivors. They were the last crew to be lost by 431. Out of the 7 aircraft lost during this raid six had collided. Only one was lost to enemy action. This 7th aircraft, Halifax NP921 L8-E, flown by Sgt R Mercier of the Free French Air Force, crashed on the island close to some barracks. The crew were initially buried close to the wreckage of their aircraft.

Only 8.3-km long (5 miles), the banana shaped island sported two airfields and heavy coastal defences, these were to be the main targets. On reaching the target area, the Master Bomber could be heard instructing the crews to bomb the centre of the red TIs. The crew of P/O Laubman in VR-Z headed in for the target at 132° at 196 mph indicated. At exactly 17:17, their fourteen 1,000-lb bombs were released, right on the TIs, from 10,800 feet. Later, at debriefing, he reported that the formation points and timings were too close and very confused. During the run-up to the target, the gaggle of aircraft wasted time to port of the IP instead of to starboard as briefed. F/O Walley's crew noted that there was some wild bombing off the western end of the Island, but in general the bombing was good.

As the raid continued and heavy smoke clouds covered the target, the MB ordered the remaining aircraft to bomb up wind of the smoke. By now the bomb-bursts could only be seen through the smoke. Due to the compact nature of the gaggle, during the bombing and photographic run, many pilots had to battle against the slipstream of the aircraft in front. F/L Short also found the aircraft too concentrated whilst over the target area, rendering accurate bombing difficult. As he was flying in towards the target, his Lancaster was thrown into a steep port bank by the slipstream of the aircraft in front. He managed to right the aircraft and continue with his bomb run.

The bombs were seen exploding in the built up areas, craters covered the airfields. At the same time, a small number of bombs undershot and fell into the water. Accompanied by S/L Powell of 6 Group PRO, S/L Hunter and his crew were flying Malton Mike on its second operational sortie. They identified the target by the TIs and the edge of the town. As the bombs left the aircraft, three of them hung up and later had to be jettisoned out to sea. The smoke hung heavy and black over the target area, climbing to above 5,000 feet.

Aerial shot of Middleton-St-George early 1945   Photo: via Geoff Hill

Having bombed from 11,200 feet, 419's C/O W/C Ferguson, flying VR-W KB851, turned for home and noticed that the station keeping of the departing gaggle of aircraft was very bad. The aircraft were spread in a disorganised gaggle a good 10 miles wide, and with the briefed heights not being adhered to. What he hadn't noticed was that when his bomb aimer had dropped his bombs Exterminator was directly below. Fortunately, the bombs missed, but only by a very short margin.

F/L Dawson also reported that the departing formation of aircraft was loose, (many of the crews had seen the collisions), and that cohesion was practically non-existent. Many of the departing crews reported that they could not hear the instructions of the formation leader. Throughout the attack, no fighters had been encountered and very little flak was thrown up. All aircraft had bombed on the upward edge of the smoke as instructed by the MB, from heights ranging from between 10,800 and 11,400 feet.

When 419 and 428 had completed their combined attack on Wangerooge, all of their aircraft returned unscathed to the thick smoke haze of Teesside. VR-K KB 884, flown by F/O Walley, was the only 419 Lancaster not to return to Middleton. Due to the bad Viz it landed at Croft instead. Not a bad effort, as this was only Walley's second solo operation. As for 428, they had N-Nan land at Croft, whilst D-Dog landed at Carnaby.

One by one the Lancasters landed and taxied to their dispersals. VR-X, KB732 Exterminator was the last Moose squadron aircraft to land after completing its 84th operation, when it touched down at 20:10. During the raid it had been flown by F/L Barny Wickham, with navigator F/O Bob Bodie (of Mynarski fame), bomb aimer F/O Bill Wright, wireless operator W/O1 Jack Lequesne, engineer Sgt Jerry Joerissen, mid-upper F/S Tommy Martin and tail gunner F/S Don McTaggart. VR-X was the squadron's oldest surviving Lancaster. It landed back last because it was by now just about clapped out and much slower than the others.

428 were to have the distinction of seeing F/L Dave Walsh's Lancaster touch down 16 minutes after Exterminator, to unknowingly create the last squeal of operational rubber on Goosepool's runways. He and his crew had dallied in the crash area, where the aircraft had collided. They circled so they could relay the exact position to the Air Sea Rescue Service.

When Walsh's Lancaster landed at 20:26, neither the crews, nor anyone else on the airfield for that matter, were aware that this had been the last operation of the war, not only for Goosepool but for all of 4 and 6 Group's bomber squadrons. 76, 78, 419, 420, and 428, along with 427, 431 and 434 at Croft would never again have to face German flak or fighters. The war was to reach its conclusion within 14 days, and despite several abortive preparations for further Ops, none were destined to come to fruition. Bad weather and poor Viz persisted until the end of the month. Still unaware that they would not be required for further Ops, both squadrons continued their flying training programs and awaited further battle orders, orders that would never come.

Canada's High Commissioner to the United Kingdom, the Honourable Vincent Massey, and Mrs Massey visited the station on the 28th, along with numerous high ranking RCAF Officers. They were shown around the airfield and introduced to members of both squadrons. Although no more of Goosepool's aircraft would ever be lost to enemy action, the Grim Reaper did however have one final card up his sleeve. Lancaster X NA-Y KB879 of 428 Squadron took off from Middleton on a training flight on the morning of April 30th. The aircraft had just returned to serviceability after the fitment of a new autopilot. During the day, word reached Middleton that the Lancaster had crashed at 11:54, at Hixton, five miles E/N/E of

F/S Edward Wright, at sixteen was the youngest Canadian airman to lose his life during WWII
Photo: courtesy of Bill and Sue, Hillman Electric Studios

Stafford, and that all the crew had been killed. It later transpired that the aircraft had broken up in flight and had dived into the ground. A subsequent enquiry into the accident revealed that the probable cause was the new autopilot, which had malfunctioned.

A doctor lived nearby and he ran to the aid of the crew. On reaching the wreckage he immediately realised that nothing could be done for any of the crew. One in particular, the tail gunner had tried to jump but the aircraft had been too low and his parachute failed to open in time. Such was the devastation at the crash site that the Doctor was severely traumatised by the whole incident and was deeply affected for the rest of his life. He retained artefacts from the crash site, which were found when he died in 1999. Local newspapers found out about the discoveries in the doctor's house and printed the story. The local council decided to erect a cairn near to the crash site during August of 1999. Members of the crew's families came to the Memorial Service. To an astonished gathering, it was revealed that the tail gunner, F/S Edward J Wright RCAF, at the time of his death had been just sixteen. He was the youngest serving airman to lose his life during WWII. At the time of the crash, F/S Wright's parents had lived in Brighton, Sussex. The Lancaster had been flown by F/L W G Campbell RCAF; he, along with Sgt Kay RCAF, F/S Berryman RCAF, WO2 Lawley RCAF, F/S Tweedy RCAF and F/S Wright were buried in Chester's Blacon Cemetery. F/S W G Ward RAF lies in Selkirk's Brierylaw Cemetery. They were the last Goosepool airmen of the war to die, with just 8 days to go to the signing of the German surrender.

May 1945

May 1945 began with a stand down for 419 and 428, with make and mend. Since their operation to Wangerooge, speculation was rife as to whether the squadrons would be called upon for any more Ops. Rumours abounded about events in Germany, and about Hitler being dead. A considerable amount of flying training was carried out during the first few days of the month. In anticipation of a possible Trans-Atlantic flight back to Canada, at 09:30 on Thursday the 3rd, all of 419's aircrew were assembled in the NAFFI for a training film on the use of airborne lifeboats. 428 were also continuing with similar tasks. One of their Lancasters had a lucky escape whilst on a fighter affiliation exercise. S/L McDonnell RCAF was flying through a Cu-Nim when his aircraft turned turtle. Normally, Lancasters are not intended to fly upside down, and the huge bomber was lucky to come out of the cloud with only a slightly strained airframe. During the excitement, F/S Hunchberger RCAF decided for reasons better known to himself to bale out. Although he injured himself slightly in the process, he managed to land ok and was admitted to the hospital at Church Broughton.

At that time, the newspapers were reporting that Germany was being over-run by the Allies and it was felt that the war wouldn't last much longer. It was slowly being realised by everyone that the bombing of German targets had to be definitely over.

On May 5th, the day dawned wet and cold. Crews were practising navigation over the sea, and a large amount of ground training was being carried out. Although a more relaxed atmosphere permeated the camp, discipline was not allowed to be relaxed. The Station Commander instructed the Service Police to report anyone who tried to leave the station wearing battledress. An officer and three NCOs fell foul of this order and were duly charged with being improperly dressed and were given extra duties.

The local newspapers, including Darlington's Northern Echo, reported stories of peace offers and an unconditional surrender being proposed by the Germans. VE[127] Day was anticipated at any hour. Indications received the next day suggested that an intensive training programme was to begin in order for the aircraft to be flown back to Canada in the near future. Great excitement abounded around the airfield, all personnel on leave were recalled so they could be available to commence training. The Tiger Force was being mobilised, as Japan was still continuing the war. The squadrons would surely be required to fight on, albeit in another theatre. After the end of the war in Europe, the American continent would become the springboard from which the Allies could attack Japan.

As it was Sunday, many personnel attended the Station Chapel in the morning. The 6 Group Chaplain gave a good sermon, which was enjoyed by all.

At 22:00 on the 6th, ten of 419's Lancasters took-off for a seven hour cross-country training flight. All navigation was done by way of radio aids and astro navigation, with good results.

On Monday the 7th, it was reported that the following day was to be VE Day, and that both His Majesty the King and Prime Minister Winston Churchill were to give radio broadcasts. In anticipation of VE Day all M.T. Vehicles and aircraft at Middleton and Croft were immobilised, all guns were returned to the Station Armouries and a guard was placed on the bomb-dumps and the fuel installations to protect against damage. Meanwhile 428 lost Q-Queenie when it crash-landed between Darlington and the airfield whilst trying to land on 3 engines. No one was hurt. Great celebrations were planned, although training for the long trip home continued. The wireless operators in particular worked late into the day building up their Morse speed in anticipation of the Trans-Atlantic flight. VE day began with the announcement that a two-day stand-down was declared. All personnel headed for their various Messes to hear the broadcasts. Once they were over, everyone began to celebrate the cessation of hostilities. By 13:00 hours, both the Officers' and Sergeants' Messes were in uproar, as one and all threw convention to the wind and entered into the spirit of the occasion. For some however, the celebrations seemed a million miles away, as two Courts Martial were taking place and they were called as witnesses. It was even worse for the accused, as they were both found guilty. Many of Goosepool's personnel left the station and went off to celebrate elsewhere.

Despite the fact that it rained heavily until about 16:00 hours, the station pipe band marched around the Mess buildings, followed by a line made up of all ranks in various stages of dress/undress and levels of intoxication. In anticipation, some wore top hats and brightly coloured civilian ties. Many wore none, as scissor wielding merry makers had clipped them off. Ties were not the only things to be clipped. As the afternoon continued, F/Os Vernon and Zanic were grabbed, and much against their will, were parted from the starboard halves of their luxurious moustaches. By 20:30, the celebrations in the Officers' Mess were diverted to the Victory Dance taking place in the NAFFI. The day had been a huge success, as the realisation that the war in Europe was over slowly sank in. For the aircrew especially, the thought of no more German night fighters or flak triggered a pent-up relief valve that most of them didn't realise existed within themselves. All on the station eventually drifted off to find their beds after a very strenuous day of celebrating.

Next morning the airfield was surprisingly quiet as the hangovers and the prospects of a lie-in prevailed. The squadron C/Os and Flight Commanders of both squadrons attended a lecture in the Station Intelligence Library. This was given by S/L Staddon AFC of Transport Command, the subject 'Trans-Atlantic beam flying'. Some attended a thanksgiving church service at 10:30, after which a matinee was shown in the station cinema. During the evening, all ranks were invited to a dance in the Waffery.

By the 10th, twenty-two crews were selected from 419 to undergo training in order to fly their Lancasters home to Canada. As with 428, the crews were selected by seniority and experience, many had almost completed a tour. In the briefing rooms, the crews were given lectures on the form that their training would take. As they would be leading the Trans Atlantic Flight, W/C Gall lectured crews of 428 on the two possible routes the aircraft might take. As it turned out, the southern

<hr>

[127] Victory in Europe

FLAREPATH

Vol. I—No. 3   Middleton St. George, June, 1945   Price 2d.

MISADVENTURES OF VICTORIA BOND

STRIP TEASER CAUSES UPROAR IN AIR FORCE STATION

Victoria Bond's morals may have caused some raised eyebrows and shaking of heads, but no one can doubt that patriotic motives inspired her ill-fated attempt to put on a strip tease show on the lawn of the Sergeants' Mess.

Victoria first appeared, on this station, in the room which L.A.C. Lew Devies, the station's semi-official artist, uses as his studio. There she was prepared for the part which she was expected to play in the Eighth Victory Loan campaign. As she had no clothes, Davies proceeded to fit her out with the finest available without using clothing coupons. The assistance of L.A.C. Rossi was enlisted for this part of the task. Before any further action could be taken it was necessary to obtain the Commanding Officer's permission to proceed with the many-angled scheme. This was readily given and work proceeded apace. Dural was chosen as the most suitable material. With loving care expert artists fashioned her a wardrobe, consisting of a slinky evening gown, shere stockings, dancing slippers and silk-like unmentionables.

In the meantime, an appropriate background was prepared and erected opposite the S.H.Q. On the opening day of the bond drive, Victoria took her place upon the "stage," ready to begin her act. The plan was that as the bond sales soared, Victoria's clothing was to come off, so that she would reach her objective of (censored) at the same time as the station reached its objective of $90,000. This plan never materialized. When those responsible for the morals of the airmen discovered what was about to happen, the act was stopped. Victoria remained, however, as reminder to one and all to buy and buy plenty ; in that role, at least, she was successful.

But that was not the end of the story. On the night of the Victory Loan dance, her clothing mysteriously disappeared. The perpetrators of this heinous crime went unapprehended. Even the find of her clothing was a task which employed the station work for the better part of a morning. Nor did her misadventures end here : within a week she was again undressed. Again the culprits escaped, although it is believed in some quarters that the wind may have been responsible this time. This last misfortune was too much for Victoria, she returned to whence she came. Whether we will ever see her again no one knows.

Victoria Bond, the strip teaser who nearly scandalized an Air Force Station.

MOOSE SQUADRON OVER THE TOP IN LOAN DRIVE

The Moose Squadron, with an objective of $40,000, subscribed $60,000, to come third in the Group. The Allouette and Swordfish Squadrons were first and second. The credit for this fine show goes to F/L. Pete Tulk, who did a tremendous amount of organizing work.

POSTED

"Flarepath's" staff has been seriously depleted during the past month by postings. First to go was the Editor, L.A.C. MacDonald, formerly of the S.H.Q., and more latterly with the Personnel Counsellors. Second to go was Flight Sergeant Davidson, of the S.W.O.'s Office, the Circulation Manager. Mac has gone to the North of Scotland and Flight Davidson to South Wales. Flight Davidson acted as S.W.O. during the period between the repat. of W.O. Huestis and the arrival of W.O. Chalmers.

MAIN STORES

Victory Day plans are well afoot at our happy little establishment. Already the "Home Beautiful" is our motto as L.A.C.'s Sexton and Rothnie are spraying for peace.

Corporal Elsie Dumford is back from an extended leave in Bournemouth and she has her new "Sweet" ration book too ! W.A.A.F. Sgt. Rae Phillips is a happy new edition to our ranks and just adores posting. WANTED : One minuet or Gay 'Ninety Dancer to replace recently posted R.A.F. Airman. Apply L.A.C.W. Peggy Fields.

Wing-Commander Maxwell has officially resigned as P.S.I. President, but L.A.C. Prescott continues to balance the ledgers.

That completes the Fourth Copy action for this edition.

OBJECTIVE PASSED AND THEN SOME

Our station passed its Eighth Victory Loan objective of $90,000 by 183%, to come third in the R.C.A.F. Bomber Group. The entire R.C.A.F. passed its objective by a comparatively mere 21%.

Before the opening of the Bond Drive, Overseas Headquarters expressed a few doubts that the R.C.A.F. could do as well as they did the last time. They won't make a mistake like that again.

SUNDAY FORUM

The Discussion Group is sp[?]ing a series of talks every Sun[?] the Y.M.C.A. Lounge. Well speakers informally lecture variety of subjects, all of which or will have a definite bearing on the life of every man on this station. Recently, F/O. Gelber spoke on the Japanese War and reasons why Canada must participate. Those who were present went away with the feeling that if they are sent to the Far East they will at least have the satisfaction of knowing that they are serving to protect Canada, and not merely to regain lost colonies and protectorates for Britain, the U.S.A. and the Netherlands.

Other speakers will, in the near future, discuss various aspects of the peace settlement and kindred international problems, and closer to home, the re-establishment of veterans.

These Sunday Evening Forums are announced on the bulletin boards in the messes and are tannoyed. They are well worth an hour of anyone's time.

The sponsors, the Discussion Group, meets in the Gen Room every Tuesday evening, when personnel have an opportunity to air their views and blow off steam in general.

428 squadron Lancaster 'Q' Queenie heading back to MSG for the celebrations crashed due to engine failure between Darlington and Dinsdale on the north side of the road. There were no injuries. Photo: via Geoff Hill

route via the Azores would be chosen, rather than the northern route via Scotland, Iceland and Greenland. The navigators were concentrating on radio and astro navigation, after it was stressed that they must be extremely proficient in these disciplines. Dry swims were carried out, and navigators could be seen at all times of the day taking shots of the sun, moon and stars. As one wag put it, 'Makes a change from the usual heavenly bodies we are normally sighting.' In the early mornings too, they were out practising astro shots. The aircraft were being cleared of all snags and the groundcrews worked tirelessly to ensure that all aircraft were totally reliable for the long hop over the pond.

The wireless operators intensified their training and familiarised themselves in Department of Transport procedures. In the link trainers, pilots were receiving instruction on beam flying. Whilst 419's C/O interviewed twenty applicants for commissioning, during their slack hours, all sections were participated in volleyball matches.

Next day, 419's C/O had a two-hour conference with the crews who were detailed to fly home. Preparations for the squadron's departure continued as the navigators conducted more dry swims and received lectures on radio range procedures. 428's bomb aimers studied Loran and sat in on the navigators' lectures, covering Astro, drifts and stars. Flight engineers were shifted around, as only all-RCAF crews would be taking the trip back to Canada; the RAF engineers were to remain behind. Lectures continued for 419's aircrews during the morning of the 13th as they gathered in 428's briefing room. For training purposes, the twenty-two crews flying home were then split into two parts. At 22:00 hours, 11 crews took-off for the first of their cross-country training exercises. Over at 428, thirteen crews undertook astro navigation training flights. The weather during the second week of May had been unseasonably cold and windy, with little opportunity for outdoor recreation by the crews who were not flying. Two reporters from the Northern Echo visited the station on the 15th, to gain information for Darlington's newspapers on the activities of 419 and 428 during the war. For a change, the weather relented and was nice. Next day, the cold and wind returned, and caused the flying training to be scrubbed. Nine hundred and fifteen copies of 419's crest were forwarded to F/L Crawford of 6 Group HQ. They were to be forwarded on to the next of kin of 419's casualties. Eleven aircraft belonging to 419 took off for another training exercise. Link training continued for the pilots, whilst the navigators wandered the airfield, taking yet more sun and astro shots.

On the 18th the weather improved. During the afternoon spare aircrew members worked in the Officers' Mess and out on the front lawn, fixing things up for the great Victory Finale dance which had been organised by S/L Goldie DFC and F/O Gray DFC for the following night. This included a fantastic beer garden, the brainchild of F/L Tulk. At the same time, some of the aircrew attended a briefing by F/L Cox, the Briefing Officer from Transport Command. The dance, which lasted until 03:30, was a qualified success, despite the cold weather, which discouraged many patrons from dallying in the beer garden for too long. As a result, the Mess itself was packed, nearly 1,200 people attended. Possibly one other reason for the Mess's popularity was the large number of girls in attendance. The RCAF dance band had arrived from London to ensure that a great time was had by all.

Despite the continuing duff weather, several Transport Command Dakotas arrived on the 21st to take some of the groundcrew to Lagens, in the Azores. All anti-gas clothing was handed in and stored in Neasham Grange until it could be collected and taken away to one of the MU/s. Next day, 6 Group Operational Order 5/1945 arrived, giving details of the flight to Canada. Meanwhile, the Dakotas, complete with groundcrew, departed for the Azores. 419's Wing Commander Ferguson was accompanied by S/L Watts and two Padres on the 23rd, when he visited hospitalised squadron members in the area. During the day, a party of officers from Middleton were injured when the jeep in which they were travelling left the Croft road.

Training cross-country exercises continued. The last daylight training flight took place on the 25th. That day, the pilots were winding up their Link training. Declaration forms were handed out to all personnel, allowing them to state their future wishes as far as the RCAF was concerned. The armourers were over at the bomb dump, stencilling bombs for their return to the MU at Brafferton. At the same time, the demolition of some unserviceable explosives was being carried out. In anticipation of their departure, individual sections of 419 Squadron began cleaning out drawers and cupboards on the 26th. At 14:30, the squadron assembled and had their picture taken. First 'A' Flight then 'B' Flight posed, followed by the individual sections. Those not detailed for flying were then given a 48-hour pass.

On the 27th, ten crews took off for a cross-country training flight. Without the personnel on leave, the sections seemed very quiet. 419's C/O spent all morning compiling 1369's on all officers. On the 28th, things were still fairly quiet. That day, voting began for the Federal Elections. All personnel flying back to Canada began to hand in their baggage the next day. Four crews tookoff during the morning to complete air training for the Trans-Atlantic flight. Stockton was the venue for W/C Ferguson, S/L Hunter, S/L Watts and F/L Miller when they were invited to attend an Engineers' party later that day. An excellent chicken dinner was laid on, after which the party then moved to the Unicorn for liquid refreshments. Personnel flying home were assembled in 428's briefing room at 14:30 on the 30th. Here they were briefed on the arrangements for their baggage. All kit for the flight was weighed, stowed and checked. All aircraft were then flown on a shake down flight and final dinghy training carried out. A final lecture was given by W/C Edwards, Base Ops Control, W/C Gall and the Adjutant. Then it was off to the pubs of Darlington, Stockton and the surrounding areas for a last fling.

This was also their final chance to say goodbye to all those people who had befriended them, and who had tried to make their stay in the war-torn Northeast as comfortable as possible. Many romances had been kindled, some were to endure after the war when airmen returned to marry local girls and local girls departed England for a new home in Canada.

At 06:30 on the last day of May 1945, all crewmembers of the fifteen Lancasters flying back to Canada were called. Breakfast was at 07:00, followed by the Navigation Briefing at 07:30 and the main briefing at 08:00. The whole station turned out to see the take-off; some of the people assembled there were also from other stations. The BBC were in attendance, as were the major press. Amongst the gathered throng were Air Chief Marshall Sir Arthur Harris, Air Marshall G O Johnson and Air Vice Marshall McEwen. Also present were Air Commodore McBurney, SASO[128] 6 Group, and Air Commodore Bryans, C/O of 64 Base. They spoke to those present of the achievements of the RCAF in the European conflict, and the effect heavy bombing had on speeding the final victory over Germany. They also stated how proud they were of the Canadian air and groundcrews, and what they had done for the people of the free world. As the proceedings continued, the RCAF Overseas Band played a variety of tunes, including, 'O Canada', 'Old Lang Syne' and the RAF March.

The aircrews of 428 then climbed aboard their aircraft. Once the checks were complete, the airfield reverberated to the sound of Merlins. The crew of F/L S V Eliosoff in F-for Fox were the first to take off, followed by the other fourteen 428 Squadron Lancasters. They departed to the waves and V-signs of those left on the ground, who were to follow by sea. F/L Cox in G-George KB848 returned early as his aircraft was not loaded correctly and was nose-heavy in trim. He was unable to stop the aircraft from dropping its nose and had to call 3 other members of the crew to help him pull the control wheel back and keep the nose level, whilst others threw equipment out to lighten the load. On their return the crew related that they really thought their time was up. Once back at Middleton the problem was sorted, and it was decided that Fox and his crew would takeoff the next day for the first leg of the flight to St Morgan, Cornwall. The rest of the crews loaded their bags into their aircraft, in preparation for their departure the next day, after which they were then air-tested.

The remainder of 428's crews on airlift departed next morning, along with F/L Cox in G-George. It was also the turn of 419 Squadron, and 10 of their aircraft. The route was the same, Goosepool - St Mawgan - Lagens (Azores) – Debart, Nova Scotia.

At 12:00 hours on June 4th 1945, the distinction of being the last wartime squadron to leave Goosepool went to 419, as their 10 remaining Lancasters departed for the flight back to their homeland. 431 squadron saw the first 5 of its aircraft depart Croft at 11:30. After take-off they circled around Darlington and Croft village in formation, before overflying the airfield and setting course. All of Croft's station personnel came out to see the crews off on the first leg of their homeward journey.

Once the sound of the last Lancaster had melted into silence, Goosepool slowly began to wind down. The final social function for the RCAF was a small luncheon in the Officers' Mess later that day, in honour of Air Commodore J G Bryan's who was relinquishing command of 64 base, prior to his departure for duties in Canada. The RCAF strength at Goosepool on May 31st 1945 consisted of 18 aircrew and 53 groundcrew officers. The number of RAF officers was marked as 6 aircrew and 5 groundcrew. RAF other ranks ground personnel totalled 47. The Canadians had been given the hint that every thing that was left had to be accounted for, and all the associated bumf filled out, in triplicate. With their mother country calling to them in their hearts, and with the disposal of much of their unwanted residue delaying their departure, they hit upon a plan. Several big holes were dug on the south side of the airfield, into which much of the unwanted components of

[128] Senior Air Staff Officer

View of final gathering of Goosepool personnel and visiting dignitaries, including Bomber Harris and the mayor of Darlington, prior to the departure of 428 squadron's aircraft for Canada. Note the Glen Martin turrets on the Lancasters. Photo: via Geoff Hill

war were placed. This solved the problem of disposing of equipment that could have taken too much time if going through the proper channels. These dumps were filled, covered over and to a large extent forgotten about, their locations not entirely known to those that would follow. As you will read, it would be well into the 1990s before the secrets of the pits were to be uncovered.

At Croft on the 6th, 15 of 431's Lancasters took-off for the first leg of their flight to Canada. Next day it was 434's turn, as 15 of their aircraft departed for home. Two days later, a signal was sent to 6 Group HQ indicating that Croft was unserviceable, due to the withdrawal of all facilities. However, despite the lack of sufficient safety facilities, such as fire fighting, the odd aircraft still landed there. Despite this, on June 22nd aircraft began disposing of Croft's incendiary bombs in the North Sea. This would require 700 sorties.

Croft was typical of all of 6 Groups airfields, as it prepared for the departure of its ground staff and equipment. This had begun on June 4th and was to be completed by the 16th. All equipment had to be taken by the MT Section and loaded onto LNER trains at Darlington Railway Station by the Service Section. It all had to be along-side the SS Asbjorn at Hornby Docks, Liverpool by June 18th. The first train had 47 trucks, The second, which carried the balance of the sea pack had 18. This represented the largest amount of freight ever loaded at Darlington station. One crate alone weighed 3 tons.

The ground staff began departing on the 12th, under the command of S/L DRC McCallum. The train left Darlington at 03:55. The Asbjorn's final destination was Dartmouth Nova Scotia.

Middleton's ground crew also departed England from Liverpool. Radar mechanic David Acaster and his friends were on board the HMT Scythia, which left Liverpool on Friday June 8th at 18:30.

W/C T W Rayn arrived at Croft on the 25th from Hampstead Norris, in anticipation of Middleton and Croft being taken over by 13 OTU, which were part of 12 Group, Fighter Command. The move was necessary as Harwell and its satellites Hampstead Norris and Fimmere were having work carried out on their runways.

For the people of Durham, Teesside and North Yorkshire, the departure of the Canadians left a hollow emptiness. So many friendships were kindled during their stay. They had touched the hearts of all they met, and left an indelible gratitude for their sacrifices made in a land so far away from their own native soil.

Today they can still be seen, each year in early June they make their pilgrimage back to Goosepool. The noise of the aircraft has changed from Merlins to jets, but the St George Hotel, formerly the Officers' Mess, will always be the Venue for as long as they are able to come. And when time passes, as time surely does, their memorial outside the hotel, and this book, will remind us, and future generations, of those wonderful people who travelled so far to liberate us from German tyranny.

The last farewell   Photo: via Geoff Hill

419 losses whilst at Croft

October 2/3. 1942, Wellington Mk III, BK269 VR-C. Ops Krefeld. Took-off Croft 18:19.

Crashed at Oosterens, 3-km southeast of Uden, Holland after being shot down by Oblt Hans Dieter Frank 1./NJG1. With the exception of Sgt Nelan, the crew are buried in Uden War Cemetery.

F/S S V Stowe RCAF	K
Sgt H S Sveinson RCAF	K
P/O A B Morlidge RCAF	K
P/O H J Stuart RCAF	K
Sgt N Nelan RCAF	POW
Sgt H D Price RCAF	K

October 5/6. 1942, Wellington Mk III, Z1623 VR-V. Ops – Aachen. Took-off Croft 18:19.

Lost without trace. All are commemorated on the Runnymede Memorial.

Sgt K E Crewe	K
Sgt R Doherty RCAF	K
Sgt G E Robson RCAF	K
Sgt J H Shaw RCAF	K
Sgt S A Palmer RCAF	K

October 5/6. 1942, Wellington Mk III, BJ729 VR-R. Ops – Aachen. Took-off Croft 18:21.

Crashed at Maastricht, Holland, at 22:30. Initially the crew were buried at Venlo. They now rest in Jonkerbos War Cemetery.

F/S T E Powell RCAF	K
P/O F L Todd RCAF	K
Sgt G J McElroy RCAF	K
Sgt J L O'Grady RCAF	K
Sgt H Broom RCAF	K

October 10. 1942, Wellington Mk III, BK335 VR-Y. Training. Took-off Croft.

Caught fire and crashed at 14:43. close to the airfield. Sgt Scobie died the following day from his injuries. The three crewmen were buried in Darlington's West Cemetery on October the 13th .

Sgt L W Scobie RCAF	Inj
P/O P Campbell RCAF	Inj
Sgt G A Lloyd	Inj
Sgt R J Colvin RCAF	K
Sgt H D'Aperng RCAF	Inj
Sgt H E Hicks RCAF	K

October 13/14. 1942, Wellington Mk III, DF664 VR-E. Ops - Kiel. Took-off Croft 18:28.

Crashed into the sea off Brockeswalde, Germany. The crew are buried in Becklingen War Cemetery.

Sgt W A Wakeman RCAF	K
P/O C E Bell RCAF	K
Sgt R V Hall RCAF	K
Sgt E S Green RCAF	K
F/S J F Streeting RCAF	K

October 15/16. 1942, Wellington Mk III, BK270 VR-. Ops - Cologne. Took-off Croft 18:56

Burst into flames after crashing near Monchengladbach.

Initially the crew were buried in the town's Hauptfriedhof. Later the bodies of Sgt Anderson and Sgt Noonan were exhumed and re-buried in the Rheinberg War Cemetery. The remainder of the crew are commemorated on the Runnymede Memorial, as their bodies could not be found.

Sgt J P Jolley RCAF	K
P/O L R Scourfield RCAF	K
Sgt V O Noonan RAAF	K
F/S H A Grover RCAF	K
Sgt P J Anderton	K

Number of 419 aircraft lost whilst serving at Croft, Operational 5, Training 1.
Aircrew killed 27, POWs 1, Injured 4.

419 losses whilst at Middleton St George

November 30. 1942, Halifax Mk II, DT540 VR-C. Training. Took off MSG.

Crash-landed at Middleton during a training flight. No injuries. This was the first Halifax lost by 419 since converting on to type, and their first loss from Middleton-St-George.

F/S M O Frederick
F/S D L Moher
Sgt E Connolly
Sgt G Sayer
Sgt J Rock

419 losses 1943

January 9/10. 1943, Halifax Mk II, W7857 VR-O. Ops – Gardening. Took-off MSG 16:32.

Presumed lost over the sea. F/S Dunn and F/S Hugli are rests in Sage War Cemetery. Sgt Watson is buried in Kviberg Cemetery, Sweden. The remainder of the crew have no known graves and are commemorated on the Runnymede Memorial. This was 419's first operational loss having become part of No.6 Group on January 1 1943.

Sgt F H Barker RCAF	K
Sgt R E Sackville-Golden	K
F/S H A Dunn RCAF	K
F/S V A Hugli RCAF	K
Sgt D A Watson RCAF	K
Sgt W D Cameron RCAF	K
F/S W G Murphy RCAF	K

January 29/30. 1943, Halifax Mk II, DT623 VR-. Ops – Lorient. Took-off MSG 16:54.

This aircraft crash-landed wheels up on its return to base at 00:09, it was subsequently written off. None of the crew were injured.

F/L A P Cranswick
Sgt F E Johnstone
W/O W McRobbie
F/S J M O'Connor RCAF
F/S D McKenzie
P/O J C Garton
F/S I L Howard.

February 3 /4. 1943, Halifax Mk II, DT630 VR-T. Ops – Hamburg. Took-off MSG 18:34.

Crashed at Sleen, Holland Most likely after being shot down by a fighter. Those killed were buried at Sleen General Cemetery.

F/S J D Mackenzie RCAF	K
Sgt W P Duthie RCAF	K
Sgt W N Garnett RCAF	POW
Sgt E R Marquand RCAF	POW
Sgt R H Hill RCAF	K
Sgt L A Gonnett RCAF	K
F/S A H Milton	POW

February 18/19. 1943, Halifax Mk 11, DT639 VR-B. Ops – Gardening. Took-off MSG

Lost without trace. The crew are commemorated on the Runnymede Memorial.

F/S B A Levasseur RCAF	K
Sgt W A Robinson RCAF	K
Sgt G A Lloyd	K
Sgt J W Grant	K
Sgt H T Jacobsen RCAF	K
Sgt R P Wilson RCAF	K
F/S W R Gray RCAF	K

February 27/28. 1943, Halifax Mk 11, DT615 VR-P. Ops – Gardening. Took-off MSG 18:25.

Hit by flak whilst carrying out a mine-laying sortie to the Frisian Islands. The crew ditched and were adrift for 22 hours before being picked up uninjured by the Royal Navy.

Sgt M F Gray RCAF
Sgt C F Wilby RCAF
F/S C O Hancock RCAF
F/O W J McNicol RCAF
Sgt G H Low RCAF
Sgt M S Branff RCAF
P/O R Harling DFC RCAF

March 1 /2. 1943, Halifax Mk II, DT641 VR-R. Ops – Berlin. Took-off MSG 18:50.

Presumed lost over the sea after being shot down by Hptm Helmut Lent 1V./NJG1. The body of Sgt Cherkinsky was found the following day, on the shores of the Frisian Island of Schiermonnikoog. He was buried in Vredenhof Cemetery. Sgt Gray rests in Kiel War Cemetery. The remainder have no known graves and are commemorated on the Runnymede Memorial.

P/O A J Herriott DFM	K
Sgt A D Cherkinsky RCAF	K
Sgt W G Francis RCAF	K
Sgt A L Bateman RCAF	K
Sgt J N Gray	K
Sgt J Kowalski RCAF	K
Sgt A T Woodhouse RCAF	K

March 5/6. 1943, Halifax Mk II, DT646 VR-C. Ops – Essen. Took-off MSG 18:57.

It is thought that this aircraft crashed near Elst, half-way between Nijmegen and Arnhem at 21:37. It was first hit by flak and then shot down by a night fighter. The tail gunner F/S J R Couper may have fallen into the waters of the Waal, he had no known grave.

Sgt L Bakewell	POW
Sgt A C Turner RCAF	Evd
F/S D D Scowen RCAF	POW
F/S J E Marvel RCAF	POW
Sgt J A Bennett RCAF	POW
Sgt W J Clark RCAF	POW
F/S J R Couper	K

March 27/28. 1943. Halifax Mk II, DT634 VR-E. Ops – Berlin. Took-off MSG 20;02.

This aircraft sustained damage to one of its engines when hit by flak southwest of Bremen. The crew continue with the operation but were shot down on the way home by a night fighter north of Hamburg. F/O Porter is buried in Hamburg's Ohlsdorf War Cemetery.

F/O C E Porter Mid RCAF	K
Sgt M V Bishop RCAF	POW
Sgt A T Budinger	POW
F/O G J Sweanor RCAF	POW
Sgt J G Lanteigne RCAF	POW
Sgt D London	POW
F/S A H Taylor RCAF	POW

March 28/29. 1943. Halifax Mk II, BB283 VR-O. Ops – St Nazaire. Took-off MSG 19:40.

This aircraft crashed at Nantes, 50 km E/S/E of St-Nazaire, after being shot down. The crew are buried in Escoublac-la-Baule War Cemetery, 12 km W/N/W of the target.

Sgt R F Beckett RCAF	K
Sgt C Foster RCAF	K
Sgt D Ansley	K
Sgt R M McLeod RCAF	K
Sgt W J Boyd	K
Sgt J J Goldspink RCAF	K
Sgt G McGrath RCAF	K

March 29/30. 1943, Halifax Mk II, JB860 VR-. Ops – Berlin. Took-off MSG 21:31.

Encountered heavy icing, this aircraft crashed at 00:51, whilst landing back at base during a strong crosswind. No injuries.

P/O L P Ainsworth
Sgt H Ebbers
Sgt A Simpson
Sgt J K Oldman
Sgt S A Lagdon
Sgt W Climie
Sgt B Blount

April 3 /4. 1943, Halifax Mk II, DT617 VR-G. Ops – Essen. Took-off MSG 19:52.

Crashed at Duur, 12 km N/N/W of Deventer, Holland at 23:50, after being shot down by Hptm Herbert Lutje, 111./NJG1. The crew are buried in Duur's Olst General Cemetery.

P/O P D Boyd	K
Sgt S N Hall RCAF	K
P/O G W Lawry RCAF	K
Sgt J B Langley	K
Sgt L H Ransome	K
P/O H T Macdonald	K
Sgt B W Agar RCAF	K

**April 8/9. 1943, Halifax Mk II, BB327 VR-Q. Ops –
Duisburg. Took-off MSG 21:47.**

This aircraft crashed near Bochum. With the exception of
Sgt L E Turner, the crew were initially laid to rest at
Krefeld, later they were buried in the Reichswald Forest
War Cemetery.

P/O J H Morris RCAF	K
Sgt L E Turner RCAF	POW
Sgt K H Godbold	K
P/O A R Hickley RCAF	K
Sgt R J Amos	K
Sgt P J Ireland RCAF	K
Sgt D C Way RCAF	K

**April 20/21. 1943, Halifax Mk II, JB912 VR-B. Ops –
Stettin. Took-off MSG 21:14.**

Crashed some 47-km north-west of the target area, after
being shot down by a night fighter. F/S Watkins DFM is
buried in Berlin's 1939-1945 War Cemetery.

P/O T E Jackson RCAF	POW
Sgt J F Westerman RCAF	POW
Sgt C J Sebastian RCAF	POW
F/S J M Carlton RCAF	POW
P/O J R Fry RCAF	POW
Sgt T M Crandell RCAF	POW
F/S D A Watkins DFM	K
Sgt E Jury	POW

**April 28/29. 1943, Halifax Mk II, JB923 VR-Q. Ops -
Gardening. Took-off MSG 20:42.**

Lost without trace. All are commemorated on the
Runnymede Memorial.

Sgt G K Smallwood RCAF	K
Sgt J A Allan RCAF	K
Sgt J W Carley RCAF	K
F/S J M O'Connor RCAF	K
Sgt J G Acker RCAF	K
Sgt L J Murphy RCAF	K
F/S R R Gourde RCAF	K

**May 4/5. 1943, Halifax Mk II, W7817 VR-A. Ops –
Dortmund. Took-off MSG 23:01.**

Crashed near Zwolle, Holland. Sgt Stanley is buried in the
town's General Cemetery.

F/O C J Vaillancourt RCAF	POW
Sgt A Jaynes RCAF	POW
P/O D Grimshaw	POW
Sgt N M Douglas	POW
Sgt A S Morrison RCAF	POW
Sgt J L Peck RCAF	POW
Sgt F T Stanley	K

**May 4/5. 1944, Halifax Mk II, DT794 VR-Y. Ops –
Dortmund. Took-off MSG 22:51**

Crashed in the middle of Dortmund, in the MitteKirche,
where all the crew were buried on May 8th. After the war
they were moved to the Reichwald Forest War Cemetery.

F/O W G Elliott RCAF	K
Sgt G D Menzies RCAF	K
P/O E E Kennedy RCAF	K
P/O H M Metcalf RCAF	K
Sgt G Sandfield	K
Sgt J W McIntosh RCAF	K
Sgt J A Farrel RCAF	K

**May 12/13. 1943, Halifax Mk II, JB791 VR-X. Ops –
Duisburg. Took-off MSG 23:18.**

After leaving the target area this aircraft was hit by flak
and partially abandoned. It later crashed at Bedburg-Hau,
4 km southeast of Kleve, and only 7 km northeast of the
site of the Reichwald Forest War Cemetery, which was laid
out after the end of WWII. Sgt Alison was found critically
injured and later died. He was buried in Belgium, in
Hotton War Cemetery. W/O McMillan is buried in
Rheinburg War Cemetery.

W/O 1 G A McMillan RCAF	K
Sgt W J Howell RCAF	POW
Sgt W J Klein RCAF	POW
P/O H Enever	POW
Sgt W H Alison	Inj
P/O A R Wallace RCAF	POW
F/S H G Bees RCAF	POW

**May 12/13. 1943, Halifax Mk II, JB861 VR-C. Ops –
Duisburg. Took-off MSG 23:14.**

Crashed 02:47, near Zuidland on Putten, 4-km southwest
of Spijkenisse, Holland, after being shot down by a night
fighter. The crew were buried in Crooswijk General
Cemetery in Rotterdam.

F/S J Palmer RCAF	K
Sgt W A Simonett RCAF	K
Sgt H Walsh	K
P/O T Brown	K
Sgt R C Weedy RCAF	K
Sgt R E Ratelle RCAF	K
Sgt A J Gearing	K

**May 13/14. 1943, Halifax Mk II, DT672 VR-D. Ops –
Bochum. Took-off MSG 23:44.**

Crashed near Monchengladbach, with no survivors.
Initially the crew were buried in the town's Stadtfriedhof,
four days after the crash. They are now buried in the
Rheinberg War Cemetery.

Sgt G Adams	K
Sgt F S Neal	K
P/O E B Ruto RCAF	K
Sgt W H Bowden RCAF	K
Sgt E Kurring	K
Sgt L D McEwen RCAF	K
Sgt O J Haralson RCAF	K

**May 13/14. 1943, Halifax Mk II, JD113 VR-Z. Ops -
Bochum. Took-off MSG 23:57.**

Crashed 03:30 near Dalen, 15 km southwest of Emmen,
Holland, after being shot down on the way home by a night
fighter, flown by Hptm Herbert Lutje, 111. / NJG1.

Sgt W H Buckwell RCAF	K
Sgt F W Walkerdine RCAF	K
F/O R W Lowry RCAF	POW
Sgt W M Reid RCAF	POW
Sgt W J Duggan RCAF	POW
Sgt A E Hurteau RCAF	K
Sgt W Le R Bovaird RCAF	K

May 23/24. 1943, Halifax Mk II, BB384 VR-. Ops - Dortmund. Took-off MSG 23:01.

Crash-landed at Dinsdale, 2 miles north-west of Middleton, due to shortage of fuel. No injuries.

F/O P G Weedon RCAF
Sgt C W Nivins
F/O P Campbell
F/O R K Shields RCAF
Sgt M Wigelsworth
Sgt S Poole
Sgt D G Plyley

May 23/24. 1943, Halifax Mk 11, JB862 VR-U. Ops - Dortmund. Took-off MSG 23:00.

The starboard engine failed whilst outbound. Shortly after, the aircraft crashed near Monchengladbach, after being shot down by flak and a night fighter. Those who were killed were buried in the town's Hauptfriedhof. Later they were reburied in Rheinberg War Cemetery.

Sgt A S Green RCAF	K
Sgt F A Dunn RCAF	POW
P/O D Gartery	K
Sgt A J Brockway	K
Sgt M A Harrison	K
Sgt J F Prieur RCAF	K
Sgt G R Gowling RCAF	K

May 29/30. 1943, Halifax Mk 11, JB793 RR-X. Ops – Wuppertal. Took-off MSG 22:52.

Crashed in the Barrage de la Gileppe, 6-km southwest of Eupen, Belgium after being attacked by a night fighter. Sgt Hall, along with 3 other members of the crew, abandoned the aircraft but his parachute may not have deployed as his body was found at Jalhay, where he was buried.

Sgt F E Winegarden RCAF	K
Sgt E Hall	K
Sgt R M Mingay RCAF	POW
P/O F H Hubbs RCAF	POW
Sgt S G Ward RCAF	POW
Sgt L R Lamoure RCAF	K
Sgt R M Ricketts RCAF	K

May 29/30. 1943, Halifax Mk 11, JB805 VR-X. Ops – Wuppertal. Took-off MSG 22:48.

Crashed at Peronnes-Lez-Binche, 14-km E/S/E of Mons after being shot down by Oblt Rudolf Altendorf of 1./NjG4. Sgt Peets is buried in the town's Charbonnage Communal Cemetery. The remainder of the crew rest in Charleroi Communal Cemetery. Sgt Baker was just 18 years old.

Sgt P Johnson RCAF	K
Sgt C P Baker	K
Sgt R S Metcalf	K
Sgt T W Peets RCAF	K
Sgt G F Humphreys	K
Sgt D J Shtitz RCAF	K
Sgt E L Armstrong	K

June 11/12. 1943, Halifax Mk 11, JD143 VR-A. Ops - Dusseldorf. Took-off MSG 22:40.

Crashed 02:00 on the western edge of the Forst Xanten, at Uedemer Bruch, 3 km E/S/E of Uedem. F/O Boyce rests in Rheinberg War Cemetery, whilst W/O1 Tripp and Sgt Chambers were buried in the Reichswald Forest War Cemetery.

F/O W J Boyce RCAF	K
W/O 1 H A Tripp RCAF	K
Sgt D N Stewart	POW
F/O D I Black	POW
F/O C L Buck	POW
Sgt D E Chambers	K
Sgt R M Hall RCAF	POW
Sgt J D Gray RCAF	POW

June 13/14. 1943, Halifax Mk 11, DT616 VR-K. Ops - Bochum. Took-off MSG 23:00.

This aircraft was shot down by a Me 110 night fighter.

Sgt B D Kirkham RCAF	POW
Sgt R J Hamilton RCAF	POW
Sgt H A Taylor RCAF	POW
Sgt D B Whittaker	POW
Sgt F J Callaghan	POW
Sgt J A Mills RCAF	POW
Sgt D L Gray RCAF	POW

June 21/22. 1943, Halifax Mk 11, W1271 VR-P. Ops - Krefeld. Took-off MSG 23:42.

Crashed at De Posthoorn, 1 km south of Rucphen, Holland. The crew were from 428 squadron, attached to 419 for operational experience. The bodies of the crew were first buried at Breda, after the war they were taken to Bergen-op-Zoom.

Sgt C R Pearce DFM RNZAF	K
Sgt J J Holland RCAF	K
F/S W T Ellis RNZAF	K
Sgt G J Thompson	K
Sgt W J Randall	K
Sgt J Galloway	K
F/S E L Robson	K

June 24/25. 1943, Halifax Mk 11, JD147 VR-C. Ops - Wuppertal. Took-off MSG 22:40.

Shot down by Ofw Reinhard Kollar, 111. / NJG4 and crashed into the Hummersveld, near Harten, Holland. F/L Jost and Sgt Johnson were buried at Venlo. Later they were reburied in Jonkerbos War Cemetery. F/O Goodwin was buried in Kapel Roman Catholic Cemetery.

F/L B N Jost DFC RCAF	K
Sgt J B Johnson RCAF	K
Sgt E B Pope	POW
F/S A W Bruce RNZAF	POW
F/O R O Goodwin RCAF	K
F/S L Barker	POW
Sgt R E Austin	POW

June 24/25. 1943, Halifax Mk 11, JD214 VR-U. Ops - Wuppertal. Took-off MSG 13:07.

Crash-landed at Wageningen, Holland, at 01:00, after being attacked by Fw190s.

Sgt G V Neale RCAF	POW
Sgt R A Cleaver	POW
Sgt R S McLachlan RCAF	POW
Sgt W N Jaffray RCAF	POW
Sgt P J Griffiths	POW
Sgt D E Kenwell RCAF	POW
Sgt W F McLeod RCAF	POW

June 24/25. 1943, Halifax Mk 11, JD258 VR-K. Ops - Wuppertal. Took-off MSG 22:56.

Shot down by Hptm Hans Dieter Frank, 1. /NJG1 and crashed 01:06 at Acht, in the north-west suburbs of Eindhoven, After the war P/O Fowler and Sgt Kimber were re-buried in Groesbeek Canadian War Cemetery. This was a 428 crew, attached for operational experience.

Sgt R Whitfield	K
Sgt P Stephenson	K
P/O R J Fowler RCAF	K
P/O W A Donnelly	K
Sgt C Gorton	K
Sgt J E Dean	K
Sgt M P Kimber RCAF	K

June 28/29. 1943, Halifax Mk 11, JD215 VR-B. Ops – Cologne. Took-off MSG 23:04

Crashed 02:14 at Waalre, 6 km S/S/W of the centre of Eindhoven, after being shot down by Maj Gunter Radusch of 1. /NJG1. At least 6 of the crew were buried in Woensel General Cemetery. After 1945 P/O Agnew, P/O Mayes and Sgt Otterholm were re-buried in the Canadian War Cemetery at Groesbeek. P/O Fowler was taken to Mierlo War Cemetery. F/L Raine, the wireless operator was on his second tour.

P/O H W Fowler AFM RCAF	
Sgt J E Dickson	
P/O W B Mayes RCAF	
P/O D R Agnew RCAF	
F/L A C Raine RCAF	
Sgt W G Otterholm RCAF	
Sgt W A Hood RCAF	

July 3/4 July. 1943, Halifax Mk 11, JD159. Ops – Cologne. Took-off MSG 23:30.

Crashed at Muizan, on the outskirts of Mechelin, Belgium after being shot down by Ofw Reinhard Kollak of 7./ NJG4. The 3 crewmen that died were buried in Antwerp's Schoonslehof Cemetery.

P/O A H Bell RCAF	K
Sgt J A Anderson RCAF	K
Sgt W B Taylor RCAF	K
Sgt A O Simpson	POW
F/S R O Williston RCAF	POW
Sgt J D Arseneaut RCAF	POW
Sgt J F Graham	POW
Sgt G E Aitken RCAF	POW

July 13/14. 1943, Halifax Mk 11, BB323 VR-R. Ops – Aachen. Took-off MSG 22:56.

Crashed near Venlo, Holland, after being shot down by a night fighter. F/S Batkin was at first buried at Venlo but he now rests in Jonkerbos War Cemetery.

2nd Lt B J Furey USAAF	POW
Sgt J S Carmichael	POW
Sgt M Cottenden RCAF	POW
Sgt G C Perrett	POW
Sgt J C Gilchrist RCAF	POW
Sgt K Lasalle RCAF	POW
F/S W C Batkin	K

July 25/26. 1943, Halifax Mk 11, JD256 VR-A. Ops – Essen. Took-off MSG 22:17.

Crashed after colliding with another aircraft over the target. The crewmembers that died are buried in the Reichswald Forrest War Cemetery.

Sgt L Chapman RCAF	POW
F/O S W Handforth RCAF	K
Sgt J Stewart	K
Sgt W E Ross RCAF	K
Sgt O H Phoenix RCAF	K
Sgt G W Askew RCAF	K
Sgt L M Hill RCAF	K
Sgt A L Porter RCAF	K

August 2/3. 1943, Halifax Mk 11, DT798 VR-T. Ops – Hamburg. Took-off MSG 22:22.

This aircraft crashed after encountering heavy icing and electrical storms. Those that died are buried in Becklingen War Cemetery. Sgt Horswill has no known grave, he is commemorated on the Runnymede Memorial.

Sgt J S Sobin RCAF	K
Sgt R E Horswill	K
P/O J Sibalis RCAF	POW
Sgt J M Mahoney RCAF	POW
Sgt A W Farrow	POW
Sgt J Sadeski RCAF	K
Sgt D J McCarty RCAF	K

August 9/10. 1943, Halifax Mk 11, JD257 VR-F. Ops – Mannheim. Took-off MSG 22:47.

This aircraft crashed at Ludwigshaven. The crew rest in Durnbach War Cemetery.

F/O M T Ludlow RCAF	K
Sgt W L Scott	K
P/O C A Wright RCAF	K
Sgt A S Maclaren RCAF	K
Sgt C R Smyth RCAF	K
Sgt D R See RCAF	K
Sgt W D Molitor RCAF	K

August 17/18. 1943, Halifax Mk 11, JD158 VR-D. Ops – Peenemunde. Took-off MSG 21:27.

This aircraft crashed in the Baltic, north of the target, close to Stralsund -Gross Zicker. The bodies of 4 members of the crew were found and buried at Greifwald, 25-km southwest of the target area. They are now buried in Berlin's 1939-1945 War Cemetery. The remainder are commemorated on the Runnymede Memorial.

F/O S M Heard RCAF	K
Sgt D M Macpherson RCAF	K
Sgt G Blyth	K
Sgt G S Walter RCAF	K
Sgt P O McSween RCAF	K
Sgt J J Newbon	K
Sgt D Thornton RCAF	K
Sgt J W Dally RCAF	K

August 17/18. 1943, Halifax Mk 11, JD163 VR-N. Ops – Peenemunde. Too-off MSG 21:25.

W/T transmissions from this aircraft were last heard at 04:26 from a W/T station at Hull. Its bearing was 064∞ from Happisburgh, on the Norfolk coast. The aircraft came down in the sea, despite an extensive search of the area, no trace was found. The crew were lost without trace and are commemorated on the Runnymede memorial.

Sgt J M Batterton RCAF	K

Sgt A Dixon	K
Sgt G F Parker RCAF	K
Sgt J O Jerome RCAF	K
Sgt D A Lloyd	K
Sgt L F Power RCAF	K
Sgt H U Morris RCAF	K

August 17/18. 1943, Halifax Mk 11, JD458 VR-C. Ops – Peenemunde. Took-off MSG 21:40.

Crashed in the Baltic. With the exception of Sgt Baker and Sgt Ramm, whose bodies were recovered from the water and buried at Griefswald, the crew are commemorated on the Runnymede Memorial. Both of those buried at Griefswald were later re-buried in Berlin's 1939-1945 War Cemetery.

F/S S T Pekin RAAF	K
Sgt H C Baker	K
F/O P J Sparkes	K
Sgt J K Gilvary	K
Sgt H Price	K
Sgt F P Davis	K
Sgt E C Ramm	K

August 22. 1943, Halifax Mk 11, JB965 VR-W. Airtest.

Carried out a wheels-up crash-landing at Middleton. The undercarriage had been damaged during its first attempt to land. No injuries.

Sgt R K Metherall RCAF	
Sgt C H Pollard	
Sgt A D Chiswell	
Sgt B Edwards	
Sgt K B Kelsall	
Sgt J L Mercer	
Sgt R H Marritt	

August 30/31. 1943, Halifax Mk 11, JD381 VR-R. Ops – Monchengladbach. Took-off MSG 23:30.

This aircraft returned to base badly damaged, after being attacked by a night fighter. Due to severe damage to the bomb bay, hydraulics and nav-aids this aircraft was ordered to be struck off charge. None of the crew were injured. Sgt Ashton was to receive an immediate DFM for his actions in putting out a serious fire in the fuselage.

F/O D D Laidlaw RCAF	
Sgt H C Eyjolfson	
Sgt J N Ashton	
F/O W E Rempel RCAF	
P/O R W Kemp RCAF	
Sgt B E Brakes	
Sgt A S Miller RCAF	
Sgt G F Clarke	

August 31 – September 1. 1943, Halifax Mk 11, JD270 VR-P. Ops – Berlin. Took-off MSG 19:58.

This aircraft's port wing was clipped over the target area by a Me109 or Fw190, after which it immediately crashed. The crewmembers that died are buried in Berlin's 1939-1945 War Cemetery.

Sgt W D Cameron RCAF	K
Sgt J T Mullany	K
Sgt G E Birtch RCAF	K
Sgt V J Wintzer RCAF	K
Sgt L H Duggan	POW

Sgt B W Scharf RCAF	POW
Sgt R E Boos RCAF	POW

August 31 – September 1. 1943, Halifax Mk 11, JD331 VR-K. Ops – Berlin. Took-off MSG 19:46.

Crashed at Hillentrup, 58-km southwest of Hannover, after being shot down by a night fighter. The 3 crewmen who died are buried in Hannover War Cemetery.

F/L D J Corcoran RCAF	POW
Sgt D W Sweet	K
W/O 1 A G MacKenzie RCAF	POW
F/S A C Harris	K
W/O 2 H d'Aperng RCAF	K
Sgt W E Greensides RCAF	POW
F/O D E Larlee RCAF	POW

August 31 – September 1. 1943, Halifax Mk 11, JD464 VR-N, Ops – Berlin. Took-off MSG 19:52.

Crashed in the vicinity of the Black Forest, after being shot down by a night fighter whilst on the way home. The three who died are commemorated on the Runnymede Memorial.

F/O R Stewart RCAF	K
Sgt H R Tenny	POW
P/O S E James RCAF	POW
Sgt V A Cleveland RCAF	K
Sgt A Embley	POW
Sgt L Northcliffe RCAF	POW
Sgt D H Garland RCAF	K

September 5/6. 1943, Halifax Mk 11, JD210 VR-S. Ops – Mannheim. Took-off MSG 19:48.

Crashed at Hattenheim, on the northern bank of the Rhine, 14 km W/S/W of Wiesbaden. This crew had an average age of 22, they are all buried in Durnbach War Cemetery.

F/O J A Studer RCAF	K
Sgt A W Hallworth	K
F/O G A Shannon RCAF	K
P/O H A Danniger RCAF	K
F/S R D Hayes RCAF	K
Sgt R G James RCAF	K
Sgt G A Usher RCAF	K

September 5/6.1943, Halifax Mk 11, JD410 VR-V. Ops – Mannheim. Took-off MSG 1941.

Broke up over the target area after a direct hit by flak. Those that were killed are buried in Rheinberg War Cemetery.

Sgt F B Allan RCAF	K
Sgt H Nuttall	K
P/O J R Harris RCAF	POW
P/O R W Burke RCAF	K
Sgt A R Slaney	K
Sgt J H Kilpatrick	K
Sgt H J Hudson	K

September 16/17. 1943, Halifax Mk 11, LW420 VR-S. Ops – Modane. Took-off MSG 19:04.

Shot down by a night fighter whilst on the way home.

F/L A N Quaile	POW
Sgt E E Bowden RCAF	POW
Sgt L F Martin RCAF	Evd
P/O L E Aspinall RCAF	POW

P/O G T Grayham RCAF	Evd
F/S T J Bright	Evd
F/O H F Smith RCAF	Evd
F/L B L Kenyon	POW

September 23/24. 1943, Halifax Mk 11, JB971 VR-X. Ops – Mannheim. Took-off MSG 19:09.

No details known, only that the average age of the crew was 20. Sgt Dempster was the oldest at 22. They are all buried in the Reichswald Forest War Cemetery.

Sgt R T Griffiths RCAF	K
Sgt L G Bender	K
Sgt R Dempster RCAF	K
Sgt J E Dayton RCAF	K
Sgt C G Rolph	K
Sgt A E Willig	K
Sgt J L Rainville RCAF	K

September 23/24. 1943, Halifax Mk 11, JD457 VR-F. Ops – Mannheim. Took-off MSG 19:02.

No details known. All are buried in Rheinberg War Cemetery.

Sgt J Kelly	K
Sgt D H Pether	K
Sgt J Morris	K
Sgt W P Maher	K
Sgt R W McNally	K
Sgt S T Mills	K
Sgt H Brown	K

September 29/30. 1943, Halifax Mk 11, BB376 VR-S. Ops – Bochum. Took-off MSG 18:18.

Lost without trace, all are commemorated on the Runnymede Memorial.

P/O J R Symons RCAF	K
Sgt A W Chandler	K
F/O G E Donaldson RCAF	K
Sgt W D Miller RCAF	K
Sgt D Lucas	K
Sgt E M Cockin RCAF	K
Sgt W G Morgan	K

October 3/4. 1943, Halifax Mk 11, JB967 VR-F. Ops – Kassel. Took-off MSG 18:36.

This aircraft was attacked by a German intruder over Lincolnshire on the way home. The crew managed to reach Middleton but crash-landed at 00:50 whilst on finals. The port wing was torn off and the fuselage broke in three places. Amaisingly, only 2 of the crew were slightly injured.

F/S D T Cook	
Sgt A Simpson	Inj
F/O O W Fonger	
F/S H H Campbell RCAF	Inj
Sgt P J Packer	
Sgt A E Legault	
Sgt D W Robertson	

October 4/5. 1943, Halifax Mk 11, JD204 VR-L. Ops – Frankfurt. Took-off MSG 17:40.

Crashed at Sohren, 100 km W/S/W of the target area whilst outbound, after being shot down by a night fighter. The 4 members of the crew that were killed are buried in Rheinberg War Cemetery.

F/O W H Hamilton RCAF	K
Sgt J McEwan	POW
F/O E L Riley RCAF	POW
F/O J R Dale RCAF	K
Sgt T A Reay	POW
Sgt E H Griffin RCAF	K
F/S A Bortolussi RCAF	K

October 4/5. 1943, Halifax Mk 11, JD463 VR-D. Ops – Frankfurt. Took-off MSG 17:37.

Crashed at Ham-sur-Heure, 11 km S/S/W of Charleroi, Belgium, after being shot down on the way home by Hptm Wilhelm Herget of 1. /NJG4. With the exception of Sgt Renner, the crew are buried in Gosselies Communal Cemetery.

Sgt A R Fare	K
Sgt C R Winterbottom	K
Sgt G E Chapman	K
Sgt W L Renner RCAF	Evd
Sgt W J Boyce	K
Sgt G H Beach	K
Sgt R E Paddison RCAF	K

October 22/23. 1943, Halifax Mk 11, JD382 VR-A. Ops – Kassel. Took-off MSG 17:10.

Crashed at Lauenforde, 38 km N/N/W of the target area. The 5 that died are buried in the Hannover War Cemetery.

W/C G A McMurdy RCAF	K
F/S A B Willson RCAF	K
Sgt T Rawlings	K
F/O W C Coleman RCAF	POW
F/L R K Shields RCAF	POW
Sgt R J Woods	POW
W/O 2 F Yackison RCAF	K
F/S P W Peterkin RCAF	K

November 18/19. 1943, Halifax Mk 11, LW239 VR-K. Ops – Mannheim. Took-off MSG 16:47.

No details available, only that their average age was 22. All are buried in Rheinberg War Cemetery.

F/O E D Fog RCAF	K
Sgt F J Davidson	K
F/O G L McLaughlin RCAF	K
F/O J S Smith RCAF	K
Sgt D J MacDonald RCAF	K
Sgt W J Gerow RCAF	K
Sgt K A Farmer RCAF	K

November 18/19. 1943, Halifax Mk 11, LW328 VR-L. Ops – Mannheim. Took-off MSG 16:55.

All of the engines stopped on the way home, due to the aircraft being out of fuel, and so the crew had to abandon. It is thought that the tanks had been hit by flak. F/S Sedgwick remained behind to allow the crew to bale out, but he was unable to get out in time and was killed. He in Rheinberg War Cemetery.

F/S A L Sedgwick RCAF	K
Sgt E K Canny	POW
F/O E R Hoe RCAF	POW
Sgt J Pappas RCAF	POW
Sgt K W Dingley	POW
Sgt N McVicar RCAF	POW
Sgt D M Johnston RCAF	POW

November 22/23. 1943, Halifax Mk 11, LW231 VR-F. Ops – Berlin. Took off MSG 16:33.

Crashed in the Staats-bossen, near Diever, Holland, after being shot down by a night fighter. The crew were buried in Diever General Cemetery. This was another very young crew, their average age just 20.

Sgt W L Hunter RCAF	K
Sgt W B Jones	K
F/O R J Newman RCAF	K
Sgt M A McKellar RCAF	K
Sgt G A Howitson RCAF	K
Sgt G A May RCAF	K
F/S J A Lesage RCAF	K

November 26/27. 1943, Halifax Mk 11, LW242 VR-N. Ops – Stuttgart. Took-off MSG 17:01.

Shot down crashed at Sankt Ingbert, 10-km northeast of Saabrucken. The crew were initially buried on November 30th . After the war they were moved to the Rheinberg War Cemetery. Again the average age was 20.

Sgt S E Clarke RCAF	K
Sgt J D Whittingham	K
Sgt L P Webster RCAF	K
Sgt J V Dillon RCAF	K
Sgt J R Henderson	K
Sgt E W Chalk RCAF	K
Sgt J L Truax RCAF	K

December 19. 1943, Halifax Mk 11, JP112 VR-R. Training.

Whilst practising a 3 engined approach in a strong crosswind, this aircraft bounced and departed the runway. The undercarriage collapsed and the aircraft was damaged sufficiently to be written off. None of the crew were injured.

S/L J G Stewart RCAF

December 29/30. 1943, Halifax Mk 11, LW282 VR-X. Ops – Berlin. Took-off MSG 16:48.

The port outer lost power and burst into flames, they spread along the wing an also set fire to the port inner. The crew baled out in the general vicinity of Berlin.

F/S R L Thompson RCAF	POW
Sgt G Cooper	POW
Sgt F H Webb RCAF	POW
Sgt S J Maloney RCAF	POW
Sgt R G Bilyard	POW
Sgt A S Carrol RCAF	POW
Sgt W J Barry RCAF	POW

419 losses 1944

January 20/21. 1944, Halifax Mk11, DT731 VR-M. Ops – Berlin. Took-off MSG 15:54.

Abandoned southwest of Leipzig whilst homebound after being attacked by a night fighter.

F/S I V Hopkins RCAF	POW
Sgt J Chambers	POW
W/O 2 W E MacKenzie RCAF	POW
T/S F S Paules USAF	POW
F/O A Cormack RCAF	POW
Sgt E R Jenkins	POW
Sgt W D McCaghey RCAF	POW

January 20/21. 1944, Halifax Mk 11, HX162 VR-X. Ops – Berlin. Took-off MSG 16:03.

Crashed at Horst, 18km E/N/E of Schleswig, after being hit by flack and fighters. The fighter attack was responsible for the loss of the 2 crewmembers. Sgt Furguson is buried in Kiel War Cemetery, whilst Sgt Sanderson rests in Hamburg's Ohlsdorf Cemetery.

P/O H L Bullis RCAF	POW
Sgt D J Ferguson	K
W/O 2 A H Towers RCAF	POW
Sgt E H Boisvert USSAF	POW
F/S R Bonathan	POW
Sgt F G Sanderson RCAF	K
F/S M A Potter RCAF	POW

January 21/22. 1944, Halifax Mk 11, JD420 VR-D. Ops – Magdeburg. Took-off MSG 19:46.

Hit by flak on the way home. Several members of the crew were injured, including the navigator, Sgt Fletcher who received mortal wounds. The port outer was hit and put out of action, and so the order to abandon was given. Sgt Fletcher was unable to jump and his body was found in the wreckage by the Germans. He was buried in the Rheinberg War Cemetery.

F/S V L Hawkes RCAF	POW
Sgt D M Board	POW
F/S W J Fletcher RCAF	K
F/O F E Hovison RCAF	POW
W/O 2 D R McDevitt RCAF	POW
Sgt A M Bowman RCAF	POW
W/O 2 W H Barnes RCAF	POW

January 21/22. 1944, Halifax Mk 11, JD466 VR-E. Ops – Magdeburg. Took-off MSG 19:41.

This aircraft crashed at Borne, 20 km S/S/W of the target area, where the crew were buried. After the war they were relocated to the 1923-1945 War Cemetery in Berlin.

F/L A G Hermitage RCAF	K
Sgt J A Wilson RCAF	K
F/S R H Walton RCAF	K
F/S W B Tobin RCAF	K
W/O 2 J B Chess RCAF	K
Sgt R Shields	K
Sgt R W Edwards RCAF	K

January 28/29. 1944, Halifax Mk 11, JP119 VR-O. Ops – Berlin. Took-off MSG 23:35.

Crashed at Zuhlen, 6 km southwest of Rheinsberg. Initially all of the crew were buried at Zuhlen on January 30th. After the war 6 of the crew were buried in Berlin's 1939-1945 War Cemetery, whilst F/S Palmer and Sgt Milner are commemorated on the Runnymede Memorial.

F/S F H Palmer RCAF	K
F/O S J Gibson RCAF	K
Sgt J H Parrott	K
F/O F Forrest RCAF	K
F/O G E Lemmerick RCAF	K
F/S F P Reilly	K
Sgt E Milner RCAF	K
Sgt R Tarbet RCAF	K

February 12/13. 1944, Halifax Mk 11, HR910 VR-R. Ops – Gardening. Took-off MSG 18:06.

Lost without trace whilst carrying out minelaying off Borkum. All are commemorated on the Runnymede Memorial.

F/L D D Laidlaw RCAF	K
Sgt J N Ashton DFM	K
F/O W E Rempel RCAF	K
F/O R W Kemp RCAF	K
W/O S A Lagdon	K
Sgt A S Miller RCAF	K
W/O 1 J G Bachand RCAF	K

February 19/20. 1944, Halifax Mk 11, JD114 VR-V. Ops – Leipzig. Took-off MSG 23:12.

Lost without trace. All are commemorated on the Runnymede Memorial.

F/S D K MacLeod RCAF	K
Sgt M B Leboldus RCAF	K
F/O J R Piper RCAF	K
F/S J L Beattie RCAF	K
Sgt T Gettings	K
Sgt D C Lewthwaite RCAF	K
Sgt A H Hackbart RCAF	K

February 25/26. 1944, Halifax Mk 11, JP200 VR-G. Ops - Gardening. Took-off MSG 20:03.

Departed for mining operation in Kiel Bay and was lost without trace. All are commemorated on the Runnymede Memorial.

F/O A L Warren RCAF	K
Sgt E D Kent RCAF	K
F/S S Sutton	K
F/O H M Sherman RCAF	K
Sgt W P King	K
Sgt M Minett RCAF	K
Sgt H Crabtree	K

March 22/23. 1944, Halifax Mk 11, JD468 VR-W. Ops – Gardening. Took-off MSG 17:39.

Whilst outbound for Kiel Bay at 22:15 the port outer caught fire, whilst at 15,000 feet, the crew put out the flames and were able to continue with the operation. On the way back at 10,000 feet, the crew suffered another engine fire, this time it was the port inner. This too was extinguished, but they began to slowly loose height. The crew transmitted an S.O.S. and 10 minutes later successfully ditched in the North Sea. A search aircraft guided a trawler to the dinghy and they were rescued. The trawler then sank the floating aircraft with its gun.

P/O G R Peck RCAF	
Sgt L E Brooks	
F/O A T Paton RCAF	
F/O E R McRorie RCAF	
F/O A W Winch RCAF	
Sgt D G Curry RCAF	
Sgt L G Ringuette RCAF	

March 25/26. 1944, Halifax Mk 11, JP125 VR-L. Ops – Aulnoye. Took-off MSG 18:28.

Whilst outbound to bomb rail yards this aircraft lost power from two of its engines. The crew jettisoned the bombs off the French Coast and set course for RAF Ford, Essex.

Having reached the airfield at 21:05, As the aircraft landed it overshot the runway, crash-landed into a ploughed field and caught fire. The crew suffered only minor injuries and were treated in the SSQ.

P/O H C Eyjolfson RCAF	Inj
Sgt R D Tunstall	Inj
F/O C E Siddall RCAF	Inj
F/L D W Haseldine	Inj
Sgt J H Pattie	Inj
Sgt A E Cossar RCAF	Inj
Sgt G Gallacher	Inj

April 18/19. 1944, Halifax Mk 11, JP202 VR-T. Ops – Gardening. Took-off MSG 20:37.

Crashed into the North Sea whilst carrying out mining operations to Fakse Bay. It would be August 22 before the body of Sgt Petrina was found near the radar station at Kryle. He was laid to rest in Nysogn Cemetery. Nine days later P/O Quinn's body came ashore at Hense. He was buried in Esbjerg Cemetery, Denmark. The remainder of the crew are commemorated on the Runnymede Memorial.

P/O J D Quinn RCAF	K
Sgt M J Petrina RCAF	K
W/O 2 E J Gares RCAF	K
F/O D L Lewis-Watts	K
F/S F J Hickson	K
Sgt D F Weeks TCAF	K
W/O 1 R O Dwyer RCAF	K

April 22/23. 1944, Halifax Mk 11, HX189 VR-J. Ops – Laon. Took-off MSG 20:36.

Crashed at Couvron-et-Aumencourt, 12 km N/N/W of Leyon. Sgt Knox is buried in Couvron-et-Aumencourt Communal Cemetery.

F/O C A Thomas USAAF	Evd
Sgt J L Thompson	POW
F/S P R Linsay RCAF	Evd
P/O J A Neal RCAF	Evd
W/O 1 P J Murphy RCAF	POW
Sgt W A Greene	Evd
Sgt V A Knox RCAF	K

April 27/28. 1944, Halifax Mk 11, JN954 VR-R. Ops – Montzen. Took-off MSG 23:26.

Crashed at Heer in the southeast suburbs of Maastricht, where the crew are buried in the Communal Cemetery.

P/O R A McIvor RCAF	K
Sgt S J Rigden RCAF	K
W/O 2 J D Bremner RCAF	K
F/S S H Goulding RCAF	K
W/O1 W T Claridge RCAF	K
Sgt K D Tucker RCAF	K
Sgt E R Dujay RCAF	K

May 1/2. 1944, Lancaster Mk X, KB711 VR-C. Ops - St Ghislain. Took-off MSG 22:00.

Crashed 1-km from Gent city centre after being attacked by a night fighter. The 2 crewmembers who died are buried in Adegem Canadian War Cemetery.

P/O J C McNary RCAF	K
F/O J R Normandale	POW
Sgt A G Hill	POW
F/O F H Love RCAF	POW

F/S R C Long RCAF	POW
W/O 1 J L Chartrand RCAF	K
Sgt J J Wilson RCAF	POW
Sgt D S Sangster RCAF	POW

Sgt N F Alsop RCAF	K
Sgt F A Milne RCAF	K

May 7. 1944, Lancaster Mk X, KB716 VR-D. Training. Crash-landed 16:00.

This aircraft suffered a flat tyre and crash-landed on its return to Middleton. No injuries.

1st Lt J H Hartshorn USAAF

May 10/11. 1944, Lancaster Mk X, KB704 VR-Y. Ops – Gent. Took-off MSG 21:33.

This aircraft crash-landed on return to base. Having overshot the runway it crossed 2 ditches before coming to a halt. No injuries.

P/O G E Holmes RCAF
Sgt E J Roberts
Sgt D J Williams RCAF
F/O E C Whitney RCAF
Sgt J W Shelson RCAF
Sgt N Turner RCAF
Sgt H J Filmer RCAF

May 12/13 1944, Lancaster Mk X, KB710 VR-W Ops - Leuven, Took off MSG 21:55

Crashed at Saint-Genesius-Rode, 12 -kms south of the centre of Brussels. All rest in the town cemetery.

P/O H I Smith RCAF	K
Sgt R Bull	K
F/O J L Moore RCAF	K
F/O W R Finlayson RCAF	K
F/O W W Price RCAF	K
Sgt J C O'Connell RCAF	K
Sgt S G Livingstone RCAF	K

May 12/13 1944, Lancaster Mk X, KB713 VR-X Ops - Leuven, Took off MSG 22:00

Crashed on the outward journey and exploded at Reninge, 10 kms S/S/W of Diksmuider. P/O Smith was buried in Coxyde cemetery, the remainder of the crew rest in Adegem Canadian war cemetery.

P/O B F Edwards RCAF	K
Sgt J R Carruthers	K
F/O R R Campbell RCAF	K
P/O P Dewer RCAF	K
P/O R S Smith RCAF	K
P/O J A Webber RCAF	K
P/O H E Oddan RCAF	K

May 15/16. 1944, Lancaster Mk X, KB701 VR-B. Training. Took-off MSG 22:38.

Crashed at Potter House Farm on Helmsley Moor near RCAF Wombleton. The 5 RCAF members of the crew are buried in Harrogate's Stonefall Cemetery. 2nd Lt Fordham was laid to rest in Cambridge Military Cemetery, whilst Sgt Jones was buried in his own home town. Sgt Alsop RCAF originally came from Darlington.

F/O J G McMaster RCAF	K
Sgt G T Jones	K
P/O E M Parsons RCAF	K
2nd Lt E N Fordham USAAF	K
W/O 2 H G Grice RCAF	K

May 22/23. 1944, Lancaster Mk X, KB717 VR-E. Ops – Dortmund. Took-off MSG 22:40.

Crashed 2-km south of Monchengladbach after being shot down by a night fighter. The crew were relocated to Rheinberg War Cemetery at the end of the war, having initially been buried in Monchengladbach. The 8th man in the crew, Sgt Chawanski, was acting as mid-under gunner.

P/O C E Patterson RCAF	K
F/O W W Mitchell RCAF	K
Sgt R E Wood	K
W/O 2 W A Bailey RCAF	K
F/S D E Derbyshire RCAF	K
Sgt A P Chawanski RCAF	K
F/S O Jones	K
F/S A C Beckett RCAF	K

May 24/25. 1944, Lancaster Mk X, KB706 VR-A. Ops - Aachen. Took-off MSG 23:39.

Shot down between Loon op Zand and Tilburg, Holland, after an attack by a night fighter. Sgt Lillico was an American from New York, he died of his injuries on May 26th . The remainder of the crew are buried in Tilburg General Cemetery.

W/O 1 D M Robson RCAF	K
Sgt J Hoarty	K
F/S P S Smith RCAF	K
F/O G R Lauder RCAF	K
Sgt T H Smith	K
Sgt B R Morgan	K
Sgt W D Lillico RCAF	K

June 12/13. 1944, Lancaster Mk X, KB714 VR-Y. Ops - Cambrai. Took-off MSG 21:35.

Crashed at Courcelette, France., after being shot down by a night fighter. The crew are buried in Meharicourt Communal Cemetery.

F/O R N Wilson RCAF	K
Sgt C C White RCAF	K
F/O R N Pole RCAF	K
F/O C R McOrmond RCAF	K
F/O D J McMullen RCAF	K
Sgt M E Gates RCAF	K
Sgt R W Francis RCAF	K

June 12/13. 1944, Lancaster Mk X, KB726 VR-A. Ops – Cambrai. Took-off MSG 21:44.

Shot down by a Ju88 whilst outbound to the target, which started fires in both port engines and in the rear fuselage when the rear turret hydraulic lines were severed. The mid-upper gunner W/O 2 Andrew Mynarski, saw that the rear gunner, Sgt Brophy was trapped in his turret and went back to help him. With complete disregard for his own safety he tried to free the trapped gunner. After realising that he could not do so, he retraced his steps back through the flames and baled out. He was helped by the French but died later of his wounds. For his valour he received the posthumous VC.

F/O A De Breyne RCAF	Evd
Sgt R E Vigars	POW
F/O A R Bodie RCAF	Evd

Sgt J W Friday RCAF	POW
W/O 2 W J Kelley RCAF	Evd
W/O 2 A C Mynarski RCAF	Inj
F/O G P Brophy RCAF	Evd

June 12/13. 1944, Lancaster Mk X, KB731 VR-S. Ops – Cambrai. Took-off MSG 21:40.

Crashed near Vieux-Berquin, 30-km north-west of Lille, after being hit by flak.

F/O W M Lacey RCAF	K
Sgt B D Wilson-Law	Evd
F/O E R Lowe RCAF	K
F/O R A Frobes RCAF	Evd
Sgt D J Applin RCAF	K
Sgt M R Larkin RCAF	K
Sgt G W Cattuthers RCAF	K

June 16/17. 1944, Lancaster Mk X, KB728 VR-V. Ops – Sterkrade. Took-off MSG 23:08.

This aircraft exploded after being attacked by a night fighter. It crashed near Elden, 3-km southwest of the centre of Arnhem at 01:30. The crew were buried in the local area. After the war they were relocated to Groesbeek Canadian War Cemetery.

F/O D Morrison RCAF	K
P/O E Fahy	K
P/O A F Hupman RCAF	K
W/O 2 G E Quinne RCAF	K
P/O H Fletcher	K
P/O P J McManus	K
P/O C S Johnston RCAF	K

June 16/17. 1944, Lancaster Mk X, KB734 VR-F. Ops – Sterkrade. Took-off MSG 23:05.

Crashed at Zeist, 9 km E/S/E of Utrecht, Holland. The 5 airmen who died are buried at Amersfoort General Cemetery. F/L Smith was the recipient of the King's Commendation for Valuable Service in the Air.

F/L E S Smith RCAF	K
Sgt J W Trussler	POW
F/S W H Gardiner RCAF	K
Sgt R E Porter RCAF	Evd
W/O 1 M Baran RCAF	K
Sgt G W Taylor RCAF	K
Sgt S A Wilson RCAF	K

July 4/5. 1944, Lancaster Mk X, KB718 VR-J. Ops - Villeneuve. Took-off MSG 21:50.

Crashed at Fays, 23 km Southeast of Liege at 01:45, after being shot down by a night fighter.

F/O L W Frame RCAF	Evd
Sgt P P Barclay	Evd
F/O W C Watson RCAF	Evd
F/O W B Raynolds RCAF	POW
Sgt D High RCAF	POW
F/S J Morris RCAF	Evd
F/S H B Hayes RCAF	POW

July 4/5. 1944, Lancaster Mk X, KB723 VR-U. Ops – Villeneuve-St-Georges. Took-off MSG 22:01.

Crashed after being hit by flak. The 3 airmen that died are buried in Clichy New Communal Cemetery.

F/O C A Steepe RCAF	Evd
Sgt J P Gauthier RCAF	K
F/O D G Murphy RCAF	Evd
F/O W J Thompson RCAF	Evd
F/O G R Hodgson RCAF	K
Sgt B A Reaume RCAF	POW
Sgt A E Roe RCAF	K

July 4/5. 1944, Lancaster Mk X, KB727 VR-H. Ops – Villeneuve-St-Georges. Took-off MSG 21:51.

Crashed northeast of Chartainvillers, 12 km N/N/W of Chartres, after being attacked by a JU88.

F/O J M Stevenson RCAF	Evd
Sgt F S Vinecombe	POW
F/O J E Prudham RCAF	POW
F/O J S Smith	POW
W/O 1 L F Head RCAF	POW
Sgt J T Pett RCAF	POW
Sgt W R Gibson RCAF	POW

July 24/25. 1944, Lancaster Mk X, KB719 VR-T. Ops – Stuttgart. Took-off MSG 21:02.

Crashed near Bassu, 16-km northeast of Vitry-le-Francois, possibly after being hit by a rocket projectile. The 4 airmen that died are buried in Bassu Communal Cemetery.

F/S J A Phillis RCAF	Evd
Sgt J Norman DFM	K
F/S W H Devine RCAF	POW
Sgt R G MacKinnon RCAF	Evd
Sgt J Spevak RCAF	K
Sgt J E Searson RCAF	K
Sgt J P Short RCAF	K

August 7/8. 1944, Lancaster Mk X, KB755 VR-F. Ops – Caen. Took-off MSG 21:22

This aircraft crashed at Auberville-La-Renault, 10 kms south of Fecamp. All are buried in the Auberville-La-Renault churchyard.

F/O B D Walker AFM RCAF	K
Sgt B Jones	K
W/O 2 J C Durrant RCAF	K
F/O P W Merrick RCAF	K
W/O 1 J A Schryer RCAF	K
Sgt W Longmore	K
F/L M G Wilson RCAF	K

August 25/26. 1944, Lancaster Mk X, KB708 VR-E. Ops – Russelsheim. Took-off MSG 19:34.

Having returned to the UK this aircraft was attempting to land at RAF Boscome Down in foggy conditions. F/O Milner was not happy with the poor visibility and initiated an overshoot. As he applied full power, the engines stopped due to lack of fuel and at 04:25 the aircraft crashed into some trees near the airfield. Sgt Trotman was buried in Durrington Cemetery, whilst the remainder of those that died were laid to rest in Brookwood Military Cemetery.

F/O W A Milner RCAF	K
Sgt J L Trotman	K
F/O P E Gariepy RCAF	Inj
F/O I J Kirschner RCAF	K
F/S H F Anderson RCAF	K
Sgt L J Weston RCAF	Inj
Sgt P Wiens RCAF	Inj

August 25/26. 1944, Lancaster Mk X, KB775 VR-Y. Ops – Russelsheim. Took-off MSG 19:58.

Crashed whilst approaching the target area, after colliding with another aircraft. The aircraft broke up on the way down and F/O Witwer was thrown clear. The remainder of the crew were killed, they are buried in Durnbach War Cemetery.

F/O H D Witwer RCAF	POW
Sgt R J Boorman	K
F/S H L McKay RCAF	K
F/O A W Larson RCAF	K
W/O 1 D R Barnard RCAF	K
Sgt V Stear RCAF	K
Sgt A R Jackson RCAF	K

September 18. 1944, Lancaster Mk X, KB735 VR-O. Ops – Walcheren. Took-off MSG 15:34.

Crash-landed at 20:36, after overshooting at RCAF East Moor on the way back to base.

F/L W R Chalcraft RCAF	
Sgt J R Gunn	
F/O J E Taylor RCAF	
F/O C D Christian RCAF	
P/O P E Bourassa RCAF	
Sgt E G Legault RCAF	
F/S H C Annable RCAF	

September 19. 1944, Lancaster Mk X, KB707 VR-W. Ops – Transit. Took-off from East Moor.

Having landed at East Moor the previous day this aircraft departed for Leeming to collect 3 passengers. It then took-off for Middleton but overshot on landing and crash-landed. None on board were injured.

P/O A C Weston RCAF	
Sgt S A Musto	
F/O J H McKeller RCAF	
F/O J H MacKay RCAF	
F/S R F Clark	
W/O 1 K F McCallum RCAF	
F/S W H Murrell RCAF	

October 4. 1944. Lancaster Mk X, KB745 VR-V. Ops – Bergen. Took-off MSG 06:05.

Took off to bomb U-boat pens. The wreckage was found later by a shepherd, on a hillside at Goldscleugh, near Rothbury, Scotland

F/O G R Duncan RCAF	K
P/O J W Hall	K
F/O W G Layng RCAF	K
F/O A Gaddess RCAF	K
Sgt W R Karstens RCAF	K
Sgt D A Trott RCAF	K
Sgt T B Tierney RCAF	K

October 9/10. 1944, Lancaster Mk X, KB754 VR-C. Ops – Bochum. Took-off MSG 20:39.

Hit by JU88 after bombing run. F/S McQueen was ejected from his turret by explosion. The crew rest in Reichswald Forest War Cemetery.

P/O A I Cohen RCAF	K
Sgt R A Campbell RCAF	K
F/O G W Murphy RCAF	K
F/S J H Goldfinch RCAF	K
Sgt R F Emerson RCAF	K
F/S L F O'Hare RCAF	K
F/S J F McQueen RCAF	POW

October 14, 1944, Lancaster Mk X, KB800 VR-C. Ops – Duisburg. Took-off MSG 06:15.

Both starboard engines caught fire northwest of the target area after the aircraft hit by flak. F/O Roy was thrown clear by an explosion and became the only survivor. The rest of his crew are buried in the Reichswald Forest War Cemetery.

F/O A M Roy RCAF	POW
Sgt G Adams	K
F/S H Sigal RCAF	K
F/O J N Therreault RCAF	K
W/O 1 L C Le Vasseur RCAF	K
W/O 1 R H Bowen RCAF	K
F/S R G Manwell RCAF	K

October 23. 1944, Lancaster Mk X, KB776 VR-F. Ops – Essen. Took-off MSG 16:13.

No details. The crew are buried in the Reichswald Forest War Cemetery.

S/L W C McGuffin DFC RCAF	K
Sgt J Mallabone	K
F/OR Molloy RCAF	K
F/O J Futiranski RCAF	K
F/S R C Schlievert RCAF	K
F/S R T Neville RCAF	K
F/S E Neufeld RCAF	K

October 28. 1944, Lancaster Mk X KB712 VR-L. Ops – Cologne. Took-off MSG 13:04.

This aircraft crashed at Hurth, 12-km southwest of Cologne. The crew, whose average age was 21, are buried in the Reichswald Forest War Cemetery.

F/L A N Nelligan RCAF	K
Sgt W E Hawkings	K
F/o J R Fichtner RCAF	K
F/O J A Nafziger RCAF	K
F/S W H Herman RCAF	K
Sgt E R Smith RCAF	K
Sgt B E Greenhalgh RCAF	K

November 1/2. 1944, Lancaster Mk X KB767 VR-U. Ops – Oberhausen. Took-off MSG 17:01.

This aircraft was first hit by flak and then a few minutes later by a fighter, which injured 3 members of the crew. F/O Cox somehow managed to get the very badly damaged Lancaster back to Manston where it was crash-landed.

F/O R L Cox RCAF	
Sgt F Dennis	
F/O S B Linsay RCAF	Inj
F/O A J Palanek RCAF	
F/O L W Sitlington RCAF	Inj
Sgt J Wilkins RCAF	
F/S R A Toane RCAF	Inj

November 24. 1944, Lancaster Mk X, KB785 VR-Y. Training.

Crashed near Sedgfield, Co Durham, after catching fire in the air, due to malfunction of the fuel jettison system

F/O R G Mansfield DFC RCAF	K
Sgt D G Newland	K
W/O 2 G H Warren-Darley RCAF	K
F/O A C Hirst RCAF	K
F/S D A Gunn RCAF	K
F/S L W Toth RCAF	K
F/S J J Murphy RCAF	K

December 6/7. 1944, Lancaster Mk X, KB779 VR-B. Ops – Osnabruck. Took-off MSG 16:40.

Lost without trace. The crew are commemorated on the Runnymede Memorial. Their average age was 21.

F/O B D Hyndman RCAF	K
Sgt R D Ovis	K
F/O G R Cheesman RCAF	K
Sgt G E Smith RCAF	K
Sgt L T Graham RCAF	K
Sgt D L Marcellus RCAF	K
F/S E M Hansen RCAF	K

December 24. 1944, Lancaster Mk X, KB715 VR-T. Ops – Lohausen. Took-off MSG 12:06.

The Starboard outer engine departed the wing when it was hit by flak. This also set fire to both inner engines. The crew baled out safely but German troops shot and killed F/O Hale just after he landed. He is buried in Rheinberg War Cemetery.

F/O T H Cowtan RCAF	POW
P/O J V Tanson RCAF	POW
Sgt C W Thompson RCAF	POW
F/O J L Cartier RCAF	POW
F/O R W Hale	K
Sgt G B Little RCAF	POW
Sgt F A Hecktor RCAF	POW

December 27/28. 1944, Lancaster Mk X, KB738 VR-D. Ops – Opladen. Took-off MSG 02:57.

Crashed 02:57 at Leverkusen-Wiesdorf, where the crew were initially buried. After the war they were relocated to the Rheinberg War Cemetery.

F/O F W How RCAF	K
Sgt J Atkinson	K
F/O R K Nickle RCAF	K
W/O 2 J A MacGregor RCAF	K
P/O C D Hubley RCAF	K
P/O C R Tait RCAF	K
P/O N R Springstein RCAF	K

December 29/30. 1944, Lancaster Mk X, KB753 VR-L. Ops – Scholven-Buer. Took-off MSG 14:58.

This aircraft exploded near Essen after a direct hit by flak. W/O 2 Rogers, the tail gunner, was thrown from his turret and was the only crewmember to survive. The remainder were buried in the Reichswald Forest War Cemetery.

P/O R F Adam RCAF	K
Sgt R E Eratt	K
W/O 2 L P Wakely RCAF	K
Sgt H C Tarzwell RCAF	K
W/O 1 F S Dennis RCAF	K
F/S J C Rhind RCAF	K
W/O 2 R G Rogers RCAF	POW

December 29/30. 1944, Lancaster Mk X, KB765 VR-Q. Ops – Scholven-Buer. Took-off MSG 14:54.

Exploded over Gelsenkirchen – Buer, after being hit by

flak and cannon fire from a fighter. Those that perished were initially buried at Gelsenkirchen but were taken to the Reichswald Forest War Cemetery after the war.

F/O R A McVicar RCAF	K
Sgt J Feldman RCAF	K
F/O V A Sorrenti RCAF	K
Sgt W G Morgan RCAF	K
F/S T J Maloney RCAF	K
F/S R C Conley RCAF	K
F/S W R McLeod RCAF	POW

419 losses 1945

January 2/3. 1945, Lancaster Mk X, KB700 VR-Z, Ops - Nuremberg. Took-off MSG 14:26.

This aircraft returned to Middleton at 23:38, suffering from hydraulic trouble, which caused problems with the flaps. Due to the excessive approach speed, caused by the flaps, the Lancaster was well down the runway by the time it touched down. It bounced heavily, ran off the end of the runway and came to a halt some 50 yards beyond. The Ruhr Express was undamaged, but as the crew were trying to get back onto the perimeter track in the dark, the starboard outer propeller hit a mechanical ditch digger and the aircraft caught fire and burned out. The crew escaped unhurt.

F/L A G R Warner

January 5/6. 1945, Lancaster Mk X, KB722 VR-A. Ops – Hannover. Took-off MSG 19:07.

Hit by fire from another Lancaster whilst outbound. Course was set for Brussels but later revised to Juvincourt. Fog there made the crew head for Manston. Meanwhile, a gap in the cloud was seen and P/O Mallen crash-landed in a field near Guise, 25 km E/N/E of St Quentin.

P/O N D Mallan RCAF	Inj
Sgt P N Hall	Inj
F/O J A Miller RCAF	
Sgt R S Dickson RCAF	InJ
W/O 2 R B Cameron RCAF	
Sgt N R Poole RCAF	Inj
Sgt C Drinka RCAF	

January 14/15. 1945, Lancaster Mk X, KB769 VR-I. Ops – Leuna. Took-off MSG 18:42.

Shot down by a night fighter whilst homebound from attacking a synthetic oil plant. F/O Eddy baled out and landed in some trees and was not badly injured. After the war the graves of those that died were discovered Bad Neustadt and taken to Hannover War Cemetery.

F/L G O Tedford RCAF	K
Sgt R J Williams	K
F/O J Q Eddy RCAF	POW
F/O G D Spencer RCAF	K
P/O C S Thompson RCAF	K
F/S H M Rumball RCAF	K
F/S A G McKay RCAF	K

January 14/15. 1945, Lancaster Mk X, KB799 VR-W. Ops – Leuna. Took-off MSG 18:42.

This aircraft was hit by flak, which holed the fuel tanks. The engines failed whilst the crew were trying to reach the allied lines and so F/O Vatne gave the order to abandon.

He remained at the controls to enable his crew to escape but was unable to jump in time.

F/O N R Vatne RCAF	K
Sgt B C Mitchel RCAF	POW
F/O H R Eager RCAF	POW
F/O N V Hoas RCAF	POW
F/S E Chatwin RCAF	POW
F/S R C Woods RCAF	POW
P/O G C Woods RCAF	POW

Feb 2/3. 1945, Lancaster Mk X, KB750 VR-N. Ops – Wiesbaden. Took-off MSG 20:41.

Hit by flak whilst homebound and crashed close to the village of Wolf, 3 km N/N/W of Traben-Trabbach, 50 km S/S/W of Koblenz. Only the tail gunner, McTaggart, had time to obey the abandon signal.

P/O B W Martin RCAF	K
Sgt J McAfee	K
F/O R W Hodgson RCAF	K
F/O J A McDonald RCAF	K
F/S P F English RCAF	K
F/S R A Nesbet RCAF	K
F/S W J McTaggart RCAF	POW

February 4/5. 1945, Lancaster Mk X, KB 787 VR-M. Ops – Bonn. Took-off MSG 17:23.

Collided with a 433 squadron Lancaster in cloud whilst outbound and along with the other aircraft crashed Vielsalm in the Belgian Ardennes. The crews of both aircraft are now buried in Hotton War Cemetery.

F/L J P Barlow RCAF	K
F/O L F Edmonds	K
F/O D W Spence RCAF	K
F/L D J Buchanan DFC RCAF	K
P/O C T Sutter RCAF	
F/O J A Gibbs RCAF	K
F/L W T Kearns RCAF	K

February 20/21. 1945, Lancaster Mk X, KB804 VR-E. Ops – Dortmund. Took-off MSG 21:26.

Hit by flak. The starboard fuel tanks were set alight, and the incendiaries, causing a fire in the bomb bay. F/O Blaney gave the order to abandon but had no time to jump himself and W/O Hanna's chute did not deploy. Both airmen that died are buried in the Reichswald Forest War Cemetery.

F/O L A Blaney RCAF	K
Sgt T S Instone	POW
W/O 2 D Hanna RCAF	K
F/O P H Owen RCAF	POW
P/O A Kindret RCAF	POW
F/S L J Nozzolillo RCAF	POW
P/O R Althan RCAF	POW

March 5/6. 1945, Lancaster Mk X, KB845 VR-L. Ops – Chemnitz. Took-off MSG 16:29.

Due to severe icing conditions on the way home, this aircraft suffered control problems and crashed at Drayton Parsloe, 10 Miles N/N/E of Aylsbury, Buckinghamshire. All are buried in Brookwood Military Cemetery.

F/O C L Reitlo RCAF	K
Sgt J A King RCAF	K
P/O J E Hanley RCAF	K

F/O W N De Witt RCAF	K
P/O F R Leet RCAF	K
Sgt N R Poole RCAF	K
F/O G J Hollinger RCAF	K

March 7/8. 1945, Lancaster Mk X, KB797 VR-K. Ops – Dessau. Took-off MSG 16:57.

The 5 crewmen who died were lost without trace and are commemorated on the Runnymede Memorial.

F/O B T MacNeill RCAF	K
Sgt R T Wilson RCAF	K
F/O W E Short RCAF	K
Sgt E V Beach RCAF	K
F/S H O Cole RCAF	POW
Sgt D C Jamieson RCAF	POW
Sgt R L Mitchell RCAF	K

March 15/16. 1945, Lancaster Mk X, KB814 VR-N. Ops – Hagen. Took-off MSG 16:25.

Crashed near to Monchengladbach at 20:45, after being attacked by a night fighter. At the time, the crewmembers who lost their lives were buried in the U.S. Military Cemetery Margraten, near Maastricht. They now rest in Nederweert War Cemetery.

F/S C W Parish RCAF	K
Sgt P V Bowman RCAF	Evd
F/O H R Hennessey RCAF	K
F/S C Ginter RCAF	Evd
F/S C H Vickery RCAF	K
Sgt T J Bristow RCAF	Evd
F/S M W Bredin RCAF	K

March 15/16. 1945, Lancaster Mk X, KB870 VR-K. Ops - Hagen. Took-off MSG 16:38.

Attacked by a night fighter and shot down over territory held by allied forces. The crewmen that died were first buried at Margraten. After the war they were relocated to Nederweert War Cemetery. Those injured were initially treated at a U.S. Hospital before being flown back to the UK.

F/L M W McLaughlin RCAF	Inj
F/S W W Lightfoot RCAF	Inj
F/O H L Garriock RCAF	K
F/O B V Saunders RCAF	Inj
W/O 1 A Sutherland RCAF	K
F/O E B Carleton DFM RCAF	K
P/O J M Charbonneau RCAF	Inj

March 20/21. 1945, Lancaster Mk X, KB786 VR-P. Ops – Heide. Took-off MSG 01:51.

Crashed at Odderade, 7 km E/S/E of Hemmingstedt, after being shot down by a night fighter. Like many rear gunners, F/S Atken was thrown clear when the aircraft exploded. The remainder of the crew were buried in Hamburg's Ohlsdorf Cemetery.

F/P R W Miller RCAF	K
Sgt S D Booth	K
F/L H B Rubin DFC RCAF	K
F/O A J Palanek RCAF	K
F/S C A Elliot RCAF	K
F/O L C Croucher RCAF	K
F/S J W Aitken RCAF	POW

March 31. 1945, Lancaster Mk X, KB761 VR-H. Ops – Hamburg. Took-off MSG 06:01.

Shot down by a Me262 jet fighter. All are commemorated on the Runnymede Memorial.

F/L H A Metivier RCAF	K
Sgt W M Sommerville RCAF	K
F/O J Todd RCAF	K
F/O R O Johnson RCAF	K
F/S G Matuszewski RCAF	K
F/S H S Tulk RCAF	K
F/S E E Morphy RCAF	K

March 31. 1945, Lancaster Mk X, KB869 VR-Q. Ops – Hamburg. Took-off MSG 06:01.

Crashed 09:07 near Hittfeld, 9 km south of Harburg after being shot down by a Me262. The crewmembers that died are buried in Becklingen War Cemetery.

F/O D S Bowes RCAF	K
Sgt J Rea RCAF	K
F/S G R Berry RCAF	POW
F/O J J Gladish RCAF	K
F/S B MacClennan RCAF	K
F/S R W Rowlands RCAF	POW
F/S W H Milne RCAF	POW

April 8/9. 1945, Lancaster Mk X, KB752 VR-V. Ops – Hamburg. Took-off MSG 19:17.

The starboard inner failed on the way to the target. On the way home the starboard outer caught fire. The flames were extinguished but with two port engines out the order to abandon had to be given. Sgt McGrath managed to evade capture after landing behind enemy lines.

F/O H R Cram RCAF	
F/S J T Case	
F/O W Olenoski RCAF	
F/O F S Crawford RCAF	
W/O 2 C S Hanna RCAF	
Sgt E K McGrath RCAF	Evd
Sgt G R Hughes RCAF	

April 13/14. 1945, Lancaster Mk X, KB866 VR-M. Ops – Kiel. Took-off MSG 20:22.

Lost without trace. All are commemorated on the Runnymede Memorial.

F/S C C Maclaren RCAF	K
Sgt G A Livingstone RCAF	K
F/O C R Loft RCAF	K
F/O D W Wincott RCAF	K
W/O 1 W Henderson RCAF	K
F/S E R Wightman RCAF	K
Sgt G J Jones RCAF	K

April 23. 1945, Lancaster Mk X, KB762 VR-J. Training.

The undercarriage collapsed whilst taxiing to hangar 1 for maintenance. Although the aircraft was declared a write-off the crew were unhurt.

F/L E C Peters

Total of 419 aircraft lost from Croft. Operational - 5. Non-operational - 1. Aircrew killed - 27. POWs - 1. Injured - 4.

Total of 419 aircraft lost from Middleton, operational - 118. Non-operational - 7. Total - 125.   Aircrew killed - 515. POWs - 182. Injured - 25. Evaded - 31.

Bomber losses 428

June 11/12 1943, Wellington Mk X, HE322 NA-J, Ops - Dusseldorf. Took off MSG 22:55, Crashed.

During the take-off the aircraft crashed. The 4,000-lb 'Cookie' it was carrying exploded. With the exception of the pilot, Sgt Lachman RCAF, the crew were killed. When found, Sgt Lachman was still strapped in his seat, which had been detached from the aircraft and blown 30 yards away. After being treated by SSQ staff he was transferred to The RAF Hospital at Northallerton, Yorks.

Sgt W Lachman RCAF	Inj
P/O J C Jette RCAF	K
Sgt R Askew	K
F/S E R Marchand RCAF	K
Sgt M P Scullion RCAF	K

July 9/10 1943, Halifax Mk V, DK229 NA-W, Ops - Gelsenkirchen. Took off MSG 22:36.

Hit by flak, and abandoned near Cologne. S/L Bowden, who was close to completing his second tour, is buried in Rheinberg War Cemetery.

S/L F H Bowden DFC and Bar	K
Sgt H McGeach RCAF	POW
Sgt H N Rowe	POW
P/O R J Gritten	POW
Sgt A J Reynolds	Evd
Sgt J W Hurst	POW
P/O B McK Fitzgerald	POW

July 13/14 1943, Halifax Mk V, DK228 NA-D, Ops - Aachen. Took off MSG 23:38.

Crashed at Mesnil-St-Blaise, 32 km south of Namur, Belgium, after being shot down by a night fighter. The crew are buried in Florennes Communal Cemetery.

F/L W G Weeks RCAF	K
Sgt S Zayets RCAF	K
F/O E D Robertson RCAF	K
P/O W F Stewart RCAF	K
Sgt J R Goodfellow RCAF	K
Sgt A D Dawson	K
F/O H B Ward RCAF	K

July 13/14 1943, Halifax Mk V, DK257 NA-Q, Ops - Aachen. Took off MSG 23:45, crashed 02:00.

Crashed Genderen, 20 km north of Tilburg, Holland, after being shot down by a night fighter. The two air gunners have no known graves, and are commemorated on the Runnymede memorial.

F/L D S Morgan RCAF	POW
Sgt D Brown	POW
F/O F H Ditchburn RCAF	POW
P/O J P O'Leary RCAF	Evd
P/O B L Gillis RCAF	POW
Sgt T H Pritchard	K
Sgt M Edwards	K

July 13/14 1943, Halifax Mk V, ED209 NA-C, Ops - Aachen. Took off MSG 23:52, abandoned 02:30.

As this aircraft departed the target area, it was hit by flak, The crew managed to continue on a W/S/W course, for a further 80-km, before having to bale out near Marche-en-Famenne, Belgium.

P/O W D Ross RCAF	POW
Sgt D J Webb RCAF	Evd
Sgt W B Webber RCAF	POW
Sgt T Chiszczyk RCAF	POW
Sgt A M Winter	POW
Sgt J C Hayes RCAF	POW
Sgt E A Bridge RCAF	Evd

July 29/30 1943, Halifax Mk V, DK239 NA-Q, Ops - Hamburg. Took off MSG 22:23.

Attacked by a night fighter and exploded near Luneburg, 40 km S/S/E of Hamburg. The crew were initially buried at Luneburg, Sgt Bates now rests in Becklingen War Cemetery, whilst the remainder of those that died are buried in Hamburg's Ohlsdorf Cemetery.

Sgt D H Bates RCAF	K
Sgt T I Hughes RCAF	K
Sgt W G Arlidge RCAF	K
Sgt P Demcoe RCAF	POW
Sgt J Galloway	K
Sgt G S Nault RCAF	K
Sgt L J Pelland RCAF	K

August 2/3 1943, Halifax Mk V, EB212 NA-U, Ops - Hamburg. Took off MSG 22:34.

Presumed lost over the sea. Only the bodies of F/O Funkhouser and Sgt Lunn were found and are buried in the Neuen Friedhof at Busum.They are now buried in Kiel War Cemetery. The rest have no known graves, and are commemorated on the Runnymede Memorial.

P/O V T Sylvester RCAF	K
F/O H G Funkhouser RCAF	K
Sgt D Charlsworth	K
Sgt P J Forde	K
F/S G K Crighton-Kelly	K
Sgt T L Rose	K
Sgt J W Lunn	K
F/S E G Smith RCAF	K

August 2/3 1943, Halifax Mk V, EB274 NA-H, Ops - Hamburg. Took off MSG 22:47.

Lost without trace, The crew are commemorated on the Runnymede Memorial.

Sgt M Chepil DFM RCAF	K
F/O F L Rogers RCAF	K
Sgt S J Williams	K
Sgt A Garalick RCAF	K
Sgt M F Spencer	K
Sgt M Evans	K
Sgt J R Burfield	K
F/O E J Andrews RCAF	K

August 17/18 1943, Halifax Mk V, DK230 NA-V, Ops - Peenemunde. Took of MSG 21:09.

Crashed in the Baltic. 6 of those that died are buried in Berlin's 1939-1945 War Cemetery. Sgt Lewis's body was never found, he is remembered on the Runnymede Memorial.

F/L G W Fanson RCAF	K
Sgt R A Lewis	K
P/O D H Orr RCAF	K
Sgt J D McNeill RCAF	K
Sgt L M Banks RCAF	K
Sgt R G McCallum	K
Sgt J A Leighton RCAF	K

August 17/18 1943, Halifax Mk V, EB211 NA-F, Ops - Peenemunde. Took off MSG 21:21

This aircraft crashed into the Baltic. The crew are buried in Berlin's 1939-1945 War Cemetery.

Sgt J F Sheridan RCAF	K
Sgt D Kennedy	K
Sgt M B Murphy RCAF	K
Sgt T B Lifman RCAF	K
Sgt W L Cogger RCAF	K
Sgt N R Mitchell	K
Sgt E R Marks RCAF	K

August 17/18 1943, Halifax Mk V, DK238 NA-I, Ops - Peenemunde. Took off MSG 21:28.

Crashed on the German Coast near Barth-Velgast, 74 km W/N/W of Peenemunde. Sgt Blackmore and F/S Williams are buried in the 1939-1945 War Cemetery in Berlin.

Sgt W W Blackmore RCAF	K
Sgt F S Williams	K
Sgt N F Oliver RCAF	POW
Sgt W S Wood	POW
F/S J J Richard RCAF	POW
Sgt G F Hodgson	POW
F/S R G Seaborn RCAF	POW

August 23/24 1943, Halifax Mk V, DK267 NA-H, Ops - Berlin. Took off MSG 20:25, crashed 02:00.

Badly damaged by a night fighter outbound, some of the crew baled out. The remainder headed for Sweden, the aircraft eventually crashed near the Swedish village of Annelov, 30 km north of Malmo. Sadly, Sgt Crampton became jammed in the escape hatch and was killed.

F/S H A Read RCAF	Int
Sgt G W Patterson RCAF	POW
Sgt L S Bates RCAF	POW
F/O J J McQuade RCAF	Int
Sgt C E Crampton	K
Sgt J Taylor	POW
Sgt W S Kerr RCAF	POW

August 27/28 1943, Halifax Mk V, EB216 NA-R, Ops - Nuremberg. Took off MSG 21:17.

Shot down by a night fighter, The 5 members of the crew that died are buried in Durnbach War Cemetery.

Sgt A L Mitchell	K
F/O J A MacT McLeish RCAF	K
Sgt H A Gordon	K
Sgt G S Brown RCAF	POW
Sgt C Lunny RCAF	POW
Sgt C R Lott	POW
Sgt A E Gourd	K
Sgt J T Hamer RCAF	K

August 31 1943, Halifax Mk V, DK233 NA-X, Ops - Berlin. Took off MSG 20:20

Whilst on the way home this aircraft was hit by flak, which damaged the port inner and started a fire in the wing. The flames spread and the aircraft had to be abandoned. It crashed near Oberhaching. Those that died are commemorated on the Runnymede Memorial.

Sgt J D Este RCAF	K
Sgt H C Burdoff	POW
Sgt M Macoulay RCAF	POW
Sgt R S Dutka RCAF	POW
Sgt Haddon	POW
Sgt S E Towle RCAF	K
Sgt R W Briggs-Jude RCAF	K

August 31 1943, Halifax Mk V, DK249 NA-K, Ops - Berlin. Took off MSG 20:18.

Crashed at Holzdorf. The Crew are buried in the Berlin 1939-1945 War Cemetery.

Sgt B R Harrison RCAF	K
Sgt R Williams	K
W/O J R Prockter	K
Sgt T K Green RCAF	K
Sgt R C Bradley	K
Sgt W J Soulsby	K
Sgt G S Feakes RCAF	K

September 6/7 1943, Halifax Mk V, DK196 NA-Z, Ops - Munich. Took off MSG 19:29.

Having reached a position close to Strasbourg on the way out, the aircraft developed engine trouble, and had to turn back. The ailing bomber re-traced its steps, but after covering 227 -kms, height could not be maintained, and the Halifax crash-landed on a hillside, close to Vertus, 37 km south of Reims, France. The pilot, Sgt Brown, was killed. Although he was buried close to the crash site at the time, he now rests in the Canadian War Cemetery at Dieppe.

Sgt W McI Brown RCAF	K
Sgt H G Brown	POW
Sgt P F Elco RCAF	POW
Sgt J A Pickup RCAF	POW
Sgt J I Francis	POW
Sgt E N Bongard RCAF	POW
Sgt J T Cousineau RCAF	POW

September 15/16 1943, Halifax Mk V, LK913 NA-N, Ops - Montlucon. Took off MSG 19:58.

Hit by incendiaries dropped by another aircraft. W/C Smith carried out a crash-landing at Cerilly, 35-km N/N/E of Montlucon.

W/C D W Smith	POW
P/O E N Bell RCAF	POW
Sgt C Hayworth	Evd
F/L E B Mason RCAF	Evd
F/O H Dereniuk RCAF	POW
P/O R O Malins	POW
P/O J M Nelmes RCAF	Evd
F/L J M Forman RCAF	Evd

September 22/23 1943, Halifax Mk V, LK635 NA-H, Ops - Hannover. Took off MSG 18:28.

Lost without trace. Commemorated on the Runnymede Memorial.

F/O H E McRae RCAF	K
Sgt D E Jeffery	K
Sgt L Cotton	K
Sgt W E Dickson RCAF	K
Sgt A R Bohn	K
Sgt J Wright	K
Sgt E G Miller RCAF	K

September 22/23 1943, Halifax Mk V, LK914 NA-K, Ops - Hannover. Took off MSG 18:31.

No details available, the crew are buried in Becklingen War Cemetery.

F/O K W Jones	K
Sgt G F Fox	K
F/O W C Ingraham RCAF	K
Sgt L Pelmear	K
Sgt C W Palmer	K
Sgt V Moore	K
Sgt E G Bartram	POW

September 23/24 1943, Halifax Mk V, DK371 NA-Q, Ops - Mannheim. Took off MSG 18:57.

This aircraft was first hit by flak and soon after by a night fighter whilst at 19,000 feet. Crashed at Geinsheim, 24-km southwest of the target. The four crewmembers that died are buried in Rheinberg War Cemetery.

F/L H F Davis RCAF	POW
Sgt G R Annand RCAF	POW
Sgt N L Reed RCAF	K
Sgt F P Sharp RCAF	K
Sgt R McK Alexander	POW
P/O V A Stewart RCAF	K
P/O R T Zdan RCAF	K

September 23/24 1943, Halifax Mk V, EB207 NA-B, Ops - Mannheim. Took off MSG 18:48.

No details available. All are buried in Rheinberg War Cemetery.

P/O W A Hadden RCAF	K
Sgt J Curran	K
Sgt A F Morris	K
Sgt S A Whitby	K
Sgt P J Flower	K
Sgt C W Renwick RCAF	K
Sgt A Yuill	K

September 27/28 1943, Halifax Mk II, JB968 NA-R, Ops - Hannover. Took off MSG 19:21.

No details, The crew are buried in Hannover War Cemetery. This aircraft was the first 428 squadron Halifax Mk II to go missing.

F/O R H Sherback RCAF	K
Sgt D B Stone RCAF	K
F/O F T Manners RCAF	K
P/O E D MacMurchy RCAF	K
Sgt J Kirby	K
Sgt D W Matthews RCAF	K
Sgt W E McKee RCAF	K

September 27/28 1943, Halifax Mk V, DK252 NA-O, Ops - Hannover. Took off MSG 19:19.

After 3 hours in the air this aircraft turned back after encountering severe icing conditions. Having reached the

Humber on the way back the port inner went U/S, followed shortly after by the starboard inner. The pitot tube froze, causing the airspeed indicator to fail. After instructing the crew to abandoned the aircraft the pilot carried out a wheels up landing at RAF Ludford Magna. No injuries.

P/O M Kogan RCAF
Sgt L F Edmonds
F/O F D Jaclman RCAF
P/O M J Johnson RCAF
Sgt E O Knowles
Sgt J Silverman RCAF
Sgt J M Custeau RCAF

September 27/28 1943, Halifax Mk V, DK270 NA-U, Ops - Hannover. Took off MSG 19:20, crashed 01:09.

Crashed at Parham House Farm, Parham, 13 miles northeast of Ipswich, Suffolk, after overshooting. Sgt Mercer RCAF is buried in Cambridge City Cemetery, the remainder of the dead are buried in their own home towns. Sgt Wainwright was uninjured.

Sgt R Wilson	Inj
Sgt W F Smith	K
Sgt G V Whitley	K
P/O B W Roughton	Inj
Sgt A J Lucas	K
Sgt J D Mercer RCAF	K
Sgt E P Wainwright	

September 27/28 1943, Halifax Mk V, EB215 NA-T, Ops - Hannover. Took off MSG 19:17, crashed 00:17.

Crashed at Oosterhof, 10 km N/N/E of Apeldoorn, Holland. After being hit by flak. Those that perished are buried in Epe General Cemetery.

Sgt J E Farmer	K
Sgt J W Satchell	K
Sgt D A Griffin	POW
Sgt T Wilson	K
Sgt J T Wilson	K
Sgt E T Springett	K
Sgt A Stuart	K
Sgt W E Mussen	K

September 27/28 1943, Halifax Mk V, LK915 NA-V, Ops - Hannover. Took off MSG 19:15

It is thought that this aircraft was shot down by a night fighter. The crew are buried in Hannover War Cemetery.

F/O M G Whalley RCAF	POW
Sgt J I Jones	K
F/O C M Butcher RCAF	K
F/O W B Higgins RCAF	POW
Sgt F C Jackson	K
Sgt J M Morrison RCAF	K
Sgt E S Driscoll RCAF	K

October 3/4 1943, Halifax Mk V, EB210 NA-E, Ops - Kassel. Took off MSG 18:48, landed 01:00.

Badly damaged by a Fw 190, landed RAF Tangmere, Sussex, deemed beyond worthwhile repair. No injuries.

F/S C R Newton RAAF
Sgt J M Jacobs RCAF
Sgt J Allan
Sgt K C Marris

Sgt V Mudford RCAF
Sgt A Jackson
Sgt F Wallbridge
Sgt H P Gough

October 3/4 1943, Halifax Mk V, EB213 NA-G, Ops - Kassel. Took off MSG 18:52.

Crashed at Hofgeismer, 22 km N/N/W of the target. The 6 men that died are buried in Hannover War Cemetery.

W/O F B Edwards	K
P/O R P Goldstein RCAF	K
Sgt E R Burbage	POW
Sgt F Gration RCAF	POW
Sgt G M Herburt RCAF	K
Sgt A J Hodkins	K
Sgt J Lundy RCAF	K
Sgt A J Cadeau RCAF	K

October 3/4 1943, Halifax Mk V, EB214 NA-S, Ops - Kassel. Took off MSG 18:39.

Crashed at Sehlen, 50-km southwest of the target, after being hit by flak. Sgt's McArthur and Elliot are buried in Hannover War Cemetery. The tail gunner, Sgt McDonald, was badly injured, but eventually recovered, after spending several weeks in Hospital.

Sgt K A McArthur RCAF	K
Sgt L F Buttler RCAF	POW
F/O R A Thompson RCAF	POW
P/O T J Elliot RCAF	K
Sgt E W Ranson	POW
Sgt R R Raymond RCAF	POW
Sgt R McDonald	POW

October 4/5 1943, Halifax Mk V, LK931 NA-W, Ops - Frankfurt. Took off MSG 17:25

Crashed outbound at Ubereisenbach, 44 km N/N/E of Arlon, Belgium, after being shot down by a night fighter. The aircraft would have had a further 180 km to fly to reach the target.

F/S J Harkins	Evd
Sgt A Scott	POW
Sgt D J Richards	POW
Sgt S A Baldwin	POW
Sgt A Parkinson	POW
Sgt G P Columbus RCAF	POW
Sgt N W Lee	Evd

October 22/23 1943, Halifax Mk V, LK908, Ops - Kassel. Took off MSG 17:17, landed 23:30.

Diverted to RAF Snetterton Heath, Norfolk, after being hit by flak. The tail took much of the brunt of the flak and both gunners were hit. The tail gunner, Sgt Clemenhagen , buried in Cambridge City Cemetery. The aircraft was deemed beyond repair, and was struck off charge, 16th of November 1943.

Sgt E J Sykes	
Sgt A C Rule RCAF	
Sgt T Grayham	
Sgt C Ovenden RCAF	
Sgt G H Bibby	
Sgt P Stuart	Inj
Sgt T F Clemenhagen RCAF	K

November 3/4 1943, Halifax Mk V, LK954 NA-E, Ops - Dusseldorf. Took off MSG 16:47, crashed 21:33.

Crashed at South Kyme, 10 miles northwest of Boston, Lincolnshire. With the exception of Sgt Weigh, the crew rest in Cambridge City Cemetery.

F/O R G Eaton RCAF	K
F/O A K Hodgkinson RCAF	K
Sgt A E Moss	K
F/O L L Whitham RCAF	K
P/O B A Elmore RCAF	K
Sgt A F Weigh	K
Sgt H B Shimwell	K
P/O A E MacKenzie RCAF	K

November 19/20 1943, Halifax Mk V, LK950 NA-T, Ops - Leverkusen. Took off MSG 16:16.

This aircraft returned to the UK and was abandoned over Kent, after being hit by flak near the target. The Halifax crashed into a cemetery in Canterbury. The mid-upper gunner, Sgt McEwan RCAF, was mortally wounded when the flak hit the aircraft, he has no known grave.

F/S K Hawthorne RCAF	
Sgt C H Kirtland	
F/O F R Storen RCAF	
F/S D L Smith RCAF	
WO1 L L Fournier RCAF	
Sgt J A McEwan RCAF	K
Sgt L J Oshowy RCAF	

November 19/20 1943, Halifax Mk V, LK956 NA-S, Ops - Leverkusen. Took off MSG 16:06.

This aircraft was badly hit by flak near Bonn, whilst on the way home. The crew managed to escape the Bonn defences, and managed to reach Holland before having to bale out.

F/S H C Shepherd RCAF	POW
Sgt J M Walker	POW
F/O D R Knight RCAF	POW
F/S D K MacGillivray RCAF	Evd
Sgt S J Stevens	POW
Sgt N H Michie RCAF	Evd
Sgt S Munns	Evd

November 22/23. 1943, Halifax Mk V, LK906 NA-D. Ops – Berlin. Took-off MSG 16:38.

This aircraft crashed at Scherenbostel, 15 km N/N/W of Hannover. The crew are buried in the town's War Cemetery.

Sgt J M Jacob RCAF	K
Sgt A Auckland	K
Sgt W R Boucher	K
Sgt A B Radbourne RCAF	K
Sgt W D Bracken	K
Sgt M F Donaldson RCAF	K
Sgt G Kemp	K

November 25/26. 1943, Halifax Mk V, LK969 NA-G, Ops - Frankfurt. Took off MSG 23:33.

Whilst flying at 19,000 feet over Frankfurt, this aircraft was attacked by a night fighter, which during its first pass, set the bomber's starboard inner on fire. The second pass claimed the life of Sgt Barske RCAF. He is buried in Durnbach War Cemetery.

S/L J R Beggs RCAF	POW
Sgt T C Qualey	POW
F/S J P McMaster RCAF	POW
Sgt P J Barske RCAF	K
F/O G M Ruff RCAF	POW
Sgt F Moore RCAF	POW
Sgt G W Redwood	POW

November 26/27. 1943, Halifax Mk II, JN966 NA-V, Ops - Stuttgart. Took off MSG 16:51.

Collided on final approach to Middleton St George with a 103 Squadron Lancaster, from RAF Elsham Wolds. Unlike the 428 aircraft, the 103 Lancaster had not been cleared to land. The only survivor was Sgt S T Bowyer, from the 103 squadron aircraft, which had diverted to Middleton due to bad weather at its base.

F/S R M Buck	K
Sgt J H Muir	K
Sgt W S Bruce	K
Sgt W H Wade RCAF	K
Sgt A H Biggs	K
Sgt L J Shirvell	K
Sgt M J Lindsay RCAF	K

December 20/21 1943, Halifax Mk V, EB252 NA-P, Ops - Frankfurt. Took off MSG 16:00.

No details available. With the exception of F/O J D Elliot RCAF the crew are buried in Rheinberg War Cemetery.

P/O W J Armour DFC RAAF	K
F/O C R Sandes RCAF	K
Sgt S P Page	K
F/O J D Elliott RCAF	POW
F/S L P Coupe	K
F/S H C Dumbrill	K
F/S F C Clucas RAAF	K
F/S J J Moon RAAF	K

December 20/21 1943, Halifax Mk V, LK928 NA-B, Ops - Frankfurt. Took off MSG 16:14.

This aircraft crashed at Glees, 25 km W/N/W of Koblenz. With the exception of the pilot, F/S Keighan RCAF, and F/S Elmer Tycoles RCAF, the crew were buried on December 27th. Since the end of the war, they were relocated to their present resting place, at the Rheinberg War Cemetery. Elmer Tycoles survived the crash, but his death was recorded on December 24th, whilst at Reserve Lager – Maria Loast. Like many Canadian airmen, after the war, Elmer Tycoles was to have a Canadian lake named after him. This was the last aircraft to be lost by 428 during 1943.

F/S J L Keighan RCAF	POW
Sgt G H Jessiman RCAF	K
F/O K M Mosher RCAF	K
F/S E L Tycoles RCAF	K
Sgt J P Slater	K
Sgt G Kensall	K
Sgt T S Dagnall	K

428 losses 1944

January 20/21 1944, Halifax Mk V, LK739 NA-P. Ops - Berlin. Took off MSG 16:38.

This aircraft was shot down by flak.

F/S F F Reain RCAF	Evd
Sgt W E Fell RCAF	Evd
F/O A R Fisher RCAF	Evd
F/O Y Lavois RCAF	Evd
Sgt W T Banner	Evd
Sgt W R Wynveen RCAF	POW
Sgt L R Fryer RCAF	Evd

January 21/22 1944, Halifax Mk V, DK237 NA-L. Ops - Magdeburg. Took off MSG 19:32.

Shot down by a night fighter over the target area. The mid-upper gunner Sgt Smith was badly injured and died later in hospital. He is buried in Berlin's 1939-1945 War Cemetery.

F/S R E Terry RCAF	POW
Sgt I P Roberts RCAF	POW
F/S H L Allen RCAF	POW
Sgt A H Murdoch RCAF	POW
W/O2 O P Yarnold RCAF	POW
Sgt S J Smith RCAF	Inj
Sgt N E Gregor RCAF	POW

April 17/18 1944, Halifax Mk II, JN973 NA-U. Ops - Gardening. Took off MSG 20:32.

Lost without trace. All are commemorated on the Runnymede Memorial.

P/O G W Lillico RCAF	K
Sgt J Doyle	K
W/O2 W K Johnson RCAF	K
F/S T Zbytnuik RCAF	K
P/O J M Westlake RCAF	K
Sgt J G Manson RCAF	K
Sgt W J Olmstead RCAF	K

April 20/21 1944, Halifax Mk II, JP113 NA-A. Ops - Lens. Took off MSG 20:55.

The crew were ordered to bale out after the aircraft was damaged by a night fighter. Three did so, but the captain was able to maintain control and return to the UK. The aircraft crash-landed at 01:20 at Attlebridge airfield, Norfolk. P/O Shaw died of his injuries and is buried in Southowram Churchyard, Brighouse, Yorkshire.

F/L C G Ford RCAF	Inj
Sgt J W Carrigan	Inj
F/O N R McGregor RCAF	Evd
F/O A H Murphy RCAF	POW
F/S E S Jones	
F/O B D Ardis RCAF	Inj
P/O A Shaw MiD	Inj

April 20/21 1944, Halifax Mk II, JP199 NA-O. Ops - Gardening. Took-off MSG 21:15.

An engine caught fire whilst the aircraft was at 20,000 feet over French waters. Due to control problems the aircraft was partially abandoned, after which it crashed near Dielert Ladygrove Farm near Discot, Berkshire. S/L McGurgan and F/O England rest in Brookwood Military Cemetery.

S/L F R McGugan RCAF	K
Sgt R F Ellis	
F/O T L Steele RCAF	
F/O G A England RCAF	K
W/O2 N C Mason RCAF	

Sgt J W Eyre	
Sgt L Lapond RCAF	

April 23/24 1944, Halifax Mk II, LW285 NA-Z. Ops - Gardening. Took-off MSG 20:46.

This aircraft was attacked at 13,000 feet by a JU88 and badly damaged and Sgt Jerry was wounded. F/O Blake headed the Halifax for Sweden, where the aircraft was abandoned at 9,000 feet after F/O Blake experienced control problems.

F/O W V Blake DFC RCAF	K
Sgt J Danskin	Evd
F/O N A Bell RCAF	Evd
F/O W D Watt RCAF	Evd
W/O C Graham	Evd
Sgt T Jerry RCAF	Evd
P/O J T Houston	Evd

June 11/12 1944, Halifax Mk II, JN953 NA-. Training.

After a loss of power from its port outer engine, this aircraft was forced-landed near Claxton Hall, 7 miles northeast of York, after being partially abandoned. The Halifax was destroyed in the resulting fire. F/O Martin's injuries included 4 fractured vertebrae, a broken ankle and burns.

F/O J Martin RCAF	Inj

July 4/5 1944, Lancaster Mk X, KB756 NA-Q. Ops - Villeneuve. Took-off MSG 21:43.

This was the first Lancaster to be lost by 428. It crashed at La Mailleraye-sur-Seine, 7 km S/S/E of Caudebec-en-Caux. P/O Gay and F/S Swartz are buried in La Mailleraye-sur-Seine Communal Cemetery.

P/O W C Gay RCAF	K
Sgt P Smith	POW
F/O W C Cullen RCAF	Evd
P/O R M Woychuk RCAF	POW
F/S W S Yates	Evd
P/O A H Pritchard	Evd
F/S S J Swartz RCAF	K

July 24/25. 1944, Lancaster Mk X, KB740 NA-V. Ops – Stuttgart. Took off MSG 21:09.

Written off at 03:26, whilst attempting to land at Woodbridge, Suffolk, after colliding with another aircraft over France. No injuries.

F/O C M Corbet RCAF	
Sgt R Enfield	
F/O S F Bryans RCAF	
F/O F L Jones RCAF	
Sgt A MacNnaught RCAF	
Sgt D Daidson RCAF	
Sgt J Sanduluk RCAF	

July 28/29 1944. Lancaster Mk X, KB759 NA-K. Ops - Hamburg. Took-off MSG 22:36.

Lost without trace. All are commemorated on the Runnymede Memorial

P/O T E Magill RCAF	K
F/O R Parsons RCAF	K
Sgt A E Attewell RCAF	K
P/O J A Urquhart RCAF	K

F/S T G Murdoch RCAF	K
F/L B L Smith DFM	K
F/S H A Adams RCAF	K
F/S F B Thaine RCAF	K

August 12/13 1944. Lancaster Mk X, KB758 NA-Z. Ops - Brunswick. Took-off MSG 21:03.

Crashed at 00:15 near Winsen, a town on the river Aller, 13 km northwest of Celle. With the exception of F/O McGregor and F/O Greer, the crew are buried in Hannover's War Cemetery.

F/O J A McGregor RCAF	POW
F/S W J Hardwick	K
F/O C Greer RCAF	POW
F/O J E Spaggett RCAF	K
P/O H A Murphy RCAF	K
F/S P A Crowley RCAF	K
F/S M Sawry RCAF	K

August 16/17 1944, Lancaster Mk X, KB751 NA-Q. Ops - Stettin. Took-off MSG

Crashed into the Baltic. F/O Fairgrieve is buried in the local Cemetery, on the Danish Island of Sejero, next to F/S Dunlop of 166 squadron. F/O Srigley is buried in Farevejle Cemetery, Denmark. F/O Slater rests Varberg Church New Cemetery, Sweden. The remainder are commemorated on the Runnymede Memorial.

F/O W C Fairgrieve RCAF	K
Sgt RG Toomey RCAF	POW
F/O L G Brown RCAF	K
F/O H Slater RCAF	K
Sgt R R Boyce RCAF	K
F/O J R Srigley RCAF	K
F/S W A Lambe RCAF	K

August 18/19 1944, Lancaster Mk X, KB743 NA-I. Ops - Bremen. Took-off MSG 21:29

The tail gunner Sgt Good was fatally injured and unable to abandon the aircraft when it was shot down in flames. He rests in Sage War Cemetery.

P/O C M Corbet RCAF	POW
Sgt R G Enfield	POW
F/O S F Bryans RCAF	POW
F/O G L Jones RCAF	POW
Sgt AR MacNaught RCAF	POW
Sgt T Davidson RCAF	POW
F/S R E Good RCAF	POW

August 29/30 1944, Lancaster Mk X, KB709 NA-G. Ops - Stettin. Took-off MSG 21:19.

It is thought that this aircraft was lost somewhere over the Baltic. F/O Pluunkett was on his second tour. He is commemorated on the Runnymede Memorial. Three are buried in Sweden's Falkenberg Forest Cemetery. The other 3 members of the crew including W/O Gravelet-Chapman are buried on the Danish Island of Anholt.

F/O L S Plunkett RCAF	K
Sgt J McFarlane	K
F/O L H Gardiner DFC RCAF	K
W/O1 J B Gravelet-Chapman RCAF	K
F/O T Baillie RCAF	K
F/S H Gordon	K
Sgt D A Sparkes	K

October 14 1944, Lancaster Mk X, KB780 NA-T. Ops – Stettin. Took-off MSG 05:58.

No information as to the circumstances of this loss is available. Although all members of the crew are buried in the Reichswald Forest War Cemetery they are also commemorated on the Runnymede Memorial.

F/L W H Janney RCAF	K
Sgt L Brotherhood	K
P/O W H Killner RNZAF	K
F/O A V Batty RCAF	K
P/O A S McFeetors RCAF	K
F/S P R Jones RCAF	K
P/O F A Harrison DFC RCAF	K

November 2/3 1944, Lancaster Mk X, KB782 NA-H. Ops – Dusseldorf. Took-off MSG 16:16.

No data available, all are buried in the Reichswald Forest War Cemetery.

F/O J Holtze RCAF	K
P/O E Crossley	K
F/S J Lupinsky RCAF	K
F/S A G Samuel RCAF	K
W/O2 L J Ruhl RCAF	K
Sgt M Dorrell RCAF	K
Sgt J F Bachant RCAF	K

November 4/5 1944, Lancaster Mk X, KB742 NA-M. Ops – Bochum. Took off MSG 17:12.

On its return to Middleton at 23:31, this aircraft over-shot the runway and crash-landed. The crew were uninjured.

F/O C R Paul RCAF

December 2/3 1944, Lancaster Mk X, KB766 NA-O. Ops - Hagen. Took-off MSG 17:17.

Ran into severe icing conditions on reaching the French Coast and became uncontrollable. The crew were ordered to abandon the aircraft. Sgt Hampseed and F/O Sucharov are buried in the Canadian War Cemetery at Bretteville-sur-Laize. The remainder of the crew landed near Le Havre and were able to return home on the December 6th.

F/O L A Turner RCAF	
Sgt M Hampseed	K
F/O M S Sacharov RCAF	K

December 5/6. 1944, Lancaster Mk X, KB768 NA-E. Ops – Soest. Took-off MSG 17:50.

Crashed at 19:00, whilst outbound, near Rugby, Warwickshire, after colliding with a 426 squadron Halifax of Linton-on-Ouse. Both crews were killed. Unlike the crew of the Halifax, only F/S A G Baxter and F/O Cooper could be identified out of 428's crew. Both were buried in Brookwood Military Cemetery. The remainder of F/L Shewfelt's crew are commemorated on the Runnymede Memorial.

F/L H A Shewfelt RCAF	K
Sgt C N Collingwood	K
F/O J Reid RCAF	K
F/O S W Pechet RCAF	K
F/S J E Virag RCAF	K
F/S A G Baxter RCAF	K
F/O E E Cooper RCAF	K

December 27/28 1944, Lancaster Mk X, KB798 NA-G. Ops – Opladen. Took-off MSG 03:00.

No details available, only that the crew were lost and are buried in the Rheinberg War Cemetery.

F/O E W Page RCAF	K
Sgt G F Owen	K
F/O S D Hewson RCAF	K
F/O A A Dixon RCAF	K
F/O R A Ebber RCAF	K
F/O K O McDivitt RCAF	K
F/O A T Le Blanc RCAF	K

428 losses 1945

January 13. 1945, Lancaster Mk X, KB793 NA-E. Training. Took-off 17:49.

This aircraft suffered a fire in its port outer engine, whilst returning to base. P/O McMullen ordered 5 members of his crew to bale out, whilst he tried to complete a left-hand circuit for runway 06. He asked the engineer to remain behind and help with the engines. Whilst turning onto base leg, close to the north-eastern suburbs of Darlington, he told the engineer to jump, knowing that if he did so himself the Lancaster would fall on the town. By the time the aircraft had cleared the houses, it was too late for P/O McMullen to jump and it dived into the ground, a few yards from the farmhouse at Lingfield Farm. The mid-upper gunner, F/S Dykes, who was the second man to jump, sprained his ankle when he landed near the village of Elton, near Stockton-on-Tees. P/O McMullen was killed instantly. He rests in the Stonefall Cemetery in Harrogate, Yorkshire.

P/O W S McMullen	K
P/O W A Sage RCAF	
F/S G T Llewellin	
F/S S Ratsoy RCAF	
F/S H H Simms RCAF	
F/S Dykes RCAF	Inj
F/S Feeley RCAF	

January 28. 1945, Lancaster Mk X, KB763 NA-S. Training. Took-off MSG 14:29.

Descended out of low cloud and crashed at Elton Hall, near Stockton-on-Tees. The aircraft burst into flames and its 6-man crew were killed. Sgt Morris is buried in Bromley Cemetery. The Canadian members of the crew were buried in Harrogate's Stonefall Cemetery.

P/O H L Clark RCAF	K
Sgt P H Morris	K
F/S B Crabb RCAF	Inj
F/S J H Carter RCAF	K
Sgt S Filipchuk RCAF	K
F/S J W Ross RCAF	K

January 28/29. 1945, Lancaster Mk X, KB770 NA-D. Ops – Stuttgart. Took-off MSG 16:38.

The 5 crewmembers who died are buried in Durnbach War Cemetery.

S/L H L Kay RCAF	K
Sgt R W Gullick	K
F/O R L Stapleford RCAF	POW
F/O G J Liney RCAF	K
F/O J W Blades RCAF	K

F/S F L Jolicoeur RCAF	K
F/S E F Ossington RCAF	POW

February 2/3. 1945, Lancaster Mk X, KB725 NA-L. Ops – Wiesbaden. Took-off MSG 20:17.

Having suffered the failure of one of its engines whilst crossing the English coast outbound, this aircraft jettisoned its cookie in the sea and turned back. As it approached base, another engine failed, and the Lancaster overshot the runway and crashed at 00:37, between the two villages of Long Newton and Elton. Both gunners, died in the crash, and are buried in the Stonefall Cemetery in Harrogate. The remainder of the crew were shaken but not injured.

F/L V M Gadkin RCAF	Inj
P/O R A Playter RCAF	K
P/O J A Keating RCAF	K

February 2/3. 1945, Lancaster Mk X, KB792 NA-I. Ops – Wiesbaden. Took-off MSG 20:20.

This aircraft blew up over the target area, after being hit by flak. With the exception of the injured tail gunner, P/O Roche, the crew were buried in Durnbach War Cemetery.

F/L D E Berry AFC RCAF	K
P/O J C Harris MiD	K
F/L C J Ordin RCAF	K
P/O F E Hogan RCAF	K
F/O C Walford RCAF	K
P/O K M Hammond RCAF	K
P/O C M Roche RCAF	POW

February 20. 1945, Lancaster Mk X, KB855 NA-F. Training.

W/C Gall and an engineer took the aircraft up for a familiarisation flight. On his return to base Gall landed well into the runway and realised that he didn't have enough distance left in which to stop. He rammed the throttles open, to go-around again for another landing, but his hand missed the fourth throttle lever, which controlled the starboard outer. The aircraft swung to the right and headed for a cement mixer. Gall pulled back on the control column and the aircraft managed to hop over the mixer, but did not have sufficient flying speed to maintain height. The Lancaster settled back onto the ground and ended up on its belly amongst some trees beyond the airfield in an area near some Nissen huts, after a ditch removed the undercarriage.

W/C M W Gall RCAF

March 5/6. 1945, Lancaster Mk X, KB778 NA-Y. Ops – Chemnitz. Took-off MSG 16:44.

Iced up whilst flying over Belgium whilst homeward bound and crashed into woods at Baraque de Fraiture, 14 km northeast of La Roche-en-Ardenne., Luxembourg. The three dead crewmembers were buried in Hotton War Cemetery.

F/O W Mytruk RCAF	Inj
F/O W R Ashdown RCAF	K
Sgt C R Hazelby	K
F/O D A Wade RCAF	K
P/O E J Chevrier RCAF	
P/O E J Snell RCAF	
F/S E L Schofield RCAF	

March 15/16. 1945, Lancaster Mk X, KB846 NA-I. Ops – Hagen. Took-off MSG 16:44.

The second tour crew of this aircraft were shot down by a Ju88 over the target area. Those that perished were initially buried in Margraten. After the war they were relocated in Nederweert War Cemetery. F/L Craton and F/O Gray were back in England within two weeks of being shot down.

F/L J D Craton RCAF	
F/L R W Newton RCAF	K
F/L R C Hamill RCAF	K
F/O D C Graham RCAF	K
F/O E R Evans RCAF	K
P/O G T Liewellin RCAF	K
F/O B B Gray RCAF	

March 22. 1945, Lancaster Mk X, KB777 NA-V. Ops – Hildesheim. Took-off MSG 10:47.

This aircraft was seen flying home at low level with its port inner feathered and on fire. Two P51 Mustangs were close by. Soon after the crew abandoned the aircraft. F/L Hadley and F/O Frame are both buried in Rheinberg War Cemetery. F/S MacKenzie has no known grave and is commemorated on the Runnymede Memorial.

F/L J F Hadley RCAF	K
Sgt R R Duke RCAF	POW
F/O W J Spence RCAF	POW
F/O C A Goodier RCAF	POW
F/S J MacKenzie RCAF	K
F/O D Frame RCAF	K
F/S J W Bellamy RCAF	POW

April 6/7. 1945, Lancaster Mk X, KB795 NA-Q. Training. Landed MSG 00:24.

Swung off the runway whilst landing. The undercarriage was retracted to prevent the aircraft from crashing beyond the airfield boundary. None of the crew were injured.

F/L R La Turner RCAF

April 13/14. 1945, Lancaster Mk X, KB784 NA-K. Ops – Kiel. Took-off MSG 20:20.

This aircraft ditched due to problems with 3 of its engines, after being hit by flak, both outbound and on the way home. The crew were adrift in their dinghy for 12 days before reaching the enemy shoreline. The tail gunner, F/S Vardy, is commemorated on the Runnymede Memorial.

F/O D M Payne RCAF	POW
F/O V Banks RCAF	POW
F/O G C Riley RCAF	POW
W/O 2 E V Miller RCAF	POW
Sgt T F Sinclare RCAF	POW
F/S E R Casey RCAF	POW
F/S A E Vardy RCAF	K

April 13/14. 1945, Lancaster Mk X, KB816 NA-E. Ops – Kiel. Took-off MSG 20:18.

Overshot at 02:40, whilst diverting to Church Broughton after returning from the target. No injuries.

F/L E P Acres RCAF

April 30. 1945, Lancaster Mk X, KB879 NA-Y. Training.

Crashed at Hixton, 5 miles E/N/E of Stafford, after breaking up in the air at 11:55. It is thought that the cause of the accident was due to the malfunction of the autopilot, which had just been fitted. F/S Ward id buried in the Brierylaw Cemetery in Falkirk, Scotland. F/S Wright was just 16. He was the youngest allied airman to lose his life during WWII. This was the last wartime crew to be lost from Goosepool.

F/L W G Campbell RCAF	K
F/S W G Ward	K
F/S J H Kay RCAF	K
W/O 2 T D Lawley RCAF	K
F/S S Berryman RCAF	K
F/S J L Tweedy RCAF	K
F/S E J Wright RCAF	K

Aircraft lost 72. Ops 66. Training 6
Aircrew killed 268. POWs 105. Injured 14. Evaded 29. Interned 2

Total number of aircraft lost by 78 = 68
Aircrew that died 205, POWs 36, injured 34, evaded 2
Total number of aircraft lost by 76 = 49
Aircrew that died 165, POWs 62, injured 8, evaded 2
Total number of aircraft lost by 420 = 20
Aircrew that died 86, POWs 7, injured 6, evaded 2
Total number of aircraft lost by 419 = 131
Aircrew that died 542, POWs 183, injured 29, evaded 31
Total number of aircraft lost by 428 = 72
Aircrew that died 268, POWs 105, injured 14, evaded 29, interned 2.

Total number of aircraft lost from 76, 78, 419, 420 and 428 squadrons whilst serving at Middleton and Croft during WWII 340.
Aircrew that died 1,266, POWs 398, injured 91, evaded 66, interned 2.

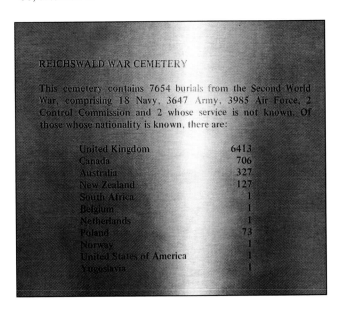

Photo: Author

CHAPTER TEN

Post War Goosepool

Post war Goosepool

With the departure of the Canadians and most of the remaining RAF ground personnel, Goosepool was put on a care and maintenance basis. This was not to be for very long however, as during July the station acquired new masters, in the form of Fighter Command.

After the hustle and bustle of wartime however, in comparison, the airfield was to enter a relatively quiet era in its history. Once again the sound of Merlins reverberated around Goosepool during July 1945 with the arrival of 13 OTU's Mosquitoes, which had flown up from Harwell. The Mosquito's tendency to swap ends during the take-off and landing stage caused a few accidents during their stay at Middleton. Barely had they arrived when, after only a few days, one of their Mosquito T3s came to grief after an engine failed on take off. Fortunately no one was seriously hurt. Two months later, one of the Mosquitoes was destroyed when it crashed near Yarm after suffering an engine fire in the circuit. Both crewmembers had managed to bale out however, and landed safely.

1946

The only fatality to take place during the unit's stay at Goosepool came the following year. On May 11th 1946, another T3, LR565, on a training exercise, crashed vertically into a pit heap near Bankdam Farm, near Thornley village, some 5 miles S/E of Durham city. This turned out to be the last accident suffered by the unit whilst at Middleton, as they departed for RAF Leeming a few days later.

1947

After a period of Care and Maintenance, a marching in and out parade on June 16th 1947 heralded Middleton's changeover from Fighter Command to Flying Training Command. The next day, the handing on certificates and No.2 forms were forwarded on to both HQ and 12 Group. On the 23rd, it was agreed that RAF Topcliffe would assume parental responsibility for Middleton St George. During the year, 608 (North Riding) Squadron of the Royal Auxiliary Air Force travelled the 5 miles from their old base at Thornaby to take up residence at Goosepool, a location they would remain at for the next 10 years. Their mounts consisted of Vampires, Mosquito NF30s and Spitfire F22s.

By July 30th, the number of care and maintenance staff on duty at Goosepool was 7 officers and 86 airman. A bombshell dropped the next day with the arrival of Air Commodore A M Proud, who had arrived to discuss the proposal that the airfield might be transferred from Flying Training Command to Technical Training Command. It was on the cards that Middleton would soon be hearing the tiny footsteps of the Rock Apes (RAF Regiment), who would possibly be moving up from RAF Wombleton. Fortunately this proposal was countermanded on August 15th, as common sense prevailed, and the idea was dropped. On September 15th, during Battle of Britain Day, Eaglescliff's Reverend S E R Fenning took part in the colour hoisting, which was presided over by F/L Moore, the Adjutant, P/O Hinson, and the Parade Warrant Officer W/O Sheridan.

On September 20th, a forward party of personnel from No.2 Air Navigation School, which operated Ansons and Wellingtons, arrived at Middleton from Bishop's Court, Northern Ireland. The main ground party departed by boat from Ardglass, Co. Down, on October 1st. W/C W H Tremear, the CFI arrived on the 13th, flying commenced on the 15th. The Station Commander at the time was G/C J C Coggle.

1948

During April 1948, 28 Air Bomber Conversion Course using Wellingtons and Ansons began at Middleton, under the command of S/L Wilberforce DFC AFC, who had been posted in on March 4th. On the 29th Middleton's former WAAF Officer's Mess, sick quarters, NAFFI and dinning room were converted into temporary married quarters. The only problem for the Wellingtons was the never-ending possibility of being struck by lightning. There were 4 such strikes on Middleton's Wellingtons during May, the first occurring on the 4th when Wellington RP570 was struck. By May 31st, Goosepool was de-WAFF'd. Sir Ralph Cockran KBE CB AFC Controller in Chief of Fighter Command visited Middleton on July 28th. On Saturday the 31st a Wellington and an Anson from Goosepool took part in an air display, organised by Darlington Aeroclub at Neasham (Croft). The Anson provided an R/T demonstration, whilst the Wellington carried out a mock bombing of a submarine. Meanwhile, training continued throughout 1948 with little cause for concern, unless you include the 64 airmen who contracted food poisoning on August 22nd. On September 4th, Middleton's Wellingtons carried out a practice daylight bombing raid on oil installations at Leicester. The next day Victoria Bridge in London was the target.

Operation 'Dagger' on September 5th and 6th sent 6 Wellingtons to 'Bomb' the Dodd and Martin seaplane factory at Grimsby, 3 did, and 3 didn't. They also carried out a 'Raid' on Leicester railway station. They must have had a thing about Leicester. Middleton had a Battle of Britain air display on September 18th. Included on the program were Lancasters, Mosquitoes and Harvards. On November 15th Middleton provided a flypast to celebrate the birth of Prince Charles. On December 21st a Wellington from Goosepool , flown by G/C Coggle flew at 2000 feet over Sunderland, along a path of searchlights. Whilst over the town the Mayor called the aircraft on the radio and passed on seasonal greetings from the people of Sunderland to the RAF.

1949

During April 1949 Middleton received its first Mk10 Wellington, which had been delivered from Boulton Paul. During August. ICI were carrying out experiments in rain making (not too difficult a task in the northeast I would have thought). Their representative flew on several occasions in one of Middleton's Wellingtons, mostly flown by F/L Otley and his navigator F/L Turner. In an attempt to persuade clouds to give up their rain, (I bet that was easy). The aircraft flew above whilst various chemicals were dropped into the clouds. The experiments worked on three occasions, (only 3?).

Also during August, a contingent of Durham policemen arrived at Middleton, to be trained in escape methods. The Battle of Britain display on Saturday the 17th included Auster, Hornet, Harvard, Hastings, Lincoln, Meteor, Tiger Moth and Wellington aircraft. Tragedy struck during the Show. The flying display began at 13:00 and went exceedingly well, until the last item on the programme. This was to be carried out by one of Middleton's Wellingtons, which was to drop dummy parachutists. The Wellington (coded J) flown by 25 year old F/O J H A MacPherson, took off and cleared to the east, then turned and commenced its run in. As it passed over the runway, the dummies began to leave the aircraft. One struck the tailplane, which jammed as the parachute's cords wrapped around it. The Wellington, which along with its regular crew was carrying trainees, nose-dived into the ground and exploded; there were no survivors. F/O MacPherson the navigator, F/L R V Wilson bomb aimer, F/L H B Tatham wireless operator, H Chapman and U/T[129] navs D Hall (age 22), and Munday (27), were all killed. The funerals of the crew took place at Darlington's West Cemetery on the 22nd, after a service at the Station Church. On the 19th, 10 students from Iraq arrived At Middleton for a nav course.

A final conference regarding rainmaking took place on October 25th, and was attended by W/C W H Tremear and Mr Murlis from ICI. On November 5th Wellington Mk B10 RP343 damaged its tailplane whilst trying to carry out a single engined approach. The aircraft suffered Cat 3 damage but non of the crew were injured. The same day, Wellington HA827 had to be abandoned out of fuel near Pocklington, the crew were uninjured but the aircraft was completely wreaked. The crew included F/L L J Otley the pilot, Major Mohammed of the Royal Iraqi Air Force who was the navigator, second nav I V Clark and Master Signaller Cameron.

On December 21st Middleton lost another Wellington when it landed wheels-up. None of the crew were injured.

1950

On January 1st 1950 Middletons Station Commander was posted and replaced by G/C D J Eayrs CBE DFC. Work had recently commenced to resurface the runways and lay a new perimeter track. Provision for new lighting was also completed in hangar 2.

On January 12th 1950 two of Goosepool's Wellingtons were dispatched on a sea search for a missing motor trawler, the 'Girl Jean'. The boat had been removed by a 14 year-old boy and taken to sea. One of the Wellingtons searched for five and a half hours, whilst the other flew for six. Both had been using the creep line ahead search pattern. Unfortunately, neither crew saw the missing vessel. By the end of the year many of Middleton's Wellingtons had been flown to 34 MU at Stoke Heath to be broken up, as their spar booms had completed their 100 hour lives.

By the end of February the work on the runways was completed. The building of married quarters then began. Wellington NC615 took off from Middleton on April 5th for a cross-country nav-ex and crashed at Horam, Sussex, killing the 4 members of its crew. This was to be the last crash suffered by 2 ANS as on April 28th they began to depart Middleton for Thorny Island. The move was completed by May 16th.

2 ANS were to be replaced on September 7th by 205 Advanced Flying Training School (AFTS), under the command of F/L D E Kingstone and F/L J E P Canaway. Meanwhile, during the period May to September, the airfield was once again put on a Care and Maintenance basis. Middleton then had a new Commander in the form of G/C W E Coles DSO DFC AFC.

205 AFTS aircraft consisted of Mk IV and Mk VII Meteors, a Persival Prentice and an Airspeed Oxford. Their policy was to give advanced jet flying training to 72 pilots, during a 959 hour flying programme.
Shortly after their arrival, Meteor Mk IV EE528 was being delivered to Middleton when one of its throttles jammed in the open position. Having stopped the engine, the pilot tried to carry out a single engined landing, but overshot, and tore off the port undercarriage. Fortunately he was uninjured.

On November 30th, 21 year old Sgt Pilot T H Seabrook was killed when he tried to abandon Meteor IV, EE559, after losing sight of the airfield and running out of fuel. The aircraft crashed and was scrapped. F/L H L Mellor was carrying out practice aerobatics on December 11th in Meteor, VT170, when he also ran out of fuel. His only option was to make a forced landing on a strip of moorland near Whitby. Mellor was uninjured but the aircraft received Cat 4 damage.

The same day, F/O McCann was practicing single engine circuits when he received a 'Red' from the runway controller. McCann had forgotten to lower his undercarriage. He opened the throttles to initiate a go-around, but there was insufficient time for the engines to spool up,[130] and the aircraft sank onto the runway. The Meteor bounced back into the air, by which time sufficient thrust from the engines allowed McCann to carry out another circuit, which was followed by a successful landing (and a good bollocking).

---

[129] Under Training
[130] In those days, up to 9 seconds

1951

On January 8th 1951, Sgt Pilot Atkinson, a pupil of 3 course, touched down at Middleton in bad visibility. The aircraft landed at excessive speed and overshot the runway into a ploughed field. Fortunately Atkinson was uninjured in the accident, but the aircraft, a Meteor Mk 4, received Cat 2 damage. Four days later, P/O I Gordon-Johnson was approaching to land in a Meteor 7 when he discovered that he did not have three 'Greens', indicating that all three wheels were not locked down. He was instructed to carry out a slow flypast to allow the control tower staff to take a look at the aircraft. Being low on fuel, he elected to stop the port engine to save fuel. When observed from the ground, the undercarriage and flaps were down and so the problem could have been nothing more than a blown bulb in the cockpit's undercarriage position indicator. Also observed from the ground was the aircraft's extremely slow speed, which on one engine caused the pilot to lose control. The aircraft crashed through the fence and travelled over the Darlington to Redcar railway line before coming to rest on the Darlington to Yarm road. The Meteor, WA719, was reduced to scrap. Fortunately, there were no fatalities.

On the 18th, Squadron Leader Butler was flying with a pupil who was carrying out the conclusion to a single engine QGH.[131] The pupil had originally cut the starboard engine prior to his approach. He then, by mistake, stopped the port engine, the result being that the Meteor struck the ground 10 yards short of the runway, breaking the undercarriage. No one was injured. At the time of the accident, the wind strength had been recorded as gusting up to 60 mph.

Yet another crash, on the 25th near Croft village, cost the life of student pilot P/O A A McKernan in Meteor 4 VW255. At 12:05, this aircraft dived into the ground near Croft Spa, shortly after take-off from Middleton, and exploded on impact. At the time the cause was unknown, and a court of enquiry was instigated to ascertain the possible cause of the accident. Presiding over the enquiry was W/C W S G Maydwell DSO DFC. The final outcome of the enquiry stated that the probable cause of the accident was due to the pilot becoming spatially disorientated in cloud, possibly causing the aircraft to become inverted. There was some attempt to recover at low altitude, but this had not been successful. Croft (often referred to as Neasham during this era) was reopened on February 19th, as Middleton's RLG,[132] used at the time by Darlington and District Aero Club. The airfield was utilised to reduce training traffic at Goosepool. On June 1st 1954, Middleton assumed the title of 4 Flying Training School.

On the 19th, the station lost another Meteor 7, VT239, when it crashed on Inglesborough Mountain, near Settle. The pilot, P/O G L Grieves, aged 20, was killed. It was thought at the time that he had suffered from anoxia.[133] On the 21st, G/C H S Darley DSO assumed command of the Station. Three days later, Meteors from Middleton took part in an exercise called Operation Dividend. During August, another Meteor Mk 4 crashed at Neasham and caught fire. P/O Valentine was killed on July 10th, when Meteor 4, VZ418, dived into the ground. It was uncertain what had caused the crash, included in the list of possibilities were lack of oxygen, structural failure and an explosion in the air. August the 1st saw No.15 course arrive at Goosepool. As they began their training, one of their number, P/O M F Rodgers, suffered a flameout on both engines whilst practicing stalls at 20,000 feet. Showing great courage and skill, he managed to land back at Middleton without engines, for which he received a Green endorsement. His glory was short lived however, as on the 20th, he slightly damaged Meteor 4 VV298 whilst carrying out an overshoot from Croft. Lady Luck was not with him that day, as, after landing back at Goosepool, he collided with a fuel bowser whilst taxiing in.

On August 23rd, Cpl Hands was travelling in one of Goosepool's 15 cwt vehicles when he was in collision with a private car on the Great North Road. One of the car's occupants was killed in the crash, and three passengers were injured. Cpl Hands received minor injuries.

On October 12th, S/L R H Golightly DFC was leading a formation of three aircraft. One of his students, F/O Tootill, had difficulty in keeping formation, and was struck in the face and received slight facial injuries when the tail of one of the other aircraft struck his canopy.

During November 1951, Goosepool suffered a series of aircraft accidents, including the loss of Mosquito Mk 36, RL258, belonging to 228 OCU at Leeming. The aircraft ground-looped whilst landing, fortunately neither the pilot, F/O Ababozynski nor the navigator, P/O Adams were injured. On the 20th, Meteor 7, WA720, failed to recover from a spin and had to be abandoned. The pilot, F/O Williams and his pupil, P/O Poppe were only slightly injured.

On November 24th, whilst part way through a refresher course, F/O R T Norman, in Meteor Mk 4, VW297, lost critical speed during a practice overshoot on runway 28. The aircraft was extensively damaged when it careered off the end of the runway and ploughed into the West Wing of the Officers' Mess.[134] Amazingly, the out of control Meteor struck P/O Norman's own private car, which was parked outside the mess. The nose of the aircraft crashed through a window[135] and came to a halt with its nose protruding into the building. Pilot Officer Norman, who was 33 years old, was not seriously injured in the crash, but in his haste to get out of the cockpit, some of the loose brickwork was dislodged, and P/O Norman was killed when it fell on him. Today, the window, with its bricked up repairs, can still be seen.

On the 4th, players from Middlesbrough football team provided a coaching demonstration in Middleton's Gym. The next day, No.17 Jet course passed out, having completed their training.

---

[131] General Handling Exercise
[132] Relief Landing Ground; as Middleton was a master Diversion Airfield (Master Div), trainee pilots were encouraged to do their circuits and bumps elsewhere tro keep the circuit clear
[133] Lack of oxygen
[134] Now the St George Hotel
[135] Possibly his own room

1952

On January 15th 1952, everyone enjoyed a variety show in the station's NAAFI, which included a hypnotist, who stole the show, and kept the audience on the edge of their seats.

Tragedy struck on the 21st, when P/O Heather was killed when his Meteor 7, WG975, crashed during his first solo.

During February, it was realised that some members of No.28 course were not reaching minimum standards. Several 'Chop' rides were flown by the Wing Commander Flying, which resulted in bags being packed, and their owners departing the station. Another Meteor was damaged on April 7th, when it landed 100 yards short of the runway at Neasham. It rolled on for 100 yards before colliding with an electrical junction box, which caused considerable damage. It ended up on the grass whilst heading for a ploughed field, from which it was later towed out.

There was no flying on the 30th, as the Station carried out the changeover from AVTUR fuel to AVTAG. During May, several windscreen failures occurred. The first was experienced by P/O Horrocks, when he suffered the failure of his windscreen whilst at 12,000 feet over the Middlesbrough area. He was able to control the Meteor and managed to land back at base. The cause of the windscreen failures was put down to the very warm weather, which everyone was enjoying at the time.

LAC Bottoms had a lucky escape on July 4th, when he was sucked into an engine, whilst the pilot was carrying out his after start checks. Due to the quick actions of the aircraft's pilot in shutting down the engine, LAC Bottoms was admitted to the SSQ suffering only minor injuries and shock.

Flying training at Goosepool continued smoothly throughout the year, but still the losses continued. On August 20th, P/O Burrows was killed in Meteor Mk 4, RA429, when it crashed at Great Stainton. P/O Caiser's body was recovered from the North Sea after he crashed in Meteor 4, EE528, on September 26th.

Winter came early to Middleton during 1952, with the result that the heating had to be put on during September. Whilst carrying out a GCA under the control of RAF Seaton Snook, P/O J M Dill was killed, when his Meteor crashed into the Cleveland Hills on October 27th. The final fatality of 1952 occurred during December, when Meteor 7, WH234, crashed soon after take-off. The student pilot, P/O D A Cox, was killed instantly.

1953

1953 was only two days old when Meteor WL365 crashed at Cotherstone, whilst night flying. The pilot, P/O Bowater, was killed.

One student who received his flying training at Middleton during the 50's was future politician Norman Tebbet, who was destined to become part of Margaret Thatcher's cabinet.

No.52 course began at Middleton on January 12th 1953, despite much snow. The Scottish firm of Mowlems arrived at the end of January to extend the existing concrete hard-standings and refuelling platforms. During February, Middlesbrough was suffering from an excess of water, due to the thawing of the vast amounts of snow experienced during the previous few weeks. Added to this was a copious amount of rain, which had followed the snow. Between the 8th and 16th, two airmen and one NCO from Middleton came to the rescue of the unfortunate householders in the Port Clarence area of Middlesbrough, and began operation 'King Canute'. Aircraft pre-heaters were pressed into service, to dry out the soggy abodes. During March however, the fickle Teesside weather changed tack completely and decided to have a drought.

On the 15th, one of Mowlem's personnel was injured when he was struck on the right side of his face by the wingtip of Meteor 7, WA711, which was being fast taxied by F/L Mellor. At the time, the worker, Mr Thomas, was working on the repair of a hardstanding. On hearing the approaching plane he had turned to look, and was immediately struck.

At Middleton during 1953, such was the efficiency of the sausage machine that a new flying course passed out every two weeks. On April 26th, the construction firm of Shepherds arrived, to begin work on the west-side of the Officers' Mess. They also started to pull down the derelict temporary married quarters buildings, leaving only one to be used as a garage by members of the Officers' Mess. Meanwhile, Middleton's new Astra cinema was still under construction by the RAF Cinema Corps.

The Grim Reaper struck yet again on May 4th, when Meteor 7, WH246, crashed, killing F/O K B Bones, aged 22, and his student F/L A Turner, aged 24.

Goosepool was sans students by May 16th, and the station was run down in anticipation of the commencement of work on the runways and the building of Nesco huts by Messrs Glossops. As the airfield would be unusable for flying for a while, 205 AFS moved over to Thornaby out of the way. To keep the instructors happy during the absence of any students, they were allowed to gain valuable experience in long distance flights by organising 'Jollies' to airfields in Germany and Malta.

Glossops began resurfacing runway 28/10 and 24/06, and had commenced the construction of new readiness platforms at the end of 24/06. The new 'Astra' cinema had its grand opening at 20:00 hours on September 17th, the opening ceremony being carried out by the Commanding Officer's wife, Mrs R I K Edwards. By December, the work at Middleton was almost complete. The runways were reopened, allowing 205 AFS to return from Thornaby. RAF Neasham was also serviceable again, having also had work carried out there.

1954

John Allinson arrived at Goosepool during July of 1954, together with 10 fellow pilots, who with John had won their wings at Moreton-in-Marsh earlier that month. They were all Pilot Officers, and included Peter Naz, Joe Hickmott, Alan Gardiner, Brian Henwood, Colin Robinson, Ken Ward, Bill Brewer, Peter Baines, Dennis Wheatley and Mick Turner.

Morton-in-Marsh had apparently been the origin of the famous post war BBC radio comedy program, 'Much-Binding-in-the-Marsh', featuring Richard Murdoch and Kenneth Horne. The weekly program, which was heard on a Sunday, portrayed the lives of RAF airman who were based at a fictitious RAF aerodrome called 'Much-Binding-in-the-Marsh'.

John Allinson, 3rd from left, with fellow course members   Photo: John Allinson

John remembers – Newly qualified pilots were being sent to a number of Jet Conversion Units, from a variety of Flying Schools, mainly in the UK. Apart from Middleton, there were others based at RAF Driffield in Yorkshire, RAF Worksop in Nottingham, and RAF Weston Zoyland in Somerset. We 'Mortonites' joined other newly qualified pilots who had just arrived from some of these Schools.

At Middleton, we flew single seat Meteor IVs, and the dual tandem seat Meteor Mk VII trainer. Nicknamed 'The Meatbox', the Meteor could be lethal. It was a good machine to fly, providing you treated it properly. That said, there were three fatal accidents during the time that I was at Middleton. Altogether we flew the Meteors for about 80 hours, divided more or less between solo and dual. Apart from familiarisation flights in the Meteor, in the middle of August we went back to ground school to learn about jet aircraft and how they operated, aspects of high level flight,

aviation medicine, etc. We were put inside a decompression chamber and shown, inter alia, the effects of a lack of oxygen at high altitude. It was interesting to see how one failed to cope with even simple tasks, a good warning to monitor one's oxygen levels and make sure that one's mask fitted properly. Flying started in earnest during September with circuits and bumps, both at Middleton and its satellite at Neasham (Croft). I can certainly remember seeing cars travelling along a nearby busy road, and thinking it odd to be so close to them.

For us, too, came the novelty of practicing single-engine landings. Very quickly you learned that there is a minimum speed below which you couldn't keep the Meteor straight with one engine out. This was due to asymmetric effect. The longer your legs, usually, the lower the speed you could hold it to, but we all aimed not to let it get below the safety speed which all pilots could maintain and which gave reasonable directional control. During this early flying, an instructor was killed practicing for the 'Battle of Britain' air show. He was last seen flying low to the south of the airfield, after which he then disappeared in the Tees Valley. The cause of the crash was not divulged to us, but there was great sadness on the station because he was well-liked. Flying continued with another novelty, high speed runs. We learned that the Meteor had a definite limit in terms of maximum speed. This was expressed in terms of a Mach number, and a juddering of the stick, when control of the aircraft could no longer be properly maintained. We also practiced 'bad weather' circuits, which were based on flying a set timed pattern at low level. This was useful later on, at times when cloud was low over Teesside and the smoke of Middlesbrough and Stockton drifted over the aerodrome. During October, we started on high level aerobatics, which could be most impressive, particularly when there was a layer of cloud far below one and the sun was really bright in a clear blue sky. We also started spinning – an interesting experience. Those were the days when a certain Polish pilot called Zurokowski used to do vertical rolls on a wing tip, so to speak, in a Meteor at the Farnborough Air Show, and how he managed it without spinning no one could ever understand. He really knew his aircraft!

Navigation exercises also started in October – both high and low level. At high level, one could see a fair chunk of England spread out below, and many features such as roads, railways and small towns virtually disappeared. It could be very difficult to decide when you were actually over a place or a turning point. Navigation at low level could be exhilarating - such as flying below the rugged cliff tops along the northeast coast. November and December saw us practicing instrument flying and learning to do letdowns in cloud, the old QGHs.

We obtained our instrument ratings during this time – a real feather in one's cap. At the same time, we were also continuing with aerobatics. Formation flying started, and this could give one a great sense of satisfaction if one stayed in 'tight', preferably for the whole flight! Low level formation flying could be dramatic, not least over the Pennines and the North York Moors, particularly if they were covered with snow. I once dropped a bit too low on of these and my instructor let it be known that I could have stayed permanently low – like on the ground that is!

I think it was during this period that a further accident occurred. A friend on another course, P/O Dickie Collingwood, crashed at night and was killed. Again we didn't hear what the cause might have been, possibly a loss of control due to disorientation or an engine flameout. It was also during this period, I seem to remember, that one of our course members, P/O Dennis Wheatley, managed to do an impressive glide from high altitude into RAF Dishforth, which was a master diversion airfield, open at all times for emergencies. Both engines had flamed out and Dennis could not re-light them, leaving him with only one option – to try to land at a suitable aerodrome. Obviously he could only make one attempt and that had to be right! He was, I believe, commended for his airmanship. He did, of course, have another option, to bale out, but history does not record how seriously he considered that!

In January, we completed a range of exercises covering what we had done so far, and also started night flying, always a fascinating experience, as one saw the lights of towns and cities spread out like glittering necklaces of pearls and diamonds. Another accident occurred, on February 1st, involving P/O Mick Turner who was on our course. He crashed near Cocklesberry Farm near Neasham in Meteor IV VT115 and was killed, having apparently lost control at altitude. It was said that his dinghy, on which he sat, might have inadvertently inflated, pushing the control column forward and making it impossible for him to recover from the ensuing dive. Before the course ended, we were all issued with knives, which were put into sheaths sewn onto our flying overalls, so we could puncture our dinghies if they accidentally inflated. We mourned Mike's loss.

February saw our final handling tests, and with their successful completion, we were setting out on our next posting. Unfortunately, there were so many pilots being trained and processed at that time in the UK (National Service was still in full swing), that many had to have their operational training postponed. So off we went to various squadrons in either Transport, Bomber or Coastal Commands, to act as supernumerary crew until the Training System could take us on again.

Whilst at Middleton we were privileged to have a fine bunch of instructors, each his own person, and each able to put over how we should do things and how we could improve, in their own inimitable style! I can still remember one of my instructors pointing out that it would be a pity if I ever left my airbrakes out again on finals, as the Meteor had been known to go inverted at approach speeds under such conditions. Of course he didn't quite put it like that, but his mixture of anger and sarcasm made its mark! Our instructors included F/Ls Kelly, Hetherington, Roe, Hall, King, Dodds, Curtis and 'Bob' Diamond, also F/Os Sands and Tony Westoby, F/Ss Hedges and Wood, Sgts Laundon and Baker.

The course was enjoyable and stimulating. So too, was the life on the station, if one joined in its activities. cars were not so plentiful in those days amongst the students, so exploring the local countryside, hostelries, cinemas, etc was not easy. There were some very good evenings in the Officers' Mess. On one occasion, after a particularly good 'dining-in' night, an Austin 7 (a sort of pre-war version of the Mini,) was somehow stripped-down and manhandled through the front doors of the Mess, and was waiting to greet breakfast-comers in the morning. The Commanding Officer was prepared to take no further action, providing the vehicle was speedily removed. This was achieved, but not without having to take the doors off first - how it was brought in with the doors in place remained a mystery.

If one was interested in sport, there were various games to take part in – football, rugby, etc – the RAF encouraged this. One of the advantages of playing for a team was the travelling to other service units and, occasionally, to civilian teams for matches. That way one got to see the world outside Middleton, and meet some interesting chaps in the process. One also invariably savoured the great northern treat of 'Fish and Chips' on the way back. - even the chips on their own were good! Talking of the RAF encouraging sport, I can remember being picked up by an Anson on a Friday night, flown down to RAF Manby in Lincolnshire for a Rugby trial of some sort, entertained well over the weekend (in addition to playing Rugby of course), and then being flown back to Middleton on Monday morning.

Another activity, amongst others on the Station, was the Theatre Club. This was great fun, not least because it was an all-ranks affair and one met and got to know more interesting and very pleasant people. The first production I was involved in was 'Sit Down a Minute Adrian', a light-hearted comedy, performed in October 1954 in the NAAFI. I seem to remember that the producer, Gordon Mitchell, had to work us quite hard, certainly his comments when he signed the programme at the end of the show seemed to reflect that – 'Never again!' However, his efforts were worthwhile, for the play seemed to be well received by the station audience. We started rehearsing for another play, to be staged sometime in 1955, but I was posted in early February, so sadly I missed that.

My final recollection of Goosepool is sitting in a very hushed anteroom in the Mess, listening to the ever-popular 'Goon Show' on the radio. Peter Naz eventually became the Air Officer Commanding the Air Training Corps, sometime in the 1980s, I think. Brian Henwood became and possibly still is a Hunter pilot on the display circuit. Peter Baines became a senior British Airways Captain, and as for me? I finished up on the management side of the Civil Aviation Authority.

1955

January 1955 had seen a change of role, from advanced flying training on jets (Meteors) of pilots already qualified to 'Wings' standard, to the new scheme of training pilots for 'Wings' standard on jet aircraft (Vampires). The first Vampire students had arrived on January 12th, for what would be a 36-week course. It was planned that a new course would commence every 6 weeks, to reach its established strength of 120 pilots by August. Meanwhile Middleton's boxing team became runners up in the 25 Group Boxing Championships. During 1955, construction of the airfield's new married quarters was well underway. On March 7th, 2 Type V houses, to be designated as Officers' Married Quarters, were completed and taken over. The Station Theatre Club gave a performance of 'Flarepath' on the 14th, whilst on the 17th, the Station Boxing Team won their match against RAF Worksop. By the 23rd, the Warrant Officer's and four Airmen's married quarters were also completed by the contractors and handed over. The Station Pig Farm was also renovated during March.

The contractors were proceeding well with the construction of the Married Quarters.[136] On May 6th, 4 more came on line.

A site conference on May 19th was held by a representative of Fighter Command, in preparation for the change over of Middleton St George from Flying Training Command to Fighter Command. Meanwhile, Vampire T11, WZ566, crashed near Stockton on June 29th, killing the pilot, P/O W C B Jenkins. On August 5th, the airfield was host to a visit by the Mayor of Darlington and his party. He was also accompanied by the Mayor of Amiens. Also at this time, Middleton became the home of 101 Jet Provost and Vampire course, which saw 9 officers pass out by September 21st. Field Marshall Viscount Montgomery of Alamein KG GCB DSO departed from Middleton by air the same day, after presenting the colours to the Green Howards at Barnard Castle. By December, married quarters buildings were being completed and released to the Station at a steady rate.

1956

On April 6th 1956, Vampire FBV, WA164, crashed on the airfield, killing the pilot, 19 year old P/O KCS Dight. Four days later, Vampire T11, WZ 609, also crashed, killing F/O Kimber and P/O P G Sharman, aged 24.

On June 8th an advance party of 4 FTS personnel under the command of S/L P J Murch departed Goosepool for their new home at RAF Worksop. The Air Party, consisting of 12 T11 Vampires and 1 Prentice T1, commanded by S/L G F Clark, departed Middleton at 15:00 hours on the 22nd, for the direct flight to Worksop, 14 miles southeast of Sheffield. The rear party, also left Middleton on the 22nd, led by F/L R Lesley. A further 8 aircraft (T11s) transferred later, along with the unit's vehicles, 2 Layland Hippos, each complete with trailer, and several 3 tonners. All aircraft remaining after 4 FTS had departed were servised and disposed of during the early part of July. They consisted of 3 Vampire FB5s (VZ273, WA288 and VZ866). They were flown to Worksop, along with a T11, VZ558. Vampire FB5, VZ318 and T11s XE887, XE828, XE873 and WZ493 were flown to 19 MU at Valley, Anglesey.

On the 23rd work began to resurface Middleton's runway and taxiways to fighter command standards. During July 1956, Messers Tarslag Ltd began to resurface Middleton's runways and taxiways. Also Messrs Tarrans began to lay the foundations of the new Radar Workshops. By the end of July Tarslag had completed 5% of the lean mixed concrete surfaces.

On June 25th, Fighter Command establishment LVE/FC/9237 became effective, which established Middleton St George as a holding party until runway resurfacing was completed, after which the Station was to became an operational 13 Group base Station. The Tech Flight, which contained elements of No.4 FTS, came under the command of F/L J C Boylan. The Administration section was to be commanded by F/L G R Griggs.

1957

By February 27th 1957, 92 and 264 Squadron, were required to leave Linton-on-Ouse and take up residence at Middleton. 264 were led by W/C J C Forbs DFM, 92 by F/L R P V Woodwood. After both squadrons had taken off they rendezvoused with 2 Meteor V111s, flown by Middleton's Station Commander G/C J Barraclough DFC AFC and W/C H F Neill DFC, O/C Flying. At 11:30 the formation of 16 aircraft from both 92 and 264, led by the two Meteors landed at Middleton. 92's element was a small one as the bulk of the squadron was on temporary detachment to Cyprus. It was expected that both squadrons were to become operational by March 1st. 92 were to undertake the role of a day squadron, whilst 264 became a night fighter squadron.

The Station Flight, under the command of F/L Woodward, was also re-formed on the 27th. Woodward's post as commander of 92's small element was taken over by F/L W W Kelly at the end of the month. 264 Squadron were equipped with Glostor Meteor NF14s, whilst 92 operated Hawker Hunter Mk F6s. During this time, work was still being carried out to improve and enlarge some of Middleton's taxiways.

From March 25th onwards, elements of 92 squadron arrived at Middleton from Cyprus, in Comets and Beverleys. A force of twelve 92 squadron Hunters, led by S/L R W T Freer, arrived on the 28th. They were met by AVM W G Cheshire CB CBE, AOC of No.12 Group.

---

[136] Which today had become the privatised Virginia Estate

History of 92 Squadron

92 (East India) Squadron was formed at London Clone, Hertfordshire on September 1st 1917 under the command of Captain P A A Leask. Its motto was Aut pugna aut morere (Either fight or die). The squadron was equipped with several different types of aircraft including the Sopwith Pup and SE5a.

By Armistice Day, the number of German aircraft destroyed by 92 Squadron during WW1 had reached 37. After the cessation of hostilities, 92 moved to Thuilles in Belgium, where routine training continued on SE5s. At this time, a captured German Fokker D-V111 was unofficially added to the squadron's strength. The squadron was officially disbanded on August 7th 1919.

92 Squadron were reformed at Tangmere on October 10th 1939 as a night-fighter squadron, and were equipped with Bristol Blenheims. These were replaced in March 1940 by Spitfires. The squadron became operational on May 9th.

In response to the Africa Corps, the Squadron was withdrawn from home duties during February 1942 and moved to Egypt. For the next year they operated across North Africa, escorting IIc Hurribombers[137] involved in harassing Rommel's lines. They also carried out sweeps and patrols. 92 assisted in the great air offensive that preceded the battle of El Alemein. After the British 8th Army's breakout of Egypt, 92 accompanied the ground forces and ensured that they had the appropriate air cover.

July 1943 saw the Squadron supporting the allied landings in Sicily from their new base on Malta. When the invasion began, 92 was to be the first RAF Squadron to operate from Sicily. They converted onto the Mk 8 Spitfire during this time, and when the invasion of Italy began they were the first squadron to operate there. 92 flew at first in a close support role for the army. As the offensive travelled north, less and less German aircraft were encountered. The squadron changed during July to a fighter bomber role, attacking the German lines with bombs and cannon. By October 1944, the squadron had reached Fino on the Adriatic Coast, where it operated until December, before moving again to Bellaria. 92 flew their last operation of WWII on May 1st 1945.

During September 1946 another move was required, this time to Zeltwig, Austria, followed a few months later by a return to England. Once home, 92 were amalgamated with 91 Squadron at Duxford on January 1st 1947 as part of Fighter Command. 92 flew various versions of the Gloster Meteor from this time until 1954, when they moved to Linton-on-Ouse and converted onto North American Sabre jets. This aircraft remained the mount of 92 until they converted onto the Hawker Hunter in February 1952.

Middleton's Operational Records Book has an interesting entry for April 1957. Rather than elaborate I have reproduced the entry verbatim: -

Records show that on two different days this month, during the early hours of the morning, an indistinct figure, wearing flying clothing, was seen walking slowly around 264's hangar. On the first occasion, 2 airmen who were working on the night shift saw the man and approached him to offer him assistance. To their consternation the figure just faded out of sight before their very eyes. As the airmen were convinced that the figure was supernatural, they reported the matter in the morning. The figure was seen again, this time by a Technical W/O of long standing, who, like most long standing W/Os, was not particularly sensitive to phenomena lying outside his normal experience. He went over to investigate, again the figure simply disappeared. Most of the squadron is convinced that it is the ghost of a former member of the squadron or station, and consequently he has been adopted by the squadron as 'Horace', the Goosepool Ghost. The record book continued: - The story of Horace has recently been the subject of an article in the local and national press.

Whilst operating as an instructor with 405 Squadron, the author met a Warrant Officer called Bill Lynass, who, in a former life, was an Aircraftsman at Middleton during the 50s. He related to me an incident that he and a fellow airman had experienced one night whilst on guard duty, and I quote - *It was a very cold winters night, with a light dusting of snow on the ground. There were no clouds, and the stars twinkled brightly. The airfield was bathed in moonlight, and as we approached the corner of one of the hangars we saw an airman dressed in full flying clothing approaching the corner of No.2 hangar. He seemed to float out of sight around the opposite side of the hangar as we challenged him. At that time of the early morning no one should have been there, so we both went to investigate. I suggested that we split up, one nipping around the left-hand side of the hangar whilst the other took the right hand side. We ran quickly and soon met up again at the opposite end of the hangar. Neither of us had come across anyone, all doors leading into the hangar were locked, there was nowhere for anyone to hide. By now we were a little shook up, and as we began to walk around the hangar, we realised one very eerie fact, there were no other footprints in the snow around the hangar - only our own!*

By June 5th, the newly re-surfaced taxiways were complete. Both squadrons took part in operation 'Vigilant', which took place between 00:12 hours on Saturday May 25th and 16:15 hours on the 27th. Both squadrons had supplied 6 singletons each to take part in this UK air defence exercise, designed to test Fighter Command's capabilities during a simulated global nuclear war. Another exercise on June 24th saw 92 Squadron exchange 4 of their Hunters with 6 from 4 Squadron, based at RAF Jevar, Germany. A De Havilland Dove landed at Goosepool during July, on board was Mr Thornton of ICI, who had arrived to discuss the possibility of the company using Middleton as a base for air travel.

264 sent an advance party to its new temporary home at Leeming on September 23rd. The squadron's main party arrived there on the 26th, along with the aircraft. The squadron was unhappy as they had heard that they were to lose their identity and were to become 33 Squadron. They finally decided that, as they were struggling to get airborne as a 264 chrysalis, it might be better to fly as a 33 butterfly.

---

[137] Ground attack/bomber versions of the Hawker Hurricane

92 sent an advance party on the 4 mile trek to its new home at Thornaby on September 25th, whilst the main party and the Hunters joined them on the 27th. From that point, Middleton assumed parenting responsibility for Thornaby and Seaton Snook. The final unit to depart was Middleton's Station Flight. Somewhat smaller than the other two squadrons, the flight needed only a day to make its move, and did so on the 30th.

The reason for their migration was the fact that the airfield was due to close to flying on October 1st to allow major civil engineering work to be carried out. Today, the huge, light-coloured concrete extensions at each end of runway 23/05 bear testimony to one of the reasons for the airfield's temporary closure. These extensions increased the main runway's length to 7,300 feet, to allow it to accommodate the English Electric Lightning and other fast jets, which would shortly be coming on line. At the same time, it was strengthened to allow heavier aircraft, such as the Vulcan, Valiant and Victor bombers, to operate from the airfield. V bombers were detached to Middleton right up to its closure, mainly Vulcans. The V Force air and groundcrew had their own self-contained accommodation at Middleton, complete with sleeping quarters, kitchen and lounge facilities. This single story complex was situated just off the taxiway at the end of runway 24. The Vulcans were parked on a bomber loop, close to the complex. This would save the need for taxiing, and allow the huge bombers to become airborne in minutes should the excrement hit the rotary cooling device and the order to scramble be given. For this was the Cold War period, when every second counted in retaliating to a threat from the Warsaw Pact.

Whilst at Thornaby, 6 of 92's Hunters joined with 6 more of 66 Squadron's, and took part in exercise 'Argus'. They were detached to Tangmere in the southern sector and took part in flying simulated bomber tracks over Belgium and France, where they were 'intercepted' by Canadian F86 Sabre Jets. F/O Fox of 92 Squadron was taking part in an air firing exercise when he flew below his break-off height and struck the flag target with his starboard wing. Fortunately the aircraft was not badly damaged and he was able to land at Acklington, Northumberland.

1958

After two weeks were lost due to bad weather, 92 detached to Cyprus on January 8th 1958. Whilst there, F/L R Higg lost his life in a flying accident. Back in the Northeast, excessive snowfalls curtailed flying. 92 remained in Cyprus until March when they returned to Thornaby.

Whilst taking off from a detachment to Horsham-St Faith on 25th April, F/L Moors in Hunter XG234 suffered a low JPT[138] and an associated loss of power. He abandoned the take-off but was unable to prevent the Hunter from running into the overshoot. Fortunately the aircraft was not damaged, just as well as he was carrying a full load of fuel and ammo. Seven of 92's Hunters took off from Thornaby, but were diverted to Acklington. During the day the airfield became 'Red', and the Hunters scrambled to attack the bogeys. During the ensuing intercepts, 92 'Splashed' 8 Vulcans, 14 Canberras and 2 Valiants.

Vampire XH296, flown by F/L Martin and F/L Davies, suffered an engine failure whilst attempting an overshoot at Dishforth on June 10th. The aircraft received Cat 3 damage, whilst Davis suffered broken vertebra. The next day S/L Hobson and his passenger S/L Wright, flying in Meteor WA671, had a flap actuating lever break. The lever punctured the upper surface of the wing skin, again causing Cat 3 damage to the aircraft. They were able to land safely without further drama. During August, 92 left Thornaby for a temporary detachment to RAF Waterbeach, to participate in a Halyard exercise.

On September 11th, having completed Halyard, 92 returned to take up residence once again at Middleton. On the 23rd, an advanced party of 33 squadron personnel (formerly 264) arrived at Middleton from Leeming. Their Gloster Javelin Mk 7s arrived on October 1st. On the same day, Goosepool welcomed a new Base Commander, with the arrival of G/C A V R Johnstone. As a Flight Lieutenant, 'Sandy' Johnstone, a pilot with 602 (City of Glasgow Squadron), was one of the first Scottish pilots to make the headlines during WWII. During 1939, he was one of the pilots who went up against the first German air raid over the Firth of Forth. He later became the C/O of 602, which he led throughout the Battle of Britain. He went on to command a Spitfire Wing during the later phases of the Battle of Malta.

As both squadrons landed back at Middleton, they found the airfield still in the throes of construction. Major work was still underway on the runways and buildings. Once settled in, both units were to take up post as air defence squadrons. Whilst at Middleton, 92 became the RAF's official aerobatic team, 'The Blue Diamonds'. On December 22nd, F/O S E Cook failed to return from a training sortie over the North Sea. An Air Sea Search by Shackletons, Sycamore helicopters and lifeboats was carried out, but only two overload wing tanks were recovered from water.

---

[138] Jet Pipe Temperature

1959

At 08:40 on May 18th 1959 Teessides first 'Airport' began operating out of Greatham airstrip near Hartlepool. A service organised by Roberts Tours Ltd of Stockton and operated by BKS Aero Charters Ltd of Southend was to be operated daily from Greatham to Northolt, London. The aircraft used for the one hour and 20 minute flights were silver and red 32 seater BKS Douglas Dakotas. The flights were aimed mainly at local businessmen. The Mayor of West Hartlepool, Counsellor J O Hewlett OBE and the Town Clerk MR E J Waggott OBE were at the airfield for the inaugural flight. Both were invided to fly, but were unable to do so, due to other commitments. Also present was Alderman J O Coxon, Chairman of the West Hartlepool Civic Airport Committee. The initial flight was flown by 35 year old Captain H W Ayre, an ex-RAF pilot.

Typical of most RAF airfields, Middleton St George was organized on a three Wing basis, Administration, Flying and Technical. Although all three Wings carried out different functions, together they worked as one, to ensure the overall smooth operation of the Station. During 1959, Middleton's Flying Wing was commanded by W/C D F M Brown AFC. He reported directly to the Station Commander, and was responsible for training and the operational efficiency of the flying squadrons based on the airfield, including the physical fitness of everyone on the airfield. Beside the two operational squadrons, 33 and 92, he also commanded Air Traffic Control and the Station Flight, which employed its own Meteor, Vampire and Anson aircraft.

As a very young Air Cadet, the author enjoyed a very happy Sunday afternoon during August 1959 when taken up with 5 of his friends on a birthday 'Hop' in the Station Flight's Anson. Having originally been promised a trip in a Meteor T7, the smiles turned to a pet lip when told just before takeoff time that it had 'gone sick'. However, the trusty Anson was pressed into service and the day was saved. In payment for my ride there was a catch. The Anson's undercarriage was wound up and down by a hand crank handle, about 200 turns I think, a most exhausting task for a young teenager, but well worth it.

The main purpose of the Station Flight was to maintain communication, gunnery training, instrument flying training and drogue towing. One of the Flight's Meteors was fitted with a half mile of steel cable, which was trailed behind the aircraft with a round, windsock looking, canvas drogue on the end. This aircraft would fly out to sea where it would be 'attacked' by the airfield's fighters. When the air-firing detail was completed, the Meteor would overfly the airfield at low level and release the cable/drogue. This was then recovered by a crew with a Landrover and brought back.

Each fighter had its cannon shells dipped in different coloured powder paint. This was to ensure that when (or if) a particular pilot successfully hit the drogue, his rounds, on passing through the canvas, would leave a telltale ring of colour around the periphery of the hole. That way, when the pilots were debriefed, the good (or bad) news about one's aim was indisputable.

Air Traffic

This was divided into Approach Control and Local Control. Approach Control, situated one floor below the glass topped bit of the control tower, took care of aircraft flying in the area surrounding the airfield, whether Middleton's aircraft or those that were simply transiting the area. If an aircraft required to recover to Middleton, it was assisted in doing so by Approach Control, who would hand over the aircraft to the Director. The pilot would then be 'Talked Down' by the controller, who was sat at his or her double-screened radar set. One display gave the aircraft's progress down the 'Glide-scope', i.e. its position on a line leading down to the runway threshold. This line was simply drawn on the glass of the radar screen to simulate an approach angle of, if I remember correctly, about four degrees.[139] The controller's job was to keep the blip coming down the line until it reached the runway. The other display gave the aircraft's position relative to the centreline of the runway (Azimuth). This time, the extended runway centreline was drawn on the glass, and the aircraft's blip (with a little help from the pilot) was kept on this line.

[139] Civilians use 3 degrees

A typical GCA would begin as the aircraft began its approach, with the pilot being told not to reply to the commands given by the controller, only to respond to them. When the approach got underway, the controller would pass instructions to the pilot as necessary such as – ' Your height is good, you are left of the centreline, turn right heading 250, maintain your rate of descent.' This would be followed a short time later by more instructions to return onto the runway heading, or, if he was above or below the Glide-Scope, to climb or dive to regain this line. On a good day, the pilot simply sat there and responded to these fly left/right, up/down commands. He would be reminded to lower flaps and undercarriage at the appropriate distance/height, just in case he had not done so himself.

Along with these commands were periodic comments as to the distance to run, such as 'You have 2 miles to run to touchdown', etc. At about half a mile it was expected that the pilot would have contact with the runway or the approach lights. If not, an overshoot would be initiated and the whole procedure started again. Not a happy thought in a Meteor with very limited poundage of fuel remaining.

It is interesting to note that GCA was still a last ditch option for non-ILS equipped approaching pilots at Middleton during the 60s and 70s, after the airfield became Teesside airport. It was of course replaced by the Instrument Landing System, which simply enough provides almost the same information seen by the ground controllers, but placed in the cockpit for the pilot to see for himself. Here the fly left/right needle on his ILS instrument panel is joined by a fly up/down needle, both displayed in the same instrument. However, to those of us who remember flying a GCA approach, there was something comforting about the soothing, reassuring voice of the controller in your earphones, which seemed to spread the load. You were not alone, and the voice in your ears gave one confidence in what could be a quite precarious situation for a fatigued pilot.

Local control

This was located in the familiar glasshouse on top of the control tower. Like Teesside's controllers of today, the local controllers were responsible for all aircraft movements within the local airfield area, both in the air and on the ground. They were also responsible, via traffic lights, pyrotechnics and Aldis lamps, for the movement of any vehicle on the airfield.

Wing Operations Centre

The Wing Operations Centre maintained the link between the Master Control Radar Station and the airfield's two fighter squadrons. During a potential war, or more usually, during training operations, Wing Ops had to keep both the aircraft and the Master Radar Station fully up to date with the minute by minute events of the current operation.

The Physical Fitness Officer

With his small staff of physical fitness instructors, the Physical Fitness Officer was responsible for maintaining the fitness of all airfield personnel. It was especially important to ensure a high state of fitness within the airfield's aircrew members, who were expected to carry out their duties at very high speed and altitudes. The Physical Fitness section was also responsible for the wide range of sporting equipment around the airfield.

Fire Fighting

At Middleton, Fire Fighting was carried out by the RAF Regiment, who were responsible for the Domestic and Flying (Fire and Crash Rescue) Fire Sections.

Technical Wing

Wing Commander P D Cherry DFC DFM commanded the Technical Wing, which supplied technical facilities and advice to all departments of the station. Both of Middleton's squadrons had their own aircraft servicing teams. The Tech Wing provided the various component-servicing bays and ran the other technical activities of the Station. Although closely linked, the Technical Wing was actually 5 separate sections, consisting of Technical Wing Headquarters, the Engineering Squadron, Armament Squadron, Signals Squadron and the Refuelling Flight.

The Headquarters Building

The HQ building was responsible for the smooth flow of technical information throughout the airfield, including letters, books, amendments etc, and for supplying the 'higher authority' with information on problems that were experienced. Headquarters staff were also responsible for the allocation of manpower on the airfield.

The Engineering Squadron

This section was responsible for the servicing of a variety of aircraft components and ground handling equipment. It was also required to service all mechanical transport on the airfield and to provide general engineering facilities in the Station Workshops.

The Armament Squadron

As the name implies, the Armament Squadron took care of aircraft armaments, along with personal weapons and anything else that went 'Bang'. This would include such strange things as cartridges for engine starting, ejection seats, and emergency canopy release systems. The Armament Squadron encompassed the Photographic Section, which covered both airborne and ground requirements.

The Signals Squadron

The Signals Squadron serviced all aircraft radio and radar equipment. They also looked after the other specialised (classified) ground to air communication systems on the airfield. Another of their requirements was to attend to the Station's teleprinters, and to provide temporary telephones circuits, other than those provided by the GPO[140]

The Refueling Flight

The Refuelling Flight's fleet of 6 tankers ensured that all aircraft were promptly refuelled after each flight. They drew a variety of fuels from several underground bulk fuel installations throughout the airfield.

The Administrative Wing

The administration of the airfield was carried out by the Administrative Wing under the command of Wing Commander J C Button DSO DFC. The 'Admin Wing' was based in the Station HQ building, and was responsible to the Station Commander for all the admin services on the station, including Station HQ, Equipment Section, Education Section, Catering Section, SSQ, RAF Police, Air Ministry Works Department and the station's Chaplains.

The Station Headquarters building housed not only the Station Commander but also the Station Accounting Staff and other secretarial departments, who were responsible for the general administration and discipline on the station as a whole. This included both service and civilian personnel.

Equipment Section

The Equipment Section was responsible for all matters relating to equipment on the station, including aircraft and MT spares, replacements, and special clothing for both air and groundcrew. They were also responsible for all stocks of fuels required on the airfield, including aviation fuels, motor fuels and solid fuel for heating. The individual items under their control were myriad, and included everything from the Station Commander's bike to the complete furnishings of the various messes and married quarters. The accounting records for these items were kept by a special section within the Equipment Section, known as the Equipment Provisioning and Supply Section.

Education Section

A wide programme of educational facilities, which all airmen were encouraged to avail themselves of, was provided by the Education Section. A well-equipped reference library was maintained, in close association with the local Education Authorities, to help with the schooling of station personnel's children. A well-appointed and comfortable information room was made available to all ranks, and contained a wide range of magazines, newspapers and periodicals, together with up-to-date information of current interests.

Messes

All messes on the Station were equipped with modern well-maintained kitchens, which were regularly inspected by the Duty Officer and regularly checked by the Medical Staff. A wide range of courses was offered at most meals. It was said at the time that the standard of catering at Middleton would rival any West End hotel.

Station Sick Quarters

The Station Sick Quarters were manned by Medical Officers responsible to the Station Commander via the Officer Commanding the Admin Wing. They were responsible for the general health and cleanliness of the station. Another of their tasks was to maintain all medical aspects of high-speed, high altitude flight. There were, of course, the day-to-day medical problems associated with the large numbers of station personnel and their families. The well-equipped SSQ contained modern, well-equipped medical and dental surgeries, together with medical inspection rooms, a dispensary and wards.

RAF Police

As part of the RAF's Provost Marshal's Department, the RAF Police Section on the airfield was required to maintain the general security and discipline of the station. The former guardroom[141] looked out towards the camp entrance. On the other side of the road stood the camp's 'Gate Guardians', a Tempest[142] and a Spitfire.

Ministry of Works Dept

The Station's Air Ministry Works Department maintained a permanent staff headed by a Clerk of Works and a Station Engineer. They were responsible for the upkeep and maintenance of all permanent buildings and installations on the station. Their responsibilities also included all electrical services, painting, plumbing and heating, both on the airfield and in its buildings, along with maintaining standby generators, grass cutting and the upkeep of the station's gardens.

Chaplains

The Station was 'Blessed' with three chaplains, who took care of the spiritual needs of all. The C of E church was located on the north side of the Station HQ Building.

---

[140] There were no BT or Cable phone suppliers in those days, only thye General Post Office (GPO). Run by the British Government, it had the monopoly on supplying the country's telephone network.
[141] A caravan showroom at the time of writing
[142] This particular Tempest is now on permanent display at the RAF Museum, Hendon

On January 14th 1959, an official visitor from British Rail arrived at Middleton to carry out exploratory discussions regarding the possibility of erecting a railway siding and halt within the precincts of the Airfield. The Station Commander, G/C Johnstone, had departed for London on January 26th to visit the High Commissioner of the Federation of Malaya, to have the Order of Johan Menku Negara conferred upon him. This was a one-of-a-kind award to be awarded to an RAF Officer.

During February 1959, Eagle Airways used a Heron aircraft on charter to ICI for a trial period of two weeks. This trial, which provided a twice-daily service, commenced on February 9th and had to be extended for another week due to Teesside's bad weather. On March 17th, F/L HO Hood landed a Vampire of the Station Flight 'Wheels up', resulting in the aircraft receiving Cat 3 damage. F/L Hood unstrapped the bits and walked away.

33 were detached to RAF Bruggen between April 7th to the 17th, to take part in operation 'Topweight'. Some wag in 92 had the idea of 'Bouncing' 33 on their return, just for the practice. As the unsuspecting 33 Squadron Javelins returned over the North Sea, they were indeed jumped on by their colleagues from Middleton. However, by all accounts they put up a good show once they realised what was going on.

A Heron of the Queen's Flight arrived on May 20th, when HRH Princess Alexandra paid a visit to Middlesbrough. She later departed Middleton, her pilot for the day being no less than Air Commodore Sir Edward Fieldon KCVO CB DFC AFC.

Late June saw 92 off to Cyprus again, and returning on July 2nd. August 20th saw the Royal Observer Corps annual 'At Home' day take place at Middleton, the area of operation for their 1,200 members being from Berwick to Lincolnshire.

During September, Goosepool was chosen to provide the Battle of Britain 'At Home' day, and this took place on Saturday the 19th. Apart from the flying displays by the airfield's Meteors, Vampires, Hunters and Javelins, there were other aircraft from various RAF stations. In those days there were no such thing as defence cuts. Today, the RAF has few types of aircraft in comparison to the 50s and 60s. Then there were Ansons, Argosies, Belfasts, Beverlys, Britannias, Bucaneers, Bulldogs, Canberras, Chipmunks, Comets, Dominies, Doves, F86 Sabres, Gnats, Hastings, Herons, HS125s, Hercules, Hunters, Javelins, Piston and Jet Provosts, Lightnings, Lincolns, Meteors (long and short nose), Oxfords, Phantoms, Shackletons, Spitfires, Twin Pioneers, Vampires, Valiants, Varsities, Valettas, VC10s, Venoms, Victors, Vulcans, - and lots of em!

Today! You can only name the American AWACS, DC10, Harrier, Hawk, Jaguar, Nimrod, Tucano, Tornado, VC10 and eventually (when they get the bugs out of it) the Eurofighter. And that's about it! They are in such short supply in comparison with the aircraft of the post war years that, if the chips were really down, they probably wouldn't be able to stop a pig in a passage. I was shocked recently when told that apparently, the RAF only have 4 squadrons of F3 Air Defence Varient Tornadoes. However, I digress!

Also present at the 'At Home Day' was the Tyne Tees Television outside broadcast unit, not only for the display, but also for the parade the next day. Imagine that now, in this football-dominated environment of ours.

September 1959 also saw 92 Squadron taking part in Army co-operation exercises on Salisbury Plain. November saw 33 on detachment to Nicosia. They were back by the 12th, just in time to enjoy the farewell party of 13 Groups AOC, AVM Earle.

HQ Fighter Command were aware that, during an international crisis, they might have to reinforce the Middle East with fighter squadrons. These would have to operate from secure and reasonably developed bases. It was decided that 92 would practice such a reinforcement between October 23rd and 28th 1959, called operation 'Sambar'. This would be accomplished by moving to the Libyan airfield of Idris and carrying out air defence operations from there, under the control of a mobile type U radar convoy. The enemy would consist of Canberras and V bombers of Bomber Command and the Middle East Airforce. S/L R H B Dixon was chosen as the Detachment Commander, S/L D F M Brown AFC was to become Director of Operations from Idris. The plan required 92 to send 10 Mk 6 Hunters from Middleton to Idris, and for Transport Command to provide 1 Beverly and 3 Hastings and a route support Varsity for air transport of the squadron.

The Hunters were to be used in the air defence role, and the exercise required each aircraft to be flown up to a maximum of three flights per day. The route was MSG – Orange – Carritat – Idris and return. Diversion airfields along the way were staged at Dijon, Decimomanu, Bigerte R/G (USAF), Luqa, Idris, Wheelus, Evreaux/Fauville (USAF), Cateroux, Deols, Marseille, Mariguore, Alghero. ETD MSG was 06:00 Zulu on October 23rd 1959. ETA Orange - 07:30, ETD Orange - 08:30, ETA Idris - 10:00 Zulu. The sections were to take off at 20-minute intervals and each section was not to contain less than two aircraft. Each section leader was responsible for route navigation and for the collection of route forecasts at MSG and all staging posts. 92's Navigation Officer was responsible for obtaining diplomatic clearances and notification procedures for the whole squadron, prior to leaving the UK for Idris. The Section Leaders were responsible for sending the arrival signals from each staging post to HQ Fighter Command, Air HQ Malta, HQ 13 Group and MSG. The signal was to contain number and type of aircraft, Section Leader's rank and name, ETA at staging post and ETD for the next intended landing point.

Air/Sea Rescue facilities for the first stage were provided by Air HQ Malta. All Hunter Mk 6s were to carry a full load of ballast ammo, 4 pylon tanks were also to be fitted. Pilots uplifting fuel at foreign airfields were to obtain receipts. They were also required to 'Check in' with Malta centre, on 119.1 m/cs. They were also required to call Malta approach on 119.7 m/cs for a weather update and instructions as to whether they were to land at Luqa or overfly and proceed to Idris. All aircraft had the option to divert to Luqa if they so desired.

The first Hunter to take off was XF521 'Alpha', flown by S/L Dixon, his air to ground call sign (AGCS) was Rafair and his air to air was Blenheim Red 1. The remaining aircraft were as follows: -

Bravo	XG238	F/L Ozanne,	Blenheim Red 2.	AGCS - Mike Alpha
Charley	XG211	F/L Bell,	Blenheim Red 3	AGCS Uncle Charley
Delta	XG520	F/L Carpenter	Blenheim Red 4	
Echo	XG231	F/L Black	Blenheim Yellow 1	
Foxtrot	XG228	F/O Buckham	Blenheim Yellow 2	
Golf	XF186	F/L Oswell	Blenheim Yellow 3	
Hotel	XF522	F/L Aylell	Blenheim Yellow 4	
Juliet	XG255	F/L Caldwell	Blenheim White 1	
Kilo	XE532	Cpt Griffin	Blenheim White 2.	

The outbound airlift used 1 Beverly and 3 Hastings transport aircraft, and provided for 85 personnel, each with 50-lbs of personal kit, and 28,000-lbs of freight consisting of

tool kit	@ 30-lbs	2,100-lbs.
10 aircraft covers	@ 80-lbs	800-lbs.
pilot's personal kit	@ 50-lbs.	500-lbs.
Spares and ground equipment		24,500-lbs.

Beverly 3203 ETA MSG 22nd - 18:00 - ETD - MSG 06:00 23rd - 18 Passengers + 18,000-lbs.
Hastings 4218 ETA MSG 22nd - 18:00 - ETD - MSG 08:00 23rd - nil Passengers + 10,000-lbs.
Hastings 4219 ETA MSG 23rd - 18:00 - ETD - MSG 09:00 23rd - 36 Passengers + Nil cargo.
Hastings 4220 ETA MSG 23rd - 18:00 - ETD - MSG 10:00 23rd - 36 Passengers + Nil cargo.

The squadron groundcrew were divided into 2 groups, A and B. The working hours for the 2 groups were 03:30 - 12:30 local Z and 12:00 - 18:00 local Z.

Full 30-mm ballast ammo was to be carried on the Hunters, but the guns were to be completely unloaded. VHF radio was fitted to all aircraft, using TR 1985/87 sets. Channel F of the Rebecca was tuned into 223 m/cs to give the aircraft a Eureka/Rebecca facility at Luca, El Adam, Idris and Treedos. DME (Distance Measuring Equipment) was also used.

1960

During January 1960, both 33 and 92 Squadrons departed Middleton for Duxford to take part in a practice mass flypast in preparation for the imminent birth of the Queen's latest child.[143] February 19th saw the re-adoption of the station by Darlington, when a plaque was presented to the station by the Mayor, Councilor Tramewan. On the same day, 92 flew in the mass flypast over Buckingham Palace in honour of the birth of the Queen's son. Throughout 1960, both squadrons took part in many detachments and exercises. On April 19th, 33 and 92 departed for Cyprus and exercise 'Fowley'.

During operation 'Yeoman' on 25th May, 2 Javelin crews flying from Leuchars, near Dundee, suffered a mid-air collision during the operation and had to be admitted to Middleton's SSQ. On the 27th, Her Majesty the Queen and Prince Phillip were visitors to the station after they visited Durham by road. They later departed in a Heron of the Queen's Flight.

33 and 92 returned to base from Cyprus on the 31st. An exchange tour to Rygge in Norway, and displays at Topcliffe, occupied 92 during June. During July, Bomber Command held a dispersed exercise at Middleton called Operation Mayflight. On Sunday the 17th, it was business as usual as both squadrons took part in a Group exercise.

On August 23rd, 92 departed for Malta on a 7-day detachment. Whilst there, they provided an aerobatic display at Takali on the 27th, arriving back at Middleton on the 29th. In their role as reserve Aerobatic Team, during September, 92 continued to give aerobatic shows up and down the country, including the Battle of Britain displays at RAF Leconfield and St Athen. On the 15th, the BBC Northern Dance Orchestra and artists performed for station personnel in the NAFFI. This performance was made the subject of two 35-minute record programs to be broadcast by the BBC. Darlington's Mayor, meanwhile Councillor J P Cottam took the salute at a station parade on the 18th.

On Wednesday October 16th, Tyne Tees Television presented 'The One O'clock Show' at the station, which was televised the following day. On November 16th, Tyne Tees Television returned to the airfield for an outside broadcast entitled 'Shield and Deter - a day in the life of RAF Middleton St George'. This title was derived from the motto depicted on the station's badge. The programme went 'On Air' at 5.30pm on ITV channel 10.

The Station Commander, G/C A V R Johnstone, was posted the following month to the Imperial Defence College. His successor was G/C Rothwell DFC, who had just completed a tour of duty as Air Attaché in Bangkok. G/C Johnstone was 'Dined Out' by the AOC of 13 Group, AVM H J Maguire CB DSO OBE. G/C Rothwell was received in the Mess on November 30th.

---

[143] Prince Andrew

1961

During January 1961, ex-111 Squadron pilots arrived at Middleton to join 92, and carried out aerobatics, as well as normal practice flying as the RAF's reserve Aerobatic Team. 92 then left for Cyprus and arrived for their detachment (code-name Leprechaun) at Nicosia on the 10th. During the transit flight, the Hunter T7 which was accompanying the single seaters suffered freezing of the vent tank's air-line, causing the aircraft to suffer a shortage of fuel. The pilots, F/O Freeman and F/L Robert, then suffered fuel transfer failure during the long leg from HalFar (Malta) to Nicosia, but managed to divert to El Adam.

Having arrived in Cyprus, 92 carried out ground firing on the Cowden range, using Rocket Projectiles (RPs), this was the first time the squadron had fired RPs. Whilst there 92 availed themselves of the lovely Cyprus weather and carried out much aerobatic practice. The team then carried out a practice display for Fighter Command's Commander-in-Chief at the end of the month.

Meanwhile 33 converted onto the Mk 9 Javelin, and on the last day of February, No. 19 squadron arrived at Middleton from Leconfield for a temporary detachment, whilst work was being carried out at their own base.

On March 3rd, 92 transitted over to Akrotiri. Tragedy nearly struck when, during a practice display, the No.2 aircraft rolled inexplicably to port, causing its port wing to collide with the No.4 aircraft's starboard wing. Fortunately both were able to land, although only one of the aircraft was able to depart when the detachment returned to the UK on March 10th. On the 27th, the C-in-C, Fighter Command, visited Middleton, to watch 92 give a full display, after which he gave his approval for them to become the RAF's official aerobatic display team for the season.

On April 15th, 92, under the command of S/L B P W Mercer gave their first display as Fighter Command's official aerobatic display team. This took place at Duxford, for Independent Television News (ITN). This was followed by more displays, which took place at North Weald, Hucknall and Yeadon (Leeds). RAF Vildenrath, Germany on the 22nd saw 92's first International Show, although poor weather forced the team to carry out a lower than normal display. At the time, the press knew the team as the Falcons.

On May 26th, all 16 of 92's Hunters departed Middleton for their new home at RAF Leconfield, near Beverly, Yorkshire, and after 4 years, ended an era for Goosepool. 33 also left for Leconfield, but they were to spend only a short time there, as they were required to re-locate to Leeming by June 1st. Although 92 had departed permanently, 33 would eventually return to Goosepool, but not for a while. The reason for their temporary move was to allow Middleton to close for the period June 1st – July 31st. This would allow yet more major civil engineering work to take place. Soon, jet noise was replaced by the sounds of huge Euclid graders, excavators, trench machines and heavy trucks. Runway over-runs were firmed up, omni-directional lighting was installed and other works services were given attention whilst the airfield was closed.

Initially Middleton's 24 hour Master Diversion Airfield (MDA) facility was maintained. By the end of June however, due to the work being carried out on the runways, Middleton's MDA status was temporarily transfured to RAF Leeming. Opportunity was taken during this period to get as many Goosepool personnel off on annual leave as possible. July was used to prepare for the return of 33 squadron and the arrival of 2 new units, the RAF's Instrument Rating Squadron and the Lightening Conversion Unit.

On July 31st the runways were opened temporarily for 6 of 33's Javelins to arrive. This was only to be a very short visit however, as they had only called in to arm with Firestrak missiles, before departing for Cyprus for a Neuralgia detachment. The next day Middleton reopened.

The Instrument Rating Squadron (IRS), arrived on August 3rd. They had formed out of 228 OCU, which had disbanded the previous month. Initially, on their arrival at Goosepool, they were equipped with only 3 Javelin T3s. The unit's C/O was S/L R Goring-Morris.

The Lightening Conversion Unit (LCU), which had formed at Coltishall on January 4th 1960, arrived on the 10th, and were under the command of S/L J M Robertson. They had no aircraft at all. Once at Middleton their nomenclare changed to the Lightening Conversion Squadron (LCS). Things were very quiet at Middleton at this time, and this was not improved by the absence of 33's Javelins. However on the 23rd, 33 returned from Cyprus and on the same day the first IRS course commenced.

On the 29th a Lightening Mk 1 flew in, to give the ground personnel experience on Lightening turn-around proceedures. It was also there to allow crash crews to receive instruction on the Lightening's rescue break-in points and the Mk 4 BS ejector seat.

On September 16/17th Middleton's Battle of Britain 'At Home' weekend took place. This was opened by non-other than G/C J B ('Willie') Taite, DSO DFC, who as you will remember, was 78 squadron's C/O during August/September 1942. The weather during the Saturday morning was not good, with cross-winds gusting up to 55 kts. This cancelled displays by a glider and paratroopers, who were to descend from a static balloon. However, this did not prevent a stunning lightening display by S/L Goodwin. During the afternoon's display, the wind did not abate, however it veered around and came within 10^0 of the runway heading.

Two Russian visitors arrived from the Soviet Embassy in London for the display. They were General Efimov, who was the Russian Military Attaché and Lt Colonel Konobeev, the assistant Air Attaché. As this period was at the height of the cold war, the RAF officer escorting both gentlemen was briefed not to divulge any sensitive information. General Efimov was very well mannered, but he was also very inquisitive. However, there was only one underhand question asked, 'How many

Lightenings do you have here at Middleton-St-George'? In case you are wondering, the RAF officer simply smiled at the General, and after giving him a knowing look, continued to talk about other things. Fortunately, the chauffeur did not speak English.

During the Sunday display 33's 'B' Flight departed for Cyprus for another one-month detachment. One of their number only managed to reach Pizza with a duff engine. Another suffered the same problem and had to land at El Adam. A replacement Javelin sent on the 25th also got no further than Pizza and it too developed engine trouble. By the end of the month 5 out of the remaining 7 Javelins also required engine changes. A detachment of Middleton's croundcrew personnel were dispatched to Pizza to fix the offending aircraft.

Also during September, the LCS were still awaiting delivery of their Lightening Mk T4 from the English Electric Factory at Warton, near Blackpool. Meanwhile, planning meetings continued at Middleton in regard to a proposal (Which never happened), to build an extra 125 married quarters.

33 Squadron took part in several deployments and exercises throughout October, including Homex, Ciano, Groupex, Windmill and Neuralgia. This particular 9 Javelin detachment to Akrotiri began on October 12th under the command of S/L Harvey, returning to Goosepool on the 21st. Operation 'Halyard' came next, when 33 detached 3 Javelins to Wattisham, between November 2nd and 9th, again under the command of S/L Harvey, the other two aircraft being flown by F/L Huppler and F/O Williams.

On October 27th, the first two students received their IRS endorsements. No. 2 IRS course began with only 1 student, G/C L A Malins DSO DFC Station Commander designate of RAF Coltishall.

At last on November 3rd, the Lightening Conversion Squadron received delivery of their long awaited Lightening T4. This was flown in after dark from Warton, by Jimmy Dell, English Electric's Deputy Chief Test Pilot. Along with him for the ride was the LCS's C/O, S/L Robertson. The formal hand-over of documents took place and the appropriate speeches and glasses of champagne were received in the crewroom. The aircraft was then handed over to the Service Squadron for an acceptance check. Due to defects in the hydraulic pipe runs in No.1 engine bay, which failed to comply with ST1, (Lightening 31), the aircraft was not accepted. On the 23rd, the joy at receiving their new toy was extinguished, when W/C Loughton, O/C Flying and S/L Goodwin quietly flew XM970 back to Warton, for further mods to the routing of the hydraulic pipes. They were told that it would be March 62, before they would get their sticky mits on their baby again.

It was doom and gloom at the LCS until they were told that an agreement had been made that would allow Middleton to carry out 200-hour inspections on Lightenings from other squadrons. This meant that they could get their hands on these Lightenings, for the test flights at least.

The first aircraft to arrive was from 56 squadron, which landed at Middleton just before the weather clamped on December 21st. There had been only 7 good flying days during December. On the 5th Bomber Command called a 'No Warning' dispersal exercise. In a hurry, the Bomber Command site at the end of runway 24 was opened up. Water, power and lighting

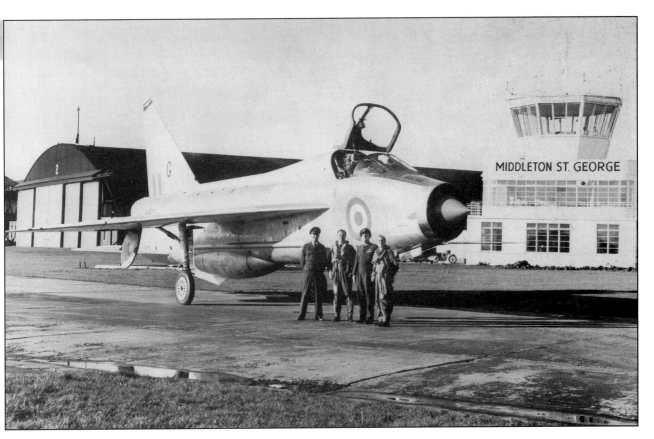

The first Lightening T4 arrives at Middleton-St-George.   Photo: PRO AIR28/1619

was turned on and the accommodation and catering facillities were prepared. In due course the Bomber Command personnel turned up to look after the Valient that arrived shortly after. It then spent the rest of the week waiting for the weather to clear.

From the 14th to the 21st, 25 squadron's Javelins were attached to Middleton for exercise 'Halyard'. This was the first time that this commitment was carried out from Middleton. From the 21st until the end of the month, Middleton's runways were 'Black', with one inch of Ice surmounted by three and a half inches of snow.

1962

During January 1962, it rained for 15 days out of the month, (Welcome to Teesside). The month also saw 33 Squadron fly 17 Javelins, both Mks 8 and 9, to Geilenkirchen, Germany. Groundcrew personnel were ferried out by RAF Britannias. The squadron was led by W/C Hughes, with S/L Porter I/C Tech Eng.

During February, with the absence of 33 and with no Lightenings for the LCS, Middleton's personnel were at a loss for something to do. The entire stock of aircraft at Middleton totalled three IRS Javelins and one T7 Meteor.

In particular this affected Air Traffic Control, who suffered much bordom, in desparation, Leeming was contacted to send over a few Jet Provost trainers to keep everyone happy. The JP students and their instructors had a whale of a time doing circuits and bumps at Middleton, a practice that continued right up to the 90's. Leeming eventually became a Master Diversion Airfield during 1964 and its JP's were discouraged from clogging up the circuit. They were banished to carry out their circuit work at Dishforth, Linton and Middleton before returning to Leeming at the end of the day.

On April 3rd, Goosepool welcomed back 15 of 33 squadrons Javelins after their jaunt to Geilenkirchen. During May Master Pilot Jack Crowther and Master Navigator Bert Farey MBE were flying in Javelin XH 755 when the aircraft began to spin uncontrollably. The crews of other aircraft flying in the formation saw both crewmembers eject and two chutes deploy. Within minutes of hitting the sea the pilot was picked up in a boat out of Aclington, having carried out a text-book landing and dinghy drill. Sadly Bert Farey was never found, despite an intensive search of the area. One possibile reason for his loss suggested at the time was that he may not have had his seat straps fastened. Bert Farey was a most popular and well respected member of the squadron. Jack Crowther returned to flying. Bert Farey's fiancée at the time lived in Geneva Road in Darlington.

On June 27th 1962 the LCS began to receive its own aircraft. The first to arrive was two-seat T4 trainer, XM970, which as you will remember had to be returned to the factory during October 1961. Once at Middleton out came the paint-brush and it was coded 'G'. By the end of October 1962 the unit would receive a further seven.

By now, The Early Warning Radar Station at Fylingdales was under construction. Middleton was visited by General Robert M Lee of the USAF. He wanted to visit the B.E.W.M.S. site at Fylingdales, and so a motorcade was organised to take him there. He returned to Middleton in the afternoon, after partaking of lunch in a country pub. He then departed for Iceland.

Royal Belgian Airforce Station Beauvechain was the venue for another liaison visit by four of 33 Squadron's Javelins on August 13th. The aircraft, flown by S/L Parker, F/L Taylor, along with F/L Huppler and P/O Chamberlain, were equipped with their 30-mm cannon, although no ammo was loaded.

On the 20th, four of 33's Javelin Mk 9s departed Middleton on a detachment to RAF Valley, Anglesey, led by W/C Gordon, to practice firing 5 telemetered missiles over the Aberporth range. The detachment occupied the 6 Javelin crews until September 7th (two aircrew members and the groundcrews travelled to Valley by private car). The aircraft flew in two sections of two aircraft each. Each Javelin carried a ventral tank, 4 Firestreaks and 2 x 30mm Aden cannons. The ammo for the detachment was to be provided by Valley, and was removed prior to their return to Goosepool. Ten missiles were airlifted to Valley from Middleton, in a ready to use state, so as to have five available. Six acquisition missiles and newly serviced ammonia cylinders were also airlifted to Valley.

Four of 33's Javelins, led by S/L J M A Parker, visited the Danish Airforce base at Skrydstrup on October 16th for a liaison visit, which was to provide an insight into the operations of other Airforces. Among the pilots along for this one was Cpt W Driver of the US Air Force, who was flying the No.2 aircraft, along with his navigator, F/L H Barker. In the third aircraft was another American Airforce officer, Cpt E Murray, who was navigating for F/L C C Taylor. Bringing up the rear was F/L A J Mackinnon and Master Navigator, F/L A Cross. As there were no squadron groundcrew available at Skrydstrup, the Aupin tank for engine starting had to be topped up after the engines were started at Middleton. The aircrew had been familiarised with the turn-around procedures for the Javelin, and for the most likely 'Snags' which might occur and which they would have to fix. The only ground equipment that could be carried was a hydraulic adapter stowed in one of the aircraft.

On October 24th 1962, word arrived at Middleton that 33 Squadron's days at Goosepool were numbered. They were to deploy to RAF Geilenkirchen by November 26th 1962, where they would become No.5 Squadron. The squadron was to transfer from Fighter Command to RAF Germany by this date, their on-route commander was to be W/C C R Gordon. The aircraft flew out in two flights, the first 9 aircraft departed Middleton on November 19th. They were followed by the remaining 8 Javelins on the 26th.

The squadron's T3 also flew out on the 19th, but returned to the UK shortly after for disposal. Their route to Geilenkirchen was as follows.

MSG to 53.36 N – 00.40E,
53.36N – 00.40E to 52.00N – 040.0E,
52.00N – 04.00E to Geilenkirchen.

Their diversion airfields were: - Leconfield, Leuchars, Coltishall, Soesterberg, Brugen, Laabruch, Wildenrath, Gutersloh.

The Javelins were to carry ventral tanks and 4 Firestreaks, ready to use or acquisition rounds.

The 33 Squadron crew list for those that were departing for Geilenkirchen was drawn up a few days prior to departure, and included: -

First Flight (pilot and nav)

W/C Gordon	S/L McCabe.
S/L Hamlin	F/L Blundell
F/L Boulton	F/L Martin
F/L Canter	F/O Smith
F/L Joyce	F/O Tilford
F/O Gardner	F/O Bradley
P/O Chamberlain	F/O Wilton
M/Pilot Crowther	M/Nav Lewis[144]
F/O Hallam	TBA

All of the squadron's ground equipment was flown out on the 19th. Each crewmember was allowed to carry a maximum of £50 Sterling for incidental expenses. All mess bills had to be paid before departure, and each aircraft had to get its own customs clearance. Also, each crewmember had to have a valid smallpox inoculation certificate. For the ferry flights to Geilenkirchen, all aircraft carried Gee, FIS Mk 2, Rebecca Mk 8 and DME. Each aircraft carried 4 missiles.

The Second flight to Geilenkirchen on the 26th consisted of:-

F/L Taylor	F/O Armiger
F/L Lundy	F/L Barker
F/L Mackinnon	F/O Cowap
F/L Packer	W/C Poole
F/L Brennan	F/L Maclochlan
F/O Watterson	F/O Baylee
F/O Gray	TBA

UHF channels for the transit began with Middleton Approach on 287.9 kilocycles.

On December 12th the Lightening Conversion Squadron suffered its first loss, when on returning from Chivenor to Middleton, XM993 ran off the runway, after the port undercarriage leg broke during the landing roll. The Lightening, Mike 93, turned over and caught fire. F/L Alan Turley and his student W/C C M Gibbs were able to escape and get clear before the aircraft burned out The aircraft ended up on its side with its port wing vertical.

1963

The Instrument Rating Squadron's No.10 and 11 Javelin Refresher Courses and No.6 Lightning Instrument Ratings Examiners Course were completed during April 1963. No.12 Javelin Conversion and Refresher Course started on the 17th with two students, who were expected to finish on May 10th.

Aircraft availability and serviceability was poor during April, with only 48.55 hours being flown. Due to a shortage of aircraft, the Standardisation visit of 41 Squadron, which was supposed to take place between April 8th and 11th, was cancelled. However, this did not deter the squadron from being able to demonstrate its aircraft to the SASO Fighter Command, and it was able to provide a formation of 2 Javelins and one Lightning for the inspection flypast.

On May 1st, Wing Commander J de M Severne MVO AFC assumed command of the Wing, when he replaced W/C Laughton who was posted to Neatishead. During the 1st and 2nd, as part of operation 'High Tide', Beverley aircraft of Transport Command operated from Middleton. Technical support was provided by the Airfield's Servicing Squadron.

There was much activity at Middleton as, at the same time, Bomber Command Vulcans operated from the airfield during Operation Mayflight. They were also scrambled due to a Bomber Command alert. Air Trooping activities continued during the month, when a force of soldiers were flown to Germany from Middleton in a Bristol Britannias, and an advance party of DLI personnel returned from Berlin on the same aircraft. This operation was taken care of by F/L Cowley, who supervised the operation from the airfield's point of view.

On May 8th, T Mk 4 Lightning XM994 was flown down to Leconfield for mods. On the same day, Lightning T Mk 4 XM971, having had its modifications carried out, returned to Middleton. Group Captain E W Wootan DFC AFC was appointed Station Commander on May 20th 1963. He replaced G/C F Rothwell, who was to attend an Air Warfare Course during July. The next day, the Commander-in–Chief of Fighter Command visited the station to familiarise himself with the Lightning. He underwent a very brief course of instruction on the Lightning, carried out over two days, which included one simulator ride and 3 flights with his instructor, F/L J S Smith. On the 23rd, 'Kingpin', an operational exercise, took place,

[144] Master Navigator

with Middleton providing 4 Lightning T Mk 4s. These were brought to readiness and scrambled, turned around and scrambled a second time. On the 27th, another exercise, 'Gano', was held, and 2 Lightning T Mk 4s were brought to readiness, scrambled, turned around and scrambled again. The next day, another Lightning T Mk 4 set off for Leconfield for mods.

Also during the month, the Simulator Flight was hard at it, with 136.20 hours of 'Sim' time being flown, despite 4.35 hours of 'Down' time, due to unserviceability. Nine pilots of No.6 Course completed 9 pre-solo conversion sorties in the simulator, 3 sortie profiles each. To add to the workload, 31.30 hours of staff simulator continuation training were carried out. No.s 10 and 11 Javelin Refresher Courses and No.6 Lightning Instrument Rating Examiner's Course were completed one student attending each course. The remaining few members of 4a Lightning conversion course completed their flying during the month, whilst 5 Course embarked upon the simulator and flying phase. By the end of May, 4 students had completed their conversion. Members of the Course included the new OC Flying Wing, W/C Severnet, and two new members of staff, F/Ls O'Donovan and Martin. It had been a busy month, with a total of 187.55 flying hours being flown. This was on top of the preparations for the AOC's inspection, when 5 aircraft were provided for the flying display. On June

33 squadron aircrew demonstrate a mock 'scramble' for the SASO's visit.   Photo: PRO AIR27/3057

1st 1963 the Lightening Conversion Squadron was re-named No. 226 OCU, soon after, it was in recept of seven ex-74 squadron F1s, which had just been overhauled by 60 MU. Whilst at Middleton the units Lightenings sported a red and white St Georges Cross livery. Also incorporated into 226 OCU was the Instrument Rating Squadron.

1964

By now the writing was on the wall for Middleton, as defence cuts necessitated the airfield's closure as it was no longer required. With this in mind, the 3 Javelins of the Instrument Rating Squadron departed for Leuchars in January 1964. 226 OCU were the last RAF unit to operate from Goosepool, but even their days were numbered. By April 1964, the winding down of Goosepool was well underway. On the 3rd, C E W Wootan DFC AFC handed over command of the Station to W/C B S Jones DSO OBE DFC. 226 OCU left for Coltishall on April 13th. By the same date, all stocks of Firestreak guided weapons were transferred to RAF Coltishall, and the station's Master Diversion Airfield commitment had been transferred to RAF Leconfield.

The Rear Party of Servicing personnel and their equipment left Goosepool the next day. Preparations then began to hand over the airfield to the Ministry of Civil Aviation on April 20th. During the first week of April, the remaining elements of 226 OTU departed to RAF Coltishall. The last remaining connection with flying, the Lightning Flight Simulator Section remained on the station, but would soon be transferred to the functional control of RAF Coltishall. To mark the end of an era, a farewell dance took place at the Airmen's Mess on the 9th. 226's pilots returned to Middleton on the 13th to fly out their aircraft. Their departure was watched by a small gathering of spectators, including members of the press. With the departure of 226's Lightnings and Javelins, the glory of being the last service aircraft to depart Goosepool went to Javelin T Mk 3 XH436, which departed on the 15th after completion of its Cat 3 repairs.

On the 18th, the station's Technical Wing ceased to exist. Meanwhile, the Education Section had been reduced to a minimum, consistent with the service required. With the exception of the main gate, which was controlled by a barrier out of working hours, all gates leading into the airfield were locked. This was to provide control of all motor traffic, both in

Flypast of Lightenings from Middleton's Lightening Conversion Squadron. View is towards Hangar 3 and the South East
Photo: PRO AIR28/1619

Flypast of two IRS Javelins and one Lightening T4 during the SASO inspection. Photo: PRO AIR28/1619

and out of the camp, with snap checks on cars and personnel being made. By mid April, the SSQ was almost completely closed and was running on bare essentials only. The medical equipment account was closed along with the Dental Centre, and all equipment returned to stores. On April 20th, the Three-Prong Station Organisation was abandoned, and the remnants of Flying Wing absorbed into SHQ, and RAF Middleton St George lost the title and establishment of 224 OCU. At the same time, the station was officially reduced to a Care and Maintenance basis, by order of Fighter Command administrative order 5164, dated 9th April 1964. The allocation of both station and Seaton Carew married quarters to RAF Catterick was well underway during April, with 8 Officers' and 27 Airmen's quarters having been allocated thus far.

At the MT Section, 14 vehicles had been dispatched, with a further 9 prepared for departure. The airfield's 6 huge fuel bowsers were to depart, prior to being put into storage. The Electronics Centre had been stripped during April and the Signals Flight moved to SHQ. To centrally control all labour, the remaining sections of the Technical Wing were organised into 6 Flights, responsible directly to the Station Commander. A total of 224 Airmen had already left during the month, leaving a total strength of 258. The Technical Wing had virtually ceased to exist, with what was left backing up the servicing and departure preparations of vehicles in the MT Section. The Corporal's Club was finally closed on April 30th.

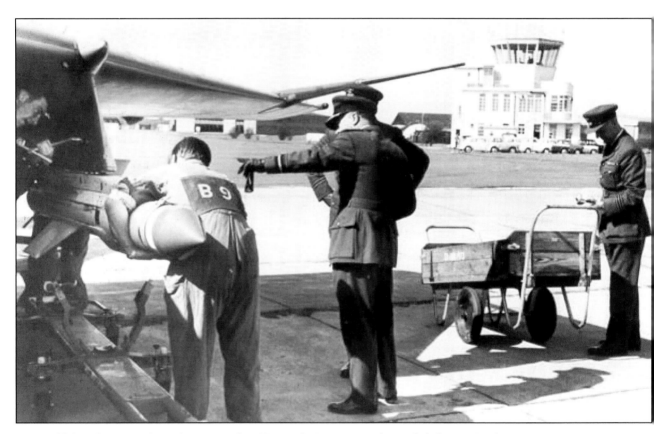

33 Squadron groundcrew demonstrate how Firestreak air to air missiles are lodad into a Javelin.   Photo: PRO AIR27/3057

By this time, a large number of buildings had been either handed over to MOA RAF Marham, or had been stripped of equipment and closed. These buildings were then subject to weatherproofing, fire precautions and security. By the end of April, practically all parenting responsibilities had been transferred over to other units.

The Sergeants' Mess was absorbed into the Officers' Mess building, and at this time, plans were in hand to incorporate the Airmen's Mess into the same building, where each of the three ranks were segregated. To facilitate the closing of buildings, all barrack equipment had been centralised in one of the hangars. By the end of April, 70% of this equipment had been withdrawn, 450 tons of stores cleared, and 14 tons of scrap sold. Meanwhile, 266 Squadron's silver was transferred to RAF Coltishall, whilst 33 Squadron's silver was sent to RAF Binbrook.

On May 25th, the Electronics Centre was placed on a C and M basis, and the Station's bulk aviation fuel was transferred to Binbrook, only tank bottoms being retained. The airmen's club was closed on May 31st, shop facilities, however, were still being provided by the grocery store, and recreational facilities were still provided by the PSI in the one remaining barrack block. By now, the bomber dispersal site had been handed over to RAF Marham. Hangars 1 and 2 were required for a few more weeks, to store the final batches of remaining barrack equipment. Meanwhile, a recommendation was being made to put the off-station VHF transmitter and receiver sites up for disposal after being stripped, as neither site was required by Bomber Command, nor MOA. The AAGW site was by now empty and was due to be closed by June 6th. The station's strength by the end of May 1964 was 18 officers, 61 W/Os and SNCO's,[145] 188 corporals and below.

Two station churches were still in use. The local Roman Catholic priest made formal application to the MOD to buy or rent the R/C church, complete with all furniture and fittings. The CO of RAF Catterick wanted to keep the C of E church as a going concern, to meet the needs of the occupants of Middleton's Married Quarters.

[145] Senior NCOs'

The remaining C and M Party during June was 13 officers, in addition to 2 officers attached for simulator duties. During the month, major items of clothing were transferred to RAF Catterick, whilst surplus barrack equipment was put on railway containers and dispatched to 7 MU. The AAGW Flight and Engineering Flight were disbanded on June 1st. All remaining technical services were by now concentrated within the MT Flight. By July, 11 officers remained on the strength, along with 2 officers attached to the simulator section. During the month, W/C B S Jones and F/L D Bensley departed Middleton for other duties. Agreement was still awaited during July from RAF Catterick, regarding the continued employment of the remainder of the full and part-time batting staff. During the month, the establishment of 4 civilian watchmen was approved. Fifteen redundancy notices for civilian personnel were issued during the month, to become effective during August. July also saw No.2 Hangar handed over to MOA on the 9th. Other buildings were emptied and handed over to the Care and Maintenance Party, including the Education Section on the 8th, the Dope Store on the 10th, workshops on the 11th, the bedding store on the 13th and the Airman's NAAFI on the 15th. When No.1 barrack block was handed over on July 17th, amongst the buildings still occupied on the domestic site were the Station HQ building (minus the majority of its officers), and the guard-room, with 1 civilian watchman occupying one room.

The fate of the Station's churches was still in hand during July. Negotiations were still under-way with Transport Command for the retention of the RC, C of E, EP, and MUB Churches by RAF Catterick. Under the temporary residents scheme, two local doctors accepted as patients the families of Goosepool's personnel who remained in married quarters. Meanwhile, during July, full security checks continued to be carried out on personnel leaving the station. On the 3rd, 13th, 15th and 23rd, representatives of No.2 Police District carried out a security check of empty buildings.

During the month, a further 11 vehicles were prepared and dispatched, whilst another was fully prepared and awaited disposal. Meanwhile, work continued on 5 other vehicles, which were to be disposed of during August. This left only 9 vehicles, which at the time remained in use. Stock disposals had been completed during July, excluding some stocks of contaminated Avtag and some uninstalled PAR equipment. The run-down of MT gas and diesel fuels was almost complete during the month, and a sale by tender of all ferrous and non-ferrous metals had been completed. With the exception of Tacan, which was to remain in operation until 1965, all ILS and ground radio equipment had been recovered, and returned to either Bomber Command or MOA. All radio related buildings were then handed over to the C and M Party. This only left the final recovery of the GPO's PBX (Main frame) and ATC (Sub-frame), and the Station's remaining telephones.

Goosepool's historic Teleprinter finally fell silent at 17:00 hours on July 24th 1964, as RAF Topcliffe assumed signals responsibility for the airfield.

At the same time, arrangements were in hand to cease switchboard operations. This was followed by No.4 Hangar and 3 Bulk Fuel Installation being transferred over on the 30th. By August 1st, 11 officers and 98 airmen remained on strength, in addition to the Bomber Command detachment party and Tacan and simulator staff, who were still on the station. During August, a further 47 airman were posted out and disposal instructions were in hand for the remainder, along with 4 civilians. The Ration Store was handed over during August. The Officers' Mess was finally vacated of service staff during September, the remaining Mess silver being transferred to RAF Coltishall on the 14th, as was the MT Section. The Equipment Section closed its doors at the end of the month. Goosepool's gate guardians, a Spitfire and a Hawker Tempest, were removed from their plinths across the road from the guardroom. Middleton's Tempest can be seen today at the RAF Museum at Hendon, where it is preserved. All clerical staff became redundant by September 22nd.

Middleton had two 'Gate Guardians', a Tempest V and a Spitfire, (shown in top photo)
Both were placed opposite the Guardroom, (now a motor-home salesroom). The particular Tempest that adorned Middleton's entrance
can be seen at the RAF Museum, Hendon. Note period bus outside the guardroom in top photo.

Photo: Mike Hooks

CHAPTER 11

Civvies

Civvies

On October 1st 1964, all remaining MOD buildings were handed over to RAF Catterick, and so Goosepool ended 23 years of faithful service as RAF Middleton St George. However, unlike the vast majority of RAF airfields built for the war, Goosepool was not destined to become an abandoned relic. For some 3 years a determined campaign had been fought by the councils of Cleveland, Durham and North Yorkshire, along with local industries, including I C I. Teesside's local councils, including those of Durham, Middlesbrough and North Yorkshire amalgamated, and aided by the Government, purchased the airfield for the amaisingly low price of £340,000. The agreement was signed with the MoD by Billingham Council's chairman, John Dyson. He became the Airport Committee chairman. The airfield was officially handed over on April the 18th 1964.

The cost of re-equipping the airfield for civil use came to about £110,000. Work to enlarge the concrete apron to enable the airport to accommodate larger airliners cost a further £144,000. The Airport's first Director was Mr Barker who ran the airfield until he was replaced by Mr C K Cole in 1969.

The Airport's first 'Employee' was Brian Champley. Brian signed up for the RAF and served at Middleton from 1956 onwards, as a driver/mechanic. When the RAF left he asked if he could stay on. Brian acquired a variety of jobs, including security, fire fighting and aircraft handling. He later went on to become Ground Services Manager. Unfortunately Brian had to retire on health grounds during 1985, after 21 years of service to the airport.

Peter Foster loved his job as a fireman at Darlington Fire Station. His interest in aviation stemmed back to his school days. Peter, like most of us at the time, would bunk off school and sit on the wooden perimeter fence by the Darlington to Redcar railway line, watching the Meteors, Vampires, Hunters, Javelins and Lightnings take off and land.

One day in June 1964, the Station Officer came to Peter and commented on his interest in aviation. He mentioned that there was a requirement for him to send 4 firemen out to the airfield at Middleton, which was soon to close and reopen in a commercial capacity as Teesside Airport. They would be required to bridge the gap between the departure of the RAF's fire-fighters and the eventual arrival of their civil counterparts.

The Station Officer asked Peter if he fancied volunteering. At first Peter was reluctant to agree. He liked what he was doing. Being called out to fires was exciting, and he made it quite clear that he had no wish to do anything else.

The Station Officer informed Peter firmly that he needed 4 volunteers, and that he was one of them. He continued by saying that it was only for a fortnight. Reluctantly Peter agreed to go for the fortnight, but made it clear that after that he would be back.

On their arrival at Middleton's Fire Section, Peter and the other 3 'Volunteers' were briefed by an RAF Flight Lieutenant, who stated that they were to eventually take over from the present RAF personnel, who were returning to RAF Catterick.

When Peter saw his close proximity to the aircraft he began to have second thoughts. Perhaps he was being a bit hasty about wanting to go back to Darlington. Such was the naivety of Peter and his fellow firemen, that at first the idea was to bring a couple of water tenders from Darlington Fire Station. After the arrival of the Civil Aviation Fire Inspectors, it was realised that foam tenders were the order of the day. One had been located at Machrihanish, Scotland.

Within a few days, the purpose built Airport Foam Tender was dispatched by road and eventually reached Goosepool. The driver duly handed over the tender to Peter and his colleagues, locked it up, and departed for Machrihanish (with the keys). So, for a week, all Peter and his oppos could do was look at the thing and give it the occasional polish. Eventually the keys were forthcoming, and soon they began to learn the intricacies of Airport Fire-Fighting.

Middleton's - sorry, Teesside Airports first Fire Crew. Left to right: T. Murray, Peter Foster, Brian Champley, Mike Waller, P. Robinson, C. White. Peter Foster and Brian Champley were destined to become two major stalwarts of the embryonic airport, and go on to give many faithfull years of service. At the time of writing; Peter was still working as hard as ever to ensure the smooth running of day to day operations.
Photo: Peter Foster

Peter's two-week stint at Middleton passed very quickly, and eventually turned into a year. His love for aviation soon overshadowed his desire to return to normal fire-fighting duties. This was somewhat encouraged during the early days by the fact that on weekends, unlike the normal Fire Service, one was paid time and a half on Saturdays, and double time on a Sunday.

A month after Peter Foster began working at Teesside, (by now the word 'Airport' had began to be omitted by most aviation-orientated personnel), a new employee took post. This was Martin Kelly, who became responsible for the upkeep of the airport's radar and Instrument Landing System equipment. His title was Senior Telecommunications Officer. Originally he had worked for the MoD and had moved over to become part of Teesside's staff.

Peters first bit of real excitement during 1964 was when four USAF F100 Super Sabres of the 79th Tactical Fighter Squadron came in for an emergency landing. The pilot of one of the Sabres, Captain Don Smith, had a problem develope with a generator in his aircraft, after leaving an exercise at the ground firing range at Otterburn in Northumberland. Captain Smith was accompanied by his wingman, Captain Lyn Dawsey. Both thaught that the airfield was still a military Master Diversion Airfield. However beggars can't be choosers and any old flat bit of landing area was good enough for them at the time. Newcastle Airport, as it was in those days, was not suitable for this type of aircraft, and so Teesside Airport was chosen as being the nearest suitable emergency airfield. As the first Sabre touched down, Captain Smith pulled the 'T'-handle to deploy his brake parachute. Instead of the chute billowing out of the tail to slow the aircraft down, it came off and fell into the undershoot at the start of the runway. The Sabre's high-speed landing run was not supposed to be retarded by brakes alone. The idea was to use aerodynamic braking at first, by way of the brake-chute (Nick-named 'the drag-bag'). After the aircraft had slowed sufficiently, the wheel brakes were to be used for the final part of the landing. On this occasion however, the brakes were all that Captain Smith had. The Sabre used up all 7,300 feet of runway to stop. The brakes were smoking quite well when the aircraft came to a hault. Peter Foster and his crew in their fire engine reached the aircraft very quickly and ensured that all was well. Two more single-seater Sabres, flown by Major John Mackey and Lieutenant Arendts, landed soon after. They were low on fuel and due to bad weather at base (Woodbridge in Suffolk) they decided to land at Teesside. The following day a USAF C47 Dakota arrived from Weatherfield, Essex, with a groundcrew party and spares to repair Captain Smith's Sabre

BKS Elizabethan during turnaround at Teesside.
Photo: Teesside International Airport (TIA) via John Waiting

Most of Peter's fellow volunteers slowly began to drift back to Darlington Fire Station, as more firemen were recruited for duty at Goosepool. By now, Peter had no intention of leaving his beloved airfield, he had become part of the fixtures and fittings. With the advent of a proper recruitment drive for permanent airport fire-fighters, Peter, like the rest, had to attend an interview in one of the fledgling airport's Nissen huts, shortly to become the airport's first terminal building. Peter met his future wife Anita at Teesside, she was the airport's first Ground Stewardess.

Eventually Peter became the airfield's Deputy Chief Fire Officer (DCFO), and realised that he would eventually become the Chief Fire Officer, once the present CFO, Joe Pallister, moved on. Sitting at a desk, and never being able to get his hands on the aeroplanes, was not Peter's idea of fun. This would never do, and when the first vacancy for Airport Duty Officer was posted he asked if he could apply.

Peter remembers talking to John Henderson, the Senior Air Traffic Control Officer (SATCO), who had recently taken over from the airport's first SATCO, John Taylor. John asked Peter if he really wanted to become a little fish in a big pond – after being a big fish in the Airport Fire Section. Peter persisted and became Duty Officer (DO). One of the first people he met was Les Bentley, the refueller. Peter's tasks were various and encompassed everything that could possibly take place on an airport.

During October of 1964, Teesside's first scheduled flight took place. This was to Manchester Ringway, and was flown in 36 minutes by a 10 seater De Havilland Devon (call-sign 'Charlie India'), belonging to Mercury Airlines. This organisation was to be short lived, as by the end of the year the company would become bankrupt and the service stopped. However, a month after Mercury undertook its first commercial flight from Teesside, BKS started twice daily flights to London Heathrow during five days of the week. They flew 55 seat Airspeed Ambassadors, of which only 20 had been built. The service went well and allowed BKS to eventually upgrade to much larger 110 seat Bristol Britannia aircraft. Unfortunately, at this time the aircraft were only operating at about 50% capacity as large numbers of passengers were not forthcoming. Eventually because of this BKS withdrew the service, although they and BEA did provide a reduced service until Autair International was granted a licence by the Air Transport Licencing Board. By the end of 1965 the number of aircraft movements (takeoffs) at Teesside had reached 12,890. This figure included operations by the flying club. The number of passengers totalled 65,756.

Autair began with scheduled flights to Luton, which began on January 1st 1967. The service to Luton was not popular with local business people, who made up a large percentage of the passengers. London Heathrow was much preferred and by September they had their way. Autair was instructed by the Board of Trade to switch to a twice-daily service to London Heathrow. This improved the situation, and the service became much more viable. This encouraged Autair to offer other scheduled services from Teesside, and for these they began to operate the 55 seat Dart Herald. Eventually the company rationalised their limited successes at Teesside. They began to concentrate on holiday charter flights, and were soon to change their name to Court Line. On their last day at Teesside, three of their Dart Heralds, Whisky Bravo, Whisky Charley, and Whisky Delta, carried out a formation flypast before flying to London where they were to be taken out of service.

British Eagle Brittania landing at Teesside.   *Photo: Mike Hooks*

View of Croft airfield taken by the author in 2002. Note the remaining runway and grass strip, home to a number of light aircraft enthusiasts including Bill Gillom. The remainder of the airfield became a motor race track in 1964
Photo: Author

British Midland Vickers Viscount taxiing in at Teesside.
Photo: Richard Bowater

Now the path was clear for the arrival of British Midland Airways, who continued to provide a daily service to Heathrow using Vickers Viscounts. This service began on November the 1st 1969, and worked well. By the end of the year the airport had seen passenger figures reach the 100,000 mark. Around this time, jet airliners such as the Trident began to permeate their way into domestic air travel, and during December of 1970, British Midland introduced the British Aircraft Corporation (BAC) 1-11 jet onto two new routes, Teesside to Jersey and Teesside to the Isle of Man.

By 1975 the number of passengers using the airport had doubled to 211,456. Aircraft movements had trippled during the last decade from 12,890 in 1965 to 36,562.

British Midland DC9 undergoing late night turnaround.
Photo: TIA via John Waiting

1976 saw the introduction of the McDonnell Douglas DC9 on British Midland's Heathrow - Teesside route. By 1985 it was anounced that the airport had reduced its working loss rate to £186,000 for the last financial year. Both Cleveland and Durham County Councils footed the bill, 60% of it being payed by Cleveland. This loss had been effectively reduced over the previous decade, and was concidered to be a reasonable figure for a subsidised airport.

In 1986, BM introduced an international business class service (Diamond Service) to routes between Heathrow and Amsterdam, Belfast, Edinburgh, Glasgow and Teesside.

Like all the airlines based at Teesside, British Midland, and more importantly its managing director Mike Bishop, relies heavily on the folks of Teesside to utilise the service provided and maintain the magic minimum of 1,500 passengers per week, as did Teesside's Airport Committee. There were times when this did not transpire, and frankly, the company struggled at times. In 2000, the number of British Midland Flights flights from Teesside were reduced. Midland really tried hard, and have persevered up to the present date to give the people of Teesside what they want. The rest, as they say, is up to them. Things are not getting any better in cash starved Britain, and British Midland, like other airlines, must continue to receive the support of everyone. They ask for only one thing, bums on seats. British Midland is a company of long standing and its resolve to provide a good service to the folk of Teesside (and beyond) is well appreciated.

British Midland's story began in 1938 with the formation of a company called Air Schools Limited, who specialised in providing flying instruction for RAF pilots. In 1949 the company formed Derby Aviation, which operated from Burnaston, Derby. Here they flew passenger and cargo charter flights, and specialised in civil aircraft maintenance and aircraft brokerage. The company also formed Wolverhampton Aviation, which also offered passenger and freight charters. Both organisations flew 8 seater De Havilland Rapides.

The company's involvement with RAF flight training ended in 1953, with July 18th of that year seeing the introduction of the company's first scheduled service, Derby – Wolverhampton – Jersey.

The following year, Wolverhampton Aviation ceased to exist. Derby Aviation however, introduced services to the Channel Islands from Birmingham and Nottingham. During 1954, the company introduced the DC3 Douglas Dakota to its fleet. All operations from Wolverhampton and Nottingham ended during 1956, the company consolidating its operations at Burnaston. During the same year, the Rapides were phased out and Derby Aviation added the Miles Marathon to its fleet. The company also began its first International route to Ostend. In 1959, Derby Aviation changed its name to Derby Airways.

By 1962, Derby Airways were at the forefront of the new and expanding package holiday industry. Along with new blue and white livery, introduced during 1964, came a new name, British Midland Airways, a name that today has become synonymous with aviation excellence. A move from Burnaston to a new base at Castle Donnington (East Midlands Airport) during 1965 was followed by the introduction of the company's first turbo-prop aircraft, the Handley Page Herald.

During 1969, British Midland Airways merged with Invicta. Later in the year BMA agreed to purchase 3 BAC 1-11s. After what was a very busy year, a Heathrow to Teesside route was inaugurated on November 1st. The following year saw the 3 BAC 1-11s enter service, and the inauguration of Teesside to Jersey and Teesside to Isle of Man services.

On October 19th 1971, Teesside Airport's new railway station was opened by Lord Crathorn. For several years an electric shuttle bus plied its way between the passenger terminal and the station. Sadly, due to indifference by the public to this method of transportation to the airport, the service was eventually withdrawn. Trains no longer stopped at the railway station.

1976 saw the introduction of the McDonnell Douglas DC9 on BMA's Heathrow - Teesside route. A second DC9 was acquired the following year, and was used on the Gatwick to Belfast route. British Midland Airways announced that it had flown its 1,000,000th passenger during 1979.

In 1985, BMA changed its name to British Midland. This involved another change in livery, to red white and blue, and the addition of their famous diamond motif. During June 1986, BM inaugurated a Heathrow to Amsterdam service. This was followed with the introduction of an international business class service (Diamond Service) to routes between Heathrow and Amsterdam, Belfast, Edinburgh, Glasgow and Teesside.

During the year the airport acquired a new and valued employee who was destined to remain at Teesside up to press. John Waiting was recruted to fill the position of Business Services Manager. One of his tasks involves liasing with airlines and tour operators with regard to promoting and developing flights from Teesside. John is highly qualified for this role and is a Fellow of the Institute of Travel and Tourism.

John Waiting, another of Teesside's long serving stalwarts.
Photo: TIA via John Waiting

On April 27th 1994, Sir Michael Bishop took delivery of the first Fokker 100. This aircraft boasted the quietest engines in its class, courtesy of Rolls Royce. This new aircraft was initially to fly the Leeds Bradford - Heathrow service. Later it would take over from the DC 9 and fly the Heathrow - Teesside service.

British Midland became the first airline to introduce an Internet reservations booking service on December 11th 1995, allowing passengers to book and pay for seats on line. This was officially known as CyberSeat. On April 10th 1996, the DC9 made its last flight from East Midlands Airport. Neil Kinnock, the EC Transport Commissioner, opened the refurbished Diamond Club lounge at Teesside on July 12th, and announced a two-year refurbishment programme. BM also unveiled a new corporate image, complete with new uniforms designed by Jaeger, which was to be launched during December. Passenger figures for Teesside during 1998 rose again to 664,093, with aircraft movements growing to 66,746.

BM announced on February 24th 1999 that it was to start code sharing with South African Airways via Heathrow to Glasgow, Edinburgh, Teesside, Manchester, and Leeds Bradford via Johannesburg.

At a large press conference at BM's hangar at Heathrow on February 1st 2000, the company unveiled its new name, corporate identity and transatlantic product. British Midland was now to be known as BMI British Midland. Sadly, since then the number of flights from Teesside to Heathrow have been reduced.

AWARDS RECEIVED BY British Midland
1983 Best UK Domestic Airline (Executive Travel)
1984 Best UK Domestic Airline (Executive Travel)
1986 Best UK Domestic Airline (Executive Travel)
1987 Best UK Domestic Airline (Executive Travel)
1989 Best UK Domestic Airline (Executive Travel)
199 0Best UK Domestic Airline (Executive Travel)
1990 Best UK Domestic Airline (Travel News Silver Globe Award)
1990 Best UK Domestic Airline (TTG & Express Newspapers)
1990 Best Airline Award (Thomson World-wide & Citybreaks)
1991 Best Scheduled Domestic Airline (Travel Bulletin)
1991 Best UK Domestic Airline (SAPP Awards)
1991/93 Best Airline Ireland - England (Irish Air Transport Users Committee)
1991 Best UK Domestic Airline (TTG & Express Newspapers)
1991 Best UK Domestic Airline (Travel Weekly Silver Globe Award)
1991Anglo-Dutch Award for Enterprise (Netherlands-British Chamber of Commerce)
1991/92 Best UK Domestic Airline (Executive Travel)
1991/92 Best Short-Haul Carrier (Executive Travel)
1992 Best Domestic Airline (TTG & Express Newspapers)
1992 Best Domestic Airline (Travel Weekly Silver Globe Award)
1992 Best Transport Supplier (Thomson City Breaks)
1992 Best UK Domestic Airline (SPAA Awards)
1993 Best UK Domestic Airline (Executive Travel)
1993 Best Short Haul Airline (Institute of Travel Managers)
1993 Best Domestic Airline (TTG & Express Newspapers)
1993 Best UK Domestic Airline (SPAA Awards)
1994 Best Domestic Airline (Executive Travel)
1994 Best Domestic Airline (Travel Weekly Awards)
1994 Best Domestic Airline (TTG & Express Newspapers)
1994 Best Short Haul Airline (Institute of Travel Managers)
1994 Best UK Domestic Airline (SPAA Awards)
1995 Best U K Domestic Airline (Travel Weekly Awards)
1995 Best Short Haul Airline (Institute of Travel Managers)
1995 Best UK Business Airline (Business Travel World)
1995 Best UK Domestic Airline (TTG and Express Newspapers)
1995 Best UK Domestic Airline (SPAA Awards)
1996 Best UK Domestic Airline (Travel Weekly Awards)
1996 Best UK Domestic Airline (TTG and Express Newspapers)
1997 Best UK Domestic Airline (Executive Travel)
1997 Best short-haul Airline (Executive Travel)
1997 Best UK Domestic Airline (Travel Weekly Awards)
1997 Top UK Domestic Airline (TTG and Express Newspapers)
1998 Best Short Haul Airline (OAG)
1999 Best UK Domestic Airline (OAG)
2000 Best UK Domestic (SPAA Awards)
1997 Passenger's Choice Award (SPAA Awards)
1997 Best Scheduled European Airline (SPAA Awards)
1998 Best UK Domestic Airline (Executive Travel)
1998 Best UK Domestic Airline (Travel Weekly Awards)
1998 International Business Airline, Western Europe (Business Travel World)
1997 Best UK Domestic Airline (SPAA Awards)
1998 Passengers' Choice Award (SPAA Awards)
1999 Best UK Domestic Airline (Travel Weekly Awards)
1999 Economy Class, Europe, Middle East and Africa (OAG)
1999 Best UK Domestic Airline, Business (Conde Nast Traveller Readers Award)
1998 Top Domestic Airline (Travel Bulletin Awards)
1999 Best UK Domestic Airline (SPAA Awards)
1999 Best UK Domestic Airline (Travel Weekly)
2000 Top Domestic Airline (Travel Bulletin)
2000 Best Short Haul Airline (Business Traveller)
2000 Best UK Airline (SPAA Awards)
2000 Best U K Domestic Airline (Travel Weekly)
2001 Best Business Short Haul Airline (Business Travel World)

There were others who tried to introduce services from Teesside, but it has to be said that the airport has not enjoyed the friends in high places that Newcastle Airport has. Newcastle has been pushed from day one as the main regional airport of the Northeast and has received the necessary funding to expand.

Sometime during the 80s, the earth moved for the pilots of Teesside. Runway 24/06, which had always pointed in that direction since the airfield was constructed, suddenly became runway 23/05. The earth precesses a little bit each year. After 40 years or so of that, it had moved on its axis enough for the CAA to notice. Oddly enough though, the other runways, 19/01 and 28/10 didn't move; strangely, they are still the same. Another thing that changed around that time was fences. Up to that point there hadn't been any, but now the airport was suffering growing pains and the Board of Trade had put their foot down. After that we had to flash our passes at everyone to allow us to go air-side.

By 1985 the airport had a new director, in the form of Ike Dawson. According to many airport employees around at the time he was not amongst the most popular of bosses. Some of the airport staff reported to me that when asked what Ike stood for, he replied, 'I Know Everything'. At one point It was reported in the local press that during a GMBATU union meeting of some 50 members of the airport's staff, including re-fuelling, fire-fighting, security and ground services, a unanimous vote of no confidence was expressed in the senior management of the airport. Ike did however strive to improve the airport's standing in the world and increase the passenger throughput.

CHAPTER TWELVE

The Flying Clubs

The Flying Clubs

As the RAF was departing from the airfield during April 1964, a small band of us attended a meeting in a pub in Darlington. The idea was to form a flying club at the new and embryonic civilian airport just down the road at Middleton St George.

The three people responsible for the formation of the first aero club (Middleton-St-George Aero Club) were Sir Edward 'Ted' Holden, who ran the club from 1964 – 1969. Ted I think was a hospital anesthetist. The second member was Alistair Craig 1964 – 1965 and Neville Balsover, 1965 - 1972 a solicitor from Teesside.

Initially Sir Edward Holden proposed the formation of the new aero club at Middleton and teamed up with Alistair Craig of Craig's Transport, which at the time was based in Harris Street, Darlington. His famous sister, Wendy Craig, went on to become the star of the TV programme 'Butterflies'. A conversation with Teesside solicitor Neville Balsover at a dinner dance enthused the latter to go along to the inaugural meeting and join Sir Edward and Alistair as the third shareholder member of the club's management. Neville suffered from vertigo at the time and thought that flying might cure him, so he agreed.

The three shareholders were responsible for the financial and spiritual leadership that allowed the club to come into existence. Alistair Craig resigned during late 1964 due to business pressures

Eventually, premises became available on the airfield, and the club was born. The club used the single story building, which ran down the side of hangar 3 as their first clubhouse. Amenities in this building were primitive, with no toilet facilities, especially for the lady members. During the war it had been a briefing room for 428 squadron. It had been from here that McMullen had been briefed before setting of on his fateful flight. It is generally excepted that the airfield's resident ghost is that of McMullen.

One Sunday in May 1964 the club members had just put the aircraft into hangar 3 as the crosswind had become too strong. The sound of a light aircraft was heard circling overhead. As it was the weekend and the control tower was unatended, the club's instructor Doug Edwards pushed one of the aircraft back out of the hangar, to allow its radio to be used to contact the visiting pilot. He informed the circling airman that he had permission to land and that some of the club members would be waiting by the side of the runway, to hold onto the wings of his aircraft and help him taxi to the hangar. When the pilot stopped the engine and jumped out it was non-other than Jimmy Edwards, who was at the time a very famous radio personality. He was in a panic to find a loo and sprinted for the clubhouse. The only toilet in the building was of the old wartime Elsan chemical variety, upon which sat Les Porter's elderly mother. After much pleading and tapping on the door he was able to persuade her to vacate her seat and allow him to utilise the facilities.

As soon as the club began to build itself up, better premises were sought. Across the taxiway, opposite hangar 3 was a much larger and more adaptable building. This was an ex-RAF single-story wooden building, which faced the runways and was in a prime site. I remember being in this building a couple of years before as an Air Cadet, watching 33 and 92 Squadron camera gun film shows (designed to keep young air cadets quiet on poor flying days). Today, the site of the original Middleton St George Aero Club is buried under FRA's Hangar 360 which was completed in April 1995. Only the concrete path leading up to the old door remains today.

Once in the new clubhouse and with the furnishings installed, the social side of the club was developed. A large bar was built, its lower part constructed out of empty beer and wine bottles, which I remember were cemented together to form quite a nice effect. The lounge area sported a dance floor and a good-sized kitchen provided for catering. Near the entrance was the pilot's briefing room, next to which was a lecture/ table-tennis room and to its right, the CFI's office. Most of the conversion was carried out on a voluntary basis by club members, as was the manning of the bar.

The aero club played an important part in promoting and developing the new airport and formed the Airport Operators Association for all of the businesses on the airport to promote and foster its development. In the early years of the airfield the club provided 90% of Teesside Airports aircraft movements, at times this figure reached almost 100%. The three clubs in operation today still do provide the lion's share of Teesside's aircraft movements (future airfield planners please note).

The first Flying Instructors were Doug Edwards, Charles Cockburn, Dennis Jackson and Norman Budden. Assistant flying instructors were Dick Dorman, Peter Pitt, Les Povey, David Hill, Al Turley and Ron Kearl.

There were many wartime pilots to swell our ranks, including Gabby Calcagni, who had been a Spitfire pilot, Les Povey an ex-RAF Halifax bomber pilot, John McVittie an ex-Swordfish pilot who had taken part in the Bismark raid, and many others. We even had two First World War pilots, John Gladish and Leonard Riddell. The Cleveland Flying School has at the time of writing a plaque presented to John and Leonard during the 70's, commemorating a combined 100 years of flying experience between them.

The late Les Porter, an architect from Stockton, and the late Alec Glover, who owned a TV shop in Catterick were among the stalwarts of the club, along with Ron Pledge, Tony Walker, Bill Walker, Geoff, Barbara and John Turner, Hank Hinks and Dave Fisher.

Many of the airfield's operational personnel were amongst the club's members. They include Mike Finley, Teesside's manager for Autair, Ann Morrison, Ground Hostess for Autair, Jack Onions the Assistant Airport Director and Freddy 'Fuselage' Fusedale the airport electrician and Ben Homan. Another member of the club was Tim Damer the manager of the newly converted St George Hotel, which had formerly been Middleton's Officer's Mess.

At first the control tower was intermittently run by an RAF holding unit, during weekdays only. One of the first to occupy the control tower was Len Taylor the Senior Air Traffic Control Officer (SATCO), a former RAF fighter pilot. He worked in the tower for several years until he departed to take up post as the SATCO of Christchurch Airport in New Zealand. He was replaced by another ex-RAF fighter pilot, John Henderson, who had flown Hawker Hunters.

I was a teenager at the time, and was one of the youngest members of the original club. I provided most of the model aircraft that hung from the ceiling in the bar, behind which I served on busy nights, as did many other members when required. The proceeds from my labours as a stand-in barman and aircraft cleaner subsidised, to a large extent, my flying training.
We had two Beagle Terrier aircraft to start with, they were originally of WWII Auster design, but were modified later by Beagle Aircraft. I remember their registrations to this day, Romeo Lima and Romeo Golf. Most of the British light aircraft around at the time were surplus military aircraft which had been used during the war. Many variants of Auster design were eventually to be configured for use in post-war general aviation (GA). These included some with different seating arrangements. We had side by side two seaters, and one with a third seat, pointing sideways, behind the two front occupants.
I remember once having a flight in an Auster with this kind of seating arrangement. Alec Glover asked me if I would like to sit in the back, as there was a spare seat, albeit facing sideways. He was going to take a new pilot up for a conversion onto type. After a few circuits and bumps we climbed up to about 3,000 feet do some upper air work. He started with steep turns, which made the whole thing that much more interesting, as I was laid on my back during right hand turns, and face down whilst steep turning to the left. This was nothing with what was to follow. Alec slowed the aircraft to stalling speed, and we fell out of the sky, sideways in my case, six times in all. Finally, just to make my day, we finished off with 3 spins.

When we taxied in and Alec had shut off the engine, I began to voice my views on this exciting sideways pointing flight. Alec's head spun around to look at me sitting close behind him, a look of horror on his face, 'Bloody hell!' he exclaimed, ' I'd forgotten you were there.' To do such steep turns, let alone stalls and spins, 3 up, was definitely not in the approved weight and balance envelope of the Auster. I thought twice before accepting any other flights with Alec, but not for long. Although based on the same Auster design, there were some quite exotic versions based at Teesside. These included an

Middleton St George Aero Club's first aircraft, Austers; Romeo Lima and Romeo Golf.
Viewed from the entrance of old club house towards Hangar 3, 1964   Photo: Neville Balsover

Auster Aiglet, which was flown by the charismatic ex racing driver Jimmy Bloumer. This aircraft had a shorter wingspan, and was beefed up for aerobatics. The Auster Autocrat was a posh version of this ubiquitous British aircraft, and later we had the dubious honour of having quite a famous example join our fleet of privately owned aircraft in hangar 3. Prior to it arriving at Teesside, a doctor from the south had used this aircraft to dump his wife's body into the North Sea. This was an act he later paid for by way of a visit from the constabulary, as I think she was later washed up on a beach somewhere.

As a student pilot, I would cadge rides in all sorts of exotic and unusual aircraft, including Les Povey's wartime Miles Messenger. Les was an ex RAF Bomber pilot with many an exciting story. Les joined 76 Squadron just after they had left Middleton for Linton. During his first Op (to Duisburg), the Halifax he was a second pilot in took some flak hits. A piece of shrapnel struck Les in the face, filling his mouth with debris, and inflicting a small amount of damage. Les was taken by a member of the crew to the rest station near the Halifax's wing spar and given comfort. The captain then brought the badly damaged Halifax safely back to base. When he was examined at the hospital, it was discovered that it was not flak at all, but pieces of Bakelite and intercom switch mechanism from Les's oxygen mask, which had been propelled into his mouth by the flak. Les spent a short time in hospital, thanking his lucky stars that the flak had not been a couple of inches further back.

During the 80s and 90s, Les was a very popular after dinner speaker, his subject - his wartime exploits. The highlight of the evening would come when Les would hold up his old flying helmet, complete with the remains of his oxygen mask intercom switch assembly.

Les recovered from his wounds, and after a few more sorties over enemy territory as a fully-fledged bomber pilot, he volunteered for SOE[146] Duties, dropping secret agents over Czechoslovakia, Yugoslavia and France. One day, he was flying an agent in a Halifax who was to be dropped in France. The trip was long, so he asked the agent, who turned out to be a young girl, if she would like to spend the flight in the cockpit, rather than down the back in the cold draughty fuselage. She accepted, and as they flew on he asked her what she was up to. 'That's for me to know, and you to wonder', she said firmly. Perhaps it was better not to know, as if they had been shot down and tortured, Les and his crew may have compromised her mission. Les explained that they would know when to drop the agents by Morse signals from a torch, held by someone on the ground. 'We got quite good at dropping agents in small places. On one occasion we had to drop one on a tennis court in an enemy held village.' On asking him how they could do that, and at what height, he replied, 'Fly over drop point at 400 feet, green light on - agent jumps - static line opens parachute - feet on the ground.'

Les Povey, aged 30, shortly after joining the RAF, at the outbreak of WWII.   Photo: Les Povey

We actually had a female pilot, Miss Thelia Adams. During the early 60s, it was extremely rare to see a female car driver, let alone a female pilot. The ladies that were on the road were usually farmer's wives, or ex wartime ambulance drivers. My-oh-my, how times have changed. Today, at times there seems to be more woman drivers on the roads than men. However, 40 years on, to see a female learning to fly at one of Teesside's 3 flying clubs is still as rare as it was in the 60s.

Flying lessons in those days (1964-65) cost £4/10s per hour,[147] a Private Pilot's Licence cost about £300. 40 hours of instruction were required for the PPL, or 35 hours for the approved course (completed within 6 months). This was a price that remained stable for a couple of years, until one day we acquired a much more modern type of aircraft. Overnight the cost of an hour's flying went up from £4/10 shillings to a whopping great £5. The culprit causing this massive price rise was a Cessna 150. This is an American, two seat, high wing, all metal aircraft, which replaced the fabric covered Austers. My logbook reminds me that this aircraft was G-ATHZ. This was soon followed by a Cessna 172 G-AVJM, which was a little bigger, had a larger engine, and 4 seats. Shortly after we also acquired a red Piper Tri-Pacer.

Although subsequent pilots have been killed after leaving Teesside, Ernie Brooks was the civilian airport's only on-field fatality, and up to July 2003, the only one since the airport was opened in 1964.

Ernie Brooks flies, hands-off, during a flyby in his gyrocopter to demonstrate its stability.
Sadly he died soon after.   Photo: via Geoff Hill

---

[146] Special Operations Executive, now SAS.
[147] £4.50 in today's money.

I remember that he was a very nice man, always cheerful and very popular in the club. He was developing a gyro-copter at his garage at Spennymoor, Co Durham. Having worked on the design for some time, it flew well. It was his intention to mass-produce this little craft, which would land in a very short distance. It was one of the fore-runners of the modern gyro-copter, similar to 'Little Nellie ' featured in the James Bond movie. Driven by a Volkswagen engine, it had a conventional rear-facing propeller, which pushed the craft along. The freewheeling rotor blades on the top simply spun as they were pushed through the air, creating lift. Ernie was in negotiations with a German firm who were looking into the possibility of acquiring some of his aircraft.

One Sunday in 1966, at about 5 pm, he took-off to demonstrate the flying characteristics of the gyro-copter to the Germans, having flown some earlier test flights during that afternoon. Eyewitnesses reported that the aircraft was seen to pull up into what looked like an aerobatic manoeuvre. The rotor on the top was pulled down by G force during the steep climb and struck the tail section. The rotor blades disintegrated, and the aircraft fell to the ground on the south side of the main runway. It landed in the middle of a wartime dispersal. Ernie died of multiple injuries.It is the aurthors understanding that a stop-lock device designed to prevent this kind of accident from hapening was not fitted to the aircraft.

The clubhouse was, as were most pubs and clubs at this time, very busy every night. The weekend would usually bring fantastic parties, many until dawn. This was the swinging sixties, and the dreaded breathalyser was a shadow of its present form. Motor cyclists did not have to contend with crash helmets, and could pass their test on a 250cc motorbike, then go out the same day and buy a 650cc BSA Super Rocket (like I did). There were far fewer cars on the road, no yellow lines, parking meters or traffic wardens. Darlington did not even boast a single traffic light. At the time, the A1M was just a dream, the old London to Edinburgh stretch of the A1 (now the A167) passed right through the centre of Darlington.

It was a much more relaxed and less mercenary Britain that we lived in, unlike today where so many rules and regulations have killed off the comparatively relaxed environment that prevailed during that great period. Today, because one must drive to the airfield, the flying clubs have no opportunity to foster real social nights as we knew them in the 60's and the 70's. One felt as though we were part of a squadron, a team, with a true kindred spirit.

My very good friend and co-pilot, the late Dick Emery.   Photo: via author

The club had many famous occasional visitors from the world of aviation and entertainment. Douglas Bader, Bob Stanford Tuck, Adolph Galland, Jimmy Edwards, Barnes Wallace of Dambuster fame, and No.1 pop group Dave, Dee, Dozy, Mick and Tich to name but a few. Sheila Scott, the former movie star and lady pilot, was also often seen at Teesside. At the time she had completed many solo record breaking flights, including a solo round the world trip.

I became a firm friend with another frequent visitor to the club, the late Dick Emery of TV fame. He will be remembered by way of his famous saying, 'You are awful - but I like you!' Dick would come up to Teesside to appear in local cabaret venues, such as The La Bamba night-club in Darlington's Grange Road, and the Fiesta in Stockton. He loved speed, and always had the latest and fastest motorbikes. As he was an accomplished pilot, Dick would base himself at the club during his stay in the area.

We did quite a bit of flying together, the club's Piper Tri-Pacer seemed to be his favourite mount. Once he pulled up at the club and demanded the keys to my Mini Cooper. He then threw me the keys to his brand new S1 Rolls Bentley, and promptly disappeared in my pride and joy, accompanied by a cloud of burning rubber. I opened the Rolls, started it up, and gingerly drove it once around the airport before parking it up in a safe place and retiring back to the with a big grin on his face. 'I'm having one of these', he said. I think he only came back because the petrol tank was empty.

At this time there were no fences at the airport, security was not a very high priority as airport terrorists had not yet been invented. Many were the times that we would let ourselves into the control tower late at night with fish and chips for the controllers. I would sit all night, keeping John Briggs and the other controllers company, whilst they covered for the late night British Eagle and Dan-Air crew-training aircraft (better known as Dan Dare after the Eagle comic, which was around at the time).

Dan Air, British Eagle and others would take full advantage of this quiet airfield, with little commercial traffic to worry about, up in the less populated Northeast. The local anti-aircraft, anti noise anti everything brigade did not invent themselves until the late 1990s. The Bristol Britannias of British Eagle were better known as 'The Whispering Giant', so quiet were they. Most locals were not aware that these huge aircraft were carrying out flying training whilst they slept. We would often cadge a ride in a Comet or a Britannia, as they were always empty, except for the Training Captain, First Officer and Engineer. Once a couple of us went on what we thought was a local flight, only to be stranded at Prestwick when the weather changed, without enough money to get back.

The only excitement regarding the Britannias was when, during a practice two engined landing, one of them departed the runway at a high rate of knots, travelled for about 80 yards, then sank up to its axles in soft mud. The only people on board were the training crew, none were injured. It took many hours for army tank recovery vehicles to get the 130-seater aircraft back on to the runway.

One night at about 1am, whilst I was in the tower, John Briggs was controlling a Dan Air Comet that was doing beacon approaches. They were using Teesside's radio approach beacon, better known as the 'Tango Delta'. After doing a touch and go landing, they would climb out again and head out to sea, ready for another practice approach. One sprog pilot was under instruction on this particular night and he got his R/T a bit wrong. He had initially called on the radio to say that he was at flight level 350 (35,000 feet). He must have become a bit busy in the cockpit, as soon after he reported to Teesside that he was requesting clearance to approach the beacon. When asked his height he replied, 'Flight level 35000.' Cool as you like, John replied, 'Roger, Alpha Papa, you are clear to fire retro rockets and splash-down in Osmotherly reservoir.' The trainee pilot had, of course, meant flight level 350, not 35000, this would have put him in earth orbit.

The trend in the sixties was for Teesside's airshow commentator to fool everyone into expecting the arrival of the aircraft from one direction, whilst it approached silently just below the speed of sound from the other. The surprise caused by a Lightning doing 600 mph at 250 feet, and coming at you from behind when you were expecting it to come down the runway, usually knocked about 5 years off your life expectancy, but you would not have missed it for the world. To see a Spitfire do a fly-by at 60 feet above your head is now a thing of the past. After the tragic events at an airshow at Ramstein in Germany during 1988, these days the CAA are up in arms if any display aircraft comes within binocular range of the spectators.

Instructors in those early days were Dennis Jackson and Charles Cockburn. Dennis was famous for his former operations out of Skegness, taking holidaymakers on joy rides from the beach when the tide was out. His favourite food whilst at Middleton was Cheese and Onion toasties, 'made with chewing gum cheese' he used to say. Dennis was a great bloke and was the kindest and most patient man I ever flew with. He tried to get everyone off on their first solo as quick as he could, 'I'm trying for the world record', he would say, 'the person with the least number of hours to go solo.' Unfortunately, like many teenagers, I had to save up for each lesson, so for me there was no continuity. I did my solo in 7 hours 50 minutes, but was beaten to the record by someone (with more money) who did it in 6 hours 30 minutes.

Charles Cockburn was much older than the other instructors. He was an ex-RAF instructor who had been doing it for too long. I remember that he was very short tempered, and although one was paying for the privilege, woe betide anyone who did anything wrong during training.

The King's Cup air races were a feature of the airshows at Teesside, and many famous air-racers came to pit their wits against each other. I remember going around the course at very low level with Eric Marsh in his Emarard, a fast little French two seater. We would fly between 250 to 500 feet, and on reaching the pylons, turn with wings nearly vertical, whilst pulling lots of Gs, before straightening out and flying off to the next pylon.

During 1969, one race was run on the Sunday, during a pre-arranged pause between air show events. Les Porter, Brian Gilbert and myself were manning the East Harlsey pylon. The other two pylons of the triangular course were at Teesside Airport (the start and finish point) and Croft Autodrome (Croft airfield). Whilst we were ensuring that all competitors didn't cheat, and flew outside our pylon during their turns, we saw a large ominous plume of black smoke to the west. This smoke appeared to be situated a few miles away, between our position and the preceding pylon at Croft. It transpired that our fears were justified, one of the racing aircraft had crashed.

The airshow taking place that year at Teesside had an English Electric Lightning as one of the highlights of the afternoon's display. The pilot of the Lightning was F/L Alan Turley, who performed a thrilling show for the crowd. Alan and his wife, Dawn who was also a pilot, owned an old Percival Proctor, a small WWII communications aircraft. She was taking part in the air races, and was standing by, engine running, whilst waiting for Alan to land after his display. The start of the race was held back a little to allow him to land, park his Lightning, and rush to join his wife at the controls of the Procter.

Once airborne, they both negotiated the first leg of the race between Teesside and Croft. During the second leg, which would take them towards us at East Harlsey, the old World War Two Gypsy engine seized, and threw a connecting rod out of the side of the engine, which immediately caught fire. With smoke and flame entering the cockpit, Alan took control of the aircraft and put it on the ground as quickly as he could. It struck three quarters of the way into field with excessive speed, only yards from the boundary hedge. Alan pulled the aircraft up and over the hedge like a horse jumping a fence, it landed once again but this time in a much smaller paddock. Fortunately it stopped about 10 feet from the garden gate of a farmhouse. The distance from the gate to the house was no more than 20 feet.

Alan dived out of the aircraft, only to realise that his wife was still in her seat. He immediately re-entered the blazing plane and freed her. Dragging her out of the inferno he sustained burns to his hands, and to a lesser degree his face and neck. Fortunately for him, he was still wearing his RAF Nomex flying suit, which saved him to some extent. His wife however, was wearing thin summer clothing and she sustained more burns. Amaisingly, a doctor happened to be visiting the farmhouse and an ambulance was passing at the same time.

The next day, I visited the site of the crash and saw the witness marks in the two fields, which showed the aircraft's path after it initially hit the ground. To see the skid-marks stop at the hedge and re-appear in the field next door, can only be described as being akin to seeing a tree on a snowy slope with a skiers tracks going either side of it. It must have taken great skill to reef the blazing aircraft off the ground again, knowing that to hit the hedge at speed was certain death. When I saw the remains of the Proctor, it was just a perfect black aeroplane shape burned into the grass. Little was left of the mostly wooden structure, only the metal parts lying in the same positions as they occupied in the aircraft. The engine and prop were at the front, with the offending con-rod sticking out of a jagged hole in the crankcase. The control cables, wiring, instrument panel and various metal brackets were still in place, as if awaiting the accident investigators. Al Turley had been awarded the Air Force Cross during 1967.

Also during 1969 Ted Holden, who you will remember formed Middleton St George Aero Club in 1964, came down with influenza, which attacked his nervous system. So bad was his condition that he went into a coma for several weeks. He survived however but was unable to take any further active part in the running of the club. His shareholding was taken over by Neville Bolsover who then became the club's sole owner.

As the 60s drew to a close, we were re-joined by ex-Halifax pilot, Les Povey, who was very popular. Les was a very good instructor, and when I was home on leave he would convert me onto the latest acquisitions of the club.

During this time we lost our first aircraft, it was G-AVJM. This aircraft had been a favourite of mine. Fred Ayres had taken Juliet Mike for a photographic sortie to Ingleby Greenhow, near Roseberry Topping in the Cleveland hills. Having completed the photography, he turned away from the village. Unfortunately he turned to the east and was heading straight for the hills which towered above his height. Due to the fact that he was in a small valley he could turn neither left or right. His only course of action was to try and out-climb the quickly approaching high ground. With the aircraft in a maximum climb and close to the stall, the steep angle of the hills won the battle and Juliet Mike struck the gorse-covered hillside. The Cessna scraped along the rough surface, at a very high angle of attack, for about 50 feet at quite low speed. When the aircraft stalled the nosewheel dug in, and she flipped over onto her back. Fortunately the only injury was a small head-wound sustained by the front passenger in the right hand seat, who hit his head on the windscreen pillar. Juliet Mike was a write-off.

As I have already stated, there were no fences at the airport at this time and we parked our cars by the side of the clubhouse. One very warm summer's day, we heard the deep throb of a diesel engine as it pulled up behind the clubhouse. We were all warned by an airport fireman to go inside the club for a few moments. Meanwhile, half a dozen off-duty air hostesses were lounging around in their bikinis on the grass at the front of the club building, oblivious to what was about to happen. It transpired that the lads in the control tower had spotted the girls and called up the Fire Section to see what they could do. Soon, from the rear of the clubhouse, came the sound of a diesel engine revving up, followed by a huge stream of water coming from a well-aimed fire hose. This had been directed by guesswork, about 50 feet into the air over the roof, and onto the unsuspecting hosties on the other side of the club. The screams were heard all over the airfield, as the cold water found its mark.

Life at the airport was very relaxed, blasting down the runway in Les Porter's Rover to see how fast it would go. Model aeroplane flying on the south side of the main runway took place, even during the arrival and departure of large aircraft.

Freddie Fusedale, the airport electrician, was a keen autogyro enthusiast. When not replacing the bulbs in the runway lights, he could be seen flying his autogyro. This aircraft had no engine, being the version that one pulled behind a Landrover or car. Freddie was able to reach a height of 100 feet or so before the string went tight. His height was dependent only on how much rope he could lay his hands on at the time. No sooner had he completed the first version of his flying machine when he began work on the Mk II.

One night, Freddie and I were in his workshop, which was located in the buildings running alongside hangar 2. We were working on the latest version of the autogyro. The door into the blacked out hangar was open. As we worked, we both suddenly felt very cold, as if someone had opened a fridge door. At the same time, a man's shadow appeared on the wall of the workshop, as if he was framed in the doorway leading into the hangar. Turning around quickly we saw no one. Then it dawned on us both, how do you get a shadow when you are in an illuminated workshop and the hangar behind you is in darkness.

We stood up, looked at each other, and dived, (well, crept), through the workshop door into the hangar. Freddie went first, the geography of the hangar being better known to him, especially in the dark. I was not scared of course, I just thought that he being older should lead the way. As he groped for the light switch box on the hangar side, there came a very loud clang in the darkness. This seemed to come from the vicinity of the hangar doors, 60 feet away, up at the end of the hangar closest to the runways. When he threw the switch, the sodium lights slowly began to glow. They took about a minute or so to reach a light intensity that enabled us to see. It would be 2 or 3 minutes before they warmed up fully and reached their full brightness. There was an object lying on the floor, close to the closed, heavy, wartime, blast-proof hangar doors.

The doors run on rails, and are opened by a large crank handle weighing 10 to 15 pounds. The object lying on the floor was this handle, which had for the best part of the evening sat in its cradle, which in turn was welded to the inside of the doors.

To remove the heavy handle from the cradle involved lifting it 6 inches or so to clear the brackets of the cradle. There was no wind, and in any case, the sand-filled doors weighed many tons, a hurricane would not have moved them. Discussing the incident later, we were both totally aware that the figure had been standing in the doorway of the workshop. Having lost the appetite for further work, we took the opportunity to retire to the club for a stiff one.

By the early seventies, the club had quite a few instructors, including Les Povey, who, as you have read earlier, was the Halifax pilot whose oxygen mask was shattered by flak. He also carried out the RT Radio license training and exams. At the turn of the new millennium, Les was still to be found at Cleveland Flying School, instructing and examining student pilots for their radio licence. Sadly, Les passed away in February 2002, but his memory never will. As per his wishes, he was buried in the churchyard at Middleton-One-Row, close to the airfield.

Other instructors during the early 70s were Dave McFerran, an ex-Australian Air Force pilot and Vietnam veteran RAF instructor Les Chamberlain from RAF Leeming. Around this time another aero club was formed, again owned by Neville Balsover, who had moved out of the old club, having sold it to the late Ron Mason, a Teesside fruit and veg merchant. Ron was to have the club for just a short time before serious illness overtook him.

Neville's new club was housed in the old RAF Astra cinema, with Norman Buddin, an ex-RAF Hunter pilot as CFI. The old club change names, Middleton-St George Aero Club became the Beacon Flying Club. Aircraft at the time included a Cherokee 140, G-AVGB, more affectionately known to us all as 'Golf Ball' or 'Getting Better'. We also had two Cessna 150s, G-AWUL, white and orange, and G-ASMS, which was white and blue. For the touring PPL. Les Povey and others opened a club right next door to the Beacon Flying Club, called The Cleveland Flying Group. This was housed in an old Nissen hut (now used by engineer Robert Thompson).

Student pilots, carrying out their navigation training, would fly a triangular cross-country exercise consisting of Teesside - Sherbern in Elmet - Sunderland - Teesside. Sherburn, near Tadcaster, has grass runways, so this was good experience for the trainee pilot. Sunderland, or Usworth as it was during the war years, had paved runways, but also had a short grass runway to be used only if the crosswind got too bad

Sunderland airfield was a very popular venue, it also had a very good club of its own. Sunny Sundays would see us take off from Teesside, head for Penshaw Monument, find the bend in the river, and drop in over the fence. Many were the times we would lay on the grass, watching strange people throw themselves out of aeroplanes and descend by parachute. Why anyone would want to do that is beyond me. Actually, Sunderland was the Mecca for parachuting in the North, and it had a school second to none.

Two unusual but very popular aircraft based at Sunderland at this time were a couple of Australian built Victor Air Tourers, G-ATCI and G-ATCL. These aircraft were somewhat unusual in having only one joystick, which was centrally placed between both pilots. The left-hand pilot flew with his right hand and the pilot in the right-hand seat flew with his left. They were realy good aircraft and flew like a dream.

Peter Metcalfe joined the club at this time, having completed his flying training at Carlisle. Peter was never out of the air, and loved long distance trips. Stavangar airport in Norway is 400 miles away, over the very inhospitable North Sea, and in a single engined aircraft this is not a trip for the squeamish. Peter did many such trips flying in a 172, and even completed the Malta air rally, his companion at the time being the very brave Mr Blenerhasset.

Peter and I would fly to Jersey for lobsters and kippers, just for the fun of it. On our return, I would leave Peter in hangar 3, boiling lobsters in a large 50-gallon drum. On one occasion he was returning alone from Jersey with a large wooden crate of lobsters on the back seat of the Cherokee. On crossing the South Coast on the way home, London Air Traffic Control instructed him to climb as conflicting traffic was approaching him at his level. This he did, and eventually levelled off at 10,000ft, with strange whistling and banging noises emanating from the back seat. Lobsters are designed to live on the bottom of the sea, and have pressurised shells, which are not designed for high altitude. It took Peter all of the next day to clean up the inside of the aircraft cockpit.

Ron Mason and Alec Glover flew a Yankee Clipper down to Jersey to be sold. This was not a very popular aircraft with club members, and had a bit of a reputation for poor spin recovery. One week later, the aircraft sale eventually fell through, and so, on September 18th, Peter and I flew Ron and Alec back to Jersey in the Cherokee to bring it home. Having picked up the Clipper, G-AYLO, Alec and Ron flew it back. Peter and I took-off shortly after, having refuelled the Cherokee. It was cloudy over the sea between Jersey and the South Coast so we climbed on top. Whilst half way across this stretch of sea we received a disturbing call from the air traffic radar controller.

Radar had detected that Alec and Ron in the Clipper were heading due west, rather than north towards the South Coast. The operator vectored Peter and I towards the other aircraft, which had, without Alec and Ron realising it, experienced a partial electrical failure, which took out the radio and radio navigation equipment. The needle on their ADF was pointing North, but they were actually heading straight for America. We managed to catch them up before they ran out of petrol, and using hand signals, persuaded them to follow us. This they did, and we played at dog fighting above the clouds until we reached the South coast.

Alec and Ron followed us to Castle Donnington airport. The last hour was in total darkness, and they only had our navigation lights to keep us in sight. We flew formation with them and saw them safely onto final approach, having used our radio to alert Castle Don's air traffic control of their predicament. Overshooting, Peter and I flew on to Teesside, arriving at 9.00pm after many hours in the air. For us, our adventure was nearly to end in tragedy. Having reached Teesside we were cleared onto left base for 24. As we were beginning our turn onto final approach at about 500 feet, a blacked out twin engined aircraft flew down the runway towards us, also at about 500-ft. It passed from left to right across our bows, no more than 30 feet away, and at exactly the same height. We heard the roar of its engines over our own as it flashed by. On showing our shocked displeasure to Teesside's air traffic, we were asked, 'What plane?' They were not aware that the other aircraft was there, nor where it had come from, or where it was going, or where it went. If we had been there one second sooner we would have collided with it and you would not be reading this. As far as I know this was a mystery that was never solved.

July 1972 saw ex-RAF Phantom pilot Mike Cairns join the club as an instructor. Later in the 70s, Mike was destined to become the leader of one of the famous Rothmans aerobatic teams (there were two). His arrival coincided with the arrival of yet another 150, G-ATYN.

One day I entered the clubhouse and saw Mike sitting at the bar. The usual Baccardi and Coke was in his hand, but he had a very angry look on his face. I enquired about his unhappy state. He told me over his drink that he and Ron Mason had just had another heated row. Trying to cheer Mike up a bit, I suggested that he might consider starting up a flying club of his own. It would seem that Mike might have taken my advice, as soon after he teamed up with Wally Linskill and in early 1973 the Cleveland Flying School was born. At first the club sported a caravan, until the clubhouse was built; it is still there today in its original location.

Les Povey, shortly after checking the author out on the Messerschmitt 209

Photo: Author

1973 was a good year, and my logbook shows Les Povey converting me onto a fantastic aeroplane called a Messerschmitt Me209, better known to the Germans as the Monsun (Monsoon). Only about 50 of these aircraft were produced in Germany by Messerschmitt - Blohm – Bolkow (MBB), between Airbus contracts, to ensure that their skilled work-force remained together and occupied. They were semi-aerobatic and very nippy, quite a change from the usual club Cessnas and Cherrytrees.

We had two examples of this fine aircraft, G-AZOC, which was blue and white, and G-AZTB, which was yellow and white. For some reason, Oscar Charley was more popular and seemed to fly better, nothing to put one's finger on, but as most pilots will tell you, no two aircraft fly exactly the same anyway. Tango Bravo had a strange quirk. Having lifted her off the runway, one would feel a strange shaking sensation, followed by a vibration. After much time and investigation it turned out that the nosewheel, spinning at high speed, was out of balance. This was fixed, but still Oscar Charley remained everyone's favourite.

A gentleman of the air. Les' 89th birthday party in 2001, just weeks before he died   *Photo: Author*

Spot landing competitions and Treasure hunts were just two of the many events organised by the club, one such hunt took us to Sedgefield-Ferryhill-Greta Bridge and back to Teesside.

Grindale, near Bridlington, had a fine aero club and parachute school at this time. The chief flying instructor was non-other than the famous wartime fighter pilot, Ginger Lacy, who was responsible for shooting down the Heinkel bomber which bombed Buckingham Palace. They would sometimes have a fly-in, and we would all depart for Grindale on a Saturday, over-flying the huge wartime emergency landing ground at Carnaby. Overnight accommodation was provided in a bunk-bed dormitory, vacated for the weekend by the parachutists.

I remember that Ginger would often come over to our club for a night out. On one occasion he flew the Monsun, and reported that it was similar to the Spitfire to fly.

The club had 2 Messerschmitt MBB 209s, known as Monsuns (German for Monsoon). Oscar Charley is shown in the foreground and Tango Bravo at the rear. Both were destined to come to untimely ends.   Photo: Author

One alleged funny story to come out of this era involved a very popular character called Doug Atherton. Doug had eventually reached the stage of his flying training when cross-country navigation exercises were being taught. The story goes that, supposedly, on one particular day around this time, Doug walked into the club and was immediately asked by one of the instructors if he would like a free flight. Jumping at the chance, he was informed that one of the club's 150s was at Leeds, having had some maintenance work carried out, and that it needed to be collected. At the time there was no maintenance organisation at Teesside, and all light aircraft in need of servicing and repair had to go to the nearest available unit, which was Northair, based at Leeds/Bradford Airport.

The plan was for Doug to receive dual nav training whilst flying the instructor to Leeds in the club's 172. He would then return solo in the slower 150. On reaching Leeds, the instructor dropped Doug off at the maintenance hangar, turned the 172 around, and headed back to Teesside.

Having checked the 150 over, Doug took off and headed for home. Halfway back, he became a bit unsure of his present position. It is worth noting at this point, that pilots never admit to getting lost, they simply become unsure of their present position. Doug remembered his lesson about obtaining a QDM, this is a course to steer to get one back to the airfield. Calling Teesside Radar, he pressed the mike button and requested a 'Quebec Delta Mike' (QDM). Doug pressed the mike switch again and continued, 'Transmitting for a fix, 1,2,3,4,5, - 5,4,3,2,1.'

The voice of Teesside's trusty Radar Controller came crisply back at him 'Are you Victor Mike Charley?' This transmission, asking Doug if he was VMC (Visual Met Conditions), would tell the controller if he was visual with the ground or flying on instruments (IMC). As there was a pause, the controller asked again, more firmly this time, 'Are you Victor Mike Charley?' Doug, trying to sound professional, instantly replied on the radio, 'Negative Teesside, I am Douglas Atherton.' - Sorry Doug! Couldn't resist it.

The only big aircraft to prang at Teesside did so on February 22nd 1973. This was a British European Airways Super BAC 1-11, which supposedly suffered an equipment failure during crew training. The 1-11 had no passengers on board, only 3 crewmembers, Captain Brian Besley, Capt R Plackett and First Officer B Jones, two of whom were Training Captains.

They had been practicing circuits and landings, each time retracting the landing gear after take-off and lowering it again for the landing, all except for the last landing that is. Unfortunately for them, the last landing was of the practice flap-less variety. Not only did they intentionally carry out a flap-less landing, but they also chose the same moment to carry out an unintentional undercarriage-less version. During the last high workload circuit and approach, it seems that someone forgot to put the wheels down. The aircraft settled onto the runway mid a shower of sparks, and obligingly slid off the runway onto the grass near the southwestern end of runway 24, thus ensuring that the runway remained open, and the airfield was not closed to further traffic. One member of the crew received slight facial injuries but the other two were unhurt. For sometime after the event, having been recovered from its resting-place on the airfield, the 1-11 was on trestles in hangar 2, sporting a charred and ragged belly. It eventually flew again after repairs.

Our second pilot to be killed, albeit away from the airfield, was Geoff Garnettt. We had a Chipmunk at the time, I remember its registration being G-AMUG, which had, I think, been owned by Austin McNamara. Geoff and Harry Pierce, who was ex-RAF wartime Spitfire pilot, took off in it on May 29th 1974 and flew south. Later that day we heard that they had been practicing aerobatics near Moulton, which is close to Flamingo Park. The aircraft had entered a spin and had failed to recover before hitting the ground. Geoff was killed, and Harry, who was in the rear cockpit, received serious injuries and was on sticks for some years.

Geoff was a great character, full of fun, and he loved flying. On more than one occasion he would accompany me in the air. Whitby and Scarborough were his favourite locations. I first met Geoff in April 1973, when I was asked by the new flying instructor and old Air Cadet chum Ken Large if I would like to take a very keen student pilot for a trip. Geoff was so keen that he would ask people to take him up between lessons, and insist on paying for the hire of the aircraft.

With the departure of Ron Mason, the old club again changed hands, and was then owned by the Cunliffe brothers. On paper it became Teesside Aviation Ltd, although for every day operational reasons, it was better known as Teesside Flying Club.

After learning to fly with the club, Charles Cunliffe decided to become a flying instructor and booked a training course at Carlisle airport. One Monday morning, Charles departed Teesside for Carlisle in one of the Monsuns (Oscar Charley) to begin his training. The next afternoon I walked into the club to see Ken Large replacing the telephone handset onto its cradle. Ken had a worried look on his face, so I asked him what the problem was. He related to me that Charles had left for Carlisle the previous morning, and that the telephone call had been from Carlisle, saying that Charles hadn't arrived and asking when he was setting off to fly over to them.

Ken and I jumped into the 172 and set off on a direct route to Carlisle to look for Charles. The other Monsun (Tango Bravo), with two other club members on board, took the dogleg route to Carlisle via the Tyne Valley. Charles could have taken either route, and we were not sure which way he had actually gone. Before taking off, he had mentioned his preference to fly the lower dog-leg route, rather than overfly the high ground found on the direct route.

Ken flew us over Hamsterly Forrest and on towards the high ground leading directly to Carlisle. Soon the weather deteriorated, and in an attempt to remain in sight of the ground we remained below the cloud. We shortly realised that to keep below the cloud, we had to fly down a valley, whose hilltops were shrouded in mist. Flying along the valley we eventually reached a dead end. Just as we thought we must climb into the cloud to avoid running into the high ground at the apex, we saw, at the last moment, a smaller valley, turning off to the left. Ken reefed the 172 into a left-hand turn and we headed down this valley, still remaining in sight of the surface. This valley was much shorter than the last, and soon, at high speed, we were again approaching a dead end. The tops of the hills were just that little lower than the previous valley however, and we were able to see a small letter-box clearing of about 100 feet between the top of the hills and the bottom of the cloud. As we over-flew the summit, there she was, sitting upright on a flat piece of ground, as if she had just landed.

The weather conditions the previous day must have been exactly the same, and had amazingly caused us to fly the same route as Charles. Perhaps the letterbox opening hadn't been there, as the Monsun had struck the gradually rising ground, somersaulted once and landed right side up again. Another 50 feet and he would have made it. We had been directly above the crashed aircraft at a height of about 50 feet when we first saw it.

Ken reduced speed and came around again for a better look, and we could see Charles in the cockpit as the canopy had shattered. There was no sign of life. We were only getting fleeting looks at the wreckage, which looked from the air as if it was largely intact. As we came around for a third time we radioed Carlisle of our find and gave our position as best we could.

At that, we suddenly became in a perilous position ourselves. The cloud had quickly swirled and descended, removing the narrow margin between the rocky crag below us, and the cloud base. Ken gunned the engine, and pulled back the control column at the same instant as the cloud descended over us. For the next few minutes, as we slowly climbed away, my eyes were transfixed by the ever so slowly moving needles of the altimeter. We were only too aware that all around, and possibly ahead, higher ground towered above us. After what seemed to be an eternity, we tentatively breathed a sigh of relief as we realised that we were (hopefully) at a height well above the highest peak.

On the way back, we popped out of the cloud into clear air, and on landing back at Teesside, we returned to the clubhouse. Only when we got back did the earlier events come fully home to us. With a heavy heart I left the airfield and drove home, leaving Ken to brief Air Traffic of our findings.

The next day, I was told that Ken, after receiving word that the searchers hadn't found the wreckage, risked his life once again, and flew back to the area after I had left. Our initial guestimated position report had been wrong, as in that isolated neck of the woods one mountain looks much the same as another. In an extreme act of bravery, Ken had again run the gauntlet of cloud and Cumulous Granite, and re-located the Monsun. His report allowed the searchers to locate Charles. We discovered later that he had been killed.

The next day, I drove to the crash-site, which was located near Allen Heads in Weardale. I was amazed to see a farmhouse, with a B road running past it, just 100 yards from the aircraft. This, too, had been shrouded in low cloud at the time of the crash, and the occupants had not seen or heard a thing.

At this time the weather was clear and sunny, totally opposite to the previous two days. I spent the afternoon picking up the wind-scattered contents and papers of Charles's briefcase, which had broken open. The aircraft itself had ended up on a flat piece of ground, upright, almost in one piece. It sounds incongruous that in a small and densely populated country like Britain during the mid-1970s, someone could lie in the wreckage of an aircraft for a day and a half, only yards from an occupied farmhouse and a well used road.

Rothmans Aerobatic Team. At the time, their mount, the famous Pitts Special was the worlds ultimate aerobatic aircraft.
Photo: Mike Hooks

During the mid 70s, Teesside, or hangar 3 to be exact, became the home of the Rothmans Aerobatic Team. They were supported there by Anvil Aviation, which was the Pitts importers at the time. Rothmans had a team which flew the world famous American Pitts Special. One of the teams was led by Marcus Edwards, and had some great aerobatic pilots. These included Brian Lacomber and Andy Legg, both of whom are still doing the rounds as solo aerobatic pilots. Brian was later to become the leader of the famous Rover Aerobatic Team, flying German Walter 300 extras. On one occasion whilst transiting back to Teesside from a display in the South, the team had to put down near Hutton Rudby, due to a shortage of fuel. As they landed in a rough field, a couple of the Pitts Specials overturned, much to the embarrassment of their pilots.

During January 27 and 28th 1978 The Rothmans Aerobatic Team gave their last ever British display at Teesside. The team had been disbanded during 1977 but were reformed by Anvil Aviation, based in hangar 3 at Teesside. The team's S2A Pitts Specials were dismantled and crated up after the display for shipment overseas, where they were to promote Rothmans cigarettes. Mike Cairns, who as you will remember was the leader of the new team and his fellow team pilots flew displays in many European and Middle-East countries. If the reader can get his or her hands on a copy of a DD Video, called 'Aerobatics' one can see 3 individual films about this team, they are well worth watching.

Rothmans Solo aerobatic pilot was David Perrin, better known to all as 'Boy Wonder'. He could make a Pitts talk, and was indeed a wonder to watch. Sadly he was killed sometime after leaving the Rothmans team, whilst working as a stunt pilot during the making of a film staring Tom Selleck called 'High Road To China'. The film was shot in Yugoslavia before its troubles. Whilst travelling back to the film-crew's hotel after filming for the day, the Yugoslavian Air Force helicopter he was travelling in crashed, killing everyone on board.

In 1979, during a lovely sunny day, the wind suddenly turned and began to blow in from the east. Although causing only a light breeze, the wind caused a sea fret to roll in over the airfield, and within 5 minutes it had fully enveloped the airfield in fog. Three of Teesside's aircraft were caught out by the suddenness of the clag and were presented with the prospects of Instrument Flying Conditions.

Amazingly, although the sea fret had blown in from the coast, some 10 miles away, Redcar racecourse was clear, and became an impromptu haven for Les Povey and his student, who were in one of the club's aircraft at the time. Les, with his good knowledge of the local area, chose to land on the racecourse, and waited there during the afternoon until the temporary fog decided to go away.

Archie Stewart, who was also a club member, tried an instrument approach into Teesside. During his first attempt he failed to see the runway, but managed to land after the second, but was down to 230 feet before making contact.

Dennis Jackson was flying as a passenger in the third aircraft, a Beagle Pup owned by Francis Blennerhassett from Hartlepool. They also tried an instrument approach but crashed whilst on the approach to runway 24, Dennis suffered a nasty head injury and was to leave us soon after this accident and retire from flying. Fortunately Francis was not seriously injured. The Pup was not so lucky.

After recovering from his injuries during the King's Cup Air Race, Alan Turley eventually found himself instructing at Teesside Flying Club. Al was also a CAA examiner, and a great guy, very popular with everyone. He went on to become General Manager of Cassair, and later flew as company pilot with Artix of Peterlee. Al flew the company's 8 seater Beech 200, G-MDJI. During one flight in 1987, his aircraft struck high ground in bad visibility around 07:00 whilst on final approach to Leeds Bradford Airport, and he was killed. He was the only one on board, having flown there to pick up passengers bound for Alicante. His aircraft had encountered fog on the approach and crashed into a beauty spot, known to the locals as 'Surprise View'. The aircraft had suffered a problem with its altimeter.

Teesside Airport became privatised on April 1st 1987, both Cleveland and Durham local Authorities, which owned the airport, retained the shares, which it was hoped would benefit local ratepayers.

The late Jack Cassidy was one of the flying club's most charismatic members. A World War Two Spitfire pilot look-alike whose cheery face, complete with handlebar moustache, and soft Scottish accent were part of the club's furniture. He also owned the Ship Inn at Low Worsal near Yarm, a fine hotel and restaurant of some notoriety. Jack went on to form Cassair, initially a small air taxi firm, which was soon to have growing pains. The company's first aircraft were to be light twins, but later would aspire to Short 360s.

Captain John Wilkinson was taking off from Teesside in the Cassair's twin engined Navajo when one of his engines failed at about 40 feet. John had not reached the aircraft's safety speed, and was unable to maintain height on the other engine. He retracted the undercarriage, and rather than land on the runway, put the aircraft down on the grass besides the runway. This reduced the

Cassair Shorts 360   Photo: TIA via John Waiting

risk of a fire. Fortunately there was no fire, and John and his three passengers from ICI Billingham, who had chartered the flight, were uninjured. The only problem was that the aircraft had been carrying a container of radio active trace materials and there was some concern that it might have been damaged, thus causing a leak. Fortunately the container was undamaged, and pronounced safe. At the time however, there was some controversy about the company's authority to carry such material.

Tango Bravo was in need of maintenance, and Ken Large had the job of flying her up to Sunderland Airport. Ken thought he would arrive in style and give a high-speed fly-by. When he reached the centre of the airfield he pulled her up to the vertical. With her nose now pointing skywards, TB chose the most inopportune moment to stop her engine. Ken (and TB) had only one way to go - and that was downwards. She bled energy and entered an incipient spin. With insufficient height to recover, Ken had little chance of recovering and the aircraft went on spinning, right into the ground.

Ken was badly injured; he broke both his legs, and as he hit the ground, his head went forward and the stick entered his mouth, breaking some of his teeth. He was removed from the aircraft by the Airport's fire crew and taken to Sunderland Hospital. Ken was out of the air for quite some time, but eventually recovered. It was a much different Ken that returned to fly again. There but for the grace of God go us all.

Only superior flying skill prevented this situation becoming a total disaster.   Photo: Ken Large

Ken went on to start his own flying club, and I, like most long-standing members at the time, followed him there. His clubhouse was located in the old RAF armoury building, which he shared with John Manning. Ken was there until the airport management decided on a one flying club on the airport policy. He decided to close and move over to work for Cleveland Flying School. At the time of writing he is still there. Ken has provided a great sevice to avaiation and has taught hundreds of budding pilots how to fly. His laid-back and friendly approach has instilled confidence and professionalism to each and every one of them.

Ken and I go back a long way, right back to our teens, when we both were Air Cadets with 405 Squadron. Then we spent Monday and Wednesday nights at the ATC HQ in Darlington, learning about principles of flight, navigation, aero engines and so on. Our HQ was two wooden huts, joined in the usual RAF way, with a centre section housing the canteen and kitchen. It was located in Poplar Road car park in Darlington, between the rear of the Empire Cinema and the river Skerne.

Another cadet there with us was Mike Lochlan, who once flew the Lightning display at Teesside's airshows. He reminded me recently of our staple Air Cadet diet during the 8-pm break from lessons, Bovril and Wagon Wheels. Today, Mike is a civilian, I/C the Tornado simulator at Leeming. During the summer we would spend time at summer camps on RAF airfields, such as Marham and Aldergrove near Belfast. However, I digress once again.

405 Squadron cadets assemble prior to departing Darlington railway station for Summer Camp at RAF Alderbrove, near Belfast. Those the Author can remember are, right to left, back row; W/O Dewar, S/L Naylor the Squadron Commander, Squadron Padre, unknown cadet, the author, Ken Large and Mark Singer, (405's present C/O). Third from right front row; Mike Thornbury, fifth from right John Edwards (now a paramedic), seventh from right Dave Ward.   Photo: Author

Peter Metcalfe was so impressed with the Rothmans Team, and the Pitts Special in particular, that he bought one and kept it at Teesside. The former owner had registered her G-BETI, and had painted a dragon spouting flames from its mouth on the engine cowling. Underneath the dragon was painted the caption, 'The Wife'. During the late 80s, I went over to Peter's house to watch some of the old Rothmans promotional videos, and I was hooked. My search for a Pitts that I could afford culminated in a part kit, which I spent the next two years building.

Peter Metcalfe with G-BETI refueling at Newcastle.   Photo: Author

The Author's first attempt at plane building, G-REAP, 'The Grim Reaper'.   Photo: Author

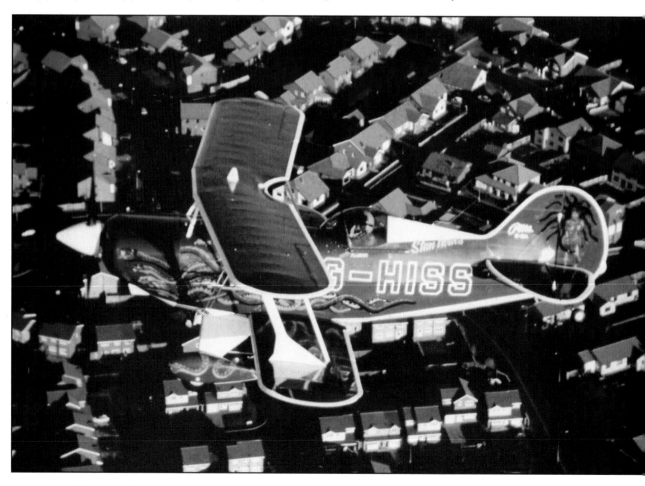

The Author's secon attempt at plane building, Pitts S-2A G-HISS, on long finals for Teesside   Photo: Keith Taylor

The old and original flying club building was pulled down during the 80s, leaving only Cleveland Flying School and the newly opened Teesside Flying Club. This new addition to the airfield was formed by Graham and Lyn Vine, and is situated on the north side of Hangar 3. The club, which formed in 1987, acquired a contract with the RAF to train Air Cadets, providing 22 hours of instruction which it was hoped would put them in good stead for a possible career in the RAF. Several intakes of Air Cadets pass through the club each year. This lucrative contract and a steady stream of new members has allowed the club to become the second longest serving on the airfield.

During the 80s, a third flying club joined the two existing ones. This was the St George Flying Club. The wheel had turned almost full circle since the first Middleton St George Aero Club, but the new club was connected by name only. Captain Eric Reed opened the club's first portacabin style building in the grounds of the St George Hotel. In more recent times, the club has progressed to a new and larger building opposite Hangar 4. The club operates a variety of aircraft, including Cessnas, Piper Warriors, and, like Teesside Aero Club, the distinctive T tailed Piper Tomahawk. The club provides a variety of flying training, including training for the commercial flying licence.

The final fatality involving an aircraft from Teesside (up to press), occurred when a student pilot, flying a PA28 belonging to Teesside Aero Club, struck a disused mast whilst carrying out a solo navigational training exercise to Carlisle.

Phil the airport fireman feeds an injured bird back to health   Photo: Phil Bikes

During 1998 I was able to gain permission from the Airport Director Bob Goldfield to dig on the site of the old Canadian wartime dump. During preparations for their exodus in May 1945, the Canadians buried much unwanted equipment in a large dump-site on the south side of the airfield. At the time a long-standing rumour existed that the remains of a Lancaster lay buried beneath this site. The story was that the Lancaster caught fire whilst being prepared for a raid close to the end of the war. Having put out the flames, which damaged a wing-tip and the port engine, the groundcrew were told to tip the remainder of the wreckage into the tip site. With the end of the war looming, it was felt that the aircraft was surplus to requirements. It was also rumored that the aircraft could also have been the remains of The Ruhr Express.

Some wreckage was growing out of the top of the site. On commencement of the dig it was soon realised that the structure was Geodetic, and part of a Wellington's bomb-bay. This turned out to be a small amount of wreckage, belonging to the Wellington, which as you have read, crashed during the Battle of Britain air display in 1949.

Having removed this from the top of the grass covered dump, a JCB was used to dig into the site. Unfortunately this did not reveal any aircraft, only a very large number of small objects. Amongst the thousands of small items dumped in haste by the Canadians were unwanted aircraft spares, tin hats, flak jackets, empty ammo belt clips, cables, rubber tubes, pipes, old crockery, bottles and a thousand and one other small items. Included in the stuff dug up was some old black cutlery, which we threw onto the side of the hole. It later turned out that during a recent reunion visit by some of Goosepool's Canadian Veterans, these blackened objects were picked up by one of their number, and after a little polish, turned out to be silver wartime Mess cutlery. Having collected them all up, the Veterans, who probably ate from them all those years ago, took them home to Canada. The only largish bit of aircraft recovered from the trenches was part of a Merlin engine cowling, complete with camouflage paint. It had been a useful exercise to explore the dump and confirm that nothing major was buried there. The site has now been filled in and landscaped.

Waiting for the return from 'Ops',
the Memorial to the airmen of Croft airfield:
Sited beside the road at Dalton
Photo: Author

*After many years of faithful service, as one of
Teesside's Duty Officers, Tom Pallister passed away in 1998.
At his request his ashes were scattered over the airfield.
This memorial stone and a seat were positioned in pride of place
beside the control tower.*
Photo: Author

*Below: The warm air rising from the firestorms over continental
Europe, caused by the bombing, elevated seeds into the lower
atmosphere, which would collect in small nooks and crannies of
the aircraft. When the bombers returned to base, rain would wash
the seeds out onto the concrete dispersal pans. When they dried
out they were blown off the concrete into the surrounding earth
by the propellers where they grew. In this photo taken during
2002, alpine flowers and maize, not indigenous to the UK can be
seen growing around the old dispersals on the south side of the
airport. This is an undeveloped area of the airfield, virtually
untouched since the war. Crews also relieved the boredom of life
between operations by planting gardens around their dispersals.
Wild roses grow around some dispersals, a legacy of life planted
during WWII by airmen long gone.*

Photo: Author

*Peter Foster during 2002 standing on a wartime concrete pop-
up ground defence gun turret on the south side of the airfield .*
Photo: G. Hill

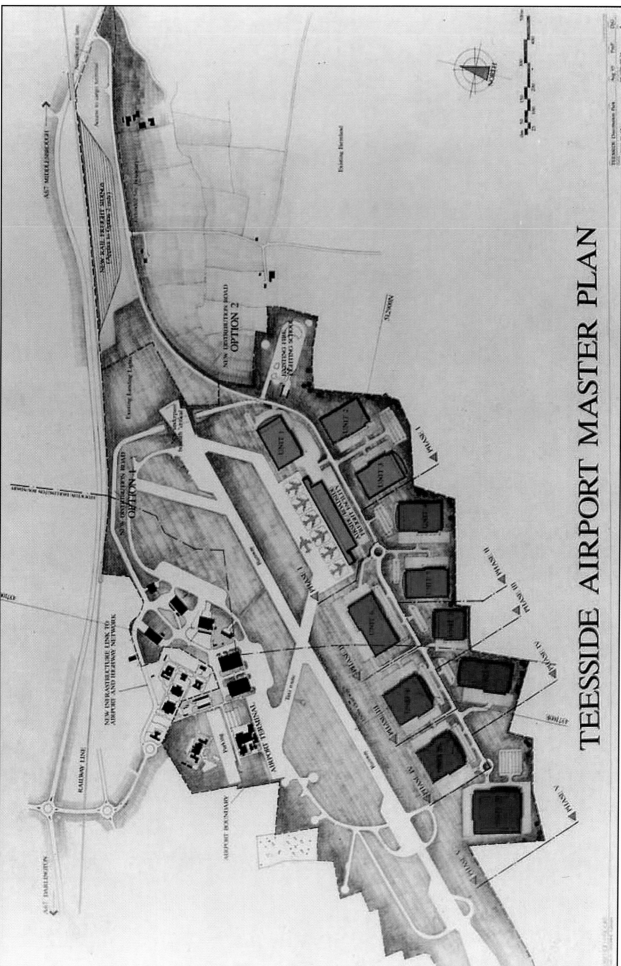

TEESSIDE AIRPORT MASTER PLAN

This proposed plan for the expansion of the Airport did not come to fruition despite much hard work by all concerned.   Photo: TIA via John Waiting

Teesside International Airport looking West. Taken from a hot air balloon Photo: Keith Taylor

Each year, hundreds of people visit the Aero Clubs, to sample the enjoyment of flying. Each club offers trial flights for a few pounds. Some are purchased simply as birthday presents, whilst others are bought by the recipient themselves, to savour the delights and freedom of flight. Many go on, having caught the bug, to win their wings, and complete the PPL course. Most budding commercial pilots begin their flying careers in this way. Others go on to expand their prowess, learning aerobatics, which allows them an even grater understanding of how to handle their aircraft in extream and unusual flight attitudes. Alan Austin, the owner of Cleveland Flying School chose air racing as his forte, he has developed his skills and has become a champion air race pilot. Along with Cleveland Flying School, the clubs, run by both Lyn and Eric, will ensure that the air minded among us will always receive the best in flying training, and the sociality to allow us to be amongst the kindred spirits we enjoy so much.

During the late 90's there was talk of a huge phased expansion program for the airfield. A service road was to be built; with its entrance to the east of the railway line, close to Urlay Nook. This solved the problem of how to access the south side of the airfield from the ring road, without having to build a bridge over the Darlington to Eaglescliffe railway line. The plan was to see the demise of runway 19/01 and the construction of a parallel taxiway. Also to be constructed over time were huge aircraft hangars and cargo handling sheds. A plan of the finished article was drawn by an artist, the author was able to acquire a copy. Sadly it all came to nought.

When this book was completed in the spring of 2003, most of the old domestic wartime buildings were still in place, and the south side of the airfield was just as it was during the war. To my knowledge the airfield was one of the most complete wartime RAF airfields still standing. There were new structures of course, including the Passenger Terminal Building, built at a cost of £506,000 and officially opened on November 1st 1966 by Princess Margaretha of Sweden. She was accompanied by the Mayor of Middlesbrough Alderman J G Boothby, who was the chairman of the Airport Committee. The Guard of Honour was provided by the RAF Regiment stationed at RAF Catterick.

During the war years 5 hangars were built at Goosepool. At the time of writing they still stand. Hangars 1 is still used for aviation related purposes. Hangar 2 has had many uses. Since British Midland began to operate from Teesside the southern end of hangar 2 has been home to their engineering and service team. For many years, until they left Teesside during the late 90's, Spray Avia utilised the northern end to carry out their role as aircraft paint sprayers. Many a civilian and military aircraft passed through their huge spray booth at the top end of Hangar 2. The HS748's of the CAA's Calibration Flight were the meat in the sandwich and utilised the middle of the hangar. The Calibration Flight was responsible for flying to various airfields and carrying out calibration tests on ILS and other electronic airfield approach and navigation equipment. The CAA Calibration Flight departed Teesside during the mid-90's. In 2001 after many years British Midland found the main part of hangar 2 surplus to requirements and decided to retain only their offices, workshop and stores along the side of the hangar for their engineering staff. In 2002 TNT Cargo took their place within the main hangar. Since the airfield became civilianised in 1964 Hangar 3 has been the home for all of the airfield's GA light aircraft, including those operated by the flying clubs and private owners. Hangar 4 has found itself outside the northern perimeter fence and has for many years been used only for storage. Hangar 5 has spent most of the post RAF years as a converted fitness centre called Top Spin, which closed during the 90's. At the time of writing its partially refurbished skeletal frame is void of any cladding and open to the elements as it awaits the continuation of its conversion into something or other, possibly another health centre and/or a hotel.

The control tower was enlarged after the war, from its original square two-story shape to the modern RAF version, complete with glazed top.

Some of the old buildings lay empty, others were occupied by various companies after the RAF left in 1964. The old H-block dormitories have been used for various purposes, including a Teachers Training College and a residential home for the elderly, known as Trees Park. The old Officers Mess became the St George Hotel soon after the RAF departed. The cost of the conversion amounting to about £250,000. Today the inside of the hotel holds testament to the wartime history of the airfield with many photographs and paintings. Large squadron crests adorn the lobby, which in 1998 was returned to its original wartime configuration. During 1999 the Author commissioned 9 paintings, depicting an aircraft of each of the wartime squadrons based at Goosepool and Croft. They now hang in the bar of the hotel. Complete with its own ghost; the hotel is the annual venue for its wartime veterans, who return each year from all over the world.

Above left:Clare Matthews in 'the tower'   Above right: 'Ali Nash in 'Radar'
Left: Dave Green. Lower left: John Rankin. Below: 'From left to right, Julian Nutting, Alison Nash,
Steve Curtis, Graeme Binnie. Both Julian and Graeme are very experienced pilots,
a great advantage in the Air Traffic business'

Photos: Author

Left: Josh Harrison and Gayle Douglas downstairs in Radar. Josh has a wealth of ATC experience, having first worked as an Air Traffic Controller
with the RAF and later at several British airports.   Right: Vincent Long and Roger Haslett   Photos: Author

CHAPTER THIRTEEN

FRA

FRA

The name, 'Cobham' is a very famous name in aviation circles. Cobham plc is based at Hurn, Bournemouth International Airport, in the south of England. Prior to 1985 one of its largest companies, Flight Refuelling Ltd had been involved in the operation, modification and maintenance of special mission aircraft since the 1930's. During April 1995 a new company was formed, FR Aviation (FRA).

During 1994 FRA began to build a hangar at Teesside, after it had won a £50 million 5-year contract with the UK Ministry of Defence, to provide Electronic Warfare (EW) Training for the Royal Air Force and the Royal Navy. Teesside was chosen for its central geographic position within the British Isles. Up to that point 360 squadron, based at RAF Wyton, had carried out EW training for the MoD in Canberra T.17s. The contract was in keeping with the British Governments policy of Contractor Owned Contractor Operated (COCO) services. This allowed civilian companies to tender for MoD contracts relating to EW Training.

FRA's Hangar, now named hangar 360, after 360 squadron, which disbanded in 1994, was completed in April 1995. FRA then began operating 6 French made Dassault Falcon 20 Jets out of Teesside, which I am told began life as air-cargo carriers for Fed-Ex. Apart from the 6 Falcons based at Teesside, two more, which had been used over the previous 10 years for navy related training tasks, were available from Hurn when required. In more recent times, a seventh Falcon was added to the Teesside fleet. In total, FRA operate a total of 20 Falcons, including the 7 from Teesside. Teesside's Falcons have customised registrations, G-FRAI, followed by J, L, S, T, U and W. The aircraft marked I, J, T and W have side cargo doors.

The Falcon was chosen over other similar aircraft, including the British BAe 125, because it is fitted with the same wing as the Dassault Mystere fighter. This wing has four hard-points, which allows the fitment of underwing stores. The Falcon also has better ground clearance than most of its contemporaries. Its crew consists of the Captain, who is normally ex-military. Because the aircraft weighs over 13 tonnes, a First Officer is required by law, he is usually a civilian pilot. The third member of the crew is the Electronic Warfare Operator (EWO).

Apart from its ex-Fed-Ex aircraft, which were acquired from North America, the company operates a second, ex- Canadian Air Force, derivative, which differs from the former. The Fed-Ex version is equipped with a flat freight floor and a large cargo door. The Falcons carry an assortment of pods under their wings, depending on the sortie. One is the ALQ-167 electronic Jammer, which is used once the emissions from enemy ground or airborne radars have been received and identified by other equipment in the aircraft. A second pod is the BOZ-3 chaff dispenser. This can sew fine particles of fibre-glass, which like wartime Window, descends very slowly and disrupts the enemy's radar capabillity. The Falcon also has on-board chaff dispensers, located at the rear of the fuselage. These fire out to each side of the fuselage, after which the chaff is dispersed by the engines. The aircraft also carries a coms jammer, which, as the title implies, disrupts enemy voice communications.

The company's Falcons operate with the forces of most NATO countries, testing the combat capability of military pilots and assisting in their training. Apart from the UK, amongst others, these include Holland, Belgium and Norway. On average, FRA's Falcons amass up to 4,000 flying-hours per year. Although most of FRA's operations are flown from Teesside, the Falcon crews can also operate as far as North America and the Far East. Much of the training is over the North Sea and involves flying against F.3 Tornadoes from Coningsby,Leeming and Leuchars. As the Tornadoes come in for the kill, the EWO works his magic, with the black boxes at his disposal, in an attempt to shake off and disrupt an impending mock attack.

FRA operates nine, three-man, civilian Falcon crews at Teesside. On occasion, Teeside's Falcons also operate buddy-style with BAC Hawks and can lay a carpet of chaff to mask them. A Hawk makes a good Exocet or stand-off missile radar trace, and is very useful for testing the defence capabilities of over the horizon warship radars. This is just one of the roles carried out by FRA. FRA's Hangar 360 facillity at Teesside services FRA's aircraft, along with those of Flight Precision Ltd. Again, most of the company's ground engineers are ex-military. At the time of writing, FRA operate 90 aircraft out of Bournemouth and Teesside

Flight Precision Ltd (FPL), formed in 1996 is a joint venture company formed by FRA and Aerodata GmbH and also operates out of Teesside. Approved by the UK CAA Safety Regulation Group, Flight Precision Ltd provides flight Inspection services, which includes the calibration of CAT III Instrument Landing Systems (ILS). For this role the company operates both Beech King Air 200 and Cessna 441 Conquest turboprop calibration aircraft. The Aerodata Flight Inspection System utilises GPS, Inertial Navigation systems and Automatic Laser Tracker Technology to ensure levels of calebration to within 2 nautical miles visibillity, even at night. Along with ILS, the Aerodata Flight Inspection System fitted to FPL's aircraft can also effectively calebrate VOR/DME, TACAN, MLS and all Air Defence, Serveillance and Precision radar systems. FPL's customers in the UK include The MoD, Air Traffic Services Ltd and all of the major Airports. The Belgian Air Force, along with many other overseas aviation authorities also avail themselves of Flight Precisions Flight Inspection Services.

FRA Falcon taxiing at Teesside. Photo: Richard Bowater

Flight Precision Ltd. operate both Cessna 441 Conquest and Beech King Air 200 calibration aircraft. Photo: Richard Bowater

Believe it or not there's a Trident 4 in there somewhere.   Photo: By kind permission of Serco International Fire Training Centre. Copyright IFTC

To the east of the threshold of runway 23 is the Fire Training Ground. It is fully equipped with various fire-fighting simulators, such as an oil-rig, complete with its own helicopter. There is also a mock-up Jumbo Jet front end. These structures are made of steel and can be used over and over again to train fire fighters, who come from all over the world to learn their trade. The school is second to none and provides fire-fighting training for oil rig, industrial and aviation fire teams. For the airfield fire fighters; old Trident airliners are used to train them in fire and passenger rescue techniques. The students come from every country in the world and during their stay they are housed in the old wartime Sergeant's Mess.

During 1996 the police North East Air Support Unit acquired a new Briton Norman Islander BN2 fixed wing aircraft and is based it at Teesside. This was in addition to a helicopter, which had been operating out of Newcastle Airport since 1990.

The Northeast Air Support Unit has recently modified its Islander with quieter propellers and exhaust stubs.   Photo: Richard Bowater

CHAPTER FOURTEEN

**Great North Air Ambulance Service
Stop Press
The Weather - Summer 2003
Not the End**

Great North Air Ambulance Service

The final unit to arrive and be based at Teesside airport is the Great North Air Ambulance Service (GNAAS). The GNAAS has recently celebrated its first year, having arrived at Teeside in June of 2002. The GNAAS has two helicopters, a twin Squirrel and a Bolkow. The Squirrel (G-NAAS) is based at Blyth, Northumberland and covers Northumberland, north Durham and north Cumbria. The Bolkow, which is based at Teesside covers south Durham, Teesside, North Yorkshire and South Cumbria. The Bolkow has a crew of 1 pilot and 2 medical staff. This may vary, between a doctor and a nurse, doctor and paramedic or 2 paramedics. Its normal cruising speed is around 140 mph.

The GNAAS is a charity and Alan Austin, who was until June 2003 the owner of Cleveland Flying School, is the Secretary of the board of Trustees. The other members of the board were chosen for their relevant skills in relation to the requirements of the charity. They include an expert in the day to day running of the ambulance service, a doctor, for medical input, an accountant and a lawyer. Alan Austin's inputs to the board are various but his long career in aviation has been harnessed for the good of the GNAAS. Alan has been responsible for the acquisition of the aircraft and for all things appertaining to the daily operational requirements of the aircraft. The Twin Squirrel, G-NAAS, was bought and donated to the North East Air Ambulance Service (NEAAS) by Dame Margaret |Barber, of Barber Jacket fame. Although the aircraft is based at Teesside the GNAAS is based in the Imperial suit within the Imperial Centre, Grange road, Darlington. The same Imperial building frequented by Goosepool's wartime airmen. Graham Pickering, a fellow ex-air cadet and 645 glider pilot (now PPL) is the Chief Executive.

The small staff of volunteers within the Imperial suit are responsible for the running and fund raising of the Organisation. A lottery, donation tins and the kindness of several dedicated volunteers provide the only financial input to the Organisation. As a charity, fundraising is vital, without it the helicopters cannot fly. Perhaps the readers of this book might spare a thought for the hard working support team who constantly battle for financial help, (Hint Hint). If this was America the funding would be provided. Sadly it is left to volunteers to do what the government wont. The GNAAS is looking ahead to acquiring new aircraft. At the top of the list is the McDonnald Douglas MD902 helicopter. Its faster and has many advantages over the Squirrel and Bolkow, including the ability to carry 2 stretchers. It also has no tail rotor, (for getting into tighter places). The MD902 also meets all the requirements of the new aviation regulations, soon to be implemented.

Alan Austin's career in aviation began with the Air Training Corps in 1958 when he began to fly as a cadet with 645 Gliding School at Middleton. 645 moved from Middleton to Catterick in 1960 when Middleton became a Master Diversion Airfield (MDA). Alan became CFI of 645 in 1966 and Commanding Officer in 1972. It was at 645 that the author first met Alan many years ago. During 1985 he went on to powered aircraft and won his Private Pilot's Licence wings at Teesside with Ken Large's flying club. Squadron Leader Alan Austin retired from The RAF VRT and 645 in August 2000. He became interested in air racing and during a race in the Isle of Man, sponsored by Manx Airlines during 1996, he won the coveted Schneider Trophy, at a speed of 153.2 mph. He went on to become the only living person to share a stamp with Her Majesty the Queen. The aircraft he used to win the trophy was G-IRIS, a Grumman AA5B Tiger. This aircraft, with Alan at the controls, was depicted on a 21p stamp in 1997. He was presented with the trophy by the granddaughter of the first winner, Howard Pixton, who had won the first Schneider seaplane race in a Sopwith Tabloid in 1913.

STOP PRESS
Weather update for summer 2003

Spring and summer 2003 was the usual mix of hot and sunny weather in the south and mediocre weather in the northeast. However, by the end of July, even the northeast was enjoying record temperatures. Not as hot as in the south, and certainly not as frequent, but still a record for the area in terms of the amount of sunny days during late July, early August. The last time Darlington had enjoyed weather like this was during the summer of 1976, 27 years previous.

Most days that turned out warm and sunny initially saw low cloud and haze cover the Darlington area during the mornings. On occasions it took until between 12-noon and 4-pm for the sky to clear. However, many an unemployed white Darlingtonian, not engaged in grappling with the aviator's 5,000-metre horizontal visibility rule, did gain a tan of sorts. The honeymoon however was to be relatively short lived.

On Sunday the 10th of August, a man died of hypothermia in the sea off Hartlepool, 15 miles to the northeast of Teesside Airport. During the morning, so thick and black were the clouds over Darlington that lights were required in homes around the area, as a horrendous storm slowly passed through. At the same time it was announced that cloud-free Heathrow Airport, 200 miles to the south, was experiencing temperatures that reached an all time British record of 101°F, (38 C). The city of York, just 40 miles to the south of Teesside Airport, also saw record temperatures and dawn to dusk roasting sunshine.

At 19° C, the temperature in Darlington was exactly half of that in the south. However, by 4-PM the rain had stopped and we did gain a small glimpse of the sky for a short time. Meanwhile, temperatures around the rest of Europe ranged between 35 and 40 degrees for weeks. Unlike the south, the cloud, and haze was still with us the next morning and remained over the following weeks, when this book went to print. By, by summer 03.

Not the End

In modern times Goosepool is no longer threatened with the wrath of the German War Machine. Instead, its foes are much more insidious, self-styled environmentalists, complaining of low flying and noisy aircraft. No one buys a house close to a railway station or a motorway then begins to complain bitterly about the noise and demands to have it closed down, so why do they do it at an airfield that has been in existence for 62 years. Airfields are rather large things, and not easily hidden. Surely with all those large jets going in and out they must have had inkling that the airfield was near-by when they bought their houses.

Surprisingly, the main complaint is not leveled at the huge and noisy jet airliners that ply their way in and out of Teesside. Instead the wingers are against the light aircraft belonging to the flying clubs. I suspect that the complainers realise that they have little chance of banning the large, prosperous and well-established airlines, so instead they attack the aero clubs, whose aircraft make a quarter of the noise of the jets. As it turns out, having got nowhere with their 'Ban the playboy pilots of the flying clubs campaign', they settled for the Police Air Support Unit's (ASU) twin-engined Islander and Squirrel helicopter.

The ASU responded by spending £50,000 on new quieter propellers and exhaust systems for their fixed wing aircraft. The Islander's role requires it to circle the Teesside and Darlington area at heights as low as 500 feet, often at silly o'clock in the morning, whilst searching for car thieves and burglars. It flies around, and around, and around, in the wee small hours, like a huge blue/black bat, searching for it's prey. This event is usually followed by the flying club's phones becoming white hot with calls from complaining residents (and parish councillors), who have mistaken the Police aircraft for the flying club variety.

During 1974 the Civil Aviation Authority proclaimed that Teesside Airport should become the airport for the north. It was almost certain that it would dwarf Newcastle. Sadly, to date, this has not yet happened. Newcastle Airport has had too many friends in high places. However, with the recent subsidence problems, caused by the old mine workings under parts of the airfield site and the, at times, serious traffic bottleneck on the A1 around the Metro Centre Shopping Complex, the airport could one day possibly fall from favour. Worries in regard to the possibility of heavy aircraft coming to grief at Newcastle due to the subsidence problem has already caused the captain of one huge Antonov AN225 transport aircraft to use Teesside Airport for a heavy load, required for the Gulf conflict during 2003.

Teesside airport enjoys no constraints and with ample room to extend the length of its main runway is destined, with the right investment, to become the North's premier International Airport. The area around the airport boasts unclogged roads any time of the day and night providing easy access for everyone from the Tyne to south Yorkshire.

During the dawn of 2003 the media announced, that at last, Teesside International Airport was to receive the funding it had been fighting for since its opening in 1964. A company called Peel Holdings PLC, which operates at Liverpool's John Lennon Airport, expressed an interest in investing over £20 million pounds in Teesside International Airport. There are expectations of enlarging the passenger terminal and turning it into a two-story complex. Also discussed is the building of a new road, stretching from the airport entrance roundabout, around the St George Hotel and up to the front of the proposed new airport terminal building.

Also envisaged is the construction of a parallel taxiway, and later, the resurrection of the northeastern service road plan. This will see the loss of 2 out of 3 of Goosepool's old runways, however the main (23/05) runway is expected to be lengthened to 10,000 feet. It is hoped that the service road, linking the Yarm road to the south-side of the airport, will open up this vast untapped area to aviation-related businesses. It is envisaged that freight handling facilities will be further developed on the north-side of the airfield. Also on the cards is a Teesside Airport Rail Terminal, which is to be built at Darlington's Bank Top railway station. Regular shuttle buses are to ply between this terminal and the proposed enlarged airport terminal building. Alas, the book is finished and cannot await the final outcome.

Let us hope that in the future, the airfield is not prostituted in the name of expedient financial survival or gain and does not eventually become yet another overgrown industrial park, or worse yet, a housing estate. Let us pray that the hangars remain hangars and do not become yet more non-aviation industrial buildings. With luck, Goosepool will remain an airfield, worthy of the legacy of glory thus far bestowed upon it. For in the not too distant future, a city or town without its own airport may itself have no future.

Here's hoping that the hard work carried out by the airport's last Managing Director, Bob Goldfield will help sustain Teesside's growth and that under the new Managing Director, Hugh Lang, the airport will at long last succeed in gaining the recognition it well deserves.

Finally, I hope that the flying clubs flock of light aircraft, which have helped Teesside through its bad times by providing high numbers of aircraft movements, when few airlines were willing to utilise the airport, will be appreciated by the airport management, both now and in the future.

Those in literary circles would have you believe that a good story must have two very important features, a good beginning and an even better ending. RAF and RCAF Middleton St George, latterly known as Teesside International Airport, certainly does have the former. One must remember however, that Goosepool's book is still open and the pen is still moving. Therefore, this story, as with the most glorious of annals, can have no ending.

To those of you that will follow us - may God bless you with happy landings.

Stanley D Howes *August 2003*

Acknowledgments

I express my deepest thanks to the following people, organisations and companies for their kind assistance, without which, this book could not have been written. Special thanks go to my old co-pilot **Larry Donnelly** for helping me with just about everything relating to the Whitley and life at Goosepool during his time there. Also to **Norman Frankish, Norman Thompson and Cyril Tuckwell** for their insight into the daily life of Middleton's groundcrew. Thanks also to **Roland Whitehorn and Robbie Robson,** who supplied info regarding their flying exploits at Goosepool. **Walter Poynter and Ron Cassells** provided in-depth information regarding the Canadian side of things. Not to be left out are **Bill Chorley and Chris Salter** of Midland Counties Publishing, for Bill's Bomber Command Losses 1939 – 1945 and his excellent book on 76 Squadron 'To See the Dawn Breaking'. Thanks too to **Nancy Rolph of Crecy ,** her assistance in allowing me to include information from **Group Captain Sawyer's** book 'Only owls and bloody fools fly at night'. **Ken Marshall** is owed special thanks for allowing me to reproduce, verbatim, a whole chapter from his book 'The Pendulum and the Scythe', relating to the loss of Chris Cheshire. I am also totally indebted to **Peter Foster** of Teesside International Airport, What Peter doesn't know about Goosepool, never happened. **Geoff Hill,** lifelong aviation enthusiast and historian provided me with much vital information, he also threw open his extensive photograph archives and allowed me to use as many as I wanted. Thanks to **Ena Bullemont** for providing me with a copy of **Vince Elmer's** 'Moose Squadron 1941 - 45'. The unsung hero in all of this is my wife Susan, who over the last 5 years, has became an extremely understanding book widow, thank god for TV soaps, that's all I can say. She also doubled up as proof reader, critic and Microsoft 'Word' spellchecker corrector, (American into proper English). The list is endless, but I must also include the following who unselfishly provided much vital information:

David Acaster, for his book 'The Silent Observer'.
John Allinson, for his exploits during the Jet years
Alan Austin of Cleveland Flying School.
Graeme Binnie, Julian Nuttal and the guys and gals from Air Traffic Control, Teesside International Airport.
Neville Balsover, who wrote to me from New Zealand and supplied historical information regarding Middleton St George Aero Club.
BMI British Midland
Anthony Bevilacua and Fred Tycoles from Canada, for photographs and information regarding Elmer Tycoles.
Canadian Services Archives
Mrs R Cassels, for sending me a copy of Ron Cassel's book, 'Ghost Squadron', and allowing me to use information therein
Darlington Memorial Hospital
Durham County Hall archives, for Dinsdale map 1938
Vince Elmer. For his most excellent book ' Moose Squadron 1942 – 1945'.
Jodi Ann Eskritt MA, Curator **RCAF Memorial Museum Trenton Astra Ontario Canada.**
FRA and Flight Precision Ltd.
Bill Gillom
Vic Hetherington, head of security, Teesside International Airport
Bill and Sue Hillman, Eclectic Studios, for information relating to the loss of F/L W G Campbell
Mike Hook, for his help with many of the photographs
Mrs Leonard, for help with information relating to Middleton's Station Sick Quarters
Imperial War Museum Photographic Archives.
IFTC Fire Training School, Teesside International Airport
Arnold Kay, my Canadian researcher.
Ken Large, (Junior and Senior) of Cleveland Flying School
Martin Middlebrook and Chris Everitt, for allowing me to use information from The Bomber Command War Diaries, and again to **Martin Middlebrook** for his book 'The Battle of Hamburg'.
MOD, for Photographs and information taken from Whitley, Halifax and Lancaster pilot's notes: **Crown Copyright/MOD. Reproduced with the kind permission of the Controller of Her Majesty's Stationery Office.**
John Morrison, for his exploits after being shot down during the Tirpitz raid.
Mike Pope, proof reader extraordinaire
Les Povey, sadly now deceased
Public Records Office, Kew, Richmond, Surrey
RAF Museum, Hendon
Cpt Eric Reed, St George Flight Training Ltd
Bob Thompson of Teesside Airport, for risking life and limb to take photos from the top of the Hangars
The late **Group Captain David Young, Michael Renaut** and **William Kimber and Co Ltd** for information from Michael Renaut's book 'Terror by Night'
Lynn Vine, Teesside Aero Club
John Waiting, Teesside International Airport.

Special thanks also go to all of the others, too many to mention, who supplied so much information, without which, this book would be much thinner. **A big thankyou to you all!**

Bibliography

A/P	Pilot's notes, Whitley V	Crown Copyright/MoD
A/P	Pilot's notes, Halifax II & V	Crown Copyright/MoD
A/P	Pilot's notes, Lancaster	Crown Copyright/MoD
	Air 27	Public Records Office, Kew
	Air 28	Public Records Office, Kew
	Air 29	Public Records Office, Kew
Acaster, David	The Silent Observer	Acaster
Cassels, Ron	Ghost squadron	Ardenlea Publishing 1991
Chorley, Bill	Bomber Command Losses 1941	Midland Counties Publishing
Chorley, Bill	Bomber Command Losses 1942	Midland Counties Publishing
Chorley, Bill	Bomber Command Losses 1943	Midland Counties Publishing
Chorley, Bill	Bomber Command Losses 1944	Midland Counties Publishing
Chorley, Bill	Bomber Command Losses 1945	Midland Counties Publishing
Chorley, Bill	To See The Dawn Breaking	Midland Counties Publishing 1981
Donnelly, Larry	The Whitley Boys	Air Research Publications 1991 & 1998
Donnelly, Larry	A Quest for Wings	Tempus publishing 2000
Marshall, Ken	The Pendulum and the Scythe	Air Research Publications 1996
Middlebrook, Martin & Everitt, Chris	Bomber Command War Diaries	Viking 1985
Middlebrook, Martin	The Battle of Hamburg	Middlebrook 1980
Renaut, Michael	Terror By Night	William Kimber 1982
Sawyer, Tom	Only Owls and Bloody Fools Fly at Night	William Kimber 1982

To the best of my knowledge the use of any copyright material has been properly acknowledged and every effort has been made to contact every information source in this regard.

This photo was taken during a street party in Brunswick Street, Darlington, on VE Day, May 1945. The baby in the photo, being held by his grandmother, is the author, age 10 months. The lady and gentleman in pyjamas with the barrel organ are Maudie and Geordie Fawbert who were well known street merchants in the town. The lady and gentleman dancing are Henry and Violet Ward. The lack of male dance partners is due to the fact that most able-bodied men had gone off to war.

Photo: The Northern Echo, via the Author